THE CAMBRIDGE
BIBLICAL HEBREW WORKBOOK

This workbook can be used together with any elementary Biblical Hebrew grammar, by students at colleges, seminaries or universities.

♦ It applies many of the tools of modern language acquisition to make learning this classical language an active and inspiring process.

♦ It uses well-known Hebrew names as a pedagogical aid to memorizing grammar and vocabulary.

♦ It focuses on original biblical texts.

♦ The exercises are based on a stock of frequently used words which is gradually enlarged.

♦ Vocabulary and grammar learnt early on are regularly revised and reinforced in later exercises.

♦ The student is carefully guided through the exercises by means of boxed notes on key points.

♦ A key to the exercises is included.

♦ The translations provided follow the Hebrew text as closely as possible.

♦ It enables students to develop their understanding of the general systematic sound changes in Biblical Hebrew, progressively providing a stable foundation and deeper insight into the language.

NAVA BERGMAN teaches Biblical and Modern Hebrew at the Department of Oriental and African Languages, Göteborg University, Sweden. In 1999 she was awarded the Göteborg University Individual Pedagogical Prize for developing her popular study-kit in Biblical Hebrew for beginners.

THE CAMBRIDGE
BIBLICAL HEBREW WORKBOOK

Introductory Level

Nava Bergman

CAMBRIDGE
UNIVERSITY PRESS

PUBLISHED BY THE PRESS SYNDICATE OF THE UNIVERSITY OF CAMBRIDGE
The Pitt Building, Trumpington Street, Cambridge, United Kingdom

CAMBRIDGE UNIVERSITY PRESS
The Edinburgh Building, Cambridge CB2 2RU, UK
40 West 20th Street, New York, NY 10011–4211, USA
10 Stamford Road, Oakleigh, VIC 3166, Australia
Ruiz de Alarcón 13, 28014 Madrid, Spain
Dock House, The Waterfront, Cape Town 8001, South Africa

http://www.cambridge.org

Originally published in Swedish as *Bibelhebreiska för Nybörjare: Övningsbok*
by Studentlitteratur, Lund, Sweden, 2000

First published in English by Cambridge University Press 2005

Printed in the United Kingdom at the University Press, Cambridge

Typeface Monotype Times

A catalogue record for this book is available from the British Library

ISBN 0 521 82631 4 Hardback
ISBN 0 521 53369 4 Paperback

For my children

Miriam, Martha, Dan, Adam and Elinor

CONTENTS

PREFACE

This workbook for introductory level is based on *Bibelhebreiska för nybörjare: Övningsbok* (in Swedish), which is the first volume of a comprehensive study-kit of Biblical Hebrew. The study-kit includes, apart from this workbook, a workbook for intermediate level, a textbook and an audio-CD package with word lists, exercises, texts and biblical songs.

The present workbook can be used together with any elementary grammar of Biblical Hebrew, whether at university, college, seminary or high school. The student is carefully guided, step by step, towards a thorough knowledge of Hebrew.

THE PEDAGOGICAL FEATURES OF THE BOOK

- Many of the tools of modern language acquisition are employed in this book to make the learning of a classical language an active and inspiring process. A classical language can be assimilated in much the same way as a modern language, namely, by diligent many-sided practice based on a wide variety of exercises and a stock of frequently used words which is gradually enlarged and repeated.
- Well-known Hebrew names are integrated in word lists, exercises and summaries throughout the book as a pedagogical aid in imprinting grammatical forms and vocabulary items on the memory.
- The method of teaching used in the book is repetitive-instructive. Main points of grammar are continually repeated, primarily by means of 'match together' exercises and 'remember and note' boxes preceding many of the exercises. Each 'remember and note' box functions as a *Prepared Table* שֻׁלְחָן עָרוּךְ which actualizes relevant data and supplies the student with practical advice and complementary information necessary for carrying out the exercise in question. This repetitive-instructive contribution makes studying effective and even enjoyable since the student does not have to disturb the flow of learning by searching for missed or forgotten data.
- In order to familiarize the student with original biblical texts, the material in most of the exercises is drawn from the Hebrew Bible.
- In order to make the student aware of the complex of problems facing the Bible translator, the translations provided in the exercises and the Key follow the Hebrew text as closely as possible. This equips the student with the tools needed to understand why various Bible translations may offer different interpretations of primarily tenses and particles.
- Concise and easily accessible material is available for review in a series of so-called *Grammatical cornerstones* רֹאשׁ פִּנָּה, in which the basic elements of the grammar of Biblical Hebrew are conveyed in a table or graphic form.

- In order to strengthen the feeling of coherence and continuity in the studies of the language, a holistic grammatical analysis is applied to parts of the material in the exercises.
- At times, simplified, somewhat transparent, grammatical terms are used to facilitate learning for students who are not at home with linguistic terminology.
- Last but not least, the studies are anchored in the common phenomena of the Hebrew language, that is, the general systematic vowel and consonant changes which occur when words are formed and inflected. Knowledge and understanding of the predictable sound changes of the language lead to a stable foundation and deeper insight in the course of the studies. It also minimizes the need to memorize grammatical forms by rote and enables the student to use a lexicon of Biblical Hebrew effectively.

THE STRUCTURE OF THE BOOK

The book consists of 28 sections followed by coherent text samples illustrating the different genres of biblical prose, three appendices (Hebrew via Hebrew names with exercises based on Hebrew names, Regular sound changes in Hebrew and Guide to grammatical terms), a Hebrew–English vocabulary, an English–Hebrew vocabulary and a key to the exercises.

Sections 3–28 are organized as follows:
- main points of grammar.
- under the heading *Memorize* one can find the cornerstones of the basic grammatical structures. Eighteen units of *Grammatical cornerstones* רֹאשׁ פִּנָּה are included in the book.
- under the heading *Hebrew via Hebrew names* עִבְרִית בְּעֶזְרַת הַשֵּׁם the knowledge of Hebrew is strengthened through Hebrew names. Sixteen units of *Hebrew via Hebrew names* are included in the book.
- under the heading *Review and application of the rules* knowledge of, above all, the regular sound changes is applied to newly introduced forms and structures.
- Word list.
- Exercises: Morphological forms are drilled first, then syntactical structures are studied individually, followed by Hebrew-to-English translation exercises and then English-to-Hebrew translation. From Section 17 onward a broad-based grammatical analysis is applied to parts of the material in the exercises.

ON THE USE OF THE BOOK

As previously mentioned, this workbook can be used together with any textbook for beginners in Biblical Hebrew. However, several sections of the book (especially Sections 1–12) can be used more or less independently. Teachers are advised to concentrate on the workbook in teaching, using the textbook as a source for additional information and complete grammatical charts.

The material in each section of the book can be divided for use in multiple class sessions according to the needs of the class and the time at one's disposal. The wide variety and broad scope of the exercises give the teacher the advantage of choosing those which are suitable for his/her students, both as a group and individually.

The following types of exercises can easily be excluded or assigned only to certain students in the group: transliteration (Sections 1–7), review and application of the sound change rules (Sections 5–28, under the heading *Review and application of the rules*) and English-to-Hebrew translations (Sections 6–28).

ACKNOWLEDGEMENTS

I wish to express my sincere gratitude to Lena-Nogah Larson and my colleague Rosmari Lillas-Schuil for helpful suggestions and proof reading of this edition. Special thanks are due to Dr. Judith Josephson for revising my English.

Gothenburg 2004   NAVA BERGMAN

THE GRAMMATICAL CORNERSTONES IN THE BOOK

ABBREVIATIONS: NAMES OF THE BOOKS IN THE HEBREW BIBLE

Gen. – Genesis		בְּרֵאשִׁית
Ex. – Exodus		שְׁמוֹת
Lev. – Leviticus		וַיִּקְרָא
Num. – Numbers		בַּמִּדְבָּר
Dt. – Deuteronomy		דְּבָרִים
Jos. – Joshua		יְהוֹשֻׁעַ
Judg. – Judges		שׁוֹפְטִים
1 Sam. – 1 Samuel	*Áleph*	שְׁמוּאֵל א׳
2 Sam. – 2 Samuel	*Bet*	שְׁמוּאֵל ב׳
1 Kings	*Áleph*	מְלָכִים א׳
2 Kings	*Bet*	מְלָכִים ב׳
Isa. – Isaiah		יְשַׁעְיָהוּ
Jer. – Jeremiah		יִרְמְיָהוּ
Ezek. – Ezekiel		יְחֶזְקֵאל
Hos. – Hosea		הוֹשֵׁעַ
Joel		יוֹאֵל
Amos		עָמוֹס
Ob. – Obadiah		עוֹבַדְיָה
Jon. – Jonah		יוֹנָה
Mic. – Micah		מִיכָה
Nah. – Nahum		נַחוּם
Hab. – Habakkuk		חֲבַקּוּק
Zeph. – Zephaniah		צְפַנְיָה
Hag. – Haggai		חַגַּי
Zech. – Zechariah		זְכַרְיָה
Mal. – Malachi		מַלְאָכִי
Ps. – Psalms		תְּהִלִּים
Prov. – Proverbs		מִשְׁלֵי
Job		אִיּוֹב
Song – Song of Songs (Song of Solomon)		שִׁיר הַשִּׁירִים
Ruth		רוּת
Lam. – Lamentations		אֵיכָה
Ecc. – Ecclesiastes		קֹהֶלֶת
Esther		אֶסְתֵּר
Dan. – Daniel		דָּנִיֵּאל
Ezra		עֶזְרָא
Neh. – Nehemiah		נְחֶמְיָה
1 Chron. – 1 Chronicles	*Áleph*	דִּבְרֵי הַיָּמִים א׳
2 Chron. – 2 Chronicles	*Bet*	דִּבְרֵי הַיָּמִים ב׳

ABBREVIATIONS: GRAMMATICAL TERMS

adj	adjective
c	common (gender)
conj	conjunction
defin art	definite article
f	feminine
gen	gender
hiph	hiphil (the H-stem)
hitp	hitpael (the HtD-stem)
huph	huphal/hophal (the Hp-stem)
imperf	imperfect
infin	infinitive
inver imperf	inverted imperfect
m	masculine
niph	niphal (the N-stem)
num	number
p, pl	plural
part	participle
perf	perfect
pers	person
pers pron	personal pronoun
pi	piel (the D-stem)
pu	pual (the Dp-stem)
suff	suffix

SECTION 1

THE HEBREW ALPHABET

Numerical value	Transliteration	Pronunciation[1]	Final form	Form	Name[2]	
1	ʔ	silent/glottal stop		א	Áleph אָלֶף	1
2	b	b as in boy		בּ	Bet בֵּית	2
	v	v as in voice		ב		
3	g	g as in gate		ג/ג	Gímel גִּימֶל	3
4	d	d as in door		ד/ד	Dálet דָּלֶת	4
5	h	h as in head		ה	He הֵא	5
6	w	v as in voice		ו	Vav וָו	6
7	z	z as in zero		ז	Záyin זַיִן	7
8	ḥ	ch as in German Bach		ח	Chet חֵית	8
9	ṭ	t as in time		ט	Tet טֵית	9
10	y	y as in year		י	Yod יוֹד	10
20	k	k as in king		כּ	Kaph כַּף	11
	x	ch as in German Bach	ך	כ		
30	l	l as in life		ל	Lámed לָמֶד	12
40	m	m as in man	ם	מ	Mem מֵים	13
50	n	n as in name	ן	נ	Nun נוּן	14
60	s	s as in son		ס	Sámech סָמֶך	15
70	ʕ	silent/glottal stop		ע	Áyin עַיִן	16
80	p	p as in peace		פּ	Pe פֵּא	17
	f	ph as in phrase	ף	פ		
90	ṣ	ts as in hearts	ץ	צ	Tsádi צָדִי	18
100	q	q as in queen		ק	Qoph קוֹף	19
200	r	r as in road		ר	Resh רֵישׁ	20
300	ś	s as in son		שׂ	Sin שִׂין	21
	š	sh as in shame		שׁ	Shin שִׁין	
400	t	t as in time		ת/ת	Tav תָּו	22

אבגדהוזחטיכךלמםנןסעפףצץקרשׁשׂת

---

[1] This reflects the normal pronunciation of modern Hebrew.
[2] For the pronunciation of vowels, see the table on p. 8.

Observe the following:

1 Hebrew is written and read from right to left.
2 All the letters represent consonants.[3]
3 There are no capital letters in Hebrew.
4 Five letters have a special form at the end of a word: ך, ם, ן, ף, ץ.
5 The difference between the ordinary forms כ, נ, פ, צ and the final forms
   ך, ן, ף, ץ is that the lower horizontal stroke of the ordinary forms is written
   vertically and therefore extends below the line, for instance,
   כ /ch/ becomes ך   and נ /n/ becomes ן .
6 An inner dot results in a different pronunciation in only three of the letters:
   ב /v/ – בּ /b/, כ /ch/ – כּ /k/, פ /f/ – פּ /p/. The other letters have the same
   sound with or without the inner dot.[4]
7 Two Hebrew letters may share the same pronunciation, e.g., both ב and ו are
   pronounced /v/. This reflects the dissimilarity prevailing between sounds and
   spelling in Hebrew.

EXERCISES

1.1 *Identify* the Hebrew letters. *Compare* the relative size and shape of the
    letters in each group. *Circle* the letters which are identical with the outlined
    letter in each line. *Pronounce* all the letters. *Note*:

> ◆ Certain letters *look alike* and can easily be confused. The following
> features will help you to distinguish between similar letters: the length
> of the vertical stroke, the presence, absence or position of a dot, the
> length of the horizontal stroke, the difference in the shape of a corner.

a Letters are distinguished by the *length of the vertical stroke*:
   ד /r/ – ך final /ch/; ו /v/ – ן final /n/; י /y/ – ו /v/.

b Letters are distinguished by the *presence, absence or position of a dot*:
   פּ /p/ – פ /f/; שׁ /sh/ – שׂ /s/; בּ /b/ – ב /v/; כּ /k/ – כ /ch/.

---

[3] י, ו, ה function as vowel letters as well, see Section 2:3.

[4] Except ו, see below Hebrew vowels, p. 8.

c Letters are distinguished by the *length of the horizontal stroke*:

נ /n/ – כ /ch/; ו /v/ – ר /r/; final ן /n/ – final ך /ch/; ז /z/ – ד /d/.

(Hebrew letter practice rows)

d Letters are distinguished by *a difference in the shape of the corner*:

ח /ch/ – ה /h/; ת /t/ – ח /ch/; ס /s/ – final ם /m/; מ /m/ – ט /t/;
צ /ts/ – ע (silent); ו /v/ – ז /z/; ר /r/ – ד /d/; נ /n/ – ג /g/;
כ /ch/ – ב /v/; א (silent) – צ /ts/.

(Hebrew letter practice rows)

1.2 *Transliterate* the Hebrew words below. *Remember*:

- Most of the Hebrew letters are transliterated as they are pronounced, except the following letters:

Form	Translit.	Pronunciation	Form	Translit.	Pronun.	Form	Translit.	Pronun.
א	ʾ	silent	שׂ	ś	s	ח	ḥ	ch
ע	ʿ	silent	שׁ	š	sh	ט	ṭ	t
ו	w	v	כ	x	ch	צ	ṣ	ts

- Transliterated Hebrew is written from left to right.
- א and ע are described as silent letters. Nevertheless, they must be rendered in transliteration.

1 אלף בית גימל דלת הא וו זין חית טית יוד כף

2 למד מים נון סמך עין פא צדי קוף ריש שין שין תו

3 אדם יעקב דבורה חוה ישראל שמואל קין לאה אסף

4 רחל בית אל שם שמעון גד יפת חנה שאול עבר לוי

5 דוד אברהם יהודה אבשלום לוט יוסף נתן שרה בנימין

1.3 *Write* the following Hebrew letters.

You may choose between two sets of letters, a set of simplified *print letters* and a set of *script letters* (used normally in handwriting).

Simplified form of print letters

Fill in each line with the Hebrew letters. The arrows indicate the starting point and direction. *Follow* the arrows step by step before writing the whole letter. *Pronounce* each letter as you write it.

נ   א silent

                                              ב v

                                              ג g

                                              ד d

                                            ה h

                                              ו v

                                            ז z

                                            ח ch

                                            ט t

                                            י y

                                            כ ch

                                            ך ch

                                            ל l

                                            מ m

                                            ם m

                                            נ n

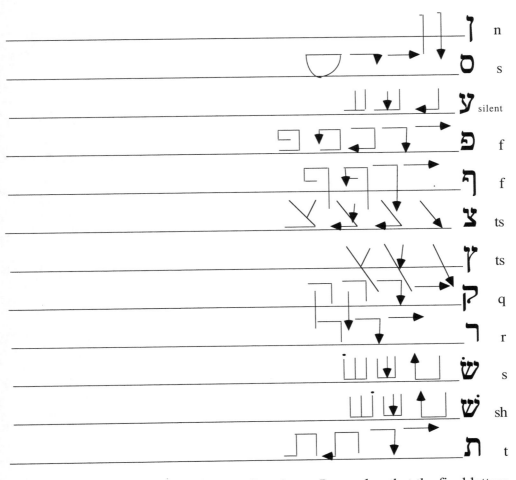

ן	n
ס	s
ע	silent
פ	f
ף	f
צ	ts
ץ	ts
ק	q
ר	r
שׂ	s
שׁ	sh
ת	t

1.4 *Write* the entire Hebrew alphabet five times. *Remember* that the final letters ץ ,ף ,ן ,ך and ק extend below the line whereas ל extends above the line. *Pronounce* each letter as you write it.

א ב ג ד ה ו ו ז ח ט י י כ ך ל מ ם נ ן ס ע פ ף צ ץ ק ר ש שׂ ת

Script letters

Arrows indicate where to start when you write each letter. *Observe* that all the letters begin either with the form c̗ , ı or 7 but the size and position of these forms vary.

	כֵ	כֵ	**א**	silent
	קֵ	בֵ	**ב**	v
	גֵ	ı	**ג**	g
		ר	**ד**	d
	הֵ	הֵ	**ה**	h
		ı	**ו**	v
	זֵ	ı	**ז**	z
	חֵ	ר	**ח**	ch
	ט	ı	**ט**	t
		ı	**י**	y
	כֵ	ר	**כ**	ch
	ךֵ	ר	**ך**	ch
	לֵ	כֵ	**ל**	l
	מ	ı	**מ**	m
	ק	ק	**ם**	m
	נ	ı	**נ**	n
		ן	**ן**	n

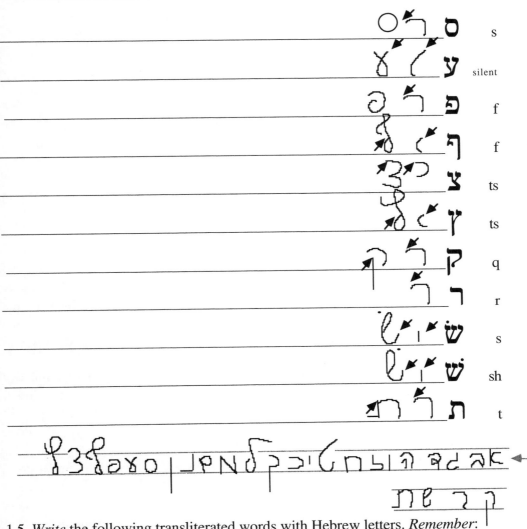

⃝ ⟍	⟨	**ס**	s
ע ⟨		**ע**	silent
⊃ ⟍		**פ**	f
⟨ ⟨		**ף**	f
⟨⊃		**צ**	ts
⟨ ⟨		**ץ**	ts
⟍ ⟍		**ק**	q
⟍		**ר**	r
ℓ⟍	⟍	**שׁ**	s
ℓ⟍	⟍	**שׁ**	sh
⟍ ⟍		**ת**	t

1.5 *Write* the following transliterated words with Hebrew letters. *Remember:*

> • Five letters have a special form at the end of a word: **כ** – **ך** /ch/,
> **מ** – **ם** /m/, **נ** – **ן** /n/, **פ** – **ף** /f/, **צ** – **ץ** /ts/.

1 nḥwm, yrwšlym, ʔmn, ʕmrm, šlm, ṣvʔwt, ywxvd, ywsf, khn, yhwntn, yhwšfṭ, qbwṣ, ptḥ tqwh, bʕl, ḥvrwn, ʔhymlx, ʕzh, rʔš pnh.

2 hllwyh, ʕmnwʔl, ṭvryh, šlwm, ʔfrym, bʔr švʕ, hr syny, mšnh, ḥzqyh, šwmrwn, tlmwd, ʕzyh, yʕl, yhwdyt, kfr nḥwm, hvh ngylh, byt ḥsdʔ.

3 yšy, ʔl ʕl, yzrʕʔl, yrdn, lwy, bryt mylh, lḥyym, mswrh, bt švʕ, yhwdh ʔyš qrywt, śdh bwqr, bny bryt, br mṣwh, glglt (glgtʔ), lmh ʕzvtny.

THE HEBREW VOWEL SIGNS AND THEIR PRONUNCIATION[5]

Vowel sound	Vowel sign (with the letter ח , pronounced /ch/)
1) /a/ as in Bathsheba	חָי/חָ/חַ
2) /e/ as in Israel	חֵי/חֶי/חֵ/חֶ
3) /i/ as in Israel	חִי/חִ
4) /o/ as in Joshua	חוֹ/חֹ/ חָ/חֳ
5) /u/ as in Joshua	חוּ/חֻ
no-vowel, zero	חְ

1 There are five vowel sounds in Hebrew. As you can see in the table above there is no agreement between the number of the vowel sounds (five) and the number of the vowel signs (seventeen above). Several vowel signs share the same pronunciation, for example, the /a/-vowel in כָּתַב katav and the /e/-vowel in עֶבֶר ʕever. Nevertheless, the vowel signs are not interchangeable.

2 The vowel sign is placed below the letter (הָגָר hagar) except for וּ /u/ and וֹ /o/ which are placed after the letter (קִבּוּץ qibbuṣ, יוֹסֵף yoseph) and the vowel ◌ֹ /o/ which is placed above and slightly left of the letter (לֹמֵד lomed).

3 A vowel sign may be followed by the letter י Yod . The presence of י Yod does not affect the sound of the vowel:[6] בֵּית אֵל bet ʔel.

4 The letter ו Vav may be combined with a vowel sign. ו Vav with an upper dot וֹ is pronounced /o/ (not 'vo'). ו Vav with an inner dot וּ (without a following vowel sign) is pronounced /u/ (not 'vu'): רוּת rut. The presence of ו Vav does not affect the sound of the vowel, e.g., both לוֹט and לֹט are pronounced 'lot'.

5 The letter ה He at the end of a word is silent: שָׂרָה śara.

6 The letter א Áleph without a following vowel sign is silent: עֶזְרָא ʕezra, יִשְׁמָעֵאל yišmaʕel.

7 In Hebrew there is a sign for no-vowel (◌ְ) which is used when a vowelless letter occurs at the beginning or in the middle of a word: שְׁמוּאֵל šmuʔel (instead of שֱׁמוּאֵל), יִשְׂרָאֵל yiśraʔel (instead of יִשְׂרָאֵל). A vowelless letter at the end of a word is normally not marked. One exception is the final letter ךְ /ch/: אַךְ ʔax.[7]

---

5 This reflects the normal pronunciation of modern Hebrew.

6 With a few exceptions which will be introduced later.

7 Another exception is תְ at the end of a word.

EXERCISES

1.6 *Read aloud. Combine* letters (consonants)[8] and vowels into syllables. *Note*:

> ◆ A syllable must begin with a consonant and should include one vowel.
> ◆ The consonant is pronounced first, followed by the vowel. הָגָר is to be pronounced h+a+g+a+r.
> ◆ The main *stress* in Hebrew usually falls on the last syllable, but sometimes on the next-to-last syllable. Stress on the last syllable is not marked: שָׁלוֹם šalóm. Stress on the next-to-last syllable is marked by the sign ⬚ above the stressed syllable: קַיִן qáyin.
> ◆ An *inner dot* in a letter does not change the pronunciation, except in ב /b/, כ /k/, פ /p/ and ו /u/ (when ו is not followed by a vowel sign).
> ◆ א *Áleph*, ה *He* and י *Yod* without a following vowel sign are silent.[9]
> ◆ א *Áleph* and ע *Áyin* without a following vowel sign are not audible. When א *Áleph* and ע *Áyin* are followed by a vowel, only the vowel is pronounced: אָב av.

a In this group of words only **the vowel /a/** is used.

הַר	תָּו	כַּף	וָו	דָּן	חַג	אָב 1
שָׁנָה	נָתַן	רַב	נָא	יָד	גַּם	אַף 2
שָׂפָה	רָעָב	אָדָם	חָכָם	לָבָן	שָׂרָה	הָגָר 3
חַמָּה	עַזָּה	אַתָּה	צָבָא	יָשָׁר	אָסָף	שַׁבָּת 4
חָכְמָה	אֲדָמָה	חַוָּה	זָהָב	אָמָה	חַנָּה	רָשָׁע 5
תַּחַת	שַׁעַר	נַעַר	בַּעַל	יַחַד	חַטָּאת	אַהֲבָה 6

b In this group of words **the vowels /a/ and /e/** are used.

בֵּית	שֵׁם	שָׁלֵם	אָמֵן	בֵּן	תֵּל	עֵת 1
אֵת	רֵישׁ	פֵּא	מֵים	טִית	חֵית	הֵא 2
יָעֵל	רָחֵל	לֵאָה	עֵשָׂו	פֶּה	זָקֵן	עֵת 3
יֶלֶד	כֶּסֶף	כֶּלֶב	דֶּלֶת	בֵּית אֵל	אֵיכָה	אֱמֶת 4
רֶגֶל	הֶבֶל	סֵפֶר	יֶפֶת	אֶבֶן	פֶּתַח	עֵבֶר 5
בֵּית לֶחֶם	בַּת שֶׁבַע	לָמֵד	דֶּלֶת	אָלֶף	פֶּסַח 6

---

[8] The word 'consonant' indicates the sound of a written letter.
[9] There are a few exceptions for י, but none of these exceptions occur in this exercise.

c In this group of words **the vowels /a/, /e/ and /i/** are used.

שִׁיר	עִיר	מִן	מִי	לִי	כִּי	בִּי 1←
דָוִד	לֵוִי	הִיא	עִם	אִם	אִישׁ	סִיר 2
חַיִּים	מִיכָה	מִלָּה	מִילָה	מִיכָאֵל	נָבִיא	אִשָּׁה 3
בַּיִת	אַיִן	חַיִל	אֵלֶיהָ	אֲנָשִׁים	צַדִּיקִים	צַדִּיק 4

d In this group of words **the vowels /a/, /e/, /i/ and /o/** are used. *Note:*

- The vowel sign ⟨ ָ ⟩ is to be pronounced /a/ throughout this section.
- The letter שׁ *Shin* shares its upper dot with a preceding /o/-vowel, e.g.,
  מֹשֶׁה *moše*, and the letter שׂ *Sin* with a following /o/-vowel: שׂנֵא *śone*.

יוֹד	דּוֹר	אוֹר	קוֹל	לוֹ	כֹּה	בּוֹ 1←
חֹק	כֹּל	דּוֹרוֹת	עוֹד	טוֹב	לוֹט	קוֹף 2
יוֹם	אוֹרוֹת	קוֹלוֹת	מָקוֹם	שָׁלוֹם	קָטֹן	טוֹבָה 3
אוֹתִי	אָדוֹן	מֹשֶׁל	מֶשֶׁךְ	שׁוֹפֵט	טוֹבִים	כּוֹכָב 4
כֹּהֵן	כָּבוֹד	קָדוֹשׁ	פֹּה	גָּדוֹל	יוֹנָה	תּוֹרָה 5
שֹׂבַע	אֹזֶן	עֹשֶׂק	אֱנוֹשׁ	אָמוֹץ	יוֹחָנָן	רֹאשׁ 6

e In this group of words **the vowels /a/, /e/, /i/, /o/ and /u/** are used.

גּוּר	כֻּלָּם	חֻקִּים	כָּתוּב	תַּמּוּז	שָׁאוּל	צוּר 1←
הוּא	פּוּרִים	חֲנֻכָּה	סֻכּוֹת	עִמָּנוּאֵל	קִבּוּץ	נַחוּם 2
לוּ	אֲנַחְנוּ	כֻּלָּנוּ	אֵלִיָּהוּ	יוֹם כִּפּוּר	שָׁבוּעוֹת	אֱלוּל 3

1.7 *Read aloud* the following proper names (names of persons and places). *Note:*

- Since several Hebrew names are pronounced differently in English, the
  English counterparts of the Hebrew names are given in the Key.
- The vowel sign ⟨ ְ ⟩ indicates no-vowel: יִשְׂרָאֵל *yiśraʔel*.

קַיִן	שְׁמוּאֵל	יִשְׂרָאֵל	חַוָּה	דְּבוֹרָה	יַעֲקֹב	אָדָם 1←
שֵׁם	שִׁמְעוֹן	בֵּית אֵל	רָחֵל	הֶבֶל	אָסָף	לֵאָה 2

3 חַנָּה יֶפֶת אַבְרָהָם שָׁאוּל עֵבֶר מֹשֶׁה גַּד

4 יְהוּדָה אַבְשָׁלוֹם יוֹסֵף שְׁלֹמֹה שָׂרָה בִּנְיָמִין נָתָן

5 הָגָר אֲבִימֶּלֶךְ יִצְחָק פַּרְעֹה חִזְקִיָּה לֶמֶךְ לֵוִי

6 יוֹחָנָן לָבָן מִרְיָם צִדְקִיָּהוּ רִבְקָה כְּנַעַן עֵשָׂו

7 מִיכָאֵל מְנַשֶּׁה יִשְׁמָעֵאל בֵּית לֶחֶם

1.8 *Rewrite*[10] the words in the tables below *and read aloud. Distinguish* between the similar letters.

Observe the length of the vertical stroke				
final /ch/ ך	/r/ ר	final /n/ ן	/v/ ו	/y/ י
לָךְ	תּוֹרָה	דָּן	תָּו	יָעֵל
אַךְ	רוּת	נָתָן	לֵוִי	יַרְדֵּן
בָּךְ	אֶסְתֵּר	יַרְדֵּן	חַוָּה	יוֹנָה

Observe the length of the horizontal strokes								
/d/ ד	/z/ ז	final /ch/ ך	final /n/ ן	/ch/ כ	/n/ נ	/r/ ר	/v/ ו	
דָּוִד	זֶה	לָךְ	נָתָן	מִיכָה	נָתָן	רָחֵל	עֵשָׂו	
דָּן	זֹאת	אַךְ	כֵּן	אֵיכָה	יוֹנָה	שָׂרָה	דָּוִד	
תּוֹדָה	מַזָּל	בָּךְ	דָּן	מְלָכִים	נַחוּם	יִשְׂרָאֵל	וָו	

---

[10] 'Rewrite' in this book means 'copy, reproduce exactly'.

Observe the difference in the shape of the corner							
/v/ ו	/z/ ז	/s/ ס	final ם /m/	/m/ מ	/t/ ט	/ch/ כ	/v/ ב
דָּוִד	מִזְרָח	עָמוֹס	שֵׁם	מָן	טוֹב	מַלְכוּ	לָבָן
לֵוִי	זֹאת	יוֹסֵף	שָׁלוֹם	מִשְׁנָה	לוֹט	מִיכָה	הֶבֶל
חַוָּה	מַזָּל	אֶסְתֵּר	מִרְיָם	תַּלְמוּד	טְבֶרְיָה	הָלְכָה	צְבָאוֹת

Observe the difference in the shape of the corner							
/d/ ד	/r/ ר	silent ע	/ts/ צ	silent א	/t/ ת	/ch/ ח	/h/ ה
אָדוֹן	רַב	עוֹד	צוּר	אַבְרָהָם	יְהוּדִית	רָחֵל	הָגָר
דְּבָרִים	רַבִּי	עַד	יִצְחָק	אֲנִי	עִבְרִית	חַנָּה	יְהוּדָה
דּוֹר	הַר	מַעֲרָב	צְבָאוֹת	צְבָאוֹת	תַּלְמוּד	חֲבַקּוּק	כֹּהֵן

1.9 *Rewrite* the names of the letters in the Hebrew alphabet on page 1 and *read aloud. Note*:

> ◆ The original Hebrew alphabet consisted of consonants only, whereas vowels were not represented in writing. The sign of each Hebrew letter was originally pictorial, representing something concrete and familiar whose initial sound indicates the sound of the letter. Thus, for instance, the picture of a head (in Hebrew רֹאשׁ **roš**) represents the sound **/r/**, the picture of a door (in Hebrew דלת **délet**) the sound **/d/** and the picture of a monkey (in Hebrew קוֹף **qof**) the sound **/q/**.

SECTION 2

1 *Dissimilarity between sounds and spelling*
   – Six pairs of letters in the Hebrew alphabet sound alike. Both ב and ו are
   pronounced /v/, ט and ת /t/, כ and ק /k/, ס and שׂ /s/, ח and כ /ch/ and א
   and ע are both silent letters.[1] The identically sounding letters are, however,
   not interchangeable.
   – Four single letters in the Hebrew alphabet have two alternative sounds,
   which is shown in writing either by the presence or absence of an inner dot,
   בּ /b/ – ב /v/, כּ /k/ – כ /ch/, פּ /p/ – פ /f/, or by the position of an upper dot,
   שׁ /sh/ – שׂ /s/.
2 *Dagesh*: The inner dot in a letter is called dagesh. It indicates either the *hard
   pronunciation* of a consonant (the *hardening dagesh*) and/or the *doubling* of
   a consonant (the *doubling dagesh*).
   – The hardening dagesh (*dagesh lene*) may appear in only six consonants:
   בּ /b/, גּ /g/, דּ /d/, כּ /k/, פּ /p/, תּ /t/. The term *BeGaDKeFaT* will help you to
   memorize these six consonants.
   – The doubling dagesh (*dagesh forte*) may appear in all consonants, except
   the gutturals (originally throat sounds: א *Áleph*, ה *He*, ח *Chet*, ע *Áyin*) and ר
   Resh. A doubled consonant is pronounced as a single one in modern Hebrew.
   – In modern Hebrew the presence of a dagesh, whether doubling or hardening,
   indicates a different sound in only three letters, ב /b/, כ /k/ and פ /p/, whereas
   a dagesh in any other letter does not change its sound.
3 *Vowel letters* ה *He*, ו *Vav* and י *Yod (matres lectionis)*: The letters ה *He*, ו *Vav*
   and י *Yod* function either as consonants (/h/, /v/ and /y/) or as vowel letters.
   – ה *He* at the end of a word (without a following vowel sign) is silent, since it
   functions as a vowel letter: חַנָּה ḥanna.
   – ו *Vav* with an inner dot וּ (without a following vowel sign) functions as an
   /u/-vowel: שָׁאוּל ša?ul. ו *Vav* with an upper dot וֹ functions as an /o/-vowel:
   שָׁלוֹם šalom.
   – י *Yod* without a following vowel sign functions as a vowel letter (except after
   /a/-, /o/- and /u/-vowels at the end of a word, see 5 below): שִׁיר šir, מִשְׁלֵי
   mišle.
4 *Silent* א *Áleph*: א *Áleph* without a following vowel sign is not audible, e.g.,
   עֶזְרָא ʕezra.
5 *Diphthongs* (vowel + the consonant י/ו *Vav/Yod*)
   – The letter י *Yod* at the *end of a word* after /a/-, /o/- and /u/-vowels (but not
   after /i/- and /e/-vowels!) functions as a consonant. The consonant י *Yod* forms,
   together with the preceding vowel, a diphthong: חַי ḥay, גוֹי goy, גָּלוּי galuy.

---

[1] This reflects the normal pronunciation of modern Hebrew. Two pairs of letters, ע–א and
   כ–ח, do not sound alike in the Sephardic pronunciation of modern Hebrew.

– The letter וֹ *Vav* was originally pronounced /w/ (not /v/ as in modern Hebrew). The letter וֹ *Vav* at the *end of a word* also functions as a consonant. וֹ *Vav* (pronounced /w/) forms, together with the preceding vowel, a diphthong: עֵשָׂו ʕeśaw, אָבִיו ʔaviw.

6 *Word stress*: The main *stress* in Hebrew usually falls on the last syllable (*ultima*), e.g., שָׁלוֹם šalóm, but sometimes it falls on the next-to-last syllable (*penultima*): קַיִן qáyin.

EXERCISES

2.1 *Rewrite* the words in the tables below and *read aloud*. *Distinguish* between the identically sounding letters. *Remember*:

> • Six pairs of letters sound alike. They have different forms but similar sound.

Both pronounced /k/		Both pronounced /t/		Both pronounced /v/	
ק	כ	ת	ט	ו	ב
קִבּוּץ	כְּפַר נַחוּם	בְּרֵאשִׁית	שׁוֹפְטִים	וַיִּקְרָא	דְּבָרִים
וַיִּקְרָא	כֹּהֵן	תַּלְמוּד	טְבֶרְיָה	לֵוִי	צְבָאוֹת
קֹהֶלֶת	כְּתוּבִים	תְּהִלִּים	שָׂטָן	חַוָּה	הָבָה נָגִילָה

Both pronounced /ch/		Both are silent letters		Both pronounced /s/	
כ	ח	ע	א	שׂ	ס
מַלְאָכִי	נַחוּם	שִׁמְעוֹן	שְׁמוּאֵל	שָׂטָן	מְסוֹרָה
שְׁכֶם	אֲחִימֶלֶךְ	עֶזְרָא	יוֹאֵל	שָׂרָה	עָמוֹס
זְכַרְיָה	נְחֶמְיָה	עוֹבַדְיָה	אֵיכָה	יִשְׂרָאֵל	בֵּית חֶסְדָּא

2.2 *Rewrite* the words in the following table and *read aloud*. *Distinguish* between hard and soft pronunciation of ב, כ, פ. *Remember*:

> • Hard pronunciation (/b/, /k/ and /p/) is shown in writing by the presence of the hardening dagesh (dagesh lene).
> • ב, כ, פ with a doubling dagesh (dagesh forte) are also hardened in pronunciation.

פ		כ		ב	
/f/ = פ	/p/ = פּ	/ch/ = כ	/k/ = כּ	/v/ = ב	/b/ = בּ
צְפַנְיָה	פִּנְחָס	מְלָכִים	כְּתוּבִים	חֶבְרוֹן	בַּר מִצְוָה
שׁוֹפְטִים	פִּנָּה	מִיכָה	כֹּהֵן	נְבִיאִים	בֵּית אֵל
אֶפְרַיִם	תֻּפִּים	אֵיכָה	מַכָּה	דְּבָרִים	שַׁבָּת

2.3 *Write* the following words with Hebrew letters. *Use* the chart of the Hebrew alphabet (column marked transliteration) on page 1. *Add* the hardening dagesh in בּ, כּ, פּ whenever necessary. *Remember*:

> * The identically sounding letters are not interchangeable.
> * Five letters have a special form at the end of a word: כ – ך /x/, מ – ם /m/, נ – ן /n/, פ – ף /f/, צ – ץ /ś/.

1 dbr ʔl ʔhrn wʔl bnyw lʔmr kh tvrxw ʔt bny yśrʔl ʔmwr lhm. yvrxx YHWH wyšmrx. yʔr YHWH pnyw ʔlyx wyḥnk. yśʔ YHWH pnyw ʔlyx wyśm lx šlwm. wśmw ʔt šmy ʕl bny yśrʔl wʔny ʔvrxm.

2 lkl zmn wʕt lxl ḥfṣ tḥt hšmym. ʕt lldt wʕt lmwt. ʕt lhrwg wʕt lrpwʔ. ʕt lšmwr wʕt lhšlyx. ʕt lʔhv wʕt lśnʔ. ʕt mlḥmh wʕt šlwm.

3 whyh bʔḥryt hymym nxwn yhyh hr byt YHWH brʔš hrym wnśʔ mgvʕwt wnhrw ʔlyw kl hgwym. whlxw ʕmym rbym wʔmrw lxw wnʕlh ʔl hr YHWH ʔl byt ʔlhy yʕqv wywrnw mdrxyw wnlxh bʔrḥtyw ky mṣywn tṣʔ twrh wdvr YHWH myrwšlm. wšfṭ byn hgwym whwxyḥ lʕmym rbym wxttw ḥrvwtm lʔtym wḥnytwtyhm lmzmrwt. lʔ yśʔ gwy ʔl gwy ḥrv wlʔ ylmdw ʕwd mlḥmh.

2.4 *Identify* the type of dagesh in the following words. *Mark* a hardening dagesh (dagesh lene) with one stroke and a doubling dagesh (dagesh forte) with two strokes. *Read aloud. Note*:

> * A hardening dagesh may appear in only six letters, the BeGaDKeFaT-letters.
> * A hardening dagesh in ב, ג, ד, כ, פ, ת is never preceded by a vowel (that is, it occurs either at the beginning of a word or, inside a word, after a consonant with the sign for no-vowel, ְ).
> * A doubling dagesh is always preceded by a vowel.

1 תּוֹרָה   דְּבָרִים   שִׁיר הַשִּׁירִים   בְּרֵאשִׁית   חֲבַקּוּק   דִּבְרֵי הַיָּמִים

2 תְּהִלִּים   חַגַּי   וַיִּקְרָא   אִיּוֹב   בַּמִּדְבָּר   אֶסְתֵּר

2.5 *Identify* and *mark* ה *He,* ו *Vav* and ' *Yod* functioning as vowel letters in the following words. *Read aloud. Remember*:

> ◆ ו *Vav* as a vowel letter is combined with a dot, וֹ /o/ or וּ /u/.
> ◆ Vowel letters are distinguished from ה *He,* ו *Vav* and ' *Yod* as consonants by the absence of a following vowel/vowel sign.[2]

1► יְהוּדִית   כְּפַר נַחוּם   יוֹכֶבֶד   צִדְקִיָּהוּ   יַרְדֵּן   צְפַנְיָה   שִׁמְשׁוֹן

2   פֶּתַח תִּקְוָה   צְבָאוֹת   אֲחִימֶלֶךְ   לֵוִי   מִשְׁנָה   שָׁלוֹם   יָעֵל

3   יְהוֹנָתָן   מְנַשֶּׁה   יוֹנָה   וַיִּקְרָא   שִׁיר הַשִּׁירִים

2.6 *Rewrite* the following words and *read aloud. Identify* the diphthongs (vowel + '/ו *Vav/Yod*). *Note*:

> ◆ Diphthongs are rare in Hebrew and normally occur at the end of a word.

Vowel + /w/ ו		Vowel + /y/ '		
/i/ + ו	/a/ + ו	/u/ + '	/o/ + '	/a/ + '
אָחִיו	יָדָיו	בָּנוּי	גּוֹי	חַי
אָבִיו	צַו	עָשׂוּי	אוֹי	אוּלַי
פִּיו	יַחְדָּו	רָאוּי	אֲבוֹי	אֲדֹנָי

2.7 *Read aloud* the following proper names/well-known Hebrew words over and over again, until you can read them rather easily. *Note*:

> ◆ Since several Hebrew names are pronounced differently in English, the English counterparts of the Hebrew names are given in the Key.

1► יְרוּשָׁלַיִם   אָמֵן   בַּת שֶׁבַע   מָסוֹרָה   שָׁלֵם   כֹּהֵן   יְהוֹנָתָן

2   יְהוֹשָׁפָט   קִבּוּץ   בַּעַל   בַּר מִצְוָה   אֲחִימֶלֶךְ   עַזָּה   עִמָּנוּאֵל

3   אֶפְרַיִם   בְּאֵר שֶׁבַע   סִינַי   מִשְׁנָה   שׁוֹמְרוֹן   תַּלְמוּד   עֻזִּיָּה

4   יָעֵל   יְהוּדִית   כְּפַר נַחוּם   הָבָה נָגִילָה   יִשַׁי   אֵל עַל   יַרְדֵּן

5   בְּרִית מִילָה   חֶבְרוֹן   לָמָה עֲזַבְתַּנִי

---

[2] An exception to this rule is a diphthong at the end of a word, see Exercise 2.6. However, no diphthongs occur in this exercise.

2.8 *Read aloud* the Hebrew names of the books in the Hebrew Bible. *Note*:

> • סֵפֶר הַסְּפָרִים is the Book of Books. The initial letters of the titles of the three parts of the Bible according to Jewish tradition are
> ת, נ, כ, pronounced הָ נָ תָּ **TaNaCH**.

(III) Writings כְּתוּבִים	(II) Prophets נְבִיאִים	(I) Law תּוֹרָה ◄
Psalms תְּהִלִּים	Joshua יְהוֹשֻׁעַ	Genesis בְּרֵאשִׁית literally: In the beginning
Proverbs מִשְׁלֵי	Judges שׁוֹפְטִים	Exodus שְׁמוֹת literally: Names
Job אִיּוֹב	1 Samuel שְׁמוּאֵל א׳ (א׳ = *Áleph*)	Leviticus וַיִּקְרָא literally: He called
Song of Songs שִׁיר הַשִּׁירִים	2 Samuel שְׁמוּאֵל ב׳ (ב׳ = *Bet*)	Numbers בַּמִּדְבָּר literally: In the desert/wilderness
Ruth רוּת	1 Kings מְלָכִים א׳	Deuteronomy דְּבָרִים literally: Words
Lamentations, literally: How אֵיכָה	2 Kings מְלָכִים ב׳	
Ecclesiastes, lit.: Preacher קֹהֶלֶת	Isaiah יְשַׁעְיָהוּ	
Esther אֶסְתֵּר	Jeremiah יִרְמְיָהוּ	
Daniel דָּנִיֵּאל	Ezekiel יְחֶזְקֵאל	
Ezra עֶזְרָא	Hosea הוֹשֵׁעַ	
Nehemiah נְחֶמְיָה	Joel יוֹאֵל	
1 Chronicles דִּבְרֵי הַיָּמִים א׳	Amos עָמוֹס	
2 Chronicles דִּבְרֵי הַיָּמִים ב׳ literally: Words/matters of the days	Obadiah עוֹבַדְיָה	
	Jonah יוֹנָה	
	Micah מִיכָה	
	Nahum נַחוּם	
	Habakkuk חֲבַקּוּק	
	Zephaniah צְפַנְיָה	
	Haggai חַגַּי	
	Zechariah זְכַרְיָה	
	Malachi מַלְאָכִי	

☆ ¹עִבְרִית בְּעֶזְרַת הַשֵּׁם ☆

The Western cultural heritage contains a nucleus that can facilitate studies of Hebrew. Well-known biblical personal names, place names and familiar Hebrew concepts and phrases, which in the course of history have been integrated into Western languages, constitute a potential gold-mine worthy of special attention. Vocabulary and grammatical structures will become more accessible if you take advantage of this readily available but often neglected resource. The material referred to as 'Hebrew names' is utilized throughout this book to enrich your knowledge of the language.

You are expected to use HEBREW NAMES AS FAMILIAR SIGNPOSTS to memorize new vocabulary and strengthen grammatical knowledge.

You have already encountered many Hebrew names, including the names of the letters of the Hebrew alphabet and the names of the books in the Hebrew Bible, in Sections 1 and 2.² Every section in this book, from Section 3 onward, includes a word list. Words that can be associated with well-known Hebrew names will be followed by the Hebrew name as pronounced in English in parentheses, preceded by a star symbol, e.g., אֵל 'god/God' (☆ Israel).

Observe that Hebrew names may be pronounced differently in English, e.g.,
– ב /v/ may be pronounced as /b/: אַבְרָהָם (Abraham).
– Gutturals (א, ה, ח, ע) are often left unpronounced: אָדָם (Adam), יְהוּדִית (Judith), יִצְחָק (Isaac), עָמוֹס (Amos).
   When the guttural ה survives, it is often pronounced as /h/: חַנָּה (Hannah).
– י /y/ is either left unpronounced, e.g., יִצְחָק (Isaac), or pronounced as /j/: יַרְדֵּן (Jordan).
– שׁ /š/ may be pronounced as /s/: שְׁמוּאֵל (Samuel).
– צ /s/ may be pronounced either as /s/, e.g., יִצְחָק (Isaac) or as /z/: צְפַנְיָה (Zephaniah).

The main points of grammar and exercises based on Hebrew names are scattered throughout this book under the title HEBREW VIA HEBREW NAMES. A comprehensive list and further exercises based on Hebrew names are found in APPENDIX I.

---

¹ עִבְרִית בְּעֶזְרַת הַשֵּׁם literally means 'Hebrew with the help of the name'. The word הַשֵּׁם 'the Name' is used by orthodox Jews as a substitute for the sacred name YHWH (the LORD), thus עִבְרִית בְּעֶזְרַת הַשֵּׁם also means 'Hebrew with the help of the LORD'.
² For the names of the Hebrew letters, see also Section 13, p. 101.

SECTION 3

1 *"Long" and "Short" Vowels*: Hebrew vowels are traditionally divided into two sets, *long and short*. However, the distinction between the two sets of vowels is probably not really one of length. The distinction has rather to do with the position of the vowel/s in relation to the stress in the word, mainly whether a vowel occurs in a stressed or an unstressed syllable. Nevertheless, since the two sets of vowels are not interchangeable, the designation long and short vowels will be retained in this book.

2 *Vowel categories*: Vowels are divided into three categories, consisting of corresponding long and short vowels in each category: A-vowels: ◌ָ ◌ַ , I/E-vowels: ◌ֵ ◌ֶ / ◌ִ , U/O-vowels: ◌וֹ ◌ֻ / ◌ָ .

3 *Full and simple vowels*: A full vowel (*plene* vowel) is a vowel written with both a vowel sign and a vowel letter (ה *He*, ו *Vav*, י *Yod*). Full vowels are regarded as long. A simple vowel is a vowel written with a vowel sign only (either long or short).

4 *Transliteration of vowels*: A long vowel is rendered in transliteration by a horizontal stroke above the vowel, for instance, נָתַן nātān, whereas a short vowel is not marked: עַם ʕam.

– The vowel letter י *Yod* (indicating an /i/- or /ē/-vowel) and the vowel letter ו *Vav* (indicating an /o/- or /u/-vowel) are rendered by a circumflex: לִי lî, בֵּית bêt, לוֹ lô, לוּ lû.

– The vowel letter י *Yod* (indicating an /ā/- or /e/-vowel), the vowel letter ה *He* and silent א *Áleph* (א with no following vowel sign) are rendered by a reduced and raised form: בָּנָיו bānāʸw, בָּנֶיהָ bāneʸhā, שָׂרָה śarā ͪ, עֶזְרָא ʕezrā ʾ.

5 *Shva (sheva, no-vowel)*: A vowelless consonant at the beginning and in the middle of a word is marked by a sign indicating absence of vowel, called *shva* ◌ְ . There are two types of shva:

– *Silent shva* (the original no-vowel), which marks the original absence of a vowel (i.e., a vowel has never existed in the position in question). Silent shva is not rendered in transliteration: אֶסְתֵּר ʔestēr.

– *Vocal shva* (shva-reduced-vowel), which marks the reduction of an original vowel (i.e., a vowel did exist but has been eliminated).[1] Vocal shva is rendered in transliteration by a reduced and raised form: דְּבָרִים dᵊvārîm.

6 *Supporting vowels for gutturals* (א *Áleph*, ה *He*, ח *Chet*, ע *Áyin*): A few vowel signs have been tailored for vowelless gutturals to facilitate their pronunciation.

– *Chateph* (shva-plus-vowel): Chateph is a shva sign combined with a short vowel, either /a/, /e/ or /o/. A guttural normally takes a chateph instead of a shva. Chateph is rendered in transliteration by a reduced and raised form: אֲבִימֶלֶךְ ʔᵃvîmelex, יַעֲקֹב yaʕᵃqōv, אֱלִיעֶזֶר ʔᵉlîʕezer, חֳדָשִׁים ḥᵒdāšîm.

---

[1] See Vowel reduction in Section 5:3.

– *The glide sound /a/ (furtive patach,* subsequently called *glide-/a/*): When a vowelless ‏ח‎ *Chet* or ‏ע‎ *Áyin* (and rarely the consonant ‏ה‎ *He*) at the end of a word is not preceded by an /a/-vowel, an additional /a/ is inserted before them. This additional (unstressed!) /a/ is written below ‏ח‎ *Chet* or ‏ע‎ *Áyin* but pronounced before them. This glide-/a/ is rendered in transliteration by a reduced and lowered form: ‏מָשִׁיחַ‎ māšiₐh, ‏הוֹשֵׁעַ‎ hôšēₐ ʕ, ‏נֹחַ‎ nōₐh.

7 *Relationship between consonants and vowels*: Certain consonants attract certain vowels since they are formed close to each other in the speech apparatus. Gutturals (‏ה‎ *He,* ‏ח‎ *Chet,* ‏ע‎ *Áyin*) often attract an /a/-vowel/s, for example, ‏בַּעַל‎ baʕal, whereas ‏י‎ *Yod* attracts an /i/-vowel: ‏קַיִן‎ qáyin.

8 *Verbless clause*: In Hebrew there are clauses with *no verb*, e.g., ‏אֲנִי כֹהֵן‎ ‘I [am/was/will be] a priest' (more about verbless clauses in Exercise 3.4).

9 *Independent personal pronouns in singular* (see word list below).

The Hebrew Vowels

Form	Transliteration	Pronunciation
‏יָ‎	āʸ	
‏הָ‎ (only at the end of a word)	āʰ	/a/ as in Bathsheba
‏ָ‎	ā	
‏ַ‎	a	
‏ֲ‎	ₐ	
‏ַ‎ (before ‏ה, ע‎ at the end of a word)	ₐ—	(glide-/a/ as in Joshua)
‏יֵ‎	ê	
‏הֵ‎ (only at the end of a word)	ēʰ	
‏ֵ‎	ē	
‏יֶ‎	eʸ	/e/ as in Israel
‏הֶ‎ (only at the end of a word)	eʰ	
‏ֶ‎	e	
‏ֱ‎	ₑ	
‏יִ‎	î	/i/ as in Israel
‏ִ‎	i	
‏וֹ‎, ‏ֹ‎	ô	
‏הֹ‎ (only at the end of a word)	ōʰ	
‏ֹ‎	ō	/o/ as in Joshua
‏ָ‎	o	
‏ֳ‎	ₒ	
‏וּ‎	û	/u/ as in Joshua
‏ֻ‎	u	
‏ְ‎ (no-vowel)	zero (not rendered)/ə	silent or a short /e/

MEMORIZE

Vowel category	LONG AND SHORT SIMPLE VOWELS	
	Long vowels	Short vowels
A	◌ָ	◌ַ
I/E	◌ֵ	◌ֶ / ◌ִ
U/O	◌ֹ	◌ָ / ◌ֻ

GRAMMATICAL CORNERSTONE 1[2] רֹאשׁ פִּנָּה

REVIEW AND APPLICATION OF THE RULES[3]

I *Match* each sound element with the Hebrew word that illustrates it. *Mark* the element in the Hebrew word clearly! Observe that the same sound element may appear in more than one word, but only one element is to be marked. Each word is to be used once!

1 Long vowel, ◌ֵ ◌ַ ◌ָ   ( ) דָּוִד

2 Short vowel, ◌ַ ◌ֶ ◌ִ ◌ֵ   ( ) לוֹט

3 Full vowel *Written with both a vowel sign and a vowel letter*   ( ) עַזָּה
   (ה *He,* ו *Vav,* י *Yod*)

4 Shva *Sign for no-vowel*   ( ) כֹּחַ

5 Chateph (shva-plus-vowel) *Supporting vowel for gutturals*   ( ) יָד
   (א *Áleph,* ה *He,* ח *Chet,* ע *Áyin*)

6 Glide-/a/ *Additional /a/-vowel before* ח *Chet or* ע *Áyin*   ( ) שְׁמוּאֵל
   at the end of a word

7 Hardening dagesh *Occurs in BeGaDKeFaT-consonants*   ( ) סִינַי
   only; never preceded by a vowel

8 Doubling dagesh *Always preceded by a vowel*   ( ) אֱלוּל

9 Silent א *Áleph,* א *is written but not pronounced*   ( ) שַׂעַר

10 Diphthong *A vowel followed by the consonant*   ( ) רֹאשׁ
   ו *Vav or* י *Yod at the end of a word*

---

[2] רֹאשׁ פִּנָּה means 'cornerstone', lit., 'head of corner': אֶבֶן מָאֲסוּ הַבּוֹנִים הָיְתָה לְרֹאשׁ פִּנָּה
   'The stone which the builders rejected has become *the head of the corner*' (Ps. 118:22).
[3] The sound change rules are referred to.

II The enlarged Hebrew word in each group below deviates from the other three words in the group. *Match* the enlarged Hebrew word with its deviant feature in the right-hand column. Observe that more than one deviation may appear in each enlarged word, but only one is referred to.

1 אֶסְתֵּר – פַּרְעֹה – **שַׁבָּת** – יַרְדֵּן

    ( ) The word does not start with a BeGaDKeFaT-letter (a letter with a hardening dagesh)

2 שָׂרָה – **הָגָר** – לֵוִי – נְחֶמְיָה

    ( ) The word ends in a consonant, not in a diphthong (a vowel plus the consonant י/ו *Vav/Yod*)

3 **שָׁאוּל** – מָשִׁיחַ – הוֹשֵׁעַ – נֹחַ

    ( ) The word ends in a vowel letter (ה *He,* ו *Vav* or י *Yod*), not in a consonant

4 **אֱלֹהִים** – בְּרִית – צְבָאוֹת – טְבֶרְיָה

    ( ) The last letter in the word does not have a special final form

5 **פֶּסַח** – חַוָּה – חַיִּים – עַזָּה

    ( ) The word ends in a consonant, not in a vowel letter (ה *He,* ו *Vav* or י *Yod*)

6 שָׁלוֹם – שִׁמְעוֹן – **שָׂטָן** – מִשְׁנָה

    ( ) The word starts with a chateph (shva-plus-vowel), not a simple shva sign

7 אָמֵן – **יָעֵל** – קִבּוּץ – מִרְיָם

    ( ) The word does not have a glide-/a/

8 אֶסְתֵּר – יַרְדֵּן – **מִשְׁלֵי** – שִׁמְשׁוֹן

    ( ) The word has a hardening dagesh (occurs in BeGaD-KeFaT-letters only!), not a doubling dagesh (occurs in all consonants, except א *Áleph,* ה *He,* ח *Chet,* ע *Áyin* and ר *Resh*)

9 דְּבוֹרָה – דָּוִד – **שְׁלֹמֹה** – בִּנְיָמִין

    ( ) The word has a doubling dagesh (which is always preceded by a vowel), not a hardening dagesh (never preceded by a vowel)

10 חַגַּי – יִשַׁי – אָבִיו – **רוּת**

    ( ) The word has שׂ *Sin,* not שׁ *Shin*

WORD LIST

Nouns   *Personal pronouns, singular*

אָב   m, father (☆ Abraham)   אֲנִי/אָנֹכִי   I

בַּעַל   m, lord, master; owner (of),   אַתָּה   m, you
       husband (☆ Baal)   אַתְּ   f, you

כֹּהֵן   m, priest (☆ Cohen)   הוּא   he

מָשִׁיחַ   m, anointed (one) (☆ Messiah)   הִיא   she

EXERCISES

3.1 *Transliterate* the words in Exercise 2.7 in Section 2. *Use* the chart of the
Hebrew alphabet on page 1 and the list of vowels on page 20. *Note*:

> • The vowel sign ◌ָ is to be transliterated /ā/ throughout Section 3.
> • The letters א *Áleph* and ע *Áyin*, although silent, are an integral part
>   of the spelling and hence must be rendered in transliteration: אֵם ʔēm,
>   עַם ʕam.
> • A letter with a doubling dagesh is to be written twice in transliteration:
>   לֹּ is the same as לֹל: הִלֵּל : לֹל hillēl.

3.2 *Transliterate* the following Hebrew words and *read aloud. Pay attention* to
the supporting vowels of the gutturals (א *Áleph,* ה *He,* ח *Chet,* ע *Áyin*).
Gutturals with supporting vowels are enlarged. *Note*:

> • *Chateph* (shva-plus-vowel): Three short vowels (/a/, /e/ and /o/)
>   may be combined with the shva sign to support a vowelless guttural,
>   e.g., אֲבִימֶלֶךְ ʔᵃvîmelex, אֱלִיעֶזֶר ʔᵉlîʕezer, חֳדָשִׁים ḥᵒdāšîm.
> • *Glide-/a/*: An additional **unstressed** /a/-vowel supports vowelless
>   ח *Chet* and ע *Áyin* at the end of a word (when not preceded by an
>   /a/-vowel), for example, הוֹשֵׁעַ hôšēₐʕ.

חֲכָמִים	אֲדָמָה	אֲנַחְנוּ	אֲנִי	אֲחִימֶלֶךְ	חֲבַקּוּק 1
אֲחָיוֹת	אֲלָפִים	חָכְמָה	עֲבָדִים	חֳרָבוֹת	אֲרָצוֹת
חֲסָדִים	חֲדָשׁוֹת	חֶזְקָה	עֲרָבִים	עֲבוֹדָה	אֲבִימֶלֶךְ
	מַחֲנֶה	מַעֲשֶׂה	יַעֲקֹב	אַחֲרֵי	אַהֲבָה 2
	אֱלִיל	אֱמוּנָה	אֱמֶת	אֱלֹהִים	אֱנוֹשׁ 3
				אֳהָלִים	חֳדָשִׁים 4
רֵעַ	מִזְבֵּחַ	מָשִׁיחַ	זְרוֹעַ	רוּחַ	הוֹשֵׁעַ 5

3.3 *Transliterate* the following Hebrew words, *mark* the stress and *read aloud.*
Pay attention to the relationship between certain consonants and certain
vowels. *Remember*:

◆ Gutturals (ה *He*, ח *Chet*, ע *Áyin*) attract an /a/-vowel/s, whereas י *Yod* attracts an /i/-vowel.

1 יַחַד   בַּעַל   נַעַר   שַׁעַר   תַּחַת   כְּנַעַן   לְמַעַן
   פַּעַם   יַעַן   פֶּתַח   שֶׁבַע   פֶּסַח   זֶרַע   שֶׁבַע

2 קַיִן   חַיִל   אַיִן   בַּיִת   מַיִם   עַיִן
   יַיִן   עֵינַיִם   שְׁנַיִם   שָׁמַיִם   מִצְרַיִם   יוֹמַיִם
   יָדַיִם   יְרוּשָׁלַיִם   אֶפְרַיִם

3.4 *Rewrite* the following verbless clauses, *read aloud* and *translate*. Proper names (names of persons and places) are enlarged. *Note*:

In a smooth translation from Hebrew to English certain Hebrew elements, words and/or constructions can be omitted, added or altered. Observe that in the Key words in parentheses render a literal translation, whereas words in square brackets are not found in the Hebrew text but added to it for the sake of good English (see, for instance, the first three points below).

◆ The verbless clause has *no time reference* of its own (*no verb* = no tense). The tense of the verbless clause is determined by the context (surrounding text). *Render* the isolated verbless clauses below in the *present tense*. *Insert* the correct form of the English verb 'to be' (am, are, is) in your translation.
◆ There is *no indefinite article* in Hebrew, for example, כֹּהֵן can be translated either '*a priest*' or 'priest'.
◆ An *additional personal pronoun* (only in the third person, הִיא or הוּא) may appear either before or after the predicate. Additional הוּא/הִיא should be left untranslated.[4]
◆ The predicate in the verbless clause may be placed either before or after the subject.
◆ The predicate agrees with the subject in gender (masculine or feminine) and number (one or many).

6 הִיא יְהוּדִית.   1 הוּא אַבְרָהָם.
7 אַתָּה שָׂטָן.   2 אֲנִי בַּעַל.
8 אַבְשָׁלוֹם כֹּהֵן הוּא.   3 אָב אָנֹכִי.
9 מָשִׁיחַ אַתָּה.   4 הוּא עַמְרָם.
10 אַתְּ פְּנִנָּה.   5 כֹּהֵן הוּא.

---

[4] This additional pronoun is described in Biblical grammars as a 'copula' (a linking element between the subject and the predicate), and/or as an element added to emphasize the subject.

SECTION 4

1 *Syllable types*: Hebrew normally permits only four types of syllables:
  – *Open syllables* (syllables ending in a vowel), which may consist of either
  'one consonant + one vowel', e.g., לְ-וִי lē-wî, or 'two consonants in a
  row + one vowel': יְהוּ-דָה yᵊhû-dāʰ.
  – *Closed syllables* (syllables ending in a consonant), which may consist of
  either 'one consonant + one vowel + one consonant', e.g., שָׁ-אוּל šā-ʔûl, or
  'two consonants in a row + one vowel + one consonant': כְּפָר kᵊfār.
  – Remember that in Hebrew *as a rule*:
  A syllable may **not** begin with a vowel, for instance, אֵל is impossible.[1]
  A syllable may **not** have more than one vowel. Diphthongs (a vowel followed
  by the consonant ו/י *Vav/Yod*, e.g., בַּיְת אֵל *bayt ʔēl) as well as triphthongs
  (the consonant ו/י *Vav/Yod* with vowels on either side, e.g., קָוַם *qāwam,
  קָנַיוּ *qānayû) are usually not tolerated in Hebrew.[2]
  A syllable may **not** begin with more than two consonants in a row, for
  example, לְשְׁמוּ-אֵל *lᵊšᵊmû-ʔēl (a syllable beginning with two vowelless
  consonants in a row) is not permitted.
  A syllable may **not** end in more than one consonant, for instance, סִפְר *sifr
  (a syllable ending in two vowelless consonants in a row) is not permitted.

2 *Consonant and vowel clusters*: Deviations from the permitted syllable types,
  called *clusters*, which often occur when words are formed, inflected or combined
  with other elements or words, are adjusted according to certain rules.
  – *A vowel cluster* (an impermissible sequence of vowels), either a *diphthong* (a
  vowel followed by the consonant י/ו *Vav/Yod*) or a *triphthong* (the consonant
  י/ו *Vav/Yod* with vowels on either side), is generally *contracted* (it becomes a
  single vowel). The consonant י/ו *Vav/Yod* in a diphthong normally becomes a
  vowel letter: בַּיְת אֵל *bayt ʔēl becomes בֵּית אֵל bêt ʔēl. The consonant י/ו
  Vav/Yod in a triphthong is generally omitted: קָוַם *qāwam becomes קָם. At
  the end of a word the triphthong becomes a full vowel, e.g., קָנַיוּ *qānayû
  becomes קָנוּ qānû.
  – *A consonant cluster* (an impermissible sequence of consonants) is normally
  broken up by inserting a *vowel* between the vowelless consonants:
  לְשְׁמוּ-אֵל *lᵊšᵊmû-ʔēl becomes לִשְׁ-מוּ-אֵל liš-mû-ʔēl and סִפְר *sifr
  becomes סֵ-פֶר sē-**fer**.

3 *Syllable division*: In order to determine the syllable division of a given word,
  it is essential to assemble *vowelless consonants* correctly. Certain vowels,
  namely chateph (ֲ , ֳ , ֱ) and the glide-/a/ (ַ), are deceptive. Their sound

---

[1] With one exception, the word 'and' (Section 8:1).
[2] An asterisk (*) before a word form indicates that the form is not attested, but is
supposed to have existed in the past. The older form of a word is reconstructed to illustrate
sound changes.

may deceive one into thinking that they are ordinary vowels that can form a syllable on their own. However, in spite of their obvious vowel sound, they cannot form a syllable on their own. Instead, they should be transferred to the adjoining syllable, together with the consonant to which they belong.

– A chateph begins a syllable: אֲבִי־מֶלֶךְ ?ᵃvî-melex.

– The glide-/a/ clings to the preceding vowel within the same syllable: נֹחַ nōₐh.

– Naturally, a consonant with the shva is considered vowelless. A silent shva (indicating an original no-vowel) closes a syllable, while a vocal shva (indicating a reduced vowel) begins a syllable. For example, in the word צְפַנְיָה sᵊfan-yāʰ the first shva is vocal and the second shva is silent.

– Please note that all the sound elements that cannot form a syllable on their own are transliterated by reduced form, either raised (vocal shva and chateph) or lowered (the glide-/a/).

4 *Qamets-/o/ (qamets chatuph) and méteg*: The vowel sign qamets $_\text{T}$ followed by a consonant with a shva $_\text{:}$ in an unstressed syllable may represent either /ā/ or /o/.

– In the Bible the presence of a short vertical stroke, called *méteg,* to the left of the vowel sign $_\text{T}$ indicates the /ā/-vowel: אָכְלוּ ?ā-xᵊlû.

– Elsewhere, a qamets followed by a consonant with a shva in an unstressed syllable indicates the /o/-vowel: גָּלְיָת gol-yāt.

5 *The basic rule of vocalization*: **All** syllables (with simple vowels) **generally** have a **long** vowel, except **an unstressed closed syllable** which **always** has a **short** vowel.

MEMORIZE

SYLLABLE TYPES
Four syllable types are permitted in Hebrew: CV, CVC, CCV, CCVC (C = consonant, V = vowel)
CLUSTERS
Clusters (impermissible sequences of consonants or vowels) are dissolved. A vowel cluster (diphthong and triphthong) is generally contracted (it is pulled together to one vowel), whereas a consonant cluster (two vowelless consonants in succession) is normally broken up by inserting a vowel.
BASIC RULE OF VOCALIZATION
All syllables (with simple vowels) generally have a long vowel, except an unstressed closed syllable, which always has a short vowel.

GRAMMATICAL CORNERSTONE 2 רֹאשׁ פִּנָּה

REVIEW AND APPLICATION OF THE RULES

I *Match* each sound element with the Hebrew word that illustrates it. *Mark* the element in the Hebrew word clearly! Observe that the same element may appear in more than one word, but only one element is to be marked. Each word is to be used once!

1 Hardening dagesh *At the beginning of a word*   (_) קֹהֶלֶת

2 Glide-/a/ *At the end of a word, below* ח *Chet or* ע *Áyin*   (_) אָנֹכִי

3 Vocal shva *Shva-reduced-vowel, at the beginning of a syllable*   (_) אֶסְתֵּר

4 Chateph *Shva-plus-vowel*   (_) הוּא

5 Doubling dagesh *Always after a vowel*   (_) אָסְנַת

6 Silent א *Áleph,* א *is not audible*   (_) נְבִיאִים

7 Long vowel,   (_) אַתָּה

$\bar{}$ $\bar{}$ $\bar{}$

8 Short vowel,   (_) אֲנִי

9 Silent shva *Original no-vowel, at the end of a syllable*   (_) כֹּהֵן

10 Diphthong *Vowel + the consonant* י/ו *Vav/Yod*   (_) פֶּתַח

11 Qamets-/o/ *In an unstressed closed syllable*   (_) יָדִי

II The enlarged Hebrew word in each group below deviates from the other three words in the group. *Match* the enlarged Hebrew word with its deviant feature. Observe that more than one deviation may appear in each enlarged word, but only one is referred to.

1 שִׁמְשׁוֹן – צְבָאוֹת – לֵוִי – שִׁמְעוֹן   (_) The word begins with a chateph (shva-plus-vowel), not a shva

2 יוֹנָה – דְּבוֹרָה – מִצְוָה – רָחֵל   (_) The word begins with a vocal shva, not a chateph

3 אֱנוֹשׁ – דְּבוֹרָה – צְפַנְיָה – צְבָאוֹת   (_) The word begins with two consonants in a row (the first one with a vocal shva), not one

4 כֹּהֵן – דָּן – אִיּוֹב – בְּרִית   (_) The word has no vowel letter

5 קֹהֶלֶת – אֲבִימֶלֶךְ – יוֹכֶבֶד – אֶסְתֵּר   (_) The word has a glide-/a/

6 שׁוֹפֵט – נְבִיאִים – יְהוּדִית – בְּרִית   (_) The word does not begin with a BeGaDKeFaT-letter (a letter with a hardening dagesh)

7 נָבִיא – וַיִּקְרָא – עֶזְרָא – עָמוֹס   (_) The word does not end in a silent א Áleph

8 אַתָּה – אֲנִי – אַתְּ – הֵם   (_) The stress in this word falls on the last syllable, not next-to-last

9 אֱלֹהִים – אֲנִי – אֲנַחְנוּ – בְּרֵאשִׁית   (_) The word begins with one consonant, not two

10 נֹחַ – אָדוֹן – בְּרִית – חַיִּים   (_) The word begins with two consonants (the first consonant with a chateph), not one

WORD LIST

Nouns

אָדוֹן   *m*, lord, master

אֵל   *m*, god; God (☆ Israel)

בְּרִית   *f*, covenant

חַיִּים   *pl*, life (☆ Lecháyim)[3]

EXERCISES

4.1 *Rewrite* the following words and *read aloud*. *Identify* the type of shva. *Mark* a silent shva (= original no-vowel) with one stroke and a vocal shva (= reduced vowel) with two strokes. *Transliterate* the words. *Note*:

> • A shva after a short vowel is silent as a rule,[4] e.g., עֶזְ-רָא ʕez-rā². Elsewhere, the shva is vocal (i.e., at the *beginning of a word* בְּרִית bᵊrît, *after a shva* נִגְ-מְרוּ nig-mᵊrû, *after a long vowel* שֹׁ-מְרִים šō-mᵊrîm, *after a vowel letter* שׁוֹ-מְרוֹן šô-mᵊrôn, *after a méteg* אָ-מְרוּ ²ā-mᵊrû).

1 אָסְפוּ   אָכְלָה   נְבִיאִים   כְּתוּבִים   בְּרֵאשִׁית   יְהוֹשֻׁעַ   שְׁמוֹת

2 שׁוֹפְטִים   תְּהִלִּים   וַיִּקְרָא   שְׁמוּאֵל   בַּמִּדְבָּר   מְלָכִים   יִרְמְיָהוּ

3 דְּבָרִים   יְשַׁעְיָהוּ   אָכְלָה

4.2 *Rewrite* the words in Exercise 3.2 (Section 3, except group 2), *divide* into syllables and *read aloud*. *Remember*:

> • Sound elements that cannot form a syllable on their own are transliterated by a reduced form, either raised (vocal shva and chateph) or lowered (the glide-/a/). These sound elements never take the stress.
> • A vocal shva (= reduced vowel) and a chateph (shva-plus-vowel) stand at the beginning of a syllable, while a silent shva (the original no-vowel) stands at the end of a syllable. The glide /a/ clings to the preceding vowel within the same syllable.

4.3 *Rewrite* the following words and *read aloud*. Then *transliterate* the words, *divide into syllables* and *identify* the syllable type (open or closed) and the vowel type (long or short) in each syllable. *Apply* the basic rule of vocalization to each syllable. *All syllables (with simple vowels)* **generally** have a **long** vowel, except *an* **unstressed closed** *syllable which* **always** *has a* **short** *vowel*, for instance,

אַבְ-רָ-הָם ²av-rā-hām:

– '?av' is an *unstressed closed* syllable with a short vowel (an unstressed closed syllable always has a short vowel),

---

[3] Lecháyim means 'cheers', literally, 'for life' (modern Hebrew).

[4] Except before a doubled letter.

– 'rā' is an *unstressed open* syllable with a long vowel (all syllables generally have a long vowel),

– 'hām' is a *stressed closed* syllable with a long vowel (all syllables generally have a long vowel). *Note*:

> ◆ A full vowel (a vowel written with both a vowel sign and a vowel letter) is regarded as long.
>
> ◆ A Hebrew letter with a doubling dagesh is divided into two simple letters. The first letter closes a syllable and the second one begins a syllable, e.g., קִבּוּץ (קִבּ - בוּץ).

1 שָׁלֵם אַבְשָׁלוֹם נִמְרֹד יִצְחָק עִמָּנוּאֵל אֶלְקָנָה גְּדַלְיָה

2 יוֹנָה יָעֵל יִפְתָּח בְּנֵי בְּרִית דְּבוֹרָה עַמְרָם דָּן יוֹחָנָן

3 סְדוֹם עֲמֹרָה רָחֵל שָׂטָן אָסָף יוֹסֵף נָתָן יְהוּדָה

4.4 *Rewrite* the words in Exercise 3.3 (p. 24), *divide* into syllables, *mark* the stress and *read aloud*. *Apply* the basic rule of vocalization to each syllable. *Find* the common feature of syllables with deviant vocalization. *Note*:

> ◆ An unstressed closed syllable always has a short vowel, but not all the other syllables (with simple vowels) have a long vowel. There are a few exceptions to the basic rule of vocalization.

4.5 *Rewrite* the words in Exercise 3.2 (Section 3, group 2 only!), *divide* into syllables and *read aloud*. *Apply* the basic rule of vocalization to each syllable. *Find* the common feature of syllables with deviant vocalization. *Remember*:

> ◆ A chateph always opens a syllable.

4.6 *Rewrite* the following verbless clauses, *read aloud* and *translate*. Then *transliterate* the clauses. Proper names (names of persons and places) are enlarged. *Note*:

> ◆ The Hebrew clause has *no verb* (no verb = no tense). Render these isolated verbless clauses in the present tense. The correct form of the verb 'to be' (am, are, is) must be inserted in the translation.
>
> ◆ There is *no indefinite article* in Hebrew, for example, כֹּהֵן is to be translated either '*a* priest' or 'priest'.
>
> ◆ An *additional* הִיא or הוּא in the verbless clause, either before or after the predicate, should be left untranslated.
>
> ◆ There is *no neuter form* (i.e., 'it') in Hebrew; הִיא 'she' and הוּא 'he' correspond to English 'it'.

7 אָדוֹן הוּא.   4 אָנֹכִי יוֹנָה.   1 אֶל אֲנִי.

8 בְּרִית הִיא.   5 דָּוִד הוּא אָב.   2 הִיא דְּבוֹרָה.

6 מֹשֶׁה כֹּהֵן הוּא.   3 אַתְּ לֵאָה.

4.7 *Write* the following transliterated biblical verses in Hebrew. *Examine* your spelling *after each Hebrew verse*, assisted by the check list given below. *Note*:

♦ Words ending in 'xa' are spelled ךָ (the final letter ך + /ā/).

---

1 wayyippōl ʔavrām ʕal pānāʸw wayᵊdabbēr ʔittô ʔᵉlōhîm lēʔmōr.

2 wᵊhāyîtā lᵊʔav hᵃmôn gôyim.

3 wᵊlōʔ yiqqārēʔ ʕôd ʔet šimᵊxā ʔavrām wᵊhāyāʰ šimᵊxā ʔavrāhām kî ʔav hᵃmôn gôyim nᵊtattîxā.

4 wᵊhifrētî ʔōtᵊxā bimʔōd mᵊʔōd ûnᵊtattîxā lᵊgôyim ûmᵊlāxîm mimmᵊxā yēṣēʔû.

5 wahᵃqimōtî ʔet bᵊrîtî bênî ûvênexā ûvên zarʕᵃxā ʔahᵃreʸxā lᵊdōrōtām livrît ʕôlām lihyôt lᵊxā lēʔlōhîm ûlᵊzarʕᵃxā ʔahᵃreʸxā.

6 wᵊnātattî lᵊxā ûlᵊzarʕᵃxā ʔahᵃreʸxā ʔēt ʔereṣ mᵊgureʸxā ʔēt kol ʔereṣ kᵊnaʕan laʔᵃḥuzzat ʕôlām wᵊhāyîtî lāhem lēʔlōhîm.

Examine your spelling step by step:

1 *Doubling dagesh*

Did you write a doubled letter twice? – In Hebrew a doubled letter is written once with the doubling dagesh inside it.

2 *Hardening dagesh*

Did you put the hardening dagesh in BeGaDKeFaT-letters where needed (at the beginning of a word and inside a word at the beginning of a syllable, that is, after a consonant with a silent shva)? – Although the dagesh does not change the sound of ג‎, ד‎, ת in modern Hebrew pronunciation, the hardening dagesh is part of the spelling.

3 *Shva*

Did you put the shva sign, representing a silent shva, where needed? – A silent shva (ending a syllable) is not rendered in transliteration.

4 *Final letter ך /x/*

Did you put the shva sign in the final letter ך /x/ (ךְ)? – A vowelless letter at the end of a word usually does not take the sign for no-vowel, but ך is an exception.

5 *Vowel letters* ו *Vav and* י *Yod*

Did you write the vowel letters ו *Vav* and י *Yod* where needed? – The vowel letters ו *Vav* and י *Yod* are marked in transliteration by a circumflex.

Dear student,

This book uses ACTIVE LEARNING as a method to acquire a classical language. A classical language can be assimilated in much the same way as a modern language, namely, by diligent many-sided practice. Please try to do all the exercises in the book! PRACTICE MAKES PERFECT!

The process of active learning is anchored in the common phenomena of the Hebrew language, that is, the general systematic vowel and consonant changes which occur when words are formed and inflected.

Since many words of the core vocabulary of the Hebrew Bible differ from the basic word patterns and inflections, the beginner is confronted with constant, seemingly chaotic, sound changes in many frequent words. Consequently, apart from the basic word patterns and inflections, the beginner has to memorize a considerable number of so-called exceptions.

In fact, most of the "deviant" forms are the result of regular sound changes. Therefore, knowledge and understanding of the SYSTEMATIC SOUND CHANGES constitute the framework of this book. You are supplied with a few effective tools in order to interpret the main part of the consonant and vowel changes in most of the words of the language. Systematic sound changes are drilled through constant REVIEW AND APPLICATION OF THE RULES, so that sooner or later they become engraved on your mind in the same way that you once learned the multiplication tables.

What at first glance may appear to be a concentration on superfluous details will, in fact, prove to be a short cut to the grammar of the Hebrew language. Following this method you will have to memorize only the basic word patterns and inflections (most of which are found in the Grammatical Cornerstones throughout the book). Predictable "deviations" can be recognized and understood through the knowledge and application of the rules of systematic sound changes.

There is a concise table and a detailed list of the principle sound changes in Hebrew in APPENDIX II.

SECTION 5

1 *Relationship between vowels and stress*: The position of the stress in a word determines which vowel (long or short) each of its syllables has.[1] *All syllables (i.e., stressed syllables and unstressed open syllables) generally have a long vowel, except an unstressed closed syllable which always has a short vowel.*

— The stress in Hebrew usually falls on the last syllable. This means that when a word takes an ending, as a rule the stress is automatically moved forward to the newly added ending. The shift in stress results in a rearrangement of the vowels according to the new stress position. However, not all vowels are affected by the position of the stress.

2 *Unchangeable and changeable vowels*

— A full vowel (written with both a vowel sign and a vowel letter) and a vowel followed by a silent א *Áleph* are unchangeable (not affected by the stress).

— A simple vowel (written with a vowel sign only) is changeable (affected by the stress).

3 *Regular vowel change*

— *Vowel change in open syllables*: When the stress is moved from its original position, a simple vowel in an *unstressed open syllable* is normally either *reduced* (i.e., dropped, which is shown in writing by the shva sign, see examples in 6 below) or *lengthened* (shown in writing by being transformed from a short into a long vowel within the same vowel category).[2]

— *Vowel change in closed syllables*: When the stress is moved from its original position, a simple vowel in an unstressed closed syllable is usually *shortened* (shown in writing by being transformed from a long into a short vowel within the same vowel category).

4 *Definite article*: The elementary form of the definite article is הַ, followed by a doubling dagesh in the next letter. הַ is attached to the following noun/adjective: הַנָּבִיא **hannāvî** 'the prophet'.

— Gutturals (א *Áleph*, ה *He*, ח *Chet*, ע *Áyin*) and ר *Resh* cannot be doubled. Instead, the vowel before א *Áleph*, ע *Áyin* and ר *Resh*[3] is lengthened, e.g., הָראֹשׁ 'the head' (instead of הַראֹשׁ). Before ה *He* and ח *Chet* the preceding vowel is not lengthened, e.g., הַחַיִּים '(the) life'. Before unstressed עָ, חָ, הָ (and חָ) the definite article is הֶ, e.g., הֶחָכָם 'the wise [one]'.

5 *Adjectives: Inflection of gender and number*

— The *base form* (i.e., the form with no inflection ending which is listed in lexicons and vocabularies, hence also referred to as the *lexical form* in this book) is ordinarily the masculine singular, e.g., טוֹב 'god'.[4]

— Feminine singular always takes the ending הָ ַ: טוֹבָה.

---

[1] This refers to the major stress.

[2] A vowel one step (i.e., syllable) before the stress that is not reduced is lengthened (called *pretonic lengthening*, tone = stress).

[3] And rarely ה.

[4] For the lexical forms of verbs, see Section 13:3.

– Masculine plural always takes the ending ‏ים‏ : ‏טוֹבִים‏.

– Feminine plural always takes the ending ‏וֹת‏ after the base form: ‏טוֹבוֹת‏.

6 *Nouns: Inflection of gender and number.* Nouns denote either animate beings (i.e., persons, animals) or inanimate things (e.g., day, hand). Both categories have grammatical gender in Hebrew, masculine or feminine.

– The *base form* is usually the masculine singular: ‏סוּס‏ 'horse', ‏שׁוֹפֵט‏ 'judge'.

– Feminine singular takes the ending ‏ה‏ or ‏ת‏: ‏סוּסָה‏, ‏שׁוֹפֶטֶת‏.

– Masculine plural usually takes the ending ‏ים‏ but sometimes ‏וֹת‏: ‏סוּסִים‏, ‏אָבוֹת‏ 'fathers'.

– Feminine plural usually takes the ending ‏וֹת‏ but sometimes ‏ים‏ : ‏סוּסוֹת‏, ‏נָשִׁים‏ 'women'.

– *Dual nouns*: A few nouns (both feminine and masculine) take a special ending for *dual* (two), namely expressions of time or number and parts of the body occurring in pairs: ‏יוֹמַיִם‏ 'two days' (one day is ‏יוֹם‏), ‏שְׁנַיִם‏ 'two', ‏יָדַיִם‏ 'two hands' (one hand is ‏יָד‏).[5]

Vowel reduction in nouns and adjectives due to the shift in stress: The endings ‏ה‏ and ‏וֹת/ים‏ take the stress. As a result, a simple vowel in an *open syllable,* located either one or two steps before the stress, is reduced.

– Vowel reduction **II**: Normally, a simple vowel in an open syllable **two** steps before the stress is dropped. For example, 'the base form ‏זָקֵן‏ (old) + the feminine ending ‏ה‏' results in the hypothetical form ‏זָ-קֵ-נָה‏, with the stress on the newly added last syllable. ‏זָ-קֵ-נָה‏ becomes ‏זְקֵ-נָה‏.

– Vowel reduction **I**: Less often, a simple vowel in an open syllable **one** step before the stress is dropped. For instance, 'the base form ‏שׁוֹפֵט‏ (judge) + the plural ending ‏ים‏' results in the hypothetical form ‏שׁוֹ-פֵ-טִים‏, with the stress on the newly added last syllable. ‏שׁוֹ-פֵ-טִים‏ becomes ‏שׁוֹ-פְטִים‏.

– *Insertion vowel at the end of a word* (traditionally called *segholizing*): 'The base form ‏שׁוֹפֵט‏ + the feminine ending ‏ת‏' results in the hypothetical form ‏שׁוֹ-פֵטְת‏, with a final syllable ending in two consonants. *A syllable may not end in more than one consonant.* An insertion vowel is added between the two vowelless consonants to break up the impermissible two-consonant sequence at the end of the word. As a rule, the insertion vowel is /e/ (called *segol*): ‏שׁוֹפֶטֶת‏. However, before and after (i.e., under) the gutturals ‏ה‏ *He,* ‏ח‏ *Chet,* ‏ע‏ *Áyin* the insertion vowel is not /e/ but /a/:[6] ‏יוֹדַעַת‏. *A guttural attracts an /a/-vowel/s.* After ‏י‏ *Yod* the insertion vowel is not /e/ but /i/: ‏יוֹמַיִם‏. *The consonant* ‏י‏ *Yod attracts an /i/-vowel.*

7 *Independent personal pronouns in plural* (see word list below).

_____

[5] The ending ‏ים‏ attached to words describing parts of the body occurring in pairs also indicates plural.

[6] 'The vowel after (i.e., under) the consonant/guttural' means that the vowel is *pronounced after* but *written under* the consonant/guttural in question.

MEMORIZE

REGULAR VOWEL CHANGE

When the word stress is moved from its original position, a simple vowel in an unstressed *open syllable* is normally either *reduced* (shown in writing by the shva sign) or *lengthened* (shown in writing by being transformed into a long vowel within the same vowel category), whereas a long vowel in an unstressed *closed syllable* is usually *shortened* (shown in writing by being transformed into a short vowel within the same vowel category).

When the *doubling* of a consonant *cannot be realized*, the short vowel before the non-doubled consonant is often *lengthened*.

Vowel category	Long vowels	Short vowels	Reduced vowels
A	ָ	ַ	ֲ / ְ
I/E	ֵ	ֶ / ִ	ֱ / ְ
U/O	וֹ	ָ / ׇ	ׇ / ְ

GRAMMATICAL CORNERSTONE 3   ר א שׁ פּ נ ג ה

REVIEW AND APPLICATION OF THE RULES

I *Match* each sound element with the Hebrew word that illustrates it. *Mark* the element in the Hebrew word clearly! Observe that the same sound element may appear in more than one word, but only one element is to be marked. Each word is to be used once!

1 Doubling dagesh (_) שׁוֹמַעַת
Always occurs after a vowel

2 Compensatory lengthening (_) שְׁלָמִים
ר ,ע, א *cannot be doubled; instead,*
the vowel before ר ,ע, א *is lengthened*

3 No compensatory lengthening (_) חֲלוֹמוֹת
ח ,ה *cannot be doubled but the vowel*
before ח ,ה *is not lengthened*

4 Vowel reduction II *A vowel* (_) כּוֹתֶבֶת
two *steps before the stress*
is reduced, i.e., dropped (shown in
writing by the shva sign)

5 Vowel reduction I *A vowel* (_) טוֹבָה
one *step before the stress is reduced*

6 Chateph (shva-plus-vowel) (_) הַצַּדִּיק

7 Unchangeable (_) רָאשִׁים
vowel *Not affected by the stress*

8 Silent א *Áleph* (_) קַיִן
Preceding vowel is
unchangeable

9 Insertion vowel /e/ (_) הָאֵל
Used to dissolve a sequence of two
consonants at the end of the word

10 Insertion vowel /a/ (_) קוֹרְאִים
After (i.e., under) a guttural, used
to dissolve a consonant cluster at
the end of the word

11 Insertion vowel /i/ (_) הַהֵיכָל
After י, *used to dissolve a two-consonant*
sequence at the end of the word

WORD LIST

Nouns		*Adjectives*	
אִישׁ	*m*, man (☆ Judas **Iscariot**): *pl* אֲנָשִׁים	גָּדוֹל	big, great; important (☆ **Gedaliah**)
אֱלֹהִים	*m*, God; gods	זָקֵן	old; elder (*noun*)
אִשָּׁה	*f*, woman, wife: *pl* נָשִׁים	חָכָם	wise, clever; skilful
מֶלֶךְ	*m*, king (☆ Abi**melech**): *pl* מְלָכִים (☆ **Kings**)	טוֹב	good (☆ **Tobi**jah)
נָבִיא	*m*, prophet: *pl* נְבִיאִים	יָשָׁר	straight, upright, honest
שׁוֹפֵט	*m*, judge: *pl* שׁוֹפְטִים (☆ **Judges**)	צַדִּיק	righteous (☆ **Zede**kiah)
		קָדוֹשׁ	holy
תּוֹרָה	*f*, instruction, teaching, law (☆ **Law**)	שָׁלֵם	perfect, whole, complete, sound (☆ Jeru**salem**)

Personal pronouns, plural

אֲנַחְנוּ	we
אַתֶּם	*m*, you: *f* אַתֵּן/אַתֵּנָה
הֵם/הֵמָּה	*m*, they: *f* הֵנָּה

Definite article

הַ ⊡ (הֶ, הָ, הַ)   the

EXERCISES

5.1 *Rewrite* the following words and *read aloud*. *Pay attention* to the insertion vowel /e/ (segol) that is normally added to break up an impermissible two-consonant sequence at the end of a word. *Note*:

> ◆ An insertion vowel never takes the stress. Thus, an insertion vowel which separates the consonants of a cluster at the end of a word results in words with the stress on the next-to-last syllable (penultima).

1   דֶּלֶת   כֶּלֶב   כֶּסֶף   יֶלֶד   עֵבֶר   אֶבֶן   יֶפֶת   סֵפֶר   הֶבֶל

2   שֵׁבֶט   חֶסֶד   עֶבֶד   בֹּקֶר   קֹדֶשׁ   אֹהֶל   נֵצֶר   שֶׁמֶשׁ   אֶלֶף

5.2 *Rewrite* the words in Exercise 3.3 (Section 3) and *read aloud*. *Pay attention* to the insertion vowels /a/ and /i/ that are added to dissolve an impermissible two-consonant sequence at the end of a word. *Remember*:

> ◆ Before and after (i.e., under) ה *He*, ח *Chet* and ע *Áyin* the insertion vowel dissolving a consonant cluster at the end of a word is /a/ instead of /e/.
>
> ◆ The insertion vowel after (i.e., under) י dissolving a two-consonant cluster at the end of a word is /i/ instead of /e/ (segol).

5.3 *Write* the feminine singular and then the plural (masculine and feminine) of the following adjectives. *Read* aloud. *Remember*:

> ◆ When the stress is moved forward to an ending, a vowel in an open syllable **two** steps before the stress is reduced (shown in writing by the shva sign): גָּדוֹל 'big, great' (base form), גְּדוֹלָה, גְּדוֹלִים, גְּדוֹלוֹת.
>
> ◆ Gutturals take a chateph (shva-plus-vowel) instead of a shva: חָבֵר 'friend', חֲבֵרָה, חֲבֵרִים, חֲבֵרוֹת.

_____	_____	_____	(complete) שָׁלֵם 1
_____	_____	_____	(old) זָקֵן 2
_____	_____	_____	(holy) קָדוֹשׁ 3
_____	_____	_____	(good) טוֹב 4
_____	_____	_____	(wise) חָכָם 5
_____	_____	_____	(righteous) צַדִּיק 6
_____	_____	_____	(straight, just) יָשָׁר 7

5.4 *Rewrite* and *read aloud* the following verbless clauses. *Translate orally.* Then *transliterate* the clauses and *divide* into syllables.

_____	_____	נְבִיאִים אֲנַחְנוּ. 1
_____	_____	חֲכָמִים הֵם. 2
_____	_____	אַתֵּן הַשּׁוֹפְטוֹת. 3
_____	_____	אֲדוֹנִים הֵם. 4
_____	_____	אֵלִים אַתֶּם. 5
_____	_____	צַדִּיקִים אֲנַחְנוּ. 6
_____	_____	אַתֶּם הָאָבוֹת. 7
_____	_____	אֲנַחְנוּ הַכֹּהֲנִים. 8
_____	_____	טוֹבוֹת הֵנָּה. 9
_____	_____	שְׁלֵמִים אַתֶּם. 10
_____	_____	יְשָׁרִים הַנְּבִיאִים. 11
_____	_____	הַמְּלָכִים זְקֵנִים הֵם. 12

13 גְּדוֹלִים אֲנַחְנוּ. _____ _____

14 קְדוֹשִׁים הֵם הָאֵלִים. _____ _____

15 הַנְּבִיאוֹת טוֹבוֹת הֵנָּה. _____ _____

5.5 *Transform* the verbless clauses in Exercise 5.4 above from the plural into the *singular*. Then *read aloud* and *translate*. *Note*:

> ◆ There is no indefinite article in Hebrew, for example כֹּהֵן can be translated either as 'a priest' or 'priest'.
>
> ◆ When you remove an ending, the stress is moved back to its original position. A reduced vowel (vocal shva or chateph) reverts to a long vowel. When the shva/chateph is located two steps before the stress, the long vowel is /ā/: הָרוּס --> הֲרוּסָה, גָּדוֹל --> גְּדוֹלִים. When the shva/chateph is located one step before the stress, the long vowel is /ē/: אֹהֵב --> אֹהֲבִים, שֹׁפֵט --> שֹׁפְטִים.
>
> ◆ It may be easier to transform a pronoun from the plural into the singular if you keep in mind three groups of personal pronouns:
> – 1st person (I, we) that begins with the אָנ/אֲנ– element:
> אָנֹכִי/אֲנִי (I) – אֲנַחְנוּ (we)
> – 2nd person (you) that begins with the אַתּ– element:
> אַתְּ (you, *f*) – אַתֵּן/אַתֵּנָה – אַתָּה (you, *m*), אַתֶּם
> – 3rd person (he, she, they) that begins with the ה– element:
> הִיא (she) – הֵנָּה (they, *f*), הוּא (he) – הֵם/הֵמָּה (they, *m*).
>
> ◆ An additional personal pronoun (3rd person: הוּא, הִיא, הֵם, הֵנָּה) which may appear either before or after the predicate should be left untranslated.

SECTION 6

1 *Special readings (Qere)*: יְהוָה (YHWH) are the four sacred letters of the name of God. In Jewish tradition יהוה is replaced in reading (so-called *qere*) by אֲדֹנָי ʔ^adōnāy, which literally means 'my lords', translated 'the LORD'.

In a vocalized biblical text יהוה is written either without vowels or with the vowels of the word אֲדֹנָי, which results in יְהוָה and pronounced ʔ^adōnāy (observe the vocal shva under י *Yod* instead of the chateph under the guttural א *Aleph* in אֲדֹנָי).

– Other frequent special readings are יְרוּשָׁלַיִם 'Jerusalem' (written יְרוּשָׁלִַם) and הִיא 'she' (written הוּא).

2 *Inseparable prepositions*: לְ 'to/for', כְּ 'as/like' and בְּ 'in/with' are attached to the following word and are normally vowelless, e.g., לְחַיִּים 'for life'.

Before a shva, the prepositions בְּ, כְּ, לְ take the vowel /i/: כִּשְׁמוּאֵל.

Before a chateph (shva-plus-vowel), the prepositions בְּ, כְּ, לְ take the vowel that matches the vowel of the chateph: לֶאֱנוֹשׁ, בַּאֲבִי.

– The hard sound of a BeGaDKeFaT-consonant becomes soft after a vocal shva (shva-reduced-vowel), e.g., 'בְּ + בַּיִת' results in בְּבַיִת 'in a house'.

– When בְּ, כְּ, לְ are attached to the definite article, e.g., לְהַבַּיִת 'to the house', the consonant ה *He* is dropped and its vowel is transferred to the preceding vowelless consonant: לַבַּיִת. The doubling of the following consonant is retained.

– The preposition מִן 'from' is attached to the following word either directly, with the form מִ⟨·⟩, e.g., מִיִּשְׂרָאֵל (originally מִנְיִשְׂרָאֵל), or by a hyphen (called *maqqeph*): מִן־יִשְׂרָאֵל.

– A vowelless נ at the end of a syllable is assimilated to (that is, absorbed in) the sound of the next letter which, in turn, is doubled (shown in writing by the doubling dagesh): מִנְיִשְׂרָאֵל becomes מִיְּשְׂרָאֵל, written מִיִּשְׂרָאֵל. Gutturals and ר *Resh* cannot be doubled. Instead, the short vowel before א *Aleph*, ה *He*, ח *Chet*, ע *Ayin* and ר *Resh* is lengthened, e.g., מֵהַבַּיִת 'from the house' (instead of מִהַבַּיִת), מֵרָחֵל 'from Rachel' (not מִרָּחֵל)

– A vowelless י *Yod* after מִ⟨·⟩ becomes silent, being transformed into a vowel letter: מִיְהוּדָה becomes מִיהוּדָה.

3 *Usage of adjectives*: An adjective may be used as a *noun*, e.g., הַזָּקֵן 'the old [one]', as an *attribute* describing a noun, e.g., הַכֹּהֵן הַזָּקֵן 'the *old* priest', or as a *predicate* in a verbless clause: הַכֹּהֵן זָקֵן 'the priest is *old*'.

– *Comparison* is expressed by using a preposition after the adjective.

גָּדוֹל כַּכֹּהֵן means '*as* great *as* a priest', literally, 'great as priest',

גָּדוֹל מִכֹּהֵן means '*greater than* a priest', literally, '*great than* priest'.

– *Superlative* is expressed by using the definite article before the adjective: דָּוִד (הוּא) הַגָּדוֹל 'David is *the greatest*', literally, 'David (he) *the great*.'

4 *Accent signs and pause*: Apart from vowel signs, the biblical text has *accent signs*. Accent signs mark word stress as well as the punctuation of the biblical verse. The two major stops in reading (called *pause*) are at the end of the verse and in the middle of the verse. Words in pause may undergo vowel and/or stress changes (see Exercises 6.3 and 6.4).

MEMORIZE

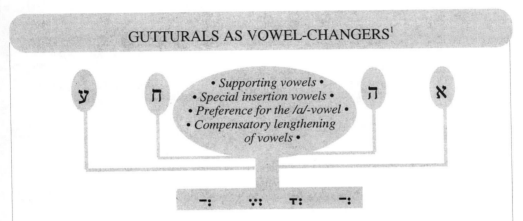

GUTTURALS AS VOWEL-CHANGERS[1]

Vowelless gutturals require supporting vowels:
– The *chateph* (shva-plus-vowel), e.g., חֲכָמִים (instead of חְכָמִים),
　יַעֲקֹב (instead of יַעְקֹב)
– The *glide-/a/*, e.g., מָשִׁיחַ (instead of מָשִׁיחְ).

The special insertion vowels used to break up clusters are as follows:
– The insertion vowel before and after (i.e., under)[2] a guttural with a chateph matches the vowel of the chateph, e.g., כַּאֲשֶׁר (instead of כְּאֲשֶׁר), תַּעֲבְדִי (instead of תְּעֲבְדִי).
– The insertion vowel before and after a guttural at the end of a word is /a/, e.g., פָּתַח (from פָּתְחָ), בַּעַל (from בַּעְל).

Gutturals may change a preceding I/E- or U/O-vowel into an /a/-vowel: שָׁמַעַת (from שָׁמְעַת)

Since gutturals (and ר *Resh*) cannot be doubled, the preceding short vowel is often lengthened: הָאִישׁ (instead of הַאִישׁ).

GRAMMATICAL CORNERSTONE 4　ר א שׁ פְּ נָ ה

---
[1] For gutturals as vowel-changers via Hebrew names, see Sections 23 and 24.
[2] 'The vowel after (i.e., under) the guttural' means that the vowel is *pronounced after* but *written under* the guttural in question.

REVIEW AND APPLICATION OF THE RULES

I *Match* each sound element with the Hebrew word that illustrates it. *Mark* the element in the Hebrew word clearly! Observe that the same sound element may appear in more than one word, but only one element is to be marked. Each word is to be used once!

1 **Doubling dagesh** (_) עֵינַיִם
Always occurs after a vowel

2 **Compensatory lengthening** (_) מְנַבִּיא
Gutturals and ר *Resh cannot be doubled. Instead, the preceding vowel is lengthened*

3 **Vowel reduction II** *A vowel* (_) לֹא
two *steps before the stress is reduced (shown in writing by the shva sign)*

4 **Vowel reduction II** *A vowel* (_) נַעַר
under a guttural **two** *steps before the stress is reduced (shown in writing by the chateph)*

5 **Vowel reduction I** *A vowel* (_) קָדוֹשׁ
one *step before the stress is reduced (shown in writing by the shva sign)*

6 **Full vowel** *With a vowel* (_) שֹׁמְרִים
letter, not affected by the stress

7 **Insertion vowel /e/** (_) סֵפֶר
(segol) Normally used to dissolve an impermissible two-consonant sequence at the end of a word

8 **Insertion vowel /a/** (_) סְפָרִים
After (i.e., under) a guttural, used to dissolve a two-consonant cluster at the end of a word

9 **Insertion vowel /i/** (_) עֲבוֹדוֹת
After (i.e., under) י *Yod, used to dissolve a two-consonant cluster at the end of a word*

10 **Silent** א *Áleph,* א *is left* (_) מֵאָדָם
unpronounced. The preceding vowel is not affected by the position of the stress in the word

II *Memorize* the names of the following Hebrew letters: א *Áleph,* ה *He,* ו *Vav,* י *Yod,* ח *Chet,* ע *Áyin* and ר *Resh.*

WORD LIST

Nouns

אָדָם *m,* person, man; mankind (☆ **Adam**)

אָח *m,* brother: *pl* אַחִים (☆ **Ahimelech**)

יהוה YHWH: the LORD, pronounced אֲדֹנָי ?ªdōnāy (☆ **Elijah, Jonathan**)[5]

מִצְוָה *f,* commandment: *pl* מִצְוֹת (miṣ wō t)(☆ Bar **mitzvah**)

סֵפֶר *m,* book: *pl* סְפָרִים

צָבָא *m,* army, host: *pl* צְבָאוֹת

שִׁיר *m,* song

Particles[3]

בְּ in, at, within, among; with, by (בְּ, בֵּ, בֶּ, בַ, בָּ)

כְּ like, as, according to (כְּ, כֵּ, כֶּ, כַ, כָּ) (☆ **Michael**)[4]

לְ to, for; of (לְ, לֵ, לֶ, לַ, לָ)

לֹא no, not

מִן/מִ from, out of; than (מֵ)

---

[3] This grammatical category includes *short words* מִלִּיּוֹת, that is, the definite article, prepositions, conjunctions, interjections and adverbs.

[4] The name Michael means 'Who is *like* God'.

[5] The elements 'Jah' and 'Jo' in the names Elijah and Jonathan are shortened forms of the divine name יהוה YHWH, the LORD (see p. 52).

EXERCISES

6.1 *Rewrite* the following clauses. *Read aloud* and *translate*. Proper names are enlarged. *Note*:

> ◆ The definite article may take various vowels: הָ, הַ or הֶ.
>
> ◆ An adjective describing a noun is always placed *after the noun* and *agrees* with it in *gender*, *number* and *definiteness* (both noun and adjective are either definite or indefinite): הָאִשָּׁה הַגְּדוֹלָה 'the great woman', literally, '*the* woman *the* great' or אִשָּׁה גְדוֹלָה '*a great woman*'.
>
> ◆ A proper name is considered definite (without the def. article), thus a following adjective takes the definite article: מִרְיָם הַגְּדוֹלָה 'Miriam the great'.
>
> ◆ An adjective used as a predicate is placed either *before or after* the subject and agrees with it in gender and number, but it *never takes the definite article*: גְּדוֹלָה הָאִשָּׁה or הָאִשָּׁה גְדוֹלָה 'the woman is *great*'.
>
> ◆ An additional personal pronoun (3ʳᵈ person: הוּא, הִיא, הֵם, הֵנָּה) which may appear either before or after the predicate should be left untranslated.
>
> ◆ The arrow shows you where to insert the correct form of the verb 'to be' (am, are, is) when you translate into English.

1   אִישׁ גָּדוֹל ← בְּיִשְׂרָאֵל.

  הָאִישׁ הַגָּדוֹל ← בְּיִשְׂרָאֵל.

2   שְׁלֹמֹה ← מֶלֶךְ גָּדוֹל.

3   קְדוֹשָׁה הִיא ← הַתּוֹרָה.

4   נֹחַ ← אִישׁ צַדִּיק.

5   גְּדוֹלִים הֵם ← הַצְּבָאוֹת.

6   שְׁלֹמֹה הַגָּדוֹל ← מֶלֶךְ.

7   הֶחָכָם ← מִבֵּית לֶחֶם.

  חָכָם ← מִבֵּית לֶחֶם.

8   יָשָׁר ← הַמֶּלֶךְ הֶחָכָם.

9   הַצַּדִּיק ← אִישׁ טוֹב הוּא.

  צַדִּיק ← הָאִישׁ הַטּוֹב.

10   הָאָדוֹן הַזָּקֵן ← מִבְּאֵר שֶׁבַע.

  זָקֵן ← הָאָדוֹן מִבְּאֵר שֶׁבַע.

6.2 Each group of clauses below contains an *adjective as predicate*. In the first clause the adjective is in the *positive* degree (e.g., טוֹב 'good'), in the second clause in the *comparative* (e.g., טוֹב מְ 'better') and in the third clause in the *superlative* (e.g., הַטוֹב 'best'). *Fill in* the blanks with the missing words according to the following examples. *Read* the clauses and *translate*. Proper names are enlarged. *Note*:

> - The form of the definite article is normally הַ, followed by a doubling dagesh in the following consonant. Before א *Áleph*, ע *Áyin* and ר *Resh* the form is הָ. Before ה *He* and ח *Chet* it is הַ (without a following doubling dagesh) and before unstressed הָ, חָ, עָ it is הֶ.
> - When the definite article follows בְּ, כְּ, לְ, the consonant ה *He* is omitted, its vowel being "inherited" by the preceding vowelless consonant, for example, כַּתּוֹרָה (instead of כְּהַתּוֹרָה).
> - מְ before gutturals and ר *Resh* becomes מֵ: מֵרָחֵל (not מְרָחֵל).
> - הִיא 'she' and הוּא 'he' correspond to English 'it'.
> - Superlative may also be expressed by the construction 'noun + הַ + the same noun in the plural': שִׁיר הַשִּׁירִים 'song of songs' (= the finest song).

The song is *as good as* a commandment.	טוֹב הַשִּׁיר כְּמִצְוָה
Literally, '*Good* the song *as* commandment'.	
The song is *better than* a commandment.	טוֹב הַשִּׁיר מִמִּצְוָה
Lit., '*Good* the song *than* commandment'.	
The song is *best*.	הַשִּׁיר הוּא הַטוֹב
Lit., 'The song, it *the good*'.	
The song is the *best* of songs.	הַשִּׁיר הוּא הַטוֹב בַּשִּׁירִים
Lit., 'The song, it the good among the songs'.	
It is the *song of songs* (= the finest song).	הוּא שִׁיר הַשִּׁירִים
Lit., 'It song the songs'.	

3 גְּדוֹלָה הַתּוֹרָה כַּתַּלְמוּד.　　1 צַדִּיקִים הַנְּבִיאִים כַּמְּלָכִים.

גְּדוֹלָה הַתּוֹרָה _____　　צַדִּיקִים הַנְּבִיאִים _____

הַתּוֹרָה הִיא _____ בַּ _____　　הַנְּבִיאִים הֵם _____

4 חָכָם שְׁלֹמֹה כְּדָוִד.　　2 חֲכָמִים הַשּׁוֹפְטִים כִּמְלָכִים.

חָכָם שְׁלֹמֹה _____　　חֲכָמִים הַשּׁוֹפְטִים _____

שְׁלֹמֹה הוּא _____　　הַשּׁוֹפְטִים הֵם _____

5 שָׁלֵם הָאָדָם כָּאֵל.

אֱלֹהִים שָׁלֵם _____

אֱלֹהִים הוּא _____

8 טוֹב הַסֵּפֶר כְּשִׁיר.

טוֹב הַסֵּפֶר _____

הַסֵּפֶר הוּא _____

הוּא _____ _____

6 זָקֵן הַמֶּלֶךְ כַּכֹּהֵן.

זָקֵן הַמֶּלֶךְ _____

הַמֶּלֶךְ הוּא _____ בַּ _____

9 יָשָׁר הַנָּבִיא כְּמֶלֶךְ.

יָשָׁר הַנָּבִיא _____

הַנָּבִיא הוּא _____

7 קָדוֹשׁ אֵל כָּאָדָם.

קָדוֹשׁ אֵל _____

הָאֵל הוּא _____

10 יְרוּשָׁלַיִם גְּדוֹלָה כְּאַשְׁקְלוֹן.

יְרוּשָׁלַיִם גְּדוֹלָה _____

יְרוּשָׁלַיִם הִיא _____

6.3 *Read* the following verse segments, drawn from the Hebrew Bible, and *translate*. *Render* these isolated verbless clauses in the present tense. However, in the Key they are rendered in the tense required by the context in which they appear in the Bible. Proper names are enlarged. *Note*:

- A vocalized biblical text includes, apart from the vowel signs, also *accent signs*, written above and below the letters, indicating the position of the stress in the word and the punctuation of the verse.
 – The end of the verse (*soph pasuq*) is marked by the sign ⬚ ⃥ .
 – The two major breaks in reading (called *pause*) are at the *end* and in the *middle of the verse*. The break at the end of the verse is marked by a vertical stroke, called *silluq* ⬚ , placed either to the left of the vowel sign or directly under the consonant of the stressed syllable in the word. The silluq is always followed by the sign for *soph pasuq*: אֲנִי, הוּא. The break in the middle of the verse is marked by *atnach* צְבָאוֹת, הָאִישׁ. The accent signs silluq and atnach are not rendered in this book.
- A word in pause may undergo sound changes (more about sound changes in pausal forms in Exercise 12.8).

(1 Chron. 23:1) דָּוִיד זָקֵן 9 **II**	(Dan. 8:21) הוּא הַמֶּלֶךְ 1 **I**
(Gen. 13:8) אַחִים אֲנָחְנוּ: 10	(Ex. 11:3) הָאִישׁ מֹשֶׁה גָּדוֹל 2
(Jer. 12:1) צַדִּיק אַתָּה יהוה 11	(2 Sam. 12:7) אַתָּה הָאִישׁ 3
(Prov. 30:24) הֵמָּה חֲכָמִים 12	(Gen. 28:13) אֲנִי יהוה 4
(Gen. 20:7) נָבִיא הוּא 13	(Gen. 6:9) נֹחַ אִישׁ צַדִּיק 5
(Num. 23:19) לֹא אִישׁ אֵל 14	(1 Kings 18:39) יהוה הוּא הָאֱלֹהִים: 6
(Lev.11:45) קָדוֹשׁ אָנִי: 15	(Jer. 8:8) חֲכָמִים אֲנַחְנוּ 7
חָכָם אַתָּה מִדָּנִאֵל 16	קָדוֹשׁ קָדוֹשׁ קָדוֹשׁ יהוה צְבָאוֹת 8
(Ezek. 28:3)	(Isa. 6:3)

6.4 *Compare* the normal vowel pattern of the word אֲנַחְנוּ 'we' in clause 7 in Exercise 6.3 above and its form in pause in clause 10 אֲנָחְנוּ:. Then *compare* the normal vowel and stress pattern of the word אֲנִי 'I' in clause 4 and its form in pause in clause 15 אָנִי:. *Describe* the vowel and stress change which occur in the words in pause.

6.5 *Reread* clauses 1–8 (group **I**) in Exercise 6.3 above and *translate* again *orally*. Then *translate* clauses 1–5 (group **I**) below into Hebrew, assisted by the Hebrew clauses in Exercise 6.3. *Proceed* to clauses 9–16 (group **II**) in Exercise 6.3, following the same procedure. *Remember*:

> ◆ The word אֱלֹהִים indicating God takes adjectives and predicates in the singular.
> ◆ The predicate in the verbless clause may be placed either before or after the subject.

I 1 I am righteous.
 2 You *(m, s)* are a wise king.
 3 God is great.
 4 The armies are big.
 5 We are holy.

II 6 You *(m, p)* are old.
 7 He is older than David.
 8 They *(m)* are the righteous prophets.
 9 You are *(m, pl)* better than the king.
 10 The LORD (YHWH) is the best.

SECTION 7

1 *Word formation in general*: Words in Hebrew generally have *three root consonants* placed in various *word patterns*. A word pattern is composed of vowels, possible additional elements and/or a doubled middle root consonant.

2 *Unchangeable and changeable consonants*: In reality, a consonant is not always a completely isolated sound unit, but may either affect or be affected by surrounding sounds.

– *Unchangeable consonants (strong consonants)*: The majority of consonants are not substantially affected by the surrounding sound units. These consonants are called unchangeable. An unchangeable consonant is *audible in pronunciation and visible in writing* in all word patterns and inflections.

– *Gutturals* (א, ה, ח, ע) are *unchangeable* consonants. They affect, however, the surrounding vowels, which results in words with *deviant vowel patterns* (see Grammatical cornerstone 4).

– *BeGaDKeFaT-consonants* (ב, ג, ד, כ, פ, ת) are also regarded as *unchangeable*. They are, however, affected by an immediately preceding vowel or a reduced vowel. The hard sound of the BeGaDKeFaT-consonants becomes soft after a vowel/reduced vowel (shown in writing by the absence of the hardening dagesh), e.g., הֶבֶל hevel.

– *Changeable consonants (weak consonants)*: א[1], ה, ו, י, נ and doubled consonants are changeable (that is, they undergo sound changes, see 3 below). They are liable to sound changes when words are formed, inflected or combined with other elements or words. א, ה, ו, י, נ and doubled consonants are changeable mostly when there is no vowel preceding or following them (shva is regarded as no-vowel!). However, when they are surrounded by vowels, no sound changes occur.

3 *Regular consonant change*: A changeable consonant may be either *silenced* (the consonant is not heard but remains in writing), *omitted* (the consonant disappears also in writing), totally *assimilated* (the consonant becomes identical with the following consonant) or *simplified* (the consonant loses its doubling). See Grammatical cornerstone 5 below.

– Observe that a doubled consonant without a following vowel at the end of a word results in an impermissible two-consonant sequence. *A syllable may not end in more than one consonant.* The consonant cluster is dissolved by *simplification* (the doubling dagesh is removed, e.g., לּ becomes ל).

A vowelless doubled consonant within the word (often י) also tends to lose its doubling, e.g., וַיְּדַבֵּר 'he talked' becomes וַיְדַבֵּר.

4 *Unchangeable and changeable root types*: Word roots with the same kind of consonants behave the same way. Word roots are divided into unchangeable and changeable root types.

---

[1] א and ה either affect the surrounding vowels (as gutturals) or undergo sound change.

– *Unchangeable root types* retain their root consonants unchanged in all word patterns and inflections. They are designated שְׁלֵמִים which means 'complete, sound' with regard to their survival in a 'complete' state in all formations and inflections.

– *Changeable root types* include changeable consonant/s and/or guttural/s. The presence of a changeable consonant/s and/or guttural/s in a word root results in forms that deviate from the normal word patterns and inflections in the language. The sound changes are, however, predictable (see Grammatical cornerstone 5 below). Changeable root types are classified in groups according to the changeable consonant/guttural and its place in the word root, i.e., first, second or third. In the word root נפל, for example, the changeable consonant נ constitutes the first root consonant and therefore the root is classified as I-נ (= first root consonant is Nun).

5 *Inseparable prepositions* לְ, כְּ, בְּ, *followed by* יהוה *YHWH and* אֱלֹהִים

– בְּ, כְּ, לְ attached to the *divine name* יהוה (pronounced אֲדֹנָי 'the Lᴏʀᴅ') results in a cluster, thus בְּאֲדֹנָי becomes בַּאֲדֹנָי. The consonant א irregularly loses its chateph, being transformed into a silent א: בַּאדֹנָי (written בַּיהוה).

– בְּ, כְּ, לְ attached to the divine name אֱלֹהִים 'God' results in a cluster as well, thus בְּאֱלֹהִים becomes בַּאֱלֹהִים. Here also the consonant א irregularly loses its chateph, being transformed into a silent א: בַּאלֹהִים. The silencing of א is compensated by lengthening the preceding vowel: בַּאלֹהִים becomes בֵּאלֹהִים (however, no lengthening occurs before יהוה: בַּיהוה).

MEMORIZE

REGULAR CONSONANT CHANGE[2]

Only א, ה, ו, י, נ, the so-called weak consonants, and doubled consonants are changeable. Sound changes occur primarily when there is no vowel either before or after the changeable consonant.

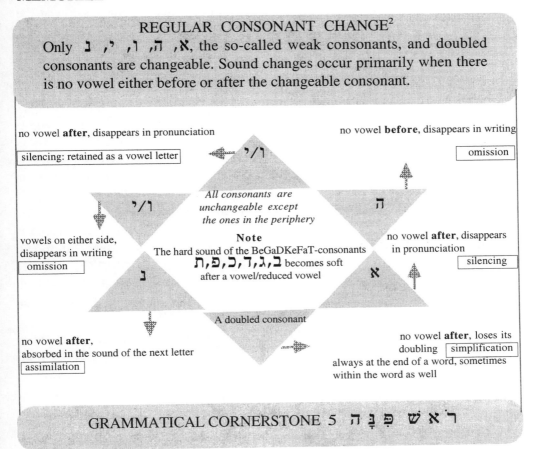

no vowel **after**, disappears in pronunciation

silencing: retained as a vowel letter

ו/י

no vowel **before**, disappears in writing

omission

ו/י

All consonants are
unchangeable except
the ones in the periphery

ה

vowels on either side,
disappears in writing

omission

נ

Note
The hard sound of the BeGaDKeFaT-consonants
ב,ג,ד,כ,פ,ת becomes soft
after a vowel/reduced vowel

no vowel **after**, disappears
in pronunciation

silencing

א

no vowel **after**,
absorbed in the sound of the next letter

assimilation

A doubled consonant

no vowel **after**, loses its
doubling   simplification
always at the end of a word, sometimes
within the word as well

GRAMMATICAL CORNERSTONE 5 ר א שׁ פּ נ ה

REVIEW AND APPLICATION OF THE RULES

I *Study* the sound change rules listed below and *vocalize* the vowelless inseparable prepositions בְּ, כְּ, לְ, מְ ⊡. *Add* the doubling dagesh in the next letter wherever necessary. *Indicate* the relevant sound change rule/s from the list below. *Note*:

- All the inseparable prepositions below undergo vowel change/s.
- The consonant after the preposition may also undergo sound change/s.

---

[2] For consonant change via Hebrew names, see Sections 23 and 24.

SOUND CHANGE RULES

1 A sequence of two vowelless consonants in immediate succession at the beginning of a syllable is not permitted, e.g., כְּבְרִית *kᵉvᵉrît. *A syllable may not begin with more than two consonants.* The impermissible consonant sequence is broken up by inserting a vowel between the two vowelless consonants, normally an /i/-vowel: כְּבְרִית becomes כְּבִ-רִית.[3]

2 The insertion vowel before a guttural with a chateph (shva-plus-vowel) matches the vowel of the chateph, e.g., בְּאָבִי becomes בַּ-אֲבִי, לְאֱנוֹשׁ becomes לֶ-אֱנוֹשׁ.

3 The consonant נ at the end of a syllable is generally assimilated to (absorbed in) the sound of the next consonant, which, in turn, is doubled (shown in writing by the doubling dagesh): מִנְטְבֶרְיָה becomes מִטְּבֶרְיָה.

4 The consonant י/ו at the end of a syllable forms a diphthong, e.g., לְיְ-הוּדָה. *A syllable may not have more than one vowel.* The vowel cluster is normally adjusted by the silencing of י/ו. That is, י/ו disappears in pronunciation but is retained in writing as a vowel letter: לְיְ-הוּדָה becomes לִיהוּדָה.

5 The consonant ה after a vowelless consonant is sometimes omitted, its vowel being "inherited" by the preceding consonant. The doubling in the following letter is, however, retained: כְּהַתּוֹרָה becomes כַּתּוֹרָה.

6 Gutturals and ר cannot be doubled. Instead of doubling, the preceding short vowel is often lengthened: הָרֹאשׁ (not הַרֹּאשׁ), מֵרָחֵל (not מִרָּחֵל).

7 The hard sound of a BeGaDKeFaT-consonant becomes soft after a vowel or a reduced vowel (vocal shva or chateph), which is shown in writing by the absence of the hardening dagesh: לְבַיִת (not לְבַּיִת).

7	בְּ + חֲרָבוֹת --> בַּחֲרָבוֹת			1	לְ + נְבִיאָה --> לִנְבִיאָה	
8	מִן + הַשִּׁיר --> מֵהַשִּׁיר			2	כְּ + כְּלִי --> כִּכְלִי	
9	לְ + עֲבָדִים --> לַעֲבָדִים			3	מִן + סֵפֶר --> מִסֵּפֶר	
10	כְּ + הָאִישׁ --> כָּאִישׁ			4	בְּ + יְרוּשָׁלַיִם --> בִּירוּשָׁלַיִם (Jerusalem)	
11	לְ + צְבָאוֹת --> לִצְבָאוֹת			5	כְּ + אֲדָמָה --> כַּאֲדָמָה	
12	בְּ + בְּרִית --> בִּבְרִית			6	לְ + הַצָּבָא --> לַצָּבָא	

II *Match* each sound element with the Hebrew word that illustrates it. *Mark* the element in the Hebrew word clearly! Observe that the same sound element may appear in more than one word, but only one element is to be marked. Each word is to be used once!

---

[3] This rule is known in some grammars of Biblical Hebrew as *The Rule of Sheva.*

1 Vowel reduction **I** *A vowel*   (_) כֹּתֶבֶת
  one *step before the stress is reduced*

2 Vowel reduction **II** *A vowel*   (_) מִזְקֵן
  two *steps before the stress is reduced*

3 Vowel reduction **II** *A vowel*   (_) הֹלְכִים
  under a guttural **two** *steps before*
  the stress is reduced

4 Insertion vowel /i/ *at the*   (_) מְלָכִים
  beginning of a syllable To dissolve
  a three-consonant sequence

5 Insertion vowel /a/ *at the*   (_) כֵּאלֹהִים
  beginning of a syllable Before a guttural,
  to dissolve a three-consonant sequence

6 The consonant י *is*   (_) עֲזוּבִים
  transformed into a vowel letter
  To adjust a diphthong

7 Silent א *Before the*   (_) לִיהוּדָה
  word 'God'

8 Vowel lengthening (_) לִנְבִיאִים
  Instead of doubling a guttural or ר

9 Insertion vowel /e/ (_) בַּעַל
  To dissolve a cluster at
  the end of a word

10 Insertion vowel /a/ (_) לַעֲבוֹדָה
  Under a guttural, to dissolve
  a cluster at the end of a word

11 Assimilation of נ   (_) בַּשִּׁיר
  closing a syllable The next
  consonant takes a doubling dagesh

12 The consonant ה   (_) מֵהַמֶּלֶךְ
  is omitted After a
  vowelless consonant

III *Match* each root type with the Hebrew word that illustrates it. *Remember:*

> - An *unchangeable consonant* in a word root is *audible* in pronunciation and *visible* in writing in all word patterns and inflections.
> - A *guttural* in a word root may *affect* the surrounding *vowels*.
> - A *changeable consonant* (א, ה, ו, י, נ) in a word root may be either *omitted or altered* (i.e., *silenced or assimilated*).

1 שְׁלֵמִים (unchangeable)(_) יָשָׁר, ישׁר

2 I (= 1ˢᵗ)-guttural   (_) דָּבָר, דבר

3 II (= 2ⁿᵈ)-guttural   (_) שִׁיר, שׁיר

4 III (= 3ʳᵈ)-guttural   (_) מָוֶת, מות

5 I-י (1ˢᵗ Yod)   (_) כֹּהֵן, כהן

6 II-י (2ⁿᵈ Yod)   (_) חָכָם, חכם

7 II-ו (2ⁿᵈ Vav)   (_) רָשָׁע, רשׁע

8 III-י (3ʳᵈ Yod)   (_) כְּלִי, כלי

WORD LIST

Nouns

אֲדָמָה	*f,* ground, soil; earth (✡ Adam)
אֶרֶץ	*f,* earth; land, country: *pl* אֲרָצוֹת, *with definite article* הָאָרֶץ
דָּבָר	*m,* word; thing; matter, affair
דֶּרֶךְ	*c⁴,* way, road: *pl* דְּרָכִים
חֶרֶב	*f,* sword: *pl* חֲרָבוֹת

יוֹם	*m,* day: *pl* יָמִים
כְּלִי	*m,* vessel, utensil: *pl* כֵּלִים
לֶחֶם	*m,* bread, food (✡ Bethlehem)
מָוֶת	*m,* death

⁴ Common gender, both masculine and feminine.

Adjectives   *Particles*

חָדָשׁ   new   מְאֹד   very, exceedingly
רָשָׁע   wicked, criminal, impious, sinful

EXERCISES

7.1 *Check* (and *correct* if needed) the vowels inserted before the nouns in
REVIEW AND APPLICATION OF THE RULES I. Then *rewrite* the words with
the preceding inseparable preposition, *transliterate* and *divide into syllables*.
Read and *translate*. Note:

> ◆ Two vowelless consonants at the beginning of a syllable become a
>   *closed syllable* by means of an insertion vowel, normally an /i/-vowel.
>   A BeGaDKeFaT-consonant immediately after this closed syllable retains
>   its soft sound: לְנְבִי-אִים becomes לִנ-בִי-אִים.
> ◆ The insertion vowel breaking up a cluster before a guttural with a
>   chateph (shva-plus-vowel) is a short vowel that matches the vowel of the
>   chateph: לֶ-אֱלִי-שָׁ-בַע, לַ-אֲבִי-מֶ-לֶךְ (chateph always begins a syllable).[5]

7.2 *Read* the following clauses and *translate orally*. Then *substitute* the enlarged
words in each group of clauses with the word given in parentheses and
change the clauses accordingly. *Translate*. Remember:

> ◆ The predicate should agree with the subject in gender and number.
> ◆ The adjective should agree with the noun in gender, number and definiteness.
> ◆ The arrow shows you where to insert the proper form of the verb 'to
>   be' (am, are, is) when you translate into English.

1 הַמֶּלֶךְ הַצַּדִּיק ↽ זָקֵן. (הַמְּלָכִים) _____

הַמֶּלֶךְ הַצַּדִּיק ↽ זָקֵן מֵהָאִישׁ הָרָשָׁע. _____

הַמֶּלֶךְ הַצַּדִּיק ↽ זָקֵן מְאֹד. _____

2 הַחַיִּים בִּירוּשָׁלַיִם ↽ טוֹבִים. (Jerusalem) (הַבְּרִית) _____

הַחַיִּים ↽ טוֹבִים מֵהַמָּוֶת. _____

הַחַיִּים בִּירוּשָׁלַיִם הַקְּדוֹשָׁה ↽ טוֹבִים מְאֹד. _____

3 הָאִישׁ ↽ חָכָם כְּנָבִיא. (הַנָּשִׁים) _____

הָאִישׁ מִיהוּדָה ↽ יָשָׁר מִנָּבִיא. (Judah) _____

הָאִישׁ הַיָּשָׁר מִיהוּדָה ↽ בַּצָּבָא. _____

---

[5] Actually, the syllable division should have been לֶ-אֱלִי-שֶׁבַע, לַ-אֲבִי-מֶלֶךְ (with the consonant
with the chateph, after the insertion vowel, closing the syllable), as in לִנ-בִיאִים. However, for
practical reasons, we let the chateph open the next syllable.

4 הַצָּבָא הַגָּדוֹל ↤ בָּאָרֶץ. (הָאִשָּׁה)

הַצָּבָא ↤ בָּאָרֶץ הַגְּדוֹלָה.

הַצָּבָא בָּאָרֶץ ↤ הוּא הַגָּדוֹל בַּצְּבָאוֹת.

5 הַתּוֹרָה ↤ קְדוֹשָׁה מְאֹד. (הַדָּבָר)

הַתּוֹרָה ↤ קְדוֹשָׁה מֵהַשִּׁיר.

הַתּוֹרָה הִיא ↤ הַקְּדוֹשָׁה בַּסְּפָרִים.

7.3 *Transform* the following clauses from the singular into the *plural*. Then *read aloud* and *translate*. Proper names are enlarged. *Remember*:

> • When a word takes an ending, the stress is usually moved forward to the newly added ending. As a result, a vowel in an open syllable either one or two steps before the stress is reduced: גָּדוֹל --> גְּדוֹלָה, שָׁמַר --> שֹׁמְרִים.
>
> • Gutturals take a chateph (shva-plus-vowel) instead of a shva: חָבֵר --> חֲבֵרִים.

1 אָב זָקֵן הוּא.

2 הָאָב הַזָּקֵן בָּאָרֶץ הַטּוֹבָה.

3 אַתָּה לֹא צַדִּיק, רָשָׁע אַתָּה מְאֹד.

4 אַתְּ הַשּׁוֹפֶטֶת הַגְּדוֹלָה מִיִשְׂרָאֵל.

5 אֲנִי נָבִיא בִּירוּשָׁלַיִם הַקְּדוֹשָׁה.

6 דֶּרֶךְ חֲדָשָׁה הִיא.

7 הַדֶּרֶךְ הַחֲדָשָׁה טוֹבָה מְאֹד.

8 כְּלִי גָּדוֹל הוּא.

9 הָאִישׁ הָרָשָׁע מֵאֶרֶץ טוֹבָה.

10 קָדוֹשׁ הָאֵל.

7.4 *Translate* the following clauses into Hebrew.
  1 The words are very good.
  2 God is wiser than man.
  3 The new sword is big.
  4 The holy soil is very big.
  5 The road in the holy land is good.
  6 It is a great day.
  7 The commandments in the Law are very good.
  8 The judge is as upright as a king.
  9 The elders from Zion are righteous.
  10 The master is the best of masters (= among the masters).

☆ עִבְרִית בְּעֶזְרַת הַשֵּׁם ☆

As previously mentioned in Section 1, the original Hebrew alphabet consisted of consonants only, whereas vowels (and dagesh) were not represented in writing. When Hebrew names are used as a learning aid, you must keep in mind that the fundamental meaning of a Hebrew word is conveyed by the consonants, whereas the vowels play a secondary role, specifying the meaning.

From word list 8 onwards only the root consonants of the Hebrew names will be marked, for instance, כֹּהֵן (☆ Cohen). If all three root consonants are not pronounced and/or they are altered in English pronunciation, the three root consonants of the Hebrew name will be given after the name in the parentheses: שָׁאוּל (☆ Saul, š.ʔ.l).

Observe that the vowel pattern (inclusive the dagesh) of a Hebrew name does not always correspond to the English pronunciation. For instance, שְׁמוּאֵל is pronounced Samuel (the /a/-vowel after שׁ is not reduced). רִבְקָה is pronounced Rebekah (the vowel after ר is /e/ instead of /i/, the /e/-vowel after ב is not reduced and ב has a hard instead of a soft sound, namely /b/). פַּרְעֹה is pronounced Pharaoh (the פ has a soft instead of a hard sound, namely /f/, and the /a/-vowel after ר is not reduced).

Furthermore, a number of Hebrew names end in an additional 'n' or 's', which are Greek endings: שְׁלֹמֹה (Solomon) or מֹשֶׁה (Moses).

There are *five types of Hebrew names*: דֶּרֶךְ
1 *Noun*: יָעֵל (Jael, y.ʕ.l, 'steinbock').
2 *Adjective*: דָּוִד (David, d.w.d 'beloved').
3 *Noun chain*: בְּאֵר שֶׁבַע (Beer-sheba: b.ʔ.r + š.b.ʕ 'well of oath').
4 *Verb*: יִצְחָק (Isaac, s.h.q 'he laughs').
5 *Clause*, either verbless or verbal, often with the divine name as subject, either אֵל (God) or יָהּ/יָהוּ/יוֹ (elements denoting YHWH, the Lord): אֵלִיָּה/אֵלִיָּהוּ (Elijah, 'The Lord is my God'), רְפָאֵל (Rephael, 'God cured'), יוֹנָתָן (Jonathan, 'The Lord gave').

SECTION 8

1   *Conjunction* וְ *'and'*: The basic form is וְ. The conjunction וְ is attached to the following word: כֹּהֵן וְנָבִיא 'a priest *and* a prophet'. In certain positions וְ undergoes vowel changes identical to those occurring in בְּ, כְּ, לְ in the same positions, except in the following three cases:
  – Before a consonant with a shva וְ becomes וּ: וּשְׁלֹמֹה (compare לִשְׁלֹמֹה 'to Solomon').
  – Before the consonants ב, מ, פ the conjunction וְ also becomes וּ: וּמִרְיָם (compare כְּמִרְיָם 'like Miriam').
  Observe that וּ 'and' is the only exception to the rule that a syllable may not begin with a vowel and may not consist of a vowel only: וּ-שְׁלֹ-מֹה û-šᵊlō-mō^h, וּ-מִרְ-יָם û-mir-yām.
  – A definite article after וְ retains its ה: וְהַבַּיִת (compare בַּבַּיִת 'in the house', from the hypothetical form בְּהַבַּיִת).

2   *Demonstrative pronouns*
  זֶה 'this', *m*; זֹאת 'this', *f*; אֵלֶּה 'these', *c* (common gender; both *m* and *f*).
  הַהוּא 'that', *m*; הַהִיא 'that', *f*; הָהֵם/הָהֵמָּה 'those', *m*; הָהֵנָּה 'those', *f*.
  – The demonstrative pronouns without the definite article function as ordinary pronouns: זֶה כֹּהֵן *'This* is a priest', הוּא כֹּהֵן *'He* is a priest'.
  – The demonstrative pronouns with the definite article function as adjectives describing nouns: הַכֹּהֵן הַזֶּה טוֹב *'This* priest is good', הַכֹּהֵן הַהוּא טוֹב 'That priest is good' (compare הַכֹּהֵן הַטּוֹב בַּבַּיִת 'The *good* priest is in the house').

3   *Noun types*: There are five noun types in Hebrew: regular masculine nouns, regular feminine nouns, penultimate nouns (nouns with the stress on the next-to-last syllable), twin-consonant nouns (nouns whose last two consonants are identical) and irregular nouns.

4   *Regular masculine nouns*: Regular masculine nouns include both unchangeable and changeable nouns, e.g., דָּבָר 'word', מִשְׁפָּט 'judgement', קוֹל 'voice', צָבָא 'army'. Regular masculine nouns are vocalized in accordance with the basic rule of vocalization and in the course of inflection they undergo regular vowel and consonant change (see Grammatical cornerstones 2–5).

5   *Regular feminine nouns*: Regular feminine nouns include both unchangeable and changeable nouns that normally end in ה‎ָ or ת, e.g., מִצְוָה, תּוֹרָה 'law', 'commandment', בְּרִית 'covenant'. Regular feminine nouns are vocalized in accordance with the basic rule of vocalization and in the course of inflection they undergo regular vowel and consonant change (see Grammatical cornerstones 2–5).

6   *Penultimate nouns*: Penultimate nouns consist of nouns with the stress on the next-to-last syllable, i.e., the penultimate. Two groups can be distinguished, masculine nouns and feminine nouns.

– *Masculine penultimate nouns* (traditionally called *segolates*)[1] occur in three vowel patterns with an insertion vowel before the last consonant to dissolve an impermissible two-consonant sequence at the end of the word. The insertion vowel is normally /e/, segol (hence the name *segolates*): מֶלֶךְ 'king' (from the original form *malk), סֵפֶר 'book' (originally *sifr) and בֹּקֶר 'morning' (originally *buqr).

Before and after a guttural the insertion vowel is not /e/ but /a/. *Gutturals attract an /a/-vowel/s*: בַּעַל 'owner' (from the original form *baʕl), פֶּתַח 'opening' (originally *pitḥ).

After ' the insertion vowel is /i/. *' attracts an /i/-vowel*: יַיִן 'wine' (from the original form *yayn).

Penultimate nouns with the insertion vowel /e/ and /a/ (regardless of vowel pattern) share the same pattern in the plural, – – – ים/וֹת:
מְלָכִים 'kings', סְפָרִים 'books', בְּעָלִים 'owners', אֲרָצוֹת 'lands'.

– *Feminine penultimate nouns* are derived either from the original form of a masculine penultimate noun or from a regular masculine noun ending in a consonant.

Feminine nouns derived from the original form of a masculine penultimate noun (e.g., *malk 'king') take the feminine ending ה ָ:
מַלְכָּה 'queen' (from *malk 'king'), יַלְדָּה 'girl' (from *yald 'boy'). The plural follows the pattern – – ְ – וֹת: מְלָכוֹת 'queens', יְלָדוֹת 'girls'.

Feminine nouns derived from a regular masculine noun ending in a consonant take the feminine ending ת: שׁוֹפֵט + the feminine ending ת' results in שׁוֹפֵ-טְת, with a final syllable ending in two consonants. The consonants of the cluster are separated by inserting a vowel, normally /e/ (segol): שׁוֹפֶטֶת. However, after the gutturals ה, ח, ע the insertion vowel is not /e/ but /a/: שׁוֹפֶטֶת and יוֹדַעַת. יוֹדַעַת share the same pattern in plural, שֹׁפְטוֹת, יוֹדְעוֹת: – – ְ – וֹ-/ – – ְ – וֹת.

---

[1] A few feminine nouns, however, are included in this group.

MEMORIZE

PRONOUNS I							
Independent Personal Pronouns				Demonstrative Pronouns			
Singular		Plural		Singular			Plural
I	אָנֹכִי/אֲנִי	we	אֲנַ֫חְנוּ	this, *m*	זֶה	these, *c*	אֵ֫לֶּה
you, *m*	אַתָּה	you, *m*	אַתֶּם	this, *f*	זֹאת		
you, *f*	אַתְּ	you, *f*	אַתֵּן/אַתֵּ֫נָה				
he	הוּא	they, *m*	הֵם/הֵ֫מָּה	that, *m*	הַהוּא	those, *m*	הָהֵם/הָהֵ֫מָּה
she	הִיא	they, *f*	הֵ֫נָּה	that, *f*	הַהִיא	those, *f*	הָהֵ֫נָּה

GRAMMATICAL CORNERSTONE 6   ר א שׁ פּ בּ ג ה

REVIEW AND APPLICATION OF THE RULES

I *Match* each sound element with the Hebrew word that illustrates it. *Mark* the element in the Hebrew word clearly! Observe that the same sound element may appear in more than one word, but only one element is to be marked. Each word is to be used once!

1 Vowel reduction **I** *A vowel one step before the stress is reduced*

2 Vowel reduction **I** *A vowel under a guttural one step before the stress is reduced*

3 Vowel reduction **II** *A vowel two steps before the stress is reduced*

4 Vowel reduction **II** *A vowel under a guttural two steps before the stress is reduced*

5 ו 'and' before ב, מ, פ

6 Insertion vowel /a/ at the beginning of a syllable *Before a guttural, to dissolve a three-consonant sequence*

7 The consonant י becomes a vowel letter *To eliminate a diphthong*

(_) אֲרָצוֹת **8** Silent א *Before the* (_) וִיהוּדָה *divine name 'God'*

(_) וֵאלֹהִים **9** Insertion vowel /e/ (_) זֶ֫בַח *To dissolve a two-consonant sequence at the end of a word*

(_) עַ֫יִן **10** Vowel lengthening *Instead of* (_) וּנְבִיאִים *doubling a guttural or* ר

(_) בַּדֶּ֫רֶךְ **11** Insertion vowel /i/ (_) וּפַרְעֹה *Separating two vowelless consonants at the end of a word*

(_) דֶּ֫רֶךְ **12** ו before a shva (_) וַעֲבוֹדָה

(_) מֵאֶ֫רֶץ **13** Insertion vowel /a/ (_) שְׁפָטוֹת *To dissolve a two-consonant sequence at the end of a word*

(_) כֹּהֲנִים **14** ה is omitted (_) דְּרָכִים *Its vowel is transferred to the preceding vowelless consonant*

II The enlarged Hebrew word in each group below deviates from the other three words in the group. *Match* the enlarged Hebrew word with its deviant feature. Observe that more than one deviation may appear in each enlarged word, but only one is referred to.

1 דְּבָרִים - נְבִיאִים - **שׁוֹפְטִים** - צְבָאוֹת ( ) The word has the insertion vowel /e/ in the final syllable, not /a/

2 בַּגַּת - בְּיִשְׂרָאֵל - בְּעֻזָּה - **בִּטְבֶרְיָה** ( ) ה after the vowelless consonant is retained, not omitted

3 אֱלֹהִים - אֲנִי - **אָדָם** - אֲדָמָה ( ) The guttural takes a chateph (shva-plus-vowel) instead of a shva

4 חֲכָמִים - גְּדוֹלִים - קְדוֹשִׁים - **זְקֵנִים** ( ) The word starts with one consonant, not two (chateph is not regarded as a vowel!)

5 בַּעַל - פֶּתַח - **מֶלֶךְ** - שַׁעַר ( ) The vowel before the guttural is lengthened (since a guttural cannot be doubled)

6 **הָאִשָּׁה** - הַבַּעַל - הַכֹּהֵן - הַמִּצְוָה ( ) The vowel one step (not two!) before the stress is reduced (shown in writing by the shva sign)

7 וְהַיַּרְדֵּן - לַכִּנֶּרֶת - בַּגָּלִיל - כַּצָּבָא ( ) The vowel before ר is lengthened (since ר cannot be doubled)

8 מִיָּעֵל - מִלָּבָן - **מֵרָחֵל** - מִדָּוִד ( ) The word has a syllable with an abnormal structure (וְ 'and')

9 סֵפֶר - יָעֵל - מֶלֶךְ - **לֶחֶם** ( ) The word has the stress on the last syllable, not next-to-last

10 וְדָוִד - וְשָׁאוּל - וּפַרְעֹה - **וְאֶפְרַיִם** ( ) The word has an insertion vowel breaking up a three-consonant sequence at the beginning of the word

III *Match* each root type with the Hebrew word that illustrates it.

1 I-guttural   ( ) גָּדוֹל, גדל   5 I-י (1st Yod) ( ) מִשְׁנָה, שׁנה

2 II-guttural   ( ) מָקוֹם, קום   6 II-י (2nd Yod) ( ) נַעַר, נער

3 III-guttural   ( ) יְלָדִים, ילד   7 II-ו (2nd Vav) ( ) בַּיִת, בית

4 Unchangeable שְׁלֵמִים ( ) פֶּתַח, פתח   8 III-ה (3rd He) ( ) עֲבָדִים, עבד

WORD LIST

Nouns

מִשְׁפָּט   *m,* judgement, legal decision, ordinance; justice

נַעַר   *m,* lad, young man: *pl* נְעָרִים

עֶבֶד   *m,* servant, slave: pl עֲבָדִים
(☆ Obadiah, ʕ.b.d)

עַיִן   *f,* eye: *dual* עֵינַיִם
(☆ the letter Áyin, ʕ.y.n)

פֶּתַח   *m,* opening, entrance: *pl* פְּתָחִים

רוּחַ   *f,* spirit; wind: *pl* רוּחוֹת

שַׁעַר   *m,* gate: *pl* שְׁעָרִים

Demonstrative pronouns

זֶה   *m,* this: הַהוּא that

זֹאת   *f,* this: הַהִיא that

אֵלֶּה   *c,* these: הָהֵם/הָהֵמָּה those *(m)*
הָהֵנָּה those *(f)*

Particles

וְ (וּ, וֶ, וִ, וַ, וֵ, וֹ)
   and (also 'but; or')

EXERCISES

8.1 *Fill in* the blanks with the correct demonstrative pronoun (זֶה, זֹאת, אֵלֶּה) in the manner of the example given below. *Read* the clauses and *translate*. *Note*:

> - The basic form of the definite article is הַ followed by a doubling dagesh in the next consonant. Before א, ע, ר the form is הָ and before ה, ח it is הַ (without a following doubling dagesh).
> - The gender of the adjective in the second clause in each group will help you to determine the gender of the noun and hence to choose the correct demonstrative pronoun (זֶה or זֹאת).
>   The *base form* of the adjective is the masculine singular: טוֹב 'god'. Feminine singular **always** takes the ending ה ָ: טוֹבָה. Masculine plural **always** takes the ending ים ִ: טוֹבִים. Feminine plural **always** takes the ending וֹת added to the base form: טוֹבוֹת.
> - An additional personal pronoun (3rd person: הוּא, הִיא, הֵם, הֵנָּה), which may appear either before or after the predicate, should be left untranslated.

This is a slave.	זֶה עֶבֶד.
Literally, '*This* slave'.	
This slave is new.	הָעֶבֶד הַזֶּה חָדָשׁ.
Lit., 'The slave, *this*, new'.	

2 _____ דֶּרֶךְ.   1 _____ חֶרֶב.

_____ יְשָׁרָה.   גְּדוֹלָה הִיא.

נַעַר.	_____	7	מִצְוֹת (miṣvōt).	_____	3
יָשָׁר הוּא.	_____		טוֹבוֹת.	_____	
שַׂעַר.	_____	8	אֲדָמָה.	_____	4
הוּא שָׁלֵם.	_____		טוֹבָה.	_____	
כְּלִי.	_____	9	רוּחוֹת.	_____	5
חָדָשׁ הוּא.	_____		טוֹבוֹת.	_____	
אֶרֶץ.	_____ 10		שׁוֹפְטִים.	_____	6
הִיא קְדוֹשָׁה.	_____		רְשָׁעִים.	_____	

8.2 *Read* the following clauses and *translate*. Then *transform* the clauses from the singular into the plural. *Note*:

> ♦ The arrow shows you where to insert the correct form of the verb 'to be' (am, are, is) when you translate into English.
> ♦ When the stress is moved forward to a newly added ending, the vowel in an open syllable either one or two steps before the stress is reduced (shown in writing by the shva sign).
> ♦ The plural pattern of penultimate nouns (nouns with the stress on the next-to-last syllable) is - ֶ - ִ -ים/וֹת .
> ♦ The definite article is הָ in הָהֵם/הָהֵמָּה   הַהוּא/הַהִיא 'that' but הָ in הָהֵם (m) and הָהֵנָּה (f) 'those'.

1 הַבַּעַל הַהוּא ← זָקֵן.   _____

2 שָׁלֵם ← הַדָּבָר.   _____

3 הַנְּבִיאָה הִיא ← הַגְּדוֹלָה.   _____

4 הַסֵּפֶר הַטוֹב הַזֶּה ← קָדוֹשׁ.   _____

5 הַשּׁוֹפֵט ← יָשָׁר מֵהַנָּבִיא.   _____

6 הַנָּבִיא הַזֶּה ← טוֹב.   _____

7 קְדוֹשָׁה ← הַבְּרִית הַהִיא.   _____

8 טוֹבָה ← הָאָרֶץ.   _____

9 הַנָּבִיא הַזֶּה ← חָכָם מֵהַמֶּלֶךְ הַהוּא.   _____

10 הַפֶּתַח הַזֶּה ← גָּדוֹל כַּפֶּתַח הַהוּא.   _____

8.3 *Rewrite* the following biblical verse segments, *read aloud* and *translate*. Proper names are enlarged.

I	1	וְהַמֶּ֫לֶךְ זָקֵן מְאֹד (1 Kings 1:15)
	2	אִישׁ חָכָם מְאֹד: (2 Sam. 13:3)
	3	הָאִישׁ מֹשֶׁה גָּדוֹל מְאֹד (Ex. 11:3)
	4	קָדוֹשׁ הַיּוֹם (Neh. 8:10)
	5	זֶה הוּא: (1 Sam. 16:12)
	6	זֶה סֵ֫פֶר (Gen. 5:1)
	7	זֶה הַיּוֹם (Judg. 4:14)
	8	זֶה־הַשַּׁ֫עַר לַיהוָה (Ps. 118:20)
	9	אִישׁ־טוֹב זֶה (2 Sam. 18:27)
	10	אֵ֫לֶּה הַדְּבָרִים (Zech. 8:16)
II	11	טוֹב־הַדָּבָר (Dt. 1:14)
	12	אֵ֫לֶּה הַמִּצְוֹת וְהַמִּשְׁפָּטִים (Num. 36:13)
	13	טוֹבָה הָאָ֫רֶץ מְאֹד מְאֹד: (Num. 14:7)
	14	טוֹב לְיִשְׂרָאֵל אֱלֹהִים (Ps. 73:1)
	15	טוֹב־וְיָשָׁר יְהוָה (Ps. 25:8)
	16	צַדִּיק וְיָשָׁר הוּא: (Dt. 32:4)
	17	אֵל אָנֹכִי וְלֹא־אִישׁ (Hos. 11:9)
	18	לֹא־נָבִיא אָנֹ֫כִי (Amos 7:14)

8.4 *Reread* clauses 1–10 (group **I**) in Exercise 8.3 above and *translate* again *orally*. Then *translate* clauses 1–5 (group **I**) below into Hebrew, assisted by the Hebrew clauses in Exercise 8.3. *Proceed* to clauses 11–18 (group **II**) in Exercise 8.3, following the same procedure.

I   1   This is a man. He is old.
    2   This day is good.
    3   These kings are very wise.
    4   The gates are big.
    5   These words are very holy.

II   6   I am not a king.
    7   This man is righteous.
    8   The king and the prophet are upright.
    9   That king and that prophet are old.
   10   The Lord is upright and holy.

SECTION 9

1 *Twin-consonant nouns* (*geminates*): These nouns end in two identical consonants (shown in writing by one consonant with a doubling dagesh, e.g., לּ). When the doubled consonant occurs at the end of a word without a following vowel, it forms an impermissible two-consonant sequence. *A syllable may not end in more than one consonant.* The consonant cluster is dissolved by *simplification,* i.e., the doubled consonant becomes a single one (shown in writing by the absence of the doubling dagesh: לּ becomes ל). There are two types of twin-consonant nouns:

– Nouns consisting of one closed syllable. These nouns occur in three vowel patterns: עַם 'nation' (from the original form *ʕamm), אֵם 'mother' (from *ʔimm), חֹק 'law' (from *ḥuqq).[1]

– There are, however, also twin-consonant nouns consisting of more than one syllable, for example, מָגֵן 'shield', אָדֹם 'red', עִבְרִי 'Hebrew, a Hebrew'.

– When followed by a vowel, the original doubled consonant remains intact: עַמִּים ʕam-mîm 'nations', אִמּוֹת ʔim-môt 'mothers', חֻקִּים ḥuq-qîm 'laws', מָגִנִּים mā-gin-nîm 'shields', אֲדֻמּוֹת ʔᵃdum-môt 'red', עִבְרִיָּה ʕiv-riy-yāʰ 'Hebrew, a Hebrew' (s, f).

Observe that the vowel change in מָגֵן/מָגִנִּים, אֵם/אִמּוֹת and חֹק/חֻקִּים, אָדֹם/אֲדֻמּוֹת is within the same vowel category (i.e., I/E-vowel, U/O-vowel).

2 *Irregular nouns*: This group of nouns consists of original old nouns, some with only two root consonants. Irregular nouns do not follow predictable vocalization and/or inflection patterns, for instance, אָח 'brother' (plural אַחִים), אִשָּׁה 'woman' (plural נָשִׁים).

3 *Formation of nouns and adjectives*: Nouns are either primary (original) or derived from another word or word root.

– Derived nouns and adjectives consist of three root consonants placed in various word patterns. The word patterns are composed of vowels, possible prefix (an element added before the root consonants, i.e., אַ, תַּ, מֵ), possible suffix (an ending, i.e., וֹן, וּת, יִם, ־ית, ־ה, ־י) and/or a doubled middle root consonant, e.g., תִּקְוָה 'hope' (from קוה), עִבְרִי 'Hebrew, a Hebrew' (from עֵבֶר), טוֹבָה 'kindness' (from טוב), קִבּוּץ 'assembly' (from קבץ).

4 *Vowel raising* (traditionally called *attenuation*): An /a/-vowel in an unstressed closed syllable changes (thins out/is raised, see diagram below, Grammatical cornerstone 7) to an /i/-vowel, for example, תַּקְ-וָה 'hope' becomes תִּקְ-וָה. However, before and after a guttural the original /a/-vowel is either retained as in מַחְ-מָד 'desirable [one]' or raised halfway to an /e/-vowel, for instance, אַצְ-בַּע 'finger' becomes אֶצְ-בַּע.

5 *Existence/non-existence* is expressed by the particles יֵשׁ (corresponds to English 'there is/are') and אַיִן (corresponds to English 'there is/are not/no').

---

[1] There are a few twin-consonant adjectives as well, e.g., עַז 'strong' (from the original form *ʕazz).

– A clause with יֵשׁ/אֵין has no time reference of its own; its tense is determined by the context: יֵשׁ מֶלֶךְ 'There is/was/will be (= יֵשׁ) a king', אֵין מֶלֶךְ 'There is not/was not/will not be (= אֵין) a king'.

– אֵין also negates the verbless clause: אֵין הַמֶּלֶךְ שָׁם 'The king is *not* there'.

6 *Have/have not*: There is no verb in Hebrew to express 'have'. Possession is expressed by the preposition לְ attached to a noun that is the possessor, with or without the particle יֵשׁ: (יֵשׁ) לְדָוִד בֵּן 'David has a son', lit., 'There is/was/will be (= יֵשׁ) to David son'. 'Have not' is expressed by the particle אֵין together with the preposition לְ attached to a following noun:

אֵין לְדָוִד בֵּן 'David does not have a son', lit., 'There is not/was not/will not be (= אֵין) to David son'.

7 *Full and defective writing (spelling)*: The use of the vowel letters (ה, ו, י) in the Bible is not completely consistent. A vowel letter may unexpectedly appear or disappear in certain positions, compare גְּדוֹלָה (full writing) and גְּדֹלָה (defective writing), דָּוִיד (full writing) and דָּוִד (defective writing).

MEMORIZE

VOWEL RAISING – "ATTENUATION"

An original **A-vowel** in an **unstressed** originally **closed** syllable is raised (thins out) to an **I/E-vowel**, ordinarily to /i/, e.g., תַּקְוָה becomes תִּקְוָה, but before or after a guttural the original /a/-vowel is either retained or raised halfway to an /e/-vowel. The vowel diagram below represents the position of the tongue in the mouth when vowels are pronounced.

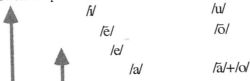

GRAMMATICAL CORNERSTONE 7 ר א שׁ פְּ נָ בְ ה

☆ VOWEL RAISING VIA HEBREW NAMES (3)

יִצְחָק (**I**saac) From the original form אַ-חָק (an original /a/-vowel is raised to /i/)

אֶפְרַיִם (**E**phraim) From the original form אַפְרַ-יִם (an original /a/-vowel is raised halfway, to /e/, due to the presence of the guttural)

יַעֲקֹב (**J**acob) The original /a/-vowel is retained in יַעֲקֹב (originally יַ-קֹב) due to the presence of the guttural.[2]

---

[2] For a chateph at the end of the syllable, see Section 7, footnote 5.

☆ NOUNS VIA THE NAMES OF THE BOOKS IN THE HEBREW BIBLE (4)

I *Identify* the following sound elements in the Hebrew names below and *count* them: doubling dagesh, hardening dagesh, silent shva, vocal shva, silent א, omitted ה. *Memorize* the Hebrew names. *Remember*:

> • You are expected to master the names of the books in the Hebrew Bible and then use them as familiar signposts to strengthen grammatical knowledge.

תּוֹרָה	Law: a derived noun consisting of the prefix תּ + the root consonants ירה 'lay a cornerstone, found; instruct, teach' (regular feminine noun).[3]
בְּרֵאשִׁית	Genesis, lit., 'in the beginning': בְּ 'in' + the derived noun רֵאשִׁית consisting of the irregular noun רֹאשׁ 'head' + the ending ית denoting an abstract noun (regular feminine noun).
שְׁמוֹת	Exodus, lit., 'names', singular שֵׁם (irregular noun).
בַּמִּדְבָּר	Numbers, lit., 'in the wilderness/desert': בְּ 'in' + the definite article הַ + the derived noun מִדְבָּר consisting of the prefix מ + the root consonants דבר (regular masculine noun).
דְּבָרִים	Deuteronomy, lit., 'words', singular דָּבָר (regular masculine noun).
שׁוֹפְטִים	Judges, singular שׁוֹפֵט (regular masculine noun).
מְלָכִים	Kings, singular מֶלֶךְ (penultimate noun).
קֹהֶלֶת	Ecclesiastes, 'preacher' (penultimate noun).
תְּהִלִּים	Psalms: a derived noun consisting of the prefix תּ + the root consonants הלל 'praise, glory' + the ending ים

WORD LIST

Nouns

אֶבֶן	f, stone: pl אֲבָנִים	מָקוֹם, קום	m, place: pl מְקוֹמוֹת
אֶחָד	m, one: f אַחַת	נֶפֶשׁ	f, soul, living thing,
אַיִן	nothing, naught		person; life: pl נְפָשׁוֹת
אֵם, אמם	mother: pl אִמּוֹת	עִיר	f, city: pl עָרִים
בַּיִת	m, house: pl בָּתִּים	עַם, עמם	m, nation, a people:
	(☆ the letter **Bet**,		pl עַמִּים, with
	Bethlehem, b.y.t)		definite article הָעָם
בֵּן	son: pl בָּנִים (☆ **Benjamin**)	רֹאשׁ	m, head: pl רָאשִׁים
בַּת	daughter: pl בָּנוֹת (☆ **Bathsheba**)		(☆ the letter **Resh**,
טוֹבָה, טוב	f, kindness, goodwill (☆ **Tobijah**)		**Rosh Pinna**, r.?.š)
יָד	f, hand: dual יָדַיִם	שְׁנַיִם	m, two: f שְׁתַּיִם
	(☆ the letter **Yod**)	תִּקְוָה, קוה	f, hope
יֶלֶד	m, child, boy: pl יְלָדִים		

---

[3] For the transformation of ו into י at the beginning of a word, see Section 21:4.

Adjectives

חַי, חיה   living (also 'alive'): *pl* חַיִּים   רַע, רעע   evil, bad, wicked:
עַז, עזז   strong, mighty: *pl* עַזִּים   *pl* רָעִים
רַב, רבב   numerous, many; great:
        pl רַבִּים (☆ **Rabbi**)

Particles

אֵין   [there is/are] nót/no (non-existence) יֵשׁ   there is/are (existence)
אֵין לְ   someone has not   יֵשׁ לְ   someone has

EXERCISES

9.1 *Fill in* the blanks with the missing words according to the example given
     below. *Read* the clauses and *translate*. Note:

> ◆ When a twin-consonant adjective such as עַז is followed by a vowel,
>   the doubled consonant remains intact (shown in writing by the presence
>   of the doubling dagesh): עַזָּה, עַזִּים, עַזּוֹת.
> ◆ Gutturals and ר cannot be doubled. Instead, the preceding vowel is
>   lengthened, compare רַע and רָעָה (not רַעָּה).
> ◆ Many of the nouns in this exercise are irregular. These nouns are
>   frequent. Therefore, their plural forms should be memorized.

The men are strong. עַזִּים הָאֲנָשִׁים.   The man is strong. עַז הָאִישׁ.
The women are strong. עַזּוֹת הַנָּשִׁים.   The hand is strong. עַזָּה הַיָּד.

_____ _____ הַבָּנִים   1   הַבֵּן הוּא רַע.
_____ _____ הַבָּנוֹת   _____ _____ הַבַּת

_____ הַבָּתִּים.   2   רַב הָעָם.
_____ הֶעָרִים.   _____ הַטּוֹבָה.
_____ הָאַחִים.   3   חַי הַבֵּן.
_____ הַנְּפָשׁוֹת.   _____ הַנֶּפֶשׁ.
_____ הָרָאשִׁים.   4   גָּדוֹל הַכְּלִי.
_____ הַנָּשִׁים.   _____ הָעִיר.

_____ _____ הַיָּמִים   5   הַיּוֹם טוֹב הוּא.
_____ _____ הַבָּנוֹת   _____ _____ הָאֵם

9.2 *Read* the following clauses and *translate*. Then *transform* the clauses from the singular into the plural. *Note*:

---

* An additional personal pronoun (3rd person: הוּא, הִיא, הֵם, הֵנָּה),
  which may appear either before or after the predicate, should be left
  untranslated.
* The arrow shows you where to insert the correct form of the verb
  'to be' (am, are, is) when you translate into English.
* An adjective always takes the ending יִם in the masculine plural and
  וֹת in the feminine plural, but plural nouns may take either יִם or וֹת,
  e.g., אָבוֹת 'fathers', נָשִׁים 'women'.
* Dual nouns take plural adjectives, e.g., יָדַיִם טוֹבוֹת 'good hands'.
* When a word takes an ending, the stress is normally moved forward
  to the newly added last syllable, which may result in a vowel reduction.

---

11 אִשָּׁה רָעָה ← אַתְּ.

12 טוֹב ← אַתָּה מִבֵּן וּמִבַּת.

13 שָׁלֵם ← הַיּוֹם.

14 הוּא ← אִישׁ זָקֵן.

15 הִיא ← הַבַּת הַחֲכָמָה.

16 אָח רַע ← אַתָּה.

17 אַתְּ ← הָאִשָּׁה הַחֲדָשָׁה.

18 עֶבֶד יָשָׁר ← אָנֹכִי.

19 זֹאת ← הָאָרֶץ הַטּוֹבָה.

20 אֵל חַי ← הוּא.

1 הוּא ← הַבֵּן הָעַז.

2 הָעַיִן ← גְּדוֹלָה הִיא.

3 זֶה ← הָאָב הַטּוֹב.

4 נֶפֶשׁ חַיָּה ← אֲנִי.

5 הַמָּקוֹם הַזֶּה ← קָדוֹשׁ הוּא.

6 זֶה ← בַּיִת חָדָשׁ.

7 זֹאת ← הָרוּחַ הָרָעָה.

8 הָעִיר הִיא ← קְדוֹשָׁה.

9 זֶה ← רֹאשׁ גָּדוֹל.

10 אַתָּה ← הָאִישׁ הָרָשָׁע.

9.3 *Read* the following clauses with יֵשׁ/אֵין and *translate*. *Render* these isolated
verbless clause in the present tense. *Remember*:

---

* יֵשׁ corresponds to 'there is/are' and אֵין to 'there is/are not/no'.
  (יֵשׁ) לְ corresponds to 'someone has' and אֵין לְ to 'someone has
  not/no'.
* The particle אֵין also negates the verbless clause: אֵין הָאִשָּׁה בַּשָּׂדֶה
  'The woman is *not* in the field'.

1 אֵין הָאִישׁ בָּעִיר.   8 לָאִשָּׁה אִישׁ בַּשַּׁעַר.

2 יֵשׁ אִשָּׁה בָּעִיר.   9 יֵשׁ אֶבֶן בַּפֶּתַח.

3 לָאִשָּׁה בֵּן.   10 אֵין סֵפֶר בַּדֶּרֶךְ.

4 אֵין לָאִישׁ בַּת.   11 יֵשׁ לַמֶּלֶךְ חֶרֶב.

5 אֵין אִשָּׁה בַּבַּיִת.   12 לַיהוָה עַם.

6 לָאִישׁ בֵּן.   13 יֵשׁ לַנָּבִיא סֵפֶר.

7 אֵין עַם בָּאָרֶץ.   14 אֵין בַּמָּקוֹם עֶבֶד.

9.4 In each pair of the phrases/clauses below there is one word spelled once with the vowel letter י/ו and once without י/ו. *Compare* the words and *mark* full writing (with י/ו) with one stroke and defective writing (without י/ו) with two strokes. *Translate* the phrases/clauses. Proper names are enlarged.

1 וְדָוִיד זָקֵן (1 Chron. 23:1)   זֶה דָוִד (1 Sam. 21:12)

2 אִשָּׁה גְדוֹלָה (2 Kings 4:8)   וְהָאֶבֶן גְּדֹלָה (Gen. 29:2)

3 קָדוֹשׁ הַיּוֹם (Neh. 8:10)   הַמָּקוֹם קָדֹשׁ: (Ezek. 42:13)

9.5 *Read* the following biblical verse segments, *rewrite* them and *translate*. Proper names are enlarged.

I 1 עַם קָדוֹשׁ אַתָּה לַיהוה (Dt. 7:6) _____

2 הִוא הָעִיר הַגְּדֹלָה: (Gen. 10:12) _____

3 טוֹבִים הַשְּׁנַיִם מִן־הָאֶחָד (Ecc. 4:9) _____

4 יֵשׁ יהוה בַּמָּקוֹם הַזֶּה (Gen. 28:16) _____

5 אֵל גָּדוֹל יהוה (Ps. 95:3) _____

6 וַאֲנַחְנוּ רַבִּים (Ezek. 33:24) _____

7 אֵלֶּה רְשָׁעִים (Ps. 73:12) _____

8 אֵין כַּיהוה (Ex. 8:6) _____

9 וְעֵינַיִם יֵשׁ (Isa. 43:8) _____

II 10 יהוה אֶחָד: (Dt. 6:4) _____

11 בַּיָּמִים הָהֵם אֵין מֶלֶךְ בְּיִשְׂרָאֵל (Judg. 17:6) _____

12 יֵשׁ אֱלֹהִים לְיִשְׂרָאֵל: (1 Sam. 17:46) _____

13 יֵשׁ נָבִיא בְּיִשְׂרָאֵל: (2 Kings 5:8) _____

14 לִפְנִנָּה יְלָדִים וּלְחַנָּה _____

אֵין יְלָדִים: (1 Sam. 1:2) _____

15 אֵין־טוֹב לָאָדָם (Ecc. 8:15) _____

16 וְאִישׁ אֵין בָּאָרֶץ (Gen. 19:31) _____

9.6 *Reread* clauses 1–9 (group **I**) in Exercise 9.5 above and *translate* again *orally*. Then *translate* clauses 1–7 (group **I**) below into Hebrew, assisted by the Hebrew clauses in Exercise 9.5. *Proceed* to clauses 10–16 (group **II**) in Exercise 9.5, following the same procedure.

I 1 They are many.
   2 There are many men.
   3 There are no big men in this place.
   4 There is a holy place in the city.
   5 You (*m, pl*) are sinful.
   6 There are sinful men in this city.
   7 There are not many women like Leah (לֵאָה).

II 8 The sons have no eyes.
   9 There are good kings in the place.
   10 There are not many prophets in Israel.
   11 Israel has strong sons.
   12 The man has children.
   13 The judges have good wives.
   14 This child is bigger than that child.

SECTION 10

1 *Nouns: Free and bound forms* (called forms in the *absolute and construct state*)
   Nouns have two forms, a *free form* (the form listed in lexicons and vocabularies)
   and a *bound form* (the form a noun has when it is followed by another noun).
   See examples in the table below.

2 *Noun chains (construct relationship/chain)*: When two nouns (occasionally
   more than two) occur together in immediate succession, they form a noun
   chain. A noun chain is *a single grammatical and sound unit* that usually
   denotes possession. The first noun in a noun chain is the possessed and the
   second noun is the possessor.

Noun: Gender/ number/type	Noun: Free form	Ending	Noun: Bound form	Ending
Masculine singular	שִׁיר 'song'	—	שִׁיר תְּהִלָּה 'a song of praise'	—
Feminine singular	תּוֹרָה 'law'	ָה	תּוֹרַת נָבִיא 'a law of a prophet'	ת ַ
Dual	עֵינַיִם 'eyes'	ַיִם	עֵינֵי אִשָּׁה 'eyes of a woman'	ֵי
Masculine plural	שִׁירִים 'songs'	ִים	שִׁירֵי תְּהִלָּה 'songs of praise'	ֵי
Feminine plural	תּוֹרוֹת 'laws'	וֹת	תּוֹרוֹת נָבִיא 'laws of a prophet'	וֹת
Penultimate noun	מֶלֶךְ 'king'	—	מֶלֶךְ יִשְׂרָאֵל 'the king of Israel'	—
Twin-conson. noun	עַם 'people'	—	עַם יִשְׂרָאֵל 'the people of Israel'	—
Irregular noun	אָב 'father'	—	אֲבִי אַבְרָהָם 'the father of Abraham'	ִי
Noun/adj ending in ה	שָׂדֶה 'field'	ֶה	שְׂדֵה הָאִישׁ 'the field of the man'	ֵה

– Being a single grammatical unit the noun chain has only *one definite article*,
attached to the last noun in the chain: תּוֹרַת הַנָּבִיא 'the law of *the* prophet'.
When the last noun is a proper name, the whole noun chain is definite without
the definite article: עַם יִשְׂרָאֵל 'the people of *Israel*'.
– Being a single sound unit the noun chain has only *one* (main) *stress*, falling
on the last noun in the chain: בֶּן־הַמֶּלֶךְ 'the son of the king' (observe that the
noun chain has one main stress also without the maqqeph, i.e., hyphen, see
examples in the table above). The bound noun that loses its stress undergoes
regular sound changes (see Exercises 10.1 and 10.2).
– Penultimate nouns (of the type מֶלֶךְ) and twin-consonant nouns (of the type
עַם) retain their free forms when they are attached to a following noun (see
examples in the table above).
– Please remember that the bound forms of the irregular nouns אָב 'father',
אָח 'brother' and פֶּה 'mouth' are אֲבִי, אֲחִי and פִּי.

– Since the nouns in a noun chain form a single grammatical unit, they cannot be separated. An adjective describing a noun in the chain is placed after the entire chain: תּוֹרַת הַנָּבִיא הַטּוֹבָה 'the *good* law of the prophet'.

– Apart from possession a noun chain may express other meanings, e.g., שִׁיר תְּהִלָּה 'a song *of* praise' actually means 'a song *with* praise', תּוֹרַת אָדָם 'a law *for* man/mankind', אַנְשֵׁי הַבַּיִת 'the men *in* the house'. A noun chain may also express *superlative*, e.g., שִׁיר הַשִּׁירִים 'the song *of* songs = the *best/finest* song', or a construction of an *adjective describing a noun*, e.g., הַר קֹדֶשׁ 'a mount *of* holiness = a *holy* mountain'.

בֵּן/בַּת 'son/daughter' attached to a proper name in a noun chain denotes a *member of a group*: בֶּן־יִשְׂרָאֵל 'a son *of* Israel = *Israelite*'.

3 *Adjective-plus-noun chain*: An adjective may be combined with a following noun: טוֹב מַרְאֶה 'good in appearance = *good*-looking', יְפֵה עֵינַיִם (the free form of יְפֵה is יָפֶה) '*beautiful* of eyes = with *beautiful* eyes'.

4 *Quantifier* כֹּל 'every/each, the whole, all': The noun כֹּל 'totality, everything' is used as a quantifier, usually joined to a following noun by a maqqeph (hyphen), ־כָּל (see Exercise 10.4).

☆ NOUN CHAINS VIA THE NAMES OF THE BOOKS IN THE HEBREW BIBLE (5)

> ◆ The names of the books in the Hebrew Bible given below (1, 2, 4–6) are either complete or incomplete *noun chains. Memorize* them.

1 דִּבְרֵי הַיָּמִים   Chronicles, lit., 'the words/matters *of* the days': דִּבְרֵי is the bound noun (the free form is דְּבָרִים, singular דָּבָר) and the independent (= free) noun is הַיָּמִים (singular יוֹם). Since הַיָּמִים, the last noun in the chain, is definite, the whole chain is definite. The last noun הַיָּמִים also takes the stress. The bound noun that loses its stress undergoes regular vowel changes.

2 שִׁיר הַשִּׁירִים   Song *of* songs, which means '*the best/finest song*': The bound noun שִׁיר (the free form is also שִׁיר) undergoes no vowel changes, since a full vowel (vowel sign + ׳/ו) is not affected by the stress.

3 סֵפֶר הַסְּפָרִים   Bible, lit., 'book *of* books = *the best book*': Observe that a bound penultimate noun retains its free form.

4 שְׁמוֹת   Exodus, lit., 'names': The entire noun chain consists of three nouns שְׁמוֹת בְּנֵי יִשְׂרָאֵל 'the names *of* the sons *of* Israel' (Ex. 1:1). בְּנֵי יִשְׂרָאֵל means 'Israelites', lit., 'sons/children *of* Israel'. The first bound noun in the chain is שְׁמוֹת (the free form is שֵׁמוֹת, singular שֵׁם), the second

bound noun is בְּנֵי (the free form is בָּנִים, singular בֵּן) and the last noun יִשְׂרָאֵל is independent. Since the last noun in the chain is definite (יִשְׂרָאֵל, a proper name, is considered definite) the entire chain is definite. The last noun also takes the stress. The loss of stress in the bound nouns results in regular vowel changes.

מִשְׁלֵי 5   Proverbs: The entire noun chain consists of two nouns מִשְׁלֵי שְׁלֹמֹה 'the proverbs *of* Solomon'. The bound noun is מִשְׁלֵי (the free form is מְשָׁלִים, singular מָשָׁל) and the independent noun is שְׁלֹמֹה.

עוֹבַדְיָה 6   Obadiah, which means 'the servant *of* the LORD': The bound noun is עוֹבֵד and the independent noun is YHWH, represented by יָה (יהוה, a proper name, is considered definite).

WORD LIST

Nouns

הַר, הרר	*m*, mountain: *pl* הָרִים, with *definite article* הָהָר
חֶסֶד	*m*, goodness, kindness, grace; faithfulness: *pl* חֲסָדִים evidences of kindness
חק, חקק	*m*, statute, law: *pl* חֻקִּים
יַיִן	*m*, wine
כּוֹכָב	*m*, star
כֹּל/כָּל-, כלל	totality, everything; all, the whole, each, every
לֵב, לבב	*m*, heart: *pl* לִבּוֹת
מִזְבֵּחַ, זבח	*m*, altar: *pl* מִזְבְּחוֹת
מַיִם	*pl*, water (☆ the letter **Mem**, m.y.m)

מִקְדָּשׁ, קדשׁ	*m*, sanctuary
מַרְאֶה, ראה	*m*, sight; appearance: *pl* מַרְאוֹת
מָשָׁל	*m*, proverb, parable
פָּנִים	*pl*, face
קֹדֶשׁ	*m*, holiness: *pl* קָדָשִׁים or קֳדָשִׁים (qamets-/o/, qo-)
קוֹל	*m*, voice, sound: *pl* קוֹלוֹת
שָׂדֶה	*m*, field: *pl* שָׂדוֹת
שֶׁבַע	*f*, seven: *m* שִׁבְעָה (☆ Bathsheba, š.b.ʕ)
שֵׁם	*m*, name: *pl* שֵׁמוֹת (☆ **Shem, Samuel**)
שָׁמַיִם	heaven/s, sky

Adjectives

יָפֶה	beautiful, handsome: *f* יָפָה
רִאשׁוֹן	first: *derived from* רֹאשׁ (☆ the letter **Resh**, r.ʔ.š)
רָם, רום	high

Particles

עַל	on, over, upon

EXERCISES

10.1 *Mark* the stress in each noun chain in the following table. *Read, explain* the sound changes in the bound nouns according to the examples given in the following table and *translate*. All the bound nouns in this exercise are in the singular. *Note:*

> • The feminine ending הָ (free form) is changed to תְ in the bound form: מִצְוָה יהוה <-- מִצְוַת יהוה 'the commandment of the LORD'. Masculine singular nouns have no special ending when they are followed by another noun.
>
> • A noun chain is a single sound unit. The stress falls on the last noun in the noun chain. In the noun chains in this exercise the stress falls on the last syllable (of the last noun in the chain), except in words ending in a closed syllable with a short vowel, e.g., דֶּרֶךְ 'way', עַיִן 'eye', בַּעַל 'master'.
>
> • The bound noun that loses its stress undergoes *regular vowel changes*:
>
> – A vowel in an unstressed *open syllable is reduced*, e.g., צָבָא --> צְבָא הַמֶּלֶךְ 'the army of the king'.
>
> – When a vowel reduction results in an impermissible consonant sequence, the *consonants of the cluster are separated by the addition of a vowel*, normally /i/. An insertion vowel after a guttural with a chateph matches the vowel of the chateph: אֲדָמָה --> אַדְמַת הַמֶּלֶךְ 'the soil of the king' (instead of אַדְמַת).
>
> – A long vowel in an unstressed *closed syllable is shortened*: ā (ָ) becomes a (ַ), ē (ֵ) becomes i/e (ִ/ֶ) and ō (ֹ) becomes o/u (ְֹ/ֻ), e.g., כְּפָר --> כְּפַר נַחוּם 'Capernaum'.
>
> • A full vowel, a vowel followed by a silent א and a short vowel in a closed syllable are unchangeable (that is, not affected by the position of the stress): קוֹל --> קוֹל יִשְׂרָאֵל 'the voice of Israel', רֹאשׁ --> רֹאשׁ פִּנָּה 'cornerstone', מִקְדָּשׁ --> מִקְדַּשׁ יהוה 'the sanctuary of the LORD'.
>
> • The consonant י/ו in nouns of the type בַּיִת and מָוֶת (from the original forms *bayt and *mawt, with a diphthong) is silenced, being transformed into a vowel letter: *bayt --> בֵּית לֶחֶם 'Bethlehem', *mawt --> מוֹת הַמֶּלֶךְ 'the death of the king'.

Translation	Sound changes in the bound nouns					Noun chain	Lexical (free) form	
	Insertion vowel which dissolves a cluster	ו/י is transformed into a vowel letter	Short-ened vowel	Reduced vowel	Unchan-geable vowel			
the song of the king					šîr	שִׁיר הַמֶּלֶךְ	שִׁיר	1
the star of/ in the sky		xav			kô	כּוֹכַב הַשָּׁמַיִם	כּוֹכָב	2
the place of the altar				mᵊ	qôm	מְקוֹם הַמִּזְבֵּחַ	מָקוֹם	3
the soil of the land	ʔad		maṭ			אֲדְמַת הָאָרֶץ	אֲדָמָה	4
			paṭ		miš	מִשְׁפַּט הַתּוֹרָה	מִשְׁפָּט	5
... of Solomon						מְשַׁל שְׁלֹמֹה	מָשָׁל	6
						מוֹת הַנָּבִיא	מָוֶת	7
... of Abraham						בֶּן־אַבְרָהָם	בֵּן	8
every ...						כָּל־נַעַר	כֹּל	9
						חֲכַם לֵב	חָכָם	10
						תִּקְוַת הָעָם	תִּקְוָה	11
						תּוֹרַת הָאָדָם	תּוֹרָה	12
						נְבִיא הָאֵל	נָבִיא	13
						צְבָא אֱלֹהִים	צָבָא	14
						דְּבַר יהוה	דָּבָר	15
						רוּחַ הַקֹּדֶשׁ	רוּחַ	16
						עֵין הָאִישׁ	עַיִן	17

10.2 All the bound nouns in the following table are either in the plural or dual. *Read, explain* the vowel changes in the bound nouns according to the examples given in the table and *translate. Note*:

> - The endings ◌ִים ◌ַ and ◌ַיִם (free forms) are changed to ◌ֵי in the bound forms. The ending וֹת (free form) remains unchanged in the bound form.
> - The bound noun that loses its stress undergoes regular vowel changes:
>   – A vowel in an unstressed *open syllable is reduced.*
>   – When a vowel reduction results in an impermissible sequence of two vowelless consonants at the beginning of a syllable the *consonants of the cluster are separated by inserting a vowel*, normally /i/: דִּבְרֵי הַמֶּלֶךְ 'the words of the king' (not דְּבְרֵי, free form: דְּבָרִים). The insertion vowel after (i.e., under) a guttural with a chateph matches the vowel of the chateph: חַכְמֵי הָעָם 'the wise [ones] of the people' (not חֲכְמֵי, free form: חֲכָמִים).
> - The insertion vowel in a bound penultimate noun corresponds to the vowel of the original form: מַלְכֵי יִשְׂרָאֵל 'the kings of Israel' (not מְלְכֵי, free form: מְלָכִים). מַלְכֵי takes the original /a/-vowel in *malk.
>   סִפְרֵי הַגּוֹיִם 'the books of the nations' (not סְפְרֵי, free form: סְפָרִים). סִפְרֵי takes the original /i/-vowel in *sifr.
> - A full vowel, a vowel sign followed by a silent א as well as a short vowel in a closed syllable are unchangeable (that is, not affected by the position of the stress), e.g., שִׁירֵי יִשְׂרָאֵל --> שִׁירִים 'the songs of Israel', מִקְדְּשֵׁי יִשְׂרָאֵל --> מִקְדָּשִׁים 'the sanctuaries of Israel'.

Translation	Vowel changes in the bound nouns			Noun chain	Noun: Free form, plural	Noun: Lexical (free) form, singular	
	Insertion vowel which dissolves a cluster	Reduced vowel	Unchangeable vowel				
the statutes of the Law			ḥuq-qê	חֻקֵּי הַתּוֹרָה	חֻקִּים	חֹק	1
the elders of the nation	ziq		nê	זִקְנֵי הָעָם	זְקֵנִים	זָקֵן	2
				שְׁנֵי אֲנָשִׁים	שְׁנַיִם	שְׁנַיִם	3
				קוֹלוֹת הָעָם	קוֹלוֹת	קוֹל	4
... of Solomon				מִשְׁלֵי שְׁלֹמֹה	מְשָׁלִים	מָשָׁל	5
the tops of...				רָאשֵׁי הֶהָרִים	רָאשִׁים	רֹאשׁ	6
... of Jerusalem				בְּנוֹת יְרוּשָׁלַיִם	בָּנוֹת	בַּת	7
			miṣ-wōt	מִצְוֹת הַתּוֹרָה	מִצְוֹת	מִצְוָה	8
				עֵינֵי הָאִשָּׁה	עֵינַיִם	עַיִן	9
				אַרְצוֹת הָעַמִּים	אֲרָצוֹת	אֶרֶץ	10
				נַפְשׁוֹת הַנְּבִיאִים	נְפָשׁוֹת	נֶפֶשׁ	11
				בְּנֵי בְּרִית	בָּנִים	בֵּן	12
				דִּבְרֵי הַשּׁוֹפֵט	דְּבָרִים	דָּבָר	13
				חַכְמֵי הַמָּקוֹם	חֲכָמִים	חָכָם	14
				מֵי הָעִיר	מַיִם	מַיִם	15
... of Judah				הָרֵי יְהוּדָה [1]	הָרִים	הַר	16
				שְׁמֵי הָאָרֶץ	שָׁמַיִם	שָׁמַיִם	17
... of Esau				יְדֵי עֵשָׂו	יָדַיִם	יָד	18
				עַמֵּי הָאֲרָצוֹת	עַמִּים	עַם	19

---

[1] A short vowel that has undergone compensatory lengthening cannot be reduced.

10.3 *Read* the following groups of verbless clauses and *translate*. *Write* the free form of the bound adjectives in the adjective-plus-noun chains. Then *transform* the clauses from the singular into the plural. *Note*:

> ◆ The first clause in each group contains an adjective-plus-noun chain,
>   e.g., הָאִישׁ טוֹב לֵב 'The man is *happy/joyous*', lit., '*good* at heart'.
>   – The second clause in each group contains יֵשׁ/אֵין or
>   יֵשׁ אִישׁ בַּבַּיִת (יֵשׁ) לְ/אֵין לְ, e.g., 'There is a man in the house'.
>   – The third clause in each group combines the first two clauses into
>   one clause: יֵשׁ אִישׁ טוֹב לֵב בַּבַּיִת 'There is a happy man in the
>   house'.
> ◆ In an adjective-plus-noun chain only the adjective is inflected in number
>   and gender, e.g., טוֹבֵי לֵב <-- טוֹב לֵב.
> ◆ A noun/adjective ending in הָ , e.g., שָׂדֶה 'field', drops the ending הָ
>   before the plural ending is added: שָׂדוֹת.
>   The bound form ends in הֵ : שְׂדֵה.

_____	(adj: free form) _____	1 הַבֵּן עַז פָּנִים.
_____		אֵין בֵּן בַּדֶּרֶךְ.
_____		אֵין בֵּן עַז פָּנִים בַּדֶּרֶךְ.
_____	(adj: free form) _____	2 הָאִשָּׁה יְפַת מַרְאֶה.
_____		יֵשׁ אִשָּׁה בָּעִיר.
_____		יֵשׁ אִשָּׁה יְפַת מַרְאֶה בָּעִיר.
_____	(adj: free form) _____	3 הָאִישׁ חֲכַם לֵב.
_____		יֵשׁ לָאִישׁ חֶרֶב.
_____		יֵשׁ לָאִישׁ חֲכַם הַלֵּב חֶרֶב.
_____	(adj: free form) _____	4 הָאִישׁ יְפֵה עֵינַיִם.
_____		אֵין אִישׁ בַּמָּקוֹם הַזֶּה.
_____		אֵין אִישׁ יְפֵה עֵינַיִם בַּמָּקוֹם הַזֶּה.
_____	(adj: free form) _____	5 הָעֶבֶד יְשַׁר לֵב.
_____		אֵין בַּשָּׂדֶה עֶבֶד.
_____		אֵין בַּשָּׂדֶה עֶבֶד יְשַׁר לֵב.
_____	(adj: free form) _____	6 הַבַּת רָעַת מַרְאֶה.
_____		יֵשׁ בַּת בַּבַּיִת.
_____		יֵשׁ בַּת רָעַת מַרְאֶה בַּבַּיִת.

10.4 *Read* the following clauses with כָּל־ and *translate*. *Note*:

> - Before a *definite noun in the singular* כָּל־ means '*the whole*': כָּל־הַיּוֹם '*the whole* day'. Before an *indefinite noun in the singular* כָּל־ means '*each, every*': כָּל־יוֹם '*each/every* day'. Before a *definite noun in the plural* כָּל־ means '*all*': כָּל־הַיָּמִים '*all (of) the* days'.
> - The arrow shows you where to insert the proper form of the verb 'to be' (am, are, is) when you translate into English.

6 כָּל־הַנָּשִׁים בַּמָּקוֹם.		1 כָּל־יוֹם הוּא יוֹם חָדָשׁ.
7 כָּל־הַבַּיִת לָאִישׁ.		2 כָּל־הַבָּתִּים חֲדָשִׁים.
8 כָּל־הַמִּקְדָּשִׁים לֵאלֹהִים.		3 לַיהוה כָּל־הָאָרֶץ.
9 טוֹבִים כָּל־הַחֻקִּים וְהַמִּשְׁפָּטִים.		4 כָּל־אִישׁ בַּשָּׂדֶה.
10 כָּל־נֶפֶשׁ חַיָּה ← בָּאָרֶץ.		5 כָּל־אִשָּׁה בַּבַּיִת.

10.5 *Read* the following verses/verse segments and *translate*. *Write* the free form of the bound nouns/adjectives in the noun/noun-plus-adjective chains. Proper names are enlarged. *Note*:

> - The ending תְ of the bound form is changed to ה ָ in the free form and the ending יְ is changed to either יִם or יַ ִ .
> - Apply the basic rule of vocalization when you vocalize the free forms: *All syllables generally have a long vowel, except an unstressed closed syllable which always has a short vowel.*

I

1   וְזֹאת תּוֹרַת הָאָדָם (2 Sam. 7:19)   _____

2   הַקֹּל קוֹל יַעֲקֹב וְהַיָּדַיִם יְדֵי עֵשָׂו: (Gen. 27:22)   _____

3   וְאֵלֶּה דִּבְרֵי הַסֵּפֶר (Jer. 29:1)   _____

4   וּדְבַר־יהוה מִירוּשָׁלָםִ: (Isa. 2:3)   _____

5   וְחֶרֶב אֵין בְּיַד־דָּוִד: (1 Sam. 17:50)   _____

6   דִּבְרֵי קֹהֶלֶת בֶּן־דָּוִד (Ecc. 1:1)   _____   _____

7   טוֹב לֵב־הַמֶּלֶךְ בַּיָּיִן (Esther 1:10)   _____

8   מִיַּד הָאֱלֹהִים הִיא:[2] (Ecc. 2:24)   _____

---

[2] The word הִיא here and in clause 10 means 'it'.

9 יהוה צְבָאוֹת אֱלֹהֵי יִשְׂרָאֵל (Isa. 37:16) _____

10 II מִצְוַת הַמֶּלֶךְ הִיא (Isa. 36:21) _____

11 וְאֵלֶּה שְׁמוֹת בְּנֵי יִשְׂרָאֵל (Ex. 1:1) _____ _____

12 מֹשֶׁה אִישׁ הָאֱלֹהִים (Dt. 33:1) _____

13 מַלְכֵי חֶסֶד הֵם (1 Kings 20:31) _____

14 טוֹבַת מַרְאֶה הִיא: (Esther 1:11) _____

15 אַתָּה אֲדֹנָי טוֹב... וְרַב־חֶסֶד (Ps. 86:5) _____

16 יהוה בְּצִיּוֹן גָּדוֹל

וְרָם הוּא עַל־כָּל־הָעַמִּים: (Ps. 99:2) _____

17 זֶה כָּל־הָאָדָם: (Ecc. 12:13) _____

18 גָּדוֹל יהוה מִכָּל־הָאֱלֹהִים (Ex. 18:11) _____

10.6 *Reread* clauses 1–9 (group **I**) in Exercise 10.5 above and *translate* again *orally*. Then *translate* clauses 1–8 (group **I**) below into Hebrew, assisted by the Hebrew clauses in Exercise 10.5. *Proceed* to clauses 10–18 (group **II**) in Exercise 10.5, following the same procedure.

I 1 David is a king. He is the king of Jerusalem.
2 And the LORD (YHWH) is the God of Israel.
3 She is a king's daughter.
4 The men are good. They are good-looking (= good in appearance).
5 The man is a prophet. He is the prophet of the LORD.
6 The sword is in the hands of the man.
7 The words of God are in the sanctuary of God.
8 The armies of the LORD (YHWH) are strong.

II 9 The kindness of God is upon this nation.
10 This is the commandment of the father.
11 The houses are beautiful (= beautiful in appearance).
12 The whole field is beautiful.
13 All the women are good in appearance.
14 All the commandments of the LORD (YHWH) are good.
15 The Israelites (= sons of Israel) are in Zion.
16 Every nation has a king.
17 Every child has a mother and a father.

SECTION 11

1 *Pronouns: Attached forms* (called *pronominal suffixes*)
Pronouns not only have independent forms (אַתָּה‎ ,אֲנִי etc.), but also attached forms that are added to different words, usually as suffixes (see below, Grammatical cornerstone 8). The attached pronouns are closely related to the independent pronouns (see Exercise 11.1 below).
– There are two sets of attached pronouns, one set attached to preceding singular nouns and one set attached to preceding plural nouns.
– Prepositions take either the "singular" or the "plural" set of the attached pronouns, with no difference in meaning between the two sets.
– The attached pronoun is linked to a preceding word either directly or by a *linking vowel* (/e/ or /a/).
– When a word ends in the vowel letter י‎/ו, the attached pronoun is linked to it directly, without any linking vowel, e.g., כָּמוֹנוּ 'like us'.
– Elsewhere, the attached pronoun is preceded by a linking vowel, which, in turn, is either retained or reduced. For example, in the construction 'ל + the linking vowel /a/ + אֲנַחְנוּ' the linking vowel is retained: לָנוּ 'to us'. In the construction 'ל + /a/ + אַתָּה' the linking vowel is reduced: לְךָ 'to you'.

2 *Prepositions and adverbs with the "singular" set of attached pronouns*
– Attached pronouns in units of preposition-plus-pronoun function as *indirect objects*, e.g., לָהֶם 'to/for them'.
– Attached pronouns in units of adverb-plus-pronoun function as *subjects*, for instance, אֵינֶהָ corresponds to אֵין הִיא 'she is not'.

3 *Nouns in singular with attached pronouns*
– Attached pronouns in units of noun-plus-pronoun function as *possessive pronoun*s (my, your, his…). A construction of a noun-plus-pronoun, like a combination of nouns in a noun chain, is a single grammatical and sound unit in which the noun is the possessed and the pronoun is the possessor: שִׁירֵנוּ 'a song *of ours* = *our* song', תּוֹרָתֵנוּ 'a law *of ours* = *our* law'.
– *Form*: In the construction of noun-plus-pronoun the attached pronoun is added to the *bound form* of the noun, e.g., תּוֹרַת (the free form is תּוֹרָה).
– *Stress*: Since the construction of a noun-plus-pronoun is a single grammatical unit, it has one (main) stress which falls either on the linking vowel, e.g., שִׁירֵנוּ, or, when the linking vowel is reduced, on the attached pronoun: שִׁירְכֶם 'your song' (*m, p*).
– *Sound changes*: Since the bound noun in a unit of a noun-plus-pronoun loses its stress, the noun undergoes regular sound changes (see Exercise 11.2).
– *Definiteness*: The unit of noun-plus-pronoun is definite. Hence, a following adjective takes the definite article: שִׁירִי הַטּוֹב 'my good song'.

– Penultimate nouns of the type מֶלֶךְ, סֵפֶר, בֹּקֶר (from the original forms *malk, *sifr and *buqr) and twin-consonant nouns of the type עַם, אֵם, חֹק (from the original forms *ʕamm, *ʔimm and *ḥuqq) retain their original forms before the attached pronoun. For example, 'מֶלֶךְ' (from *malk, – מַלְכ) + the attached pronoun 'ִי' results in מַלְכִּי 'my king' and 'עַם' (from *ʕamm, – עַמ) + the attached pronoun 'ִי' results in עַמִּי 'my people'.

MEMORIZE

PRONOUNS II			
	Pronouns attached to singular nouns		
Independent personal pronouns	after a noun ending in the vowel letter ו/י	after a noun ending in a consonant	Meaning: possessive pronouns
אָנֹכִי/אֲנִי	־ִי	־ִי	my
אַתָּה	־ְךָ	־ְךָ	your, m
		־ֶ֫ךָ	pausal form
אַתְּ	־ֵךְ	־ֵךְ׃	your, f
הוּא	־ֹהוּ/־וֹ	־וֹ	his
הִיא	־ָהָ	־ָהּ	her
אֲנַ֫חְנוּ	־ֵ֫נוּ	־ֵ֫נוּ	our
אַתֶּם	־ֶכֶם	־ְכֶם	your, m
אַתֵּן/אַתֵּ֫נָה	־ֶכֶן	־ְכֶן	your, f
הֵם/הֵ֫מָּה	־ֶהֶם	־ָם	their, m
הֵ֫נָּה	־ֶהֶן	־ָן	their, f
GRAMMATICAL CORNERSTONE 8 ר א שׁ פ בַּ נַ הַ			

☆ EXCEPTIONS TO THE BASIC RULE OF VOCALIZATION VIA HEBREW NAMES (6)

I *Find* exceptions to the basic rule of vocalization in the word list of Section 12. *Indicate* from the list below the grammatical category to which each word with deviant vocalization belongs. *Gather* words that do not fit into any of the mentioned categories under the title *other categories/odd exceptions. Remember*:

> ♦ *All* syllables with simple vowels *generally (**not always!**)* have a *long vowel*, except an unstressed closed syllable which **always** has a *short* vowel. That is to say, exceptions to the basic rule of vocalization apply to syllables with a short instead of a long vowel.

1 *Rabbi* רַב: *Stressed closed* syllable with a short instead of a long vowel. The deviation applies to an /a/-vowel in twin-consonant nouns and adjectives: עַם, עַז, חַי.

2 *Haggai* חַגַּי: *Stressed closed* syllable with a short instead of a long vowel. The deviation applies to an /a/-vowel in a diphthong with the consonant י at the end of a word.

3 *Qohelet* קֹהֶלֶת: *Stressed open* syllable with a short instead of a long vowel. The deviation applies to an /e/-vowel in words with the stress on the next-to-last syllable: מֶלֶךְ, אֶרֶץ, פֶּתַח

4 *Baal* בַּעַל: *Stressed open* syllable with a short instead of a long vowel. The deviation applies to an /a/-vowel in words with the stress on the next-to-last syllable: נַעַר, שַׁעַר.

5 *Jerusalem* יְרוּשָׁלַיִם (see Baal above): שְׁנַיִם, עַיִן, בַּיִת.

6 *Jacob* יַעֲקֹב: *Unstressed open* syllable with a short instead of a long vowel. The deviation applies to a short vowel immediately before a chateph (shva-plus-vowel): וֶאֱנוֹשׁ, וַאֲרָצוֹת, כַּחֲרָבוֹת, לַעֲבָדִים.[1]

REVIEW AND APPLICATION OF THE RULES

I All the enlarged particles (בְּ, מִ⬚ , וְ, לְ, הַ ⬚) in the verse segments below have a deviant form. *Study* the sound change rules listed below and *indicate* the relevant sound change rule/s in each case. Then *read* the clauses and *translate* (new vocabulary is found in the word list below).

SOUND CHANGE RULES

1 A sequence of two vowelless consonants in a row at the beginning of a syllable results in an impermissible three-consonant sequence, e.g., לִשְׁמוּ-אֵל. *A syllable may not begin with more than two consonants.* The consonant cluster is broken up by inserting a vowel between the two vowelless consonants, normally /i/: לְשְׁמוּ-אֵל becomes לִשְׁ-מוּ-אֵל.

---

[1] For syllable division before a chateph, see Section 7, footnote 5.

2 The insertion vowel which dissolves a three-consonant sequence before a guttural with a chateph matches the vowel of the chateph: לְאַרְ-צוֹת becomes לַ-אֲרָ-צוֹת.

3 The consonant י/ו at the end of a syllable forms a diphthong, e.g., לְאַ-הוֹדָה. *A syllable may not have more than one vowel.* The vowel cluster is normally adjusted by the silencing of י/ו, i.e., י/ו disappears in pronunciation but is retained in writing as a vowel letter: לְאַ-הוֹדָה becomes לִיהוּדָה.

4 ה after a vowelless consonant sometimes disappears in writing, its vowel being transferred to the preceding vowelless consonant. The doubling in the following letter is, however, retained: כְּהַתּוֹרָה becomes כַּתּוֹרָה.

5 Gutturals and ר cannot be doubled. Instead of doubling, the preceding short vowel is often lengthened: הָרֹאשׁ (not הַרֹּאשׁ), מֵרָחֵל (not מִרָּחֵל).

6 The hard sound of a BeGaDKeFaT-consonant becomes soft after a vowel or a reduced vowel (vocal shva or chateph), which is shown in writing by the absence of the hardening dagesh: לְבַיִת (not לְבַּיִת).

1 אֲנִי קֹהֶלֶת ...(Qohelet) מֶלֶךְ עַל-יִשְׂרָאֵל (Israel) בִּירוּשָׁלָםִ: (Jerusalem) (Ecc. 1:12)

2 לַכֹּל... עֵת... תַּחַת הַשָּׁמָיִם: (Ecc. 3:1)

3 יֵשׁ רָעָה... תַּחַת הַשֶּׁמֶשׁ וְרַבָּה הִיא עַל-הָאָדָם: (Ecc. 6:1)

4 הַיָּמִים הָרִאשׁנִים... טוֹבִים מֵאֵלֶּה (Ecc. 7:10)

5 לִפְנִנָּה (Peninnah) יְלָדִים (1 Sam. 1:2)

6 בַּיָּמִים הָהֵם אֵין מֶלֶךְ בְּיִשְׂרָאֵל (Israel) (Judg. 17:6)

7 וַאֲנַחְנוּ רַבִּים (Ezek. 33:24)

8 וְאִישׁ אֵין בָּאָרֶץ (Gen. 19:31)

WORD LIST

Nouns

אוֹר	*m*, light
זָהָב	*m*, gold
כֶּסֶף	*m*, silver; money
מַלְאָךְ, לאך	*m*, messenger; angel (☆ Malachi, l.ʔ.k)
עֵת,עתת	*f*, time: *pl* עִתִּים/עִתּוֹת
פֶּה	*m*, mouth: *pl* פִּיּוֹת, with suff פִּיךָ (☆ the letter **Pe**)
פְּרִי	*m*, fruit: *pl* פֵּרוֹת, with suff פִּרְיִי
רָעָה	*f*, evil, trouble, disaster
שֶׁמֶשׁ	*f*, sun (☆ Samson, š.m.š)
שָׁנָה	*f*, year: *pl* שָׁנִים/שָׁנוֹת

Particles

אֶל-	to, toward
אֵת/אֶת-	with, together with: *with suff* אִתִּי
כְּמוֹ	as, like (= כְּ): *with suff* כָּמוֹנִי, כָּכֶם
עוֹד	again, yet, still: *with suff* עוֹדֶנִּי/עוֹדִי
עָם	with, together with: *with suff* עִמִּי (☆ Immanuel, ʕ.m.m)
תַּחַת	under; instead of, in place of

EXERCISES

11.1 *Read* and *fill in* the blanks with the missing data according to the example in the table below. *Note*:

- The attached pronouns are shortened forms of the independent pronouns:
  - אָנֹכִי/אֲנִי: The יִ or נִי element is kept in the attached pronoun, e.g., אֵינֶנִּי, לִי
  - אֲנַחְנוּ: The נוּ element is kept in the attached pronoun, e.g., לָנוּ.
  - The ת in אַתְּ, אַתָּה, אַתֶּם, אַתֶּן is replaced by כ in the attached pronoun: לְךָ, לָךְ, לָכֶם, לָכֶן.
  - The ה in הוּא, הִיא, הֵם, הֵנָּה, הֵנָּה is either kept in the attached pronoun as in לָהּ, לָהֶם, לָהֶן or omitted as in לוֹ 'to him', אִתָּם 'with them' (*m*). Compare וְהַבֵּן in which the ה is retained and לַבֵּן in which the ה is omitted (not לְהַבֵּן).
- The consonant ה at the end of a word is distinguished from the vowel letter ה by a dot, called *mappiq*. Compare יַלְדָהּ 'her child' and יַלְדָה 'girl'.
- The particles (כְּ=כְּמוֹ) 'as, like', מִן 'from' and אַיִן 'non-existence' with attached pronouns have irregular forms. Nevertheless, it is not difficult to identify them.

Translation	Particle: Lexical (free) form	Independent personal pronoun	Particle-plus-pronoun		Translation	Particle: Lexical (free) form	Independent personal pronoun	Particle-plus-pronoun	
			אִתָּנוּ	11	with us	עִם	אֲנַחְנוּ	עִמָּנוּ	1
			מִמֶּנָּה	12				בִּי	2
			לְךָ	13				לָכֶם	3
			בָּהּ	14				לוֹ	4
			לָנוּ	15		מִן		מִמְּךָ	5
		הוּא/אֲנַחְנוּ	אֵינֶנּוּ	16				לָהֶם	6
			בָּם	17				אֵינוֹ	7
			כָּמוֹהוּ	18				עִמָּהּ	8
		הוּא/אֲנַחְנוּ	מִמֶּנּוּ	19		כְּ/כְּמוֹ		כָּמוֹנִי	9
			אִתּוֹ	20				אֵינְכֶן	10

11.2 *Study* the examples of the units of noun-plus-pronoun below. *Pay attention to the vowel changes occurring in the nouns. Remember*:

> + The attached pronouns are added to the bound form of the noun: מְצַוֺת (the free form is מִצְוָה) + 'אֲנִי' results in מִצְוָתִי, which is adjusted to מִצְוָתִי in accordance with the basic rule of vocalization. *All syllables generally have a **long** vowel except an **unstressed closed** syllable which always has a **short** vowel.*
> + Penultimate nouns and twin-consonant nouns retain their original forms before the attached pronoun.

Vowel changes in nouns in the units of noun-plus-pronoun, compared to the corresponding bound forms without the atttached pronoun	Noun: Bound form	Translation: Noun-plus-pronoun	Independent personal pronoun	Noun-plus-pronoun	Noun: Lexical (free) form
1) A full vowel (with the vowel letter י/ו) and a vowel followed by a silent א is unchangeable (i.e., not affected by the position of the stress).	אִישׁ	her husband	הִיא	אִישָׁהּ	אִישׁ
2) A short vowel in an open syllable immediately before the stress is lengthened.	יַד	your hand	אַתְּ	יָדֵךְ	יָד
3) A short vowel in an unstressed closed syllable is unchangeable (i.e., not affected by the position of the stress). See also 1 above (a full vowel with י/ו is unchangeable).	כּוֹכַב	your star	אַתֶּם	כּוֹכַבְכֶם	כּוֹכָב
4) The original form of a twin-consonant noun with a short vowel followed by a doubled consonant remains intact (e.g., 'ʔimm').	אֵם	my mother	אָנֹכִי	אִמִּי	אֵם
5) The original form of a penultimate noun with a short vowel followed by two vowelless consonants remains intact (e.g., 'nafš').	נֶפֶשׁ	your soul	אַתָּה	נַפְשְׁךָ	נֶפֶשׁ
See 3 and 2 above.	אַדְמַת	our soil	אֲנַחְנוּ	אַדְמָתֵנוּ	אֲדָמָה
See 2 above.	זְהַב	their gold	הֵם	זְהָבָם	זָהָב

11.3 *Read* and *fill in* the blanks with the missing data according to the example given in the table below.

Vowel changes (according to the examples given in Exercise 11.2)	Noun: Bound form	Translation: Noun-plus-pronoun	Independent personal pronoun	Noun-plus-pronoun	Noun: Lexical (free) form	
3, 2	מַלְאַךְ	my messenger	אֲנִי	מַלְאָכִי	מַלְאָךְ	1
	מוֹת			מוֹתֵנוּ	מָוֶת	2
				חֻקָּה	חֹק	3
				אַדְמָתְךָ	אֲדָמָה	4
				בְּרִיתוֹ	בְּרִית	5
				מְשִׁיחָם	מָשִׁיחַ	6
				מִצְוָתָהּ	מִצְוָה	7
				אוֹרֶךָ	אוֹר	8
				אֲדוֹנְכֶם	אָדוֹן	9
				סִפְרְכֶם	סֵפֶר	10
				נְבִיאֶךָ	נָבִיא	11
				תּוֹרָתוֹ	תּוֹרָה	12
				רֹאשָׁם	רֹאשׁ	13
				מַלְכֵּנוּ	מֶלֶךְ	14
				תִּקְוָתִי	תִּקְוָה	15
				קָדְשְׁךָ	קֹדֶשׁ	16
	עֵין			עֵינָהּ	עַיִן	17
				עַמִּי	עַם	18

11.4 *Cover* the English translation, *read* and *translate* as much as you can on your own. Then *fill in* the blanks with the missing pronouns in the following translation and *check/complete* your translation against it. *Remember*:

> • In a smooth translation from Hebrew to English certain Hebrew elements, words and/or constructions can be omitted, added or altered. Observe that words in parentheses render a literal translation, whereas words in square brackets are not found in the Hebrew clause but added to it for the sake of good English.
> • 'Fill in' exercises of this type are intended to help you to repeat your growing vocabulary and at the same time to show you how to translate Hebrew clauses, staying as close as possible to the original Hebrew text. Thus, you are **not** supposed to **fill in** the missing words **mechanically!**

1 שִׁמְךָ בְּכָל־הָאָרֶץ _____ name [is] in all the earth (Ps. 8:2)

2 גָּדוֹל שְׁמוֹ: _____ name [is] great (Ps. 76:2)

3 הִיא טוֹבָה לָךְ מִשִּׁבְעָה בָּנִים: _____ [is] better (= good) to _____ than seven sons (Ruth 4:15)

4 אַתָּה אָבִינוּ _____ [are] _____ father (Isa. 63:16)

5 וַיהוה אֱלֹהֵי צְבָאוֹת עִמּוֹ: And the Lord, the God of hosts, [was]² with _____ (2 Sam. 5:10)

6 אֵין טוֹב בָּם [There is] no good in _____ (Ecc. 3:12)

7 אַחַת הִיא לְאִמָּה _____ [is only] one of (= לְ) _____ mother (Song 6:9)

8 אַתֶּם בְּיָדִי בֵּית יִשְׂרָאֵל: _____ [are] in _____ hand, [O] house of Israel (Jer. 18:6)

9 אָחִי הוּא _____ [is] _____ brother (Gen. 20:5)

10 בֵּן אֵין־לָהּ וְאִישָׁהּ זָקֵן: _____ has no (= not to _____) son and _____ husband [is] old (2 Kings 4:14)

11 יֶשׁ־לָנוּ אָב זָקֵן _____ have (= יֵשׁ to _____) [an] old father (Gen. 44:20)

12 לִי הַכֶּסֶף וְלִי הַזָּהָב _____ have (= to _____) the silver and _____ have (= to _____) the gold (Hag. 2:8)

---

² Remember that a verbless clause has no tense of its own, hence its time reference is determined by the context (surrounding text).

13 אֵין לָהּ אָב וָאֵם _____ has no (= not to _____) father and [no] mother

(Esther 2:7)

14 אֲנִי בִּנְךָ _____ [am] _____ son (Gen. 27:32)

11.5 *Read* the following verse segments and *translate*. Proper names are enlarged.

9 זֹאת תּוֹרַת הַבָּיִת (Ezek. 43:12)   1 אָבִינוּ זָקֵן (Gen. 19:31)

10 יָפָה הִוא מְאֹד: (Gen. 12:14)   2 יהוה צְבָאוֹת עִמָּנוּ (Ps. 46:12)

11 וְכָל־אַנְשֵׁי בֵיתוֹ (Gen. 17:27)   3 עִמָּנוּ אֵל: (Isa. 8:10)

12 בֵּן וָאָח אֵין־לוֹ (Ecc. 4:8)   4 לִי כָּל־הָאָרֶץ: (Ex. 19:5)

13 בִּשְׁנַת־מוֹת הַמֶּלֶךְ (Isa. 6:1)   5 וּבְבֵיתִי אֵין לֶחֶם (Isa. 3:7)

14 אֱלֹהֵי אָבִי אַבְרָהָם (Gen. 32:10)   6 אָבִי אָתָּה (Ps. 89:27)

15 יְשָׁרִים דַּרְכֵי יהוה (Hos. 14:10)   7 טוֹב חַסְדְּךָ מֵחַיִּים (Ps. 63:4)

8 זֶה דְּבַר־יהוה אֶל־זְרֻבָּבֶל (Zech. 4:6)

11.6 *Reread* the phrases/clauses in Exercise 11.5 above and *translate* again *orally*. Then *translate* the following clauses into Hebrew, assisted by the clauses in Exercise 11.5.

1 Your father (*m, s*) is with us.
2 The Law of the Lord is our law.
3 You (*f, s*) have (= שׁ? to you) sons and daughters in your house.
4 I have (= שׁ? to me) a son like him. He has no (= אֵין to him) brothers.
5 The army of the king is strong. He has (= שׁ? to him) a strong army.
6 God is the greatest. His kindness is great toward (= עַל) his nation.
7 Each nation has (= to each nation) a sanctuary. All the sanctuaries are holy.
8 All the men are in the big field.
9 I am not in her beautiful house.
10 You (*m, p*) are not in our good city.
11 This is a big country. There are many people (= men) in it. It is bigger than your (*m, p*) country.
12 Their (*m*) father is older than their mother. He is older than she.
13 Your (*m, s*) word is our statute.
14 The way of God is good. My life (= soul) is in the hands of God.
15 Your (*m, p*) brother is not with me.

SECTION 12

1 *Prepositions with the "plural" set of attached pronouns*: Certain prepositions take the "plural" set of attached pronouns, for instance, עֲלֵיכֶם 'on/over *you*'.

2 *Nouns in plural with attached pronouns*

  – The bound form of both the plural ending ◌ִים and the dual ending ◌ַיִם is ◌ֵי. The י of the ending ◌ֵי appears in all the attached "plural" pronouns, thus serving as a *plural marker*, for instance, דְּבָרֵינוּ 'our *words*' (compare the singular דְּבָרֵנוּ without a י, 'our *word*').

  – The "plural" set of attached pronouns with the plural marker י is also attached to plural nouns ending in וֹת. Thus, plural nouns ending in וֹת have both י and וֹת as plural markers: תּוֹרֹתֵינוּ 'our *laws*'.

3 *Questions*: A yes-or-no question is sometimes not marked in Hebrew. An isolated clause like טוֹב הָאִישׁ may be interpreted both as 'The man is good' and 'Is the man good?'

  – *Question marker* הֲ: The particle הֲ functions as a *question mark* in a yes-or-no question: הֲטוֹב הָאִישׁ 'Is the man good?'

  Before a shva, הֲ is changed to הַ: הַמְלָכִים הֵם 'Are they kings?'

  Before a guttural (except unstressed עָ ,חָ ,הָ ,אָ), the question marker is also הֲ: הֶעֶבֶד הָאִישׁ 'Is the man a slave?' Before unstressed עָ ,חָ ,הָ ,אָ, the form is הֶ: הֶאָדוֹן הָאִישׁ 'Is the man a master?'

  – הֲלוֹא (הֲ + לוֹא) often introduces a rhetorical question: הֲלוֹא מְלָכִים הֵם 'Are they not kings!'

  – *Interrogative pronouns* מִי 'who' and מַה/מָה⸱ 'what'

  מִי אַתָּה 'Who are you?' מַה־דְּבַר הָאִישׁ 'What is the word of the man?'

  מָה is commonly joined to the following word by a maqqeph, מַה־. מַה־ is vocalized like the definite article הַ, that is, with an /a/-vowel followed by a doubling dagesh in the next consonant (see Exercise 12.5 below).

  – A question may be intensified by זֶה/זֹאת:

  מִי זֶה פֹּה 'Who is *this* here?' (compare מִי פֹּה 'Who is here?')

  מַה־זֶּה פֹּה 'What is *this/that* here?'

  הַאַתָּה זֶה 'Is *this [really]* you?'

4 *Sound changes across word boundaries*: Two sound units may affect each other across word boundaries.

  – A final vowel in one word may soften the sound of a BeGaDKeFaT-consonant beginning the next word, when the words are read together without a break (softening is shown in writing by the absence of the hardening dagesh): לֹא בֶן־נָבִיא (lōˀven nāvîˀ).

  – A doubling dagesh, usually preceded by a maqqeph, may unite a word ending in the vowel letter ה with the following word: מַה־זֶּה (maʰ**zz**eʰ).

5 *More about sound changes in words in pause* (see Exercise 12.8).

MEMORIZE (this table is to be used as reference)

NOUN TYPES[1]

	Singular				Plural				
	Noun: Lexical (free) form	Noun: Bound form	Noun-plus-pronoun	Noun-plus-pronoun with כֶם/ן, הֶם/ן	Noun: Free form	Noun: Bound form	Noun-plus-pronoun	Noun-plus-pronoun with כֶם/ן, הֶם/ן	
I	דָּבָר	דְּבַר	דְּבָרִי	דְּבַרְכֶם	דְּבָרִים	דִּבְרֵי	דְּבָרַי	דִּבְרֵיכֶם	I
	שָׂדֶה	שְׂדֵה	שָׂדִי	שַׂדְכֶם²	שָׂדוֹת	שְׂדוֹת	שְׂדוֹתַי	שְׂדוֹתֵיכֶם	
II	תּוֹרָה	תּוֹרַת	תּוֹרָתִי	תּוֹרַתְכֶם	תּוֹרוֹת	תּוֹרוֹת	תּוֹרוֹתַי	תּוֹרוֹתֵיכֶם	II
	בְּרִית	בְּרִית	בְּרִיתִי	בְּרִיתְכֶם	בְּרִיתוֹת	בְּרִיתוֹת	בְּרִיתוֹתַי	בְּרִיתוֹתֵיכֶם	
III	מֶלֶךְ	מֶלֶךְ	מַלְכִּי	מַלְכְּכֶם	מְלָכִים	מַלְכֵי	מְלָכַי	מַלְכֵיכֶם	III
	סֵפֶר	סֵפֶר	סִפְרִי	סִפְרְכֶם	סְפָרִים	סִפְרֵי	סְפָרַי	סְפָרֵיכֶם	
	בֹּקֶר	בֹּקֶר	בָּקְרִי	בָּקְרְכֶם	בְּקָרִים	בָּקְרֵי	בְּקָרַי	בְּקָרֵיכֶם	
	מַלְכָּה	מַלְכַּת	מַלְכָּתִי	מַלְכַּתְכֶם	מְלָכוֹת	מַלְכוֹת	מַלְכוֹתַי	מַלְכוֹתֵיכֶם	
	שֹׁפֶטֶת	שֹׁפֶטֶת	שֹׁפַטְתִּי	שֹׁפַטְתְּכֶם	שֹׁפְטוֹת	שֹׁפְטוֹת	שֹׁפְטוֹתַי	שֹׁפְטוֹתֵיכֶם	
	מִלְחָמָה³	מִלְחֶמֶת	מִלְחַמְתִּי	מִלְחַמְתְּכֶם	מִלְחָמוֹת	מִלְחֲמוֹת	מִלְחֲמוֹתַי	מִלְחֲמוֹתֵיכֶם	
IV	עַם	עַם	עַמִּי	עַמְּכֶם	עַמִּים	עַמֵּי	עַמַּי	עַמֵּיכֶם	IV
	אֵם	אֵם	אִמִּי	אִמְּכֶם	אִמּוֹת	אִמּוֹת	אִמּוֹתַי	אִמּוֹתֵיכֶם	
	חֹק	חֹק	חֻקִּי	חָקְכֶם	חֻקִּים	חֻקֵּי	חֻקַּי	חֻקֵּיכֶם	
V	אָב	אֲבִי	אָבִי	אֲבִיכֶם	אָבוֹת	אֲבוֹת	אֲבוֹתַי	אֲבוֹתֵיכֶם	V
	אָח	אֲחִי	אָחִי	אֲחִיכֶם	אַחִים	אֲחֵי	אַחַי	אֲחֵיכֶם	
	פֶּה	פִּי	פִּי	פִּיכֶם	פִּיּוֹת/פֵּיוֹת				

GRAMMATICAL CORNERSTONE 9   ר א שׁ פָּ נָ ה

---

[1] **I** – Regular masculine nouns, **II** – Regular feminine nouns, **III** – Penultimate nouns,
    IV – Twin-consonant nouns, **V** – Irregular nouns.

[2] Also שְׁדֶכֶם.

[3] מִלְחָמָה 'war, battle'.

☆ NOUN TYPES VIA HEBREW NAMES (7)

Noun type	Hebrew name	English pronunciation	Lexical (free) form	Bound form	Form with attached pronoun	Plural: Free form	Meaning: Lexical form
I Regular masculine	אַבְשָׁלוֹם	**Abs**alom	שָׁלוֹם	שְׁלוֹם	שְׁלוֹמִי	_____	peace, well-being
	מַלְאָכִי	**Malach**i	מַלְאָךְ	מַלְאַךְ	מַלְאָכִי	מַלְאָכִים	messenger, angel
II Regular feminine	דְּבוֹרָה	Deborah	דְּבוֹרָה	דְּבוֹרַת	דְּבוֹרָתִי	דְּבוֹרִים	bee
	תּוֹרָה	Torah	תּוֹרָה	תּוֹרַת	תּוֹרָתִי	תּוֹרוֹת	law
	יָעֵל	Jael	יָעֵל	יָעֵל	יַעֲלִי	יְעֵלִים	steinbock
III Penultimate	אֲבִימֶלֶךְ	Abi**melech**	מֶלֶךְ	מֶלֶךְ	מַלְכִּי	מְלָכִים	king
	בַּת שֶׁבַע	**Bathsheba**	שֶׁבַע	שֶׁבַע	_____	_____	seven, oath
	נָעֳמִי	**Naom**i	נֹעַם	נֹעַם	נָעֳמִי	_____	kindness
IV Twin-consonant	חַגַּי	**Hagg**ai	חַג	חַג	חַגִּי	חַגִּים	feast
	תֵּל אָבִיב	**Tel** Aviv	תֵּל	תֵּל	תִּלִּי	תִּלִּים	mound of ruins
	עֻזִּיָּה	**Uzz**iah	עֹז	עֹז	עֻזִּי	_____	strength
V Irregular	אַבְרָהָם	**Ab**raham	אָב	אֲבִי	אָבִי	אָבוֹת	father
	אֲחִימֶלֶךְ	**Ahi**melech	אָח	אֲחִי	אָחִי	אַחִים	brother
	בִּנְיָמִין	**Benj**amin	בֵּן	בֵּן/בֶּן	בְּנִי	בָּנִים	son
	בַּת שֶׁבַע	**Bath**sheba	בַּת	בַּת	בִּתִּי	בָּנוֹת	daughter
	אִישׁ־קְרִיּוֹת	**Iscariot**	אִישׁ	אִישׁ	אִישִׁי	אֲנָשִׁים	man, person
	בֵּית אֵל	**Beth**el	בַּיִת	בֵּית	בֵּיתִי	בָּתִּים	house
	שֵׁם	Shem	שֵׁם	שֵׁם	שְׁמִי	שֵׁמוֹת	name

WORD LIST

Nouns		Adjectives	
אֹזֶן	f, ear: dual אָזְנַיִם, with suff אָזְנִי	חָזָק	strong, mighty
אָחוֹת	f, sister: pl אֲחָיוֹת	מְעַט	a little, few:
אֶלֶף	m, thousand: dual אַלְפַּיִם,		pl מְעַטִּים
	pl אֲלָפִים (☆ the letter Áleph, ʔ.l.p)	קָטֹן, קָטָן	small, young, un-
אֱמֶת, אָמַן	f, truth (☆ Amen, ʔ.m.n)		important: f קְטַנָּה
בֹּקֶר	m, morning: pl בְּקָרִים,		
	with suff בְּקָרִי	Particles	
בְּרָכָה	f, blessing		
הֵיכָל	m, palace, temple: pl הֵיכָלוֹת	אַחַר/אַחֲרֵי	after, behind:
זֶרַע	m, seed, offspring: pl זְרָעִים,		with suff אַחֲרֵי
	with suff זַרְעִי	אֵי/־אַיֵּה	where?
חַג, חֹגֵג	m, feast, festival: with defin art	אֵי־זֶה	which?
	הֶחָג, pl חַגִּים (☆ Haggai, ḥ.g.g)	אֵיפֹה (אֵי + פֹּה)	where?
חַיִל	m, strength, power, army;	הֲ	question marker
	capacity, valour: pl חֲיָלִים	הֲ ....אִם	whether… or
כִּסֵּא	m, throne, seat: pl כִּסְאוֹת	לִפְנֵי (לְ + פָּנִים)	before, in front
מַעֲשֶׂה, עֹשֶׂה	m, deed, act		of: with suff לְפָנַי
מִצְרַיִם	f, Egypt	מֵאַיִן (מִן + אַיִן)	where from?
עוֹלָם	m, eternity: לְעוֹלָם, עַד־עוֹלָם,		whence?
	לְעוֹלָם וָעֶד forever	מָה, מַה־ ☐	what?
צֶדֶק	m, righteousness, justice: with	מִי	who?
	suff צִדְקִי (☆ Zedekiah, ṣ.d.q)	עַד	to, up to, until:
צְדָקָה, צֶדֶק	f, righteousness		with suff עָדַי
רֶגֶל	f, foot: dual רַגְלַיִם, with suff רַגְלִי	פֹּה	here
שָׁלוֹם	m, peace; well-being (☆ Solomon, š.l.m)		

EXERCISES

12.1 *Fill in* the blanks with the missing data according to the example in the
   following table. All the prepositions in the table below take the "plural" set
   of the attached pronouns. *Remember*:

> • ׳ functions as a plural marker in the "plural" set of the attached
>   pronouns:

my	ִ י	[áy]	our	ֵ ינוּ	[ênû]
your, m	ֶ יךָ	[éʸxā]	your, m	ֵ יכֶם	[êxém]
your, f	ַ יִךְ	[áyix]	your, f	ֵ יכֶן	[êxén]
his	ָ יו	[āʸw]	their, m	ֵ יהֶם	[êhém]
her	ֶ יהָ	[éʸhā]	their, f	ֵ יהֶן	[êhén]

Translation	Preposition: Lexical form	Independent personal pronoun	Preposition-plus-pronoun	
to/towards us	אֶל	אֲנַחְנוּ	אֵלֵינוּ	1
			עָלַי	2
			אֵלָיו	3
			עֲלֵיכֶם	4
			אֲלֵיהֶן	5
			עָלָיו	6
			עָלֶיךָ	7
			לְפָנֵינוּ	8
			עָלֶיהָ	9
			אַחֲרֶיךָ	10
			תַּחְתַּי	11
			לְפָנֶיךָ	12
			אַחֲרֶיהָ	13
			תַּחְתֶּיךָ	14
			אַחֲרָיו	15
			לִפְנֵיכֶם	16
			אַחֲרֵיהֶם	17
			לְפָנַי	18

12.2 *Fill in* the blanks with the data according to the examples in the following table. *Remember*:

> ◆ Plural nouns ending in וֹת have two plural markers, both וֹת and ־ִי, e.g., תּוֹרוֹתֵיכֶם 'your laws'.

Translation: Noun-plus-pronoun	Noun: Singular, lexical (free) form	Noun: Plural, free form	Independent personal pronoun	Noun-plus-pronoun	
my festivals	חַג	חַגִּים	אֲנִי/אָנֹכִי	חַגַּי	1
				מְקוֹמוֹתַי	2
his women/ wives	אִשָּׁה	נָשִׁים	הוּא	נָשָׁיו	3
				מִשְׁלֵיכֶם	4
				עַמֵּינוּ	5
				אֲבוֹתָיו	6
				שְׂדוֹתֵיכֶם	7
				שִׁירֶיהָ	8
				כּוֹכָבֶיךָ	9
				בְּקָרֶיךָ	10
				מִצְוֹתֵיהֶם	11
				חֻקָּיו	12
				אָזְנֵינוּ	13
				עֵינֵיהֶם	14
				בָּתֶּיךָ	15
				רַגְלַיִךְ	16
				פָּנֵינוּ	17
				הֵיכָלוֹתַי	18

12.3 *Match* each Hebrew question with the correct English translation.

> This is how you are expected to work with this type of exercise: First read the Hebrew text and **try to translate** as much as you can **on your own**. Then match each Hebrew verse segment with the correct English translation and check your translation against it.

1 הֲיֵשׁ לָכֶם אָח   ( ) Whose daughter (= daughter of who) [are] you? (Gen. 24:23)

2 מִי אַתָּה בְּנִי: ( ) Where [is] Abel, your brother? (Gen. 4:9)

3 לְמִי־אַתָּה   ( ) Where [are] Samuel and David? (1 Sam. 19:22)

4 הַעֶבֶד יִשְׂרָאֵל   ( ) Have we not all (= not to all of us) one father! (Mal. 2:10)

5 אַיֵּה אֱלֹהֶיךָ:   ( ) What [is] this trouble? (Judg. 20:12)

6 בַּת־מִי אַתְּ   ( ) Do you have (= יֵשׁ to you) [a] brother? (Gen. 43:7)

7 אַיֵּה שָׂרָה אִשְׁתֶּךָ   ( ) Where [is] their God? (Joel 2:17)

8 הֲלוֹא לָנוּ הֵם   ( ) [Is] this your youngest (= the young) brother? (Gen. 43:29)

9 הֲזֶה אֲחִיכֶם הַקָּטֹן   ( ) Where [is] Sarah, your wife? (Gen. 18:9)

10 אַחַי מֵאַיִן אַתֶּם   ( ) [Are] they not ours (= to us)! (Gen. 34:23)

11 מָה הָרָעָה הַזֹּאת   ( ) Who [is a] God like you? (Mic. 7:18)

12 אֵיפֹה שְׁמוּאֵל וְדָוִד   ( ) [Is] Israel [a] slave? (Jer. 2:14)

13 מִי־אֵל כָּמוֹךָ   ( ) My brothers, where [are] you from? (Gen. 29:4)

14 אַיֵּה אֱלֹהֵיהֶם: ( ) To whom (= to who) [do] you [belong]? (Gen 32:17)

15 אֵי הֶבֶל אָחִיךָ   ( ) Who [are] you, my son? (Gen. 27:18)

16 הֲלוֹא אָב אֶחָד לְכֻלָּנוּ   ( ) Where [is] your God? (Ps. 42:4)

12.4 *Insert* the correct vowel after (i.e., under) the question marker ה (normally vocalized הֲ). *Read* the questions and *translate*. Proper names are enlarged. *Remember*:

> - הֲ ...אִם means 'whether... or': הֲקָטֹן הוּא אִם גָּדוֹל 'Is he/it little or big?'
> - Before a shva הֲ becomes הַ. *A syllable may not begin with more than two consonants in a row. The consonants of the cluster are separated by the addition of an insertion vowel that matches the vowel of the chateph*: הַמְלָכִים (not הֲמְלָכִים).
> – Before a guttural הֲ becomes הַ, but before unstressed עָ ,הָ ,אָ it is הֶ.

1	הַאַתָּה אִישׁ־הָאֱלֹהִים (1 Kings 13:14) _____
2	הַעוֹד אֲבִיכֶם חַי (Gen. 43:7) _____
3	הַבְרָכָה אַחַת הִוא־לְךָ אָבִי (Gen. 27:38) _____
4	הֲלוֹא־אָח עֵשָׂו לְיַעֲקֹב (Mal. 1:2) _____
5	הַטוֹבָה הִוא אִם־רָעָה (Num. 13:19) _____
6	הֲזֹאת נָעֳמִי: (Ruth 1:19) _____
7	הַמְעַט הוּא אִם־רָב: (Num. 13:18) _____
8	הַאֵין פֹּה נָבִיא (2 Kings 3:11) _____
9	הַאֱלֹהִים אָנִי (2 Kings 5:7) _____
10	הֶחָזָק הוּא (Num. 13:18) _____

12.5 *Insert* the correct vowel after the letter מ in the word מָה 'what'. *Read* the questions and *translate*. *Remember*:

> - מָה is usually joined to the following word by a maqqeph and it is *vocalized like the definite article*, i.e., normally מַה־◌ּ (compare הַ ◌ּ).
> – Before ר ,ע ,א (and rarely ה) the form is מָה־ (compare הָ). *Gutturals and* ר *cannot be doubled. Instead, the preceding vowel is lengthened.*
> – Before ח ,ה the form is normally מַה־ (compare הַ); neither doubling of the following consonant nor lengthening of the preceding vowel occurs.
> – Before unstressed עָ ,חָ ,הָ the form is מֶה (compare הֶ).

1	מַה־הִיא (Zech. 5:6) _____
2	מַה־שְּׁמוֹ וּמַה־שֶּׁם־בְּנוֹ (Prov. 30:4) _____

3   מַה־שְּׁמֶ֫ךָ (Gen. 32:28)   _____

4   מָה הֶעָרִים הָאֵ֫לֶּה (1 Kings 9:13)   _____

5   מָה־הַדָּבָר הָרָע הַזֶּה (Neh. 13:17)   _____

6   מָה־אָדָם (Ps. 144:3)   _____

7   מַה אַרְצֶ֫ךָ (Jon. 1:8)   _____

12.6   *Cover* the English translation, *read* and *translate*. Then *fill in* the blanks with the missing pronouns in the following translation and *check/complete* your translation against it. *Remember*:

> • יֵשׁ is rendered by 'there is/was/will be' and אֵין by 'there is not/was not/will not be', as the context requires.

1   יהוה אֱלֹהֵ֫ינוּ יהוה אֶחָד: The LORD [is] _____ God. The LORD [is] one (Dt. 6:4)

2   מִשְׁפָּטֶ֫יךָ טוֹבִים: _____ legal decisions [are] good (Ps. 119:39)

3   וְאָחִ֫ינוּ הַקָּטֹן אֵינֶ֫נּוּ אִתָּ֫נוּ: And _____ youngest (= the young) brother, (_____) [is] not with _____ (Gen. 44:26)

4   אֶ֫רֶץ מִצְרַ֫יִם לְפָנֶ֫יךָ The land of Egypt [is] before _____ (Gen. 47:6)

5   מִפִּ֫יךָ וּמִפִּי זַרְעֶ֫ךָ From _____ mouth and from the mouth of _____ offspring (Isa. 59:21)

6   וְיֵשׁ־בָּם אַנְשֵׁי־חַ֫יִל And there [is] (= יֵשׁ) among _____ powerful men (men of power) (Gen. 47:6)

7   אֵין־כָּמ֫וֹךָ בָאֱלֹהִים אֲדֹנָי וְאֵין כְּמַעֲשֶׂ֫יךָ: [There is] none like _____ among the gods, [O] LORD, and [there are] no deeds like _____ (Ps. 86:8)

8   וְלִבְּךָ אֵין אִתִּי And _____ heart [is] not with _____ (Judg. 16:15)

9   לְעוֹלָם חַסְדּוֹ: _____ kindness [endures] forever (Ps. 136:3)

10   אָחוֹת לָ֫נוּ קְטַנָּה _____ have (= to _____) [a] little sister (Song 8:8)

11   יהוה אֱלֹהֵי אֲבֹתֶ֫יךָ The LORD, the God of _____ fathers (Dt. 1:21)

12   אֲנִי נָבִיא כָּמ֫וֹךָ _____ [am a] prophet like _____ (1 Kings 13:18)

13 צַדִּיק אַתָּה מִמֶּ֫נִּי _____ [are more] righteous than _____

(1 Sam. 24:18)

14 יהוה בְּהֵיכַל קָדְשׁוֹ יהוה בַּשָּׁמַ֫יִם כִּסְאוֹ The Lord [is] in _____ holy

temple (temple of holiness); the Lord, in the heavens [is] _____

throne (Ps. 11:4)

15 וּמָנ֫וֹחַ אִישָׁהּ אֵין עִמָּהּ: And Manoah, _____ husband, [was] not

with _____ (Judg. 13:9)

16 צִדְקָתְךָ צֶ֫דֶק לְעוֹלָם וְתוֹרָתְךָ אֱמֶת: _____ righteousness [is a]

righteousness forever and _____ law [is] truth (Ps. 119:142)

17 יהוה אֱלֹהֵ֫ינוּ עִמָּ֫נוּ The Lord, _____ God, [is] with _____

(1 Kings 8:57)

12.7 *Mark* the softened BeGaDKeFaT-consonants at the beginning of a word in
the verse segments below. *Read* the phrases/clauses and *translate*. Proper
names are enlarged. *Remember*:

> • A final vowel in one word may soften the sound of a BeGaDKeFaT-
> consonant beginning the next word, when the words are read together
> without a break.

1 לִי בְנֵי־יִשְׂרָאֵל עֲבָדִים (Lev. 25:55)

_____

2 הֲלֹא כָל־הָאָ֫רֶץ לְפָנֶ֫יךָ (Gen. 13:9)

_____

3 כָּל־עַבְדֵי פַרְעֹה זִקְנֵי בֵיתוֹ

וְכֹל זִקְנֵי אֶ֫רֶץ־מִצְרָ֫יִם: (Gen. 50:7)

_____

4 אַבְשָׁלוֹם אַבְשָׁלוֹם בְּנִי בְנִי: (2 Sam. 19:5)

_____

5 יהוה מִי כָמ֫וֹךָ (Ps. 35:10)

_____

6 מִי־לִי בַשָּׁמָ֫יִם (Ps. 73:25)

_____

7 הֲלוֹא־אִישׁ אַתָּה וּמִי כָמ֫וֹךָ בְּיִשְׂרָאֵל

(1 Sam. 26:15)

_____

12.8 The enlarged word in each verse/verse segment below is in pausal form. *Write* the normal form of these words. *Indicate* the relevant sound change/s occurring in them using the list given below. *Read* the phrases/clauses and translate. Remember:

> ♦ Words in pause sometimes undergo sound changes (see below).
> ♦ The break in reading *(pause)* at the end of the verse is marked by *silluq* ⸣ . The silluq is always followed by the sign for *soph pasuq* (end of the verse) ⸽ , e.g., הוּא׃ אָנִי. The break in the middle of the verse is marked by *atnach* ⸢ , e.g., צְבָאוֹת, הָאִישׁ.
> ♦ Certain minor breaks in reading may also cause sound changes, which are marked, for instance, by *zaqeph qaton* ⸠ אַרְצֶךָ and *revia* ⸋ אַרְצֶךָ.
> ♦ The accent signs are not rendered in this book.

SOUND CHANGES IN WORDS IN PAUSE

1 A short vowel in the stressed syllable of a word is lengthened: עַם 'nation' becomes עָם, יָדַי 'my hands' becomes יָדָי (pronounced 'yaday'), מַיִם becomes מָיִם.

2 The stress is moved backward from the last to the next-to-last syllable. In addition, the short vowel in the stressed next-to-last syllable is lengthened: אַתָּה becomes אָתָּה.

3 The original linking vowel /e/ replaces a vocal shva. The linking vowel takes the stress: עַמְךָ 'your nation' *(m, s)* becomes עַמֶּךָ.

4 The original linking vowel /a/ replaces a vocal shva: לְךָ 'to you' *(m, s)* becomes לָךְ, which is identical in form with the feminine pronoun לָךְ *(f, s)*.

5 An original short vowel replaces a chateph. The original vowel takes the stress and is lengthened: אֲנִי becomes אָנִי.

6 The original /a/-vowel in a penultimate noun replaces the /e/-vowel: מֶלֶךְ becomes מַלֶךְ. Besides, the original /a/-vowel is lengthened: מָלֶךְ.

_____	1 מַה אַרְצֶךָ (Jon. 1:8)
_____	2 מִי־לִי בַשָּׁמָיִם (Ps. 73:25)
_____	3 יֵשׁ רָעָה... תַּחַת הַשֶּׁמֶשׁ וְרַבָּה הִיא עַל־הָאָדָם׃ (Ecc. 6:1)
_____	4 מַה־שְּׁמֶךָ (Gen. 32:28)
_____	5 מִי הָאֲנָשִׁים הָאֵלֶּה עִמָּךְ׃ (Num. 22:9)
_____	6 הֲשָׁלוֹם לָךְ הֲשָׁלוֹם לְאִישֵׁךְ הֲשָׁלוֹם לַיָּלֶד (2 Kings 4:26)

7 חַסְדְּךָ גָּדוֹל עָלָי (Ps. 86:13) _____

8 כָּל־קְדֹשָׁיו בְּיָדֶךָ (Dt. 33:3) _____

9 טוֹב־לִי תוֹרַת־פִּיךָ מֵאַלְפֵי זָהָב וָכָסֶף: (Ps. 119:72) _____

10 אֵשֶׁת חַיִל אָתְּ: (Ruth 3:11) _____

11 זֹאת תּוֹרַת הַבָּיִת (Ezek. 43:12) _____

12 אָבִי אָתָּה (Ps. 89:27) _____

13 מֶלֶךְ גָּדוֹל אָנִי (Mal. 1:14) _____

14 אַחִים אֲנָחְנוּ: (Gen. 13:8) _____

15 וּדְבַר־יהוה מִירוּשָׁלָ͏ִם: (Isa. 2:3) _____

12.9 *Translate* the following clauses into Hebrew. *Do not use* pausal forms.

1 Where are the children?
2 Where are these men from (= from where are…)?
3 What is your (*m, s*) law?
4 Who is your (*f, s*) master? Is he good?
5 Who is here and who is in the temple of God?
6 Is he not your (*m, s*) brother!
7 Do you (*m, p*) have a sister? Where is she?
8 Are all your (*m, s*) daughters in your (*m, s*) house?
9 My throne is in the country forever.
10 Where are all my children?

SECTION 13

1 *Verb system*

– *Formation of verbs*: Verbs, like other words in Hebrew, generally consist of *three root consonants* placed in various *patterns*. A verb pattern consists of vowels, possible prefix and/or a doubled middle root consonant.

– *Finite and non-finite verb forms*: Hebrew has *two finite verb forms*, the *perfect* and *imperfect*, and *two non-finite verb forms*, the *participle* and the *infinitive*. A finite verb form indicates the time in which an action/event takes place, whereas a non-finite verb form has no time reference of its own, hence its time is indicated by the surrounding text.

– *Seven verb types (stems)*: There are *seven* verb patterns in Hebrew, one basic, called the *G-stem* (from German 'Grundstamm'), and six derived stems.

– *Basic stem (Qal)*: The basic verb type consists of a vowel pattern only, ־ ־ ־, thus called *Qal*, which means 'easy, light; simple'. Qal carries the basic meaning of the verb root, which is slightly altered in the derived stems.

– *Model verb* פָּעַל: The root consonants of the model verb פָּעַל 'do, make' are traditionally placed in the verb patterns to indicate the names of the verb stems, e.g., 'פעל + the vowel pattern of Qal ־ ־ ־' results in the traditional name פָּעַל, 'פעל + the pattern ־ ־ ־ נִ' results in נִפְעַל etc.

הָפְעַל	הִפְעִיל	הִתְפַּעֵל	פֻּעַל	פִּעֵל	נִפְעַל

ל ע פ

– *Two inflection patterns*: There are two inflection patterns, one consisting of a set of attached *suffixed pronouns* (called the *perfect*, denoting mainly past time) and the other one consisting of a set of *prefixed pronouns* (called the *imperfect*, denoting mainly non-past, that is, present and future).[1] All seven verb types share the same inflection patterns.

The suffixed and prefixed pronouns attached to verbs function as *subjects*, indicating person, gender and number.

– *Unchangeable and changeable root types*: All seven verb types include both unchangeable root types (שְׁלֵמִים 'complete, sound', traditionally called *strong*) and changeable root types (*weak*).

– Verb roots with changeable consonants/gutturals are divided into root types according to the changeable consonant/guttural and its place in the verb root, i.e., first, second or third.

– Traditionally, the root letters of the model verb פעל are used to label the place of the changeable consonant/guttural in the verb root: פ *Pe* = I (first), ע

---

[1] However, certain prefixed pronouns are followed by an ending.

Áyin = II (second), לְ *Lámed* = III (third). In the verb root עָמַד, for example, the guttural עְ *Áyin* constitutes the first root consonant and therefore the root is classified as פ״ג *Pe-Gímel* (= I-guttural: ג is the initial letter of the word גְּרוֹנִית 'guttural').

2 *Perfect in general: Form and meaning*
   – *Form*: The perfect is formed by the addition of a set of pronouns attached to the root consonants as endings. They are called *suffixed pronouns (sufformatives)*. The only form of verbs in the perfect that does not take a suffixed pronoun is the 3rd *person masculine singular* (i.e., 3ms הוּא). Thus, the 3ms functions as the *base form* of the perfect. Observe that not all suffixed pronouns take the stress. *Normally, when a word takes an ending, the stress is automatically moved forwards to the newly added ending.* For the inflection of the perfect, see Grammatical cornerstone 10 below.
   – *Meaning*: The perfect is a *finite* verb form expressing *completed actions* which normally denote *past time*. However, certain verbs in the perfect may correspond to other English tenses (see 'note', Exercise 14.5).

3 פָּעַל *(Qal, the G-stem) perfect: Basic forms (unchangeable verbs,* שְׁלֵמִים*)*
   – *Lexical form*: The 3ms of פָּעַל is the form under which the verb is listed in the lexicon, e.g., שָׁמַר 'he guarded' corresponds to English '(to) guard'. The derived verb stems are listed in the lexicon under פָּעַל.
   – *Three vowel patterns*: פָּעַל perfect occurs in three vowel patterns, in which the vowel under the second root consonant, called *stem vowel*, varies. It is either an /a/-vowel (called *perfect-/a/ verbs*, often verbs which express an action, e.g., שָׁמַר 'guard'), an /e/- or an /o/-vowel (called *perfect-/e/* and *perfect-/o/ verbs*, often verbs which express a *state of being*, e.g., זָקֵן 'be/become old', קָטֹן 'be/become small').
   – *Vowel change*: Certain suffixed pronouns take the stress, which results in regular vowel reductions due to the shift in stress (see Exercise 13.2).

4 פָּעַל perfect of verbs with gutturals and ל״א *Lámed-Áleph* (III-א)-*verbs* undergo regular sound changes.

5 פָּעַל perfect of the irregular verb נָתַן 'give': The *third* root consonant נ *Nun* at the end of a syllable in נָתַן is *irregularly* assimilated to (absorbed in) the following consonant:[2] נָתַנְתִּי becomes נָתַתִּי.

6 *Vowel lowering* (known as *Philippi's law*): An original I/E-vowel in a stressed (originally) closed syllable is ordinarily changed into an /a/-vowel (see diagram in Section 14, Grammatical cornerstone 11). Vowel lowering applies to all forms of the perfect-/e/ verbs except the 3ms (הוּא), e.g., זָקֵנְתִּי becomes זָקַנְתִּי (whereas the /ē/-vowel in זָקֵן remains intact).

7 *Verbal clause* (see Exercise 13.5).

---

[2] However, in I-נ *Nun* verbs, the consonant נ *Nun* at the end of a syllable is *regularly* assimilated to the following consonant.

MEMORIZE

<table>
<tr><td colspan="8" align="center">PRONOUNS III</td></tr>
<tr><td></td><td colspan="3" align="center">Subject pronouns</td><td colspan="4" align="center">Possessive pronouns</td></tr>
<tr>
<td>Person</td>
<td></td>
<td>Independent</td>
<td>Attached to verbs in the perfect</td>
<td></td>
<td>Attached to nouns in singular
(after ʾ/ו)</td>
<td>Attached to nouns in singular
(after a consonant)</td>
<td>Attached to nouns in plural</td>
</tr>
<tr><td>3ms</td><td>he</td><td>הוּא</td><td>– – –</td><td>his</td><td>הוּ–/ו–</td><td>וֹ–</td><td>יו–</td></tr>
<tr><td>3fs</td><td>she</td><td>הִיא</td><td>ה– – –</td><td>her</td><td>הָ–</td><td>הָ–</td><td>יהָ–</td></tr>
<tr><td>2ms</td><td>you, m</td><td>אַתָּה</td><td>תָּ– – –</td><td>your</td><td>ךָ–</td><td>ךְ–</td><td>יךָ–</td></tr>
<tr><td>2fs</td><td>you, f</td><td>אַתְּ</td><td>תְּ– – –</td><td>your</td><td>ךְ–</td><td>ךְ–</td><td>יךְ–</td></tr>
<tr><td>1cs</td><td>I</td><td>אָנֹכִי/אֲנִי</td><td>תִּי– – –</td><td>my</td><td>י–</td><td>י–</td><td>י–</td></tr>
<tr><td>3mp</td><td>they, m</td><td>הֵם/הֵמָּה</td><td>וּ– – –</td><td>their</td><td>הֶם–</td><td>ם–</td><td>יהֶם–</td></tr>
<tr><td>3fp</td><td>they, f</td><td>הֵנָּה</td><td>וּ– – –</td><td>their</td><td>הֶן–</td><td>ן–</td><td>יהֶן–</td></tr>
<tr><td>2mp</td><td>you, m</td><td>אַתֶּם</td><td>תֶּם– – –</td><td>your</td><td>כֶם–</td><td>כֶם–</td><td>יכֶם–</td></tr>
<tr><td>2fp</td><td>you, f</td><td>אַתֵּן/אַתֵּנָה</td><td>תֶּן– – –</td><td>your</td><td>כֶן–</td><td>כֶן–</td><td>יכֶן–</td></tr>
<tr><td>1cp</td><td>we</td><td>אֲנַחְנוּ</td><td>נוּ– – –</td><td>our</td><td>נוּ–</td><td>נוּ–</td><td>ינוּ–</td></tr>
<tr><td colspan="8" align="center">GRAMMATICAL CORNERSTONE 10   ר א שׁ פֶּ נָ בְּ ה</td></tr>
</table>

☆ HEBREW VIA THE NAMES OF THE HEBREW ALPHABET (8)

I   The names of the Hebrew letters represent Hebrew words. *Memorize* the names and meaning of the following Hebrew letters. *Remember*:

- The sign of each Hebrew letter was originally pictorial, representing something concrete and familiar whose initial sound indicates the sound of the letter, e.g., the picture of a head (in Hebrew רֹאשׁ) represents the sound **/r/**.
- The traditional names of the changeable root types are a combination of a root letter of the model verb פָּעַל (indicating the place of the guttural/changeable letter in the verb root: פ *Pe* = I, ע *Áyin* = II, ל *Lámed* = III) and either the letter ג (indicating a guttural) or א, ה, ו, י, נ (the changeable letter in question), e.g., ע״ג *Áyin-Gímel* (II-guttural), פ״י *Pe-Yod* (I-י). A verb root with identical second and third root letters is called ע״ע *Áyin-Áyin*. The double apostrophe between two letters indicates an abbreviation, e.g., פ״י is פֶּא and יוֹד.

Name of letter	Hebrew word	Translation: Hebrew word	Name of letter	Hebrew word	Translation: Hebrew word
אָלֶף	אֶלֶף	ox; thousand	כַּף	כַּף	palm (of hand/foot)
בֵּית	בַּיִת	house	מֵים	מַיִם	water
גִּימֶל	גָּמָל	camel	עַיִן	עַיִן	eye
דָּלֶת	דֶּלֶת	door	פֵּא	פֶּה	mouth
וָו	וָו	nail (hook)	רֵישׁ	רֹאשׁ	head
יוֹד	יָד	hand	שִׁין	שֵׁן	tooth
			תָּו	תָּו	mark

REVIEW AND APPLICATION OF THE RULES

I *Match* each root type with the Hebrew verb that illustrates it. *Pronounce* the names of the Hebrew letters indicating the root types, assisted by HEBREW VIA THE NAMES OF THE HEBREW ALPHABET above. *Remember*:

> - All the verb forms below are in the **3**rd person **m**asculine singular (3ms, הוּא). The 3ms of פָּעַל perfect is the form under which the verb is listed in the lexicon and thus is called the *lexical form* in this book. שָׁמַר (lit., 'he guarded'), for example, corresponds to English '(to) guard'.
> - In the unchangeable root types (שְׁלֵמִים) all three root consonants are audible and visible in writing in all forms and inflections. Therefore, unchangeable root types fit into the normal formation and inflection patterns of the Hebrew language.
>   – In root types with gutturals (ע, ח, ה, א) the root consonants are also audible and visible in writing in all forms and inflections, but the normal vowel patterns are sometimes changed (in accordance with the sound change rules).
>   – In root types with changeable root consonants (א, ה, ו, י, נ or a doubled consonant) the changeable root consonant/s may be omitted or altered (in accordance with the sound change rules).
>   – The consonants א and ה either affect the surrounding vowels (as gutturals) or undergo sound change.
> - There are *ten changeable root types* in Hebrew: I-guttural, II-guttural, III-guttural, I-א, I-י/ו, I-נ Nun, II-י/ו, twin-consonant (geminate) verbs, III-א and III-ה (III-י/ו).

1 שְׁלֵמִים 'complete, sound' (_) שָׁמַע	5 פ״א, I-א (_) עָבַד
(unchangeable)	6 פ״י, I-י (_) שָׁתָה
2 פ״ג, I-guttural (_) כָּתַב	7 פ״נ, I-נ (1st Nun) (_) גָּאַל
3 ע״ג, II-guttural (_) נָפַל	8 ל״א, III-א (_) אָכַל
4 ל״ג, III-guttural (_) יָשַׁר	9 ל״ה, III-ה (3rd He) (_) קָרָא

II *Study* the sound change rules listed below. *Indicate* the relevant sound change/s occurring in each deviant verb form (on the left side) by comparing it with the corresponding normal form (on the right side). *Indicate* to which root type each deviant verb form belongs. *Remember*:

> • The gutturals/changeable consonants are liable to sound changes when there is no vowel either before or after them. *Shva is considered no-vowel!* However, when surrounded by vowels, no sound changes occur.
> • The sound change rules give the deviant forms a see-through structure. It is easiest to detect the deviant feature/s of a given form by placing the consonants of the deviant form, e.g., קָרָאתִי, in the corresponding normal verb pattern, i.e., ־ ־ ־תִּי, and ask, "Why is it קָרָאתִי instead of קָרָאתִּי (as in שָׁמַרְתִּי)?" Sound change rules 4 and 5 below answer the question.

SOUND CHANGE RULES

1 Two identical letters without an intervening vowel are rendered by one letter with a doubling dagesh: כָּרַתְתִּי is written כָּרַתִּי. *It is actually a rule of spelling rather than a sound change rule.*

2 A guttural takes a chateph (shva-plus-vowel) instead of a shva.

3 A guttural attracts an /a/-vowel/s.

4 A vowelless א at the end of a syllable is silenced, that is, א disappears in pronunciation but is retained in writing. The silencing of א is compensated by the lengthening of the preceding vowel (if it is not already long).

5 The hard sound of a BeGaDKeFaT-consonant becomes soft after a vowel (shown in writing by the absence of the hardening dagesh).

_____	שָׁמַרְתָּ – כָּרַתָּ	5	4, 5	שָׁמַרְתִּי – קָרָאתִי	1
_____	שְׁמַרְתֶּן – קְרָאתֶן	6	_____	שָׁמְרָה – מָאֲסָה	2
_____	שָׁמְרוּ – גָּאֲלוּ	7	_____	שָׁמַרְתָּ – שָׁמַעַתָּ³	3
_____	שָׁמַרְנוּ – נָתַנּוּ	8	_____	שְׁמַרְתֶּם – עֲבַדְתֶּם	4

WORD LIST

Nouns

גּוֹי — *m*, nation, a people: *pl* גּוֹיִם

יָשַׁר — be/become straight, upright

Verbs

אָהַב — love

אָמַר — say

גָּאַל — redeem

זָכַר — remember (☆ **Zechariah**)

זָקֵן — be/become old

כָּרַת — cut: כָּרַת בְּרִית make a covenant

כָּתַב — write

מָלַךְ — reign (as king) (☆ Abimelech)

מָשַׁח — anoint (☆ **Messiah**, m.š.ḥ)

נָתַן — give, set, put; appoint; allow, permit (☆ **Nathan**)

---

³ The form שָׁמַעַתָ would be expected (without a hardening dagesh in the ת after a vowel).

עָבַד	work, serve (☆ Obadiah, ʕ.b.d)	שָׁמַע	hear, listen; understand: שָׁמַע בְּקוֹל/לְקוֹל obey (☆ Simeon, š.m.ʕ)
קָטַל	kill, slay	שָׁמַר	guard, keep, watch (☆ Samaria)
קָטֹן	be/become small, unimportant		
קָרָא	call, proclaim, name (followed by לְ), summon; read		

Particles

אָז — then (= at that time)

לָמֶּה/לָמָה (לְ + מֶה) — why? (for + what)

EXERCISES

13.1 *Fill in* the table below with the missing forms of פָּעַל perfect. *Read* all the verb forms and *translate* orally. For practical reasons, render the perfect as simple past. *Write* the meaning of the lexical forms. *Note*:

- None of the attached pronouns in this exercise is stressed. Since there is no shift in stress, no vowel changes occur.
- Several suffixed pronouns are shortened forms of the independent pronouns:
  – אֲנִי/אָנֹכִי: The יִ element is kept in the attached pronoun, e.g., שָׁמַרְתִּי.
  – אֲנַחְנוּ: The נוּ element is kept in the attached pronoun, e.g., שָׁמַרְנוּ.
  – אַתָּה, אַתְּ: The תָּ/תְּ element is kept in the attached pronoun, e.g., שָׁמַרְתָּ/שָׁמַרְתְּ.

Meaning: Lexical form	אֲנַחְנוּ	אַתְּ	אַתָּה	אָנֹכִי/אֲנִי	Lexical form (3ms, 'he')	
write				כָּתַבְתִּי	כָּתַב	1
			שָׁמַרְתָּ		שָׁמַר	2
		מָלַכְתְּ			מָלַךְ	3
	אָהַבְנוּ				אָהַב	4
					אָמַר	5
					גָּאַל	6
					עָבַד	7

13.2 *Fill in* the blanks with the missing forms of פָּעַל perfect in the table below. *Read* all the verb forms and *translate* orally. *Write* the meaning of the lexical forms. *Note*:

> ◆ All the attached pronouns in this exercise take the stress. When the stress is moved forward to the attached pronoun, the vowel in the open syllable either one or two steps before the stress is reduced: 'הֵם + כָּתַב + הִיא' results in כָּתַבָה which becomes כָּתְבָה, 'כָּתַב + הֵם' results in כָּתַבוּ which becomes כָּתְבוּ, 'כָּתַב + אַתֶּם' results in כָּתַבְתֶּם which becomes כְּתַבְתֶּם.
> ◆ A guttural takes a chateph instead of the shva: אֲמַרְתֶּם.
> ◆ Several attached pronouns are shortened forms of the independent pronouns:
> – אַתֶּם, אַתֶּן: The תֶּם/תֶּן element is kept in the attached pronoun, e.g., שְׁמַרְתֶּם, שְׁמַרְתֶּן.
> – The ending ה ָ in הִיא, e.g., שָׁמְרָה, should be associated with the feminine ending ה ָ in nouns and adjectives, e.g., טוֹבָה, סוּסָה.

Meaning: Lexical form	אַתֶּן	אַתֶּם	הֵם/הֵנָּה	היא	Lexical form (3ms, 'he')	
				כָּרְתָה	כָּרַת	1
			שָׁמְרוּ		שָׁמַר	2
		מְלַכְתֶּם			מָלַךְ	3
	עֲבַדְתֶּן				עָבַד	4
					אָהֵב	5
					גָּאַל	6
					שָׁמַע	7

13.3 *Fill in* the blanks with the missing data according to the example given in the table below. *Read* and *translate*.

Translation	Verb: Lexical form (3ms, 'he')	Independent personal pronoun	Verb-plus-pronoun	
we wrote	כָּתַב	אֲנַחְנוּ	כָּתַבְנוּ	1
			זָכַרְתִּי	2
			עָבַדְתָּ	3
			שָׁמַעַתְּ	4
			אָהֲבָה	5
			קְרָאתֶם	6
			קְרָאנוּ	7
			אָמְרוּ	8
			שְׁמַעְתֶּם	9
			שָׁמַרְתָּ	10
			נָתְנָה	11
			אָמְרָה	12
			עֲבַדְנוּ	13
			מָלְכוּ	14
			קָרָאתִי	15
			נָתַתָּ	16
			מָשְׁחָה	17
			אֲהַבְתֶּן	18

13.4 *Attach* the correct suffixed pronouns to the verb roots below. *Vocalize, mark* the stress, *read* and *translate*. *Note*:

> - The basic vowel pattern of פָּעַל perfect is ־ ֿ ֿ, e.g., כָּתַב.
> - An /a/-vowel in a stressed closed syllable in finite verb forms is usually *short*, e.g., כָּתַב, which is an exception to the basic rule of vocalization. *All syllables (with simple vowels)* **generally** have a **long** vowel, *except an* **unstressed closed** *syllable which* **always** *has a* **short** *vowel*.
> - Attached suffixed pronouns consisting of a vowel only (called *vocalic suffixes*, that is, הָ and וּ) and the suffixes תֶּן/תֶּם (called *heavy suffixes*) commonly take the stress, which results in a vowel reduction. A vowel in an open syllable either one or two steps before the stress is reduced, e.g., 'כָּתַב + הִיא' results in כָּתְבָה which becomes כָּתְבָה, 'כָּתַב + אַתֶּם' results in כָּתַבְתֶּם which becomes כְּתַבְתֶּם.
> - A guttural takes a chateph (shva-plus-vowel) instead of a shva: אֲהַבְתֶּם.

Translation	Verb-plus-pronoun	
I anointed	מָשַׁחְתִּי	1 אֲנִי (משׁח)
————	————	2 אַתֶּן (אמר)
————	————	3 אַתְּ (קרא)
————	————	4 הוּא (שׁמע)
————	————	5 הִיא (אהב)
————	————	6 הֵם/הֵנָּה (כתב)
————	————	7 אַתֶּם (עבד)
————	————	8 אַתָּה (אמר)
————	————	9 אֲנַחְנוּ (מלך)
————	————	10 הוּא (זכר)
————	————	11 אָנֹכִי (שׁמר)
————	————	12 הֵם/הֵנָּה (קרא)
————	————	13 אַתֶּם (שׁמע)
————	————	14 הִיא (עבד)

13.5 *Translate* the verbal clauses below. Proper names are enlarged. *Note*:

> - The word order of the verbal clause is normally *Verb-Subject-Object* (VSO): אָמַר מֹשֶׁה לָעָם 'Moses said to the people'. Adverbials of time are placed first in the clause: בַּיּוֹם הַהוּא אָמַר מֹשֶׁה לָעָם 'At that day Moses said to the people'.
> - The perfect is negated by לֹא: לֹא כָּתַבְנוּ 'We did *not* write'.
> - Although the perfect may be rendered in English translation by various tenses (e.g., נָתַן may mean 'he gave, has given, had given, had been giving, did give, gives, will give' etc.), for practical reasons, *render* the perfect as simple past (e.g., נָתַן 'he gave'). However, in the Key the verbs are interpreted according to the context in which they appear in the Bible.[4]

1 לָמָּה לֹא־שָׁמַעְתָּ בְּקוֹל יהוה (1 Sam. 15:19)

2 וּמִמִּצְרַיִם קָרָאתִי לִבְנִי: (Hos. 11:1)

3 יהוה אֱלֹהֵינוּ כָּרַת עִמָּנוּ בְּרִית בְּחֹרֵב: (Dt. 5:2)

4 לֹא־שָׁמַע עַמִּי לְקוֹלִי (Ps. 81:12)

5 לֹא שָׁמְרוּ בְּרִית אֱלֹהִים (Ps. 78:10)

6 לֹא שָׁמַעְתָּ בְּקוֹל יהוה אֱלֹהֶיךָ (Dt. 28:45)

7 אָמַרְתִּי לַיהוה אֵלִי אָתָּה (Ps. 140:7)

8 קָרָאתָ לִי (1 Sam. 3:8)

9 אָז שָׁמַע הַמֶּלֶךְ אֲלֵיהֶם: (2 Chron. 24:17)

10 מָלַךְ אֱלֹהִים עַל־גּוֹיִם (Ps. 47:9)

13.6 *Translate* the clauses below into Hebrew. *Remember*:

> - The normal word order of the verbal clause in Biblical Hebrew is '(Adverbial of time) + **Verb–Subject–Object**'.

1 We said to him, "You are our king."
2 The woman heard a voice from heaven.
3 The man obeyed (= listened in the voice of) God.
4 I read a book about a wise man.
5 At that time (= then) the king ruled over many countries.
6 At that day you (*m, s*) called (+ to) me from the city of David (דָּוִד).
7 God made (= cut) a covenant with his people (= nation).
8 Why did the Lord give (+ to) me gold and silver?
9 You (*m, s*) worked in my city.
10 The Israelites (= sons of Israel) worked in Egypt.

---

[4] Various Bible translations may offer different tense interpretations.

SECTION 14

1 *Object marker* **אֶת/אֵת־**: אֵת is usually attached to a following noun by a maqqef, **אֶת־**. The particle **אֶת/אֵת־** has a double function:
   – *Object marker*: Before a definite direct object אֵת serves as an *object marker*, e.g., קָרָאתָ אֶת־הַסֵּפֶר 'You read *the book*' (**אֶת־** is not rendered in translation). The object marker אֵת before an attached pronoun takes the form **אֹת/אוֹת־**, for instance, 'אֵת + אֲנִי' results in אֹתִי/אוֹתִי (me).
   – *Preposition*: אֵת also serves as the preposition 'with'. The preposition אֵת (**אֶת־**) before an attached pronoun takes the form **אִת־**, for instance, 'אֵת + אֲנִי' results in אִתִּי 'with me' (Section 11).

2 *Direction marker* ה ָ : The unstressed ending ה ָ attached to nouns, place names and certain adverbs usually indicates *motion towards* (a place): 'הַבַּיִת (the house) + ה ָ ' results in הַבַּיְתָה 'to/towards the house', 'מִצְרַיִם (Egypt) + ה ָ ' results in מִצְרַיְמָה 'to/towards Egypt', 'שָׁם (there) + ה ָ ' results in שָׁמָּה 'thither' (though sometimes 'there').

3 *Verbal clause with variant word order* (the usual word order is considered to be **Verb–Subject–Object**): An element in the clause can be emphasized by placing it in initial position: אֶת־קוֹלְךָ שָׁמַעְתִּי. '*It was your voice* that I heard', lit., '*Your voice* I heard'. Compare שָׁמַעְתִּי אֶת־קוֹלְךָ. 'I heard your voice'.
   – *The construction* 'ו + *noun/pronoun* + *verb in the perfect*': A verbal clause beginning with *a noun/pronoun* and followed by a *verb in the perfect* is quite often preceded by ו in the Hebrew Bible. ו in this position separates the information given in the preceding clause/s from the following information, thus marking a *break in the story-telling*. This construction can be used for various reasons, e.g., to introduce a *new segment in the story*, to highlight a *contrast* or to supply *additional information* related to the main line of the story. In this position ו may be rendered in English translation by 'and, but, now, whereas, because, although' etc., as the context requires, e.g., וְהָאִישׁ יָדַע אֶת־הַדָּבָר '*Now/but/and/whereas/because/ for* (etc.) the man knew the matter'.

4 *Verbal clause with an additional personal pronoun*: An independent personal pronoun may precede the verb in a verbal clause in spite of the fact that a pronoun is already included in the verb form. This additional personal pronoun usually *emphasizes the subject* of the clause: אֲנִי שָׁמַעְתִּי אֶת־קוֹלְךָ '*I myself/It was I who* heard your voice', lit., 'I – I heard your voice'. Compare שָׁמַעְתִּי אֶת־קוֹלְךָ 'I heard your voice'.

5 *Particles-as-intensifiers*: Certain particles are used to intensify a following word, phrase or entire clause. A particle-as-intensifier can be rendered in English by various intensifying adverbs and adverbial constructions, e.g., אָמְנָם/הִנֵּה שָׁמַעְתִּי 'I have *surely/truly/indeed/no doubt* (and the like) heard'.

6 *Denoting immediate presence by* הִנֵּה (and rarely הֵן): Apart from being a particle-as-intensifier (see 5 above) הִנֵּה is frequently used to express the *immediate presence* of someone/something. הִנֵּה is often rendered in English by '*behold/look/here/now…*'. הִנֵּה can take attached pronouns, e.g., 'אַתָּה + הִנֵּה' results in הִנְּךָ '*Behold/look/here* you [are]…'.

MEMORIZE

VOWEL LOWERING – PHILIPPI'S LAW

An original **I/E-vowel** in a **stressed**, originally **closed** syllable is lowered to an **A-vowel**, e.g., זִקַנְתִּי becomes זָקַנְתִּי. The vowel diagram below represents the position of the tongue in the mouth when vowels are pronounced.

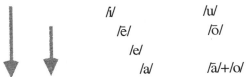

/i/	/u/
/ē/	/ō/
/e/	
/a/	/ā/+/o/

GRAMMATICAL CORNERSTONE 11   ר א שׁ פּ ה ב ב

☆ פָּעַל (QAL) PERFECT VIA HEBREW NAMES I (9)

	Verb form	Vowel pattern	Hebrew name	English pronunciation	Meaning: Lexical form
Perfect	Perf-/a/ (שָׁמַר)	– – ַ	נָתַן[1]	Nathan	give
	Perf-/e/ (זָקֵן)	– – ֵ	שָׁלֵם	Jeru**salem**	be/become whole, complete

REVIEW AND APPLICATION OF THE RULES

I *Match* each root type with the verb form that illustrates it. *Pronounce* the names of the Hebrew letters indicating the root types. *Note*:

- All the following verb forms are in the 3rd person masculine singular (הוּא). The 3ms of פָּעַל perfect is the form under which the verb is listed in the lexicon, e.g., שָׁמַר corresponds to English '(to) guard'.
- A verb root may be related to more than one root type.

---

[1] Note that when a verb form is used as a proper name, the short /a/-vowel in a stressed closed syllable (e.g., the verb form נָתַן) should be rendered by /ā/ (e.g., the name נָתָן). However, for pedagogical reasons, the names are vocalized as if they were verb forms, i.e., with a short instead of a long /a/-vowel.

1 שְׁלֵמִים 'complete', unchangeable (_) בָּחַר   7 פ״י, I-י   (_) עָמַד

2 ע״ג, II-guttural   (_) עָשָׂה   8 פ״נ, I-נ   (_) יָשַׁב

3 פ״י, I-י + ל״א, III-א   (_) אָבַד   9 ל״א, III-א   (_) גָּלָה

4 פ״ג, I-guttural + ל״ה, III-ה   (_) נָפַל   10 פ״ג, I-guttural   (_) יָדַע

5 פ״י, I-י and ל״ג + III-guttural (_) יָרֵא   11 פ״א, I-א   (_) שָׁלַח

6 ל״ה, III-ה   (_) מָלֵא   12 ל״ג, III-guttural   (_) זָכַר

II *Study* the sound change rules listed below. *Indicate* the relevant sound change/s occurring in each deviant verb form (on the left side) by comparing it with the corresponding normal form (on the right side). *Indicate* to which root type each deviant verb form belongs. *Note*:

> ◆ The consonants א and ה may function either as *gutturals* (affecting the normal vowel patterns of words) or as *changeable consonants* (being omitted or altered).
>
> – ה/א as the *third* root consonant in a word root is changeable, thus classified as III-א and III-ה (= III-י/ו, see Section 15:3) respectively.
>
> – ה/א as the *second* root consonant in a word root functions as a *guttural*, thus classified as II-guttural.
>
> – א as the *first* root consonant in a word root may function *either* as a *guttural* (affecting the vowels), thus classified as I-guttural, *or* as a *changeable consonant* (being silenced), thus classified as I-א. ה as the *first* root consonant in a word root always functions as a *guttural*, thus classified as I-guttural.

SOUND CHANGE RULES

1 Two identical letters without an intervening vowel are rendered by one letter with a doubling dagesh: כָּרַתְּתִי is written כָּרַתִּי. *It is actually a rule of spelling rather than a sound change rule.*

2 A guttural takes a chateph (shva-plus-vowel) instead of a shva.

3 A guttural attracts an /a/-vowel/s.

4 A vowelless א at the end of a syllable is silenced. That is, א disappears in pronunciation but is retained in writing. The silencing of א is compensated by the lengthening of the preceding vowel (if it is not already long).

5 The hard sound of a BeGaDKeFaT-consonant becomes soft after a vowel (shown in writing by the absence of the hardening dagesh).

_____ עֲזַרְתֶּם – שְׁמַרְתֶּם 5   _____ מָלֵא – זָקֵן 1

_____ שָׁלַחַתְּ – שָׁמַרְתְּ 6   _____ עֲמַדְתֶּן – שְׁמַרְתֶּן 2

_____ בָּחֲרוּ – שָׁמְרוּ 7   _____ כָּרַתָּ – שָׁמַרְתָּ 3

_____ יָצָאתִי – שָׁמַרְתִּי 8   _____ בָּחֲרָה – שָׁמְרָה 4

III *Match* each sound element with the Hebrew word that illustrates it. *Mark* the element in the Hebrew word clearly! Observe that the same sound element may appear in more than one word, but only one element is to be marked. Each word is to be used once!

1 Vowel reduction **I** *A vowel* (_) קָרָא
 one step before the stress is reduced

2 Vowel reduction **II** *A vowel* (_) כָּתַב
 two steps before the stress is reduced

3 Vowel reduction **I** *A vowel* (_) נָתַתִּי
 under a gutteral **one** step
 before the stress is reduced

4 Vowel reduction **II** *A vowel* (_) שָׁמְרָה
 under a gutteral **two** steps before
 the stress is reduced

5 Vowel lengthening (_) בָּחֲרוּ
 Before a silent א

6 Exception to the (_) שָׁמַרְתְּ
 basic rule of vocalization

7 Abnormal two- (_) כְּתַבְתֶּם
 consonant sequence
 at the end of a word

8 Doubling dagesh (_) עֲבַדְתֶּם
 נ *is assimilated to the*
 next consonant

WORD LIST

Nouns

יוֹנָה   *f*, dove: *pl* יוֹנִים (☆ Jonah)

יִרְאָה, ירא *f*, fear

כָּבוֹד, כבד *m*, glory, honour

לַיְלָה   *m*, night: *pl* לֵילוֹת

מִשְׁכָּן, שכן *m*, dwelling-place; tabernacle:
 pl מִשְׁכָּנוֹת

עִבְרִי, עבר *m*, a Hebrew (also Hebrew, adj):
 f עִבְרִיָּה, *pl* עִבְרִים (☆ Eber, ʕ.b.r)

Verbs

אָכַל   eat

בָּחַר   choose (followed by בְּ)

הָלַךְ   go, walk

יָדַע   know

יָצָא   come/go out, come/go forth

יָרֵא   fear, be afraid

יָשַׁב   sit; dwell, reside

לָקַח   take

מָלֵא   be full/filled (with)

מָצָא   find

עָמַד   stand

שָׁלַח   send; *with* יָד stretch out one's hand

Particles[2]

אַךְ   only; surely (intensifier)

אָכֵן   truly, indeed (intensifier)

אִם   if; surely (intensifier)

אָמְנָם, אמן   surely (intensifier)
 (☆ Amen, ʔ.m.n)

אָן/אָנָה   where? where to?

אֶת/אֶת־ marker of a direct
 definite object; with

גַּם   also, too, even;
 moreover (intensifier)

הֵן/הִנֵּה indeed (intensifier);
 behold! look! here!
 with suff הִנְנִי/הִנֵּנִי

כֹּה   so, thus: כֹּה אָמַר יהוה
 'Thus says/said the Lord'
 (prophetic formula)

כִּי   undoubtedly (intensifier)

כֵּן   so, thus; rightly

רַק   only, except; surely
 (intensifier)

שָׁם   there

---

[2] Particles-as-intensifiers can be rendered in English translation by various intensifying adverbs and adverbial constructions. The suggested translation above can be substituted by other intensifying adverbs/adverbial constructions.

EXERCISES

14.1 *Fill in* the table below with the missing forms of פָּעַל perfect. *Read* all the verb forms and *translate* orally. For practical reasons, render the perfect as simple past. *Write* the meaning of the lexical forms. *Note*:

> ♦ None of the attached (suffixed) pronouns in this exercise is stressed. Since there is no shift in stress, no vowel changes occur.

Meaning: Lexical form	אֲנַחְנוּ	אַתְּ	אַתָּה	אָנֹכִי/אֲנִי	Lexical form הוּא	
remember	זָכַרְנוּ	זָכַרְתְּ	זָכַרְתָּ	זָכַרְתִּי	זָכַר	1
				כָּרַתִּי	כָּרַת	2
					אָכַל	3
					יָדַע	4
					הָלַךְ	5
					יָרֵא	6
					יָצָא	7
					יָשַׁב	8
					בָּחַר	9
					מָשַׁח	10
	נָתַנּוּ			נָתַתִּי	נָתַן	11
	קָטֹנּוּ				קָטֹן	12
					קָרָא	13
					שָׁמַע	14
					לָקַח	15
					שָׁלַח	16
					מָצָא	17

14.2 *Fill in* the table below with the missing forms of פָּעַל perfect. *Read* all the verb forms and *translate* orally. For practical reasons, render the perfect as simple past. *Write* the meaning of the lexical forms. *Note*:

> ● All the attached pronouns in this exercise take the stress. When the stress is moved forward to the attached pronoun, the vowel in the open syllable either one or two steps before the stress is reduced: 'הֵם + כָּתַב' results in כָּתְבָה which becomes כָּתְבָה, 'הִיא + כָּתַב' results in כָּתְבוּ which becomes כָּתְבוּ, 'אַתֶּם + כָּתַב' results in כָּתַבְתֶּם which becomes כְּתַבְתֶּם.
> ● A guttural takes a chateph instead of the shva: אֲמַרְתֶּם

Meaning: Lexical form	אַתֶּן	אַתֶּם	הֵם/הֵנָּה	הִיא	הוּא	
remember	זְכַרְתֶּן	זְכַרְתֶּם	זָכְרוּ	זָכְרָה	זָכַר	1
					עָמַד	2
					אָכַל	3
					בָּחַר	4
					שָׁלַח	5
					יָדַע	6
					מָצָא	7
					מָלֵא	8
					שָׁמַע	9
					לָקַח	10
					נָתַן	11
					קָטֹן	12
					אָהֵב	13
					קָרָא	14

14.3 *Read* and *fill in* the blanks with the missing data according to the example given in the table below. For practical reasons, render the perfect as simple past.

Translation: Verb-plus-pronoun	Root type	Lexical form (3ms, 'he')	Independent personal pronoun	Verb-plus-pronoun	
I was full/filled (with)	א״ל/III-א	מָלֵא	אֲנִי/אָנֹכִי	מָלֵאתִי	1
				אֲכַלְתֶּם	2
				זָכַרְתָּ	3
				כָּרַתְנוּ	4
				לָקַחַתְּ	5
				יָשְׁבָה	6
				בָּחֲרוּ	7
				יָדַע	8
				יְצָאתֶן	9
				אֲכָלְנוּ	10
				הָלְכָה	11
				בָּחַרְתְּ	12
				שְׁלַחְתֶּם	13
				מָצְאוּ	14
				מָלֵאתָ	15
				עָמַדְתִּי	16
				יָרֵא	17
				יְדַעְתֶּן	18

14.4 *Attach* the correct suffixed pronouns to the verb roots below. *Vocalize,* *mark* the stress, *read* and *translate. Remember*:

- The basic vowel patterns of פָּעַל perfect are ‐ ‐ ָ (often verbs expressing an action) and ‐ ‐ ָ / ‐ ֵ ָ (often verbs expressing a state of being).
- Suffixed pronouns consisting of a vowel only (הָ and וֹ) and the suffixes תֶּם/תֶּן commonly take the stress, which results in a vowel reduction. The vowel in an open syllable either one or two steps before the stress is reduced, e.g., 'כָּתַב + הֶם' results in כָּתַבוּ which becomes כָּתְבוּ, 'כָּתַב + אַתֶּם' results in כָּתַבְתֶּם which becomes כְּתַבְתֶּם.
- A guttural takes a chateph (shva-plus-vowel) instead of a shva: בָּחֲרוּ.
- א at the end of a syllable is silenced. The silencing of א is compensated by the lengthening of the preceding vowel (if it is not already long): קָרָא

Translation	Verb-plus-pronoun	
_____	_____	1 אֲנִי (ידע)
_____	_____	2 אַתָּה (כרת)
_____	_____	3 אַתְּ (יצא)
_____	_____	4 הוּא (ישב)
_____	_____	5 הִיא (בחר)
_____	_____	6 אֲנַחְנוּ (זכר)
_____	_____	7 אַתֶּם (שלח)
_____	_____	8 אַתֶּן (אכל)
_____	_____	9 הֵם/הֵנָּה (הלך)
_____	_____	10 אַתָּה (מלא)
_____	_____	11 אֲנַחְנוּ (נתן)
_____	_____	12 הוּא (עמד)
_____	_____	13 אָנֹכִי (ירא)
_____	_____	14 אַתְּ (אכל)
_____	_____	15 אַתֶּם (אמר)
_____	_____	16 הִיא (לקח)
_____	_____	17 הֵם/הֵנָּה (אהב)
_____	_____	18 אַתֶּן (מצא)

14.5 Each verse segment below includes a *verb form in* פָּעַל *perfect. Cover* the English translation, *read* and *translate* as much as you can on your own. Then *fill in* the blanks with the missing pronouns in the following translation and *check/complete* your translation against it. *Pay attention* to the meaning of the perfect and to variant word order. *Note*:

> ◆ You were previously requested to render the perfect as simple past. However, certain verbs in the perfect may also correspond to other English tenses.
> – In the translation given in this book the perfect (and the other verb forms) are interpreted according to the context in which they appear in the Bible. However, be aware of the fact that the various Bible translations may offer different tense interpretations.
> ◆ The meaning of the perfect:
> – The perfect expresses *completed actions,* which normally denote *past*, e.g., שָׁמַר corresponds to English 'he guarded' or 'he has/had guarded'.
> – The perfect may correspond to *English present* in verbs expressing a state of being, e.g., זָקַנְתִּי 'I *am* old', as well as in verbs expressing an attitude, experience or perception such as 'know, love, understand, remember', e.g., יָדַעְתִּי 'I *know*'.
> – The perfect may correspond to *English future* when something (such as a *promise* or a *prophecy*) is considered by the speaker to be *certain*.
> ◆ Word order: The usual word order of the verbal clause is **Verb–Subject–Object**. Variant word order and an additional independent personal pronoun often signal emphasis, which is rendered in English translation by corresponding emphatic constructions.

1 הֲלֹא יְדַעְתֶּם מָה־אֵלֶּה Do _____ not know _____ _____ [things are]! (Ezek. 17:12)

2 אָבִיו וְאִמּוֹ לֹא יָדְעוּ _____ [own] father and _____ [own] mother did not know (Judg. 14:4)

3 עָמַדְתָּ לִפְנֵי יהוה אֱלֹהֶיךָ _____ stood before the Lord, _____ God (Dt. 4:10)

4 נָתַתִּי בְיָדְךָ אֶת־סִיחֹן מֶלֶךְ־חֶשְׁבּוֹן הָאֱמֹרִי וְאֶת־אַרְצוֹ _____ have given _____ (= into _____ hand) Sihon, the king of Heshbon, the Amorite, and _____ land (Dt. 2:24)

5 עֵשָׂו לָקַח אֶת־נָשָׁיו מִבְּנוֹת כְּנָעַן Esau took _____ wives from the daughters of Canaan (Gen. 36:2)

6 כַּסְפִּי וּזְהָבִי לְקַחְתֶּם ＿＿＿ have taken ＿＿＿ [own] silver and ＿＿＿ [own] gold (Joel 4:5)

7 שְׁנֵיהֶם עָמְדוּ עַל־הַיַּרְדֵּן: The two of ＿＿＿ stood by (= עַל) the Jordan (2 Kings 2:7)

8 לֹא יָדַעְתִּי אִי מִזֶּה הֵמָּה: ＿＿＿ do not know from where actually (= זֶה) ＿＿＿ [are] (1 Sam. 25:11)

9 הִנֵּה אַתָּה זָקַנְתָּ וּבָנֶיךָ לֹא הָלְכוּ בִּדְרָכֶיךָ See, ＿＿＿ are old and ＿＿＿ sons – ＿＿＿ have not walked in ＿＿＿ ways (1 Sam. 8:5)

10 לֹא שְׁמַעְתֶּם בְּקֹלוֹ: ＿＿＿ did not obey ＿＿＿ (= listened in ＿＿＿ voice) (Dt. 9:23)

11 זָכַר לְעוֹלָם בְּרִיתוֹ ＿＿＿ remembers ＿＿＿ covenant forever (Ps. 105:8)

12 אֲנִי זָקַנְתִּי ＿＿＿ am old (1 Sam. 12:2)

13 מָצָאתִי דָוִד עַבְדִּי ＿＿＿ have found David, ＿＿＿ servant (Ps. 89:21)

14 מָה־אָמַר לָכֶם שְׁמוּאֵל: ＿＿＿ did Samuel say to ＿＿＿? (1 Sam. 10:15)

14.6 Each verb segment below includes a *verb form in* פָּעַל *perfect. Match* each Hebrew clause with the correct English translation. *Remember:*

> ◆ Variant word order and an additional personal pronoun quite often signal emphasis.

I 1 לֹא שָׁמְעוּ בְּקוֹלִי: ( ) [The] way of peace they did not know (Isa. 59:8)

2 וְלֹא־שָׁמַע הַמֶּלֶךְ אֶל־הָעָם ( ) indeed (= כִּי), I have not dwelt in [a] house (2 Sam. 7:6)

3 הִנֵּה נָתַתִּי לְךָ לֵב חָכָם ( ) Thus said/says the LORD, the God of Israel (1 Sam. 10:18)

4 וְלֹא הָלַךְ בְּדֶרֶךְ יהוה: ( ) He had not eaten food (= bread) the whole day and the whole night (1 Sam. 28:20)

5 דֶּרֶךְ שָׁלוֹם לֹא יָדְעוּ ( ) And the king did not listen to the people (1 Kings 12:15)

6 נָתַתִּי רוּחִי עָלָיו ( ) Look, I shall certainly give (= נָתַתִּי) you [a] wise heart (1 Kings 3:12)

7 אָן הֲלַכְתֶּם ( ) And he did not walk in the way of the LORD (2 Kings 21:22)

8 כֹּה־אָמַר יהוה אֱלֹהֵי יִשְׂרָאֵל ( ) They did not obey me (= listened in my voice) (Num. 14:22)

9 לֹא אָכַל לֶחֶם כָּל־הַיּוֹם וְכָל־הַלָּיְלָה: ( ) Where did you go? (1 Sam. 10:14)

10 כִּי לֹא יָשַׁבְתִּי בְּבַיִת ( ) I have put my spirit upon him (Isa. 42:1)

II

1　יְהוָה נָתַן וַיהוָה לָקָח 　( ) From the Lᴏʀᴅ this (= הַ) matter came out (Gen. 24:50)

2　וְאָנֹכִי עָמַדְתִּי בָהָר 　( ) Israel did not take the land of Moab (Judg. 11:15)

3　לֶחֶם לֹא אָכַלְתִּי 　( ) The Lᴏʀᴅ has given and the Lᴏʀᴅ has taken [away] (Job 1:21)

4　מֵיהוָה יָצָא הַדָּבָר 　( ) I have become/I am old, I do not know (= יָדַעְתִּי) the day of my death (Gen. 27:2)

5　זָקַנְתִּי לֹא יָדַעְתִּי יוֹם מוֹתִי: 　( ) The Lᴏʀᴅ has put over you [a] king (1 Sam. 12:13)

6　וְגַם־שָׁאוּל הָלַךְ לְבֵיתוֹ 　( ) The glory of the Lᴏʀᴅ filled the tabernacle (Ex. 40:34)

7　כְּבוֹד יהוה מָלֵא אֶת־הַמִּשְׁכָּן: 　( ) Why did you not guard your lord (= lords, pl of majesty), the king? (1 Sam. 26:15)

8　לֹא־לָקַח יִשְׂרָאֵל אֶת־אֶרֶץ מוֹאָב 　( ) And I – I stood on (= בְּ) the mountain (Dt. 10:10)

9　לָמָּה לֹא שְׁמַרְתָּ אֶל־אֲדֹנֶיךָ הַמֶּלֶךְ 　( ) And Saul – he also went to his home (1 Sam. 10:26)

10　נָתַן יהוה עֲלֵיכֶם מֶלֶךְ: 　( ) Bread I did not eat (Dt. 9:9)

14.7　Each verse segment below includes *the particle* אֵת (אֶת־). *Read and translate. Pay attention* to the usage of אֵת. Proper names are enlarged. *Remember:*

◆ אֵת (אֶת־) before a definite direct object is not rendered in translation into English. The object marker אֵת (אֶת־) before an attached pronoun usually takes the form אֵת/אוֹת−, e.g., אֹתִי/אוֹתִי 'me', but before the 2ⁿᵈ person plural (you) it takes the form אֶת−, e.g., אֶתְכֶם 'you'.

– An object is definite when it is either preceded by the definite article or followed by a possessive pronoun. Proper names are considered definite in Hebrew.

◆ The preposition אֵת (אֶת־) 'with' before an attached pronoun takes the form אִתּ−, e.g., אִתִּי 'with me'.

1　לֹא שָׁמַרְתָּ אֶת־מִצְוַת יהוה אֱלֹהֶיךָ (1 Sam.13:13)

2　לֹא־שָׁמְרוּ אֲבוֹתֵינוּ אֶת־דְּבַר יהוה (2 Chron. 34:21)

3　וְאָבִיו שָׁמַר אֶת־הַדָּבָר: (Gen. 37:11)

4 וְאֶת־קֹלוֹ שָׁמַ֫עְנוּ (Dt. 5:24)

5 נָתַן יהוה לָכֶם אֶת־הָאָ֫רֶץ (Jos. 2:9)

6 נָתְנוּ לוֹ אֶת־הָעִיר (Jos. 19:50)

7 אֹתוֹ אָהַב אֲבִיהֶם מִכָּל־אֶחָיו (Gen. 37:4)

8 אָהַ֫בְתִּי אֶתְכֶם (Mal. 1:2)

9 אֲדֹנִי לֹא־יָדַע אִתִּי מַה־בַּבָּ֫יִת (Gen. 39:8)

10 וְשָׁם אִתָּ֫נוּ נַ֫עַר עִבְרִי (Gen. 41:12)

11 חֲכָמִים אֲנַ֫חְנוּ וְתוֹרַת יהוה אִתָּ֫נוּ (Jer. 8:8)

12 אֹתוֹ מָשְׁחוּ לְמֶ֫לֶךְ תַּ֫חַת אָבִ֫יהוּ (1 Kings 5:15)

13 וְאֶת־בִּנְיָמִין אֲחִי יוֹסֵף לֹא־שָׁלַח יַעֲקֹב אֶת־אֶחָיו (Gen. 42:4)

14 בַּיּוֹם הַהוּא כָּרַת יהוה אֶת־אַבְרָם בְּרִית (Gen. 15:18)

15 אֲמַרְתֶּם כָּרַ֫תְנוּ בְרִית אֶת־מָ֫וֶת (Isa. 28:15)

16 לֹא אֶת־אֲבֹתֵ֫ינוּ כָּרַת יהוה אֶת־הַבְּרִית הַזֹּאת (Dt. 5:3)

17 וְאֶת־כָּל־אֶחָיו נָתַ֫תִּי לוֹ לַעֲבָדִים (Gen. 27:37)

18 אֶת־קֹלְךָ שָׁמַ֫עְתִּי (Gen. 3:10)

19 לֹא־שָׁלַ֫חְתִּי אֶת־הַנְּבִאִים (Jer. 23:21)

20 מָצָא חִלְקִיָּ֫הוּ הַכֹּהֵן אֶת־סֵ֫פֶר תּוֹרַת־יהוה (2 Chron. 34:14)

21 וַיהוה אִתָּ֫נוּ (Num. 14:9)

14.8 Each verse segment below includes at least one *particle-as-intensifier* (enlarged in the Hebrew text and italicized in the translation). *Cover* the English translation, *read* and *translate* as much as you can on your own. Then *fill in* the blanks with the missing pronouns in the following translation and *check/complete* your translation against it. *Remember*:

> - Particles-as-intensifiers may be rendered in English translation by various intensifying adverbs and adverbial constructions, such as '*surely, truly, undoubtedly, indeed, really, no doubt*' and the like.
> - The particle-as-intensifier הִנֵּה is also used to denote the immediate presence of something/someone. Thus הִנֵּה is often rendered by 'behold/look/here'. הִנֵּה takes attached pronouns.
> - A question may be intensified by זֶה/זֹאת.

1   הִנְּךָ יָפֶה   Look, _____ [are] handsome (Song 1:16)

2   הִנָּךְ יָפָה עֵינַיִךְ יוֹנִים: Behold, _____ [are] beautiful, _____ eyes [are] doves (Song 1:15)

3   הִנֵּה אַתָּה זָקַנְתָּ   Look, _____ are/have grown old (1 Sam. 8:5)

4   גַּם הִנֵּה עַבְדְּךָ יַעֲקֹב אַחֲרֵינוּ   Moreover, look, _____ servant Jacob [is] behind ____ (Gen. 32:21)

5   אָכֵן יֵשׁ יהוה בַּמָּקוֹם הַזֶּה   Surely, the LORD is (= יֵשׁ) in _____ place (Gen. 28:16)

6   אָכֵן שָׁמַעְתָּ   Surely, _____ have heard (Ps. 31:23)

7   רַק אֵין־יִרְאַת אֱלֹהִים בַּמָּקוֹם הַזֶּה   Certainly, [there is] no fear of God in _____ place (Gen. 20:11)

8   אַךְ מֶלֶךְ־יִשְׂרָאֵל הוּא   Undoubtedly, _____ [is] the king of Israel (1 Kings 22:32)

9   אָמְנָם כִּי אַתֶּם־עָם   Absolutely doubtless (כִּי + אָמְנָם), _____ [are the] people (Job 12:2)

10   הַאַתָּה זֶה אֲדֹנִי אֵלִיָּהוּ:   [Is] this _____ , _____ lord, Elijah? (1 Kings 18:7)

11   הַאַתָּה זֶה בְּנִי עֵשָׂו אִם־לֹא: [Is] it (= זֶה) _____ , _____ son Esau or (= אִם) not? (Gen. 27:21)

12   מִי זֶה מֶלֶךְ הַכָּבוֹד   _____ [is] this the king of glory? (Ps. 24:8)

13   הַאַתָּה זֶה עֲשָׂהאֵל   [Is] that _____ , Asahel? (2 Sam. 2:20)

14   הִנֵּה שָׁמַעְתִּי בְקֹלְכֶם   Behold, _____ have listened to _____ (= in _____ voice) (1 Sam. 12:1)

14.9 *Translate* into Hebrew. *Repeat* carefully the word list of this section before you start to translate. *Remember*:

> ◆ The *unstressed* ending הָ   attached to nouns, place names and certain adverbs usually indicates *motion towards* (a place):
> 'הַבַּיִת (the house) + הָ   ' results in הַבַּיְתָה '*to/towards* the house'.
> ◆ The particle אֵת (אֶת־) should be inserted before a *definite direct object*. An object is definite when it is either preceded by the definite article or followed by a possessive pronoun. Proper names are considered definite in Hebrew.
> ◆ The normal word order of the verbal clause is **Verb–Subject–Object**.
> ◆ The construction 'וְ + noun/pronoun + verb in the perfect' may be used to highlight a contrast or to supply *additional information* related to the main line of the story. In this position וְ may be rendered in English by 'but, whereas, while, when, because, although' etc. (instead of 'and').

1 The man ate his bread at night (= the night), whereas (= וְ) his wife ate her bread in the morning.
2 The people (= nation) in the land of Egypt (מִצְרַיִם) ate bread, but (= וְ) the Hebrews in the land of Canaan (כְּנַעַן) did not eat [any] bread.
3 The woman went toward the house.
4 You (*m, s*) took the bread and ate it.
5 You (*m, p*) stood on the mountain and streched out (= שָׁלַח) your hands toward the sky.
6 You are (*f, s*) in the palace with them (*m*).
7 A Hebrew woman went out of (= from) the house to (= אֶל־) her husband in the field.
8 God has chosen him (בְּ + suffixed pronoun) to [be a] prophet there.
9 The tabernacle was filled with (= בְּ) the glory of the LORD. We fear (observe, verb in the perfect!) the LORD.
10 Thus says (= said) the LORD, 'I have sent you (*m, p*) to Egypt to (= אֶל־) your brother'.
11 Where (= where to) did my people (= nation) go on (= בְּ) that day?
12 Look, I have found a wife for you (= [1]for you [2]wife).

SECTION 15

Root type	Perfect: 3ms	Perfect: 2ms
1 *II-י/ו Hollow verbs* (קוּם)	קָם stand up	קַמְתָּ
2 *Twin-consonant verbs* (סבב), *transitive*	סָבַב go around	סַבּוֹתָ
(קלל), *intransitive*	קַל be/become light	קַלּוֹתָ
3 *III-י/ו* (בנה, *III-*ה)	בָּנָה build	בָּנִיתָ

1 **פָּעַל** *perfect of II-י/ו verbs* (ע״ו, called *Hollow verbs*)
 – *Lexical form*: The lexical form of a II-י/ו verb is not the 3ms (הוּא) of פָּעַל perfect but *the infinitive*, for instance, קוּם 'stand up', שִׂים 'put'.
 – *Inflection*: The consonant י/ו in verbs such as קוּם and שִׂים forms a triphthong (י/ו with vowels on either side). The י/ו in the triphthong is ordinarily omitted. Since the middle root consonant י/ו is omitted, only the first and third root consonants of a II-י/ו verb are apparent in writing, e.g., קָם (from the hypothetical form קָוַם *qāwam).[1]

2 **פָּעַל** *perfect of twin-consonant verbs* (ע״ע, called *geminate verbs*)
 – *Lexical form*: The lexical form is not the 3ms of פָּעַל perfect but *the three root letters without any vowels*, e.g., קלל 'be/become light'.
 – *Inflection of the 3rd person* (he, she, they): Transitive twin-consonant verbs (that is, verbs that can take a direct object) are often inflected like שְׁלֵמִים (unchangeable verbs), e.g., סָבַב 'go around' (compare שָׁמַר), סָבְבָה, סָבְבוּ. *Intransitive* twin-consonant verbs (verbs that cannot take a direct object) undergo simplification of the doubled consonant when it occurs at the end of a word without a following vowel, e.g., קַלְל *qall beomes קַל qal. However, when the doubled consonant is followed by a vowel, the doubling remains intact: קַלְּה, קַלּוּ.
 – *Inflection of the 1st and 2nd persons* (I, we; you): In the 1st and 2nd persons both verbs such as סָבַב and קלל take the *linking vowel /ô/* before the attached pronoun, e.g., *qalltî becomes קַלּוֹתִי and *sabbtî סַבּוֹתִי.

3 **פָּעַל** *perfect of III-י/ו verbs* (ל״י/ו, called ל״ה/III-ה): The original third root consonant of most of the so-called III-ה verbs is actually not ה but י/ו.[2]
 – *Inflection of the 3rd person* (he, they): The 3ms (הוּא) and the 3cp (הֵם/הֵנָּה) originally ended in a triphthong (י/ו with vowels on either side). The י/ו in the triphthong is ordinarily omitted. Since the third root consonant י/ו is omitted, only the first and second root consonants of a III-י/ו verb are apparent in writing, e.g., בָּנָה 'he built' (the ה is a vowel letter).[3]
 – The 3fs (הִיא) of III-י/ו verbs takes a double gender marker, both ת (which is the original feminine ending) and ה ָ: בָּנְתָה

---
[1] Some grammarians consider forms like קָם and שָׂם as original two-consonant forms rather than original three-consonant forms with י/ו as the middle root consonant.
[2] There are, however, a few original III-ה verbs. None of these verbs occur in this book.
[3] The 3ms originally ends in a short /a/-vowel, e.g.,*ban⟨aya⟩ which becomes בָּנָה bānāʰ.

– *Inflection of the 1ˢᵗ and 2ⁿᵈ persons* (I, we; you): The consonant **י/ו** before an attached pronoun beginning with a consonant forms a diphthong. The consonant **י/ו** in a diphthong ordinarily becomes a vowel letter, e.g., **בָּנִיתִי** (from the hypothetical form **בָּנַיְתִי** *banaytî*).

4 *Relative clauses*: A relative clause in Hebrew is usually introduced by the particle **אֲשֶׁר** that corresponds to English relative pronouns such as '*who, whom, which, whose, that; the one who/whom…*' or '*what, where*', depending on the context. There are *two types* of relative clauses:

– Relative clauses which *describe a noun* in a clause (called *attributive relative clauses*): **הַמֶּלֶךְ אֲשֶׁר בְּחַרְתֶּם חָכָם** 'The king *whom you have chosen* is wise'.

– Relative clauses which *replace a noun* in a clause, e.g.,

אֲשֶׁר בְּחַרְתֶּם חָכָם '[The one] *whom you have chosen* is wise'.

– *"Redundant" attached pronoun*: A relative clause often contains an attached pronoun that refers back to the described/replaced noun. This pronoun is not rendered in English translation: **הַמֶּלֶךְ אֲשֶׁר בְּחַרְתֶּם בּוֹ חָכָם** 'The king *whom you have chosen* is wise', lit., 'The king **אֲשֶׁר** *you have chosen him* [is] wise'.

5 *Usage of the verb* **הָיָה** '*be*': The verbless clause has normally no time reference of its own. The verb **הָיָה** may, however, be used to specify the time of the verbless clause. **הָיָה** may correspond to English '*was, had, happened, became, came*' (see Exercise 15.7).

☆ **פָּעַל** PERFECT VIA HEBREW NAMES II (10)

	Verb form	Vowel pattern	Hebrew name	English pronunciation	Root type	Meaning: Lexical form
Perfect	Perf-/a/ (**שָׁמַר**)	– – ָ	**נָתַן**	Nathan	I-**נ** (irregular)	give
	Perf-/e/ (**זָקֵן**)	– – ֵ ָ	**שָׁלֵם**	Jerusalem	**שְׁלֵמִים** unchangeable	be/become whole, complete
	Perf-/a/ (**קָם**)	– ָ	**דָּן**	Dan	II- **י/ו** **עו״י** Hollow	judge

REVIEW AND APPLICATION OF THE RULES

I *Match* each root type with the verb form that illustrates it. *Pronounce* the names of the Hebrew letters indicating the root types. *Remember*:

- The lexical form of a Hollow verb (II-**י/ו**, **עו״י**) is the infinitive (of **פָּעַל**), e.g., **קוּם** 'stand up', and the lexical form of a twin-consonant verb is the three root letters without any vowels, e.g., **קלל** 'be/become light'.
- A verb root may be related to more than one root type.

1 ע״ע, Twin-consonant verb (_) בָּרָא		6 ו/י-III, (ל״ה) לו״י (_) פלל
2 ע״י, Hollow verb, II-י (_) עָבַר		7 ג״פ, I-guttural (_) שׁוּב
3 ע״ו, Hollow verb, II-ו (_) עָלָה		8 ל״א, III-א (_) בָּנָה
4 ע״ו, II-ו + ל״א, III-א (_) רָאָה		9 ע״ג, II-guttural (_) בּוֹא
5 ג״פ, I-guttural + (_) שִׁיר		10 ע״ג, II-guttural + (_) בָּחַר
ו/י-III (ל״ה) לו״י		ו/י-III, (ל״ה) לו״י

II *Study* the sound change rules listed below. *Indicate* the relevant sound change/s occurring in each deviant verb form (on the left side) by comparing it with the corresponding normal form (on the right side). *Indicate* to which root type each deviant verb form belongs. *Remember*:

> ◆ The knowledge and application of the sound change rules give the deviant forms a see-through structure. It is easiest to detect the deviant feature/s of a given form by placing the consonants of the deviant form, e.g., קָרָאתִי, in the corresponding normal verb pattern, that is, תִּי - ַ - ָ, and ask, "Why is it קָרָאתִי instead of קָרָאְתִי as in שָׁמַרְתִּי?" Sound change rules 2 and 5 below answer the question.
>
> ◆ Sound changes mostly occur when the guttural/changeable consonant is vowelless. However, when surrounded by vowels, no sound changes occur.
>
> ◆ A verb form may have more than one deviant feature.

SOUND CHANGE RULES

1 A guttural takes a chateph (shva-plus-vowel) instead of a shva.

2 A vowelless א at the end of a syllable is silenced. The silencing of א is compensated by the lengthening of the preceding vowel (if it is not already long).

3 The consonant י at the end of a syllable forms a diphthong, which is normally contracted to one vowel. That is, י disappears in pronunciation but is retained in writing as a vowel letter.

4 **a.** The consonant י/ו with vowels on either side forms a triphthong. The consonant י/ו in a triphthong inside the word is omitted.
   b. At the end of a word the triphthong (י/ו with vowels on either side) is replaced by a full vowel (with either the vowel letter י/ו or ה).

5 The hard sound of a BeGaDKeFaT-consonant becomes soft after a vowel (shown in writing by the absence of the hardening dagesh).

5 שָׁמַר – עָלָה _____		1 שָׁמַרְתִּי – עָשִׂיתִי _____
6 שָׁמַרְנוּ – מָצָאנוּ _____		2 שְׁמַרְתֶּם – עֲלִיתֶם _____
7 שָׁמַר – קָם _____		3 שָׁמְרָה – קָמָה _____
8 שְׁמַרְתֶּם – רְאִיתֶם _____		4 שָׁמְרוּ – עָלוּ _____

III *Match* each grammatical element with the Hebrew word that illustrates it. *Mark* the element in the Hebrew word clearly! Observe that the same element may appear in more than one word, but only one element is to be marked. Each word is to be used once!

1 Vowel reduction **II** *A vowel*   קַלּוּ (__)
  two steps before the stress is reduced

2 Vowel reduction **II** *A vowel under a* (__) בָּאנוּ
  guttural two steps before the stress is reduced

3 Contraction of a diphthong *The*   (__) סַבּוֹתִי
  consonant י/ו *at the end of a syllable becomes a vowel letter*

4 Contraction of a triphthong.   (__) קַמְתִּי
  The consonant י/ו *with vowels on either side is omitted (in a II-*י/ו *verb)*

5 Linking vowel *Before the attached*   (__) קָם
  pronoun

6 Silent א   בָּנָה (__)

7 Vowel letter ה   בָּנִיתִי (__)
  *In a III-*י/ו *verb, 3ms 'he'*

8 Doubling dagesh (__) בָּנְתָה

9 Exception to the (__) בְּנִיתֶם
  basic rule of vocalization
  A stressed closed syllable has a short instead of a long vowel

10 Gender is marked (__) עֲלִיתֶם
  twice *In a III-*י/ו *verb, 3fs 'she'*

WORD LIST

Nouns

לֵבָב   *m*, heart (also לֵב): *pl* לְבָבוֹת

עֵץ   *m*, tree, wood, stick: *pl* עֵצִים

רֵאשִׁית   *f*, beginning (derived from רֹאשׁ)

Adjectives

אַחֵר   another, other

תָּמִים/תַּם   perfect, complete, whole

Verbs

בּוֹא   come, enter, go in: *perf* בָּא

בָּנָה   build

בָּרָא   create

הָיָה   be; become (followed by לְ); happen

חָיָה   live (☆ Lecháyim, ḥ.y.y/ḥ.y.h)[4]

מָכַר   sell

עָבַר   cross, pass over; transgress (☆ Eber, ʕ.b.r)

עָלָה   go up, ascend

עָשָׂה   do, make

קוּם   stand up, rise up: *perf* קָם (☆ Jehoiakim, q.w.m)

קָלַל   be/become light, unimportant, despised: *perf* קַל (☆ the verb type **Qal**, q.l.l)

רָאָה   see

שִׂים   put, set; appoint: *perf* שָׂם

שׁוּב   return, come back: *perf* שָׁב

שָׁכַן   dwell

Particles

אֵיךְ   how?

אֲשֶׁר   who, which, that; the one who...; what, where (☆ Asher, ʔ.š.r)

---

[4] Lecháyim means 'cheers', literally, 'for life' (modern Hebrew).

EXERCISES

15.1 *Fill in* the table below with the missing forms of פָּעַל perfect. *Read* all the verb forms and *translate* orally. For practical reasons, render the perfect as simple past. *Indicate* the root type and the meaning of the lexical forms. *Note*:

> ◆ The 3fs (הִיא) of III- י/ו verbs takes a double gender marker, both ת (the original feminine ending) and ה ָ, e.g., בָּנְתָה 'she built'.
> ◆ Certain forms of II-י/ו verbs and III-י/ו (III-ה) verbs are identical. The stress pattern will help you to identify the root type. Compare שָׁבוּ (II-י/ו) 'they returned' and שָׁבוּ (III-י/ו) 'they took captive', שָׁבָה (II-י/ו) 'she returned' and שָׁבָה (III-י/ו) 'he took captive'.
> ◆ In the irregular verbs הָיָה 'be' and חָיָה 'live' the middle root consonant י is retained in all forms.

Meaning: Lexical form	Root type	הֵם/הֵנָּה	אַתֶּם/אַתֶּן	הִיא	הוּא	
			קַמְתֶּם/תֶּן	קָמָה		1
				עָלְתָה	עָלָה	2
		בָּנוּ				3
			הֱיִיתֶם/תֶן			4
					בָּא	5
			רְאִיתֶם/תֶן			6
		קָלוּ				7
		עָשׂוּ				8
			חֲיִיתֶם/תֶן			9
		שָׁבוּ				10
				שָׂמָה		11

15.2 *Fill in* the blanks with the missing data according to the example given in the table below. *Read* and *translate*. *Remember*:

- The lexical form of II-י/ו verbs is the infinitive, e.g., קוּם.
- The lexical form of the twin-consonant verbs is the three root letters without any vowels, e.g., קלל.

Translation	Root type	Verb: Lexical form	Independent personal pronoun	Verb-plus-pronoun	
I was	irregular	הָיָה	אֲנִי/אָנֹכִי	הָיִיתִי	1
				בָּנִיתָ	2
				קָמָה	3
				עָלָה	4
				עָשְׂתָה	5
				רָאִינוּ	6
				שַׂמְתֶּם	7
				עֲלִיתֶן	8
				שָׁבוּ	9
she went around				סָבְבָה	10
				בָּאת	11
				הָיִינוּ	12
				חֲיִיתֶם	13
				קַלּוֹתִי	14
				בָּרָאתָ	15
				עֲשִׂיתֶן	16
				עָלוּ	17

15.3 *Attach* the correct suffixed pronouns to the verb roots below. *Vocalize,* *mark* the stress, *read* and *translate. Note*:

> • II-ו/י verbs (the so-called Hollow verbs):
> – The middle root consonant ו/י is omitted. Therefore, only the first and the third root consonants are visible in writing, e.g., קָם.
> – Unlike other root types, the vocalic suffixes of II-ו/י verbs are unstressed: קָמָה, קָמוּ.
> – The perfect of the 1ˢᵗ and 2ⁿᵈ persons (I, we; you) takes a patach (/a/) instead of the ordinary qamets (/ā/) under the first root consonant. Compare שָׁמַרְתִּי and קַמְתִּי.
> • III-ו/י (the so-called III-ה) verbs:
> – In the 1ˢᵗ and 2ⁿᵈ persons (I, we; you) the consonant ו/י becomes a vowel letter, e.g., עָלִיתִי (not עָלַיְתִּי).
> – In the 3ʳᵈ person (he, she, they) the consonant ו/י is omitted. Hence, only the first and the second root consonants are visible in writing: עָלָה, עָלְתָה, עָלוּ.
> – The 3fs (she) takes a double gender marker, both ת and ה ָ : עָלְתָה.

Translation	Verb-plus-pronoun	
_____	_____	1 אֲנִי (עלה)
_____	_____	2 אַתָּה (היה)
_____	_____	3 אַתְּ (בנה)
_____	_____	4 הוּא (קום)
_____	_____	5 הִיא (שוב)
_____	_____	6 אֲנַחְנוּ (ראה)
_____	_____	7 אַתֶּם (חיה)
_____	_____	8 אַתֶּן (בוא)
_____	_____	9 הֵם/הֵנָּה (היה)
_____	_____	10 אַתָּה (עשה)
_____	_____	11 אַתֶּם (ראה)
_____	_____	12 הוּא (בנה)
_____	_____	13 הִיא (היה)
_____	_____	14 אֲנַחְנוּ (עלה)
_____	_____	15 אָנֹכִי (חיה)
_____	_____	16 אַתְּ (שים)

15.4 Each verse segment below includes a *verb form in* פָּעַל *perfect. Cover* the English translation, *read* and *translate* as much as you can on your own. Then *match* each Hebrew clause with the correct English translation below and *check/complete* your translation against it. *Pay attention* to the meaning of the verbs in the perfect. *Remember*:

> ◆ The perfect expresses *completed actions,* which normally denote the *past.* Thus שָׁמַר, for example, usually means 'he guarded, he has/had guarded'.
> – The perfect may correspond to the *English present* in verbs describing a state of being, e.g., זָקַנְתִּי 'I *am* old', as well as in verbs describing an attitude, experience or perception such as 'know, love, understand, remember', e.g., יָדַעְתִּי 'I *know'.*
> – The perfect may correspond to the *English future* when something (such as a *promise* or a *prophecy*) is considered by the speaker to be *certain.*

I 1 הֶן־כֹּל רָאֲתָה עֵינִי שָׁמְעָה אָזְנִי ( ) And Abraham returned to his place (Gen. 18:33)

2 לֹא יָדַעְתִּי מִי עָשָׂה אֶת־הַדָּבָר הַזֶּה ( ) To your offspring/seed I will give (= נָתַתִּי) this land (Gen. 15:18)

3 מַה־זֹּאת עָשִׂית ( ) How [come] you said she [is] my sister? (Gen. 26:9)

4 אֵיךְ אָמַרְתָּ אֲחֹתִי הִוא ( ) What [is] this [that] God has done to us? (Gen. 42:28)

5 לְזַרְעֲךָ נָתַתִּי אֶת־הָאָרֶץ הַזֹּאת ( ) Look, my eye has seen everything, my ear has heard (Job 13:1)

6 וְאַבְרָהָם שָׁב לִמְקֹמוֹ: ( ) What [is] this [that] you have done? (Gen. 3:13)

7 מַה־זֹּאת עָשָׂה אֱלֹהִים לָנוּ: ( ) I do not know (= יָדַעְתִּי) who did this thing (Gen. 21:26)

II 1   אָהַבְתָּ רָע מִטּוֹב

( ) The word went out from the mouth of the king (Esther 7:8)

2   אַתֶּם עֲשִׂיתֶם אֵת כָּל־הָרָעָה הַזֹּאת

( ) See, the king's sons have come (2 Sam. 13:35)

3   הִנֵּה בְנֵי־הַמֶּלֶךְ בָּאוּ

( ) You love (= אָהַבְתָּ) evil [more] than good (Ps. 52:5)

4   אֵי־זֶה הַדֶּרֶךְ הָלָךְ

( ) You – you have done all this evil (1 Sam. 12:20)

5   אַחֲרָיו לֹא־קָם כָּמֹהוּ׃

( ) Look, I myself (= I – I) also have seen (Jer. 7:11)

6   גַּם אָנֹכִי הִנֵּה רָאִיתִי

( ) After him did not arise [anybody] like him (2 Kings 23:25)

7   אֵי־מִזֶּה עַם אָתָּה׃

( ) Which (= אֵי־זֶה) way (= the way) did he go? (1 Kings 13:12)

8   הַדָּבָר יָצָא מִפִּי הַמֶּלֶךְ

( ) From which (= אֵי־מִזֶּה) people [are] you? (Jon. 1:8)

15.5   *Translate* the clauses below. Proper names are enlarged.

1   הוּא נָתְנָה לִּי מִן־הָעֵץ (Gen. 3:12)

2   אָמַרְתִּי לַיהוה אֵלִי אָתָּה (Ps. 140:7)

3   וְלֹא הָלַךְ בְּדֶרֶךְ יהוה׃ (2 Kings 21:22)

4   אֵי הֶבֶל אָחִיךָ (Gen. 4:9)

5   וְאֶת־אִשְׁתּוֹ לָקַחְתָּ לְּךָ לְאִשָּׁה (2 Sam. 12:9)

6   שָׁמַע אֱלֹהִים אֶל־קוֹל הַנַּעַר (Gen. 21:17)

7   וְיַעֲקֹב נָתַן לְעֵשָׂו לֶחֶם (Gen. 25:34)

8   רָאָה יַעֲקֹב אֶת־רָחֵל (Gen. 29:10)

9   אַבְרָם יָשַׁב בְּאֶרֶץ־כְּנַעַן (Gen. 13:12)

10   מַה־יָּדַעְתָּ (Job 15:9)

11   מֶה עָשִׂיתָ (1 Sam. 13:11)

12   בְּרֵאשִׁית בָּרָא אֱלֹהִים אֵת הַשָּׁמַיִם וְאֵת הָאָרֶץ׃ (Gen. 1:1)

15.6 Each verse/verse segment below includes a *relative clause*. *Cover* the English translation, *read* and *translate* as much as you can on your own. Then *fill in* the blanks with the missing words in the following translation and *check/complete* your translation against it. *Remember*:

> • A relative clause is usually introduced by the particle אֲשֶׁר.
> • There are two types of relative clauses, attributive (*describing a noun*; אֲשֶׁר is rendered by 'who, whom, which, whose, that') and independent (*replacing a noun*; אֲשֶׁר is rendered by 'the one that/who/whom/which/whose, what, where').
> • A relative clause often contains an attached pronoun that refers back to the described/replaced noun. This pronoun is attached either to a preposition, the particle אֶת־ or a verb and it is not rendered in translation into English.
> – Observe that the relative clauses which replace a noun in the main clause are enlarged. In the relative clauses which describe a noun in the main clause the particle אֲשֶׁר, the described noun and the possible pronoun referring back to the described noun are enlarged.

1 אֲנִי יוֹסֵף אֲחִיכֶם אֲשֶׁר־מְכַרְתֶּם אֹתִי מִצְרָיְמָה: _____ [am] Joseph,

_____ brother, whom _____ sold (אֹתִי 'me', which refers back to

אֲנִי, is left untranslated) into Egypt (Gen. 45:4)

2 הַרְאִיתֶם אֲשֶׁר בָּחַר־בּוֹ יהוה כִּי אֵין כָּמֹהוּ בְּכָל־הָעָם Have _____

seen the one whom (= אֲשֶׁר) the Lord has chosen (בּוֹ the pronoun

'him', which refers to 'the one whom…', is left untranslated)? Certainly,

(= כִּי) [there is] none like _____ among _____ the people (1 Sam.10:24)

3 כֹּל אֲשֶׁר הָיָה⁵ לְשָׁאוּל וּלְכָל־בֵּיתוֹ נָתַתִּי לְבֶן־אֲדֹנֶיךָ: _____ that

belonged to (= was to) Saul and to _____ of _____ house _____ have

given to the son of _____ master (= masters, plural of majesty)

(2 Sam. 9:9)

4 זֶה הַיּוֹם אֲשֶׁר נָתַן יהוה אֶת־סִיסְרָא בְּיָדֶךָ הֲלֹא יהוה יָצָא לְפָנֶיךָ

_____ [is] the day [in] which the Lord will certainly give (= נָתַן) Sisera

in _____ hand. Has not the Lord gone out before _____! (Judg. 4:14)

5 אַיֵּה הָאֲנָשִׁים אֲשֶׁר־בָּאוּ אֵלֶיךָ הַלָּיְלָה Where [are] the men who

came to _____ tonight (= the night) ? (Gen. 19:5)

⁵The pronoun 'it' is included in the verb הָיָה (and likewise 'he' in יָדַע in entry 8 below).

6 וְזֹאת הַתּוֹרָה אֲשֶׁר־שָׂם מֹשֶׁה לִפְנֵי בְּנֵי יִשְׂרָאֵל: And _____ [is] the law that Moses set before the Israelites (= sons of Israel) (Dt. 4:44)

7 אַתֶּם רְאִיתֶם אֲשֶׁר עָשִׂיתִי לְמִצְרָיִם _____ _____ have seen what _____ did to Egypt (Ex. 19:4)

8 מֶלֶךְ־חָדָשׁ עַל־מִצְרָיִם אֲשֶׁר לֹא־יָדַע אֶת־יוֹסֵף: [A] new king over Egypt who did not know Joseph (Ex. 1:8)

9 הִנֵּה שָׁמַעְתִּי בְקֹלְכֶם לְכֹל אֲשֶׁר־אֲמַרְתֶּם לִי See, _____ have listened to _____ (= in _____ voice), in (= ־לְ) _____ that _____ have said to _____ (1 Sam. 12:1)

10 וְהַלֵּוִי אֲשֶׁר־בִּשְׁעָרֶיךָ And the Levite who [is] within _____ gates (Dt. 14:27)

11 אֱלֹהִים אֲחֵרִים אֲשֶׁר לֹא יָדַעְתָּ אַתָּה וַאֲבֹתֶיךָ: Other gods whom neither (= לֹא) _____ nor (= וְ) _____ fathers have known (Dt. 13:7)

12 קָטֹנְתִּי מִכֹּל הַחֲסָדִים וּמִכָּל־הָאֱמֶת אֲשֶׁר עָשִׂיתָ אֶת־עַבְדֶּךָ _____ am unworthy of (= קָטֹנְתִּי מִ) _____ the kindness (= evidences of kindness) and of (= מִ) _____ the faithfulness that _____ have done for (= אֶת־) _____ servant (Gen. 32:10)

15.7 Each verse segment below includes *the verb* הָיָה. *Cover* the English translation, *read* and *translate* as much as you can on your own. Then *fill in* the blanks with the missing words in the following translation and *check/complete* your translation against it. *Note*:

> • The verb הָיָה specifies the time of the verbless clause. Compare אֲנִי כֹהֵן 'I [am/was/will be] a priest' and הָיִיתִי כֹהֵן 'I *was* a priest'.
> – The construction 'הָיָה לְ + definite noun/attached pronoun' denotes possession in the past, e.g., הָיָה לָהּ בֵּן 'She *had* a son', lit., '*Was to* her son'.
> • הָיָה corresponds sometimes to English 'happen': מֶה־הָיָה לָאִישׁ 'What *happened* to the man?' (or 'What *did* the man *have*?')
> • 'הָיָה לְ + noun' may correspond to English '*become*', e.g., הָיָה לְאָדוֹן 'He *became* a master'.
> • In the formula הָיָה דְבַר יְהֹוָה אֶל־ 'The word of the Lord הָיָה to…' the verb הָיָה means '*came*'.

1 וּבַגּוֹיִם הָרַבִּים לֹא־הָיָה מֶלֶךְ כָּמֹהוּ And among the many nations [there] was no king like _____ (Neh. 13:26)

2 הָיְתָה יְהוּדָה לְקָדְשׁוֹ Judah became _____ holy [place] (= holiness) (Ps. 114:2)

3 וְהָיָה הָאִישׁ הַהוּא תָּם וְיָשָׁר And _____ man was blameless (= perfect) and upright (Job 1:1)

4 לְכָל־בְּנֵי יִשְׂרָאֵל הָיָה אוֹר _____ the Israelites had light (= to _____ the sons of Israel was light) (Ex. 10:23)

5 הֶהָיְתָה זֹּאת בִּימֵיכֶם וְאִם בִּימֵי אֲבֹתֵיכֶם: Has _____ happened in _____ days or (= וְאִם) in the days of _____ fathers? (Joel 1:2)

6 לֹא יָדַעְנוּ מֶה־הָיָה לוֹ: _____ do not know (= יָדַעְנוּ) _____ has happened to _____ (Ex. 32:1)

7 מַה־זֶּה הָיָה לְבֶן־קִישׁ _____ is _____ [that] has happened to the son of Kish? (1 Sam. 10:11)

8 אַחַר הַדְּבָרִים הָאֵלֶּה הָיָה דְבַר־יהוה אֶל־אַבְרָם After _____ things the word of the LORD came (= was) to Abram (Gen. 15:1)

9 אֱמֶת הָיָה הַדָּבָר אֲשֶׁר שָׁמַעְתִּי בְּאַרְצִי עַל־דְּבָרֶיךָ The word was true which _____ have heard in _____ land about (= עַל) _____ affairs/matters (1 Kings 10:6)

10 וְכָמֹהוּ לֹא־הָיָה לְפָנָיו מֶלֶךְ אֲשֶׁר־שָׁב אֶל־יהוה בְּכָל־לְבָבוֹ וּבְכָל־נַפְשׁוֹ And before _____ [there] was no king like _____ who returned to the LORD with _____ _____ heart and with _____ _____ soul (2 Kings 23:25)

11 גַּם יַד־יהוה הָיְתָה בָּם Indeed (= גַּם), the hand of the LORD was against (= בְּ) _____ (Dt. 2:15)

12 וְהוּא הָיָה לְאָבֶן: And _____ became as (= to) [a] stone (1 Sam 25:37)

15.8 *Translate* into Hebrew. *Note*:

> ◆ The verb הָיָה agrees with the noun it refers to in gender and
>   number: הָיוּ אֲנָשִׁים/נָשִׁים, הָיְתָה אִשָּׁה, הָיָה אִישׁ.
> ◆ The normal word order of the verbal clause is **V**erb–**S**ubject–**O**bject
>   (VSO).

1 You (*m, s*) dwelt in this land. Your father was a slave. You dwelt in the land in which (= אֲשֶׁר + in it) your father was a slave.

2 I came to (= אֶל־) a holy place. There were many trees in that place. There were many trees in the place to which (= אֲשֶׁר + to it) I came.

3 The old king built a house for the Lord. The house of the Lord was very beautiful. The house which the king built for the Lord was very beautiful.

4 The man had no (= were not to the man) children. He had (= were to him) two wives. The man (= to the man) who had (= אֲשֶׁר + were to him) two wives had no (= were not) children until the day of his death.

5 God has given you (*f, s*) (= to you) a wise heart. You had (= were to you) also other things. God has given to the woman, who had (= were to her) many things, also a good heart.

6 Each people had (= were to every nation) silver/money. The silver was in the palace. The people who had (= אֲשֶׁר + were to it) silver in the palace are (+ הוּא) the people of the Lord.

SECTION 16

1 *Imperfect in general: Form and meaning*
   – *Form*: The imperfect is formed by the addition of a set of pronouns attached to the beginning of the root consonants, called *prefixed pronouns (preformatives)*. Certain prefixed pronouns are, in addition, followed by an ending. The 3ms functions as the *base form* of the imperfect. For the inflection of the imperfect, see Grammatical cornerstone 12 below.
   – *Meaning*: Like the perfect, the imperfect is a *finite* verb form. The imperfect expresses *uncompleted actions,* which normally denote *non-past,* i.e., *future* (and sometimes *present*). However, certain verbs in the imperfect may correspond to other English tenses (see Exercise 16.6, 2nd note).

2 פָּעַל *imperfect: Basic forms (unchangeable verbs,* שְׁלֵמִים)
   The basic pattern of פָּעַל imperfect can be recognized in the base form (3ms), e.g., יִשְׁמֹר 'he will guard'.
   – *Prefix vowel*: The prefix vowel is normally /i/, e.g., יִשְׁמֹר, except the 1cs (אֲנִי) which takes an /e/-vowel: אֶשְׁמֹר. The prefix vowels /i/ and /e/ are the result of vowel raising ("attenuation"). *An original /a/-vowel in an unstressed closed syllable is usually raised to an /i/-vowel. However, before and after a guttural the original /a/-vowel is either retained or raised only halfway to an /e/-vowel:* יַשְׁמֹר *becomes* יִשְׁמֹר *and* אַשְׁמֹר *becomes* אֶשְׁמֹר.
   – *Three vowel patterns*: Like the perfect, the imperfect occurs in three vowel patterns, in which the vowel under the second root consonant, called *stem vowel,* varies (either an /o/-, /e/- or /a/-vowel).

Perfect	*Imperfect*	*Perfect*	*Imperfect*
שָׁמַר perf-/a/	יִשְׁמֹר imperf-/o/	קָטֹן perf-/o/	יִקְטַן imperf-/a/
נָתַן perf-/a/	יִתֵּן imperf-/e/	זָקֵן perf-/e/	יִזְקַן imperf-/a/

   – Note that perf-/a/ verbs (usually verbs expressing an action) normally take an /o/-vowel (and rarely an /e/-vowel) under the second root consonant in the imperfect, whereas perf-/e/ and perf-/o/ verbs (usually verbs expressing a state of being) normally take an /a/-vowel as stem vowel in the imperfect.
   – *Vowel change*: Certain endings take the stress, which results in regular vowel reductions due to the shift in stress (see Exercise 16.2).

3 פָּעַל *imperfect of I-guttural* (פ''ג) *verbs*: Before the gutturals ה, ח, ע, the original /a/-vowel of the prefix is retained, e.g., יַעֲבֹד, whereas before א it is raised only halfway, to an /e/-vowel, e.g., יֶאֱסֹף.[1]
   – The silent shva (the original no-vowel) at the close of the first syllable in, for instance, יַ-עְ-בֹד and יֶ-אְ-סֹף, is usually replaced by a chateph. The vowel of the chateph corresponds to the preceding prefix vowel: יַעֲבֹד, יֶאֱסֹף. *Remember that for practical reasons we always let the chateph open the syllable:* יַ-עֲ-בֹד, יֶ-אֱ-סֹף.

---

[1] However, before ח the prefix vowel is sometimes /e/.

4 **פָּעַל** *imperfect of II-guttural (ע״ג) verbs, III-guttural (ל״ג) verbs and III-א
(ל״א) verbs*: Verbs of action normally take an /o/-vowel under the second root
consonant in the imperfect (imperf-/o/ verbs), but II-guttural, III-guttural and
III-א verbs take an /a/-vowel instead, e.g., יִפְעַל 'do', יִשְׁמַע 'hear', יִקְרָא
'read'. *Gutturals attract the /a/-vowel.* In addition, the consonant א at the end of a
syllable in a III-א verb is silenced. The silencing of א is compensated by the
lengthening of the preceding vowel: יִקְרַא becomes יִקְרָא.

5 **פָּעַל** *imperfect of the irregular verbs* נָתַן 'give' *and* לָקַח 'take'
    – נָתַן: The first root consonant נ *Nun* at the end of a syllable is *regularly*
assimilated to the following consonant, which is doubled (shown in writing by
the doubling dagesh), e.g., יִנְתֵן becomes יִתֵּן.
    – לָקַח: The first root consonant ל *Lámed* at the end of a syllable is *irregularly*
assimilated to the following consonant, which is doubled (shown in writing by
the doubling dagesh), e.g., יִלְקַח becomes יִקַּח.

MEMORIZE

PRONOUNS IV						
	Subject pronouns			**Possessive pronouns**		
Person	Independent	Attached to verbs in the perfect	Attached to verbs in the imperfect	Attached to nouns in singular (after ׳/ו)	Attached to nouns in singular (after a consonant)	Attached to nouns in plural
3ms, he	הוּא	– – –	י– – –	his	־הוּ/ו–	ו–	יו ָ–
3fs, she	הִיא	־ה – –	תּ– – –	her	־הָ	־הָ	־יהָ
2ms, you	אַתָּה	־ָתּ– –	תּ– – –	your	־ךָ	־ךָ	־יךָ
2fs, you	אַתְּ	תְּ– – –	־י– – תּ	your	־ך	־ך	־יִך
1cs, I	אָנֹכִי/אֲנִי	־תִּי – –	א– – –	my	־י	־י	־י
3mp, they	הֵם/הֵמָּה	ו– – –	יו– – –	their	־הֶם	־ם	־יהֶם
3fp, they	הֵן/הֵנָּה	ו– – –	־נָה– – תּ	their	־הֶן	־ן	־יהֶן
2mp, you	אַתֶּם	־תֶּם– –	ו– – – תּ	your	־כֶם	־כֶם	־יכֶם
2fp, you	אַתֶּן/אַתֵּנָה	־תֶּן – –	־נָה– – תּ	your	־כֶן	־כֶן	־יכֶן
1cp, we	אֲנַחְנוּ	־נוּ – –	נ– – –	our	־נוּ	־נוּ	־ינוּ
GRAMMATICAL CORNERSTONE 12 ר א שׁ פּ נ ה						

REVIEW AND APPLICATION OF THE RULES

I *Study* the sound change rules listed below. *Indicate* the relevant sound change/s occurring in each deviant verb form (on the left side) by comparing it with the corresponding normal form (on the right side). *Indicate* to which root type each deviant verb form belongs. *Remember*:

> ◆ The knowledge and application of the sound change rules give the deviant forms a see-through structure. It is easiest to detect the deviant feature/s of a given form by placing the consonants of the deviant form, e.g., תִּשְׁאֲלִי, in the corresponding normal pattern, that is, תִּ - ־ְ - ־ִי, and ask, "Why is it תִּשְׁאֲלִי instead of תִּשְׁאָלִי (as in תִּשְׁמְרִי)?" Sound change rule 1 below answers the question.

SOUND CHANGE RULES

1 A guttural takes a chateph (shva-plus-vowel) instead of a shva.
2 A guttural attracts an /a/-vowel instead of the I/E- or U/O-vowel.
3 The insertion vowel used to break up a consonant cluster after (i.e., under) a guttural with a chateph is the vowel of the chateph, e.g., תַּעֲמֹד + the ending וּ results in תַּעֲמֹדוּ, which after the vowel reduction becomes תַּ - עֲמֹדוּ becomes תַּ - עַמְדוּ. תַּ - עַמְדוּ.
4 Vowel raising ("attenuation") before a guttural is not realized. That is, the original /a/-vowel before a guttural in an unstressed closed syllable is retained, e.g., תַּעֲמֹד.
5 Vowel raising ("attenuation") before a guttural is realized halfway. That is, the original /a/-vowel before a guttural in an unstressed closed syllable is raised to /e/, e.g., תֵּאָסֵף.
6 A vowelless א at the end of a syllable is silenced. The silencing of א is compensated by the lengthening of the preceding vowel (if it is not already long).

_____	5 יִשְׁמֹר – יִקְרָא	_____	1 יִשְׁמֹר – יִשְׁלַח
_____	6 תִּשְׁמֹרְנָה – תַּעֲבֹדְנָה	_____	2 יִשְׁמֹר – יַעֲמֹד
_____	7 תִּשְׁמְרוּ – תִּבְחֲרוּ	_____	3 יִשְׁמֹר – יֶאֱסֹף
_____	8 נִשְׁמֹר – נִבְחַר	_____	4 תִּשְׁמְרִי – תַּעַבְרִי

WORD LIST

Nouns

מִלְחָמָה	f, war, battle	רָצַח	kill: *imperf* יִרְצַח

Verbs

אָסַף   gather: *imperf* יֶאֱסֹף (☆ **Asaph**, ʔ.s.p)

שָׁאַל   ask, inquire; request: *imperf* יִשְׁאַל (☆ **Saul**, š.ʔ.1)

גָּדֵל/גָּדַל   be/become great/big, grow: *imperf* יִגְדַּל (☆ **Gedal**jah)

שָׁפַט   judge: *imperf* יִשְׁפֹּט

דָּרַשׁ   seek; inquire: *imperf* יִדְרֹשׁ

לָמַד   learn: *imperf* יִלְמַד (☆ the letter **Lámed**)

Particles

בֵּין   between: *with suff in sing* בֵּינִי, *with suffix in pl* בֵּינֵינוּ

EXERCISES

16.1   *Fill in* the table below with the missing forms of פָּעַל imperfect. *Indicate* the root type. *Read* all the verb forms and *translate* orally. For practical reasons, render the imperfect as simple future, e.g., יִשְׁפֹּט 'he will judge'. *Note*:

> ♦ The ending נָה (2–3fp) is not stressed. Since there is no shift in stress, no vowel changes occur.

Root type	אַתֵּן/הֵנָּה	אֲנַחְנוּ	אַתָּה/הִיא	אָנֹכִי/אֲנִי	Base form הוּא	
					יִכְתֹּב	1
				אֶכְרֹת		2
		נִשְׁפֹּט				3
			תִּזְכֹּר			4
				אֶעֱבֹר		5
	תִּשְׁלַחְנָה					6
					יַעֲבֹד	7
	תִּגְדַּלְנָה					8
			תִּרְצַח			9
		נִשְׁאַל				10
					יֶאֱסֹף	11
	תִּקְרֶאנָה					12

SECTION 16   139

16.2 *Fill in* the table below with the missing forms of פָּעַל imperfect. *Read* all the verb forms and *translate* orally. For practical reasons, render the imperfect as simple future. *Indicate* the root type and the meaning of the lexical forms. *Remember*:

- All the attached pronouns in this exercise take the stress. When the stress is moved forward, a vowel in an open syllable is reduced, e.g., 'תִּכְתֹּב + the ending 'יָ ' results in תִּכְאָבִי which becomes תִּכְתְּבִי.
- The insertion vowel used to break up a consonant cluster after (i.e., under) a guttural with a chateph is the vowel of the chateph, e.g.,'תַּעֲמֹד + the ending 'וּ' results in תַּעֲמֹדוּ, which after the vowel reduction becomes תַּ-עֲמְדוּ. The shva-plus-vowel in תַּ-עֲמְדוּ is replaced by the /a/-vowel of the chateph: תַּ-עֲמְדוּ.
- A BeGaDKeFaT-consonant immediately after a closed syllable with an insertion vowel does not take a hardening dagesh: תַּ-עֲמְ-דוּ.

Meaning: Lexical form	Root type	הֵם	אַתֶּם	אַתְּ	Base form הוא	
write					יִכְתֹּב	1
				תִּכְרְתִי		2
			תִּזְכְּרוּ			3
		יִשְׁפְּטוּ				4
					יִשְׁלַח	5
		יַאַסְפוּ				6
				תַּעֲבְדִי		7
			תַּעֲבְרוּ			8
		יִשְׁאֲלוּ				9

16.3 *Fill in* the blanks with the missing data according to the example given in the table below. *Read* and *translate*. For practical reasons, render the imperfect as simple future.

Translation	Lexical form (3ms, perfect)	Base form (3ms, imperfect)	Independent personal pronoun	Pronoun-plus-verb	
he will write	כָּתַב	יִכְתֹּב	הוּא	יִכְתֹּב	1
				אֶשְׁמֹר	2
				תִּמְלֹךְ	3
				תִּזְכְּרִי	4
				נִקְרָא	5
				תַּעַבְדוּ	6
				תִּשְׁלַחְנָה	7
				יִשְׁמְעוּ	8
				תִּבְחַרְנָה	9
				תִּגְדַּל	10
				יִמְצָא	11
				תִּשְׁאֲלִי	12
				אֶשְׁפֹּט	13
				תִּמְשְׁחוּ	14
				תִּשְׁמֹרְנָה	15
				יִקְרְאוּ	16
				נִשְׁלַח	17
				תַּאַסְפִי	18

16.4 *Attach* the correct prefixed pronouns (and the endings where necessary) to the verb roots below. *Vocalize, mark* the stress, *read* and *translate*. All the verb roots in this exercise are unchangeable (שְׁלֵמִים). *Remember*:

> • The basic vowel pattern of פָּעַל imperfect is יִ־ ־ ־ (imperf-/o/ verbs, often expressing an action) and יִ־ ־ ־ (imperf-/a/ verbs, often expressing a state of being).
>
> • All the imperfect forms take a prefix. The 2fs (אַתְּ) and 2-3 pl (הֵם/הֵנָּה and אַתֶּם/אַתֶּן) take both a prefix and an ending, e.g., תִּשְׁמְרִי, תִּשְׁמֹרְנָה.
>
> • The set of prefixed pronouns consists of four letters: אית״ן. The term EYTaN will help you to memorize these letters. Associate the EYTaN-letters with the corresponding independent personal pronouns and the suffixed pronouns.
>   – אָנֹכִי/אֲנִי: The א is kept in the prefixed pronoun, e.g., אֶשְׁמֹר.
>   – אֲנַ֫חְנוּ: The נ is kept in the prefixed pronoun, e.g., נִשְׁמֹר (compare שָׁמַ֫רְנוּ).
>   – אַתָּה, אַתְּ, אַתֶּם, אַתֶּן: The ת is kept in the prefixed pronouns, e.g., תִּשְׁמֹר, תִּשְׁמְרוּ (compare שָׁמַ֫רְתָּ, שָׁמַ֫רְתְּ).
>
> • אַתָּה תִּשְׁמֹר is identical in form with הִיא תִּשְׁמֹר.
>
> • Endings consisting of a vowel only, e.g., ־ִי, normally take the stress, which results in a vowel reduction, e.g., תִּשְׁמֹר + the ending ־ִי results in תִּשְׁמֹרִי which becomes תִּשְׁמְרִי.

Translation	Pronoun-plus-verb	
I will judge	_____	1 אֲנִי (שפט)
_____	_____	2 אַתָּה (שמר)
_____	_____	3 אַתְּ (זכר)
_____	_____	4 הוּא (מלך)
_____	_____	5 הִיא (כתב)
_____	_____	6 אֲנַ֫חְנוּ (כרת)
_____	_____	7 אַתֶּם (כתב)
_____	_____	8 הֵם (זכר)

16.5 *Attach* the correct prefixed pronouns (and the necessary endings) to the verb roots below. *Vocalize, mark* the stress, *read* and *translate*. All the verb roots in this exercise include a guttural. *Remember*:

> - II-guttural and III-guttural verbs take an /a/- instead of an /o/-vowel under the second root consonant, e.g., תִּבְחַר (compare תִּשְׁמֹר).
> - A guttural takes a chateph (shva-plus-vowel) instead of a shva: תִּבְחֲרוּ (compare תִּשְׁמְרוּ).
> - III-א verbs also take an /a/- instead of an /o/-vowel under the second root consonant. Further, the consonant א at the end of a syllable is silenced. The silencing of א is compensated by the lengthening of the preceding vowel (if it is not already long), e.g., תִּקְרָא.

Translation	Pronoun-plus-verb	
_____	_____	1 הוּא (בחר)
_____	_____	2 אֲנַחְנוּ (שׁלח)
_____	_____	3 אַתָּה (גאל)
_____	_____	4 אַתְּ (קרא)
_____	_____	5 אֲנִי (שׁאל)
_____	_____	6 אֲנִי (קרא)
_____	_____	7 אַתֶּם (שׁמע)
_____	_____	8 הִיא (בחר)
_____	_____	9 הֵם (משׁח)
_____	_____	10 אֲנַחְנוּ (מצא)

16.6   Each verse segment below includes an *enlarged verb form in* פָּעַל *imperfect*. *Cover* the English translation, *read* and *translate* as much as you can on your own. Then *fill in* the blanks with the missing words in the following translation and *check/complete* your translation against it. *Pay attention* to the meaning of the imperfect. *Note*:

> ◆ You were previously requested to render the imperfect as simple future. However, certain verbs in the imperfect may also correspond to other English tenses.
> – In the translations given in this book the imperfect (and other verb forms) are interpreted according to the context in which they appear in the Bible. However, be aware of the fact that the various Bible translations may offer different tense interpretations.
> ◆ The meaning of the imperfect:
> – The imperfect expresses *uncompleted actions* which normally denote *non-past*, i.e., *future* and sometimes *present*. Thus יִשְׁמֹר, for instance, usually means 'he will guard' and sometimes 'he guards'.
> – The imperfect may also express an *ongoing action/event* (e.g., 'he is/will be guarding') and a *repeated* or a *customary action* (e.g., 'he sometimes/usually guards').
> – The imperfect is also used when an *action/event* is considered by the speaker to be *uncertain*, which applies, for example, to *questions* and *expressions of wish* (e.g., 'he might/would/should guard, may he guard').
> ◆ The 2fs (אַתְּ), 2mp (אַתֶּם) and 3mp (הֵם) of the imperfect are sometimes followed by נ, e.g., תִּשְׁמְרוּן.

1   זֹאת בְּרִיתִי אֲשֶׁר **תִּשְׁמְרוּ** בֵּינִי וּבֵינֵיכֶם וּבֵין זַרְעֲךָ אַחֲרֶיךָ

[is] _____ covenant _____ _____ will keep, between _____ and (between)

_____ and (between) _____ offspring/seed after _____ (Gen. 17:10)

2   זֹאת הַבְּרִית אֲשֶׁר **אֶכְרֹת** אֶת־בֵּית יִשְׂרָאֵל אַחֲרֵי הַיָּמִים הָהֵם

[is] the covenant _____ _____ will make (= cut) with the house of

Israel after _____ days (Jer. 31:33)

3   לָמָּה זֶּה **תִּשְׁאַל** לִשְׁמִי   Why [is] _____ [that] _____ inquire for _____

name? (Gen. 32:29)

4   **יִשְׁמְעוּן** אֶת־שִׁמְךָ הַגָּדוֹל   _____ will hear _____ great name

(1 Kings 8:42)

5   וְאֶת־אַהֲרֹן וְאֶת־בָּנָיו **תִּמְשָׁח**   And Aaron and _____ sons _____ will

anoint (Ex. 30:30)

6 מִי־יִשְׁכֹּן בְּהַר קָדְשֶׁךָ: _____ will dwell on (= בְּ) _____ holy mountain (mountain of _____ holiness)? (Ps. 15:1)

7 אֵשֶׁת־חַיִל מִי יִמְצָא [A] capable wife (wife of valour/capacity) _____ would find? (Prov. 31:10)

8 הָאִישׁ אֲשֶׁר־יִבְחַר יהוה הוּא הַקָּדוֹשׁ The man _____ the LORD will choose, _____ [is] the holy [one] (Num 16:7)

9 הָעֵצִים אֲשֶׁר־תִּכְתֹּב עֲלֵיהֶם בְּיָדְךָ לְעֵינֵיהֶם: The sticks on _____ _____ write [are] in _____ hand before (= לְ)_____ eyes (Ezek. 37:20)

10 אֶשְׁלַח אֶת־עֲבָדַי אֵלֶיךָ _____ will send _____ servants to _____ (1 Kings 20:6)

16.7 Each verse segment below includes an *enlarged form in* פָּעַל *imperfect*. *Cover* the English translation, *read* and *translate* as much as you can on your own. Then *match* each verse segment with the correct English translation. *Check/complete* your translation against the translation given in the book. *Pay attention* to the meaning of the verbs in the imperfect.

1 וְאֶת־מִצְוֺתַי תִּשְׁמֹרוּ   ( ) How would Pharaoh listen to me? (Ex. 6:30)

2 וְלֹא־יִלְמְדוּ עוֹד מִלְחָמָה: ( ) And your ears will hear [a] word (Isa. 30:21)

3 וְאָזְנֶיךָ תִּשְׁמַעְנָה דָבָר   ( ) He will remember his covenant forever (Ps. 111:5)

4 עַד־יִגְדַּל שֵׁלָה בְנִי   ( ) And they shall not learn war [any] more (Isa. 2:4)

5 הוּא יִשְׁלַח מַלְאָכוֹ לְפָנֶיךָ   ( ) And your name will become great forever (2 Sam. 7:26)

6 שָׁאוּל יִמְלֹךְ עָלֵינוּ   ( ) And my commandments – you will keep [them] (Lev. 26:3)

7 וּבְשֵׁם יהוה אֶקְרָא: ( ) And on (= בְּ) the name of the LORD I will call (Ps. 116:17)

8 וִיגַדַּל שִׁמְךָ עַד־עוֹלָם   ( ) It is he who will send (= he – he will send) his angel before you (Gen. 24:7)

9 יִזְכֹּר לְעוֹלָם בְּרִיתוֹ:   ( ) Shall Saul be king over us? (1 Sam. 11:12)

10 אֵיךְ יִשְׁמַע אֵלַי פַּרְעֹה: ( ) Until Shelah, my son, grows (Gen. 38:11)

16.8 *Rewrite* the enlarged Hebrew verb forms in the imperfect in Exercises
      16.6 and 16.7 above and then *transform* them into the perfect.

16.9 *Translate* into Hebrew. *Remember*:

> ◆ The normal word order of the verbal clause is **Verb–Subject–Object**.
> ◆ Variant word order often signals emphasis.

1 The LORD will make (= cut) a covenant with his people (= nation)
   forever.
2 His sons will remember his words and keep the commandments of God.
3 I will write a book for my children (= [1] for my children [2] book), in
   which (אֲשֶׁר + in it) they will read every day. My children will learn the
   laws of the LORD and remember them.
4 You (*m, s*) will hear a voice from heaven.
5 Thus says the LORD, 'It is you whom I will send to Egypt and it is you
   who will stand before the king.'
6 You (*m, pl*) will choose a king and I will anoint him.

SECTION 17

1 פָּעַל *imperative*: The imperative occurs *only in the 2nd person (you)*. The masculine singular functions as the *base form* of the imperative. The imperative is formed like the imperfect, only without the prefix תּ, e.g., תִּשְׁמֹר (2ms, imperfect) becomes שְׁמֹר (ms) 'guard!'

	Imperfect	Imperative	
2ms (imperf-/o/)	תִּשְׁמֹר	שְׁמֹר/שָׁמְרָה (šomrā^h)	'guard!'
(imperf-/a/)	תִּשְׁכַּב	שְׁכַב/שִׁכְבָה	'lie down!'
2fs	תִּשְׁמְרִי/תִּשְׁכְּבִי	שִׁמְרִי/שִׁכְבִי (not שְׁמְרִי/שְׁכְבִי)	
2mp	תִּשְׁמְרוּ/תִּשְׁכְּבוּ	שִׁמְרוּ/שִׁכְבוּ (not שְׁמְרוּ/שְׁכְבוּ)	
2fp	תִּשְׁמֹרְנָה/תִּשְׁכַּבְנָה	שְׁמֹרְנָה/שְׁכַבְנָה	

– The masculine singular may occur with the ending ה‸ : שְׁמֹר (imperf-/o/ verb) + the ending ה‸ ' results in שָׁמְרָה (pronounced šomrā^h with a qamets-/o/). Both forms mean 'guard!'. שְׁכַב (imperf-/a/ verb) + ה‸ ' results in שִׁכְבָה 'lie down!' שְׁלַח (a III-guttural verb) + ה‸ ' results in שְׁלָחָה 'send!'.

– The impermissible three-consonant sequence at the beginning of a syllable in the fs (אֱתֵ) and mp (אֱתֶם) is ordinarily broken up by inserting an /i/-vowel, e.g., שְׁמְרִי becomes שִׁמְרִי and שְׁמְרוּ becomes שִׁמְרוּ.

2 *Lengthened imperfect* (called *cohortative*): The lengthened imperfect is used as a *mild imperative* expressing a wish in the *1st person (I, we)*. The lengthened imperfect is formed by the addition of the ending ה‸ to the ordinary imperfect, e.g., 'אֶשְׁמֹר + ה‸ ' results in אֶשְׁמֹרָה, which becomes אֶשְׁמְרָה. The lengthened imperfect is usually rendered in English by 'may/let me/us' before the verb in question: אֶשְׁמְרָה 'let me/may I guard'.

3 *Shortened imperfect* (called *jussive*): The shortened imperfect is used as a *mild imperative* expressing a wish in the *3rd person (he, she, they)*. Observe that the shortened imperfect of unchangeable root types (שְׁלֵמִים) and most of the changeable root types is *identical in form with the ordinary imperfect*. Like the lengthened imperfect, the shortened imperfect is usually rendered in English by 'may/let' before the verb in question: יִשְׁמֹר יְהוָה אֹתְךָ 'May/let the LORD guard you'.

4 *Negative commands and prohibitions*
   – 'The particle אַל + shortened imperfect' expresses an *immediate specific command*, e.g., אַל תִּשְׁמֹר (ms) 'do not guard!'
   – 'The particle לֹא + ordinary imperfect' expresses a *permanent absolute command* (that is, a *prohibition*), e.g., לֹא תִשְׁמֹר 'you *shall* not guard!'

5 *Particle-as-intensifier* נָא: The particle נָא often follows a verb form in the imperative, lengthened imperfect or shortened imperfect, to intensify the effect of request in those verb forms.

– The particle נָא also occurs after the particles אַל 'not' and הִנֵּה 'look, here, now' to intensify their meaning. נָא is often rendered in English translation by *'please'* or *'I/we pray'*, but נָא may also be rendered by other intensifying constructions or it may be left untranslated.

☆ פָּעַל IMPERFECT VIA HEBREW NAMES (11)

Verb form		Vowel pattern: Base form	Hebrew name	English pronunciation	Root type	Meaning: Lexical form
Imperf	Imperf-/o/ (יִשְׁמֹר)	־ ־ ־ יִ	נִמְרֹד	Nimrod	unchangeable שְׁלֵמִים	revolt, rebel
	Imperf-/o/ (יַעֲבֹד)	־ ־ ־ יַ	יַעֲקֹב	Jacob	I-guttural פ"ג	grasp by the heel, cheat
	Imperf-/a/ (יִבְחַר)	־ ־ ־ יִ	יִצְחַק	Isaac	II-guttural ע"ג	laugh

The lengthened imperf + particle-as-intensifier נָא: הוֹשִׁיעָה נָּא אָ Hosi**anna** 'Do save, please!'

REVIEW AND APPLICATION OF THE RULES

I *Study* the sound change rules listed below. *Indicate* the relevant sound change/s occurring in each deviant verb form (on the left side) by comparing it with the corresponding normal form (on the right side). *Indicate* to which root type each deviant verb form belongs.

SOUND CHANGE RULES

1 A guttural takes a chateph (shva-plus-vowel) instead of a shva.
2 A guttural attracts an /a/-vowel instead of an I/E- or U/O-vowel.
3 The insertion vowel before a guttural with a chateph (shva-plus-vowel) matches the vowel of the chateph, e.g., גָּאַל + the ending וּ' results in גָּאֲלוּ, which after the vowel reduction becomes גָּאֲלוּ. גָּאֲלוּ becomes גַּאֲלוּ.
4 A vowelless א at the end of a syllable is silenced. The silencing of א is compensated by the lengthening of the preceding vowel (if it is not already long).

1 שָׁמַר – שָׁלַח _____	4 שָׁמֹר – קָרָא _____
2 שָׁמַר – עָמַד _____	5 שָׁמְרָנָה – עֲבֹדְנָה _____
3 שִׁמְרִי – שַׁאֲלִי _____	6 שָׁמְרוּ – בַּחֲרוּ _____

WORD LIST

Nouns

חֵן   agreeableness, charm, favour: *with suff* חִנִּי

תְּפִלָּה, פלל *f*, prayer

Particles

אַל   no, not (followed by the shortened imperf)

נָא   please, I/we pray (intensifier) (☆ Hosi**anna**)

EXERCISES

17.1 *Fill in* the table below with the missing forms of פָּעַל *imperative*. *Read* all the verb forms and *translate. Remember*:

> ◆ When a word takes an ending, the stress is usually moved forward to that newly added ending. As a result, a vowel in an open syllable is reduced, e.g., 'שְׁמֹר + ִי.' results in שִׁמְרִי. Two vowelless consonants at the beginning of a syllable become a *closed syllable* by means of an insertion vowel, normally /i/: שְׁמְרִי becomes שִׁמְרִי.
>
> ◆ A BeGaDKeFaT-consonant immediately after a closed syllable with an insertion vowel retains its soft sound: כְּתֻבִי becomes כִּתְ-בִי 'write!'.
>
> ◆ Before a guttural with a chateph (shva-plus-vowel), the insertion vowel matches the vowel of the chateph, e.g., בְּחֲרִי becomes בַּחֲרִי 'choose!'.

Translation: Imperative	אַתֵּן	אַתֶּם	אַתְּ	אַתָּה	
send!				שְׁלַח	1
			עִבְדִי		2
				אֱסֹף	3
		כִּרְתוּ			4
	שְׁפֹטְנָה				5
	שְׁאַלְנָה				6
	קְרֶאנָה				7

17.2 *Fill in* the table below with the missing forms of פָּעַל in the *ordinary* and the *lengthened imperfect*. *Read* all the verb forms and *translate* orally. For practical reasons, render the ordinary imperfect as simple future. *Remember*:

> ◆ The endings added to the forms in this exercise take the stress. As a result, the vowel in an open syllable one step before the stress is reduced, e.g., 'אֶשְׁמֹר + ָה' results in אֶשְׁמֹרָה which becomes אֶשְׁמְרָה.
>
> ◆ A guttural takes a chateph instead of a shva; אֶבְחֲרָה

Lengthened imperfect		Ordinary imperfect				
אֲנַחְנוּ	אֲנִי/אָנֹכִי	הֵם	אַתֶּם	אַתְּ	הוּא Base form	
	אֶשְׁמְעָה				יִשְׁמַע	1
נִבְחֲרָה				תִּבְחֲרִי		2
			תִּקְרָאוּ			3
		יִדְרְשׁוּ				4
					יְלַמַד	5
				תִּגְאָלִי		6

17.3   Each verse segment below includes an *enlarged verb form in* פָּעַל *imperative, lengthened or shortened imperfect. Read* the clauses and *translate*. Then *match* each Hebrew clause with the correct English translation. *Remember*:

- 'The particle אַל + shortened imperfect' expresses an *immediate specific command*, e.g., אַל תִּשְׁמֹר (*ms*) '*do not* guard!'
- 'The particle לֹא + ordinary imperfect' expresses a *permanent command* (= *prohibition*), e.g., לֹא תִשְׁמֹר 'you *shall not* guard!'

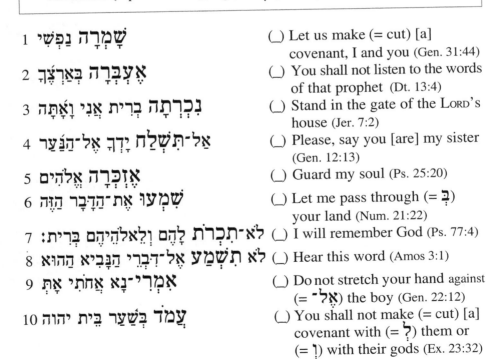

1 שָׁמְרָה נַפְשִׁי	( ) Let us make (= cut) [a] covenant, I and you (Gen. 31:44)
2 אֶעְבְּרָה בְאַרְצֶךָ	( ) You shall not listen to the words of that prophet (Dt. 13:4)
3 נִכְרְתָה בְרִית אֲנִי וָאַתָּה	( ) Stand in the gate of the LORD's house (Jer. 7:2)
4 אַל־תִּשְׁלַח יָדְךָ אֶל־הַנַּעַר	( ) Please, say you [are] my sister (Gen. 12:13)
5 אֶזְכְּרָה אֱלֹהִים	( ) Guard my soul (Ps. 25:20)
6 שִׁמְעוּ אֶת־הַדָּבָר הַזֶּה	( ) Let me pass through (= בְּ) your land (Num. 21:22)
7 לֹא־תִכְרֹת לָהֶם וְלֵאלֹהֵיהֶם בְּרִית:	( ) I will remember God (Ps. 77:4)
8 לֹא תִשְׁמַע אֶל־דִּבְרֵי הַנָּבִיא הַהוּא	( ) Hear this word (Amos 3:1)
9 אִמְרִי־נָא אֲחֹתִי אָתְּ	( ) Do not stretch your hand against (= אֶל־) the boy (Gen. 22:12)
10 עֲמֹד בְּשַׁעַר בֵּית יהוה	( ) You shall not make (= cut) [a] covenant with (= לְ) them or (= וְ) with their gods (Ex. 23:32)

17.4 *Transform* the verbs in Exercise 17.3 above from the imperative/imperfect into the perfect. Then *write down* the entire clauses with the transformed verb forms. *Exclude* the particle נָא in entry 9. *Remember*:

> - The imperative always refers to the 2nd person (you). Thus, for instance, שְׁמֹר/שָׁמְרָה (imperative) should be transformed into שָׁמַרְתָּ (2ms, perfect).
> - The perfect is negated by לֹא.

17.5 Each verse/verse segment below includes a verb form in פָּעַל *imperative*. *Read* and *translate*. Then *negate* the imperative forms according to the example given below. Proper names are enlarged. *Remember*:

> - The imperative is negated by the particle אַל followed by the shortened imperfect (jussive), e.g., אַל תִּשְׁמֹר (ms) 'do not guard!'. The so-called shortened imperfect is often identical in form with the ordinary imperfect.
> - The imperative (only the ms, e.g., שְׁמֹר) may occur with the ending הָ : 'שְׁמֹר + הָ ' results in שָׁמְרָה 'guard!' (pronounced šomrā^h), 'שְׁמַע (III-guttural verb) + הָ ' results in שָׁמְעָה 'listen!'

1 שַׁאֲלוּ שְׁלוֹם יְרוּשָׁלָם (Ps. 122:6)   אַל תִּשְׁאֲלוּ

2 שְׁמַע יִשְׂרָאֵל יהוה אֱלֹהֵינוּ יהוה אֶחָד: (Dt. 6:4)   _____

3 אֶרֶץ אֶרֶץ אָרֶץ שִׁמְעִי דְּבַר־יהוה: (Jer. 22:29)   _____

4 אֱלֹהִים שָׁפְטָה הָאָרֶץ (Ps. 82:8)   _____

5 שִׁלְחָה אֵלַי אֶת־דָּוִד בִּנְךָ (1 Sam. 16:19)   _____

6 יהוה אֱלֹהִים צְבָאוֹת שִׁמְעָה תְפִלָּתִי (Ps. 84:9)   _____

7 בֶּן־אָדָם עֲמֹד עַל־רַגְלֶיךָ (Ezek. 2:1)   _____

8 וּכְתֹב עָלֶיהָ אֵת כָּל־הַדְּבָרִים הָרִאשֹׁנִים (Jer. 36:28)   _____

9 שִׁמְרוּ וְדִרְשׁוּ כָּל־מִצְוֹת יהוה (1 Chron. 28:8)   _____

17.6 Each verse segment below includes *the particle* נָא (often rendered by 'please, I/we pray'). *Read* the clauses and *translate*. Then *transform* the clauses from the singular into the plural according to the example given below.

1 הִנֵּה־נָא זָקַנְתִּי לֹא יָדַעְתִּי יוֹם מוֹתִי: (Gen. 27:2)

Plural: הִנֵּה־נָא זָקַנּוּ, לֹא יָדַעְנוּ יוֹם מוֹתֵנוּ.

2 אִם־נָא מָצָאתִי חֵן בְּעֵינֶיךָ אַל־נָא תַעֲבֹר מֵעַל עַבְדֶּךָ׃ (Gen. 18:3)

3 הִנֵּה־נָא עָשִׂיתִי אֶת־הַדָּבָר הַזֶּה (2 Sam. 14:21)

4 הִנֵּה־נָא פָּתַחְתִּי פִי (Job 33:2)

5 אֶעְבְּרָה־נָּא בְאַרְצֶךָ וְלֹא שָׁמַע מֶלֶךְ אֱדוֹם (Edom) (Judg. 11:17)

6 יַעֲבָר־ (yaʕᵃvor) נָא אֲדֹנִי לִפְנֵי עַבְדּוֹ (Gen. 33:14)

17.7 *Match* each grammatical element from Exercise 17.6 above with the Hebrew word/construction that illustrates it. *Mark* the element in the Hebrew word/construction clearly. Observe that the same grammatical element may appear more than once, but only one occurrence is to be marked. Each Hebrew word/construction is to be used once!

1 Definite direct object marker   מֵעַל (_)

2 Silent א   אֶת־הַדָּבָר (_)

3 Omitted hardening dagesh *Preceding word ends in a vowel*   יַעֲבָר־נָא (_)

4 Particle used to negate an imperative   אַל־תַּעֲבֹר (_)

5 Pausal form *With segol (/e/) instead of a shva in the normal form* אֶעְבְּרָה־נָּא (_)

6 Linking doubling dagesh *Joins two words into one sound unit* עַבְדֶּךָ (_)

7 Compensatory lengthening of a vowel *Since a guttural* מָצָאתִי (_)

   cannot be doubled

8 Qamets-/o/ *A word before a maqqeph (hyphen) loses its stress* פָּתַחְתִּי פִי (_)

17.8 Each verse segment below includes an *enlarged word in pause*. *Read* the clauses and *translate*. Then *write* the normal form of the words in pause. *Indicate* from the list given below the relevant sound change/s which occur in the words in pause (see 'note' in Exercises 6.3 and 12.8).

SOUND CHANGES (occurring in the words in pause)

1 A short vowel in the stressed syllable of a word is lengthened, e.g., שָׁמַר becomes שָׁמָר, יִשְׁמַע becomes יִשְׁמָע.

2 The original linking vowel /e/ replaces a reduced vowel (shva or chateph) and takes the stress, e.g., עַמְּךָ 'your nation' (*m, s*) becomes עַמֶּךָ.

3 An original vowel replaces a reduced vowel (shva or chateph). The original vowel takes the stress and is lengthened (if it is not already long), e.g., יִשְׁמְרוּ becomes יִשְׁמֹרוּ, יִשְׁמְעוּ becomes יִשְׁמָעוּ.

4 The original /a/-vowel in a penultimate noun replaces the /e/-vowel and, in addition, is lengthened, e.g., מֶלֶךְ becomes מָלֶךְ.

———	1 נַעְבְּרָה־נָּא בְאַרְצֶ֫ךָ (Num. 20:17)
———	2 אֶת־יהוה אֱלֹהֵ֫ינוּ נַעֲבֹד וּבְקוֹלוֹ נִשְׁמָע: (Jos. 24:24)
———	3 וְגַם אֶת־הַגּוֹי אֲשֶׁר יַעֲבֹ֫דוּ (Gen. 15:14)
———	4 אַל־נָא תַעֲבֹר מֵעַל עַבְדֶּ֫ךָ: (Gen. 18:3)
———	5 אֶת־יהוה זָכָ֫רְתִּי (Jon. 2:8)
———	6 לֹא־הָ֫יָה לָהּ יָ֫לֶד עַד יוֹם מוֹתָהּ: (2 Sam. 6:23)
———	7 אָמַ֫רְתְּ לֹא אֶשְׁמָע (Jer. 22:21)
——— ———	8 וְאֶת־מִצְוֹתָיו תִּשְׁמֹ֫רוּ וּבְקֹלוֹ תִשְׁמָ֫עוּ וְאֹתוֹ תַעֲבֹ֫דוּ (Dt. 13:5)
———	9 דִּבְרֵיכֶם אֲנִי שָׁמָ֫עְתִּי: (Ezek. 35:13)
———	10 וְאַתָּה מִשָּׁמַ֫יִם תִּשְׁמָע (Neh. 9:27)
———	11 וּבְכָל־אֶ֫רֶץ מִצְרַ֫יִם הָיָה לָ֑חֶם: (Gen. 41:54)
———	12 בִּי מְלָכִים יִמְלֹ֫כוּ (Prov. 8:15)

17.9 *Transform* the verbs in the imperfect in Exercise 17.8 above (except entries 6 and 11 and the verb אמר in entry 7) into the perfect and the verbs in the perfect into the imperfect.

17.10 *Translate* into Hebrew. Do not use pausal forms.

1 Serve (*m, s*) the LORD. Do not serve other gods.
2 Listen (*m, s*) to the words of the prophet who will dwell (שׁכן) in your land.
3 Please, remember (*f, s*) your land and your people. Do not listen to that vicious man.
4 May the LORD remember you (*m, s*) and your children.
5 Let us make (= cut) a covenant with this king.
6 Please, write (*m, p*) all these statutes and ordinances in the chronicles (= the words of the days).
7 May the king rule over us and over all the people of Israel.
8 Please, send (*m, p*) us to the land which God has given (+ to) our fathers. Let us serve the LORD there.

SECTION 18

1 *Participles in general*: Unlike the perfect and the imperfect, the participle is a *non-finite* verb form, which means that it has no time reference of its own, hence the time reference is specified by the context. The 3ms functions as the *base form* of the participle.
   – There are two types of participles, *active* and *passive*.
   – The participle in Hebrew shares the *qualities of both nouns and verbs*:
   Like the noun, the participle is *inflected only in gender and number* and it can take the definite article or a possessive pronoun (see Exercise 18.2).
   Being a verb form, the participle can replace a finite verb denoting an ongoing action and/or take an object (see Exercises 18.3–4).

2 *Participles of* פָּעַל: שְׁלֵמִים *(unchangeable verbs) and* II-י/ו (עו״י) *verbs*

	ms	fs	mp	fp	Voice	Meaning
Perf-/a/ (שָׁמַר)	שֹׁמֵר (שֹׁמְרָה)	שֹׁמֶרֶת	שֹׁמְרִים	שֹׁמְרוֹת	active	guarding
	שָׁמוּר	שְׁמוּרָה	שְׁמוּרִים	שְׁמוּרוֹת	passive	guarded
Perf-/a/ (קָם)	קָם (II-י/ו)	קָמָה	קָמִים	קָמוֹת	active	standing up
Perf-/e/ (זָקֵן)	זָקֵן	זְקֵנָה	זְקֵנִים	זְקֵנוֹת		aged/old
Perf-/o/ (יָכֹל)	יָכֹל	יְכֹלָה	יְכֹלִים	יְכֹלוֹת		able/capable

   – Only transitive perf-/a/ verbs (verbs that can take a direct object) of פָּעַל usually have both an active and a passive participle, e.g., שֹׁמֵר 'guarding' and שָׁמוּר 'guarded'. All other verbs have either an active participle, e.g., קָם 'standing up', or a passive participle, e.g., זָקֵן 'aged'.
   – The base form (ms) of participles of the perf-/e/ verbs (e.g., זָקֵן), the perf-/o/ verbs (e.g., יָכֹל) and the II-י/ו verbs (e.g., קָם) is identical with the 3ms of the perfect.
   – The passive participle of the perf-/a/ verbs, e.g., שָׁמוּר, and many of the perf-/e/ and perf-/o/ verbs correspond to English adjectives, e.g., זָקֵן 'old'.

3 *Participles with deviant form*: The presence of a changeable consonant and/or a guttural in a verb root normally results in regular sound changes.

4 *Usage of participles*: Participles function like adjectives. The participle can be used either as a *noun* (הַשֹּׁמֵר lit., 'the *guarding/keeping [one]* = the guard/keeper', compare הַטּוֹב 'the *good [one]*'), an *attribute* describing a noun (הָאִישׁ הַשֹּׁמֵר, lit., '*the guarding* man = the man *who* [is, was, will be] guarding', compare הָאִישׁ הַטּוֹב 'the *good* man') or a *predicate* (הָאִישׁ שֹׁמֵר 'The man *[is, was, will be]* guarding', compare הָאִישׁ טוֹב 'the man [is, was, will be] *good*').

5 *Negation of participles*: Like other verbless clauses, a clause with a participle as predicate is negated by אֵין: אֵין הָאִישׁ שֹׁמֵר 'The man [is, was, will] *not* [be] *guarding*'

6 *Participles with tense markers*: The time reference of the participle can be specified by the verb היה 'be' and the particle הִנֵּה 'see, now, here'.

– The verb הָיָה (in the perfect) signals *past time*, e.g., הָיָה שָׁמַר 'He *guarded*'.
– The particle הִנֵּה signals a *near future*: הִנֵּה הוּא שָׁמַר 'He *is about to*/Soon he *will* guard'.

7 *Conjunctions* כִּי *and* אֲשֶׁר

– The conjunction כִּי: Apart from being a particle-as-intensifier, כִּי is frequently used as a conjunction which introduces various types of subordinate clauses. The most frequent clauses introduced by כִּי are as follows:

Clauses expressing a *cause* (כִּי corresponds to 'because, for, since').

After verbs of saying (such as 'say, declare, announce' etc.), כִּי introduces *indirect speech*, e.g., אָמַר כִּי 'He said *that*…'.

After verbs expressing an attitude, experience or perception (such as 'know, love, understand, remember' etc.) כִּי introduces a *statement/fact* related to the preceding verb, e.g., רָאָה/יָדַע כִּי 'He saw/knew *that*…'.

כִּי often occurs combined with other particles, e.g., יַעַן כִּי 'because'.

– The conjunction אֲשֶׁר: Apart from introducing a relative clause, אֲשֶׁר introduces various types of subordinate clauses, especially clauses expressing a *cause* or *purpose*.

אֲשֶׁר often occurs combined with other particles, e.g., יַעַן אֲשֶׁר 'because'.

MEMORIZE

THE INFLECTION SYSTEM OF THE VERB					
All verb types share the same inflection					
	Independent personal pronoun	Perfect	Imperfect	Imperative	Participle (inflected only in gender and number)
he	הוּא	– – –	יְ– – –		– – –
she	הִיא	– – –ָה	תְ– – –		– –ֶ–ת (–ָ–– ה)
you, *m*	אַתָּה	–ְ–ַ–תָּ	תְ– – –	– – –	– – –
you, *f*	אַתְּ	–ְ– –תְּ	תְ– – –ִי	–ְ– –ִי	– –ֶ–ת (–ָ–– ה)
I	אָנֹכִי/אֲנִי	–ַ–ְ–תִּי	אֶ– – –	–ֶ–/ –ת (ה ָ–)
they, *m*	הֵם/הֵמָּה	– – –וּ	יְ– – –וּ		– –ִים
they, *f*	הֵנָּה	– – –וּ	תְ–ֹ–ְ–נָה		– – –וֹת
you, *m*	אַתֶּם	– – –תֶּם	תְ– – –וּ	– – –וּ	– –ִים
you, *f*	אַתֵּן/אַתֵּנָה	– – –תֶּן	תְ–ֹ–ְ–נָה	–ְ–ֹ–נָה	– – –וֹת
we	אֲנַחְנוּ	–ַ–ְ–נוּ	נְ– – –		– – –ִים/וֹת

| GRAMMATICAL CORNERSTONE 13   ר א שׁ פָּ נֶ ה |

☆ PARTICIPLES OF פָּעַל VIA HEBREW NAMES (12)

Verb form		Voice	Vowel pattern	Hebrew name	English pronunciation	Root type	Translation: Participle
Parti-ciple	שׁוֹמֵר/שֹׁמֵר Perf-/a/	Active	-וֹ-ֵ-/ -ֹ-ֵ-	יוֹסֵף	Joseph[1]	I-ו/י, פו״י	adding
	קָם Perf-/a/	Active	-ָ-	דָּן	Dan	II-ו/י, עו״י	judging
	שָׁמוּר Perf-/a/	Passive	-ָ-וּ-	שָׁאוּל	Saul[1]	II-ג, ע״ג	wished for, required, asked
	זָקֵן Perf-/e/	Passive	-ָ-ֵ-	שָׁלֵם	Jeru**salem**	unchangeable שְׁלֵמִים	complete, whole, sound

REVIEW AND APPLICATION OF THE RULES

I *Study* the sound change rules listed below. *Indicate* the relevant sound change/s occurring in each deviant verb form (on the left side) by comparing it with the corresponding normal form (on the right side). *Indicate* to which root type each deviant verb form belongs.

SOUND CHANGE RULES

1. A guttural usually takes a chateph (shva-plus-vowel) instead of a shva.
2. A guttural attracts an /a/-vowel instead of an I/E- or U/O-vowel.
3. After (i.e., under) a guttural the insertion vowel added to break up an impermissible two-consonant sequence at the end of a word is /a/ instead of /e/ (segol).
4. A guttural (ע ,ח) at the end of a word that is not preceded by an /a/-vowel attracts a glide-/a/, e.g., שֹׁמֵעַ šōmē$_a$ʕ.
5. A vowelless א at the end of a syllable is silenced. That is, א disappears in pronunciation but is retained in writing. The silencing of א is compensated by the lengthening of the preceding vowel (if it is not already long).
6. The consonant ו/י in a triphthong (i.e., ו/י with vowels on either side) is omitted, which results in a form with two root consonants instead of three.

1 שֹׁמֵר - שֹׁלֵחַ ______

2 זָקֵן - יָרֵא ______

3 שְׁמוּרָה - עֲזוּבָה ______

4 שֹׁמֵר - קֹרֵא ______

5 שֹׁמְרִים - בֹּנִים ______

6 שׁוֹמֶרֶת - שׁוֹמַעַת ______

7 בְּנוּיִים - עֲשׂוּיִים ______

8 שֹׁמְרוֹת - שֹׁאֲלוֹת ______

---

[1] Although the root type is changeable, the vowel pattern of the name reflects the normal pattern of the relevant verb form. *Remember that sound changes normally occur when there is no vowel (marked by shva) before or after the changeable consonant/guttural.*

II Match each grammatical element with the Hebrew word that illustrates it. Mark the element in the Hebrew word clearly! Observe that the same element may appear in more than one word, but only one element is to be marked. Each word is to be used once!

1 Vowel reduction **I** *A vowel under* (_) עֲזוּבִים **6** Insertion vowel /a/ (_) בֹּחֲרִים
   a guttural **one** *step before the stress*   *Under a guttural, used to dissolve*
   is reduced   *a two-consonant sequence*

2 Vowel reduction **I** *A vowel* (_) כֹּתֶבֶת   *at the end of a word*
   one *step before the stress is reduced*   **7** Glide-/a/ *Under* ע/ח (_) קֹרֵאת

3 Vowel reduction **II** *A vowel* (_) שׁוֹמַעַת   *at the end of a word*
   two *steps before the stress is reduced*   **8** Diphthong   (_) בָּנִים

4 Vowel reduction **II** *A vowel under* (_) מַלְכוּת   *A vowel + the consonant* י/ו
   a guttural **two** *steps before the stress*   **9** Contraction of a   (_) בָּנוּי
   is reduced   triphthong, י/ו *with vowels*

5 Insertion vowel /e/ *Used to* (_) שְׁמוּרָה   *on either side is omitted*
   dissolve a two-consonant sequence   **10** Silent א   (_) שֹׁמֵעַ
   at the end of a word

WORD LIST

Nouns   *Particles*

סֹפֵר   *m*, scribe   אֲשֶׁר   for, because (conj)
עֲבוֹדָה, עֶבֶד *f*, work, service   (☆ Asher, ʔ.š.r)
             (☆ Obadiah, ʕ.b.d)   יַעַן   because: often followed

Verbs[2]   by כִּי/אֲשֶׁר
ארר   curse: *passive part* אָרוּר   כַּאֲשֶׁר   as; when
ברך   bless: *in Qal only*   כִּי   that; because, since, for;
             passive part בָּרוּךְ   when (conj)
כָּבֵד   be/become heavy: לְבַד   alone
             imperf יִכְבַּד   עֵקֶב   because: often followed by
רָדַף   pursue, persecute: כִּי/אֲשֶׁר (☆ Jacob, ʕ.q.b)
             imperf יִרְדֹּף   עַתָּה   now
שָׁכַב   lie down: *imperf* יִשְׁכַּב

---
[2] The lexical form of verbs that only partially or never occur in פָּעַל consists of the three root consonants without any vowels.

EXERCISES

18.1 *Fill in* the blanks with the missing data according to the example given in the table below. *Remember*:

> • Only transitive פָּעַל verbs (verbs taking a direct object), e.g., שָׁמַר, usually have both an active participle (שֹׁמֵר/שׁוֹמֵר 'guarding') and a passive participle (שָׁמוּר 'guarded'). All other verbs have either an active participle, e.g., קָם 'standing up', or a passive participle, e.g., זָקֵן 'aged/old'.
> • When the stress is moved forward, the vowel in an open syllable either one or two steps before the stress is reduced.

Root type	Lexical form	Participle: Basic meaning	Voice	Feminine plural	Masculine plural	Feminine singular	Masculine singular	
שְׁלֵמִים	שָׁמַר	guarding	active	שׁוֹמְרוֹת	שׁוֹמְרִים	שׁוֹמֶרֶת	שׁוֹמֵר	1
							אֹכֶלֶת	2
				אֲהוּבוֹת				3
					לְקֻחִים			4
	קוּם						קָם	5
		fearing/ being afraid	active/ passive			יְרֵאָה		6
				נְתֻנוֹת				7
							יוֹדֵעַ	8
						עֹשָׂה	עֹשֶׂה	9
					קֹרְאִים			10
	בּוֹא			בָּאוֹת				11
						שׁוֹמַעַת		12
					רֹאִים			13
							בָּנוּי	14
						זְקֵנָה		15

18.2 Each verse segment below includes an *active participle* (enlarged in the Hebrew text and italicized in the translation) *used as a **noun**. Read* and *translate* as much as you can on your own. Then *check* your translation against the following translation. *Fill in* the blanks with the following data: **a)** Participle: Free form **b)** Participle: Gender and number **c)** Participle: Basic meaning **d)** Lexical form (normally the 3ms of פָּעַל perfect). *Note:*

- A participle used as a noun represents *the one who performs an action*. Thus, שֹׁמֵר corresponds to 'one who [is, was, will be] guarding/keeping = *guard/keeper*'.
- The participle, like the noun, can take the definite article, e.g., הַשֹּׁמֵר 'the guard', or a possessive pronoun: שֹׁמְרִי '*my* guard'.
- The participle can be combined with other noun/s in a noun chain and, like the noun, the participle has two forms, *free* and *bound*, e.g., יַד הַשֹּׁמֵר 'the hand of the *guard*', שֹׁמֵר הַבְּרִית 'the *keeper of* the covenant', often translated as 'the one (e.g., he, you) *who* [is, was, will be] *keeping* the covenant' or 'the one *who keeps, kept (etc.)* the covenant'. The tense of the participle is determined by the context.

---

1 רַבִּים רֹדְפַי Many [are] *my persecutors* (Ps. 119:157)

   a) _____ b) _____ c) _____ d) _____

2 שָׁלַח הַמֶּלֶךְ אֶת־שָׁפָן בֶּן־אֲצַלְיָהוּ בֶן־מְשֻׁלָּם הַסֹּפֵר The king sent Shaphan, the son of Azaliah, the son of Meshullam, *the scribe*

   (2 Kings 22:3) a) _____ b) _____ c) _____ d) _____

3 הֲשֹׁפֵט כָּל־הָאָרֶץ לֹא יַעֲשֶׂה מִשְׁפָּט: Shall not *the judge* of all the earth do justice? (Gen. 18:25)

   a) _____ b) _____ c) _____ d) _____

4 שִׁמְעוּ אֵלַי רֹדְפֵי צֶדֶק Listen to me, *you who pursue* (= pursuers of) righteousness (Isa. 51:1)

   a) _____ b) _____ c) _____ d) _____

5 בָּרוּךְ הַבָּא בְּשֵׁם יהוה Blessed [be] *he who enters* in the name of the LORD (Ps. 118:26)

   a) _____ b) _____ c) _____ d) _____

6 הֲשֹׁמֵ֖ר אָחִ֥י אָנֹֽכִי׃ [Am] I the *guardian* of my brother? (Gen. 4:9)

a) _____ b) _____ c) _____ d) _____

18.3 Each verse segment below includes an *active participle* (enlarged in the Hebrew text) *used as an **attribute describing a noun**. Read* and *translate* as much as you can on your own. For practical reasons, *render* the participles below in the present tense. Then *complete* the missing words in the following translation and *check/complete* your translation against it. *Note*:

> - הָאִישׁ הַשֹּׁמֵר literally means 'the *guarding* man' (compare הָאִישׁ הַטּוֹב 'the *good* man'). However, the construction 'הַ + participle' after a definite noun is usually rendered in English translation by a *relative clause*: הָאִישׁ הַשֹּׁמֵר 'the man *who* [is, was, will be] *guarding*' or 'the man *who guards, guarded (etc.)*'.
> - In the Key the participles are rendered in the tense required by the context in which they appear in the Bible.
> - A participle can *take an object*.

1 בֶּן־מָ֙וֶת֙ הָאִ֣ישׁ הָעֹשֶׂ֥ה זֹֽאת׃ The man _____ deserves to die (= son of death) (2 Sam. 12:5)

2 הָֽאֲנָשִׁ֛ים הָעֹלִ֖ים מִמִּצְרַ֑יִם The men _____ (Num. 32:11)

3 הַרְּאִיתֶם֙ הָאִ֤ישׁ הָֽעֹלֶה֙ הַזֶּ֔ה Have you seen this man _____? (1 Sam. 17:25)

4 הָאִ֣ישׁ הַשֹּׁכֵ֣ב עִם־הָֽאִשָּׁ֗ה The man _____ (Dt. 22:22)

5 מֶ֣לֶךְ יְהוּדָ֔ה הַמֹּלֵ֖ךְ תַּ֣חַת יֹֽאשִׁיָּ֥הוּ אָבִ֖יו
The king of Judah _____ Josiah, his father (Jer. 22:11)

18.4 Each verse/verse segment below includes a *participle* (enlarged in the Hebrew text and italicized in the translation) *used as a* **predicate**. *Read* and *translate* as much as you can on your own. *Complete* the missing pronouns in the following translation and *check/complete* your translation against it. Then *fill in* the blanks with the following data:
a) Participle: Free form   **b)** Participle: Gender and number   **c)** Participle: Voice (active/passive) **d)** Participle: Basic meaning **e)** Lexical form. *Note:*

- An active participle used as a predicate replaces a verb expressing an *ongoing action either in the past, the present or the future*. Since the participle has no time reference of its own, the tense is specified by the context, e.g., הָאִישׁ שֹׁמֵר 'the man [is, was, will be] guarding' or 'the man *guards, guarded (etc)'*.
- A participle can *take an object*: הָאִישׁ שֹׁמֵר אֶת־הַמָּקוֹם
- A passive participle used as a predicate corresponds to an English adjective, e.g., הַמָּקוֹם שָׁמוּר 'the place [is, was, will be] *guarded'*.

---

1 בְּרוּכָה אַתְּ לַיהוה בִּתִּי *Blessed* [may] _____ [be] by (= לְ) the LORD, _____ daughter (Ruth 3:10)

a) _____ b) _____ c) _____ d) _____ e) _____

2 הֲלֹא־הִיא כְתוּבָה עַל־סֵפֶר הַיָּשָׁר [Is] _____ not *written* in (= עַל) the Book of Jashar? (Jos. 10:13)

a) _____ b) _____ c) _____ d) _____ e) _____

3 בֶּן־אָדָם שׁוֹלֵחַ אֲנִי אוֹתְךָ אֶל־בְּנֵי יִשְׂרָאֵל Son of man, _____ *send* (= sending) _____ to the Israelites (= sons of Israel) (Ezek. 2:3)

a) _____ b) _____ c) _____ d) _____ e) _____

4 אָנֹכִי עֹמֵד בֵּין־יהוה וּבֵינֵיכֶם בָּעֵת הַהוּא _____ *stood* (= standing) between the LORD and (between) _____ at _____ time (Dt. 5:5)

a) _____ b) _____ c) _____ d) _____ e) _____

5 לֹא אִתְּכֶם לְבַדְּכֶם אָנֹכִי כֹּרֵת אֶת־הַבְּרִית הַזֹּאת [It is] not with _____ alone [that] _____ *make* (= cutting) _____ covenant (Dt. 29:13)

a) _____ b) _____ c) _____ d) _____ e) _____

6 כַּאֲשֶׁר כָּתוּב בְּתוֹרַת מֹשֶׁה As it [is] *written* in the law of Moses (Dan. 9:13)

a) _____ b) _____ c) _____ d) _____ e) _____

7 הִנְנִי נֹתֵן דְּבָרַי בְּפִיךָ Look, _____ [am] putting _____ words in

_____ mouth (Jer. 5:14)

a) _____ b) _____ c) _____ d) _____ e) _____

8 הִנְּךָ שֹׁכֵב עִם־אֲבֹתֶיךָ Look, [soon] _____ [will be] lying down with

_____ fathers (Dt. 31:16)

a) _____ b) _____ c) _____ d) _____ e) _____

9 לָמָּה זֶּה אֲדֹנִי רֹדֵף אַחֲרֵי עַבְדּוֹ Why [is] this [that] _____ lord [is]

pursuing after _____ servant? (1 Sam. 26:18)

a) _____ b) _____ c) _____ d) _____ e) _____

10 אָרוּר אַתָּה בָּעִיר וְאָרוּר אַתָּה בַּשָּׂדֶה: Cursed [shall] _____ [be] in

the city and cursed [shall] _____ [be] in the field (Dt. 28:16)

a) _____ b) _____ c) _____ d) _____ e) _____

18.5 *Translate* into English. Proper names are enlarged.

1 אֵלֶּה שְׁמוֹת בְּנֵי יִשְׂרָאֵל הַבָּאִים מִצְרָיְמָה אֵת יַעֲקֹב (Ex. 1:1)

2 יהוה אֱלֹהֵי יִשְׂרָאֵל אֵין כָּמוֹךָ אֱלֹהִים בַּשָּׁמַיִם... וְעַל־הָאָרֶץ מִתָּחַת
שֹׁמֵר הַבְּרִית וְהַחֶסֶד לַעֲבָדֶיךָ הַהֹלְכִים לְפָנֶיךָ בְּכָל־לִבָּם: (1 Kings 8:23)

3 הַמָּקוֹם אֲשֶׁר אַתָּה עוֹמֵד עָלָיו אַדְמַת־קֹדֶשׁ הוּא: (Ex. 3:5)

4 וְכָל־הָעָם רֹאִים אֶת־הַקּוֹלֹת (Ex. 20:15)

5 מֶלֶךְ בָּבֶל אֲשֶׁר־אַתֶּם יְרֵאִים מִפָּנָיו (Jer. 42:11)

6 אַבְרָהָם הֹלֵךְ עִמָּם (Gen. 18:16)

7 בְּרוּכִים אַתֶּם לַיהוה (1 Sam. 23:21)

8 הַשֹּׁמְרִים הֵם אֶת־דֶּרֶךְ יהוה (Judg. 2:22)

9 מָה־הַדָּבָר הַזֶּה אֲשֶׁר אַתָּה עֹשֶׂה לָעָם (Ex. 18:14)

10 וּדְבוֹרָה אִשָּׁה נְבִיאָה אֵשֶׁת לַפִּידוֹת
הִיא שֹׁפְטָה אֶת־יִשְׂרָאֵל בָּעֵת הַהִיא: (Judg. 4:4)

11 אַחֲרֵי מִי אַתָּה רֹדֵף (1 Sam. 24:15)

12 שְׁמוּאֵל שֹׁכֵב בְּהֵיכַל יהוה (1 Sam. 3:3)

18.6 *Transform* the clauses in entries 1, 7, 8 in Exercise 18.5 above from the singular into the plural and the clauses in entries 3, 9, 11 from the plural into the singular. *Read* and *translate* orally.

18.7 *Match* each grammatical element from Exercise 18.5 above with the Hebrew word/construction that illustrates it. *Mark* the element in the Hebrew word/construction clearly. Observe that the same grammatical element may appear more than once, but only one occurrence is to be marked. Each Hebrew word/construction is to be used once!

1 Definite direct object marker *Left untranslated in English*   ( ) הַבָּאִים

2 No compensatory lengthening of a preceding vowel occurs

   Normally before the gutturals ה, ח   ( ) אֶת־דֶּרֶךְ

3 Maqqeph *Two words joined by a maqqeph form a single*   ( ) הַשֹּׁמְרִים

   sound unit with one (main) stress

4 Particle introducing a relative clause   ( ) מִצְרַיְמָה

   Rendered in English by 'which, that, who' etc.

5 Particle introducing a question   ( ) הַהֹלְכִים

   Rendered in translation by a question mark

6 Defective writing *The vowel letter* ו *is unexpectedly omitted*   ( ) וְעַל־הָאָרֶץ

7 Direction marker *The unstressed ending* ָה, *rendered in*   ( ) אֲשֶׁר

   English by 'to/toward'

8 Participle of a II-ו/י verb *Hollow verb*   ( ) הַקּוֹלֹת

18.8 *Translate* into Hebrew. *Remember*:

> ♦ The normal word order of a clause with a participle as predicate is 'Subject + Participle + Object'.

1 The men [are] coming to the house with their wives.
2 They (*m*) [are] going to the temple of God and now we [are] guarding (+ עַל) their houses.
3 Whom (אֶת־ + who) do you (*m, s*) judge (= judging) today (= the day)?
4 Why [are] you (*m, p*) afraid of (+ אֶת־) the LORD? The LORD loves (*participle*) you.
5 What [is] he doing in this land?
6 She sees (= seeing) all the people (= nation) standing there.
7 Who [is] the man who (= הַ) persecutes (= persecuting) you (*f, s*)?
8 The woman who (= הַ) sits (= sitting) in the temple of God is a prophetess.

18.9 Each verse segment below includes *the conjunction* כִּי. *Read* and *translate* as much as you can on your own. Then *match* each Hebrew clause with the correct English translation below and *check/complete* your translation against it. *Pay attention* to the function of the conjunction כִּי. *Remember:*

- כִּי expressing a *cause* is rendered by '*because, for, since*', e.g., כִּי שָׁמַרְתָּ '*because/for/since* you guarded'.
- כִּי after verbs of saying ('say, declare' etc.) and verbs such as 'know, feel, hear, see' is rendered by '*that*': אָמַרְתָּ / רָאִיתָ כִּי 'You said/saw *that*…'.

---

1 כִּי יוֹדֵעַ כָּל־שַׁעַר עַמִּי
    כִּי אֵשֶׁת חַיִל אָתְּ:

( ) That I [am] judging his house forever (1 Sam. 3:13)

2 עַתָּה זֶה יָדַעְתִּי
    כִּי אִישׁ אֱלֹהִים אָתָּה

( ) For now I know (= יָדַעְתִּי) that you fear (= fearing) God (Gen. 22:12)

3 יָדַעְתִּי כִּי־נָתַן יהוה
    לָכֶם אֶת־הָאָרֶץ

( ) For thus said the LORD concerning (= אֶל) Shallum, the son of Josiah (Jer. 22:11)

4 אָז יָדַע מָנוֹחַ
    כִּי־מַלְאַךְ יהוה הוּא:

( ) Now indeed (= זֶה) I know (= יָדַעְתִּי) that you [are a] man of God (1 Kings 17:24)

5 יָדַעְתִּי כִּי אִשָּׁה
    יְפַת־מַרְאֶה אָתְּ:

( ) For everyone in the gate (= every gate) of my people knows that you [are an] excellent woman (woman of worth) (Ruth 3:11)

6 כִּי־כָבְדָה הָעֲבֹדָה
    עַל־הָעָם הַזֶּה:

( ) I know (= יָדַעְתִּי) that the LORD will give (= נָתַן) you (= to you) the land (Jos. 2:9)

7 כִּי עַתָּה יָדַעְתִּי
    כִּי־יְרֵא אֱלֹהִים אָתָּה

( ) For Hiram had always (= all the days) been [a] friend (אֹהֵב = one who loves) of (= לְ) David (1 Kings 5:15)

8 כִּי כֹה אָמַר יהוה
    אֶל־שַׁלֻּם בֶּן־יֹאשִׁיָּהוּ

( ) I know (= יָדַעְתִּי) that you [are a] beautiful (= beautiful in appearance) woman (Gen. 12:11)

9 כִּי אֲנִי יהוה אֹהֵב מִשְׁפָּט

( ) Then Manoah knew that he [was] the angel of the LORD (Judg. 13:21)

10 כִּי־שֹׁפֵט אֲנִי אֶת־בֵּיתוֹ
     עַד־עוֹלָם

( ) For the LORD [is] our judge (Isa. 33:22)

11 כִּי יהוה שֹׁפְטֵנוּ

( ) Because the work was heavy upon this people (Neh. 5:18)

12 כִּי אֹהֵב הָיָה חִירָם
     לְדָוִד כָּל־הַיָּמִים:

( ) For I, the LORD, love (*participle*) justice (Isa. 61:8)

SECTION 19

1 *Infinitives in general*: The infinitive, like the participle, is a *non-finite* verb form.

– There are *two types* of infinitives in Hebrew:

Ordinary infinitive (traditionally called the *infinitive construct*) and in this book it will also be referred to merely as the *infinitive*): The ordinary infinitive corresponds to the English infinitive or gerund, e.g., *'guard/guarding'*. It is usually identical in form with the base form (ms) of the imperative.

Infinitive-as-intensifier (traditionally called the *infinitive absolute*): The main function of the infinitive-as-intensifier is to intensify the meaning of a following (and sometimes a preceding) finite verb. The infinitive-as-intensifier corresponds to English intensifying adverbs and adverbial constructions.

– Like the participle, the infinitive shares the *qualities of both nouns and verbs*. Like the noun the infinitive can be preceded by a preposition and followed by a noun/pronoun. Like the verb the infinitive can take an object.

2 *Infinitives of* פָּעַל שְׁלֵמִים (*unchangeable verbs*)

– The basic form of the *ordinary infinitive* is שְׁמֹר 'guard/ing' (compare שְׁמֹר, imperative ms: 'guard!'). It is often preceded by a preposition and followed by a noun or an attached pronoun, e.g., בִּשְׁמֹר יִשְׂרָאֵל, lit., 'in Israel's guarding', בְּשָׁמְרֵנוּ, lit., 'in our guarding' ('בִּשְׁמֹר + the linking vowel /e/ + the attached pronoun 'נוּ', pronounced bᵊšomrēnû).

– The basic form of the *infinitive-as-intensifier* is שָׁמוֹר. The infinitive-as-intensifier cannot be combined with other elements and words.

3 *Infinitives with deviant form*: The presence of a changeable consonant and/or a guttural in the word root results in regular sound changes.

4 *Usage of the (ordinary) infinitive*

– When the infinitive occurs without any attached element, it functions as an English *infinitive/gerund*, e.g., טוֹב זְכֹר מִשְּׁכֹחַ *'Remembering/[to] remember is better than forgetting/[to] forget'*.

– The construction 'בְּ/כְּ + infinitive + noun/attached pronoun' corresponds to an English *temporal clause*. Since the infinitive has no time reference of its own, the time reference is specified by the context, e.g., בִּשְׁמֹר יִשְׂרָאֵל 'in Israel's guarding' and is usually translated as '*when* Israel [is, was, will be] guarding' or '*when* Israel guards, guarded (etc.)', כְּשָׁמְרֵנוּ 'as our guarding' is rendered by '*while/when* we [are, were, will be] guarding' or '*while/when* we guard, guarded (etc.)'.

– Like the *verb*, the infinitive can take an object: בְּשָׁמְרִי אֶת־הַמָּקוֹם 'When I [am, was, will be] guarding /guard, guarded (etc.) *the place*'.

– The construction 'לְ + infinitive' corresponds to the English construction *'to + infinitive'* or to an English *phrase expressing purpose*: לִשְׁמֹר אֶת־הַמָּקוֹם means *'to keep'* or *'in order to keep'* the place'.

5 *Usage of the infinitive-as-intensifier*: The infinitive-as-intensifier frequently precedes a finite verb (in the perfect, imperfect or imperative) of the same root to *intensify its meaning*: שָׁמֹר שָׁמַר 'He *really/indeed* (and the like) guarded'. For other functions of the so-called infinitive-as-intensifier see Exercise 19.2.

6 *Negation of infinitives*: The infinitive-as-intensifier cannot be negated. The (ordinary) infinitive is negated by בִּלְתִּי/לְבִלְתִּי:

לְבִלְתִּי שְׁמֹר אֶת הַשַּׁבָּת 'not to keep/keeping the sabbath day'.

7 *Quotation marker* לֵאמֹר (לְ + אֱמֹר), lit., 'to say/saying': לֵאמֹר is often used in the Bible to introduce direct speech. לֵאמֹר is rendered in English by '*saying*' which corresponds to 'as follows', but לֵאמֹר may also be left untranslated.

☆ FOUR FORMS OF פָּעַל VIA HEBREW NAMES (13)

Verb form		Vowel pattern: Base form	Hebrew name	English pronunciation	Root type	Meaning: Lexical form
Perfect	Perf-/a/	– – ָ–	נָתַן	Nathan[1]	I-נ (irregular)	give
	Perf-/e/	– – ֵ–	שָׁלֵם	Jerusalem	unchangeable	be/become complete
Imperfect	Imperf-/o/	–ֹ – – יִ	נִמְרֹד	Nimrod	unchangeable	rebel
	Imperf-/o/	–ֹ – ֲ– יַ	יַעֲקֹב	Jacob	I-guttural	grasp by the heel
	Imperf-/a/	– – ְ– יִ	יִצְחָק	Isaac	II-guttural	laugh
Participle	Active part (perf-/a/)	–ֵ –וֹ–	יוֹסֵף	Joseph[1]	I-י/ו	add
	Active part (perf-/a/)	– ָ–	דָּן	Dan	II-י/ו	judge
	Passive part (perf-/a/)	–וּ– ָ–	שָׁאוּל	Saul[1]	II-guttural	request, ask
	Passive part (perf-/e/)	– – ֵ–	שָׁלֵם	Jerusalem	unchangeable	be/become complete
Infinitive	Infinitive-as-intensifier	–וֹ– ָ–	עָמוֹס	Amos[1]	I-guttural	load

---

[1] Although the root type is changeable, the vowel pattern of the name reflects the normal pattern of the relevant verb form. *Remember that sound changes normally occur when there is no vowel before or after the changeable consonant/guttural.*

☆ VERB ROOTS AND PARTICLES VIA HEBREW NAMES (14)

I Each Hebrew name below (names of books in the Hebrew Bible) includes a *verb form. Identify* the root letters of each verb form and *indicate* to which root type it belongs. *Write* the basic meaning of the verb roots you recognize. *Note:*

- As previously mentioned, many Hebrew names constitute a whole clause, often with the divine name as subject, either אֵל (God) or יָה/יָהוּ/יוֹ (elements denoting YHWH, the LORD), e.g., רְפָאֵל Rephael 'God cured', יוֹנָתָן Jonathan 'The LORD gave'.
- In order to find the three root letters of the verb form in a Hebrew name, it is necessary to identify and remove additional elements, such as
  - letters indicating the divine name, e.g., יו in יוֹנָתָן, אל in רְפָאֵל,
  - letters of a prefixed or suffixed pronoun, e.g., י in יִצְחָק, and
  - vowel letters, e.g., ו in שָׁאוּל.
- If after the removal of the additional elements, only two letters are left, the missing root letter in the names given below is י/ו.

---

5 עוֹבַדְיָה	4 עָמוֹס	3 יְחֶזְקֵאל	2 יִרְמְיָהוּ	1 יְשַׁעְיָהוּ
10 נְחֶמְיָה	9 דָּנִיֵּאל	8 זְכַרְיָה	7 צְפַנְיָה	6 נַחוּם

II Each Hebrew name below (names of books in the Hebrew Bible) includes at least one *particle. Identify* the particle/s, *write* them and *translate.*

5 אֵיכָה	4 מִיכָה	3 בַּמִּדְבָּר	2 וַיִּקְרָא	1 בְּרֵאשִׁית

WORD LIST

Nouns

אָרוֹן	*m*, chest, ark (of the covenant): *with def art* הָאָרוֹן	מוּת	die: *perf* מֵת
בָּשָׂר	*m*, flesh, meat	מָשַׁל	rule: *imperf* יִמְשֹׁל, followed by בְּ
דָּם	*m*, blood	עָזַר	help: *imperf* יַעֲזֹר,
זֶבַח	*m*, sacrifice: *pl* זְבָחִים, *with suff* זִבְחִי		followed by לְ (☆ Ezra, ʕ.z.r)
זְרוֹעַ	*f*, arm; strength	פָּקַד	remember; pay attention, take care of; watch over: *imperf* יִפְקֹד
נָהָר	*m*, river: *pl* נְהָרוֹת	קָבַר	bury: *imperf* יִקְבֹּר

Verbs

בָּכָה	weep	שָׁכַח	forget: *imperf* יִשְׁכַּח
בָּרַח	flee: *imperf* יִבְרַח		
יָכֹל	be able/capable		

Particles

בִּלְתִּי/לְבִלְתִּי   not, not to (negates an infinitive)

EXERCISES

19.1 *Fill in* the blanks with the missing data according to the examples given in the table below. *Note*:

> ◆ The (ordinary) infinitive is often identical in form with the ms of the imperative, e.g., שְׁמֹר. Observe, however, the following exceptions:
> – The II-guttural, III-guttural and III-א verbs, compare נְחֹל '[to] inherit/inheriting' and נְחַל 'inherit!', שְׁמֹעַ '[to] listen/listening' and שְׁמַע 'listen!', קְרֹא '[to] read/reading' and קְרָא 'read!'
> – The infinitive of III-י/ו verbs (e.g., בָּנָה 'build') ends in וֹת: בְּנוֹת.
> ◆ The infinitive of II-י/ו verbs, e.g., קוּם 'stand up', שִׂים 'put', בּוֹא 'come', functions as the lexical form.

Infinitive-as-intensifier	Ordinary infinitive	Imperative: Base form, ms	Root type	Meaning: Lexical form	Lexical form	
שָׁפוֹט	שְׁפֹט	שְׁפֹט	unchangeable	judge	שָׁפַט	1
בּוֹא	בּוֹא	בּוֹא	II-י/ו + III- א	come	בּוֹא	2
		אֱמֹר			אָמַר	3
עֲלֹה	עֲלוֹת	עֲלֵה			עָלָה	4
					עָשָׂה	5
		קְרָא			קָרָא	6
		רְאֵה			רָאָה	7
שָׁלוֹחַ	שְׁלֹחַ	שְׁלַח			שָׁלַח	8
					שָׁמַע	9
מוֹת					מוּת	10
					בָּנָה	11
					זָכַר	12
					כָּתַב	13
					מָצָא	14
					עָבַד	15
					שׁוּב	16

19.2 Each verse segment below includes an *infinitive-as-intensifier* (enlarged in the Hebrew text and italicized in the translation). *Read* and *translate* as much as you can on your own. Then *fill in* the blanks with the missing verbs in the following translation and *check* your translation against it. *Note*:

> * The infinitive-as-intensifier usually precedes (but occasionally follows) a verb in the perfect, imperfect or imperative (rarely a participle) of the same root to intensify its meaning: שָׁמַר שָׁמוֹר 'He *really/indeed* (and the like) guarded'.
> * After a finite verb, the so-called infinitive-as-intensifier may express *duration*: שָׁמוֹר יִשְׁמֹר 'He will *continually/all the time* (and the like) guard'.
> * The so-called infinitive-as-intensifier can replace a finite verb, primarily an *imperative*: שָׁמוֹר אֶת־יוֹם הַשַּׁבָּת '*Keep/observe* the sabbath day!'.
> * The 2fs (אַתְּ), 2mp (אַתֶּם) and 3mp (הֵם) of the imperfect are sometimes followed by נ, e.g., תִּשְׁמְרוּן.

1 וֵאלֹהִים פָּקֹד יִפְקֹד אֶתְכֶם But (= וְ) God will *surely* _____ you (Gen. 50:24)

2 הֲמָלֹךְ תִּמְלֹךְ עָלֵינוּ אִם־מָשׁוֹל תִּמְשֹׁל בָּנוּ Are you *indeed* going to _____ over us, or (= אִם) are you *really* going to _____ over (= בְּ) us? (Gen. 37:8)

3 שָׁמוֹר תִּשְׁמְרוּן אֶת־מִצְוֹת יהוה אֱלֹהֵיכֶם You must *diligently* _____ the commandments of the Lᴏʀᴅ, your God (Dt. 6:17)

4 הַכֹּהֲנִים... לִפְנֵי אֲרוֹן יהוה הֹלְכִים הָלוֹךְ The priests... [were] *all the time* _____ before the ark of the Lᴏʀᴅ (Jos. 6:13)

5 אִם־לָמֹד יִלְמְדוּ אֶת־דַּרְכֵי עַמִּי If they will *diligently* _____ the ways of my people (Jer. 12:16)

6 שִׁמְעוּ שָׁמוֹעַ אֵלַי _____ *carefully* to me (Isa. 55:2)

7 שָׁמֹר אֶת־כָּל־הַמִּצְוָה _____ all the commandment (Dt. 27:1)

19.3 Each verse segment below includes an *(ordinary) infinitive* (enlarged in the Hebrew text). *Read* and *translate* as much as you can on your own. Then *match* each verse segment with the correct English translation below and *check/complete* your translation against it. *Remember*:

> - The Hebrew infinitive corresponds to the English *infinitive/gerund*, e.g., שָׁמֹר '[to] guard/guarding'.
> - The construction 'בְּ/כְּ + infinitive + noun/attached pronoun' corresponds to an English *temporal clause*. Since the infinitive has no time reference of its own, its tense is determined by the context: בְּ/כִּשְׁמֹר יִשְׂרָאֵל 'in/as Israel's guarding' corresponds to 'when/while Israel [is, was, will be] guarding/guards, guarded (ect)'.
> - The construction 'לְ + infinitive' corresponds to English '*to + infinitive*' or to an English *phrase expressing a purpose*: לִשְׁמֹר 'to guard' or 'in order to guard'

1 לִשְׁפֹּט אֶת־עַמְּךָ   ( ) When (= כְּ) my lord the king lies (= lying) down with his fathers (1 Kings 1:21)

2 כִּשְׁכַב אֲדֹנִי־הַמֶּלֶךְ עִם־אֲבֹתָיו   ( ) To bury his father (Gen. 50:7)

3 לִזְכֹּר בְּרִית עוֹלָם בֵּין אֱלֹהִים וּבֵין כָּל־נֶפֶשׁ חַיָּה   ( ) To judge your people (1 Kings 3:9)

4 בְּיוֹם עֲשׂוֹת יהוה אֱלֹהִים אֶרֶץ וְשָׁמָיִם: ( ) Not to eat the blood, because the blood [is] the soul (Dt. 12:23)

5 לִרְדֹף אַחֲרֵיהֶם   ( ) [It is the] time to seek the LORD (Hos. 10:12)

6 לִקְבֹּר אֶת־אָבִיו   ( ) To keep the commandments of the LORD, your God (Dt. 4:2)

7 עֵת לִדְרוֹשׁ אֶת־יהוה   ( ) To chase after (= pursue) them (Jos. 8:16)

8 לִשְׁמֹר אֶת־מִצְוֹת יהוה אֱלֹהֵיכֶם   ( ) [It is] not good [for] man (= the man) [to] be alone (Gen. 2:18)

9 לְבִלְתִּי אֲכֹל הַדָּם כִּי הַדָּם הוּא הַנָּפֶשׁ   ( ) In the day [that] the LORD God made (= making) earth and heaven (Gen. 2:4)

10 לֹא־טוֹב הֱיוֹת הָאָדָם לְבַדּוֹ   ( ) To remember [the] everlasting covenant between God and (between) every living creature (= soul) (Gen. 9:16)

19.4 *Match* each grammatical element from Exercise 19.3 above with the Hebrew word/construction that illustrates it. *Mark* the element in the Hebrew word/construction clearly. Observe that the same grammatical element may occur more than once, but only one occurrence is to be marked. Each Hebrew word/construction is to be used once!

1 Definite direct object marker *Left untranslated in English* ( ) כְּשֶׁכַב

2 Infinitive as the first term in a noun chain ( ) בְּרִית

3 Feminine noun *Ends in* ת ( ) עֲשׂוֹת

4 Pausal form *With a long instead of a short vowel* ( ) אָרֶץ

5 Penultimate noun *The last syllable is closed and has a short vowel* ( ) וְשָׁמַיִם

6 Particle/s negating an infinitive ( ) כִּי

7 Twin-consonant noun *With identical second and third root consonants* ( ) לְבִלְתִּי אֲכָל

8 Insertion vowel used to dissolve a three-consonant cluster at the beginning of a syllable *Normally an /i/-vowel* ( ) הֱיוֹת הָאָדָם

9 Infinitive of a III-י/ו (III-ה) verb *The first two root consonants are followed by* וֹת ( ) עִמָּךְ

10 Particle introducing a causal clause *'Because, since'* ( ) אֶת־אָבִיו

19.5 *Attach* the correct suffixed pronouns to the *infinitives* according to the example given below. *Vocalize*, *mark* the stress, *read* and *translate*. *Note*:

> ◆ The infinitive takes the "singular" set of the attached possessive pronouns. The stress falls on the next-to-last syllable only in the 1cp (we), e.g., שָׁמְרֵנוּ šomrēnû, 'our guarding'.
> ◆ The suffixed pronoun is attached to the form שָׁמְר– – ־ ־ ־, e.g., šomr– (with a qamets-/o/): שָׁמְרֵנוּ šomrēnû.
> ◆ The infinitive of III-י/ו verbs (e.g., בְּנוֹת) and II-י/ו verbs (e.g., קוּם) undergoes no vowel change before the attached pronoun, e.g., 'בְּנוֹת + י ָ' results in בְּנוֹתִי 'my building' and 'קוּם + י ָ' results in קוּמִי 'my standing up'.

Translation	Infinitive-plus-pronoun	
our guarding	שָׁמְרֵנוּ	1 שָׁמֹר (אֲנַחְנוּ)
_____	_____	2 שָׁפֹט (אֲנִי)
_____	_____	3 עֲזֹר (אַתָּה)
_____	_____	4 זְכֹר (אַתְּ)
_____	_____	5 אֲכֹל (הוּא)

‏_____‏	‏_____‏	6 ‏כְּתֹב (הִיא)‏
‏_____‏	‏_____‏	7 ‏בְּנוֹת (אַתֶּם)‏
‏_____‏	‏_____‏	8 ‏קְרֹא (הִיא)‏
‏_____‏	‏_____‏	9 ‏שְׁמֹעַ (הֵם)‏
‏_____‏	‏_____‏	10 ‏קוּם (הֵנָּה)‏
‏_____‏	‏_____‏	11 ‏מוּת (אַתָּה)‏
‏_____‏	‏_____‏	12 ‏שְׁכֹחַ (הוּא)‏
‏_____‏	‏_____‏	13 ‏עֲשׂוֹת (אֲנַחְנוּ)‏
‏_____‏	‏_____‏	14 ‏בּוֹא (אַתֶּם)‏

19.6 Each verse/verse segment below includes an *infinitive preceded by a preposition and followed by an attached pronoun* (enlarged in the Hebrew text). *Read* and *translate* on your own. Then *fill in* the blanks with the missing words in the following translation and *check* your translation against it. *Note*:

> * Since the infinitive has no time reference of its own, its tense is specified by the context. Like the verb, the infinitive in Hebrew can take an object.
> * The attached pronoun in the construction '‏בְּ/כְּ‏ + infinitive + attached pronoun' usually functions as *subject*, e.g., ‏בְּ/כְּשָׁמְרוֹ‏ 'when/while *he* [is, was, will be] guarding' (lit., 'in/as his guarding'), whereas in the construction '‏לְ‏ + infinitive + attached pronoun' the attached pronoun functions as *object*: ‏לְשָׁמְרוֹ‏ 'to/in order to guard *him*'.

---

1 ‏בִּכְתֹב אֶת־הַדְּבָרִים הָאֵלֶּה עַל־סֵפֶר מִפִּי יִרְמְיָהוּ‏ When _____ wrote (= *in* _____ *writing*) _____ words in (= ‏עַל‏) [a] book from the mouth of Jeremiah (Jer. 45:1)

2 ‏עִמּוֹ זְרוֹעַ בָּשָׂר וְעִמָּנוּ יהוה אֱלֹהֵינוּ לְעָזְרֵנוּ‏ With _____ [is an] arm of flesh, but (= ‏וְ‏) with _____ [is] the LORD, _____ God, to help _____ (2 Chron. 32:8)

3 ‏בְּיוֹם אֲכָלְךָ מִמֶּנּוּ‏ In the day _____ eat (= *in the day of* _____ *eating*) from _____ (Gen. 2:17)

4 ‏בְּבָרְחוֹ מִפְּנֵי אַבְשָׁלוֹם בְּנוֹ:‏ When _____ fled (= *in* _____ *fleeing*) from (the face of) _____ son, Absalom (Ps. 3:1)

5 ‏עַד שׁוּבִי בְשָׁלוֹם:‏ Until _____ return (= *until* _____ *returning*) in peace (2 Chron. 18:26)

6 (‏עַל‏ =) By ‏עַל נַהֲרוֹת בָּבֶל שָׁם יָשַׁבְנוּ גַּם־בָּכִינוּ בְּזָכְרֵנוּ אֶת־צִיּוֹן:‏ the rivers of Babylon – there _____ sat, _____ also wept, when _____ remembered (= *in* _____ *remembering*) Zion (Ps. 137:1)

7 ‏לִשְׁמָרְךָ בְּכָל־דְּרָכֶיךָ:‏ To guard _____ in _____ _____ ways (Ps. 91:11)

8 ‏בְּכָל־הַדֶּרֶךְ אֲשֶׁר הֲלַכְתֶּם עַד־בֹּאֲכֶם עַד־הַמָּקוֹם הַזֶּה:‏ In _____ the way _____ _____ walked until _____ came (= *until* _____ *coming*) to _____ place (Dt. 1:31)

9 ‏עַל־רָדְפוֹ בַחֶרֶב אָחִיו‏ Because (= ‏עַל‏) _____ pursued (= *on* _____ *pursuing*) _____ brother with the sword (Am. 1:11)

19.7 *Transform* the infinitives in entries 1, 3, 4, 5, 7, 9 in Exercise 19.6 above from the singular into the plural and the infinitives in entries 2, 6, 8 from the plural into the singular.

19.8 *Translate* into English. Proper names are enlarged.

1 ‏לִשְׁמֹר אֶת־דֶּרֶךְ עֵץ הַחַיִּים:‏ (Gen. 3:24)

2 ‏בִּהְיוֹת יְהוֹשֻׁעַ בִּירִיחוֹ‏ (Jos. 5:13)

3 ‏לִכְתֹּב אֶת־דִּבְרֵי הַתּוֹרָה־הַזֹּאת עַל־סֵפֶר‏ (Dt. 31:24)

4 ‏בשמעו (כִּשְׁמֹעַ) אֶת־הַדְּבָרִים הָאֵלֶּה‏ (1 Sam. 11:6)

5 ‏יהוה יִשְׁמַע בְּקָרְאִי אֵלָיו:‏ (Ps. 4:4)

6 ‏בְּשָׁכְבְּךָ תִּשְׁמֹר עָלֶיךָ‏ (Prov. 6:22)

7 ‏לְבִלְתִּי שְׁמֹר מִצְוֹתָיו וּמִשְׁפָּטָיו‏ (Dt. 8:11)

8 ‏אִם־שָׁכֹחַ תִּשְׁכַּח אֶת־יהוה אֱלֹהֶיךָ‏ (Dt. 8:19)

9 ‏זָכוֹר אֶת־הַיּוֹם הַזֶּה אֲשֶׁר יְצָאתֶם מִמִּצְרַיִם מִבֵּית עֲבָדִים‏ (Ex. 13:3)

10 ‏הָלוֹךְ... אֶל־דָּוִד כֹּה אָמַר יהוה‏ (2 Sam. 24:12)

11 וְאִם רַע בְּעֵינֵיכֶם לַעֲבֹד אֶת־יהוה בַּחֲרוּ לָכֶם הַיּוֹם אֶת־מִי תַעֲבֹדוּן

אִם אֶת־אֱלֹהִים אֲשֶׁר־עָבְדוּ אֲבוֹתֵיכֶם... וְאִם אֶת־אֱלֹהֵי הָאֱמֹרִי אֲשֶׁר

אַתֶּם יֹשְׁבִים בְּאַרְצָם וְאָנֹכִי וּבֵיתִי נַעֲבֹד אֶת־יהוה: (Jos. 24:15)

12 אַתָּה יָדַעְתָּ אֶת־דָּוִד אָבִי כִּי לֹא יָכֹל לִבְנוֹת בַּיִת לְשֵׁם יהוה אֱלֹהָיו

(1 Kings 5:17)

13 וּכְשָׁמְעוֹ אֶת־דִּבְרֵי רִבְקָה אֲחֹתוֹ לֵאמֹר (Gen. 24:30)

14 הִנֵּה אַתָּה זָקַנְתָּ וּבָנֶיךָ לֹא הָלְכוּ בִּדְרָכֶיךָ

עַתָּה שִׂימָה־לָּנוּ מֶלֶךְ לְשָׁפְטֵנוּ כְּכָל־הַגּוֹיִם: (1 Sam 8:5)

19.9 *Read aloud* Ecc. 1:4, 7; 3:2, 3, 6, 8 in Text **III.2** in the **FOUR STYLES OF BIBLICAL PROSE: TEXT SAMPLES** (after Section 28) and then:
a) *List* all the participles in Ecc. 1:4, 7 and *translate* them. *Indicate* the root type to which each participle belongs.
b) *List* only the infinitives that you can identify in Ecc. 3:2, 3, 6, 8 and *translate* them. *Indicate* the root type to which each infinitive belongs and the corresponding participle/s, e.g., the participles which correspond to שְׁמֹר are שֹׁמֵר and שָׁמוּר.

19.10 *Translate* into Hebrew.

1 When I was writing (= in my writing) a book about (= עַל) the prophets, my servant was not in the house.
2 Your father will help (+ לְ) you, when you (*m, s*) keep (= in your keeping) the commandments of the LORD.
3 When she sent (= in her sending) her husband to (= אֶל) the priest, the priest was standing (= stood) at the entrance of the temple.
4 As soon as you (*f, s*) came (= as your coming), the woman gave (+ לְ) you bread.
5 When he made (= in his making) the gate, his father was not in the city.
6 I came to help (+ לְ) my people (= nation).
7 You (*m, s*) went out of the country to find a wife for your son.

19.11 *Check* (and *correct* if needed) your translation of Exercise 19.10 above. Then *transform* the Hebrew clauses (verbs as well as nouns and pronouns) from the singular into the plural.

SECTION 20

1   *Verb chains with* וְ/וַ: Two verbs or more in succession linked together by וְ/וַ form a *verb chain*. The most frequent types of verb chains in the Hebrew Bible are as follows:

– '*Verb in the perfect* + וַ + *verb/s in the shortened imperfect*', e.g., קָרָא וַיִּכְתֹּב 'He read and *wrote*'. The tense of וַיִּכְתֹּב, the second verb in the chain, is changed from non-past into past time.

Remember that the shortened imperfect of unchangeable root types (שְׁלֵמִים) as well as of many changeable root types is identical in form with the ordinary imperfect.

– '*Verb in the imperfect/imperative (occasionally a participle)* + וְ + *verb/s in the perfect*', e.g., יִקְרָא וְכָתַב 'He *will* read and *write*'. The tense of וְכָתַב, the second verb in the chain, is changed from past into *future time*.

2   *Inverting-Vav* (traditionally called the *Vav/Waw-consecutive/conversive*)

– The inverting וַ before a verb in the imperfect (shortened!) signals *past time*. It is vocalized like the definite article הַ, that is, with an /a/-vowel followed by a doubling dagesh in the next consonant, e.g., וַיִּכְתֹּב.

– The inverting וְ before a verb in the perfect (after a verb in the imperfect/imperative) signals *future time*. It is vocalized like the conjunction וְ, e.g., וְכָתַב.

– *Shift in stress after the inverting-Vav*: After the inverting-Vav, the word stress in certain verb forms is moved either forwards or backwards.

After the inverting וְ the stress in the 1cs (אֲנִי) and 2ms (אַתָּה) forms of the perfect is thrown forwards to the last syllable, that is, to the attached pronoun, e.g., וְכָתַבְתָּ, וְכָתַבְתִּי (though no vowel change occurs).

After the inverting וַ the stress in certain imperfect forms is thrown backwards (for specification, see Section 25).

3   *Usage of verb chains*

– Verb chains with the *inverted imperfect* are used in the Bible primarily to describe *past events in chronological or logical order*. Thus, the inverting וַ is not always rendered in English translation by 'and' but also by adverbs indicating either time sequence, such as 'then, afterwards, now' (and the like), or logical sequence, such as 'thus, so, hence' (and the like), as required by the context. The inverting וַ may also be left untranslated.

– Verb chains with the *inverted perfect* are used in the Bible mainly in *direct speech*. The inverting וְ is often rendered by 'and' or is left untranslated. Sometimes, however, the inverting וְ is rendered by other conjunctions, such as 'in order that' or 'so that'.

4   *Expression of purpose and result*: Purpose and result phrases/clauses are identical in form, hence the precise meaning (whether a purpose or a result) is determined by the context. The most frequent constructions are as follows:

– 'לְ + infinitive': יָשַׁב לִקְרֹא 'He sat down *to read* (= *in order that, i.e., with the goal that/so that he may read*').

– '(אֲשֶׁר/כִּי) + לְמַעַן/בַּעֲבוּר + verb in the imperfect', e.g.,
יָשַׁב לְמַעַן/בַּעֲבוּר (אֲשֶׁר/כִּי) יִקְרָא 'He sat down *in order that/so that he may read*'.

– 'אֲשֶׁר + verb in the imperfect', e.g., יָשַׁב אֲשֶׁר יִקְרָא 'He sat down *in order that/so that* he may read'.

– *Negation of clauses of purpose/result*: Clauses of purpose/result are negated either by לְמַעַן/בַּעֲבוּר לֹא or פֶּן־, e.g., לְמַעַן לֹא/פֶּן־יִקְרָא '*lest/in order that/so that* he may *not* read'.

5   **פָּעַל** *perfect with attached object pronouns*: Apart from the independent object pronouns (אֹתִי, אֹתְךָ etc.), the verb can take a set of attached object pronouns. The attached object pronouns are identical in form with the possessive pronouns, except the 1cs (אֲנִי). Compare זְכָרַנִי 'he remembered *me*' and דְּבָרִי '*my* word'. There is no difference in meaning between the independent object pronouns and the attached object pronouns. Both זְכָרַנִי and זָכַר אֹתִי mean 'he remembered *me*'.

– *Sound changes*: When the object pronoun is attached to a verb form, the stress is thrown forwards either to the linking vowel or to the attached pronoun. The shift in stress usually results in regular sound changes.

MEMORIZE

Observe that the model verb קטל 'kill' is normally used in grammatical charts.

VERB TYPES I (unchangeable root types, i.e., *strong* שְׁלֵמִים)		פָּעַל (Qal, G-stem)
Finite	Perfect	קָטַל/קָטֵל/קָטֹל
	Imperfect	יִקְטֹל/יִקְטַל
	Imperative	קְטֹל/קְטַל
Non-finite	Infinitive (ordinary)	קְטֹל
	Infinitive-as-intensifier	קָטוֹל
	Participle: Active	קֹטֵל/קוֹטֵל
	Participle: Passive	קָטוּל/קָטֵל/קָטֹל
GRAMMATICAL CORNERSTONE 14 ר א שׁ פָּ נָ ה		

WORD LIST

Nouns   *Verbs*

אַהֲבָה   *f,* loving, love   חָטָא   sin: *imperf* יֶחֱטָא/יֶחֱטָא

אוֹת   *f,* sign, omen   יָלַד   bear (child), give birth

אֵשׁ   *f,* fire   עָזַב   leave, abandon:

דּוֹר   *m,* generation: *pl* דּוֹרוֹת   *imperf* יַעֲזֹב

זֵכֶר   *m,* mention (of a name):   שָׂנֵא   hate: *imperf* יִשְׂנָא

          med suff זִכְרִי (☆ Zechariah)   שָׂרַף   burn: *imperf* יִשְׂרֹף

חַיָּה   *f,* living thing, beast, animal

חֻקָּה, חקק   *f,* statute   *Particles*

מִדְבָּר, דבר   *m,* wilderness; desert   בַּעֲבוּר (בְּ + עָבוּר)   in order that/so

מוֹלֶדֶת, ילד   *f,* birth   that; for the sake of

עֵדָה   *f,* congregation, assembly   לְמַעַן (לְ + מַעַן)   in order that/so

שִׂנְאָה, שׂנא   *f,* hatred   that; for the sake of

שַׁבָּת   *f,* day of rest, Sabbath   פֶּן   lest, in order not/so that not

EXERCISES

20.1 *Insert* the missing vowel under each inverting-Vav in the table below. *Add* the doubling dagesh in the following consonant wherever necessary. *Study* the sound change rules listed below. *Indicate* (from the list below) the relevant sound change occurring in each deviant form of the inverting-Vav. *Read* the verb forms and *translate. Remember*:

> - The inverting ◌ַו signals *past time* and the inverting וֹ signals *future time.*
> - The vocalization of the inverting ◌ַו is similar to the vocalization of the definite article, e.g., וַיִּקְרָא (☆ Leviticus, lit., 'he called'). The inverting וֹ is vocalized like the conjunction וְ, e.g., וְכָתַב.
> - The tense of the inverted verb forms in a verb chain corresponds to the tense of the first verb in the chain.

SOUND CHANGE RULES

1 Gutturals and ר cannot be doubled. Instead, the preceding short vowel is often lengthened, e.g., וָאֶכְתֹּב (not וַאֶכְתֹּב).

2 Two vowelless consonants in a row at the beginning of a syllable result in an impermissible three-consonant sequence, e.g., וְכְתַבְתֶּם. The consonant cluster is broken up by changing the וְ to וּ: וְכְתַבְתֶּם becomes וּכְתַבְתֶּם.

3 The insertion vowel used to break up a three-consonant sequence before a guttural with a chateph matches the vowel of the chateph, e.g., וְעֲמַדְתֶּם becomes וַעֲמַדְתֶּם.

4 Before the consonants פ, מ, ב (called *labials*) וְ is changed to וּ, e.g., וּבָחַר (not וְבָחַר).

Translation (perf = inverted imperf; imperf = inverted perf)	Sound change rule (relevant to the deviant form of the inverting-Vav)	Inverted perfect/ imperfect	Perfect/ imperfect	
		וָאֶקְרָא	קָרָ֫אתִי	1
		וּקְרָאתֶם	תִּקְרְאוּ	2
		וַעֲבַדְתֶּם	תַּעַבְדוּ	3
		וּמָלַךְ	יִמְלֹךְ	4
		וְשָׁכַבְתָּ/וּשְׁכִבָה	תִּשְׁכַּב	5
		וַיִּכְתֹּב	כָּתַב	6
		וַתִּכְתֹּב	כָּתַ֫בְתָּ	7
		וַיִּכְרְתוּ	כָּרְתוּ	8
		וַיִּשְׁכֹּן	שָׁכַן	9
		וְעָמַדְתִּי	אֶעֱמֹד	10
		וַיַּעַבְרוּ	עָבְרוּ	11
		וּשְׁמַעְנוּ	נִשְׁמַע	12
		וְתִזְכְּרִי	זָכַרְתְּ	13
		וַתִּשְׁמְרוּ	שְׁמַרְתֶּם	14
		וּשְׁמַעְתֶּן	תִּשְׁמַ֫עְנָה	15
		וָאֶזְכֹּר	זָכַ֫רְתִּי	16
		וַיִּשְׁמֹר	שָׁמַר	17
		וּשְׂרַפְנוּ	נִשְׂרֹף	18

20.2 Each verse segment below includes an *inverted verb form. Read* and *translate*. Then *transform* the verb forms in the inverted imperfect into the perfect and the verb forms in the inverted perfect into the imperfect. Proper names are enlarged.

———	1 וַיִּקְרָא יהוה אֱלֹהִים אֶל־הָאָדָם (Gen. 3:9)
———	2 וּמָלַךְ יהוה עֲלֵיהֶם בְּהַר צִיּוֹן מֵעַתָּה וְעַד־עוֹלָם: (Mic. 4:7)
———	3 וַעֲבַדְתֶּם אֹתָנוּ: (1 Sam. 17:9)
———	4 וַיִּכְתֹּב בְּשֵׁם הַמֶּלֶךְ (Esther 8:10)
———	5 וַיִּכְתֹּב בַּסֵּפֶר (1 Sam. 10:25)
———	6 וַיִּכְרְתוּ בְרִית בִּבְאֵר שָׁבַע (Gen. 21:32)
———	7 וָאֶזְכֹּר אֶת־בְּרִיתִי: (Ex. 6:5)
———	8 וַיִּשְׂרְפוּ אוֹתָהּ וְאֶת־אָבִיהָ בָּאֵשׁ: (Judg. 15:6)
———	9 וַיִּשְׁכַּב דָּוִד עִם־אֲבֹתָיו (1 Kings 2:10)
———	10 וַיִּשְׁמֹר מִצְוֹתָיו (2 Kings 18:6)
———	11 וַיִּשְׁכֹּן כְּבוֹד־יהוה עַל־הַר סִינַי (Ex. 24:16)
———	12 וַיִּשְׂרֹף אֶת־בֵּית־יהוה וְאֶת־בֵּית הַמֶּלֶךְ וְאֵת כָּל־בָּתֵּי יְרוּשָׁלַ͏ִם (2 Kings 25:9)
———	13 וַיִּזְכֹּר אֱלֹהִים אֶת־נֹחַ (Gen. 8:1)

20.3 Each verse segment below includes either a positive or a negative *phrase/clause of purpose or result* (the particle/s introducing the phrase/clause of purpose/result are enlarged in the Hebrew text and italicized in the translation). *Read* the phrases/clauses and *translate* on your own. Then *fill in* the blanks with the missing words in the following translation and *check* your translation against it. *Note*:

> ◆ Since a phrase/clause of purpose/result expresses an *uncertain event/action* (that is, it does not express a fact but an intention, wish, hope etc.), the verb is in the imperfect. The imperfect form is rendered in English translation by 'may/might + infinitive'.

1 **פֶּן־**יִשְׁלַח יָדוֹ וְלָקַח גַּם מֵעֵץ הַחַיִּים וְאָכַל *In order that* _____ may *not* stretch out _____ hand and take also from the tree of life and eat (Gen. 3:22)

2 **לְמַעַן** לֹא אֶחֱטָא־לָךְ: *In order that* _____ may *not* sin against (= לְ) _____ (Ps. 119:11)

3 **לְמַעַן** אֶלְמַד חֻקֶּיךָ: *In order that* _____ may learn _____ laws (Ps. 119:71)

פֶּן־תִּשְׁכַּח אֶת־יהוה אֱלֹהֶיךָ לְבִלְתִּי שְׁמֹר מִצְוֹתָיו וּמִשְׁפָּטָיו וְחֻקֹּתָיו 4

Lest _____ forget the LORD, _____ God, [by] not keeping _____

commandments and _____ ordinances and _____ statutes (Dt. 8:11)

לְמַעַן יִשְׁמְעוּ כָּל־עֲדַת בְּנֵי יִשְׂרָאֵל: 5 *So that* the _____ congregation

of the Israelites may listen (Num. 27:20)

בַּעֲבוּר יְהוֹנָתָן אָבִיךָ 6 *For the sake of* Jonathan, _____ father

(2 Sam. 9:7)

20.4 *Write* the corresponding independent form of each attached object pronoun
below. *Read* the constructions and *translate*. *Note*:

> - When a verb is followed by two attached pronouns, the *last
>   attached pronoun* is the *object* of the clause and the *next-to-last
>   pronoun* is the *subject*.
> - The linking vowel between a verb form in the perfect and the
>   attached pronoun is /a/, e.g., זְכָרַנִי 'he remembered me'.
> - The attached object pronouns are identical in form with the
>   possessive pronouns, except the 1cs (אֲנִי). Compare זְכָרַנִי and
>   דְּבָרִי 'my word'.
> - Before the attached pronoun of the 3fs (הִיא), the verb form in
>   the perfect is שָׁמַרת– (not שָׁמְרָה): שָׁמַרת + 'נִי' results in
>   שְׁמָרַתְנִי 'she guarded me'.

Translation	Independent object pronoun	Verb	
he appointed me	אֹתִי	שָׂם	שָׂמַנִי 1
_____	_____	יָדַעְתִּי	יְדַעְתִּיךָ 2
_____	_____	יָלְדָה	יְלָדַתְנִי 3
_____	_____	שָׁלַח	שְׁלָחֲךָ 4
_____	_____	לָקַח	לְקָחַנִי 5
_____	_____	מָשַׁחְתִּי	מְשַׁחְתִּיךָ 6
_____	_____	אָכְלָה	אֲכָלַתְהוּ 7
_____	_____	עָזְבוּ	עֲזָבוּנִי 8
_____	_____	שָׁלַחְתִּי	שְׁלַחְתִּיךָ 9
_____	_____	עָזְבְתְּ	עֲזַבְתְּנִי 10
_____	_____	שָׂנֵא	שְׂנֵאָה 11

_____	_____	אָהַב (אָהַב)	12 אַהֲבָה
_____	_____	בָּחַרְתִּי	13 בְּחַרְתִּיךָ
_____	_____	שָׁלַחְתִּי	14 שְׁלַחְתִּיו
_____	_____	שָׁלַחְתִּי	15 שְׁלַחְתִּים
_____	_____	אָהַבְתָּ	16 אֲהַבְתָּנוּ
_____	_____	שָׁלַח	17 שְׁלָחַנִי

20.5 Each verse/verse segment below contains a *verb in the perfect followed by an attached object pronoun. Read* and *translate.* Then *fill in* the blanks with the missing words in the following translation and *check* your translation against it.

1 כֹּה אָמַר בִּנְךָ יוֹסֵף שָׂמַנִי אֱלֹהִים לְאָדוֹן לְכָל־מִצְרָיִם Thus said _____ son Joseph, 'God has appointed (= שָׂם לְ) _____ lord for _____ Egypt' (Gen. 45:9)

2 אֲנִי יְדַעְתִּיךָ בַּמִּדְבָּר It was _____ who (= _____ – _____) knew _____ in the wilderness (Hos. 13:5)

3 שְׁמַע־נָא חֲנַנְיָה לֹא־שְׁלָחֲךָ יהוה Listen, please, Hananiah, the Lord has not sent _____ (Jer. 28:15)

4 יהוה אֱלֹהֵי הַשָּׁמַיִם אֲשֶׁר לְקָחַנִי מִבֵּית אָבִי וּמֵאֶרֶץ מוֹלַדְתִּי The Lord, the God of the heavens, _____ took _____ from _____ father's house and from the land of _____ birth (Gen. 24:7)

5 כֹּה־אָמַר יהוה אֱלֹהֵי יִשְׂרָאֵל אָנֹכִי מְשַׁחְתִּיךָ לְמֶלֶךְ עַל־יִשְׂרָאֵל Thus says (= אָמַר) the Lord, the God of Israel, '_____ _____ anointed _____ (+ לְ) king over Israel' (2 Sam. 12:7)

6 חַיָּה רָעָה אֲכָלָתְהוּ [A] vicious beast devoured _____ (Gen. 37:20)

7 וְזֶה־לְּךָ הָאוֹת כִּי אָנֹכִי שְׁלַחְתִּיךָ And _____ [shall be] the sign for _____ that it was _____ who (= _____ – _____) sent _____ (Ex. 3:12)

8 כִּי גְדוֹלָה הַשִּׂנְאָה אֲשֶׁר שְׂנֵאָהּ מֵאַהֲבָה אֲשֶׁר אֲהֵבָהּ Indeed, the hatred [with] which _____ hated _____ [was] great[er] than [the] love [with] which _____ had loved _____ (2 Sam. 13:15)

9 וְאַתָּה יִשְׂרָאֵל עַבְדִּי יַעֲקֹב אֲשֶׁר בְּחַרְתִּיךָ זֶרַע אַבְרָהָם אֹהֲבִי׃ But

(= וְ) _____, Israel, [are] _____ servant, [you] Jacob, whom _____ have

chosen (+ _____, this pronoun is redundant in English translation), the

offspring (= seed) of Abraham, _____ friend (= [the one] loving _____)

(Isa. 41:8)

10 אֲנִי לֹא שְׁלַחְתִּיו It was not _____ who (= _____ – _____) sent _____

(Jer. 29:31)

11 אֲנִי לֹא־שְׁלַחְתִּים It was not _____ who (= _____ – _____) sent

_____ (Jer. 14:15)

12 אָהַבְתִּי אֶתְכֶם אָמַר יהוה וַאֲמַרְתֶּם בַּמָּה אֲהַבְתָּנוּ '_____ have loved

_____', said the Lord, and _____ said, 'In what [way] _____ loved

_____ ?' (Mal. 1:2)

13 יהוה אֱלֹהֵי הָעִבְרִים שְׁלָחַנִי אֵלֶיךָ The Lord, the God of the Hebrews,

sent _____ to _____ (Ex. 7:16)

20.6 *Translate* into English. Proper names are enlarged.

1 אֵלִי אֵלִי לָמָה עֲזַבְתָּנִי (Ps. 22:2)

2 הִנֵּה אָנֹכִי בָא אֶל־בְּנֵי יִשְׂרָאֵל וְאָמַרְתִּי לָהֶם אֱלֹהֵי אֲבוֹתֵיכֶם
שְׁלָחַנִי אֲלֵיכֶם וְאָמְרוּ־לִי מַה־שְּׁמוֹ (Ex. 3:13)

3 יהוה אֱלֹהֵי אֲבֹתֵיכֶם אֱלֹהֵי אַבְרָהָם אֱלֹהֵי יִצְחָק וֵאלֹהֵי יַעֲקֹב
שְׁלָחַנִי אֲלֵיכֶם זֶה־שְּׁמִי לְעֹלָם... (Ex. 3:15)

4 פָּקֹד פָּקַדְתִּי אֶתְכֶם וְאֶת־הֶעָשׂוּי לָכֶם בְּמִצְרָיִם׃ (Ex. 3:16)

5 וְשָׁמְרוּ בְנֵי־יִשְׂרָאֵל אֶת־הַשַּׁבָּת לַעֲשׂוֹת אֶת־הַשַּׁבָּת לְדֹרֹתָם
בְּרִית עוֹלָם׃ (Ex. 31:16)

6 אֶפְתַּח אֶת־פִּיךָ וְאָמַרְתָּ אֲלֵיהֶם כֹּה אָמַר אֲדֹנָי יֱהֹוִה
(= אֱלֹהִים special reading הַשֹּׁמֵעַ יִשְׁמָע) (Ezek. 3:27)

7 כִּי כָל־הָעֵדָה כֻּלָּם קְדֹשִׁים (Num. 16:3)

8 וַיִּשְׁמְעוּ אֵלָיו בְּנֵי־יִשְׂרָאֵל... וְלֹא־קָם נָבִיא עוֹד בְּיִשְׂרָאֵל כְּמֹשֶׁה
אֲשֶׁר יְדָעוֹ יהוה פָּנִים אֶל־פָּנִים: לְכָל־הָאֹתוֹת... אֲשֶׁר שְׁלָחוֹ יהוה
לַעֲשׂוֹת בְּאֶרֶץ מִצְרַיִם לְפַרְעֹה וּלְכָל־עֲבָדָיו וּלְכָל־אַרְצוֹ:

(Dt. 34:9–11)

9 פֶּן־נִשְׂרֹף אוֹתָךְ וְאֶת־בֵּית אָבִיךְ בָּאֵשׁ (Judg. 14:15)

20.7 *Match* each grammatical element (from Exercise 20.6 above) with the
Hebrew word/construction that illustrates it. *Mark* the element in the Hebrew
word/construction clearly. Observe that the same grammatical element
may appear more than once, but only one occurrence is to be marked.
Each Hebrew word/construction is to be used once!

1 Definite direct object marker *Left untranslated in English*   (_) עֲזַבְתָּנִי
2 Infinitive-as-intensifier *Followed by a finite verb*   (_) אָנֹכִי בָא
3 Particle introducing a relative clause *Rendered in English*   (_) שְׁלָחַנִי
   by 'which, that, who' etc.
4 Pausal form *The stressed syllable has a long instead*   (_) אֲבֹתֵיכֶם
   of a short vowel
5 Penultimate noun followed by an attached pronoun   (_) זֶה־שְּׁמִי
   The original form is retained before the attached pronoun
6 Passive participle of a III- י/ו (III-ה) verb   (_) פָּקוֹד פָּקַדְתִּי
7 Linking vowel *Joins a verb to an attached pronoun*   (_) הֶעָשׂוּי
8 Defective writing *The vowel letter ו is unexpectedly omitted*   (_) לַעֲשׂוֹת
9 Infinitive of a III-י/ו (III-ה) verb *The first two root*   (_) אֲשֶׁר יְדָעוֹ
   consonants are followed by וֹת
10 Particle introducing a causal clause *Denotes a reason*   (_) אֶתְכֶם
11 Omitted hardening dagesh *Preceding word ends in a vowel*   (_) כִּי
12 Linking doubling dagesh *Joins two words into a single*   (_) אַרְצוֹ
   sound unit

20.8 *Read aloud* Gen. 16:15–16, 17:1–10 in Text **I.2** in the **FOUR STYLES OF
BIBLICAL PROSE: TEXT SAMPLES** (after Section 28). *Mark* all the forms
of the particle וְ (וַ ,וֶ ,וְ ,וָ ,וֹ ,וּ), inclusive the inverting-Vav, in the above
mentioned verses and *count* them. *Note*:

♦ The particle וְ is the most frequent particle in the Hebrew Bible. וְ
  has many functions in Hebrew, hence וְ can be rendered in English
  translation by 'and, but, or, then, afterwards, now, while, when,
  because, in order that, so that, though' etc., as required by the
  context. וְ can also be left untranslated.

20.9 *Read aloud* Gen. 22:3–11 (including verse 11!) in Text **I.3** in the **FOUR STYLES OF BIBLICAL PROSE: TEXT SAMPLES**. *List* all the inverted imperfect forms and *count* them. *Note*:

> ♦ The inverted imperfect (that is, the shortened imperfect preceded by ·1) is the most frequent verb form in the Hebrew Bible.
> ♦ The inverting ·1 is vocalized like the definite article, e.g., וַיִּכְתֹּב. Before the guttural א the vowel is /ā/ instead of /a/, e.g., וָאֶכְתֹּב.
> ♦ A doubled ׳ with a shva (preceded by 1) generally loses its doubling (shown in writing by the absence of the doubling dagesh), e.g., וַיְּדַבֵּר becomes וַיְדַבֵּר (compare הַיְשׁוּעָה that becomes הַיְשׁוּעָה).

20.10 *Translate* into Hebrew. *Remember*:

> ♦ A verb chain beginning with a verb in the perfect should be continued by verb/s in the inverted imperfect. The words corresponding to the inverting ·1 such as 'and, then, now, thus' etc., are italicized in the exercise below.
> ♦ No element can be inserted between the inverting-Vav and the following verb form.

1 The prophet went to the people (= nation) *and* read to them (= in their ears) the law of the LORD. *Then* the prophet stood up (עָמַד), chose a king for the people *and* anointed him. *Now* the king obeyed the LORD (= listened in voice of the LORD), his God, *and* remembered all his commandments all the days of his life. *Thus* he reigned a long time (= many days).

2 The judge wrote all the laws and the commandments of the LORD (= all the laws of the LORD and his commandments). *As a result*, the people served the LORD *and* kept his commandments.

3 The messenger/angel found the woman in the field *and* asked her who gave her (= to her) bread.

20.11 *Check* (and *correct* if needed) your translation of Exercise 20.10 above. Then *transform* the Hebrew clauses (verbs as well as nouns and pronouns) from the singular into the plural.

SECTION 21

1 נִפְעַל (the *N-stem*): *Basic forms (unchangeable verbs,* שְׁלֵמִים)

Perfect	Imperfect	Imperative	Infinitive (ordinary)	Infinitive (as-intensifier)	Participle
נִשְׁמַר ←	יִשָּׁמֵר	הִשָּׁמֵר	הִשָּׁמֹר	הִשָּׁמֹר/נִשְׁמֹר	נִשְׁמָר

– The basic pattern (שְׁלֵמִים) of נִפְעַל perfect is נִ‍ ַ‍ ־‍ ־. The characteristic feature of נִפְעַל is the consonant נ of the prefix, which is either apparent, e.g., נִשְׁמַר, or assimilated to the following consonant (shown in writing by the doubling dagesh), e.g., יִשָּׁמֵר (instead of יִנְשָׁמֵר). Therefore, נִפְעַל is also called the *N-stem*.

– *Prefix vowel*: The prefix vowel of נִפְעַל is normally /i/, which is a result of vowel raising ("attenuation"). *An original /a/-vowel in an unstressed closed syllable is usually raised to an /i/-vowel*, e.g., נִשְׁמַר (from the original form נַשְׁמַר).

– *Vowel lowering*: In the 2fp אַתֵּן and the 3fp הֵנָּה the /ē/ vowel in a stressed closed syllable is changed into an /a/-vowel in accordance with Philippi's law. *An original I/E-vowel in a stressed originally closed syllable is lowered to an /a/-vowel,* e.g., תִּשָּׁמֵרְנָה becomes תִּשָּׁמַרְנָה (compare זָקֵנְתִּי which becomes זָקַנְתִּי, Section 13:6).

2 נִפְעַל *verbs with deviant form*: Verbs with changeable consonants and/or gutturals undergo regular sound changes in accordance with the sound change rules (see examples below).

a *I-guttural* (פ״ג) *verbs*: "Attenuation" (vowel raising) before the guttural is realized halfway, that is, to an /e/-vowel, e.g., נֶעֱמַד (from the original form נַעֲמַד). The silent shva (the original no-vowel) of the first syllable is often replaced by a chateph. The vowel of the chateph corresponds to the vowel of the preceding prefix, e.g., נֶעֱמַד (compare יַעֲבֹד, יֶאֱסֹף, Section 16:3).

– In the imperfect, imperative and infinitive the prefix vowel before a guttural (and ר) is not /i/ but /ē/. *Gutturals and ר cannot be doubled. Instead, the preceding vowel is lengthened,* e.g., יִעָעֵבֵד becomes יֵעָבֵד (not יֶעָבֵד).

b *I-י/ו* (פו״י) *verbs*: Most of the word roots which begin with the consonant originally had ו as the first root consonant, but ו at the beginning of a word is replaced by י. However, the original ו is retained when it is preceded by a prefix, e.g., יִוָּלֵד 'he will be born' (the root letters are ילד).

– The consonant ו at the end of a syllable forms, together with the preceding vowel, a diphthong. The diphthong is ordinarily contracted (being pulled together to one vowel). That is, ו disappears in pronunciation but is retained in writing as a vowel letter, e.g., נַוְלַד becomes נוֹלַד.

3 *Meaning of the derived stems*: The basic meaning of a verb root, that is, the simple active meaning, is usually expressed by פָּעַל. The six derived verb stems normally modify the basic meaning of the action expressed by פָּעַל.

– The derived stems may express nuances in meaning such as passive, reflexive, reciprocal (mutual) or causative (see, for instance, 4 below).

– Not all verbs occur in פָּעַל. The basic meaning of verbs that do not occur in פָּעַל is expressed by one of the derived stems.

4 *Meaning of נִפְעַל verbs*: נִפְעַל serves mainly to express a *passive* nuance of פָּעַל verbs. It may also express a *reflexive* or *reciprocal* (mutual) meaning of פָּעַל verbs, e.g., שָׁמְרוּ (פָּעַל) means 'they guarded' whereas נִשְׁמְרוּ (נִפְעַל) means either 'they *were guarded*' (passive nuance) 'they *guarded themselves/they were on their guard*' (reflexive nuance) or 'they *guarded each other*' (reciprocal nuance), as required by the context.

– Certain נִפְעַל verbs express a simple active meaning, e.g., נִשְׁבַּע 'he swore'.

5 פָּעַל *imperfect and imperative with attached object pronouns*: The imperfect and the imperative take the same set of suffixed pronouns as are taken by verbs in the perfect, but the linking vowel is not /a/ (שְׁמָרַנִי) but /e/ (יִשְׁמְרֵנִי).

– *Additional* נ *before the object pronouns*: Certain object pronouns attached to imperfect or imperative forms are preceded by a נ, which is normally assimilated to the next consonant, e.g., יִשְׁמְרָנְךָ becomes יִשְׁמָרְךָ.

MEMORIZE

VERB TYPES II (unchangeable root types, i.e., *strong* שְׁלֵמִים)		
	G-stem	N-stem
Verb form	פָּעַל	נִפְעַל
Finite	Perfect	קָטַל/קָטֵל/קָטֹל	נִקְטַל
	Imperfect	יִקְטֹל/יִקְטַל	יִקָּטֵל
	Imperative	קְטֹל/קְטַל	הִקָּטֵל
Non-finite	Infinitive (ordinary)	קְטֹל	הִקָּטֵל
	Infinitive (as-intensifier)	קָטוֹל	הִקָּטֹל/נִקְטֹל
	Participle	קֹטֵל/קָטוּל	נִקְטָל

| GRAMMATICAL CORNERSTONE 15 ר א שׁ נ פ ב ה |

REVIEW AND APPLICATION OF THE RULES

I *Study* the sound change rules listed below. *Indicate* the relevant sound change/s occurring in each deviant verb form (on the left side) by comparing it with the corresponding normal form (on the right side). *Indicate* to which root type each deviant verb form belongs.

SOUND CHANGE RULES

A 1 A guttural usually takes a chateph (shva-plus-vowel) instead of a shva.

2 A guttural attracts an /a/-vowel instead of an original I/E- or U/O-vowel.

3 After (i.e., under) a guttural, the insertion vowel added to break up an impermissible two-consonant sequence at the end of a word is /a/ instead of /e/ (segol).

4 Gutturals and ר cannot be doubled. Instead, the preceding short vowel is often lengthened.

5 A vowelless א at the end of a syllable is silenced. That is, א disappears in pronunciation but is retained in writing. The silencing of א is compensated by the lengthening of the preceding vowel (if it is not already long).

5 הִשָּׁמֵר – הַמָּצֵא		1 נִשְׁמֶרֶת – נִשְׁמַעַת
6 יִשָּׁמֵר – יִשָּׁלַח		2 נִשְׁמְרוּ – נִגְאֲלוּ
7 תִּשָּׁמֵר – תֵּחָשֵׁב		3 הִשָּׁמֵר – הִשָּׁבַע
		4 הִשָּׁמְרִי – הִלָּחֲמִי

B 1 Vowel raising ("attenuation") before a guttural is realized halfway. That is, the original /a/-vowel before a guttural in an unstressed closed syllable is raised to /e/.

2 A guttural often takes a chateph (shva-plus-vowel) instead of a shva.

3 The insertion vowel after (i.e., under) a guttural with a chateph is the vowel of the chateph.

4 The consonant י/ו at the end of a syllable forms a diphthong. The diphthong is normally contracted to one vowel. That is, י/ו disappears in pronunciation but is retained in writing as a vowel letter.

5 The consonant י/ו with vowels on either side forms a triphthong. The י/ו in a triphthong is omitted. The contraction of a triphthong at the end of a word results in a full vowel (with either the vowel letter י/ו or ה).

6 The hard sound of a BeGaDKeFaT-consonant becomes soft after a vowel (shown in writing by the absence of the hardening dagesh).

5 נִשְׁמַר – נִבְנָה		1 נִשְׁמָר – נֶחְשָׁב
6 תִּשָּׁמְרִי – תִּבָּנִי		2 נִשְׁמַרְתָּ – נִבְנֵיתָ
7 נִשְׁמְרוּ – נֶעֶמְדוּ		3 נִשְׁמַר – נֶאֱכַל
		4 נִשְׁמְרָה – נוֹלְדָה

WORD LIST

Nouns

אֱנוֹשׁ	*m*, man (☆ Enosh, ʔ.n.š)	שׁבע	*niph* נִשְׁבַּע swear, take an
מִשְׁפָּחָה	*f*, family, clan:		oath: *imperf* יִשָּׁבַע
	bound form מִשְׁפַּחַת		(☆ Bathsheba, š.b.ʕ)
עָוֹן	*m*, offence, sin: *pl* עֲוֹנוֹת	שָׁבַר	break: *imperf* יִשְׁבֹּר
תָּוֶךְ	*m*, midst, middle:		
	bound form תּוֹךְ		

Adjectives

נִפְעַל *verbs* (familiar vocabulary)

קָרוֹב	near, close	נִבְרַךְ	be blessed
		נִזְכַּר	remember, be remembered:

Verbs[1]

imperf יִזָּכֵר

הָרַג	kill, slay: *imperf* יַהֲרֹג	נִכְרַת	be cut off: *imperf* יִכָּרֵת
כלם	*niph* נִכְלַם be/feel ashamed:	נִמְצָא	be found: *imperf* יִמָּצֵא
	imperfect יִכָּלֵם	נִפְתַּח	be opened: *imperf* יִפָּתַח
לחם	*niph* נִלְחַם fight: *imperf* יִלָּחֵם	נִקְבַּר	be buried: *imperf* יִקָּבֵר
	(☆ Bethlehem, l.ḥ.m)	נִקְרָא	be called, be read:
מלט	*niph* נִמְלַט escape:		*imperf* יִקָּרֵא
	imperfect יִמָּלֵט	נִשְׁבַּר	be broken: *imperf* יִשָּׁבֵר
פָּתַח	open: *imperf* יִפְתַּח	נִשְׁמַר	be guarded, be on one's guard,
	(☆ Jephthah, p.t.ḥ)		be careful: *imperf* יִשָּׁמֵר

EXERCISES

21.1 *Fill in* the the table below with the missing forms of נִפְעַל perfect and
imperfect. *Read* all the verb forms and *translate* orally. *Remember*:

> - All verb stems share the same inflection patterns. Hence נִפְעַל is
>   inflected like פָּעַל.
> - The characteristic feature of נִפְעַל is the consonant נ of the
>   prefix, which is either visible, e.g., נִשְׁמַר, or assimilated to the next
>   consonant, e.g., יִשָּׁמֵר (from the original form יִנְשָׁמֵר).
> - The prefix vowel of נִפְעַל is normally /i/, except the 1cs (I) of the
>   imperfect that usually takes an /e/-vowel, e.g., אֶשָּׁמֵר (though
>   occasionally the /i/-vowel also occurs, e.g., אִוָּלֵד).
> - When the stress is moved forward, the vowel in the open syllable
>   one step before the stress is reduced, e.g., תִּשָּׁמְרִי becomes תִּשָּׁמֵרִי.
> - A guttural usually takes a chateph (shva-plus-vowel) instead of a
>   shva, e.g., תִּגָּאֲלִי (instead of תִּגָּאְלִי).

---

[1] The lexical form of verbs that only partially or never occur in פָּעַל is the three root
consonants without any vowels.

Imperfect	Perfect	Imperfect	Perfect	Imperfect	Perfect	Pronoun
	נִלְחַם		נִזְכַּר	יִשָּׁמֵר	נִשְׁמַר	הוּא
				תִּשָּׁמֵר	נִשְׁמְרָה	הִיא
				תִּשָּׁמֵר	נִשְׁמַרְתָּ	אַתָּה
				תִּשָּׁמְרִי	נִשְׁמַרְתְּ	אַתְּ
נִלְחַמְתִּי		נִזְכַּרְתִּי		אֶשָּׁמֵר	נִשְׁמַרְתִּי	אֲנִי
				יִשָּׁמְרוּ	נִשְׁמְרוּ	הֵם
				תִּשָּׁמַרְנָה	נִשְׁמְרוּ	הֵנָּה
				תִּשָּׁמְרוּ	נִשְׁמַרְתֶּם	אַתֶּם
				תִּשָּׁמַרְנָה	נִשְׁמַרְתֶּן	אַתֶּן
				נִשָּׁמֵר	נִשְׁמַרְנוּ	אֲנַחְנוּ

21.2 *Fill in* the blanks with the missing imperative forms of נִפְעַל. *Read* all the forms and *translate*.

Translation: Imperative	אַתֶּן	אַתֶּם	אַתְּ	אַתָּה	
be on your guard/be careful!				הִשָּׁמֵר	1
			הִכָּלְמִי		2
				הִלָּחֵם	3
		הִשָּׁבְעוּ			4
	הִזָּכַרְנָה				5
			הִמָּלְטִי		6

21.3 *Fill in* the table below with the missing participle forms of נִפְעַל. *Read* all the forms and *translate. Note*:

- The only difference in form between the base form of the perfect (נִשְׁמַר) and the base form of the participle (נִשְׁמָר) is the stem vowel (the vowel under the second root consonant). The perfect has a patach (/a/), whereas the participle has a qamets (/ā/).
- Most of the participles of נִפְעַל below express a passive nuance of פָּעַל verbs, which the passive participle of פָּעַל also does. The difference between שָׁמוּר (the passive participle of פָּעַל) and נִשְׁמָר (the participle of נִפְעַל) is that נִשְׁמָר denotes the action itself 'being guarded', whereas שָׁמוּר denotes the result of the action, 'guarded'.

Translation: Participle	fp	mp	fs	ms	
being guarded				נִשְׁמָר	1
fighting			נִלְחֶמֶת		2
		נִכְרָתִים			3
	נִקְבָּרוֹת				4
		נִמְצָאִים			5
remembering, being remembered				נִזְכָּר	6
swearing			נִשְׁבַּעַת		7
				נִפְתָּח	8
			נִכְתֶּבֶת		9
	נִשְׁפָּטוֹת				10

21.4 *Fill in* the blanks with the missing forms of נִפְעַל from the list given below (the missing forms are italicized in the translation). Then *read* the entire Hebrew text and *translate* on your own. *Check* your translation against the translation in the book. *Pay attention* to the meaning of נִפְעַל. Finally *analyze* the verb forms as follows:

a) tense   b) root consonants   c) person/gender/number. *Remember*:

> • נִפְעַל serves to express a *passive, reflexive* or *reciprocal* (mutual) nuance of an *action* of פָּעַל verbs, e.g., שָׁמְרוּ (פָּעַל) means 'they guarded', whereas נִשְׁמְרוּ (נִפְעַל) means either 'they *were guarded*' (passive nuance), 'they *guarded themselves = they were careful*' (reflexive nuance) or 'they *guarded each other*' (reciprocal nuance). – Certain נִפְעַל verbs express, however, a *simple active* meaning, e.g., נִשְׁבַּע 'swear'.

וְנִבְרְכוּ   נִמְצְאוּ   יִזָּכֵר   תִּלָּחֲמוּ   תִּמָּלֵט   יִלָּחֵם   יִזָּכְרוּ   נִשְׁבָּר
יִכָּרֵתוּ (pausal form)   נִקְרָא   הִכָּלֵם   נִשְׁבְּרֵי

1 עֲוֹן אֲבֹתָיו אֶל־יהוה _____ May the sin of his fathers *be remembered*

before (= אֶל־) the Lord (Ps. 109:14)

a) _____   b) _____   c) _____

2 _____ וּרְשָׁעִים מֵאֶרֶץ But (= וְ) the wicked *will be cut off* from

[the] earth (Prov. 2:22) a) _____   b) _____   c) _____

3 עוֹד _____ וְלֹא And *they will* no more *be remembered*

(Zech. 13:2) a) _____   b) _____   c) _____

4 לֵב־ _____ קָרוֹב יהוה לְ The Lord [is] close to [the] *broken*hearted

(Ps. 34:19) a) _____   b) _____   c) _____

5 לָכֶם _____ יהוה The Lord *will fight* for you (Ex. 14:14)

a) _____   b) _____   c) _____

6 בְּנֵי יִשְׂרָאֵל אַל־ _____ עִם־יהוה אֱלֹהֵי־אֲבֹתֵיכֶם

Israelites (= sons of Israel), do not *fight* against (= עִם־) the Lord, the

God of your fathers (2 Chron. 13:12)

a) _____   b) _____   c) _____

7 לֹא יָדָעוּ _____ They did not know [how to] *feel ashamed*

(Jer. 8:12) a) _____   b) _____   c) _____

8 מִיָּדוֹ _____ וְאַתָּה לֹא And you – *you will* not *escape* out of

(= מ) his hand (Jer. 34:3) a) _____   b) _____   c) _____

9 _____ זִבְחֵי אֱלֹהִים רוּחַ נִשְׁבָּרָה לֵב־ The sacrifices to God [are

a] broken spirit, [a] *broken* heart (Ps. 51:19)

a) _____   b) _____   c) _____

10 דְּבָרֶיךָ _____ Your words *were found* (Jer. 15:16)

   a) _____ b) _____ c) _____

11 שִׁמְךָ עָלַי _____ כִּי־ For your name *has been called* upon me

   (Jer. 15:16) a) _____ b) _____ c) _____

12 בְךָ כֹּל מִשְׁפְּחֹת הָאֲדָמָה: _____ And all the families of the earth

   will be blessed by [means of] you (Gen. 12:3)

   a) _____ b) _____ c) _____

21.5 *Write* the corresponding independent form of each attached object pronoun below. *Read* the constructions and *translate. Remember*:

> ◆ Certain attached object pronouns are preceded by the consonant נ, which is normally assimilated to the next consonant (shown in writing by the doubling dagesh), e.g., יִשְׁמָרְנְךָ becomes יִשְׁמָרְךָ.
>   – When preceded by נ, the attached object pronouns of the 3ms (he) and the 1cp (we) are identical in form, e.g., יִשְׁמָרֶנּוּ means either 'he guarded *him*' or 'he guarded *us*' (compare מִמֶּנּוּ 'from him/us' and אֵינֶנּוּ 'he is/we are not').
> ◆ The linking vowel between a verb form, in the imperfect/imperative and the attached pronoun is /e/, e.g., יִשְׁמְרֵנִי.
> ◆ A qamets in an unstressed closed syllable is a qamets-/o/, e.g., כָּתְבֵם (kotvēm).

Translation	Independent object pronoun	Verb		
serve him!	אֹתוֹ	עֲבֹד	עָבְדֵהוּ	1
_____	_____	שְׁפֹט	שְׁפָטֵנִי	2
_____	_____	שְׁלַח	שְׁלָחַנִי	3
_____	_____	כְּתֹב	כָּתְבֵם	4
_____	_____	זְכֹר	זָכְרֵנִי	5
_____	_____	שְׁמֹר	שְׁמָרֵם	6
_____	_____	קְבֹרוּ	קְבָרוּהָ	7
_____	_____	תִּקְבֹּר	תִּקְבְּרֶנּוּ	8
_____	_____	תִּקְבֹּר	תִּקְבְּרֵנִי	9
_____	_____	יִשְׁמֹר	יִשְׁמָרְךָ	10
_____	_____	יִשְׁלַח	יִשְׁלָחֵנִי	11
_____	_____	יִקְבֹּרוּ	יִקְבְּרוּהוּ	12

21.6 Each verse/verse segment below contains a verb form in פָּעַל *imperfect/imperative followed by an attached object pronoun. Read* and *translate* on your own. Then *fill in* the blanks with the missing pronouns in the following translation and *check* your translation against it. *Note*:

> ◆ The attached pronouns are translated in the Key as required by the context in which they appear in the Bible.

1 זָכְרֵנִי נָא Remember _____, I pray (Judg. 16:28)

2 וַיִּשְׂרְפָהּ בָּאֵשׁ And _____ had burnt _____ with fire (= the fire)
(1 Kings 9:16)

3 שָׁמָּה תִּקְבְּרֵנִי There _____ shall bury _____ (Gen. 50:5)

4 מָה־אֱנוֹשׁ כִּי־תִזְכְּרֶנּוּ וּבֶן־אָדָם כִּי תִפְקְדֶנּוּ: _____ [is] man that _____ remember _____, [mortal] man (= and son of man) that _____ take care of _____? (Ps. 8:5)

5 וַיִּרְדְּפֵם יִשְׂרָאֵל And Israel pursued _____ (1 Kings 20:20)

6 אַךְ טוֹב וָחֶסֶד יִרְדְּפוּנִי כָּל־יְמֵי חַיָּי Surely/only goodness and kindness will follow _____ all the days of _____ life (Ps. 23:6)

7 לֹא הֲרַגְתִּיךָ _____ did not kill _____ (1 Sam. 24:12)

8 לֹא הֲרַגְתָּנִי: _____ did not kill _____ (1 Sam. 24:19)

9 וְלֹא הֲרָגוּם: And _____ did not kill _____ (Jos. 9:26)

10 אַל־נָא תִקְבְּרֵנִי בְּמִצְרָיִם: Please, do not bury _____ in Egypt (Gen. 47:29)

11 כִּי־קָבוֹר תִּקְבְּרֶנּוּ בַּיּוֹם הַהוּא Indeed (= כִּי), _____ should by all means/indeed (= קָבוֹר) bury _____ on _____ day (Dt. 21:23)

12 שָׁמְרֵם בְּתוֹךְ לְבָבֶךָ: Keep _____ in the midst of _____ heart (Prov. 4:21)

13 מָכֹר לֹא־תִמְכְּרֶנָּה בַּכֶּסֶף _____ should definitely (= מָכֹר) not sell _____ for (= בְּ) money (= the money) (Dt. 21:14)

21.7 *Translate* into English. Proper names are enlarged.

1 וְשָׁם תִּקָּבֵר אַתָּה וְכָל־אֹהֲבֶיךָ (Jer. 20:6)

2 נִפְתְּחוּ הַשָּׁמַיִם (Ezek. 1:1)

3 וְנִכְרַת מֵעַמָּיו: (Ex. 30:33)

4 וְלֹא־תִלָּחֲמוּ עִם־אֲחֵיכֶם (2 Chron. 11:4)

5 וְלֹא־יִזָּכֵר שֵׁם־יִשְׂרָאֵל עוֹד: (Ps. 83:5)

6 ²⁹ דִּבְרֵי רְחַבְעָם וְכָל־אֲשֶׁר עָשָׂה הֲלֹא־הֵמָּה כְתוּבִים עַל־סֵפֶר דִּבְרֵי הַיָּמִים לְמַלְכֵי יְהוּדָה: ³⁰ וּמִלְחָמָה הָיְתָה בֵין־רְחַבְעָם וּבֵין יָרָבְעָם כָּל־הַיָּמִים: ³¹ וַיִּשְׁכַּב רְחַבְעָם עִם־אֲבֹתָיו וַיִּקָּבֵר עִם־אֲבֹתָיו בְּעִיר דָּוִד וְשֵׁם אִמּוֹ נַעֲמָה הָעַמֹּנִית וַיִּמְלֹךְ אֲבִיָּם בְּנוֹ תַּחְתָּיו:

(1 Kings 14:29-31)

7 פִּקְדוּ־נָא אֶת־הָאֲרוּרָה הַזֹּאת וְקִבְרוּהָ כִּי בַת־מֶלֶךְ הִיא:

(2 Kings 9:34)

8 וַיִּקְבְּרֻהוּ בְּבֵיתוֹ (1 Sam. 25:1)

9 וַיִּשְׁלָחֵנִי אֱלֹהִים לִפְנֵיכֶם (Gen. 45:7)

10 יהוה יִשְׁמָרְךָ מִכָּל־רָע, יִשְׁמֹר אֶת־נַפְשֶׁךָ: (Ps. 121:7)

11 וְאַתֶּם כִּתְבוּ עַל־הַיְּהוּדִים (Jews) כַּטּוֹב בְּעֵינֵיכֶם בְּשֵׁם הַמֶּלֶךְ... כִּי־... אֲשֶׁר־נִכְתָּב בְּשֵׁם הַמֶּלֶךְ (Esther 8:8)

21.8 *Match* each grammatical element (from Exercise 21.7 above) with the Hebrew word/construction that illustrates it. *Mark* the element in the Hebrew word/construction clearly. Observe that the same grammatical element may appear more than once, but only one occurrence is to be marked. Each Hebrew word/construction is to be used once!

1 Qamets-/o/   אֹהֲבֶיךָ ( )

2 Participle of **נִפְעַל** (ms) *With a qamets under the second root consonant*   לֹא־תִלָּחֲמוּ ( )

3 Perfect of **נִפְעַל** (3ms) *With a patach (/a/) under the second root consonant*   סֵפֶר דִּבְרֵי הַיָּמִים ( )

4 Prohibition 'לֹא + *(ordinary) imperfect*'   הֲלֹא ( )

5 Noun chain *Consisting of three nouns*   נִכְתָּב ( )

6 Passive participle of **פָּעַל** (fs)   פִּקְדוּ־נָא ( )

7 Particle introducing a causal clause *Denotes a reason*   הָאֲרוּרָה ( )

8 Defective writing *The vowel letter ו is unexpectedly omitted*   וְנִכְרַת ( )

9 Particle of request *Follows an imperative*   וַיִּקְבְּרֻהוּ ( )

10 Rhetorical question marker *The question marker הֲ followed by לֹא*   כִּי בַת־מֶלֶךְ הִיא ( )

11 Active participle of **פָּעַל** (mp)   וַיִּשְׁלָחֵנִי ( )

12 Linking vowel *Before an object pronoun*   יִשְׁמָרְךָ ( )

21.9 *Translate* into Hebrew.

    1 His sons were found after the war. When they were found (בְּ + infinitive + attached pronoun), they had no (= there was not to them) water and [no] bread. His sons were not killed by their (= the hands of their) pursuers (= pursuing, *m, p*), because they escaped from the place in the morning. The sons swore to return to the battlefield.

    2 The men were killed and buried with their fathers.

    3 The books were found in the temple of the LORD and they were read to the men (= in the ears of the men) in the temple.

    4 The guards found us when we were (בְּ + infinitive + attached pronoun) there.

    5 Be on your *(m, p)* guard in order that you may not forget the LORD.

21.10 *Check* (and *correct* if needed) your translation of Exercise 21.9 above. Then *transform* the clauses (verbs as well as nouns and pronouns) from the plural into the singular.

21.11 *Check* (and *correct* if needed) Exercise 21.10 above. Then *transform* the verbs in the perfect into the imperfect.

SECTION 22

1 פִּעֵל, פֻּעַל (the *D-* and *Dp-stems*): *Basic forms (unchangeable verbs,* שְׁלֵמִים)

	Perfect	Imperfect	Imperative	Infinitive (ordinary)	Infinitive (as-intensifier)	Participle
→ פִּעֵל	קִדֵּשׁ	יְקַדֵּשׁ	קַדֵּשׁ	קַדֵּשׁ	קַדֵּשׁ	מְקַדֵּשׁ
פֻּעַל	קֻדַּשׁ	יְקֻדַּשׁ	—	—	קֻדַּשׁ	מְקֻדָּשׁ

– The characteristic feature of פִּעֵל is the doubled middle root consonant, e.g., קִדֵּשׁ 'sanctify'. Therefore, פִּעֵל is also called the *D-stem* (D = **d**ouble).

– פֻּעַל is also a *D-stem* (i.e., it has a doubled middle root consonant), e.g., קֻדַּשׁ 'be sanctified'. A further characteristic feature of פֻּעַל is the /u/-vowel under the first root consonant: קֻדַּשׁ. The /u/-vowel should be associated with *passive forms*, compare שָׁמוּר (the passive participle of פָּעַל). Therefore, פֻּעַל is also called the *Dp-stem* (p = **p**assive).

– *Prefix vowel*: The prefix vowel of פִּעֵל and פֻּעַל is shva, e.g., יְקַדֵּשׁ, מְקַדֵּשׁ.

– *Sound changes*

a) *Vowel lowering*: In the 1ˢᵗ and the 2ⁿᵈ persons (I, we; you) of פִּעֵל the /ē/-vowel in a stressed originally closed syllable is replaced by an /a/-vowel in accordance with Philippi's law. *An original I/E-vowel in a stressed originally closed syllable is changed into an /a/-vowel, e.g.,* הִלַּלְתִּי becomes הִלַּלְתִּי 'I praised' (compare זָקַנְתִּי in פָּעַל and תִּשְׁמַ֫רְנָה in נִפְעַל).

b) *Simplification of a vowelless doubled consonant*: When the doubled middle root consonant is followed by a shva, it sometimes loses its doubling, e.g., הִתְהַלְלָה becomes הִתְהַלְלָה. A vowelless doubled י (י with a shva) after the inverting-Vav usually loses its doubling, e.g., וַיְקַדֵּשׁ becomes וַיְקַדֵּשׁ.

2 פִּעֵל *and* פֻּעַל *verbs with deviant form*: Verbs with changeable consonants and/or gutturals undergo regular sound changes in accordance with the sound change rules (see examples below).

– II-*guttural* (ע׳׳ג) *verbs* (ר *Resh* is included in this group): Since gutturals and ר cannot be doubled, the preceding short vowel before א and ר is lengthened, e.g., מֵאֵן 'refuse' (instead of מֵאֵּן). No vowel lengthening occurs before ח, e.g., נִחַם 'comfort'. Before ה och ע vowel lengthening occurs only in פֻּעַל.

3 *Meaning of* פִּעֵל *and* פֻּעַל *verbs*: פִּעֵל serves mainly to express a *causative* nuance of intransitive פָּעַל verbs (verbs that cannot take a direct object) or adjectives, e.g., קִדֵּשׁ 'make/let something become holy = sanctify' (from קָדוֹשׁ 'holy').[1]

– פִּעֵל is also used to express the intensified or repeated action of פָּעַל verbs, e.g., סִפֵּר 'recount' (סָפַר 'count').

– פֻּעַל, which is rarely used in the Bible, serves as the passive counterpart of פִּעֵל verbs, e.g., מְקֻדָּשׁ 'sanctified' (compare מְקַדֵּשׁ 'sanctifying').

---

[1] The exact term used to denote an intransitive verb which has been transformed into a transitive one is *factitive*.

MEMORIZE

VERB TYPES III (unchangeable root types, i.e., *strong* שְׁלֵמִים)				
Verb form		G-stem	N-stem	D-stems
		פָּעַל	נִפְעַל	(D) פִּעֵל	(Dp) פֻּעַל
Finite	Perfect	קָטַל/קָטֵל/קָטֹל	נִקְטַל	קִטֵּל	קֻטַּל
	Imperfect	יִקְטֹל/יִקְטַל	יִקָּטֵל	יְקַטֵּל	יְקֻטַּל
	Imperative	קְטֹל/קְטַל	הִקָּטֵל	קַטֵּל	—
Non-finite	Infinitive (ordinary)	קְטֹל	הִקָּטֵל	קַטֵּל	—
	Infinitive (as-intensifier)	קָטוֹל	הִקָּטֹל/נִקְטֹל	קַטֵּל/קַטֹּל	קֻטֹּל
	Participle	קֹטֵל/קָטוּל	נִקְטָל	מְקַטֵּל	מְקֻטָּל
GRAMMATICAL CORNERSTONE 16 ר א שׁ פ נ ה				

REVIEW AND APPLICATION OF THE RULES

I *Study* the sound change rules listed below. *Indicate* the relevant sound change/s occurring in each deviant form (on the left side) by comparing it with the corresponding normal form (on the right side). *Indicate* the root type to which each deviant form belongs.

SOUND CHANGE RULES

1 A guttural usually takes a chateph (shva-plus-vowel) instead of a shva.
2 A guttural (and occasionally ר) attracts an /a/-vowel/s.
3 Gutturals and ר cannot be doubled. Instead, the preceding short vowel is often lengthened.
4 The consonant י/ו in a diphthong normally disappears in pronunciation but is retained in writing as a vowel letter.
5 The consonant י/ו in a triphthong (י/ו with vowels on either side) is omitted.
6 Vowelless א at the end of a syllable is silenced. The silencing of א is compensated by the lengthening of the preceding vowel (if it is not already long).
7 A doubled consonant with a shva sometimes loses its doubling (shown in writing by the absence of the doubling dagesh).

1 יְקַדְּשׁוּ – יְכַסּוּ   4 קַדֵּשׁ – שַׁלַּח   7 קִדְּשׁוּ – מֵאֲנוּ

2 מְקַדֵּשׁ – מְבָרֵךְ   5 קִדֵּשׁ – בֵּרַךְ   8 קְדֹשׁ – מָלֵא

3 קִדַּשְׁנוּ – כִּסִּינוּ   6 מְקֻדֶּשֶׁת – מְשֻׁלַּחַת   9 מְקַדְּשִׁים – מְבַקְשִׁים

II *Match* each sound element with the Hebrew word that illustrates it. *Mark* the element in the Hebrew word clearly! Observe that the same sound element may appear more than once, but only one instance is to be marked. Each Hebrew word is to be used once!

1 Vowel reduction **I** *A vowel* מְהַלְלִים (_)   **6** Glide-/a/ *Before* ע, ח (_) מְבָרֵךְ
  one *step before the stress is reduced*   *at the end of a word*

2 Vowel reduction **I** *A vowel under a* (_) מִלֵּאנוּ   **7** Vowel lowering   (_) כִּסִּיתָ
  guttural **one** *step before the stress*   *In a stressed (originally)*
  is reduced   *closed syllable* /ē/ *becomes* /a/

3 Compensatory lengthening of a (_) דִּבְּרָה   **8** Contraction of a   (_) נֶחֱמוּ
  vowel Gutturals and ר *cannot be*   diphthong *The consonant*
  doubled. Instead, the preceding short   י / ו *at the end of syllable*
  vowel is lengthened: /a/ *becomes* /ā/   *becomes a vowel letter*

4 Compensatory lengthening of a (_) דִּבַּרְתִּי   **9** Simplification of a (_) פֵּאֵר
  vowel Gutturals and ר *cannot be*   doubled consonant with
  doubled. Instead, the preceding short   a shva *Shown in writing by the*
  vowel is lengthened: /i/ *becomes* /ē/   *absence of the doubling dagesh*

5 Compensatory lengthening of a (_) יְמָאֵן   **10** Silent א   מְשֻׁלַּח (_)
  vowel Instead of doubling, /u/ *becomes* /ō/

III *Review* EXCEPTIONS TO THE BASIC RULE OF VOCALIZATION VIA HEBREW NAMES in Section 11 on page 79. Then in the following words *find* exceptions to the basic rule of vocalization. *Mark* the syllables with the deviant vocalization and *indicate* from the list below the grammatical category to which each deviant form belongs. *Remember*:

> ◆ *All* syllables with simple vowels *generally* (**not always!**) have a *long vowel*,
> except an unstressed closed syllable which **always** has a *short* vowel.

SYLLABLES WITH A SHORT INSTEAD OF A LONG VOWEL

1 *Stressed closed syllables*
a An /a/-vowel followed by the consonant י (that is, a diphthong) at the end of a word, e.g., יָדִי.
b An /a/-vowel in finite verb forms, e.g., שָׁמַר, יִלְמַד.
2 *Stressed open syllables*
a An /e/- or /a/-vowel in words with the stress on the next-to-last syllable, e.g., פֶּתַח, נַעַר.

b The linking vowels /e/ and /a/ in a stressed open syllable: שְׁמָרַ֫נִי, לְבָבְךָ.

3 *Unstressed open syllables*

a Before a chateph (shva-plus-vowel), e.g., תֵּ-אָסֵף, לַ-עֲבָדִים.

b Before a consonant which has been simplified, e.g., הַיְלָדִים, or when an expected doubling is not realized, e.g., הַחַיִּים (shown in writing by the absence of the dagesh).

5 אֲבוֹתַי	4 וַיֶּחֱזַק	3 יַעֲבֹד	2 בִּקְשָׁה	1 נִשְׁמַ֫עַת
10 יָדֵךְ	9 זְכָרֹ֫נוּ	8 מְדַבֶּ֫רֶת	7 עֲזָבַ֫נִי	6 נֹאכַל
15 יֵאָסֵף	14 טְהַר	13 יִשְׁכַּב	12 הַלְלוּ	11 יָדַ֫עְנוּ

WORD LIST

Nouns

חָכְמָה, חכם *f,* wisdom

Verbs[2]

בקש	*pi* בִּקֵּשׁ seek; require: *imperf* יְבַקֵּשׁ
דבר	*pi* דִּבֵּר speak, talk: *imperf* יְדַבֵּר
הלל	*pi* הִלֵּל praise: *imperf* יְהַלֵּל
חָזַק	be/become strong, hard: *imperf* יֶחֱזַק (☆ Ezekiel, ḥ.z.q)
יָרַד	go down, descend (☆ **Jordan**)
כסה	*pi* כִּסָּה cover, conceal
כפר	*pi* כִּפֶּר atone for: *imperf* יְכַפֵּר (☆ Yom Kippur)
מאן	*pi* מֵאֵן refuse: *imperf* יְמָאֵן
נחם	*pi* נִחַם comfort, console: *imperf* יְנַחֵם (☆ Nahum, Nehemiah, n.ḥ.m)
סָפַר	count: *pi* סִפֵּר recount, tell: *imperf* יְסַפֵּר
פלט	*pi* פִּלֵּט let escape: *imperf* יְפַלֵּט
צוה	*pi* צִוָּה command, order (☆ Bar mitzvah, ṣ.w.h)

קדשׁ	*pi* קִדֵּשׁ sanctify (make sacred/holy): *imperf* יְקַדֵּשׁ
שרת	*pi* שֵׁרֵת serve, minister: *imperf* יְשָׁרֵת

פָּעֵל *verbs* (familiar vocabulary)

בֵּרַךְ	*pi* bless: *imperf* יְבָרֵךְ
חִזֵּק	*pi* make strong: *imperf* יְחַזֵּק
כִּבֵּד	*pi* make weighty, honour: *imperf* יְכַבֵּד
לִמֵּד	*pi* make learn, teach: *imperf* יְלַמֵּד (☆ the letter **Lámed**)
מִלֵּא	*pi* cause to be full (with), fill: *imperf* יְמַלֵּא
שִׁלַּח	*pi* send away, let go: *imperf* יְשַׁלַּח

Particles

אֵצֶל	near, beside, by: *with suff* אֶצְלִי
לָכֵן	therefore
נֶגֶד	before, in front of, opposite to: *with suff* נֶגְדִּי

---

[2] The lexical form of verbs that only partially or never occur in פָּעַל is the three root consonants without any vowels.

EXERCISES

22.1 *Fill in* the the table below with the missing forms of פִּעֵל perfect and imperfect. *Read* all the verb forms and *translate* orally. *Remember*:

> ◆ The characteristic feature of פִּעֵל is the doubled middle root consonant (D).
>
> ◆ The doubled middle root consonant of פִּעֵל tends to lose its doubling when it is followed by a shva (except for the BeGaDKeFaT-consonants which never lose their dagesh), e.g., הִתְהַלְלָה becomes הִתְהַלְלָה.
>
> ◆ The prefix vowel of פִּעֵל is shva.

Imperfect	Perfect	Imperfect	Perfect	Imperfect	Perfect	Pronoun
		יְדַבֵּר	דִּבֶּר		קִדֵּשׁ	הוּא
				תְּקַדֵּשׁ		הִיא
תְּבַקֵּשׁ						אַתָּה
		תְּדַבְּרִי				אַתְּ
	בִּקַּשְׁתִּי			אֲקַדֵּשׁ		אֲנִי
יְבַקְשׁוּ						הֵם
		תְּדַבֵּרְנָה				הֵנָּה
		תְּדַבְּרוּ				אַתֶּם
תְּבַקֵּשְׁנָה						אַתֶּן
				נְקַדֵּשׁ		אֲנַחְנוּ

22.2 *Fill in* the blanks with the missing imperative forms of פִּעֵל. *Read* all the verb forms and *translate*.

Translation	אַתֵּן	אַתֶּם	אַתְּ	אַתָּה	
speak!				דַּבֵּר	1
			קַדְּשִׁי		2
		סַפְּרוּ			3
			בַּקְּשִׁי		4
		כַּבְּדוּ			5
				הַלֵּל	6
	לַמֵּדְנָה				7

22.3 *Fill in* the blanks with the missing participle forms of פִּעֵל. *Read* all the verb forms and *translate*.

Translation	fp	mp	fs	ms	
strengthening				מְחַזֵּק	1
	מְכַבְּדוֹת				2
			מְסַפֶּרֶת		3
		מְבַקְשִׁים			4
				מְלַמֵּד	5

22.4 *Fill in* the the table below with the missing forms of פִּעֵל. *Read* all the verb forms and *translate* orally. *Remember*:

- The characteristic features of פִּעֵל are the doubled middle root consonant (D) and the /u/-vowel under the first root consonant (p). The doubled middle root consonant sometimes loses its doubling when it is followed by a shva (except for the BeGaDKeFaT-consonants that never lose their dagesh).
- The prefix vowel of פִּעֵל is shva.

Imperfect	Perfect	Imperfect	Perfect	Imperfect	Perfect	Pronoun
	כֻּפַּר		חֻזַּק	יְכֻבַּד		הוּא
				תְּכֻבַּד		הִיא
				תְּכֻבַּד		אַתָּה
				תְּכֻבְּדִי		אַתְּ
				אֲכֻבַּד		אָנֹכִי
			חֻזְּקוּ	יְכֻבְּדוּ		הֵם
				תְּכֻבַּדְנָה		הֵנָּה
				תְּכֻבְּדוּ		אַתֶּם
				תְּכֻבַּדְנָה		אַתֶּן
				נְכֻבַּד		אֲנַחְנוּ

22.5 Each verse/verse segment below contains a verb form in פִּעֵל (enlarged in the Hebrew text and italicized in the translation). *Read* the Hebrew text and *translate* on your own. Then *fill in* the blanks with the missing words in the following translation and *check* your translation against it. *Note*:

> * פִּעֵל serves mainly to give a *causative* meaning to intransitive פָּעַל verbs (verbs that cannot take a direct object) or adjectives, e.g., קִדֵּשׁ 'make/let something become holy = sanctify' (from קָדוֹשׁ 'holy').
> – פִּעֵל is also used to express an intensified or repeated action of פָּעַל verbs, e.g., סִפֵּר 'recount' (סָפַר 'count').
> – Certain פִּעֵל verbs that do not occur in פָּעַל express, however, a simple active meaning, e.g., הִלֵּל 'praise'.

1 אֱלֹהַי פַּלְּטֵנִי מִיַּד רָשָׁע _____ God, let _____ *escape* from hand of [the] wicked (Ps. 71:4)

2 וְכָל־הָאָרֶץ מְבַקְשִׁים אֶת־פְּנֵי שְׁלֹמֹה לִשְׁמֹעַ אֶת־חָכְמָתוֹ אֲשֶׁר־נָתַן אֱלֹהִים בְּלִבּוֹ: And the _____ earth [were] *seeking* Solomon (= the face of Solomon) to hear _____ wisdom _____ God had put in _____ heart (1 Kings 10:24)

3 וַיִּשְׁמַע יהוה אֶת־קוֹל דִּבְרֵיכֶם בְּדַבֶּרְכֶם אֵלָי And the Lᴏʀᴅ heard _____ words (= the voice of _____ words) when _____ spoke (= in _____ speaking) to _____ (Dt. 5:28)

4 כְּדַבְּרָהּ אֶל־יוֹסֵף יוֹם וְלֹא־שָׁמַע אֵלֶיהָ לִשְׁכַּב אֶצְלָהּ [Thus] although (= כְּ) _____ spoke (= as _____ speaking) to Joseph day [after] day, (and) _____ did not listened to _____ to lie with (= אֵצֶל) _____ (Gen. 39:10)

5 אָמַרְתִּי כַּבֵּד אֲכַבֶּדְךָ _____ said, '_____ will certainly (= כַּבֵּד) honour _____' (Num. 24:11)

6 וּבְדַבְּרִי אוֹתְךָ (read אִתְּךָ) אֶפְתַּח אֶת־פִּיךָ וְאָמַרְתָּ אֲלֵיהֶם כֹּה אָמַר אֲדֹנָי יֱהוִֹה (special reading אֱלֹהִים =) And when _____ speak (= in _____ speaking) with _____, _____ will open _____ mouth, so that (= וְ) _____ will say to _____, 'Thus says (= אָמַר) the Lᴏʀᴅ God' (Ezek. 3:27)

7 וּבְדַבְּרוֹ עִמִּי אֶת־הַדָּבָר הַזֶּה עָמַדְתִּי And when _____ [was] speaking (= in _____ speaking) with _____ _____ word, _____ did stand up (Dan. 10:11)

8 אֶת־אַחַי אָנֹכִי מְבַקֵּשׁ [It is] _____ brothers _____ [am] seeking (Gen. 37:16)

9 יַד־אֱלֹהֵינוּ עַל־כָּל־מְבַקְשָׁיו The hand of _____ God [is] upon _____ [those] seeking _____ (Ezra 8:22)

10 כִּי־מְכַבְּדַי אֲכַבֵּד For [those] honouring _____, _____ will honour (1 Sam. 2:30)

11 אַתֶּם רְאִיתֶם כִּי מִן־הַשָּׁמַיִם דִּבַּרְתִּי עִמָּכֶם: _____ _____ have seen that [it was] from the heavens _____ spoke with _____ (Ex. 20:22)

22.6 *Fill in* the blanks with the missing forms of פִּעֵל from the list given below (the missing forms are italicized in the translation). Then *read* the entire Hebrew text and *translate* on your own. *Check* your translation against the translation in the book. *Pay attention* to the meaning of פִּעֵל. Finally *analyze* the verb forms as follows:

a) tense   **b)** root consonants   **c)** person/gender/number

---

צֻוָּה   מְדַבֵּר   בֵּרַךְ   מְבַקְשִׁים   הַלְלִי   כַּבֵּד   וְדִבַּרְתִּי   צֻוָּה   יְכַבֵּד

---

1 אָב וְעֶבֶד אֲדֹנָיו _____ בֵּן [A] son *honours* [his] father and [a]

servant his master (= masters, plural of majesty) (Mal. 1:6)

a) _____ b) _____ c) _____

2 עִמְּךָ שָׁם _____ וְיָרַדְתִּי And I *will* come down and *speak* with

you there (Num. 11:17)

a) _____ b) _____ c) _____

3 אֶת־אָבִיךָ וְאֶת־אִמֶּךָ _____ *Honour* your father and your mother

(Dt. 5:16) a) _____ b) _____ c) _____

4 אֵלֶּה דִבְרֵי הַבְּרִית אֲשֶׁר־ _____ יהוה אֶת־מֹשֶׁה לִכְרֹת אֶת־בְּנֵי

יִשְׂרָאֵל These [are] the words of the covenant which the LORD *commanded*

Moses to make (= cut) with the Israelites (Dt. 28:69)

a) _____ b) _____ c) _____

5 אֶת־נַפְשֶׁךָ: _____ הָאֲנָשִׁים הָאֵלֶּה אֲשֶׁר These men who [are]

seeking your life (= soul) (Jer. 38:16)

a) _____ b) _____ c) _____

6 נַפְשִׁי אֶת־יהוה: _____ הַלְלוּ־יָהּ Praise the LORD (= Jah), *praise*

the LORD, my soul (Ps. 146:1)

a) _____ b) _____ c) _____

7 עִמָּם וְהִנֵּה הַמַּלְאָךְ יֹרֵד אֵלָיו _____ עוֹדֶנּוּ [While] he [was] still

speaking with them, here (= וְהִנֵּה) [was] the messenger coming down

to him (2 Kings 6:33)

a) _____ b) _____ c) _____

8 וְזֹאת הַבְּרָכָה אֲשֶׁר _____ מֹשֶׁה אִישׁ הָאֱלֹהִים אֶת־בְּנֵי יִשְׂרָאֵל

לִפְנֵי מוֹתוֹ: Now (= וְ) this [is] the blessing [with] which Moses, the

man of God, *blessed* the Israelites before his death (Dt. 33:1)

a) _____ b) _____ c) _____

9 לִפְנֵי מוֹתוֹ _____ אָבִיךָ Your father *commanded* before his

death (Gen. 50:16) a) _____ b) _____ c) _____

22.7 Each verse segment below contains a form of פִּעֵל. *Read* and *translate* on your own. Then *match* each verse segment with the correct English translation. *Check/complete* your translation against the translation in the book.

1 מְלַמֵּד יָדַי לַמִּלְחָמָה

( ) The work (= deed) of his hands you have blessed (Job 1:10)

2 קוֹל אֱלֹהִים חַיִּים מְדַבֵּר מִתּוֹךְ־הָאֵשׁ

( ) Praise the Lord (Jah)! Praise God in his sanctuary (= holiness) (Ps. 150:1)

3 וְעַתָּה דַּבֶּר־נָא אֶל־הַמֶּלֶךְ

( ) Hear, my people, and I will speak (Ps. 50:7)

4 בַּקֵּשׁ שָׁלוֹם וְרָדְפֵהוּ:

( ) Honour me, please, in front of the elders of my people (1 Sam. 15:30)

5 כַּבְּדֵנִי נָא נֶגֶד זִקְנֵי־עַמִּי

( ) He [is] teaching my hands for war[fare] (= the war) (2 Sam. 22:35)

6 הַלְלוּ יָהּ הַלְלוּ־אֵל בְּקָדְשׁוֹ

( ) And now speak, please, to the king (2 Sam. 13:13)

7 זָכְרֵנִי נָא וְחַזְּקֵנִי נָא

( ) Seek peace and pursue it (Ps. 34:15)

8 וַיְבַקֵּשׁ לַהֲרֹג אֶת־מֹשֶׁה

( ) And the boy started to serve (= was serving) the Lord (1 Sam. 2:11)

9 מַעֲשֵׂה יָדָיו בֵּרַכְתָּ

( ) The voice of [the] living God speaking out of (= מִ) the middle of the fire (Dt. 5:23)

10 שִׁמְעָה עַמִּי וַאֲדַבֵּרָה

( ) Remember me, please, and strengthen me, please (Judg. 16:28)

11 וְהַנַּעַר הָיָה מְשָׁרֵת אֶת־יהוה ( ) He sought to kill Moses (Ex. 2:15)

22.8 *Match* each grammatical element (from Exercise 22.7 above) with the Hebrew word/construction that illustrates it. *Mark* the element in the Hebrew word/construction clearly. Observe that the same grammatical element may appear more than once, but only one instance is to be marked. Each Hebrew word/construction is to be used once!

1 Qamets-/o/ *In an unstressed closed syllable*   ( ) דַּבֶּר־נָא

2 פִּעֵל: Participle (ms) *Prefix מְ + doubled middle root letter*   ( ) וַאֲדַבֵּרָה

3 פִּעֵל: Imperative (ms) *Followed by an attached object pronoun*   ( ) וַיְבַקֵּשׁ

4 פָּעַל: Imperative (ms) *Followed by an attached object pronoun*   ( ) הַלְלוּ

5 Simplification of the doubled consonant *After an inverting-Vav* ( ) וְרָדְפֵהוּ

6 Simplification of the doubled middle root consonant   ( ) מְלַמֵּד

7 Mappiq *A dot indicating that ה at the end of a word is a consonant* ( ) כַּבְּדֵנִי

8 פִּעֵל: Lengthened imperfect (1cs) *Imperfect + the ending ָה*   ( ) בְּקָדְשׁוֹ

9 Particle of request *Follows an imperative*   ( ) יָהּ

22.9 *Translate* into English. Proper names are enlarged.

1 וּבָרֵךְ אֶת־עַמְּךָ אֶת־יִשְׂרָאֵל וְאֵת הָאֲדָמָה אֲשֶׁר נָתַתָּה לָנוּ כַּאֲשֶׁר
נִשְׁבַּעְתָּ לַאֲבֹתֵינוּ... הַיּוֹם הַזֶּה יהוה אֱלֹהֶיךָ מְצַוְּךָ לַעֲשׂוֹת אֶת־
הַחֻקִּים הָאֵלֶּה וְאֶת־הַמִּשְׁפָּטִים וְשָׁמַרְתָּ וְעָשִׂיתָ אוֹתָם בְּכָל־לְבָבְךָ
וּבְכָל־נַפְשֶׁךָ׃ (Dt. 26:15–16)

2 וַיִּמְצָאֵהוּ אִישׁ... בַּשָּׂדֶה וַיִּשְׁאָלֵהוּ הָאִישׁ לֵאמֹר מַה־תְּבַקֵּשׁ׃ וַיֹּאמֶר
אֶת־אַחַי אָנֹכִי מְבַקֵּשׁ (Gen. 37:15)

3 הֲלֹא־זֶה הַדָּבָר אֲשֶׁר דִּבַּרְנוּ אֵלֶיךָ בְמִצְרַיִם לֵאמֹר (Ex. 14:12)

4 כִּי־מֵתוּ כָּל־הָאֲנָשִׁים הַמְבַקְשִׁים אֶת־נַפְשֶׁךָ׃ (Ex. 4:19)

5 הֲנִשְׁמַע כָּמֹהוּ׃ הֲשָׁמַע עָם קוֹל אֱלֹהִים מְדַבֵּר מִתּוֹךְ־הָאֵשׁ כַּאֲשֶׁר־שָׁמַעְתָּ
אַתָּה (Dt. 4:32-33)

6 הַאַתָּה הָאִישׁ אֲשֶׁר־דִּבַּרְתָּ אֶל־הָאִשָּׁה וַיֹּאמֶר אָנִי׃ (Judg. 13:11)

7 וּמְהַלְלִים לַיהוה יוֹם בְּיוֹם הַלְוִיִּם וְהַכֹּהֲנִים (2 Chron. 30:21)

8 וְאַבְרָהָם הֹלֵךְ עִמָּם לְשַׁלְּחָם׃ וַיהוה אָמַר הַמְכַסֶּה אֲנִי מֵאַבְרָהָם
אֲשֶׁר אֲנִי עֹשֶׂה׃ (Gen. 18:16–17)

9 לָכֵן בְּזֹאת יְכֻפַּר עֲוֹן־יַעֲקֹב (Isa. 27:9)

22.10 *Reread* the text of Exercise 22.9 and *translate* again orally. Then *match* each grammatical element from the Exercise above with the Hebrew word/construction that illustrates it. *Mark* the element in the Hebrew word/construction clearly. Observe that the same grammatical element may appear more than once, but only one occurrence is to be marked. Each Hebrew word/construction is to be used once!

I 1 Defective writing *The vowel letter* י *is unexpectedly omitted* ( ) עֹשֶׂה
   2 Full writing *The vowel letter* ה *is unexpectedly added* ( ) לֵאמֹר
   3 פָּעַל: Infinitive *Followed by an attached pronoun* ( ) נָתַתָּה
   4 פָּעַל: Inverted imperfect *Followed by an attached pronoun* ( ) הַמְבַקְשִׁים
   5 פָּעַל: Participle *Followed by an attached pronoun* ( ) וַיִּמְצָאֵהוּ
   6 פָּעַל: Participle of a III-י/ו (ה) verb (ms) ( ) וּבָרֵךְ
   7 פָּעַל: Infinitive of a III-י/ו (ה) verb *Ends in* ות ( ) לְשַׁלְּחָם
   8 Simplification of doubled consonants (two cases!) ( ) לַעֲשׂוֹת
      Shown in writing by the absence of the doubling dagesh
   9 Quotation marker *Literally, 'to + say/ing';* ( ) מְצַוְּךָ
      introduces direct speech
   10 Compensatory lengthening of a vowel, פָּעַל *verb, 3ms* ( ) הַלְוִיִּם

II 1 Relative clause describing a noun in a main clause (_) הָאֲנָשִׁים
    Introduced by אֲשֶׁר *'which, who, that' etc.* הַמְבַקְשִׁים אֶת...

   2 Relative clause replacing a noun in a clause (_) כִּי־מֵתוּ
    Introduced by אֲשֶׁר *'[the thing] that/which, what' etc.* כָּל־הָאֲנָשִׁים

   3 Participle describing a noun in a clause (_) וְאַבְרָהָם הֹלֵךְ
    'ה + participle' corresponds to an English relative clause עִמָּם

   4 Participle replacing a verb *Follows the subject* (_) הַאַתָּה הָאִישׁ
    and has no time reference of its own

   5 Yes/no question *The particle* הַ *functions as a* (_) הַדָּבָר אֲשֶׁר
    question mark דִּבַּרְנוּ

   6 Question marker הַ before a shva (_) הֲנִשְׁמַע כָּמֹהוּ

   7 Question marker הַ before a guttural (_) הֲלֹא־זֶה הַדָּבָר

   8 Particle introducing a causal clause (_) הַמְכַסֶּה אֲנִי
    'Because, for, since'

   9 Rhetorical question *Introduced by the* (_)... הַמְכַסֶּה אֲנִי
    question marker הַ *and followed by* לֹא אֲשֶׁר אֲנִי עֹשֶׂה

22.11 *Translate into Hebrew. Remember*:

  ♦ The normal word order of the verbal clause is **Verb–Subject–Object** (VSO).

  ♦ The construction 'ו + noun/pronoun + verb in the perfect' is used, among other things, to highlight a contrast. In this position ו is usually rendered in English translation by 'but, however, whereas' (and the like) instead of 'and'.

---

1 My father commanded me not to do these things, but (= ו) I did not obey him (= listened in his voice).

2 The LORD blessed his people (= nation), whereas (= ו) the people refused to remember his laws and (+ to) keep his commandments.

3 The king of Egypt sent the Israelites away out of (= from) his land. Then (= ו) Moses taught them the Law in the wilderness/desert, in Sinai (בְּסִינַי).

4 The man praised the LORD, his God, and served (שׁרת) him with all his heart and with all his soul.

1 הִתְפַּעֵל (the *HtD-stem*): *Basic forms (unchangeable verbs,* שְׁלֵמִים)

	Perfect	Imperfect	Imperative	Infinitive (ordinary)	Infinitive (as-intensifier)	Participle
➤	הִתְפַּעֵל הִתְקַדֵּשׁ	יִתְקַדֵּשׁ	הִתְקַדֵּשׁ	הִתְקַדֵּשׁ	הִתְקַדֵּשׁ	מִתְקַדֵּשׁ

– The characteristic feature of הִתְפַּעֵל, apart from the *doubled middle root consonant*, is the prefix הִת, e.g., הִתְקַדֵּשׁ 'sanctify oneself'. Therefore, הִתְפַּעֵל is also called the *HtD-stem*. The consonant ה of the prefix is either visible, e.g., הִתְקַדֵּשׁ, or omitted, e.g., יִתְקַדֵּשׁ (from the hypothetical form יִהְתְקַדֵּשׁ, compare בְּהַמָּקוֹם that becomes בַּמָּקוֹם).
– *Prefix vowel*: The prefix vowel of הִתְפַּעֵל is /i/:
מִתְקַדֵּשׁ, הִתְקַדֵּשׁ, יִתְקַדֵּשׁ.

2 *On sound changes of* הִתְפַּעֵל *verbs*: Unchangeable and changeable הִתְפַּעֵל verbs undergo sound changes identical to those occurring in פִּעֵל verbs (review Section 22:1–2).
– *Compensatory lengthening of vowels in the D-stems*: Since gutturals and ר cannot be doubled, the preceding short vowel may be lengthened according to the following scheme (**CL** = Compensatory **L**engthening):

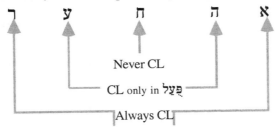

Vowel category	Vowel change	
	Short vowel	Long vowel
A	ֱ	ָ
I/E	ִ	ֵ
U/O	ֻ	ֹ

– *Sound changes in the* הִתְפַּעֵל *marker* ת *Tav*
When ת is followed by ז, ס, שׁ, שׂ, צ (consonants pronounced with a hissing sound, called *sibilants*), the sibilant and the ת change places, e.g., הִתְסַתֵּר becomes הִסְתַּתֵּר.
– When the first root consonant is צ *Tsádi* the הִתְפַּעֵל marker ת becomes ט *Tet*: הִצְטַדֵּק (instead of הִצְתַדֵּק).

– Further, when the first root consonant is ט *Tet* or ד *Dálet*, the הִתְפַּעֵל marker ת is assimilated to the first consonant, which in turn is doubled (shown in writing by the doubling dagesh), e.g., הִטַּהֵר (instead of הִתְטַהֵר).

3 *Meaning of* הִתְפַּעֵל *verbs*: הִתְפַּעֵל serves mainly to express a reflexive nuance of פָּעַל or פִּעֵל verbs, e.g., הִתְקַדֵּשׁ 'make *oneself* holy'. הִתְפַּעֵל is also used to express a reciprocal (mutual) or repeated nuance of פָּעַל verbs, e.g., הִתְרָאָה 'see *one another*', הִתְהַלֵּךְ 'walk *around*'.

MEMORIZE

VERB TYPES IV (unchangeable root types, i.e., *strong* שְׁלֵמִים)					
Verb form	G-stem	N-stem	D-stems		
	פָּעַל	נִפְעַל	פִּעֵל D	פֻּעַל Dp	הִתְפַּעֵל HtD
Finite — Perfect	קָטַל / קָטֵל / קָטֹל	נִקְטַל	קִטֵּל	קֻטַּל	הִתְקַטֵּל
Finite — Imperfect	יִקְטֹל / יִקְטַל	יִקָּטֵל	יְקַטֵּל	יְקֻטַּל	יִתְקַטֵּל
Finite — Imperative	קְטֹל / קְטַל	הִקָּטֵל	קַטֵּל	——	הִתְקַטֵּל
Non-finite — Infinitive (ordinary)	קְטֹל	הִקָּטֵל	קַטֵּל	——	הִתְקַטֵּל
Non-finite — Infinitive (as-intensifier)	קָטוֹל	הִקָּטֹל / נִקְטֹל	קַטֵּל / קַטֹּל	קֻטַּל	הִתְקַטֵּל
Non-finite — Participle	קֹטֵל / קָטוּל	נִקְטָל	מְקַטֵּל	מְקֻטָּל	מִתְקַטֵּל

GRAMMATICAL CORNERSTONE 17 ר א שׁ נָּ פִּ ה

☆ SOUND CHANGE RULES VIA HEBREW NAMES I (15)

I The Hebrew names below illustrate regular sound changes in Hebrew. *Study* the sound change rules in **Appendix II**. Then *indicate* the relevant sound change/s occurring in the enlarged element of each name. *Rewrite* the Hebrew names and *add* after each name two Hebrew words/constructions that illustrate the relevant sound change/s occurring in the name.

1 *Abraham* אַבְרָהָם

2 *Ezra* עֶזְרָא[1]

3 *Abimélech* אֲבִימֶלֶךְ

4 *Baal* בַּעַל
(from *baʕl)

5 *Dan* דָּן
(דון)

6 *Jacob* יַעֲקֹב
(not יַעְקֹב)

7 *Jacob* יַעֲקֹב
(not אַעְקֹב)

8 *Messiah* מָשִׁיחַ

9 *Tel Aviv* תֵּל אָבִיב
(תלל)

10 *Sarah* שָׂרָה
(שׂרר)

11 *Joseph* יוֹסֵף (G-verb, participle)

12 *Jonathan* יוֹנָתָן[2]
(from יְהוֹנָתָן)[3]

13 *Michael* מִיכָאֵל

14 *Bethlehem* בֵּית לֶחֶם
(from *bayt)

15 *Mazal tov* מַזָּל טוֹב[4]
(not *manzal)

REVIEW AND APPLICATION OF THE RULES

I *Study* the sound change rules listed below. *Indicate* the relevant sound change/s occurring in each deviant form (on the left side) by comparing it with the corresponding normal form (on the right side). *Indicate* the root type to which each deviant form belongs.

SOUND CHANGE RULES

1 A guttural attracts an /a/-vowel/s.

2 Gutturals and ר cannot be doubled. Instead, the preceding short vowel is often lengthened.

3 The consonant י/ו in a diphthong normally disappears in pronunciation but is retained in writing as a vowel letter.

4 The consonant י/ו in a triphthong (י/ו with vowels on either side) is omitted. A triphthong at the end of a word is replaced by a full vowel (either with the vowel letter י/ו or ה).

5 Vowelless א at the end of a syllable is silenced. The silencing of א is compensated by the lengthening of the preceding vowel (if it is not already long).

6 A doubled consonant with a shva sometimes loses its doubling (shown in writing by the absence of the doubling dagesh).

7 The hard sound of a BeGaDKeFaT-consonant becomes soft after a vowel (shown in writing by the absence of the hardening dagesh).

---

[1] Actually Aramaic spelling.

[2] Note that when a verb form is used as a proper name, the short /a/-vowel in a stressed closed syllable (e.g., the verb form נָתַן) is replaced by a qamets, /ā/ (e.g., the name נָתָן).

[3] Both forms, יוֹנָתָן (without ה) and יְהוֹנָתָן (with ה), occur in the Bible.

[4] מַזָּל טוֹב means 'congratulations' (modern Hebrew).

1 תִּתְקַדְּשִׁי – תִּתְכַּסִּי   4 מִתְקַדְּשִׁים – מִתְהַלְלִים   7 הִתְקַדֵּשׁ – הִתְפַּתַּח

2 מִתְקַדֵּשׁ – מִתְבָּרֵךְ   5 הִתְקַדֵּשׁ – הִתְמַלֵּא   8 הִתְקַדֵּשׁ – הִתְכַּסָּה

3 הִתְקַדַּשְׁתָּ – הִתְכַּסִּיתָ   6 מִתְקַדֶּשֶׁת – מִתְפַּתַּחַת

II *Match* each sound element with the Hebrew word that illustrates it. *Mark* the element in the Hebrew word clearly! Observe that the same sound element may appear in more than one word, but only one instance is to be marked. Each Hebrew word is to be used once!

1 Vowel reduction **I** *A vowel* **one** *step before the stress is reduced*   ( ) הִתְנַחֲמוּ

6 Glide-/a/ *Before* ע,ח( )   הִתְפָּאֵר *at the end of a word*

2 Vowel reduction **I** *A vowel under a guttural* **one** *step before the stress is reduced*   ( ) הִתְפַּלַּלְתִּי

7 Contraction of a   ( ) הִתְהַלְלִי *diphthong The consonant* י/ו *becomes a vowel letter*

3 Compensatory lengthening of a vowel *Gutturals and* ר *cannot be doubled. Instead, the preceding vowel is often lengthened,* /a/ *becomes* /ā/   ( ) יִשְׁתַּמֵּר

8 Insertion vowel   ( ) הִתְמַלֵּאתִי *Used to break up an impermissible two-consonant sequence at the end of a word*

4 Simplification of a doubled consonant *Shown in writing by the absence of the doubling dagesh*   ( ) הִתְהַלְכוּ

9 Vowel lowering   ( ) מִתְפַּתַּחַת *The vowel* /ē/ *in a stressed originally closed syllable becomes* /a/

5 The הִתְפָּעֵל marker ת stands ( ) *after the first root consonant A sibilant:* ז, ס, שׂ, שׁ, צ   התְעַנִּינוּ

10 Silent א   ( ) מִתְפַּתֵּחַ א *not audible*

WORD LIST

Verbs

טָהֵר	be/become clean, pure: *imperf* יִטְהַר	הִטַּהֵר, טהר	*hitp* cleanse/purify oneself: *imperf* יִטַּהֵר
סתר	*hitp* הִסְתַּתֵּר hide oneself: *imperf* יִסְתַּתֵּר	הִצְטַדֵּק, צדק	*hitp* prove oneself to be right, innocent: *imperf* יִצְטַדֵּק
פלל	*hitp* הִתְפַּלֵּל pray: *imperf* יִתְפַּלֵּל	הִתְקַדֵּשׁ, קדש	*hitp* sanctify oneself: *imperf* יִתְקַדֵּשׁ
צָדֵק	be just, righteous: *imperf* יִצְדַּק (☆ **Zedekiah**, ṣ.d.q)	הִשְׁתַּמֵּר, שׁמר	*hitp* be on one's guard, be careful: *imperf* יִשְׁתַּמֵּר

הִתְפָּעֵל *verbs* (familiar vocabulary)

הִתְהַלֵּךְ, הלך   *hitp* walk/go around: *imperf* יִתְהַלֵּךְ

Particles

בְּעַד (בְּ + עַד)   for (the sake of), on behalf of

EXERCISES

23.1 *Fill in* the table below with the missing forms of הִתְפַּעֵל perfect and imperfect. *Read* all the verb forms and *translate* orally. *Remember*:

> - The characteristic features of הִתְפַּעֵל are the doubled middle root consonant (D) and the ת *Tav* of the prefix.
> - The prefix vowel of הִתְפַּעֵל is /i/.
> - The doubled middle root consonant of the D-stems sometimes loses its doubling when it is followed by a shva (except for the BeGaDKeFaT-consonants which never lose their dagesh), e.g., הִתְהַלְלָה becomes הִתְהַלֲלָה.

Imperfect	Perfect	Imperfect	Perfect	Imperfect	Perfect	Pronoun
	הִתְהַלֵּךְ		הִסְתַּתֵּר	יִתְפַּלֵּל		הוּא
				תִּתְפַּלֵּל		הִיא
				תִּתְפַּלֵּל		אַתָּה
				תִּתְפַּלְלִי		אַתְּ
				אֶתְפַּלֵּל		אָנֹכִי
				יִתְפַּלְלוּ		הֵם
				תִּתְפַּלֵּלְנָה		הֵנָּה
				תִּתְפַּלְלוּ		אַתֶּם
				תִּתְפַּלֵּלְנָה		אַתֶּן
				נִתְפַּלֵּל		אֲנַחְנוּ

23.2 *Fill in* the blanks with the missing participle forms of פִּעֵל and הִתְפַּעֵל. *Read* all the verb forms and *translate*.

Translation	fp	mp	fs	ms	
blessing				מְבָרֵךְ	1
	מִסְתַּתְּרוֹת				2
			מְהַלֶּלֶת		3
		מְבַקְשִׁים			4
				מִתְפַּלֵּל	5

23.3 *Fill in* the blanks with the missing forms of the imperative of פִּעֵל and הִתְפַּעֵל. *Read* all the verb forms and *translate*.

Translation	אַתֵּן	אַתֶּם	אַתְּ	אַתָּה	
go around!				הִתְהַלֵּךְ	1
			הִסְתַּתְּרִי		2
		הִתְפַּלְלוּ			3
	מַלֵּאנָה				4
		חַזְּקוּ			5
			שַׁלְּחִי	שַׁלַּח	6
				כַּפֵּר	7

23.4 *Fill in* the blanks with the missing forms of הִתְפַּעֵל from the list given below (the missing forms are italicized in the translation). Then *read* the entire Hebrew text and *translate* on your own. *Check* your translation against the translation in the book. *Pay attention* to the meaning of הִתְפַּעֵל. Finally *analyze* the verb forms as follows:
a) tense **b)** verb root **c)** person/gender/number. *Remember*:

> • הִתְפַּעֵל serves mainly to express a reflexive nuance of פִּעֵל or פָּעַל verbs, e.g., הִתְקַדֵּשׁ 'make *oneself* holy'. הִתְפַּעֵל is also used to express a reciprocal (mutual) or repeated nuance of פָּעַל verbs, e.g., הִתְרָאָה 'see *one another*', הִתְהַלֵּךְ 'walk *around*'.

מִתְהַלֵּךְ וְהִתְהַלֵּךְ תִּתְפַּלֵּל וַיִּתְהַלֵּךְ וָאֶשְׁתַּמְּרָה וְהִתְהַלֵּךְ
הִתְהַלְּכוּ מִסְתַּתֵּר הִתְפַּלֵּל

1 בְּעַד־הָעָם הַזֶּה _____ אַל־ וְאַתָּה And [as for] you, do not *pray*
on behalf of this people (Jer. 11:14)

a) _____ b) _____ c) _____

2 אֱלֹהִים: אֹתוֹ לָקַח־כִּי וְאֵינֶנּוּ הָאֱלֹהִים אֶת־חֲנוֹךְ _____ Enoch
walked with God (= the God); then (= וְ) he [was] no [more], for God
took him (Gen. 5:24) a) _____ b) _____ c) _____

3 עִמָּנוּ _____ דָוִד הֲלוֹא [Is] not David *hiding* among (= עִם) us!
(1 Sam. 23:19) a) _____ b) _____ c) _____

4 הַזֶּה: אֶל־הַבַּיִת _____ וּבָא And *he will* come and *pray* toward
this house (1 Kings 8:42)

a) _____ b) _____ c) _____

5 אֱלֹהֶיךָ אֶל־יְהוה עֲבָדֶיךָ בְּעַד־ _____ *Pray* for your servants to
the LORD, your God (1 Sam. 12:19)

a) _____ b) _____ c) _____

6 כָּל־הַיָּמִים: לִפְנֵי־מְשִׁיחִי _____ And *he will walk* before my
anointed forever (= all the days) (1 Sam. 2:35)

a) _____ b) _____ c) _____

7 _____ אֱלֹהִים יהוה אֶת־קוֹל וַיִּשְׁמְעוּ Later (= וַ) they heard the
voice of the LORD God *walking* (Gen. 3:8)

a) _____ b) _____ c) _____

8 וַאֲחִיכֶם אַתֶּם _____ *Sanctify yourselves,* you and your brothers
(1 Chron. 15:12) a) _____ b) _____ c) _____

9 מֵעֲוֹנִי: _____ And *I will keep myself* from sin (= my sin)
(2 Sam. 22:24) a) _____ b) _____ c) _____

10 אוֹתָהּ וְכִתְבוּ בָאָרֶץ _____ *Walk around* in the country and map
(= write) it (Jos. 18:8) a) _____ b) _____ c) _____

23.5 Each verse segment below contains a פָּעַל or הִתְפָּעֵל form. *Read* the Hebrew text and *translate* on your own. Then *match* each Hebrew verse segment with the correct English translation. *Check/complete* your translation against the translation in the book.

1 אָכֵן אַתָּה אֵל מִסְתַּתֵּר   ( ) To teach them war[fare] (Judg. 3:2)

2 כַּאֲשֶׁר צִוָּה אֱלֹהִים אֶת־נֹחַ:   ( ) As for me (= וַאֲנִי), look, I [am] hardening the heart of the Egyptians (= Egypt) (Ex. 14:17)

3 רָחֵל מְבַכָּה עַל־בָּנֶיהָ   ( ) Hear, please, and I will speak (Job 42:4)

4 וַאֲנִי הִנְנִי מְחַזֵּק אֶת־לֵב מִצְרַיִם   ( ) Rachel [is] weeping over her sons (Jer. 31:15)

5 כִּי הִטַּהֲרוּ הַכֹּהֲנִים וְהַלְוִיִּם כְּאֶחָד   ( ) The heavens [are] telling [the] glory of God (Ps. 19:2)

6 דַּבֶּר־נָא בְּאָזְנֵי הָעָם   ( ) As God had commanded Noah (Gen. 7:9)

7 בַּקְּשׁוּ פָנָיו   ( ) Seek him (= his face) (Ps. 105:4)

8 שְׁמַע־נָא וְאָנֹכִי אֲדַבֵּר   ( ) For the priests and the Levites had purified themselves as one [group] (Ezra 6:20)

9 לְלַמְּדָם מִלְחָמָה   ( ) Speak, please, to the people (= in the ears of the people) (Ex. 11:2)

10 הַשָּׁמַיִם מְסַפְּרִים כְּבוֹד־אֵל   ( ) Truly, you [are a] God [who] concealed (= concealing) himself (Isa. 45:15)

23.6 *Translate* into English. Proper names are enlarged. Then *study* carefully the characteristics of the different verb types in Grammatical cornerstone 18 in Section 24. *Analyze* the verb forms as follows:
a) tense b) root consonants c) verb type.

1 וְאַבְרָהָם זָקֵן בָּא בַּיָּמִים וַיהוה בֵּרַךְ אֶת־אַבְרָהָם בַּכֹּל: וַיֹּאמֶר (said)
אַבְרָהָם אֶל־עַבְדּוֹ זְקַן בֵּיתוֹ הַמֹּשֵׁל בְּכָל־אֲשֶׁר־לוֹ (Gen. 24:1–2)

a) _____ b) _____ c) _____   בֵּרַךְ

2 וְאָכַל (pausal form) בַּעֲבוּר אֲשֶׁר יְבָרֶכְךָ לִפְנֵי מוֹתוֹ: (Gen. 27:10)

a) _____ b) _____ c) _____   וְאָכַל

3   וְהִתְבָּרֲכוּ בְזַרְעֲךָ כֹּל גּוֹיֵי הָאָרֶץ עֵקֶב אֲשֶׁר שָׁמַעְתָּ בְּקֹלִי:

(Gen. 22:18)

שָׁמַעְתָּ   a) _____ b) _____ c) _____

4   יהוה אֲשֶׁר־הִתְהַלַּכְתִּי לְפָנָיו יִשְׁלַח מַלְאָכוֹ אִתָּךְ (Gen. 24:40)

יִשְׁלַח   a) _____ b) _____ c) _____

5   אָמוֹר אָמַרְתִּי בֵּיתְךָ וּבֵית אָבִיךָ יִתְהַלְּכוּ לְפָנַי עַד־עוֹלָם (1 Sam. 2:30)

אָמוֹר   a) _____ b) _____ c) _____

6   בְּהַר קֹדֶשׁ אֱלֹהִים הָיִיתָ בְּתוֹךְ אַבְנֵי־אֵשׁ הִתְהַלָּכְתָּ: (Ezek. 28:14)

הָיִיתָ   a) _____ b) _____ c) _____

7   מַה־נְּדַבֵּר וּמַה־נִּצְטַדָּק הָאֱלֹהִים מָצָא אֶת־עֲוֺן עֲבָדֶיךָ הִנֶּנּוּ עֲבָדִים

לַאדֹנִי (Gen. 44:16)

נְדַבֵּר   a) _____ b) _____ c) _____

8   הַמְעַט־לָנוּ אֶת־עֲוֺן פְּעוֹר אֲשֶׁר לֹא־הִטַּהַרְנוּ מִמֶּנּוּ עַד הַיּוֹם הַזֶּה

(Jos. 22:17)

הִטַּהַרְנוּ   a) _____ b) _____ c) _____

9   אָמְנָם יָדַעְתִּי כִי־כֵן וּמַה־יִּצְדַּק אֱנוֹשׁ עִם־אֵל: (Job 9:2)

יָדַעְתִּי   a) _____ b) _____ c) _____

10   וַיהוה בֵּרַךְ אֶת־אֲדֹנִי מְאֹד וַיִּגְדָּל (Gen. 24:35)

11   וַיְחַזֵּק יהוה אֶת־לֵב פַּרְעֹה מֶלֶךְ מִצְרַיִם וַיִּרְדֹּף אַחֲרֵי בְּנֵי יִשְׂרָאֵל

וּבְנֵי יִשְׂרָאֵל יֹצְאִים בְּיָד רָמָה: וַיִּרְדְּפוּ מִצְרַיִם אַחֲרֵיהֶם (Ex. 14:8–9)

וַיְחַזֵּק   a) _____ b) _____ c) _____

וַיִּרְדְּפוּ   a) _____ b) _____ c) _____

12   שִׁמְעוּנִי הַלְוִיִּם עַתָּה הִתְקַדְּשׁוּ וְקַדְּשׁוּ אֶת־בֵּית יהוה אֱלֹהֵי אֲבֹתֵיכֶם

(2 Chron. 29:5)

קַדְּשׁוּ   a) _____ b) _____ c) _____

23.7 *Reread* the text of Exercise 23.6 and *translate* again orally. Then *match* each grammatical element from the Exercise above with the Hebrew word/construction that illustrates it. *Mark* the element in the Hebrew word/construction clearly. Observe that the same grammatical element may appear more than once, but only one occurrence is to be marked. Each Hebrew word/construction is to be used once!

I   1   הִנֵּה 'Look, here, now', followed by an attached pronoun   ( ) אֶת־אַבְרָהָם

   2   פָּעַל: Infinitive-as-intensifier   ( ) יְבָרֶכְךָ

   3   פָּעַל: Imperative *Followed by an attached object pronoun*   ( ) וְיִתְבָּרְכוּ

   4   פָּעַל: Imperfect *Followed by an attached object pronoun*   ( ) אֱמֹר

   5   Simplification of a doubled consonant *After inverting-Vav*   ( ) הִגַּנּוּ

   6   Particle-as-intensifier   ( ) אֲבֹתֵיכֶם

   7   ר *Resh* with a chateph (shva-plus-vowel) instead of a shva   ( ) אָמְנָם

   8   Omitted hardening dagesh *Preceding word ends in a vowel*   ( ) אֶת־עֲוֹן עֲבָדֶיךָ

   9   Defective writing *The vowel letter ו is unexpectedly omitted*   ( ) יָדַעְתִּי כִּי־כֵן

  10   Definite direct object marker *A proper name is definite*   ( ) וַיֶּחֱזַק

  11   Definite direct object marker *A unit of a*   ( ) שְׁמָעוּנִי
       noun-plus-pronoun is definite

II   1   Relative clause describing a noun in a main   ( ) וּבְנֵי יִשְׂרָאֵל יֹצְאִים
       clause *Introduced by* אֲשֶׁר 'which, who, that' etc.

   2   Clause expressing purpose *Introduced by a particle*   ( ) עֵקֶב אֲשֶׁר שָׁמַעְתָּ בְּקֹלִי
       followed by אֲשֶׁר 'for, in order that' + a verb in the imperfect

   3   Participle replacing a verb in a clause   ( ) עֲוֹן פְּעוֹר אֲשֶׁר
       The time reference of the participle is determined by the   לֹא־הִטַּהַרְנוּ מִמֶּנּוּ
       context. The word order is Subject–Predicate

   4   Participle describing a noun in a clause   ( ) הַמְעַט־לָנוּ
       'ה + participle' *corresponds to an English relative clause*

   5   Yes/no question *The particle* ה *functions as*   ( ) יהוה אֲשֶׁר־
       a question mark (observe, הֲ *before a shva!)*   הִתְהַלַּכְתִּי לְפָנָיו

   6   The particle כִּי introduces a statement   ( ) בְּכָל־אֲשֶׁר־לוֹ
       After the verb 'know', rendered by ' that.'

   7   Clause expressing cause 'Because, since',   ( ) זָקֵן בֵּיתוֹ הַמֹּשֵׁל
       introduced by a particle followed by אֲשֶׁר +   בְּכָל־אֲשֶׁר...
       a verb in the perfect

   8   The preposition לְ denoting possession *Corresponds* ( ) יָדַעְתִּי כִּי־כֵן
       to English 'have'

   9   "Redundant" attached pronoun in a relative   ( ) בַּעֲבוּר אֲשֶׁר
       clause *Refers back to a noun in the main clause.*   יְבָרֶכְךָ
       Not rendered in English translation

23.8 *Find* in Exercise 23.6 above five words that undergo sound changes in pause and *write* them. Then *write* down the corresponding normal forms of the words in pause.

23.9 *Translate* into Hebrew.

  1 The priest went to the temple to serve the LORD and (+ to) pray. He asked *(inverted imperf)* (+ from) the LORD [for] well-being (= peace) for himself, (+ for) his wife, (+ for) his son, (+ for) his daughter and (+ for) his people.

  2 The man killed the prophet of the LORD. The king sent *(inverted imperf)* a guard to find the man who killed the prophet, but (וֹ) he did not find him. The man who had done this evil thing hid himself *(inverted imperf)* at his brother's house a long time (= many days), because the king sought (בְּקֵשׁ) his life (= soul).

  3 The prophets spoke to their nations as follows (= לְ + say/ing), "Bless God and praise him. Teach your children (= sons) the commandments of the LORD in order that they may keep them all their life (= the days of their life)."

23.10 *Check* (and *correct* if needed) your translation of Exercise 23.9 above. Then *transform* units 1–2 from the singular into the plural (verbs as well as nouns and pronouns) and unit 3 from the plural into the singular.

SECTION 24

1 הִפְעִיל, הָפְעַל (הֻפְעַל) (the *H-* and *Hp-stems*): *Basic forms (unchangeable verbs,* שְׁלֵמִים)

	Perfect	Imperfect (ordinary)	Imperfect (shortened)	Imperative	Infinitive (ordinary)	Infinitive (as-intensifier)	Participle
→	הִפְעִיל הִמְלִיךְ	יַמְלִיךְ	יַמְלֵךְ	הַמְלֵךְ	הַמְלִיךְ	הַמְלֵךְ	מַמְלִיךְ
	הָפְעַל הָמְלַךְ	יָמְלַךְ	יָמְלַךְ	⸻	⸻	הָמְלֵךְ	מָמְלָךְ
							מָמְלָךְ

– The characteristic feature of הִפְעִיל and הָפְעַל/הֻפְעַל is the consonant ה *He* of the prefix, either visible, e.g., הִמְלִיךְ, הָ/הָמְלַךְ, or omitted, e.g., יַמְלִיךְ (not יַהְמְלִיךְ, compare בַּבַּיִת instead of בְּהַבַּיִת), מָמְלָךְ (not מָהְמְלָךְ). Therefore, הִפְעִיל and הָ/הֻפְעַל are also called the *H-stems*.
– הָפְעַל/הֻפְעַל has, in addition, the /u/- or /o/-vowel (qamets-/o/!) of the prefix as a characteristic feature, e.g., הָמְלַךְ/הֻמְלַךְ. The /u/-vowel is to be associated with *passive forms*, compare שָׁמוּר (the passive participle of פָּעַל) and קֻדַּשׁ (the Dp-stem). Hence הָפְעַל/הֻפְעַל is also called the *Hp-stem*.
– *Prefix vowel*: The prefix vowel of the imperfect and the participle of הִפְעִיל is /a/, e.g., מַ, יַמְלִיךְ, and of הָפְעַל/הֻפְעַל it is either /u/ or /o/ (qamets-/o/), e.g., יֻמְלַךְ/יָמְלַךְ.
– *Vowel lowering*: In the 1st and 2nd persons (I, we; you) of הִפְעִיל the /î/-vowel in a stressed originally closed syllable is changed into an /a/-vowel in accordance with Philippi's law, e.g., הִמְלַכְתִּי 'crown' (not הִמְלִיכְתִּי).

2 הִפְעִיל *shortened imperfect (jussive) of* שְׁלֵמִים *(unchangeable verbs)*
Unlike all other stems (root type שְׁלֵמִים) whose shortened imperf forms are identical with the forms of the ordinary imperf, הִפְעִיל has two distinct forms of the imperf, the ordinary and the shortened. The shortened imperf occurs only in forms that are not followed by an ending, compare יַמְלִיךְ (ordinary imperf) and יַמְלֵךְ (shortened imperf).

3 הִפְעִיל *and* הָפְעַל *verbs with deviant form*: Verbs with changeable consonants and/or gutturals undergo regular sound changes in accordance with the sound change rules (see examples below).

a *I-guttural* (פ"ג) *verbs*: The original prefix vowel of הִפְעִיל perfect, like נִפְעַל perfect, is /a/. An /a/-vowel in an unstressed originally closed syllable is ordinarily changed into an /i/-vowel, e.g., הַמְלִיךְ becomes הִמְלִיךְ. Before a guttural the original /a/-vowel is raised halfway, that is, to an /e/-vowel, e.g., הַעֲמִיד becomes הֶעֱמִיד (compare נַעֲמַד that becomes נֶעֱמַד).
– The original silent shva at the end of the syllable in, for instance, הֶעֱמִיד, often takes a chateph (shva-plus-vowel). The vowel of the chateph corresponds to the vowel of the preceding prefix, e.g., הֶעֱמִיד (compare יַעֲבֹד, יֶאֱסֹף and נֶעֱמַד).

b I-י/ו (פו״י) *verbs*: Most of the word roots which begin with the consonant י originally had ו as the first root consonant, but ו at the beginning of a word has been replaced by י. However, the original ו is retained, when it is preceded by a prefix, e.g., הַוְלִיד which becomes הוֹלִיד, הַוְלַד which becomes הוּלַד, compare נַוְלַד (נִפְעַל) which becomes נוֹלַד (the verb root is ילד).

4 *Meaning of* הִפְעִיל *and* הָפְעַל *verbs*: הִפְעִיל serves mainly to express a *causative nuance* of פָּעַל verbs, e.g., הִמְלִיךְ 'let someone be/make someone king = crown', whereas מָלַךְ means 'be/become king'.

– הָפְעַל, which is rarely used in the Bible, serves as the passive counterpart of הִפְעִיל, e.g., הָמְלַךְ 'be made king = crowned'.

MEMORIZE

VERB TYPES V (unchangeable root types, i.e., *strong* שְׁלֵמִים)							
Verb form	G-stem	N-stem	D-stems			H-stems	
	פָּעַל	נִפְעַל	D פִּעַל	Dp פֻּעַל	HtD הִתְפָּעֵל	H הִפְעִיל	Hp הָפְעַל
Perfect	קָטַל/ קָטֵל/קָטֹל	נִקְטַל	קִטֵּל	קֻטַּל	הִתְקַטֵּל	הִקְטִיל	הָקְטַל/ הֻקְטַל
Characteristics of the perfect	Qamets under the first root letter	Prefix נ	Doubled middle root letter	/u/-vowel + doubled middle root letter	Prefix הִת + doubled middle root letter	Prefix ה	Prefix הָ or הֻ (ho)
Imperfect (ordinary)	יִקְטֹל/ יִקְטַל	יִקָּטֵל	יְקַטֵּל	יְקֻטַּל	יִתְקַטֵּל	יַקְטִיל	יָקְטַל/ יֻקְטַל
Imperfect (shortened)	Same as ordinary imperfect	Same as ordinary imperfect	Same as ordinary imperfect	Same as ordinary imperfect	Same as ordinary imperfect	יַקְטֵל	Same as ordinary imperfect
Characteristics of the imperfect	Prefix vowel /i/	Prefix vowel /i/ + doubled first root letter	Prefix vowel shva + doubled middle root letter	Prefix vowel shva + /u/-vowel + doubled middle root letter	Prefix vowel /i/ + ת + doubled middle root letter	Prefix vowel /a/ + stem vowel /i/ (ordinary imperfect)	Prefix vowel /u/ or /o/
Imperative	קְטֹל	הִקָּטֵל	קַטֵּל	——	הִתְקַטֵּל	הַקְטֵל	——
Infinitive (ordinary)	קְטֹל	הִקָּטֵל	קַטֵּל	——	הִתְקַטֵּל	הַקְטִיל	——
Infinitive (as-intensifier)	קָטוֹל	הִקָּטֹל/ נִקְטֹל	קַטֵּל/ קַטֹּל	קֻטֹּל	הִתְקַטֵּל	הַקְטֵל	הָקְטֵל/ הֻקְטֵל
Participle	קֹטֵל קָטוּל	נִקְטָל	מְקַטֵּל	מְקֻטָּל	מִתְקַטֵּל	מַקְטִיל	מָקְטָל/ מֻקְטָל
Characteristics of the participle	No prefix	Prefix נ	Prefix מְ + doubled middle root letter	Prefix מְ + /u/-vowel + doubled middle root letter	Prefix מִת + doubled middle root letter	Prefix מַ + stem vowel /i/	Prefix מָ or מֻ (mo)
Meaning expressed by each verb type	Active simple	Passive (of G-stem), reflexive, reciprocal	Active causative (factitive) intensive-repetitive	Passive (of D-stem)	Reflexive (of G & D-stems), repetitive, reciprocal	Active causative	Passive (of H-stem)

GRAMMATICAL CORNERSTONE 18   רֹ א שׁ פְּ נָ ה

Remember:

> • In the 1ˢᵗ and 2ⁿᵈ persons (I, we; you) of פָּעֵל, הִתְפַּעֵל and הִפְעִיל the
> I/E-vowel under the second root consonant (that is, the stem vowel) in a
> stressed originally closed syllable is changed to an /a/-vowel in accordance
> with Philippi's law, e.g., הִמְלַכְתִּי 'crown' becomes הִמְלַכְתִּי.

☆ SOUND CHANGE RULES VIA HEBREW NAMES II (16)

I The Hebrew names below illustrate regular sound changes in Hebrew.
Study the sound change rules in **Appendix II**. Then *indicate* the relevant
sound change/s occurring in the enlarged element of each name. *Rewrite* the
Hebrew names and *add* after each name two Hebrew words/constructions that
illustrate the relevant sound change/s occurring in the name.

1 *Naomi* נָעֳמִי (not נָעְמִי)   6 *Zephaniah* צְפַנְיָה   11 *Nimrod* נִמְרֹד

2 *Noah* נֹחַ   7 *Eliézer* אֱלִיעֶזֶר   12 *Ephraim* אֶפְרָיִם

3 *Ham* חָם (חמם)   8 *Joshua* יְהוֹשֻׁעַ   13 *Hallelujah* הַלְלוּיָה (D-verb)

4 *Obadiah* עוֹבַדְיָה   9 *Bathsheba* בַּת שֶׁבַע   14 *Isaac* יִצְחָק
(instead of עוֹבֵד)[1]   (from *šibʕ)   (from *yashaq)

5 *Hosea* הוֹשֵׁעַ   10 *Torah* תּוֹרָה   15 *Joseph* יוֹסֵף (H-verb,
(from *hawšēₐʕ, יש״,   (from *tawrāʰ, ירה,   shortened imperfect, 'may he
compare *Jesus* יֵשׁוּעַ)   compare יְרוּשָׁלַם)[2]   add', from *yawsef, יסף)

REVIEW AND APPLICATION OF THE RULES

I *Study* the sound change rules listed below. *Indicate* the relevant sound
change/s occurring in each deviant form (on the left side) by comparing it with
the corresponding normal form (on the right side). *Indicate* the root type to
which each deviant form belongs.

SOUND CHANGE RULES

A 1 A guttural usually takes a chateph (shva-plus-vowel) instead of a shva.
  2 A guttural attracts an /a/-vowel/s.
  3 The insertion vowel after (i.e., under) a guttural with a chateph is the vowel
    of the chateph.
  4 Vowel raising ("attenuation") before/after a guttural is realized only halfway.
    That is, the original /a/-vowel in an unstressed originally closed syllable is
    changed to an /e/-vowel.
  5 Vowelless א at the end of a syllable is transformed into a silent letter. The
    silencing of א is compensated by the lengthening of the preceding vowel (if
    it is not already long).

---

[1] The name Obadiah 'servant of the Lᴏʀᴅ' consists of two nouns, the participle עוֹבֵד
(serving) and יהוה (YHWH).

[2] The name Jerusalem is interpreted here as 'found by Salem', which consists of two elements,
ירה 'found' + Salem.

1   מַמְלֶכֶת – מַשְׁמַעַת   4   הִמְלִיכוּ – הֶעֱמִידוּ   7   הִמְלִיךְ – הִשְׁמִיעַ

2   תַּמְלִיכִי – תַּאֲזִינִי   5   הַמֶּלֶךְ – הַשְׁמַע   8   מַמְלִיךְ – מַקְרִיא

3   הִמְלִיכָה – הֶאֱזִינָה   6   הָמְלְכָה – הָעָמְדָה

B 1 The consonant י/ו at the end of a syllable forms a diphthong. The diphthong is normally contracted to one full vowel. That is, י/ו disappears in pronunciation but is retained in writing as a vowel letter.

  2 The consonant י/ו with vowels on either side forms a triphthong. The י/ו in a triphthong is omitted. At the end of a word the triphthong becomes a full vowel (with either the vowel letter י/ו or ה).

  3 The consonant נ at the end of a syllable is assimilated to (absorbed in) the next consonant, which, in turn, is doubled (shown in writing by the doubling dagesh).

1   הִמְלַכְנוּ – הִגְלֵינוּ   4   תַּמְלִיכִי – תַּגְלִי   7   יַמְלִיךְ – יֵיטִיב

2   מַמְלִיכִים – מוֹשִׁיעִים   5   הִמְלַכְתָּ – הִגַּדְתָּ   8   יַמְלִיכוּ – יַכּוּ

3   תַּמְלִיכוּ – תּוֹלִידוּ   6   יַמְלִיכוּ – יַעֲלוּ   9   אַמְלִיךְ – אוֹרִישׁ

WORD LIST

Nouns

אָבִיב   *m*, ears (of grain); month of year (Mar/Apr) (☆ Tel **Aviv**, ?.b.b)

בּוֹר   *m*, pit; cistern

חֹדֶשׁ   *m*, new moon, month: *pl* חֳדָשִׁים, *with suff* חָדְשֵׁי

מַכָּה, נכה   *f*, stroke; plague; defeat

עָפָר   *m*, dust

שָׁלֹשׁ   *f*, three: *m* שְׁלֹשָׁה

Verbs

אזן   *hiph* הֶאֱזִין listen: *imperf* יַאֲזִין, *inverted imperf* וַיַּאֲזֵן (from אֹזֶן 'ear')

אמן   *niph* נֶאֱמַן be confirmed, verified, trustworthy: *imperf* יֵאָמֵן (☆ **Amen**, ?.m.n)

בדל   *hiph* הִבְדִּיל separate, distinguish: *imperf* יַבְדִּיל, *inverted imperf* וַיַּבְדֵּל

גלה   uncover, reveal; go into exile

ירשׁ   inherit

ישׁע   *hiph* הוֹשִׁיעַ save, deliver: *imperf* יוֹשִׁיעַ (☆ **Hosea, Isaiah** y.š.ʕ)

נגד   *hiph* הִגִּיד tell, report: *imperf* יַגִּיד (followed by לְ), *huph* הֻגַּד be told/reported

נכה   *hiph* הִכָּה hit, strike, smite; defeat

קרב   come near, approach: *imperf* יִקְרַב

שלך   *hiph* הִשְׁלִיךְ throw, cast: *imperf* יַשְׁלִיךְ, *inverted imperf* וַיַּשְׁלֵךְ

הִפְעִיל verbs (familiar vocabulary)

הֶאֱכִיל, אכל	cause to eat, feed: *imperf* יַאֲכִיל, *inverted imperf* וַיַּאֲכֵל
הִגְלָה, גלה	cause to go into exile, send into exile
הִזְכִּיר, זכר	make someone remember, remind, mention: *imperf* יַזְכִּיר, *inverted imperf* וַיַּזְכֵּר
הוֹלִיד, ילד	cause to have a child, beget, become the father of
הוֹצִיא, יצא	cause to go out, bring out: *imperf* יוֹצִיא
הוֹרִישׁ, ירשׁ	make someone inherit: *imperf* יוֹרִישׁ
הוֹשִׁיב, ישׁב	make someone sit, set, settle, populate (a city): *imperf* יוֹשִׁיב
הִכְרִית, כרת	cause to cut off, eliminate: *imperf* יַכְרִית, *inverted imperf* וַיַּכְרֵת
הִמְלִיךְ, מלך	make someone king, crown: *imperf* יַמְלִיךְ, *inverted imperf* וַיַּמְלֵךְ
הִסְתִּיר, סתר	hide, conceal: *imperf* יַסְתִּיר, *inverted imperf* וַיַּסְתֵּר
הֶעֱלָה, עלה	cause to go up, bring up, lead up
הֶעֱמִיד, עמד	cause to stand, set upright, set someone standing: *imperf* יַעֲמִיד, *inverted imperf* וַיַּעֲמֵד
הִקְרִיב, קרב	make come near, bring (near), offer: *imperf* יַקְרִיב, *inverted imperf* וַיַּקְרֵב
הִשְׁמִיעַ, שׁמע	cause to hear, announce: *imperf* יַשְׁמִיעַ, *inverted imperf* וַיַּשְׁמַע

EXERCISES

24.1 *Fill in* the table below with the missing forms of הִפְעִיל perfect and imperfect. *Read* all the verb forms and *translate* orally. *Remember*:

- The characteristic features of הִפְעִיל are the ה of the prefix and the full stem vowel /i/ (the vowel under the second root consonant).
- The prefix vowel of הִפְעִיל (except in the perfect) is /a/.
- Unlike other verb types, the vocalic endings of the finite forms of הִפְעִיל (perf, imperf and imperative) are not stressed, e.g., הִבְדִּילָה, הַבְדִּילִי, יַבְדִּילוּ (compare שָׁמְרָה, יִשְׁמְרוּ, שָׁמְרִי).
- Unlike other verb types, הִפְעִיל (only forms without an ending) has two distinct forms of the imperfect, ordinary, e.g., יַמְלִיךְ 'he will crown' and shortened (jussive): יַמְלֵךְ 'may he crown'.
- The shortened imperf occurs only in the 2nd and 3rd persons.

Imperfect: Shortened	Imperfect: Ordinary	Imperfect: Shortened	Imperfect: Ordinary	Imperfect: Shortened	Imperfect: Ordinary	
יַזְכֵּר			יַסְתִּיר	יַמְלֵךְ	יַמְלִיךְ	הוּא
					תַּמְלִיךְ	הִיא
					תַּמְלִיךְ	אַתָּה
				Same as ordinary imperf	תַּמְלִיכִי	אַתְּ
				——	אַמְלִיךְ	אֲנִי
				Same as ordinary imperf	יַמְלִיכוּ	הֵם
				Same as ordinary imperf	תַּמְלֵכְנָה	הֵנָּה
				Same as ordinary imperf	תַּמְלִיכוּ	אַתֶּם
				Same as ordinary imperf	תַּמְלֵכְנָה	אַתֶּן
				——	נַמְלִיךְ	אֲנַחְנוּ

24.2 *Fill in* the blanks with the missing forms of the imperative of הִפְעִיל. *Read* all the verb forms and *translate. Note*:

- Like נִפְעַל verbs, the imperative and the infinitive forms of הִפְעִיל verbs begin with the consonant ה, compare הִשָּׁמֵר (נִפְעַל, usually with the prefix vowel /i/ followed by the doubling dagesh in the first root consonant) and הַמְלֵךְ (הִפְעִיל, usually with the prefix vowel /a/).
- None of the endings of הִפְעִיל imperative is stressed.

Translation	אַתֶּן	אַתֶּם	אַתְּ	אַתָּה	
crown!				הַמְלֵךְ	1
			הַשְׁלִיכִי		2
		הַכְרִיתוּ			3
	הַבְדֵּלְנָה				4
		הַקְרִיבוּ			5
				הַסְתֵּר	6

24.3 *Fill in* the table below with the missing forms of הָפְעַל. *Read* all the verb forms and *translate* orally. *Remember*:

> • The characteristic feature of הָפְעַל is the prefix ה, either with a qamets-/o/ or an /u/-vowel.
> • Two identical consonants without an intervening vowel are rendered in writing as one consonant with a doubling dagesh, e.g., הָכְרַ֫תָּ (the root is כרת).
> • הָפְעַל serves as the passive counterpart of הִפְעִיל, e.g., הָמְלַךְ 'he was made king/crowned'.

Imperfect	Perfect	Imperfect	Perfect	Imperfect	Perfect	Pronoun
יָבְדֵל			הָקְרַב	יָכְרַת	הָכְרַת	הוּא
				תִּכְרַת	הָכְרְתָה	הִיא
				תִּכְרַת	הָכְרַ֫תָּ	אַתָּה
				תָּכְרְתִי	הָכְרַתּ	אַתְּ
				אָכְרַת	הָכְרַ֫תִּי	אֲנִי
				יָכְרְתוּ	הָכְרְתוּ	הֵם
				תָּכְרַ֫תְנָה	הָכְרְתוּ	הֵ֫נָּה
				תָּכְרְתוּ	הָכְרַתֶּם	אַתֶּם
				תָּכְרַ֫תְנָה	הָכְרַתֶּן	אַתֶּן
				נָכְרַת	הָכְרַתְנוּ	אֲנַ֫חְנוּ

24.4 *Fill in* the table below with the missing participle forms of הִפְעִיל/הָפְעַל. *Read* all the forms and *translate*.

Translation	fp	mp	fs	ms	
casted				מָשְׁלָךְ mošlāx	1
casting			מַשְׁלִיכָה		2
		מַקְרִיבִים			3
	מָכְרָתוֹת				4
	מַבְדִּילוֹת				5
				מַסְתִּיר	6
			מָעֳמֶדֶת		7

24.5 *Fill in* the blanks with the missing forms of הִפְעִיל (and the one הָפְעַל form) from the list given below (the missing forms are italicized in the translation). Then *read* the Hebrew text and *translate* on your own. *Check* your translation against the translation in the book. *Pay attention* to the meaning of הִפְעִיל. Finally *analyze* the verb forms as follows:
a) tense b) root consonants c) person/gender/number. *Remember*:

> ◆ הִפְעִיל serves to express a *causative* nuance of פָּעַל verbs, e.g.,
> הִמְלִיךְ 'let someone be/make someone king = crown',
> whereas מָלַךְ (פָּעַל) means 'be/become king'.

הוֹשִׁיעַ   מוֹצָאִים   הִגִּידוּ   מַעֲלֶה   תַּסְתִּיר   מַכִּים   תַּבְדִּיל
הִשְׁלִיכוּ   הַגֵּד   הַסְתֵּר   אַזְכִּירָה

1 וּלְכָל־הָעָם _____ And *they* told (+ to) all the people as follows (= לֵאמֹר), "Look, the king [is] sitting in the gate[way]" (2 Sam. 19:9) לֵאמֹר הִנֵּה הַמֶּלֶךְ יוֹשֵׁב בַּשַּׁעַר

a) _____ b) _____ c) _____

2 אֵלֶּה הֵם הָאֱלֹהִים הַ _____ אֶת־מִצְרַיִם בְּכָל־מַכָּה בַּמִּדְבָּר: This (= these) [is] the God who (= הַ) smote (= *smiting*) Egypt with every [sort of] plague in the wilderness (1 Sam. 4:8)

a) _____ b) _____ c) _____

3 אֶתְכֶם _____ כִּי־אִתְּכֶם אָנִי לְ For I [am] with you to *save*

you (Jer. 42:11) a) _____ b) _____ c) _____

4 לַאדֹנִי _____ הֲלֹא־ Has not my lord *been told* (= told to)!

(1 Kings 18:13)

a) _____ b) _____ c) _____

5 אֶת־פָּנֶיךָ מִמֶּנִּי: _____ עַד־אָנָה How long (= until where)

will you conceal your face from me? (Ps. 13:2)

a) _____ b) _____ c) _____

6 לְךָ בְּתוֹךְ אַרְצֶךָ _____ שָׁלוֹשׁ עָרִים Three cities *you will set*

apart (= *distinguish*) for yourself in the middle of your land (Dt. 19:2)

a) _____ b) _____ c) _____

7 אֹתוֹ אֶל־הַבּוֹר הַזֶּה _____ *Cast* him into (= אֶל־) this pit

(Gen. 37:22)

a) _____ b) _____ c) _____

8 שִׁמְךָ בְּכָל־דֹּר וָדֹר _____ *Let me mention* your name in all

generations (= in every generation and generation) (Ps. 45:18)

a) _____ b) _____ c) _____

9 אַסְתִּיר פָּנַי בַּיּוֹם הַהוּא _____ וְאָנֹכִי But (= וְ) I will *surely* hide

my face on (= בְּ) that day (Dt. 31:18)

a) _____ b) _____ c) _____

10 אֹתָנוּ מֵאֶרֶץ מִצְרָיִם _____ הַ יהוה אַיֵּה אָמְרוּ וְלֹא And they

did not say, "Where [is] the LORD who (= הַ) *brought* (= *bringing*) us

up from the land of Egypt" (Jer. 2:6)

a) _____ b) _____ c) _____

11 אֶל־הַכַּשְׂדִּים _____ בָּנֶיךָ וְאֶת־ נָשֶׁיךָ וְאֶת־כָּל־ And all your

wives and your sons [they] *shall lead out* (= *leading/bringing out*) to

the Chaldeans (Jer. 38:23)

a) _____ b) _____ c) _____

24.6 *Match* each grammatical construction with the Hebrew phrase/clause (from Exercise 24.5 above) that illustrates it. *Read* and *translate* orally. Observe that the same grammatical construction may appear more than once, but only one instance is to be noted. Each Hebrew phrase/clause is to be used once!

1 Participle describing a noun in a clause ( ) הֲלֹא־הֻגַּד לַאדֹנִי
   'הַ + *participle' corresponds to an*
   English relative clause

2 Rhetorical question *Introduced by* הֲלֹא ( ) הַסְתֵּר אַסְתִּיר פָּנַי

3 Verbal clause: Emphasis is signalled ( ) וְאֶת־בָּנֶיךָ
   by variant word order *The normal*
   word order is said to be **Verb–Subject–Object**

4 Verbal clause: Emphasis is signalled ( ) אֶתְכֶם אָנִי לְהוֹשִׁיעַ אֶתְכֶם
   by an additional independent pronoun

5 Definite direct object marker ( ) וּלְכָל־הָעָם הִגִּידוּ לֵאמֹר

6 Infinitive-as-intensifier ( ) הָאֱלֹהִים הַמַּכִּים אֶת־מִצְרַיִם

7 Particle-as-intensifier *Usually rendered* ( ) שָׁלוֹשׁ עָרִים תַּבְדִּיל לָךְ
   in English by 'look'

8 Quotation marker *Literally 'to + say/ing',* ( ) וְאָנֹכִי אַסְתִּיר פָּנַי
   introduces direct speech

9 Phrase expressing purpose, ( ) אַזְכִּירָה שְׁמֶךָ
   לְ *'to/in order to' + ordinary infinitive*

10 Imperfect expressing a wish ( ) הִנֵּה הַמֶּלֶךְ יוֹשֵׁב
   Lengthened imperfect (1ˢᵗ person),
   'let me/us, may I/we…'

24.7 Each Hebrew verse/verse segment below contains a form of הִפְעִיל (enlarged in the Hebrew text). *Read* and *translate* on your own. *Fill in* the blanks with the missing words in the following translation and *check/complete* your translation against it.

1 אַסְתִּירָה פָּנַי מֵהֶם Let _____ conceal _____ (= _____ face) from
   _____ (Dt. 32:20)

2 בְּחֹדֶשׁ הָאָבִיב הוֹצִיאֲךָ יהוה אֱלֹהֶיךָ מִמִּצְרַיִם לָיְלָה: In the month
   of Abib the LORD, _____ God, brought _____ out of (= מִ) Egypt [by]
   night (Dt. 16:1)

3 כִּשְׁמֹעַ כָּל־יִשְׂרָאֵל כִּי־שָׁב יָרָבְעָם וַיִּשְׁלְחוּ וַיִּקְרְאוּ אֹתוֹ אֶל־הָעֵדָה

וַיַּמְלִיכוּ אֹתוֹ עַל־כָּל־יִשְׂרָאֵל As [soon as] _____ Israel heard

(= hearing) that Jeroboam had returned, _____ sent and called _____

_____ the assembly and made _____ king over _____ Israel

(1 Kings 12:20)

4 יְהוָה אֱלֹהִים יֵאָמֵן דְּבָרְךָ עִם דָּוִיד אָבִי כִּי אַתָּה הִמְלַכְתַּנִי

עַל־עַם רַב כַּעֲפַר הָאָרֶץ: [O] Lord God, let _____ word to (= עִם)

David _____ father be confirmed, _____ [it was] _____ [who]

(= _____ – _____) have made _____ king _____ [a] people [as]

numerous as the dust of the earth (2 Chron. 1:9)

5 יְהוָה הַמַּסְתִּיר פָּנָיו מִבֵּית יַעֲקֹב The Lord who (= הַ) [is] concealing

_____ (= _____face) _____ the house of Jacob (Isa. 8:17)

6 אַל־תַּשְׁלִיכֵנִי מִלְּפָנֶיךָ Do not cast _____ from (= מִלְּ) _____ presence

(= _____ face) (Ps. 51:13)

7 הִגִּיד לְךָ אָדָם מַה־טּוֹב וּמָה־יְהוָה דּוֹרֵשׁ מִמְּךָ _____ told _____,

man, _____ [is] good and _____ the Lord [is] requiring of (= מִ) _____

(Mic. 6:8)

8 כִּי אֲנִי יְהוָה אֱלֹהֶיךָ קְדוֹשׁ יִשְׂרָאֵל מוֹשִׁיעֶךָ For _____ [am] the

Lord, _____ God, the Holy [One] of Israel, _____ Saviour (Isa. 43:3)

9 מַה־זֹּאת עָשִׂיתָ לִי לָמָּה לֹא־הִגַּדְתָּ לִי כִּי אִשְׁתְּךָ הִוא: _____ [is]

_____ _____ have done to _____? _____ did _____ _____ tell (= tell

to) _____ that _____ [is] _____ wife? (Gen. 12:18)

10 אֵת אוּרִיָּה הַחִתִּי הִכִּיתָ בַחֶרֶב וְאֶת־אִשְׁתּוֹ לָקַחְתָּ לְּךָ לְאִשָּׁה וְאֹתוֹ

הָרַגְתָּ בְּחֶרֶב בְּנֵי עַמּוֹן: Uriah the Hittite _____ smote with the sword

and _____ wife _____ took to [be] _____ wife (= for _____ to wife)

and _____ _____ killed by the sword of the Ammonites (= sons of

Ammon) (2 Sam. 12:9)

24.8 *Match* each grammatical construction (from Exercise 24.7 above) with the Hebrew phrase/clause that illustrates it. *Read* and *translate* orally. Observe that the same grammatical construction may appear more than once, but only one occurrence is to be noted. Each Hebrew phrase/clause is to be used once!

1 Participle describing a noun in a clause (__) וַיִּקְרְאוּ אֹתוֹ אֶל־הָעֵדָה
'*הַ* + participle' corresponds to an English relative clause

2 Subordinate clause of cause (__) וְאֹתוֹ הָרַגְתָּ
Begins with כִּי '*because, for*'

3 Verbal clause: Emphasis is signalled (__) אַל־תַּשְׁלִיכֵנִי
by variant word order *The normal word order is said to be **Verb–Subject–Object***

4 Verbal clause: Emphasis is signalled (__) אֱלֹהִים יֵאָמֵן דְּבָרְךָ עִם דָּוִיד
by an additional independent pronoun

5 Adverbial of time (__) כִּי אַתָּה הִמְלַכְתַּנִי
Usually placed first in the clause

6 Verbal clause with normal word (__) אַסְתִּירָה פָּנַי
order *That is, **Verb–Subject–Object***

7 זֹאת intensifying a question (__) יהוה הַמַּסְתִּיר פָּנָיו

8 Temporal phrase 'כְּ *(while)* + (__) אַתָּה הִמְלַכְתַּנִי
ordinary infinitive + noun/pronoun', *corresponds to an English temporal clause*

9 Doubling dagesh linking (__) מַה־זֹּאת עָשִׂיתָ
two words together

10 Imperfect expressing a wish *Lengthened* (__) כִּשְׁמֹעַ כָּל־יִשְׂרָאֵל
imperfect (1ˢᵗ person), 'may I/we, let me/us…'

11 Imperfect expressing a wish *Shortened* (__) עָשִׂיתָ לִּי
imperfect, identical in form with the ordinary imperf (occurs in the 2ⁿᵈ and 3ʳᵈ persons)

12 Negative command, 'אַל + *shortened imperf*' (__) בְּחֹדֶשׁ הָאָבִיב הוֹצִיאֲךָ יהוה

24.9 *Translate* into English. Proper names are enlarged. Then *study* carefully the characteristics of the different verb types in Grammatical cornerstone 18 above. *Analyze* the verb forms as follows:
a) tense b) root consonants c) verb type. *Remember*:

> • All verb types except פָּעַל (called Qal, 'light') include characteristic additional consonant/s and/or a doubling dagesh.
> • Find the root consonants of the verbs as follows:
> – *Identify* and *remove* any attached pronoun/s.
> – *Identify* and *remove* any characteristic additional element/s.

1 וַיהוה הִשְׁלִיךְ עֲלֵיהֶם אֲבָנִים גְּדֹלוֹת מִן־הַשָּׁמַיִם עַד־**עֲזֵקָה** (Jos. 10:11)

2 הַבְדֵּל יַבְדִּילַנִי יהוה מֵעַל (read מֵ) עַמּוֹ (Isa. 56:3)

3 אָנֹכִי הִגַּדְתִּי וְהוֹשַׁעְתִּי וְהִשְׁמַעְתִּי (Isa. 43:12)

וְהוֹשַׁעְתִּי

a) _____ b) _____ c) _____

4 עַתָּה יָדַעְתִּי כִּי הוֹשִׁיעַ יהוה מְשִׁיחוֹ (Ps. 20:7)

יָדַעְתִּי

a) _____ b) _____ c) _____

5 לְךָ אָמַר לִבִּי בַּקְּשׁוּ פָנָי אֶת־פָּנֶיךָ יהוה אֲבַקֵּשׁ: אַל־תַּסְתֵּר פָּנֶיךָ

מִמֶּנִּי (Ps. 27:8–9) אֲבַקֵּשׁ

a) _____ b) _____ c) _____

6 הַסְתֵּר פָּנֶיךָ מֵחֲטָאָי (Ps. 51:11)

7 הִגִּידוּ הַשָּׁמַיִם צִדְקוֹ וְרָאוּ כָל־הָעַמִּים כְּבוֹדוֹ: (Ps. 97:6)

הִגִּידוּ

a) _____ b) _____ c) _____

8 אַל־תַּסְתֵּר מִמֶּנִּי מִצְוֹתֶיךָ: (Ps. 119:19)

תַּסְתֵּר

a) _____ b) _____ c) _____

9 אָמַר שְׁמוּאֵל אֶל־כָּל־יִשְׂרָאֵל הִנֵּה שָׁמַעְתִּי בְקֹלְכֶם לְכֹל אֲשֶׁר־
אֲמַרְתֶּם לִי וָאַמְלִיךְ עֲלֵיכֶם מֶלֶךְ: וְעַתָּה הִנֵּה הַמֶּלֶךְ מִתְהַלֵּךְ לִפְנֵיכֶם
וַאֲנִי זָקַנְתִּי... וּבָנַי הִנָּם אִתְּכֶם וַאֲנִי הִתְהַלַּכְתִּי לִפְנֵיכֶם (1 Sam. 12:1–2)

מִתְהַלֵּךְ

a) _____ b) _____ c) _____

24.10 *Translate* into Hebrew. *Render* the English simple past by the Hebrew perfect.

1 The son inherited the house. His father made him inherit
(יָרֵשׁ, הִפְעִיל¹⁾ + לְ²⁾ + ³⁾him) it. The house was beautiful.

2 The woman bore a child. The child was born (יָלַד, נִפְעַל) in the city.
The son became the father of/begot (יָלַד, הִפְעִיל) many children.

3 The people (= nation) went from its land into exile. It was the LORD
who sent the people (= caused the people to go) into exile
(גָּלָה, הִפְעִיל).

4 The son ate. The woman fed him (= caused him to eat אָכַל, הִפְעִיל).

5 The man did not remember the commandment of the LORD. The
priest reminded him of (זָכַר, הִפְעִיל¹⁾ + לְ²⁾ + ³⁾him) this commandment.

6 The nation dwelt in this good land. It was God who made the nation
dwell (יָשַׁב, הִפְעִיל) there.

24.11 *Check* (and *correct* if needed) your translation of Exercise 24.10 above.
Then *transform* the clauses from the singular into the plural (verbs as well
as nouns and pronouns).

SECTION 25

פָּעַל verbs	Perf	Imperf: Ordinary	Imperf: Shortened	Imperf: Inverted	Imperative	Infinitive: Ordinary
1 I-א (פ״א)	אָכַל eat	יֹאכַל	יֹאכַל	וַיֹּאכַל	אֱכֹל	אֱכֹל
	אָמַר say	יֹאמַר	יֹאמַר	וַיֹּאמֶר (!)	אֱמֹר	אֱמֹר
2 I-י (פ״י)	____ be/come good	יִיטַב	יִיטַב	וַיִּיטַב		
I-ו (inflected as I-י)	יָרַשׁ inherit	יִירַשׁ	יִירַשׁ	וַיִּירַשׁ	רַשׁ/רֵשׁ	רֶשֶׁת
Irregular	יָכֹל be able	יוּכַל	יוּכַל	וַיּוּכַל		יְכֹלֶת
I-ו (פ״ו)	יָשַׁב sit, dwell	יֵשֵׁב	יֵשֵׁב	וַיֵּשֶׁב	שֵׁב	שֶׁבֶת
Irregular	הָלַךְ walk	יֵלֵךְ	יֵלֵךְ	וַיֵּלֶךְ	לֵךְ	לֶכֶת
3 I-נ (פ״נ)	נָפַל fall	יִפֹּל	יִפֹּל	וַיִּפֹּל	נְפֹל	נְפֹל
(imperf -/a/)	____ come near	יִגַּשׁ	יִגַּשׁ	וַיִּגַּשׁ	גַּשׁ	גֶּשֶׁת
Irregular	נָתַן give	יִתֵּן	יִתֵּן	וַיִּתֵּן	תֵּן	תֵּת
Irregular	לָקַח take	יִקַּח	יִקַּח	וַיִּקַּח	קַח	קַחַת
I-נ + II-ג	נָחַל possess	יִנְחַל	יִנְחַל	וַיִּנְחַל	נְחַל	נְחֹל
4 III-י/ו (לו״י)	בָּנָה build	יִבְנֶה	יִבֶן	וַיִּבֶן	בְּנֵה	בְּנוֹת
	בָּכָה weep	יִבְכֶּה	not attested	וַיֵּבְךְּ (!)	בְּכֵה	בְּכוֹת
	רָאָה see	יִרְאֶה	יֵרֶא	וַיַּרְא (!)	רְאֵה	רְאוֹת
Irregular	הָיָה be	יִהְיֶה	יְהִי	וַיְהִי (!)	הֱיֵה	הֱיוֹת
Irregular	חָיָה live	יִחְיֶה	יְחִי	וַיְחִי (!)	חֲיֵה	חֲיוֹת

1 פָּעַל *imperfect of* I-א (פ״א) *verbs*: Most of the verbs which begin with א belong to the I-guttural (ג״פ) root type (verbs with changeable vowels), e.g., אסף 'gather' (imperf יֶאֱסֹף). However, in a few פָּעַל verbs, whose most frequent are אָמַר 'say' and אָכַל 'eat', the consonant א at the end of a syllable is silenced and the prefix vowel is /o/, e.g., יֹאמַר. The stem vowel is /a/: יֹאמַר. The inverted imperfect of אָמַר is וַיֹּאמֶר. *Observe that the stress is thrown back from the last to the next-to-last syllable.*

2 פָּעַל *imperfect, imperative and infinitive of* I-י/ו (פו״י) *verbs*

a *Imperfect*: In פ״י-verbs (verbs with an original י as the first root consonant) the consonant י at the end of a syllable forms a diphthong. י ordinarily becomes a vowel letter, e.g., אֱיטַב becomes יִיטַב.

– Certain פ״ו-verbs (verbs with an original ו as the first root consonant), whose most frequent are יָרַשׁ 'inherit' and יָרֵא 'fear', are inflected like the פ״י-verbs, e.g., אֱיְרַשׁ becomes יִירַשׁ.

– פ״ו-verbs: The original consonant ו at the beginning of a word is replaced by י, e.g., יָשַׁב 'sit, dwell'. The imperf is formed without the first root consonant and both the stem- and the prefix vowels are /e/: יֵשֵׁב. The inverted imperf is וַיֵּשֶׁב. *Note that the stress is thrown back from the last to the next-to-last syllable.*

– *The irregular verb* הָלַךְ:הלךְ 'go' is inflected like יֵשֵׁב, e.g., וַיֵּלֶךְ.

b *Imperative*: The imperative of I-ו verbs, like the imperf, is formed without the first root consonant, e.g., שֵׁב (ישׁב) 'sit!', לֵךְ (הלך) 'go!'.

c *Infinitive*: The infinitive of I-ו verbs is also formed without the first root consonant, but the consonant ת is added after the third root consonant, which results in an impermissible two-consonant sequence at the end of the word, e.g., שֶׁבְתּ. The cluster is broken up by inserting a vowel, normally /e/, but after a guttural /a/, e.g., שֶׁבְתּ becomes שֶׁבֶת, דֵּעְתּ becomes דֵּעַת 'know' (ידע).

3 פָּעַל *imperfect, imperative and infinitive of* I-נ (פ"נ) *verbs*

a *Imperfect*: The consonant נ at the end of a syllable is assimilated to the following consonant, which in turn is doubled, e.g., יַנְפֹּל becomes יִפֹּל.
– Before a guttural, however, the נ is retained: יִנְחַל .
– *The irregular verb* לקח:לָקַח is inflected like I-נ verbs, e.g., יִלְקַח becomes יִקַּח.

b *Imperative*: The imperative of imperf-/a/ and imperf-/e/ verbs is formed without the first root consonant, e.g., גַּשׁ (נגשׁ) 'come near!', קַח (לקח) 'take!'.

c *Infinitive*: The infinitive of imperf-/a/ and imperf-/e/ verbs is also formed without the first root consonant, but the consonant ת is added after the third root consonant, which results in a two-consonant cluster at the end of the word. The consonant cluster is broken up by inserting a vowel, normally /e/, but after a guttural /a/, e.g., גְּשְׁתּ becomes גֶּשֶׁת, קְחְתּ becomes קַחַת.

4 פָּעַל *imperfect of* III-י/ו (ל"י/ו) *verbs*: III-י/ו (III-ה) verbs have two forms of the imperfect, ordinary and shortened.
– *Ordinary imperfect*: The third root consonant י/ו with vowels on either side forms a triphthong, which is ordinarily contracted to one full vowel (either with the vowel letter י/ו or ה), e.g., the hypothetical form יִבְנַיְ becomes יִבְנוּ and יִבְנַיְ becomes יִבְנֶה.[1]
– *Shortened imperfect* (only forms without an ending!) is formed without the last syllable with the vowel letter ה, e.g., יִבֶּן, יַעַל 'go up' (compare יִבְנֶה and יַעֲלֶה). The consonants of the clusters at the end of the words are separated by an insertion vowel, normally /e/, but after a guttural /a/, thus יִבֶּן becomes יִבֶן and יַעַל becomes יַעַל.
– Sometimes the cluster at the end of the word is retained, e.g., יִבְךְּ.
– *The irregular verbs* הָיָה 'be' *and* חָיָה 'live': The ordinary imperfect is יִהְיֶה and יִחְיֶה ("attenuation" takes place in spite of the following guttural). The shortened imperfect is יְהִי, יְחִי. A vowelless particle, e.g., לְ, followed by the infinitive of הֱיוֹת/חֲיוֹת results in לִהְיוֹת/לִחְיוֹת.

---

[1] Note that historically most of the words in Hebrew (including the ordinary imperf) ended in a vowel, either short or long, but at a certain stage in the history of the language the original short vowels at the end of words fell away. However, the suffixless forms of the shortened imperf did not end in a vowel.

REVIEW AND APPLICATION OF THE RULES

I *Match* each grammatical element with the Hebrew word that illustrates it. *Mark* the element in the Hebrew word clearly! Observe that the same element may appear more than once, but only one occurrence is to be marked. Each Hebrew word is to be used once!

1 Vowel reduction **I** *A vowel* (__) יוּכַל   **7** Vowel raising ("attenuation") (__) תֹּאמְרִי
  one step before the stress is reduced   before a guttural is not realized
        The original /a/-vowel remains intact

2 Vowel reduction **I** *A vowel* (__) וַיִּבֶן   **8** Contraction of a (__) וַיֵּשְׁתְּ
  under a guttural **one** *step before the*   diphthong *The consonant*
  stress is reduced   ' *becomes a vowel letter*

3 Two-consonant sequence (__) יֵשְׁבוּ   **9** Doubling dagesh *Since* נ (__) תִּנְחֲלוּ
  at the end of a word, *III-*י*/*ו *verb*   is assimilated to the next consonant

4 Infinitive of I-י/ו verb (__) יִפֹּל   **10** Contraction of a (__) יִיטַב
  Without the first root consonant י*/*ו;   diphthong *The consonant*
  ת *is added after the third root consonant*   ו *becomes a vowel letter*

5 Insertion vowel (segol) *Used* (__) יִבְנוּ   **11** Insertion vowel after a (__) יַעֲנוּ
  to break up an impermissible two-consonant   guttural *Used to break up a*
  *sequence at the end of a word, III-*י*/*ו *verb*   *two-consonant sequence at the end of a word*

6 Silent א (__) וַיִּעַן   **12** Contraction of a (__) רֶדֶת
        triphthong, ו*/*י *is omitted*

II The verb forms below (from Exercise 25.4) undergo regular sound changes. *Study* the sound change rules in **Appendix II**. Then *indicate* the relevant sound change/s occurring in the enlarged element/s of each verb form. *Translate.*

1 וַיְדַבֵּר, מָצָאתִי, מֵת, אֶעֱלֶה, קָבֹר, וַיַּעַל, וַיַּעֲלוּ (G-stem, compare וַיִּשְׁמְרוּ)

2 וַיַּעֲנוּ (G-stem), הֻגַּד, וַנִּירָא, וַיַּעַשׂ, וַיִּצֶל, הָרְגוּם   **3** וְעָשִׂיתָ   **4** וַיִּשָּׁבַע

WORD LIST

Nouns

נְאֻם	*m*, utterance, oracle: נְאֻם יְהֹוָה 'utterance of the LORD' (prophetic formula)	נצל	*hiph* הִצִּיל save, rescue: *imperf* יַצִּיל, *inverted imperf* וַיַּצֵּל
עֶרֶב	*m*, evening: *pl* עֲרָבִים, *with suff* עַרְבִּי	נָשָׂא	lift up, raise, carry: *imperf* יִשָּׂא

Verbs

		סָגַר	shut, close: *imperf* יִסְגֹּר
חָרֵב	be/become dried up, wasted, desolated: *imperf* יֶחֱרַב	עָנָה	answer, respond: *imperf* יַעֲנֶה, *inverted imperf* וַיַּעַן
נָפַל	fall: *imperf* יִפֹּל		

Derived verbs (familiar vocabulary)

הוּרַד ,ירד *huph* be brought down: הִשְׁבִּיעַ ,שׁבע *hiph* make swear,
    imperf יוּרַד   *imperf* יַשְׁבִּיעַ

נִרְאָה ,ראה *niph* become visible, appear: שִׁכֵּן ,שׁכן *pi* make dwell:
    imperf יֵרָאָה, *hiph* הִרְאָה   *imperf* יְשַׁכֵּן
    cause to see, show: *imperf* יַרְאָה

EXERCISES

25.1 Each verse/verse segment below contains a הִפְעִיל form of either a I-א,
I-י/ו, I-נ or III-י/ו (III-ה) verb. *Read* the Hebrew text and *translate* on
your own. Then *match* each Hebrew verse/verse segment with the correct
English translation below and *check/complete* your translation against it.
Analyze the verbs as follows:
a) verb type **b**) verb root **c**) tense **d**) person/gender/number. *Note*:

> ◆ The inverted imperf of רָאָה (פָּעַל) is identical in form with the
> inverted imperf of הִפְעִיל: וַיַּרְא means either 'he saw' (פָּעַל) or 'he
> showed' (הִפְעִיל).

I 1 וַיֹּאמֶר אֱלֹהִים יְהִי אוֹר וַיְהִי־אוֹר: (_) I myself will go down with
    a) וַיֹּאמֶר   b) _____   you to Egypt (Gen. 46:4)
    c) _____   d) _____

   2 וַיַּרְא אֹתָם אֶת־בֶּן־הַמֶּלֶךְ:   (_) Make for us gods who will go
    a) וַיַּרְא   b) _____   before us (Ex. 32:1)
    c) _____   d) _____

   3 וְרוּחַ קָדְשְׁךָ אַל־תִּקַּח מִמֶּנִּי: (_) You shall not see me
    a) תִּקַּח   b) _____   (= my face) (2 Sam. 3:13)
    c) _____   d) _____

   4 לֹא־תִרְאֶה אֶת־פָּנַי   (_) God said, "Let [there] be
    a) תִרְאֶה   b) _____   light", and [there] was light
    c) _____   d) _____   (Gen. 1:3)

   5 אָנֹכִי אֵרֵד עִמְּךָ מִצְרַיְמָה   (_) And in this place I will give
    a) אֵרֵד   b) _____   prosperity (= peace), [is] the
    c) _____   d) _____   utterance of the LORD (Hag. 2:9)

   6 עֲשֵׂה־לָנוּ אֱלֹהִים אֲשֶׁר יֵלְכוּ לְפָנֵינוּ   (_) The LORD gave and the LORD has
    a) יֵלְכוּ   b) _____   taken [away]. Let the name of
    c) _____   d) _____   the LORD be blessed (Job 1:21)

   7 וּבַמָּקוֹם הַזֶּה אֶתֵּן שָׁלוֹם נְאֻם יהוה   (_) And your holy spirit, do not
    a) אֶתֵּן   b) _____   take [away] from me
    c) _____   d) _____   (Ps. 51:13)

   8 יהוה נָתַן וַיהוה לָקָח יְהִי שֵׁם יהוה   (_) And he showed them the
    מְבֹרָךְ:   king's son (2 Kings 11:4)
    a) יְהִי   b) _____
    c) _____   d) _____

II 1 כִּי מִי יוּכַל לִשְׁפֹּט אֶת־עַמְּךָ   ( ) To give them one heart
יוּכַל   a) _____ b) _____   (2 Chron. 30:12)
       c) _____ d) _____

2 וַיֹּאמֶר אֱלֹהִים אֶל־מֹשֶׁה   ( ) And his glory will be seen
אֶהְיֶה אֲשֶׁר אֶהְיֶה   upon you (Isa. 60:2)
אֶהְיֶה   a) _____ b) _____
       c) _____ d) _____

3 לָתֵת לָהֶם לֵב אֶחָד   ( ) Let not all the people go up
תֵּת   a) _____ b) _____   (Jos. 7:3)
       c) _____ d) _____

4 אַל־יַעַל כָּל־הָעָם   ( ) God said to Moses, "I am who
יַעַל   a) _____ b) _____   I am" (Ex. 3:14)
       c) _____ d) _____

5 וּכְבוֹדוֹ עָלַיִךְ יֵרָאֶה: ( ) For who is able to judge your
יֵרָאֶה   a) _____ b) _____   people? (1 Kings 3:9)
       c) _____ d) _____

6 וַיֻּגַּד לְיוֹאָב הִנֵּה הַמֶּלֶךְ בֹּכֶה   ( ) Nation shall not lift up sword
וַיֻּגַּד   a) _____ b) _____   against (= אֶל־) nation (Isa. 2:4)
       c) _____ d) _____

7 לֹא־יִשָּׂא גוֹי אֶל־גּוֹי חֶרֶב   ( ) Now (= וְ) Joseph was brought
יִשָּׂא   a) _____ b) _____   down to Egypt (Gen. 39:1)
       c) _____ d) _____

8 וְיוֹסֵף הוּרַד מִצְרָיְמָה   ( ) Later (= וְ) it was reported to
הוּרַד   a) _____ b) _____   Joab, "Look, the king [is]
       c) _____ d) _____   weeping" (2 Sam. 19:2)

25.2 *Match* each grammatical phenomenon (from Exercise 25.1 above) with the Hebrew word/construction that illustrates it. *Read* and *translate* orally. Observe that the same grammatical phenomenon may appear more than once, but only one instance is to be noted. Each Hebrew word/construction is to be used once!

I 1 Penultimate noun   ( ) קָדְשְׁךָ
   2 Twin-consonant noun   ( ) מִצְרָיְמָה
   3 Direction marker ◌ָה   ( ) עַמְּךָ
   4 Shortened imperfect III-י/ו verb   ( ) לֹא־תֵרָאֶה
   5 Qamets-/o/   ( ) חֶרֶב
   6 Noun chain   ( ) לָקַח
   7 Omitted hardening dagesh   ( ) וַיִּרְא אַתֶּם
      Preceding word ends in a vowel   אֶת־בֶּן־הַמֶּלֶךְ
   8 Pausal form *With long instead of a short vowel*   ( ) יַעַל
   9 Two direct objects in succession   ( ) נְאֻם יהוה
      Signalled by the particle אֵת

II   1 Negative command, 'אַל + *shortened imperf'*   ( ) נְאֻם יהוה

      2 Prohibition 'לֹא + *ordinary imperf'*   ( ) וּבַמָּקוֹם הַזֶּה אֶתֵּן שָׁלוֹם

      3 Relative clause *Signalled by the particle* אֲשֶׁר   ( ) אַל־תִּקַּח

      4 Particle-as-intensifier *Often rendered by 'look'*   ( ) לֹא־תִרְאֶה אֶת־פָּנַי

      5 Emphasis is signalled by variant word   ( ) אָנֹכִי אֵרֵד עִמְּךָ

         order *The normal word order is*

         Verb–Subject–Object

      6 Emphasis is signalled by an additional   ( ) הִנֵּה הַמֶּלֶךְ בֹּכֶה

         independent pronoun

      7 Subordinate clause of cause *Begins with* כִּי   ( ) אֱלֹהִים אֲשֶׁר יֵלְכוּ לְפָנֵינוּ

      8 Prophetic formula   ( ) כִּי מִי יוּכַל לִשְׁפֹּט

25.3   *Study* carefully the characteristics of the different verb types in Grammatical cornerstone 18. *Fill in* the blanks with the missing Hebrew verb forms from the list given below (the missing forms are italicized in the translation). *Pay attention* to the meaning of the different verb types.

      Then *read* the entire Hebrew text and *translate* on your own. *Fill in* the blanks with the missing words in the following translation and *check* your translation against it. *Analyze* the verb forms as follows: **a)** verb type **b)** verb root **c)** tense **d)** meaning (see footnote below).[2] *Note*:

> • Very few verb roots exist in all seven stems.
>
> • The basic meaning of a verb root, i.e., *simple active*, is usually expressed by פָּעַל. Certain verbs do not occur in פָּעַל, thus the basic meaning is expressed by one of the derived stems.
>
> • Both פָּעַל and הִפְעִיל may express an *active causative* nuance of פָּעַל verbs.
>
>   – פִּעֵל serves as the causative (*factitive*)[3] counterpart of *intransitive* פָּעַל verbs (verbs that do not take a direct object), 'make something/someone *become...*'.
>
>   – הִפְעִיל serves as the causative counterpart of *transitive* פָּעַל verbs (verbs that take a direct object), 'make someone *do*/cause someone *to do...*'.

---

[2] Meaning, e.g, שׁמר 3ms, perfect: Active simple (e.g., he guarded), passive (e.g., he was guarded), active causative (e.g., he caused someone to guard), reciprocal (e.g., they guarded one another), reflexive (e.g., he guarded himself/he was on his guard = he was careful).

[3] For the term *factitive*, see Section 22, footnote 1.

I וַיִּתְמַכְּרוּ שָׁמַרְתָּ יִשָּׁגֵר הִשָּׁמְרוּ וְסָגַר וַיִּמְכְּרוּ וָאֶשְׁתַּמְּרָה
נִמְכַּר תַּסְגִּיר

1 לֹא _____ *You have* not *kept* the אֶת־מִצְוַת יהוה אֱלֹהֶיךָ אֲשֶׁר צִוָּךְ

commandment of the Lord, _____ God, _____ _____ commanded

_____ (1 Sam. 13:13)

　a) _____ b) _____ c) _____ d) _____

2 לָכֶם פֶּן־תִּשְׁכְּחוּ אֶת־בְּרִית יהוה _____ *Be careful (= be on your*

guard), _____ _____ forget the covenant of the Lord (Dt. 4:23)

　a) _____ b) _____ c) _____ d) _____

3 מֵעֲוֹנִי: _____ *I kept myself* from iniquity (= _____ iniquity)

　(2 Sam. 22:24) a) _____ b) _____ c) _____ d) _____

4 וְיָצָא _____ אֶת־הַשַּׁעַר אַחֲרֵי צֵאתוֹ: *Then (= וְ) _____ shall go out*

and *[one] shall shut* the gate _____ _____ has gone out

(= _____ going out) (Ezek. 46:12)

　a) _____ b) _____ c) _____ d) _____

5 וְיָצָא וְהַשַּׁעַר לֹא־ _____ עַד־הָעָרֶב: *Then (= וְ) _____ shall go*

out, but (= וְ) the gate *shall _____ be shut* _____ the evening

(Ezek. 46:2) a) _____ b) _____ c) _____ d) _____

6 לֹא־ _____ עֶבֶד אֶל־אֲדֹנָיו *You shall _____ hand over*

(= *cause to shut in)* [a] slave _____ _____ master (= masters, plural of

majesty) (Dt. 23:16) a) _____ b) _____ c) _____ d) _____

7 _____ וַיַּעֲלוּ אֶת־יוֹסֵף מִן־הַבּוֹר _____ אֶת־יוֹסֵף לַיִּשְׁמְעֵאלִים

lifted up Joseph _____ the pit and *they sold* Joseph _____ the Ishmaelites

(Gen. 37:28)

　a) _____ b) _____ c) _____ d) _____

8 יוֹסֵף: _____ לְעֶבֶד *Joseph was sold* _____ [be a] slave

(Ps. 105:17) a) _____ b) _____ c) _____ d) _____

9 לַעֲשׂוֹת הָרַע בְּעֵינֵי יהוה _____ *They sold themselves* _____ do

evil (= the evil) _____ the sight (= eyes) of the Lord (2 Kings 17:17)

　a) _____ b) _____ c) _____ d) _____

II יִשְׁמַע הִשְׁמִיעֲךָ הַקְרִיב וַתִּקְרֶאנָה וַיִּקְרָא וַיִּקְרַב וְנִקְרַב וּשְׁמַעְתֶּם

1 אַהֲרֹן אֶל־הַמִּזְבֵּחַ _____ So (= וְ) Aaron *drew near* _____ the altar

(Lev. 9:8)

a) _____ b) _____ c) _____ d) _____

2 בַּעַל־הַבַּיִת אֶל־הָאֱלֹהִים _____ Then (= וְ) the owner of the house *shall be brought near* _____ God (= the God) (Ex. 22:7)

a) _____ b) _____ c) _____ d) _____

3 מֹשֶׁה בְּסֵפֶר כַּכָּתוּב לַיהוה _____ לְ To *offer (= cause to bring near)* _____ the LORD, _____ it [is] written _____ the book of Moses

(2 Chron. 35:12)

a) _____ b) _____ c) _____ d) _____

4 דָוִד: אֲבִי־יִשַׁי אֲבִי הוּא עוֹבֵד שְׁמוֹ _____ לְנָעֳמִי בֵּן־יֻלַּד "A son has been born _____ Naomi." *They called* _____ name Obed; _____ [was] the father of Jesse, David's father (Ruth 4:17)

a) _____ b) _____ c) _____ d) _____

5 עַל־שְׁמָם: _____ *He was called* by (= עַל) _____ name

(Ezra 2:61)

a) _____ b) _____ c) _____ d) _____

6 בְּקֹלוֹ _____ אֹתוֹ וַעֲבַדְתֶּם *You* will serve _____ and *obey* _____ (= listen _____ _____ voice) (1 Sam. 12:14)

a) _____ b) _____ c) _____ d) _____

7 חָרֵב אֹמְרִים אַתֶּם אֲשֶׁר בַּמָּקוֹם־הַזֶּה _____ עוֹד יהוה אָמַר כֹּה הוּא _____ says (= אָמַר) the LORD, 'Again (= עוֹד) [there] (= *it*) *will be heard* in _____ place [of] which _____ say (= saying) it [is] waste/ruined'

(Jer. 33:10)

a) _____ b) _____ c) _____ d) _____

8 אֶת־קֹלוֹ _____ הַשָּׁמַיִם מִן _____ (the) heavens *he let/made you hear* _____ voice (Dt. 4:36)

a) _____ b) _____ c) _____ d) _____

25.4 *Translate* into English. Proper names are enlarged. *Remember*:

> ♦ The particle וְ can be rendered in English translation by 'and, but, or, then, afterwards, now, while, when, because, in order that, so that, though' etc., as required by the context. וְ can also be left untranslated.

1 ⁴ וַיְדַבֵּר יוֹסֵף אֶל־בֵּית פַּרְעֹה לֵאמֹר אִם־נָא מָצָאתִי חֵן בְּעֵינֵיכֶם דַּבְּרוּ־נָא בְּאָזְנֵי פַרְעֹה לֵאמֹר: ⁵ אָבִי הִשְׁבִּיעַנִי לֵאמֹר הִנֵּה אָנֹכִי מֵת... בְּאֶרֶץ כְּנַעַן שָׁמָּה תִּקְבְּרֵנִי וְעַתָּה אֶעֱלֶה־נָּא וְאֶקְבְּרָה אֶת־אָבִי... ⁶ וַיֹּאמֶר פַּרְעֹה עֲלֵה וּקְבֹר אֶת־אָבִיךָ כַּאֲשֶׁר הִשְׁבִּיעֶךָ: ⁷ וַיַּעַל יוֹסֵף לִקְבֹּר אֶת־אָבִיו וַיַּעֲלוּ אִתּוֹ כָּל־עַבְדֵי פַרְעֹה זִקְנֵי בֵיתוֹ וְכֹל זִקְנֵי אֶרֶץ־מִצְרָיִם: ⁸ וְכֹל בֵּית יוֹסֵף וְאֶחָיו וּבֵית אָבִיו (Gen. 50:4–8)

2 ²⁴ וַיַּעֲנוּ אֶת־יְהוֹשֻׁעַ וַיֹּאמְרוּ כִּי הֻגֵּד הֻגַּד לַעֲבָדֶיךָ אֵת אֲשֶׁר צִוָּה יהוה אֱלֹהֶיךָ אֶת־מֹשֶׁה עַבְדּוֹ לָתֵת לָכֶם אֶת־כָּל־הָאָרֶץ... וַנִּירָא מְאֹד לְנַפְשֹׁתֵינוּ מִפְּנֵיכֶם וַנַּעֲשֵׂה אֶת־הַדָּבָר הַזֶּה: ²⁵ וְעַתָּה הִנְנוּ בְיָדֶךָ כַּטּוֹב וְכַיָּשָׁר בְּעֵינֶיךָ לַעֲשׂוֹת לָנוּ עֲשֵׂה: ²⁶ וַיַּעַשׂ לָהֶם כֵּן וַיַּצֵּל אוֹתָם מִיַּד בְּנֵי־יִשְׂרָאֵל וְלֹא הֲרָגוּם: (Jos. 9:24–26)

3 ¹¹ בַּמָּקוֹם אֲשֶׁר יִבְחַר יהוה אֱלֹהֶיךָ לְשַׁכֵּן שְׁמוֹ שָׁם: ¹² וְזָכַרְתָּ כִּי־עֶבֶד הָיִיתָ בְּמִצְרָיִם וְשָׁמַרְתָּ וְעָשִׂיתָ אֶת־הַחֻקִּים הָאֵלֶּה: (Dt. 16:11–12)

4 ²¹ וַיִּשָּׁבַע לְבִלְתִּי עָבְרִי אֶת־הַיַּרְדֵּן וּלְבִלְתִּי־בֹא אֶל־הָאָרֶץ הַטּוֹבָה אֲשֶׁר יהוה אֱלֹהֶיךָ נֹתֵן לָךְ... : ²² כִּי אָנֹכִי מֵת בָּאָרֶץ הַזֹּאת אֵינֶנִּי עֹבֵר אֶת־הַיַּרְדֵּן וְאַתֶּם עֹבְרִים וִירִשְׁתֶּם אֶת־הָאָרֶץ הַטּוֹבָה הַזֹּאת: ²³ הִשָּׁמְרוּ לָכֶם פֶּן־תִּשְׁכְּחוּ אֶת־בְּרִית יהוה אֱלֹהֵיכֶם אֲשֶׁר כָּרַת עִמָּכֶם

(Dt. 4:21–23)

25.5 In each group of verses in Exercise 25.4 above *identify* the verb forms belonging to the following stems:

1 a) פָּעַל verbs b) פִּעֵל c) הִפְעִיל
2 a) פָּעַל verbs b) פִּעֵל c) הִפְעִיל d) הָפְעַל
3 a) פָּעַל verbs b) פִּעֵל
4 a) פָּעַל verbs b) נִפְעַל.

List the verbs under the verb types to which they belong and *count* them. *Indicate* which verb type is the most frequent one in the verses above.

25.6 In Exercise 25.4 above *identify* four *finite verb forms* (i.e., perf, imperf or imperative) *followed by an attached object pronoun*. *Write* the units of verb-plus-pronoun and *indicate* after each unit the corresponding construction of a verb followed by an independent object pronoun. *Indicate* to which verb type each verb form belongs. *Note*:

> ◆ Only the active stems (G פָּעַל, D פִּעֵל, H הִפְעִיל) take an object pronoun.

25.7 In Exercise 25.4 above *identify* seven forms of the *ordinary infinitive*. *Separate* the infinitives from any additional element/s and *write* them alone. *Indicate* to which verb type each form belongs. *Remember*:

> ◆ The ordinary infinitive is often preceded by a preposition and sometimes followed by an attached pronoun.

25.8 In Exercise 25.4 above *identify* eleven forms of the *inverted imperf, write* them and *indicate* to which verb type and root type each form belongs. *Remember*:

> ◆ הִפְעִיל (H) verbs and III-י/ו verbs of פָּעַל (only forms without an ending) have special shortened forms after the inverting-Vav.

25.9 In Exercise 25.4 above *identify* the constructions consisting of 'preposition + noun denoting a part of the body + noun/attached pronoun'. *Write* the Hebrew constructions and *translate*. *Note*:

> ◆ The above mentioned constructions are not always rendered literally in English translation. The noun denoting the part of the body may be omitted.

25.10 *Match* each grammatical phenomenon (from Exercise 25.4 above) with the Hebrew construction that illustrates it. *Read* and *translate* orally. Observe that the same phenomenon may appear more than once, but only one instance is to be noted. Each Hebrew construction is to be used once!

1 Infinitive-as-intensifier *Rendered in*   ( ) וְזָכַרְתָּ כִּי־עֶבֶד הָיִיתָ בְּמִצְרָיִם
   English by 'surely, without a doubt' etc.

2 Clause expressing cause   ( ) הִשָּׁמְרוּ לָכֶם פֶּן־תִּשְׁכְּחוּ
   Begins with כִּי *'because, for'*

3 Attributive relative clause *Introduced*   ( ) אִם־נָא מָצָאתִי חֵן בְּעֵינֵיכֶם
   by אֲשֶׁר, *describes a noun in a main clause*

4 Quotation marker *Lit., 'to + say/ing',*   ( ) הִנֵּה אָנֹכִי מֵת
   introduces direct speech

5 כִּי *introducing a statement Rendered by 'that'*( ) דַּבְּרוּ־נָא

6 Particle of request *Often follows an*   ( ) וַיַּעַל יוֹסֵף לִקְבֹּר אֶת־אָבִיו
   imperative

7 Participle with a tense marker   ( ) הֻגֵּד הֻגַּד לַעֲבָדֶיךָ
   'הִנֵּה + *participle' signals near future*

8 Phrase expressing purpose   ( ) כִּי אָנֹכִי מֵת בָּאָרֶץ הַזֹּאת
   'לְ *(to/in order to) + ordinary infinitive'*

9 Negation of infinitive   ( ) אֵינֶנִּי עֹבֵר אֶת־הַיַּרְדֵּן
   Infinitive is negated by 'בִּלְתִּי + לְ'

10 Negation of participle   ( ) בַּמָּקוֹם אֲשֶׁר יִבְחַר יהוה
   Participle is negated by אֵין

11 Request formula *Introduces a request*   ( ) וַיִּשָּׁבַע לְבִלְתִּי עָבְרִי אֶת־הַיַּרְדֵּן
   to a person higher in status than the speaker

12 Negation of a clause expressing   ( ) לֵאמֹר
   purpose/result 'פֶּן *(lest) + verb in the imperfect'*

25.11 *Translate* into Hebrew. *Use* the perfect tense. *Note:*

> ◆ The verbs in the clauses below are among the most frequent in
>   the Hebrew Bible. *Memorize* them.
> ◆ The normal word order of the verbal clause is **V**erb–**S**ubject–**O**bject.

1 The man ate bread.
2 The woman said to her husband, "Am I not your wife!"
3 The priest had (= was to the priest) a book.
4 You (*m, s*) went to the city to see the king.
5 The prophetess (*f, s*) bore two sons.
6 My father knew where the money [was].
7 The people (= nation) went out of (= from) the country.
8 The prophet sat in the sanctuary of God.
9 The servant carried the vessels of his master.
10 You (*m, s*) took the child to the house.
11 His son went up out of (= from) the land of Egypt.
12 The young man did all these things.
13 My daughter saw the army of the king.

SECTION 26

1 *'One another' in Hebrew (expression of reciprocity)*: Apart from certain נִפְעַל (N) and occasionally הִתְפַּעֵל (HtD) verbs which express a reciprocal nuance of פָּעַל (G) verbs, 'one another' is commonly expressed by the following constructions:
  – 'אִישׁ/אִשָּׁה (man/woman) + אֶת/preposition + אָחִיו/אֲחוֹתָהּ (his brother/her sister)', e.g., אָמְרוּ אִישׁ אֶל אָחִיו 'They said to one another', lit., 'They said, *man to his brother*'.
  – 'אִישׁ/אִשָּׁה (man/woman) + אֶת/preposition + רֵעֵהוּ/רְעוּתָהּ (his/her friend/companion)', e.g., אָמְרוּ אִשָּׁה אֶל רְעוּתָהּ 'They said to one another', lit., 'They said, *woman to her friend/companion/neighbour*'.

2 *Verbs with two direct objects (double transitivity)*: It is mainly הִפְעִיל (H) verbs that can take two direct objects in succession. The first object of two direct objects in succession is usually a pronoun: הֶאֱכִילוּ/הֶאֱכִיל אוֹתוֹ לֶחֶם 'He let/made *him* eat *bread*'.

3 *Time frame*: Adverbials of time are usually placed first in the clause in biblical narrative, often preceded by וְהָיָה/וַיְהִי. וְהָיָה/וַיְהִי in this position may be left untranslated in English:
  (וַיְהִי) אַחַר הַדְּבָרִים הָאֵלֶּה אָמַר הָאִישׁ 'After these things, the man said'.

4 *Expression of wish*: A wish is expressed mainly by means of the following constructions:
  – A verb in the shortened or lengthened imperf, e.g., יְהִי כֵן 'May/let/would it be so', אֲהַלְלָה אֶת־אֱלֹהַי 'May I/let me/I wish to praise my God',
  – The construction מִי יִתֵּן, lit., 'who will give/allow', or the particle לוּ. Both מִי יִתֵּן and לוּ correspond to English '*if only!/might, let…(I/we wish that)*'

5 *Adverbs and adverbial constructions*
  – *Adverbs*: There are *original* adverbs, e.g., שָׁם 'there', and *derived* adverbs, which are formed by the addition of an ending, e.g., 'אָמֵן (confirmed) + the ending ָם' results in אָמְנָם 'certainly, truly' and 'מִצְרַיִם + the direction marker הָ' results in מִצְרַיְמָה 'to/towards Egypt'.
  An *infinitive-as-intensifier* may also function as an adverb, for instance, מַהֵר (פָּעֵל D) 'quickly'.
  – *Frequent adverbial constructions*: 'Finite verb + לְ + infinitive'; the finite verb in this construction functions as an adverbial, whereas the infinitive functions as the main verb, e.g., אוֹסִיף לְדַבֵּר 'I will speak *more*', lit., 'I will add to speak/ing'.
  'Finite verb + (וְ/וַ) + finite verb': In a construction of two finite verbs in succession (either with or without וְ/וַ) the first verb usually functions as an adverbial, e.g., וָאוֹסִיף וָאֲדַבֵּר 'and I spoke *more*', lit., 'I added and spoke'.

6 הִשְׁתַּפְעֵל: *The verb* הִשְׁתַּחֲוָה (see Exercise 26.6 below).

REVIEW AND APPLICATION OF THE RULES

I The verb forms below (from Exercises 26.1, 26.5 and 26.10) undergo regular sound changes. *Study* the sound change rules in **Appendix II**. Then *indicate* the relevant sound change/s occurring in the enlarged element/s of each verb form. *Translate*.

(26.1) 1 וַיְהִי, רָאוּ 2 וַיִּשְׁאֲלוּ 4 וְנִלְחֲמוּ 5 וְהוֹדַעְתִּי

(26.5) 1 וַעֲבַדְתַּנִי 3 הֶחֱרִיבוּ 4 לְהוֹשִׁיעַ 5 הֵיטַבְתָּ

(26.10) 1 וַתִּתֵּן, הָיִיתָ, יֵאָמֵן, גָּלִיתָ, לִבְנוֹת, מָצָא

WORD LIST

Nouns

חַטָּאת	*f,* sin; pardon, sin-offering
חֹשֶׁךְ	*m,* darkness
יְשׁוּעָה, יֶשַׁע	*f,* salvation, deliverance (☆ Isaiah, y.š.ʕ)
מִשְׁמָר, שָׁמַר	*m,* guard(ing) (☆ **Samaria**)
רֵעַ	*m,* friend; companion, neighbour

Verbs

חוה	*hisht* הִשְׁתַּחֲוָה bow down, prostrate oneself, worship: *imperf* יִשְׁתַּחֲוֶה, *inverted imperf* וַיִּשְׁתַּחוּ
יטב	be/become good (perf is not used; טוֹב serves as perf to פָּעַל): *imperf* יִיטַב, *hiph* הֵיטִיב make good, treat kindly; before infinitive 'well'

יָסַף	add, continue: *hiph* הוֹסִיף add, continue; before infinitive 'again, more': *imperf* יוֹסִיף, *inverted imperf* וַיּוֹסֶף/וַיֹּסֶף (☆ **Joseph**)
מהר	*pi* מִהַר hurry; before infinitive 'quickly': *imperf* יְמַהֵר
נָחַל	inherit, take possession: *imperf* יִנְחַל
נסה	*pi* נִסָּה test, try: *imperf* יְנַסֶּה

Particles (and derived adverbs)

יוֹמָם	by day, during the day: derived from יוֹם
לוּ	if only! O that... might...
חִנָּם	without compensation, for nothing: derived from חֵן

Derived verbs (familiar vocabulary)
See Hebrew–English Vocabulary, pp. 298–310.

EXERCISES

26.1 Each verse/verse segment below contains an *enlarged expression of reciprocity* corresponding to English 'one another'. *Read* and *translate* on your own. *Fill in* the blanks with the missing words in the following translation and *check/complete* your translation against it. Then *analyze* the verb forms as follows: **a)** verb type **b)** root consonants **c)** tense

1 וַיְהִי חֹשֶׁךְ... בְּכָל־אֶרֶץ מִצְרַיִם שְׁלֹשֶׁת (שְׁלֹשָׁה free form) יָמִים: לֹא־רָאוּ אִישׁ אֶת־אָחִיו... וּלְכָל־בְּנֵי יִשְׂרָאֵל הָיָה אוֹר [There] was

   darkness… _____ _____ the land of Egypt three days. They did not see

   _____ _____ (= man _____ _____), but (= וְ) _____ the Israelites had

   (= to the Israelites was) light (Ex.10:22–23)

   רָאוּ a) _____ b) _____ c) _____

2 דַּבֶּר־נָא בְּאָזְנֵי הָעָם וְיִשְׁאֲלוּ אִישׁ מֵאֵת רֵעֵהוּ וְאִשָּׁה מֵאֵת רְעוּתָהּ כְּלֵי־כֶסֶף וּכְלֵי זָהָב: Speak, please, to (= in the ears of) the

   people that (= וְ) they will ask, [a] man of (= מֵאֵת 'from') _____ _____

   and [a] woman of _____ _____ articles (= כֵּלִים) of silver and articles

   of gold (Ex. 11:2) דַּבֶּר־ a) _____ b) _____ c) _____

3 אָז נִדְבְּרוּ יִרְאֵי יהוה אִישׁ אֶת־רֵעֵהוּ Then [those who] feared

   (= fearing of) the LORD spoke _____ _____ _____ (= נִפְעַל verb), [a]

   man _____ _____ _____ (Mal. 3:16)

   נִדְבְּרוּ a) _____ b) _____ c) _____

4 וְנִלְחֲמוּ אִישׁ־בְּאָחִיו וְאִישׁ בְּרֵעֵהוּ עִיר בְּעִיר _____ will fight

   against (= בְּ) _____ _____ (= _____ against _____ _____ and _____

   against _____ _____), _____ against _____ (Isa. 19:2)

   וְנִלְחֲמוּ a) _____ b) _____ c) _____

5 כִּי־יִהְיֶה לָהֶם דָּבָר בָּא אֵלַי וְשָׁפַטְתִּי בֵּין אִישׁ וּבֵין רֵעֵהוּ וְהוֹדַעְתִּי אֶת־חֻקֵּי הָאֱלֹהִים וְאֶת־תּוֹרֹתָיו: Whenever (= כִּי) they have [a] dispute

   (= is to them thing/word) it comes before (= _____) _____ and _____

   judge _____ [one] person and _____ (= and _____ _____ _____), and

   _____ make known the laws of God and _____ instructions (Ex. 18:16)

   יִהְיֶה a) _____ b) _____ c) _____

26.2   Each verse/verse segment below contains *two direct objects in succession*.
Read and *translate* on your own. *Mark* the objects in the Hebrew text.
Fill in the blanks with the missing words in the following translation and
check/complete your translation against it. *Analyze* the verb forms as
follows: **a)** verb type **b)** root consonants **c)** tense

1   כִּי אַתָּה תַּנְחִיל אֶת־הָעָם הַזֶּה אֶת־הָאָרֶץ אֲשֶׁר־נִשְׁבַּעְתִּי לַאֲבוֹתָם

For _____ are the one who (= _____ – _____) will cause _____ _____

to inherit _____ _____ _____ _____ swore to _____ fathers (Jos. 1:6)

נִשְׁבַּעְתִּי a) _____ b) _____ c) _____

2   אֲשֶׁר לֹא־יָדַעְתָּ (manna) אֶת־הַמָּן וַיַּאֲכִלְךָ He did let _____ eat _____

_____ _____ you did _____ know (Dt. 8:3)

וַיַּאֲכִל a) _____ b) _____ c) _____

3   יִשְׁאָלוּנִי מִשְׁפְּטֵי־צֶדֶק _____ asked [of] _____ _____ _____ (Isa. 58:2)

יִשְׁאֲלוּ a) _____ b) _____ c) _____

4   וְהוּא יַנְחִיל אוֹתָם אֶת־הָאָרֶץ And _____ is the one who (= _____ –

_____) will cause _____ to inherit _____ _____ (Dt. 3:28)

יַנְחִיל a) _____ b) _____ c) _____

26.3   Each verse/verse segment below is introduced by a *time frame*. Read and
translate on your own. *Fill in* the blanks with the missing time frame in
the following translation and *check/complete* your translation against the
translation in the book. *Analyze* the verb forms as follows:
a) verb type **b)** root consonants **c)** tense

1   וַיְהִי בִּשְׁכֹּן יִשְׂרָאֵל בָּאָרֶץ הַהוּא וַיֵּלֶךְ רְאוּבֵן וַיִּשְׁכַּב אֶת־בִּלְהָה

_____, Reuben went and lay with Bilhah (Gen. 35:22)

וַיֵּלֶךְ a) _____ b) _____ c) _____

2   וַיְהִי אַחַר הַדְּבָרִים הָאֵלֶּה וְהָאֱלֹהִים נִסָּה אֶת־אַבְרָהָם וַיֹּאמֶר אֵלָיו

אַבְרָהָם וַיֹּאמֶר הִנֵּנִי: _____, (and the) God tested

Abraham, thus (= וַ) he said to him, "Abraham!" and he said, "Here

[am] I" (Gen. 22:1) וַיֹּאמֶר a) _____ b) _____ c) _____

3   בַּיּוֹם הַהוּא יִהְיֶה מִזְבֵּחַ לַיהוה בְּתוֹךְ אֶרֶץ מִצְרָיִם

_____

[there] will be [an] altar to the Lᴏʀᴅ in the midst of the land of Egypt

(Isa. 19:19) יִהְיֶה a) _____ b) _____ c) _____

4 וַיְהִי כִשְׁמֹעַ אֲדֹנָיו אֶת־דִּבְרֵי אִשְׁתּוֹ אֲשֶׁר דִּבְּרָה אֵלָיו לֵאמֹר כַּדְּבָרִים

הָאֵלֶּה עָשָׂה לִי עַבְדֶּךָ _____, which she spoke to

him, saying, "Like this and this (= these things) your servant did to

me" (Gen. 39:19)

שָׁמֹעַ a) _____ b) _____ c) _____

5 וַיְהִי כַּאֲשֶׁר יָשַׁב דָּוִיד בְּבֵיתוֹ וַיֹּאמֶר דָּוִיד אֶל־נָתָן הַנָּבִיא הִנֵּה אָנֹכִי

יוֹשֵׁב _____, David said to Nathan, the prophet, "Look,

I [am] dwelling…" (1 Chron. 17:1)

יוֹשֵׁב a) _____ b) _____ c) _____

26.4 Each verse/verse segment below contains an *expression/s of wish* (enlarged
in the Hebrew text). *Read* and *translate* on your own. *Fill* in the blanks
with the missing words in the following translation and *check/complete*
your translation against it. *Analyze* the verb forms as follows:
a) verb type **b)** root consonants **c)** tense.

1 וַיֹּאמֶר אֱלֹהִים יְהִי אוֹר God _____, "Let [there] _____ light!"

(Gen. 1:3) יְהִי a) _____ b) _____ c) _____

2 וְחַטָּאתָם כִּי כָבְדָה מְאֹד: אֵרֲדָה־נָּא וְאֶרְאֶה And _____ sin, yes

(= כִּי), it is _____ heavy (= כָּבְדָה). Let me _____,[1] please, that (= וְ) I

may _____ (Gen. 18:20–21)

אֵרֲדָה a) _____ b) _____ c) _____

3 מִי יִתֵּן כָּל־עַם יהוה נְבִיאִים כִּי־יִתֵּן יהוה אֶת־רוּחוֹ עֲלֵיהֶם: O, I

_____ (= who might give/allow) [that] _____ the LORD's people [were]

prophets, that the LORD would put _____ spirit upon _____!

(Num. 11:29) יִתֵּן a) _____ b) _____ c) _____

4 מִי יִתֵּן מִצִּיּוֹן יְשׁוּעַת יִשְׂרָאֵל O, I _____ (= who might give/allow)

[that] the deliverance of Israel [would come] _____ Zion! (Ps. 14:7)

5 וַיֹּאמֶר לָבָן הֵן לוּ יְהִי כִדְבָרֶךָ: Laban _____, "Certainly! (= הֵן)

_____ it _____ (יְהִי + לוּ) as _____ have said (= according to/as _____

word)!" (Gen. 30:34) וַיֹּאמֶר a) _____ b) _____ c) _____

---

[1] Observe that each blank space corresponds to one Hebrew element (noun, pronoun, verb
or particle), but sometimes one Hebrew element corresponds to more than one word in
English, e.g., עָלָה 'go up'.

6 לוּ עַמִּי שֹׁמֵעַ לִי יִשְׂרָאֵל בִּדְרָכַי יְהַלֵּכוּ׃ O, _____ _____ people [would] listen (= listening) to _____, Israel would walk _____ _____ ways! (Ps. 81:14) יְהַלֵּכוּ a) _____ b) _____ c) _____

26.5 Each verse/verse segment below contains an *adverb/adverbial construction* (italicized in the translation). *Read* and *translate* on your own. *Rewrite* the Hebrew adverbs/adverbial constructions. *Fill in* the blanks with the missing pronouns in the following translation and *check/complete* your translation against it.

1 וַעֲבַדְתַּנִי חִנָּם _____ will serve _____ *for nothing* (Gen. 29:15)

2 וַנִּתְפַּלֵּל אֶל־אֱלֹהֵינוּ וַנַּעֲמִיד מִשְׁמָר עֲלֵיהֶם יוֹמָם וָלַיְלָה But (= וַ) _____ prayed to _____ God and set up [a] guard over _____ *day and night* (Neh. 4:3)

3 אָמְנָם יהוה הֶחֱרִיבוּ מַלְכֵי אַשּׁוּר אֶת־הַגּוֹיִם וְאֶת־אַרְצָם׃ *Truly,* [O] LORD, the kings of Assyria have devastated (= made dry up) the nations and _____ land (2 Kings 19:17)

4 לֹא־אוֹסִיף לְהוֹשִׁיעַ אֶתְכֶם׃ _____ will not save _____ *again* (Judg. 10:13)

5 הֵיטַבְתָּ לִרְאוֹת _____ have seen *well* (Jer. 1:12)

6 מִהַרְתָּ לִמְצֹא בְּנִי _____ have found [it] *quickly,* _____ son (Gen. 27:20)

7 וַיֹּסִפוּ בְּנֵי יִשְׂרָאֵל לַעֲשׂוֹת הָרַע בְּעֵינֵי יהוה And the Israelites *again* did what (= הַ) [was] evil in the sight (= eyes) of the LORD (Judg. 3:12)

26.6 Each verse/verse segment below contains a form of the odd verb הִשְׁתַּחֲוָה 'bow down, prostrate oneself, worship'. The verb type is הִשְׁתַּפְעֵל (הִשְׁתַּחֲוָה, יִשְׁתַּחֲוֶה, מִשְׁתַּחֲוֶה, וַיִּשְׁתַּחוּ :חוה). *Read* and *translate*. Proper names are enlarged.

1 וְהִשְׁתַּחֲוִיתָ לֵאלֹהִים אֲחֵרִים וַעֲבַדְתָּם׃ (Dt. 30:17)

2 אַתָּה־הוּא יהוה לְבַדֶּךָ אַת (= אַתָּה) עָשִׂיתָ אֶת־הַשָּׁמַיִם שְׁמֵי הַשָּׁמַיִם וְכָל־צְבָאָם הָאָרֶץ וְכָל־אֲשֶׁר עָלֶיהָ... וְאַתָּה מְחַיֶּה אֶת־כֻּלָּם וּצְבָא הַשָּׁמַיִם לְךָ מִשְׁתַּחֲוִים׃ (Neh. 9:6)

3 וַיִּשְׁתַּחוּ אַבְרָהָם לִפְנֵי עַם הָאָרֶץ׃ (Gen. 23:12)

4 וַיִּפֹּל יוֹאָב אֶל־פָּנָיו אַרְצָה וַיִּשְׁתַּחוּ וַיְבָרֶךְ אֶת־הַמֶּלֶךְ וַיֹּאמֶר יוֹאָב
הַיּוֹם יָדַע עַבְדְּךָ כִּי־מָצָאתִי חֵן בְּעֵינֶיךָ אֲדֹנִי הַמֶּלֶךְ אֲשֶׁר־עָשָׂה
הַמֶּלֶךְ אֶת־דְּבַר עבדו (= עַבְדֶּךָ): (2 Sam. 14:22)

5 וַתִּפֹּל עַל־רַגְלָיו וַתִּשְׁתַּחוּ אָרְצָה וַתִּשָּׂא אֶת־בְּנָהּ וַתֵּצֵא:
וֶאֱלִישָׁע שָׁב הַגִּלְגָּלָה (2 Kings 4:37–38)

6 וְהָיָה בַּיּוֹם הַהוּא... וְהִשְׁתַּחֲווּ לַיהוה בְּהַר הַקֹּדֶשׁ בִּירוּשָׁלָםִ: (Isa. 27:13)

7 יִשְׁתַּחֲווּ לְךָ בְּנֵי אָבִיךָ: (Gen. 49:8)

26.7 *Study* carefully the characteristics of the different verb types in Grammatical
cornerstone 18. *Fill in* the blanks with the missing Hebrew verb forms
from the list given below (the missing forms are italicized in the translation).
Read the entire Hebrew text and *translate* on your own. *Pay attention* to
the meaning of the different verb types.
Then *fill in* the blanks with the missing words in the following translation
and *check* your translation against it. *Analyze* the verb forms as follows:
a) verb type **b)** root consonants **c)** tense **d)** meaning (see Section 25,
footnote 2). *Remember*:

> • The basic meaning of a verb root, i.e., simple active, is usually
>   expressed by פָּעַל. The six derived verb types normally modify the
>   basic meaning of the action expressed by פָּעַל.
> • There are three stems expressing active meaning (voice) and
>   three expressing passive meaning: פָּעַל (active) – נִפְעַל (passive),
>   פִּעֵל (active) – פֻּעַל (passive), הִפְעִיל (active) – הָפְעַל (passive).

I יִגְלֶה וְגָלִיתָ גָּלָה נִגְלָה הִגְלֵיתִי וַיַּגֶל מַגְלִים גָּלֹה גָּלָה

1 **מִמְּקוֹמְךָ אֶל־מָקוֹם אַחֵר** _____ יוֹמָם לְעֵינֵיהֶם _____ וֹ And
(you) go into exile by day in (= לְ) _____ sight (= eyes). *You shall go
into exile* _____ _____ place _____ another place (Ezek. 12:3)

a) _____ b) _____ c) _____ d) _____

a) _____ b) _____ c) _____ d) _____

2 **בְּשִׁלֹו שְׁמוּאֵל אֶל־יהוה** _____ כִּי־ Because the Lᴏʀᴅ *revealed*
himself _____ Samuel _____ Shiloh (1 Sam. 3:21)

a) _____ b) _____ c) _____ d) _____

3 ：מֵעַל אַדְמָתוֹ _____ _____ בַּחֶרֶב יָמוּת יָרָבְעָם וְיִשְׂרָאֵל

_____ the sword Jeroboam will die and Israel *will surely go into exile*

[away] from (= מֵעַל) _____ soil (Am. 7:11)

a) _____ b) _____ c) _____ d) _____

a) _____ b) _____ c) _____ d) _____

4 ：יִשְׂרָאֵל מֵעַל אַדְמָתוֹ אַשּׁוּרָה עַד הַיּוֹם הַזֶּה _____ So (= וְ) Israel

went _____ _____ soil *into exile* _____ Assyria _____ _____ day

(2 Kings 17:23)

a) _____ b) _____ c) _____ d) _____

5 ：מִירוּשָׁלַם בָּבֶלָה _____ אֲשֶׁר־ Whom *I have caused to go into*

exile _____ Jerusalem _____ Babylon (Jer. 29:4)

a) _____ b) _____ c) _____ d) _____

6 ：בָּבֶלָה _____ הַ יְרוּשָׁלַם וִיהוּדָה Jerusalem _____ Judah who

(= הַ) [were] *being taken into exile* _____ Babylon (Jer. 40:1)

a) _____ b) _____ c) _____ d) _____

וְהוֹדַעְתֶּם נוֹדַע נֵדַע יְדַעְתֶּם רָאָה יֵרָאוּ הֵרְאָה הָרְאֵיתָ　 II

1 ：אֶת־שָׁאוּל וַיהוה עָנָהוּ _____ וּשְׁמוּאֵל When (= וְ) Samuel *saw*

Saul, then (= וְ) the LORD answered _____ (1 Sam. 9:17)

a) _____ b) _____ c) _____ d) _____

2 _____ לֹא וּפָנַי But (= וְ) _____ face *shall* not *be seen* (Ex. 33:23)

a) _____ b) _____ c) _____ d) _____

3 יהוה אֶת־מֹשֶׁה _____ כַּמַּרְאֶה אֲשֶׁר According to (= _____) the

vision (= sight) _____ the LORD *had shown* (= *caused to see*) Moses

(Num. 8:4)

a) _____ b) _____ c) _____ d) _____

4 ：בָּהָר _____ אֲשֶׁר _____ *you were shown* on (= בְּ) the mountain

(Ex. 26:30)

a) _____ b) _____ c) _____ d) _____

5 כִּי שְׁנַיִם יָלְדָה־לִּי אִשְׁתִּי: _____ אַתֶּם *You* do *know* _____

_____ wife bore two [sons] _____ _____ (Gen. 44:27)

a) _____ b) _____ c) _____ d) _____

6 אֶת־הַדָּבָר אֲשֶׁר לֹא־דִבְּרוֹ יהוה: _____ אֵיכָה _____ *may we know*

the word _____ the LORD has not spoken (_____) (Dt. 18:21)

a) _____ b) _____ c) _____ d) _____

7 מִי הִכָּהוּ: _____ לֹא *It was* not *known* _____ struck _____

(Dt. 21:1) a) _____ b) _____ c) _____ d) _____

8 אֶת־בְּנֵיכֶם לֵאמֹר _____ *You shall let* _____ children *know*, saying

(Jos. 4:22) a) _____ b) _____ c) _____ d) _____

III וְהוֹצֵאתִי וַיֵּצֵא צֵאת וְהוֹשַׁבְתִּי יֵשֵׁב הוֹשַׁבְתֶּם

1 בָּאָרֶץ _____ הַ עַז הָעָם כִּי The people _____ (= הַ) *dwell*

(= *dwelling*) _____ the land [are] really (= כִּי) strong (Num. 13:28)

a) _____ b) _____ c) _____ d) _____

2 אֶת־הֶעָרִים _____ עֲוֹנוֹתֵיכֶם מִכֹּל אֶתְכֶם טַהֲרִי בְּיוֹם When

_____ have cleansed (= in the day of _____ cleansing) _____ _____

_____ _____ iniquities, *I will populate* (= *cause to inhabit*) the cities

(Ezek. 36:33)

a) _____ b) _____ c) _____ d) _____

3 לְבַדְכֶם _____ וְ And *you have been made to dwell* by _____

(= alone) (Isa. 5:8)

a) _____ b) _____ c) _____ d) _____

4 יִשְׂרָאֵל מִמִּצְרָיִם _____ בְּ When Israel *went forth* (= in the *going*

out of Israel) _____ Egypt (Ps. 114:1)

a) _____ b) _____ c) _____ d) _____

5 נֹחַ וּבָנָיו וְאִשְׁתּוֹ וּנְשֵׁי־בָנָיו אִתּוֹ: _____ So (= וַ) Noah *went forth*

and _____ sons and _____ wife _____ _____ sons' wives with _____

(Gen. 8:18) a) _____ b) _____ c) _____ d) _____

6 אֶת־צְבְאֹתַי _____ וְלֹא־יִשְׁמַע אֲלֵכֶם פַּרְעֹה וְנָתַתִּי אֶת־יָדִי בְּמִצְרָיִם

אֶת־עַמִּי בְנֵי־יִשְׂרָאֵל מֵאֶרֶץ מִצְרָיִם And Pharaoh will _____ listen

_____ _____. Then (= וְ) *I will* lay (= put) _____ hand upon (בְּ) Egypt

and *bring forth (= cause to go out)* _____ hosts, _____ people the

Israelites, _____ the land of Egypt (Ex. 7:4)

a) _____ b) _____ c) _____ d) _____

26.8   *Check* (and *correct* if needed) your translation of Exercise 25.11 (Section 25). Then *transform* the verbs in the perfect into the inverted imperfect, assisted by the chart of verbs on page 232. *Note*:

> ◆ The transformation of the verbs from the perfect into the inverted imperf does not change the meaning of the clauses.

26.9   *Check* (and *correct* if needed) Exercise 26.8 above. Then *transform* the clauses with the verbs in the inverted imperfect from the singular into the plural (verbs as well as nouns and pronouns are to be transformed).

26.10 *Translate* into English. Proper names are enlarged. *Analyze* the verb forms as follows: a) verb type b) root consonants c) tense. *Remember*:

> ◆ The particle וְ can be rendered in English translation by 'and, but, or, then, afterwards, now, while, when, because, in order that, so that, though' etc., as required by the context. וְ can also be left untranslated.

1 ²² וַתִּתֵּן אֶת־עַמְּךָ יִשְׂרָאֵל לְךָ לְעָם עַד־עוֹלָם וְאַתָּה יהוה הָיִיתָ לָהֶם
לֵאלֹהִים: ²³ וְעַתָּה יהוה הַדָּבָר אֲשֶׁר דִּבַּרְתָּ עַל־עַבְדְּךָ וְעַל־בֵּיתוֹ
יֵאָמֵן עַד־עוֹלָם וַעֲשֵׂה כַּאֲשֶׁר דִּבַּרְתָּ: ²⁴ וְיֵאָמֵן וְיִגְדַּל שִׁמְךָ עַד־עוֹלָם
לֵאמֹר יהוה צְבָאוֹת אֱלֹהֵי יִשְׂרָאֵל אֱלֹהִים לְיִשְׂרָאֵל... ²⁵ כִּי אַתָּה
אֱלֹהַי גָּלִיתָ אֶת־אֹזֶן עַבְדְּךָ לִבְנוֹת לוֹ בָּיִת עַל־כֵּן מָצָא עַבְדְּךָ
לְהִתְפַּלֵּל לְפָנֶיךָ: ²⁶ וְעַתָּה יהוה אַתָּה־הוּא הָאֱלֹהִים (1 Chron. 17:22–26)

יֵאָמֵן a) _____ b) _____ c) _____

בְנוֹת a) _____ b) _____ c) _____

2 ¹⁴ וַיֹּאמַר² יהוה אֱלֹהֵי יִשְׂרָאֵל אֵין־כָּמוֹךָ אֱלֹהִים בַּשָּׁמַיִם וּבָאָרֶץ
שֹׁמֵר הַבְּרִית וְהַחֶסֶד לַעֲבָדֶיךָ הַהֹלְכִים לְפָנֶיךָ בְּכָל־לִבָּם: ¹⁵ אֲשֶׁר

_____
² Pausal form, marked in the Hebrew Bible by the accent sign revia.

שָׁמַרְתָּ לְעַבְדְּךָ דָוִיד אָבִי אֵת אֲשֶׁר־דִּבַּרְתָּ לּוֹ וַתְּדַבֵּר בְּפִיךָ וּבְיָדְךָ

מִלֵּאתָ כַּיּוֹם הַזֶּה: ¹⁶ וְעַתָּה יהוה אֱלֹהֵי יִשְׂרָאֵל שְׁמֹר לְעַבְדְּךָ דָוִיד

אָבִי אֵת אֲשֶׁר דִּבַּרְתָּ לּוֹ לֵאמֹר לֹא־יִכָּרֵת לְךָ אִישׁ מִלְּפָנַי יוֹשֵׁב

עַל־כִּסֵּא יִשְׂרָאֵל רַק אִם־יִשְׁמְרוּ בָנֶיךָ אֶת־דַּרְכָּם לָלֶכֶת בְּתוֹרָתִי

כַּאֲשֶׁר הָלַכְתָּ לְפָנָי: ¹⁷ וְעַתָּה יהוה אֱלֹהֵי יִשְׂרָאֵל יֵאָמֵן דְּבָרְךָ אֲשֶׁר

דִּבַּרְתָּ לְעַבְדְּךָ לְדָוִיד: ¹⁸ כִּי הַאֻמְנָם יֵשֵׁב אֱלֹהִים אֶת־הָאָדָם עַל־הָאָרֶץ

(2 Chron. 6:14–18)

a) _____ b) _____ c) _____   לֶכֶת

a) _____ b) _____ c) _____   יֵשֵׁב

26.11 In each group of verses in Exercise 26.10 above *identify* the verb forms belonging to the following stems: **1** a) פָּעַל b) נִפְעַל c) פִּעֵל d) הִתְפַּעֵל **2** a) פָּעַל b) נִפְעַל c) פִּעֵל. *List* the verbs under the verb types to which they belong and *count* them. *Indicate* which stem (verb type) is the most frequent one in the verses above.

26.12 *Translate* into Hebrew. *Remember*:

> ◆ The word order of the verbal clause is normally as follows: Adverbial of time (time frame) + **Verb–Subject–Object**.

1 Then the men went out of (= from) the house and said *(inverted imperf)* to one another (= man to his brother), "May the LORD rescue us from them (= their hand)."
2 After these things the prophets spoke again (יסף, הִפְעִיל 'add' perf + the prophets + לְ + infinitive 'speak') to the people, saying, "God is with you."
3 On that day the Israelites said, "We wish that (= who will give/allow) we would pass through your land by day (= in daytime)."
4 While he was hiding himself (= in his hiding) the guards went to the gate of the city.

26.13 *Check* (and *correct* if needed) your translation of Exercise 26.12 above. *Transform* the verbs in the perfect into the inverted imperf. Then *transform* the verbs in the inverted imperf from the plural into the singular. *Note*:

> ◆ In certain forms of the inverted imperfect (forms without an ending) the stress is thrown back from the last to the next-to-last syllable. As a result, the vowel in the unstressed closed syllable is shortened. *An unstressed closed syllable always takes a short vowel.*

SECTION 27

1 פָּעַל *imperf of* II-י/ו (עו״י) *and twin-consonant* (ע״ע) *verbs*

	Perf	Imperf: Ordinary	Imperf: Shortened	Imperf: Inverted
Hollow verbs	קָם *stand up*	יָקוּם	יָקֹם	וַיָּקָם
II-י/ו (עו״י)	שָׂם *put, set*	יָשִׂים	יָשֵׂם	וַיָּשֶׂם
Twin-consonant verbs (ע״ע)	סָבַב *go around*	יִסֹּב/יָסֹב	יִסֹּב/יָסֹב	וַיִּסֹּב/וַיָּסָב
	קַל *be light*	יֵקַל/יִקַּל	יֵקַל/יִקַּל	וַיֵּקַל/וַיִּקַּל

– II-י/ו (עו״י) *verbs*

Ordinary imperf. Apart from the 2nd and 3rd persons of the feminine plural (תָּשֵׂמְנָה, תָּקֹמְנָה) the second root consonant י/ו is visible in writing as a vowel letter, e.g., יָקוּם, יָשִׂים, יָבוֹא. The prefix vowel is /a/:
יָקוּם, יָשִׂים, יָבוֹא.

Shortened imperf. The second root consonant י/ו is omitted and the first root consonant is followed by a simple long vowel: יָקֹם, יָשֵׂם.

Inverted imperf. The stress (in forms without an ending) is thrown back from the last to the next-to-last syllable, which results in the shortening of the vowel of the closed last syllable. *An unstressed closed syllable always has a short vowel:* וַיָּקָם, וַיָּשֶׂם.

– *Twin-consonant* (ע״ע) *verbs*

Ordinary and shortened imperf. When the doubled consonant occurs at the end of the word, it is ordinarily simplified (shown in writing by the absence of the doubling dagesh), e.g., יָסֹב, יֵקַל. When the doubled consonant is followed by a vowel, the doubling is retained: יָסֹבּוּ, תֵּקַלִּי.

The prefix vowel is /a/ or /e/ יֵקַל, יָסֹב (observe the alternative forms יִסֹּב and יִקַּל which may easily be confused with the I-נ verbs!).

Inverted imperf. The stress (in forms without an ending) is thrown back from the last to the next-to-last syllable, which results in the shortening of the vowel in the closed last syllable, e.g., וַיָּסָב, וַיֵּקַל.

2 נִפְעַל (N), הִפְעִיל (H) *and* הָפְעַל (Hp) *of* II-י/ו *and twin-consonant verbs*

		Perf: 3ms	Perf: 2ms	Imperf: 3ms	Participle ms
Hollow verbs	N	נָקוֹם	נְקוּמוֹתָ	יִקּוֹם	נָקוֹם
	H	הֵקִים	הֲקִימוֹתָ	יָקִים	מֵקִים
	Hp	הוּקַם	הוּקַמְתָּ	יוּקַם	מוּקָם
Twin-consonant verbs	N	נָסַב	נְסַבּוֹתָ	יִסַּב	נָסָב
	H	הֵסֵב	הֲסִיבּוֹתָ	יָסֵב	מֵסֵב
	Hp	הוּסַב	הוּסַבּוֹתָ	יוּסַב	מוּסָב

– *Linking vowel*: Both the 1ˢᵗ and 2ⁿᵈ persons take the linking vowel /ô/ before the attached pronoun. The linking vowel takes the stress. The vowel in the open syllable two steps before the stress is regularly reduced: נְקוּמֹתִי, הֲקִימֹתִי (II-י/ו verbs); הֲסִבֹּתִי, נְסַבֹּתִי (twin-consonant verbs).

– נִפְעַל (N) *imperfect*: The consonant נ at the end of a syllable is regularly assimilated to the following consonant (shown in writing by the doubling dagesh), e.g., יִנְקוֹם becomes יִקּוֹם and יִנְסַב becomes יִסַּב.

3 פּוֹלֵל, פּוֹלַל, הִתְפּוֹלֵל *verbs*

	Perf	Imperf	Imperative	Infinitive	Participle
(קום) פּוֹלֵל	קוֹמֵם	יְקוֹמֵם	קוֹמֵם	קוֹמֵם	מְקוֹמֵם
(סבב) פּוֹלֵל	סוֹבֵב	יְסוֹבֵב	סוֹבֵב	סוֹבֵב	מְסוֹבֵב
פּוֹלַל	קוֹמַם	יְקוֹמַם	____	____	מְקוֹמָם *(likewise* סבב*)*
הִתְפּוֹלֵל	הִתְקוֹמֵם	יִתְקוֹמֵם	הִתְקוֹמֵם	הִתְקוֹמֵם	מִתְקוֹמֵם *(likewise* סבב*)*

– The odd verb patterns above, which correspond to פִּעֵל, פֻּעַל and הִתְפַּעֵל, occur in certain II-י/ו and twin-consonant verbs.

4 *Oaths*: The following oath formulae are common in the Bible:
– נִשְׁבַּע בְּ' (swear) + proper name (often יהוה/אֱלֹהִים) + אִם/אִם לֹא (אִם of oath) or כִּי (particle-as-intensifier)' followed by a statement, e.g., נִשְׁבַּעְתִּי בַּיהוה אִם אֲדַבֵּר/אִם לֹא אֲדַבֵּר 'I swear in the [name of] the Lᴏʀᴅ *not to* talk/ *to* talk'. Observe that the אִם of oath is rendered by '*not to*' (*negative* statement), whereas אִם לֹא is rendered by '*to*' (*positive* statement).
– חַי (live) + proper name (often יהוה/אֱלֹהִים) + אִם/אִם לֹא/כִּי (אִם of oath)' + statement, e.g., חַי יהוה אִם לֹא אֲדַבֵּר 'As the Lᴏʀᴅ lives, I will talk'.
– 'כֹּה יַעֲשֶׂה ל... יהוה/אֱלֹהִים' followed by כִּי/אִם/אִם לֹא (אִם of oath)' + statement, e.g., כֹּה יַעֲשֶׂה לִי אֱלֹהִים וְכֹה יוֹסִיף כִּי אֲדַבֵּר 'Thus and more may God do to me (lit., 'may God do so to me and add so'), I will certainly (= כִּי) speak'.

REVIEW AND APPLICATION OF THE RULES

I *Match* each grammatical element with the Hebrew word that illustrates it. *Mark* the element in the Hebrew word clearly! Observe that the same element may appear in more than one word, but only one element is to be marked. Each Hebrew word is to be used once!

1 Vowel reduction I *A vowel*   (_) יִסַּב   6 Simplified doubled   (_) יוּקְמוּ
   one *step before the stress is reduced*   consonant *At the end of the word*

2 Vowel reduction II *A vowel*   (_) וַיָּגָר   7 Shift in stress   (_) וַהֲקִימֹתִי
   two *steps before the stress is reduced*   *Forwards, after the inverting-Vav*

3 Vowel reduction II *After a guttural* (_) וַיָּשֶׂם 8 Shift in stress   (_) נְסַבֹּתִי
                                                                     Backwards, after the inverting-Vav

4 Cluster at the end of the word is   9 Qamets-/o/   (_) סַבּוֹתֶם
   not broken up *III-י/ו verb, G-stem*(_) יִכּוֹן 10 Assimilated נ, *N-stem*(_) וְכוֹנַנְתִּי

5 Linking vowel /ô/   (_) וַיֵּבְךְ

II The verb forms below (from Exercise 27.5) undergo regular sound changes. *Study* the sound change rules in **Appendix II**. Then *indicate* the relevant sound change/s occurring in the enlarged element/s of each verb form. *Translate.*

1 יִתֵּן   2 וַיְצַו   3 וַיַּעַבְרוּ   5 וַיִּכֹּר, עָשִׂיתִי, יִשְׁמַע   6 תּוֹכַל, שָׁב

7 וַיְהִי, וַיֹּאמְרוּ, מָצָאנוּ

WORD LIST

Nouns

אֹהֶל	*m*, tent: *pl* אֹהָלִים, with suff אֹהָלִי	כון	*niph* נָכוֹן be firm, established: *imperf* יִכּוֹן, *polel* כּוֹנֵן establish, found
אַחֲרִית	*f*, end: derived from אַחַר	נכר	*hiph* הִכִּיר recognize: *imperf* יַכִּיר, *inverted imperf* וַיַּכֵּר
מוֹעֵד, יעד	*m*, appointed time		
מָחָר	*m*, tomorrow	סבב	turn; go around, surround: *perf*
פַּעַם	*f*, step; time (= occurrence): *dual* פַּעֲמַיִם twice, *pl* פְּעָמִים		סַב/יָסֹב, *imperf* סָבַב/יָסֹב/סַב, *inverted imperf* וַיָּסֹב/וַיִּסֹב
		פרד	*hiph* הִפְרִיד separate, part: *imperf* יַפְרִיד, *inverted imperf* וַיַּפְרֵד

Adjectives

שֵׁנִי	second	רעע	be/become bad/displeasing: *perf* רַע, *imperf* יֵרַע, *inverted imperf* וַיֵּרַע, *hiph* הֵרַע cause evil, harm

Verbs

גּור	stay as foreigner/guest: *perf* גָּר, *imperf* יָגוּר, *inverted mperf* וַיָּגָר	תמם	be finished/completed: *perf* תַּם, *imperf* יִתַּם/יִתֹּם

Derived verbs (familiar vocabulary)

הֵבִיא, בוא	*hiph* cause to come, bring: *imperf* יָבִיא, *inverted imperf* וַיָּבֵא
הֵקִים, קום	*hiph* make stand, set up, maintain: *imperf* יָקִים, *inverted imperf* וַיָּקֶם
שׁוֹבֵב, שוב	*polel* cause to return, bring back, restore, refresh: *imperf* יְשׁוֹבֵב

Particles

לִקְרַאת	toward, against, to meet: *with suff* לִקְרָאתִי

EXERCISES

27.1 *Fill in* the blanks with the missing Hebrew verb forms from the list given below (the missing forms are italicized in the translation). *Read* the entire Hebrew text and *translate* on your own. Then *complete* the missing words in the following translation and *check/complete* your translation against it. *Analyze* the verb forms as follows:

a) verb type **b)** root consonants **c)** tense **d)** person/gender/number.

I   וְכֹנַנְתִּי   וַיָּקָם   וַיָּשֶׂם   מוֹת   תָּבִיאוּ   נָכוֹן   יָבֹא   יָגוּר

1   בְּאָהֳלֶךָ [bᵉʔohᵒlexā]   _____   מִי־יִשְׁכֹּן בְּהַר קָדְשֶׁךָ:   ־מִי   יהוה

[O] Lord, _____ will be guest _____ _____ tent, _____ will dwell on

(= בְּ) _____ holy mountain (mountain of holiness) ? (Ps. 15:1)

a) _____ b) _____ c) _____ d) _____

2   תָּמוּת: _____   כִּי בְּיוֹם אֲכָלְךָ מִמֶּנּוּ   For _____ the day _____ eat

(= _____ the day of _____ eating) _____ _____, _____ will _certainly_

die (Gen. 2:17)

a) _____ b) _____ c) _____ d) _____

3   חֲזַק   אֹתוֹ   שָׂמָה   _____   הוּא   יְהוֹשֻׁעַ בִּן־נוּן הָעֹמֵד לְפָנֶיךָ

אֶת־יִשְׂרָאֵל: יַנְחִלֶנָּה   כִּי־הוּא   Joshua, the son of Nun, who (= הַ) [is]

standing _____ _____, _he is the one who (= he – he) will go in_ _____.

Encourage _____ (= make _____ strong) because it is _____ who

(= _____ – _____) will cause Israel to inherit _____ (Dt. 1:38)

a) _____ b) _____ c) _____ d) _____

4   בָּאָרֶץ: יַעֲשֶׂה יהוה הַדָּבָר הַזֶּה   לֵאמֹר מָחָר   יהוה מוֹעֵד   _____

And the Lord _set_ [an] appointed time, saying, "Tomorrow the Lord will

do _____ thing _____ the _____" (Ex. 9:5)

a) _____ b) _____ c) _____ d) _____

5   בְּרֹאשׁ הֶהָרִים   יְהוָה   ־יִהְיֶה הַר בֵּית   _____   וְהָיָה בְּאַחֲרִית הַיָּמִים

It shall come to pass (= וְהָיָה), _____ the coming _____ (= the end of

the days), the mountain of the Lord's _____ shall _be established_ above

the top of (= at the head of) the mountains (Isa. 2:2)

a) _____ b) _____ c) _____ d) _____

6   וַיַּהַרְגֵהוּ:   אָחִיו   אֶל־הֶבֶל   קַיִן   _____   וַיְהִי בִּהְיוֹתָם בַּשָּׂדֶה

And when _____ were (= _____ _____ being) _____ the field, Cain

rose up against _____ _____ Abel and killed _____ (Gen. 4:8)

a) _____ b) _____ c) _____ d) _____

7 וְאֶת־אֲחִיכֶם הַקָּטֹן _____ אֵלַי וְיֵאָמְנוּ דִבְרֵיכֶם וְלֹא תָמוּתוּ
וַיַּעֲשׂוּ־כֵן: וַיֹּאמְרוּ אִישׁ אֶל־אָחִיו "But (= וְ) *you will bring (= cause
to come)* _____ young[est] (= the young) brother _____ _____, so that
(= וְ) _____ _____ may be verified and _____ will _____ die." And
_____ did so. _____ said to _____ _____ (= man to _____ _____)
(Gen. 42:20) a) _____ b) _____ c) _____ d) _____

8 הוּא יִבְנֶה־לִּי בַיִת _____ אֶת־כִּסְאוֹ עַד־עוֹלָם: _____ is the one
who (= _____ – _____) shall build [a] _____ _____ _____ and *I will
establish* _____ throne forever (1 Chron. 17:12)
a) _____ b) _____ c) _____ d) _____

II יְשׁוֹבֵב הָרָעֹת יָמֻתוּ וַהֲקִימֹתִי וַיֵּרַע מֵבִיא סָבְבוּ וַיָּסֹבּוּ

1 אֶת־בְּרִיתִי אִתְּכֶם: _____ *I will maintain (= make stand)* _____
covenant _____ _____ (Lev. 26:9)
a) _____ b) _____ c) _____ d) _____

2 לָכֵן כֹּה־אָמַר יהוה אֱלֹהֵי יִשְׂרָאֵל הִנְנִי _____ רָעָה עַל־יְרוּשָׁלַם
וִיהוּדָה Therefore, _____ _____ _____, the God of Israel, '*I* [am]
bringing [a] disaster upon Jerusalem and Judah' (2 Kings 21:12)
a) _____ b) _____ c) _____ d) _____

3 וַתְּהִי־לוֹ לְאִשָּׁה וַתֵּלֶד לוֹ בֵּן _____ הַדָּבָר אֲשֶׁר־עָשָׂה דָוִד
בְּעֵינֵי יהוה: _____ became (= וַתְּהִי־לְ) his (= to him) wife and bore to
him [a] _____. The _____ _____ David had done *displeased* the Lord
(= *was bad* in the _____ of the Lord) (2 Sam. 11:27)
a) _____ b) _____ c) _____ d) _____

4 וַיֹּאמֶר מֹשֶׁה אֶל־יהוה לָמָה _____ לְעַבְדֶּךָ Then (= וַ) Moses said
_____ the Lord, "_____ *have you caused evil* _____ _____ _____?"
(Num. 11:11) a) _____ b) _____ c) _____ d) _____

5 אֶת־הָעִיר בַּיּוֹם הַשֵּׁנִי פַּעַם אַחַת _____ On (= בְּ) the second _____
they marched (= walked) around the _____ once (= one time)
(Jos. 6:14) a) _____ b) _____ c) _____ d) _____

6 רַק בַּיּוֹם הַהוּא _____ אֶת־הָעִיר שֶׁבַע פְּעָמִים: Only _____ _____

_____ *they marched around* the _____ _____ *times* (Jos. 6:15)

a) _____ b) _____ c) _____ d) _____

7 _____ בַּמִּדְבָּר הַזֶּה יִתַּמּוּ וְשָׁם _____ _____ *wilderness* _____ *shall*

be annihilated (= *finished, come to an end*); (*and*) _____ *they shall die*

(Num. 14:35) a) _____ b) _____ c) _____ d) _____

8 _____ נַפְשִׁי _____ *soul/life he restores* (Ps. 23:3)

a) _____ b) _____ c) _____ d) _____

27.2 *Match* each grammatical phenomenon (from Exercise 27.1 above) with
the Hebrew construction that illustrates it. *Read* and *translate* orally. Observe
that the same phenomenon may appear more than once, but only one
instance is to be noted. Each Hebrew construction is to be used once!

1 Participle with a tense marker   וַיֹּאמְרוּ אִישׁ אֶל־אָחִיו ( )
   '*The verb* היה (*be*) + *participle*'

2 Clause expressing cause *Begins with* כִּי   יַנְחִלֶנָּה אֶת־יִשְׂרָאֵל ( )

3 Relative clause describing a noun in a   מוֹת תָּמוּת ( )
   main clause *Introduced by* אֲשֶׁר

4 Verbal clause with normal word   הִנְנִי מֵבִיא רָעָה ( )
   order *Adverbial of time* + *Verb–Subject–Object*

5 Participle describing a noun in a clause   בִּהְיוֹתָם בַּשָּׂדֶה ( )
   'הַ + *participle*', *rendered in English by a relative clause*

6 Phrase expressing time 'בְּ (*when*) +   הַדָּבָר אֲשֶׁר־עָשָׂה דָוִד ( )
   ordinary infinitive + *attached pronoun*',
   rendered in English by a temporal clause

7 Participle with a tense marker   יְהוֹשֻׁעַ בֶּן־נוּן הָעֹמֵד לְפָנֶיךָ ( )
   'הִנֵּה + *participle*' *signals near future*

8 Verbal clause: Emphasis is signalled   וְהָיָה בְּאַחֲרִית הַיָּמִים ( )
   by an additional independent pronoun

9 Verbal clause: Emphasis is signalled   בַּיּוֹם הַהוּא סָבְבוּ אֶת־הָעִיר ( )
   by variant word order   שֶׁבַע פְּעָמִים

10 הִפְעִיל verb with two direct objects   בַּמִּדְבָּר הַזֶּה יִתַּמּוּ ( )
   in succession *The first object is an attached pronoun*

11 Time frame *Preceded by an*   כִּי־הוּא יַנְחִלֶנָּה ( )
   inverted form of היה

12 'One another' in Hebrew *Literally,*   הוּא יַנְחִלֶנָּה ( )
   '*man + preposition + his brother*'

13 Infinitive-as-intensifier *Precedes a finite* נָכוֹן יִהְיֶה הַר בֵּית־יהוה ( )
   verb, rendered by an intensifying adverbial, e.g., '*surely*'

27.3 Each Hebrew verse/verse segment below contains an *oath formula* (enlarged
in the Hebrew text and italicized in the translation). *Read* the Hebrew text
and *translate* on your own. Then *complete* the missing verb forms in the
following translation and *check/complete* your translation against it.

1 וְכִרְאוֹת שָׁאוּל אֶת־דָּוִד יֹצֵא לִקְרַאת הַפְּלִשְׁתִּי אָמַר אֶל־אַבְנֵר שַׂר

הַצָּבָא בֶּן־מִי־זֶה הַנַּעַר אַבְנֵר וַיֹּאמֶר אַבְנֵר חֵי נַפְשְׁךָ הַמֶּלֶךְ

אִם־יָדַעְתִּי: As [soon as] Saul _____ (= _____) David _____ against

the Philistine, he _____ to Abner, the commander of the army, "Whose

son [is] that boy (= son of who this boy)?" And Abner _____, "*By

your life (= soul), O (= הַ) king, I do* not *(= אִם)* _____" (1 Sam. 17:55)

2 בַּאֲשֶׁר תָּמוּתִי אָמוּת וְשָׁם אֶקָּבֵר כֹּה יַעֲשֶׂה יהוה לִי וְכֹה יֹסִיף

כִּי הַמָּוֶת יַפְרִיד בֵּינִי וּבֵינֵךְ: Where (= **בַּאֲשֶׁר**) you _____ I will

_____, and there I will be _____. *Thus and more may the LORD do to

me (= so may the LORD do to me and add so)*, death only (= כִּי) will part

me from you (= part between me and between you) (Ruth 1:17)

3 וְהָיָה אִם־לָמֹד יִלְמְדוּ אֶת־דַּרְכֵי עַמִּי לְהִשָּׁבֵעַ בִּשְׁמִי חַי־יהוה כַּאֲשֶׁר

לִמְּדוּ אֶת־עַמִּי לְהִשָּׁבֵעַ בַּבָּעַל וְנִבְנוּ בְּתוֹךְ עַמִּי: And if they diligently

(= לָמֹד) _____ the ways of my people, to _____ by my name '*As the

LORD lives*,' as they _____ my people to _____ by Baal, then *(= וְ)* they

will be _____ in the midst of my people (Jer. 12:16)

4 לֹא־טוֹב הַדָּבָר הַזֶּה אֲשֶׁר עָשִׂיתָ חַי יהוה כִּי בְנֵי־מָוֶת אַתֶּם אֲשֶׁר

לֹא־שְׁמַרְתֶּם עַל־אֲדֹנֵיכֶם עַל־מְשִׁיחַ יהוה This thing that you have

_____ [is] not good. *As the LORD lives*, you *indeed (= כִּי)* deserve to

_____ (= you sons of _____), because you did not _____ over your

lord (= lords, plural of majesty), (+ over) the LORD's anointed

(1 Sam. 26:16)

27.4 *Match* each grammatical phenomenon (from Exercise 27.3 above) with the Hebrew construction that illustrates it. *Read* and *translate* orally. Observe that the same phenomenon may appear more than once, but only one instance is to be noted. Each Hebrew construction is to be used once!

1 Infinitive-as-intensifier *Precedes a finite* ( ) חֵי נַפְשְׁךָ הַמֶּלֶךְ אִם יָדַעְתִּי
   verb, rendered by an intensifying adverbial, e.g., 'surely'

2 Particle-as-intensifier ( ) הַדָּבָר הַזֶּה אֲשֶׁר עָשִׂיתָ

3 Clause expressing cause ( ) כִּי בְנֵי־מָוֶת אַתֶּם
   Introduced by אֲשֶׁר *'because, for'*

4 Proper name denoting a member of ( ) אֲשֶׁר לֹא־שְׁמַרְתֶּם עַל־אֲדֹנֵיכֶם
   a group 'פְּלֶשֶׁת *(Philistia) + the ending* יִ .'

5 Oath formula *'As the* LORD *lives...'* ( ) לָמֹד יִלְמְדוּ

6 Phrase expressing time 'כְּ *(as/when) +* ( ) הַפְּלִשְׁתִּי
   ordinary infinitive + noun', rendered in
   English by a temporal clause

7 אִם *of oath Rendered by* **'not'** ( ) חַי־יהוה כִּי

8 Relative clause describing a noun in a ( ) וְכִרְאוֹת שָׁאוּל אֶת־דָּוִד
   main clause *Introduced by* אֲשֶׁר

27.5 *Translate* into English. Proper names are enlarged. *Analyze* the verb forms as follows: **a**) verb type **b**) root consonants **c**) tense.

1 וַיִּבְךְ וְכֹה אָמַר בְּלֶכְתּוֹ בְּנִי אַבְשָׁלוֹם בְּנִי בְנִי אַבְשָׁלוֹם מִי־יִתֵּן
   מוּתִי אֲנִי תַחְתֶּיךָ (2 Sam. 19:1)

   a) _____ b) _____ c) _____   וַיִּבְךְ

2 וַיָּקֻמוּ הָאֲנָשִׁים וַיֵּלֵכוּ וַיְצַו יְהוֹשֻׁעַ אֶת־הַהֹלְכִים לִכְתֹּב אֶת־הָאָרֶץ
   לֵאמֹר לְכוּ וְהִתְהַלְּכוּ בָאָרֶץ וְכִתְבוּ אוֹתָהּ וְשׁוּבוּ אֵלַי (Jos. 18:8)

   a) _____ b) _____ c) _____   וַיְצַו

3 וַיֵּלְכוּ הָאֲנָשִׁים וַיַּעַבְרוּ בָאָרֶץ וַיִּכְתְּבוּהָ לֶעָרִים... עַל־סֵפֶר וַיָּבֹאוּ
   אֶל־יְהוֹשֻׁעַ אֶל־הַמַּחֲנֶה שִׁלֹה: (Jos. 18:9)

   a) _____ b) _____ c) _____   וַיֵּלְכוּ

4 וַיֹּאמֶר־לוֹ פַרְעֹה לֵךְ מֵעָלָי הִשָּׁמֶר לְךָ אַל־תֹּסֶף רְאוֹת פָּנַי כִּי בְּיוֹם
   רְאֹתְךָ פָנַי תָּמוּת: וַיֹּאמֶר מֹשֶׁה כֵּן דִּבַּרְתָּ לֹא־אֹסִף עוֹד רְאוֹת
   פָנֶיךָ: (Ex. 10:28–29)

   a) _____ b) _____ c) _____   תֹּסֶף

5 ¹⁷ וַיַּכֵּר שָׁאוּל אֶת־קוֹל דָּוִד וַיֹּאמֶר הֲקוֹלְךָ זֶה בְּנִי דָוִד וַיֹּאמֶר דָּוִד
קוֹלִי אֲדֹנִי הַמֶּלֶךְ: ¹⁸ וַיֹּאמֶר לָמָּה זֶּה אֲדֹנִי רֹדֵף אַחֲרֵי עַבְדּוֹ כִּי מֶה
עָשִׂיתִי וּמַה־בְּיָדִי רָעָה: ¹⁹ וְעַתָּה יִשְׁמַע־נָא אֲדֹנִי הַמֶּלֶךְ אֵת דִּבְרֵי
עַבְדּוֹ (1 Sam. 26:17–19)

וַיַּכֵּר   a) _____ b) _____ c) _____

6 וַיֹּאמֶר שָׁאוּל אֶל־דָּוִד בָּרוּךְ אַתָּה בְּנִי דָוִד גַּם עָשֹׂה תַעֲשֶׂה וְגַם
יָכֹל תּוּכָל (pause) וַיֵּלֶךְ דָּוִד לְדַרְכּוֹ וְשָׁאוּל שָׁב לִמְקוֹמוֹ: (1 Sam. 26:25)

תּוּכַל   a) _____ b) _____ c) _____

7 ³¹ וַיִּשָּׁבְעוּ אִישׁ לְאָחִיו וַיְשַׁלְּחֵם יִצְחָק וַיֵּלְכוּ מֵאִתּוֹ בְּשָׁלוֹם:
³² וַיְהִי בַּיּוֹם הַהוּא וַיָּבֹאוּ עַבְדֵי יִצְחָק וַיַּגִּדוּ לוֹ... וַיֹּאמְרוּ לוֹ מָצָאנוּ
מָיִם: ³³ וַיִּקְרָא אֹתָהּ שִׁבְעָה עַל־כֵּן שֵׁם־הָעִיר בְּאֵר שֶׁבַע עַד
הַיּוֹם הַזֶּה: (Gen. 26:31–33)

וַיִּשָּׁבְעוּ   a) _____ b) _____ c) _____

27.6 *Match* each grammatical phenomenon (from Exercise 27.5 above) with the Hebrew word/construction that illustrates it. *Read* and *translate* orally. Observe that the same phenomenon may appear more than once, but only one occurrence is to be noted. Each Hebrew word/construction is to be used once!

1 Infinitive-as-intensifier *Precedes a finite verb* ( ) אֹסֵף

2 Particle of request *After a verb in the imperfect* ( ) מִי־יִתֵּן מוּתִי אֲנִי תַחְתֶּיךָ

3 Defective writing *Expected י/ו is omitted* ( ) אַל־תֹּסֶף רְאוֹת פָּנַי

4 Hardening dagesh is omitted *Preceding word ends in a vowel* ( ) וְכֹה אָמַר בְּלֶכְתּוֹ

5 Phrase expressing time ( ) הֲקוֹלְךָ זֶה בְּנִי
'בְּ *(when/while) + infinitive + attached pronoun*'

6 Question marker ( ) בְּנִי בְנִי אַבְשָׁלוֹם

7 זֶה intensifying a question ( ) וַיִּשָּׁבְעוּ אִישׁ לְאָחִיו

8 הִפְעִיל verb functioning as an adverbial ( ) וְגַם יָכֹל תּוּכָל
Followed by an infinitive, rendered by 'again'

9 Expression of wish *Lit., 'who will give/allow'* ( ) וַיְהִי בַּיּוֹם הַהוּא וַיָּבֹאוּ

10 Time frame *Preceded by an inverted form of* היה (_) לָמָּה זֶּה אֲדֹנִי רֹדֵף
אַחֲרֵי עַבְדּוֹ

11 'One another' in Hebrew *Literally,* (_) יִשְׁמַע־נָא אֲדֹנִי
'man + preposition + his brother'

27.7 In Exercise 27.5 above *identify* nine infinitive forms and *write* them. Then *indicate* the corresponding participle form/s, e.g., שָׁמֹר (infinitive) corresponds to שֹׁמֵר and שָׁמוּר (participles of פָּעַל).

27.8 In Exercise 27.5 above *identify* twenty-four forms of the inverted imperfect and *write* them. Then *write* the corresponding forms in the perfect.

27.9 *Translate* into Hebrew. *Use* the perfect tense. *Note*:

> ◆ The verbs in the clauses below are among the most frequent in the Hebrew Bible. *Memorize* them.
> ◆ The normal word order of the verbal clause is **Verb–Subject–Object**.

1 The man talked to the king and said, "Please, if I have found favour in your sight (= eyes)...."
2 The woman came to see her son in the temple.
3 The LORD sent this prophet to (= אֶל) us. The old prophet died.
4 God gave the Law to his people.
5 His son read the book and put it in the house.
6 The slave went back to his master.
7 My brother saw me sitting at the gate with the elders of the city.

27.10 *Check* (and *correct* if needed) your translation of Exercise 27.9 above. Then *transform* the verbs in the perfect into the inverted imperf. *Note*:

> ◆ The meaning of the clauses will not be changed.

27.11 *Transform* the clauses with the verbs in the perfect in Exercise 27.9 above (except entry 4) from the singular into the plural (verbs as well as nouns and pronouns). *Remember*:

> ◆ Unlike other root types, the vocalic suffixes (suffixes consisting of a vowel only) of II-י/ו verbs are unstressed, e.g., קָמוּ, תָּקוּמוּ, compare שָׁמְרוּ, יִשְׁמְרוּ.

SECTION 28

1 *Numerals*

	Masculine			Feminine		
	Free form	Bound form	Ordinal	Free form	Bound form	Ordinal
one	אֶחָד	אַחַד	רִאשׁוֹן *first*	אַחַת	אַחַת	רִאשׁוֹנָה
two	שְׁנַיִם	שְׁנֵי	שֵׁנִי *second*	שְׁתַּיִם	שְׁתֵּי	שֵׁנִית
three	שְׁלֹשָׁה	שְׁלֹשֶׁת	שְׁלִישִׁי *etc.*	שָׁלֹשׁ	שְׁלֹשׁ	שְׁלִישִׁית
four	אַרְבָּעָה	אַרְבַּעַת	רְבִיעִי	אַרְבַּע	אַרְבַּע	רְבִיעִית
five	חֲמִשָּׁה	חֲמֵשֶׁת	חֲמִישִׁי	חָמֵשׁ	חֲמֵשׁ	חֲמִישִׁית
six	שִׁשָּׁה	שֵׁשֶׁת	שִׁשִּׁי	שֵׁשׁ	שֵׁשׁ	שִׁשִּׁית
seven	שִׁבְעָה	שִׁבְעַת	שְׁבִיעִי	שֶׁבַע	שְׁבַע	שְׁבִיעִית
eight	שְׁמֹנָה	שְׁמֹנַת	שְׁמִינִי	שְׁמֹנֶה	שְׁמֹנֶה	שְׁמִינִית
nine	תִּשְׁעָה	תִּשְׁעַת	תְּשִׁיעִי	תֵּשַׁע	תְּשַׁע	תְּשִׁיעִית
ten	עֲשָׂרָה	עֲשֶׂרֶת	עֲשִׂירִי	עֶשֶׂר	עֶשֶׂר	עֲשִׂירִית

– Like nouns, the numerals have free (independent) and bound forms, but unlike nouns, the base form (the form without an ending) is the feminine and not the masculine.

– The numbers 'eleven' to 'nineteen' are a combination of 'number + עָשָׂר (masculine) or עֶשְׂרֵה (feminine)'. עָשָׂר/עֶשְׂרֵה corresponds to English '-teen', e.g., שְׁלֹשָׁה עָשָׂר 'thirteen' (m) and שְׁלֹשׁ עֶשְׂרֵה 'thirteen' (f).

עֶשְׂרִים is 'twenty'. The ending ־ים corresponds to English '-ty', e.g., 'שְׁלֹשׁ (three) + ־ים' results in שְׁלֹשִׁים 'thirty'.

2 *Denoting age*: The construction 'בֵּן/בַּת (son/daughter) + number + שָׁנָה/שָׁנִים (year/s)' denotes age, e.g., בֶּן/בַּת־שֶׁבַע שָׁנִים 'seven years old', lit., 'son/daughter of seven years'.

3 *Conditional clauses*: A condition (in a conditional clause) is usually followed by a consequence in the main clause. The conditional relationship is usually expressed by means of the particles לוּ ,כִּי ,אִם.[1] There are three types of conditional clauses:

– The condition is *real*, that is, can be fulfilled, and refers to a *specific case*: 'אִם (rarely כִּי) + verb in the imperf/perf + (וְ) consequence', e.g., אִם תָּבוֹא הַיּוֹם וְהָלַכְנוּ 'If you come today, we will go'.

– The condition is *real* and does not refer to a specific instance but is *general*: 'כִּי + verb, usually in the imperf + (וְ) consequence', e.g., כִּי תָבוֹא אֵלֵךְ 'In case (whenever it happens that) you come, I will go'. This type of clause is often found in regulations and laws.

---

[1] The conditional relationship can also be expressed by the particle וְ or without any particle.

– The condition is *unreal*, that is, hypothetical, and thus cannot be fulfilled: 'לוּ (negatively לוּלֵי/לוּלֵא) + verb in the perf + (וְ) consequence', e.g.,

לוּ/לוּלֵי בָּאתָ וְהָלַכְתִּי   '*If you had/had not come*, I would have gone'.

REVIEW AND APPLICATION OF THE RULES

I   The verb forms below (from Exercises 28.8, 28.10 and 28.12) undergo regular sound changes. *Review* the sound change rules in **Appendix II**. Then *indicate* the relevant sound change/s occurring in the enlarged element/s of each verb form/construction. *Translate*.

(28.8   **1** וַיָּקָם   **2** וַיַּגֵּד, לְבַקְשׁוֹ   **3** מָצָאתִי, יִתְּנוּ

(28.10   **1** וַיְדַבֵּר   **2** וַיָּבֹא, וַיַּהֲרֹג, וַיֵּאָסְפוּ

3 וַיַּגִּידוּ, וַיַּעֲמֹד, וַיִּשָּׂא, וַיִּקְרָא, יִשְׁמַע, לִמְשֹׁחַ

(28.12   **1** לַעֲשׂוֹת, וַיְהִי   **2** בָּא, נוֹרָא, הִגִּיד, תִּשְׁתִּי   **3** וַיִּשְׁמַע

WORD LIST

Nouns

אָמָה	f, female slave
זָכָר	m, male (☆ **Zechariah**)
מֵאָה	f, hundred: *bound form* מְאַת, *dual* מָאתַיִם
מַחֲנֶה	m, camp: *pl* מַחֲנִים/מַחֲנוֹת
מַצָּה	f, unleavened bread
מַמְלָכָה, מֶלֶךְ	f, kingdom
רָעָב	m, hunger, famine

Adjectives

שְׁבִיעִי, שבע	seventh (☆ **Bathsheba**, š.b.ʕ)

Verbs

הָרָה	conceive, be pregnant: *imperf* תַּהֲרֶה, *inverted imperf* וַתַּהַר

מול	circumcise: *perf* מָל, *imperf* יָמוּל, *inverted imperf* וַיָּמָל, *niph* נִמּוֹל be circumcised
צָחַק	laugh: *imperf* יִצְחַק (☆ **Isaac**, ṣ.ḥ.q)
רוץ	run: *perf* רָץ, *imperf* יָרוּץ, *inverted imperf* וַיָּרָץ
שָׁתָה	drink: *imperf* יִשְׁתֶּה, *inverted imperf* וַיֵּשְׁתְּ

Particles

אוּלַי	perhaps
לוּלֵא/לוּלֵי	if not, unless

EXERCISES

28.1 *Memorize* the following numbers: 'one' to 'ten' (free form, feminine!), 'twenty' (עֶשְׂרִים), 'hundred' (מֵאָה) and 'thousand' (אֶלֶף). This will enable you to identify all the numbers.

28.2 Each verse/verse segment below contains a *number/s*. *Read* and *translate* on your own. Then *complete* the missing words in the following translation and *check/complete* your translation against it. *Analyze* the verb forms as follows: **a)** verb type **b)** root consonants **c)** tense. *Note*:

> • The ending ים. corresponds to English '-ty', e.g., 'שָׁלֹשׁ (three) + ים. ' results in שְׁלֹשִׁים 'thirty'.
> • The noun after the numbers 'two' to 'ten' is in the plural, e.g., שָׁלֹשׁ שָׁנִים 'three years', whereas the noun after a number higher than 'ten' is usually in the singular, e.g., שְׁלֹשִׁים שָׁנָה 'thirty years'.
> • Age is expressed by the construction 'בֶּן/בַּת + number + שָׁנָה or שָׁנִים'.

1 בָּרִאשֹׁן בְּאַרְבָּעָה עָשָׂר יוֹם לַחֹדֶשׁ בָּעֶרֶב תֹּאכְלוּ מַצֹּת עַד יוֹם הָאֶחָד

וְעֶשְׂרִים לַחֹדֶשׁ בָּעָרֶב: _____ the _____ [month], on (= בְּ) the fourteenth

day of (= לְ) the month _____ the evening _____ shall _____ unleavened

bread _____ the twenty-first _____ of the month _____ _____ evening

(Ex. 12:18) תֹּאכְלוּ a) _____ b) _____ c) _____

2 וַיְבָרֶךְ אֱלֹהִים אֶת־יוֹם הַשְּׁבִיעִי וַיְקַדֵּשׁ אֹתוֹ God _____ the _____

day and made _____ sacred (Gen. 2:3)

וַיְבָרֶךְ a) _____ b) _____ c) _____

3 בֶּן־שְׁלֹשִׁים שָׁנָה דָּוִד בְּמָלְכוֹ אַרְבָּעִים שָׁנָה מָלָךְ: בְּחֶבְרוֹן מָלַךְ

עַל־יְהוּדָה שֶׁבַע שָׁנִים וְשִׁשָּׁה חֳדָשִׁים [ḥ°dāšîm] וּבִירוּשָׁלַם מָלַךְ

שְׁלֹשִׁים וְשָׁלֹשׁ שָׁנָה עַל כָּל־יִשְׂרָאֵל וִיהוּדָה: David [was] _____ years

old (= son of _____ year) when _____ became king (= in _____

reigning as king). He reigned _____ year[s]. _____ Hebron _____

reigned _____ Judah _____ years and _____ months, and in Jerusalem

he reigned _____ (= _____ and _____) year[s] over _____ Israel and

Judah (2 Sam. 5:4–5) מָלַךְ: a) _____ b) _____ c) _____

4 וַיֹּסֶף עוֹד לְדַבֵּר אֵלָיו וַיֹּאמַר² אוּלַי יִמָּצְאוּן שָׁם אַרְבָּעִים

וַיֹּאמֶר לֹא אֶעֱשֶׂה בַּעֲבוּר הָאַרְבָּעִים: _____ spoke to him again

(= וַיֹּסֶף + עוֹד) and _____ _____, "Perhaps _____ will be found

_____?" And _____ _____, "I will not _____ [it] for the sake of the

_____" (Gen. 18:29)

וַיֹּסֶף   a) _____ b) _____ c) _____

5 וְאַבְרָם בֶּן־שְׁמֹנִים שָׁנָה וְשֵׁשׁ שָׁנִים בְּלֶדֶת־הָגָר אֶת־יִשְׁמָעֵאל

לְאַבְרָם: Abram [was] _____ years old (= son of _____ year and

_____ years) when Hagar bore (= in Hagar's bearing) Ishmael _____

Abram (Gen. 16:16)

לֶדֶת   a) _____ b) _____ c) _____

6 וַיִּפֹּל אַבְרָהָם עַל־פָּנָיו וַיִּצְחָק וַיֹּאמֶר בְּלִבּוֹ הַלְּבֶן מֵאָה־שָׁנָה יִוָּלֵד

וְאִם־שָׂרָה הֲבַת־תִּשְׁעִים שָׁנָה תֵּלֵד: Then (= וַ) Abraham fell _____

_____ _____ and laughed as (= וַ) _____ _____ to himself (= in his

heart), "Will [a child] (= he) be _____ to [a man who is a] _____

year[s] old (= son of _____ year) or (= וְאִם) will Sarah, [a woman

who is] _____ year[s] old (= daughter of _____ year), give birth?"

(Gen. 17:17) יִוָּלֵד a) _____ b) _____ c) _____

7 וְלִי נָתְנוּ הָאֲלָפִים But (= וְ) _____ _____ _____ have _____ the

_____ (1 Sam. 18:8)

נָתְנוּ   a) _____ b) _____ c) _____

8 וְאֵלֶּה יְמֵי שְׁנֵי־חַיֵּי אַבְרָהָם אֲשֶׁר־חָי מְאַת שָׁנָה וְשִׁבְעִים שָׁנָה וְחָמֵשׁ

שָׁנִים: This [was] the total span of Abraham's life (= and _____ the

_____ of the _____ of Abraham's _____ _____ he lived), [one] _____

and _____ years (= _____ year and _____ year and _____ years)

(Gen. 25:7)

חָי (pausal form חָי) a) _____ b) _____ c) _____

---

² Pausal form, marked in the Hebrew Bible by the accent sign *zaqeph qaton*.

28.3 *Match* each grammatical phenomenon (from Exercise 28.2 above) with the Hebrew word/construction that illustrates it. *Read* and *translate* orally. Observe that the same phenomenon may appear more than once, but only one occurrence is to be noted. Each Hebrew word/construction is to be used once!

1 Defective writing, י/ו *is unexpectedly omitted* ( ) וְאֵלֶּה יְמֵי־שְׁנֵי־חַיֵּי אַבְרָהָם

2 Imperfect form of נִפְעַל *followed by* נ ( ) הֲבַת־תִּשְׁעִים שָׁנָה תֵּלֵד

3 Relative clause describing a noun in a main ( ) וַיֹּסֶף... לְדַבֵּר אֵלָיו
   clause *Introduced by* אֲשֶׁר

4 Noun chain with four nouns *The first* ( ) בְּמָלְכוֹ
   three have bound forms

5 Phrase expressing time 'בְּ *(when) +* ( ) חַיֵּי אַבְרָהָם אֲשֶׁר־חָי
   ordinary infinitive + proper name', rendered
   in English by a temporal clause

6 Phrase expressing time 'בְּ *(when) +* ( ) בְּלֶדֶת־הָגָר אֶת־יִשְׁמָעֵאל
   ordinary infinitive + attached pronoun',
   rendered in English by a temporal clause

7 Question marker *Introduces yes-or-no question* ( ) בֶּן־שְׁלֹשִׁים שָׁנָה

8 Noun chain expressing age ( ) וַיְקַדֵּשׁ אֹתוֹ
   Introduced by בֵּן/בַּת

9 הִפְעִיל verb functioning as an adverbial ( ) מַצֹּת
   Followed by 'לְ + infinitive', rendered by 'again, more'

10 Penultimate noun *The plural pattern is* ־ִים ־ָ־ ( ) יִמָּצְאוּן

11 Doubling dagesh is omitted *Refers to a* ( ) הָאֲלָפִים
   consonant with a shva

28.4 Each verse/verse segment below contains *number/s*. *Read* and *translate* into English. Proper names are enlarged.

1 אוּלַי יֵשׁ חֲמִשִּׁים צַדִּיקִם בְּתוֹךְ הָעִיר (Gen. 18:24)

2 שְׁנֵים־עָשָׂר אֲנַחְנוּ אַחִים בְּנֵי אָבִינוּ הָאֶחָד אֵינֶנּוּ וְהַקָּטֹן הַיּוֹם
   אֶת־אָבִינוּ בְּאֶרֶץ כְּנָעַן: (Gen. 42:32)

3 שֵׁשֶׁת יָמִים תַּעֲבֹד... וְיוֹם הַשְּׁבִיעִי שַׁבָּת לַיהוה אֱלֹהֶיךָ (Ex. 20:9–10)

4 וְנֶפֶשׁ אָדָם שִׁשָּׁה עָשָׂר אָלֶף: (Num. 31:46)

5 וַיֹּאמֶר אֲלֵהֶם בֶּן־מֵאָה וְעֶשְׂרִים שָׁנָה אָנֹכִי הַיּוֹם (Dt. 31:2)

6 וּמֹשֶׁה בֶּן־מֵאָה וְעֶשְׂרִים שָׁנָה בְּמֹתוֹ (Dt. 34:7)

7   כִּי יָדַע עַבְדְּךָ כִּי אֲנִי חָטָאתִי וְהִנֵּה־בָאתִי הַיּוֹם רִאשׁוֹן (2 Sam. 19:21)

8   וַיְדַבֵּר שְׁלֹשֶׁת אֲלָפִים מָשָׁל וַיְהִי שִׁירוֹ חֲמִשָּׁה וָאָלֶף: (1 Kings 5:12)

9   וּשְׁנֵי חַיֵּי לֵוִי שֶׁבַע וּשְׁלֹשִׁים וּמְאַת שָׁנָה: (Ex. 6:16)

28.5 In Exercise 28.4 above *identify* three words with defective spelling (that is, the vowel letter י/ו is unexpectedly omitted). *Write* the Hebrew words and *indicate* the normal spelling.

28.6 Each Hebrew text unit below contains a *conditional clause/s* (the particles introducing the conditional clause, i.e., אִם, אִם לֹא, כִּי, לוּ, לוּלֵא/לוּלֵי, as well as the particle וְ introducing the consequence are enlarged). *Read* the Hebrew text and *translate* on your own. Then *complete* the missing words in the following translation and *check/complete* your translation against it.

1   וְהָיָה אִם־יִקְרָא אֵלֶיךָ וְאָמַרְתָּ דַּבֵּר יהוה כִּי שֹׁמֵעַ עַבְדֶּךָ

If _____ calls (+ to) _____, _____ will _____, "_____, Lord, for

_____ servant [is] _____" (1 Sam. 3:9)

2   וַיֹּאמֶר אֵלֶיהָ בָּרָק אִם־תֵּלְכִי עִמִּי וְהָלָכְתִּי וְאִם־לֹא תֵלְכִי עִמִּי

לֹא אֵלֵךְ: Barak said _____ _____, "If you will _____ with _____,

_____ will _____, but (= וְ) if _____ will not _____ _____ _____,

_____ will not _____" (Judg. 4:8)

3   וַיֹּאמְרוּ אִישׁ אֶל־רֵעֵהוּ מָה אֲנַחְנוּ יֹשְׁבִים פֹּה   עַד־מָתְנוּ:

אִם־אָמַרְנוּ   נָבוֹא הָעִיר וְהָרָעָב בָּעִיר וָמַתְנוּ שָׁם וְאִם־יָשַׁבְנוּ פֹּה

וָמָתְנוּ וְעַתָּה לְכוּ וְנִפְּלָה אֶל־מַחֲנֵה אֲרָם אִם־יְחַיֻּנוּ נִחְיֶה

וְאִם־יְמִיתֻנוּ וָמָתְנוּ: And _____ _____ to one another (= man _____

_____ _____), "Why (lit., 'what') [are] _____ _____ _____ until

_____ have _____? If _____ _____, 'Let us _____ the city and the

famine [is] _____ the city, then (= וְ) _____ shall _____ _____, and if

we _____ _____, _____ shall [also] _____. So (= וְ) _____ come on

(= לְכוּ) and let us desert (= נפל) to the Aramean camp (= camp of

Aram). If _____ let us _____, _____ shall _____; and if _____ let us

_____, we shall _____'." (2 Kings 7:3–4)

4 אִם־תִּהְיוּ כָמֹנוּ לְהִמֹּל לָכֶם כָּל־זָכָר׃ וְנָתַנּוּ אֶת־בְּנֹתֵינוּ לָכֶם וְאֶת־
בְּנֹתֵיכֶם נִקַּח־לָנוּ וְיָשַׁבְנוּ אִתְּכֶם וְהָיִינוּ לְעַם אֶחָד׃ וְאִם־לֹא
תִשְׁמְעוּ אֵלֵינוּ לְהִמּוֹל וְלָקַחְנוּ אֶת־בִּתֵּנוּ וְהָלָכְנוּ׃ If _____ will

become (= be) _____ _____, [that] _____ male of you (= לָכֶם) [will]

be (= to be) circumcised, then (= וְ) _____ will _____ _____ daughters

_____ _____, and _____ daughters _____ will _____ to ourselves, and

_____ will _____ _____ _____ and become (= הָיָה + לְ) one _____.

But (= וְ) if _____ will not _____ _____ _____, to be circumcised, then

(= וְ) _____ will _____ _____ daughter and _____ will _____

(Gen. 34:15–17)

5 כִּי־תִמְצָא אִישׁ לֹא תְבָרְכֶנּוּ וְכִי־יְבָרֶכְךָ אִישׁ לֹא תַעֲנֶנּוּ If _____

meet anyone (= find man), _____ shall not greet (= ברך) _____, and if

anyone (= man) greets _____, _____ shall not answer _____

(2 Kings 4:29)

6 אִם־יִהְיֶה אֱלֹהִים עִמָּדִי (= עִמִּי) וּשְׁמָרַנִי בַּדֶּרֶךְ הַזֶּה אֲשֶׁר אָנֹכִי הוֹלֵךְ
וְנָתַן־לִי לֶחֶם לֶאֱכֹל׃ ...וְשַׁבְתִּי בְשָׁלוֹם אֶל־בֵּית אָבִי וְהָיָה יהוה
לִי לֵאלֹהִים׃ If God will _____ _____ _____ and will _____ _____ in

_____ way, [on] which I [am] _____, and will _____ (+ to) _____

bread to _____..., so that (= וְ) _____ will return in peace _____ the

_____ of _____ _____, then (= וְ) the Lord shall be _____ God (= God

to _____) (Gen. 28:20–21)

7 וְכִי־יִמְכֹּר אִישׁ אֶת־בִּתּוֹ לְאָמָה לֹא תֵצֵא כְּצֵאת הָעֲבָדִים׃ And in

case/when [a] _____ sells _____ daughter as (= to) [a] slave, _____

will not be freed (= go out) as the male slaves do (= as the going out of

the male slaves) (Ex. 21:7)

8 כִּי־יִמָּכֵר לְךָ אָחִיךָ הָעִבְרִי... וַעֲבָדְךָ שֵׁשׁ שָׁנִים וּבַשָּׁנָה הַשְּׁבִיעֵת
תְּשַׁלְּחֶנּוּ... מֵעִמָּךְ׃ In case/when [a] fellow Hebrew (= your Hebrew

brother) is sold _____ _____, _____ shall serve _____ _____ years,

and in the _____ year _____ shall let _____ go... _____ _____ (Dt. 15:12)

9 וְהָיָה כִּי־יֹאמַר אֵלֶיךָ לֹא אֵצֵא מֵעִמָּךְ כִּי אֲהֵבְךָ וְאֶת־בֵּיתֶךָ כִּי־טוֹב

לוֹ עִמָּךְ: וְלָקַחְתָּ   But (= וְ) if/in case he says _____ _____, '_____

will not go out _____ _____ ' for he loves _____ and _____ house[hold],

for he [is] happy (= good to him) with _____, then (= וְ) _____ shall

_____ ... (Dt. 15:16–17)

10 כִּי־יִקַּח אִישׁ אִשָּׁה חֲדָשָׁה לֹא יֵצֵא בַּצָּבָא   In case/when [a] man is

newly married (= _____ new _____), _____ shall not go out with (= בְּ)

the _____ (Dt. 24:5)

28.7 In Exercise 28.6 above *identify* eight finite verb forms (perf, imperf and
imperative) followed by attached object pronouns. *Write* the Hebrew verbs
with the attached pronouns. Then *write* the verb forms alone with the
corresponding independent object pronouns, e.g., יִשְׁמְרוּ/יִשְׁמְרֶנּוּ
corresponds to יִשְׁמֹר אֹתוֹ 'he will guard him'.

28.8 *Translate* into English. Proper names are enlarged. *Analyze* the verb forms
as follows: **a)** verb type **b)** root consonants **c)** tense.

1 ² וַיָּקָם דָּוִד וַיַּעֲבֹר הוּא וְשֵׁשׁ־מֵאוֹת אִישׁ אֲשֶׁר עִמּוֹ אֶל־אָכִישׁ
בֶּן־מָעוֹךְ מֶלֶךְ גַּת: ³ וַיֵּשֶׁב דָּוִד עִם־אָכִישׁ בְּגַת הוּא וַאֲנָשָׁיו
אִישׁ וּבֵיתוֹ דָּוִד וּשְׁתֵּי נָשָׁיו אֲחִינֹעַם הַיִּזְרְעֵאלִית וַאֲבִיגַיִל
אֵשֶׁת־נָבָל הַכַּרְמְלִית:

a) _____ b) _____ c) _____   וַיָּקָם

a) _____ b) _____ c) _____   וַיַּעֲבֹר

2 ⁴ וַיֻּגַּד לְשָׁאוּל כִּי־בָרַח דָּוִד גַּת לְגַת (read) וְלֹא־יוֹסַף (= יָסַף) עוֹד
לְבַקְשׁוֹ:

a) _____ b) _____ c) _____   וַיֻּגַּד

3 ⁵ וַיֹּאמֶר דָּוִד אֶל־אָכִישׁ אִם־נָא מָצָאתִי חֵן בְּעֵינֶיךָ יִתְּנוּ־לִי מָקוֹם
בְּאַחַת עָרֵי הַשָּׂדֶה וְאֵשְׁבָה שָּׁם וְלָמָּה יֵשֵׁב עַבְדְּךָ בְּעִיר הַמַּמְלָכָה
עִמָּךְ: ⁶ וַיִּתֶּן־לוֹ אָכִישׁ בַּיּוֹם הַהוּא אֶת־צִקְלָג לָכֵן הָיְתָה צִקְלַג
לְמַלְכֵי יְהוּדָה עַד הַיּוֹם הַזֶּה: (1 Sam. 27:2–6)

a) _____ b) _____ c) _____   יִתְּנוּ

a) _____ b) _____ c) _____   אֵשְׁבָה

28.9 *Match* each grammatical phenomenon (from Exercise 28.8 above) with the Hebrew construction that illustrates it. *Read* and *translate* orally. Observe that the same grammatical phenomenon may appear more than once, but only one occurrence is to be noted. Each Hebrew construction is to be used once!

1 Request formula *Introduces a request to a person higher in status than the speaker*   הָיְתָה צִקְלַג לְמַלְכֵי יְהוּדָה (_)

2 Formula indicating reported speech *'The verb* נגד *(3ms,* הֻפְעַל *Hp) +* לְ *+ noun'*   וְשֵׁשׁ־מֵאוֹת אִישׁ אֲשֶׁר עִמּוֹ (_)

3 Relative clause describing a noun in a main clause *Introduced by the particle* אֲשֶׁר   אֲחִינֹעַם הַיִּזְרְעֵאלִית (_)

4 Hardening dagesh is omitted *Preceding word ends in a vowel*   וַיֻּגַּד לְשָׁאוּל כִּי־ (_)

5 Qamets-/o/   כִּי־בָרַח (_)

6 Possession (past time) *Expressed by* 'היה *+* לְ*', corresponds to English 'belonged to', lit. 'was to'*   וְלֹא־יוֹסֵף (יָסַף) לְבַקְשׁוֹ (_)

7 Noun chain *Rendered by the construction 'adjective + noun'*   אִם־נָא מָצָאתִי חֵן בְּעֵינֶיךָ (_)

8 Verb functioning as an adverbial *Followed by* 'לְ *+ infinitive', rendered by 'again, more'*   וַיָּקָם דָּוִד (_)

9 Proper name denoting a member of a group *'Place name + the ending* י*.'*   עִיר הַמַּמְלָכָה (_)

28.10 *Translate* into English. Proper names are enlarged. *Analyze* the verb forms as follows: **a)** verb type **b)** root consonants **c)** tense.

1 ¹ וַיֵּלֶךְ אֲבִימֶלֶךְ בֶּן־יְרֻבַּעַל שְׁכֶמָה אֶל־אֲחֵי אִמּוֹ וַיְדַבֵּר אֲלֵיהֶם וְאֶל־כָּל־מִשְׁפַּחַת בֵּית־אֲבִי אִמּוֹ לֵאמֹר: ² דַּבְּרוּ־נָא בְּאָזְנֵי כָל־בַּעֲלֵי שְׁכֶם מַה־טּוֹב לָכֶם הַמְשֹׁל בָּכֶם שִׁבְעִים אִישׁ כֹּל בְּנֵי יְרֻבַּעַל אִם־מְשֹׁל בָּכֶם אִישׁ אֶחָד...

a) _____ b) _____ c) _____   וַיֵּלֶךְ

2 ³...וַיְדַבְּרוּ אֲחֵי־אִמּוֹ עָלָיו בְּאָזְנֵי כָל־בַּעֲלֵי שְׁכֶם אֵת כָּל־הַדְּבָרִים הָאֵלֶּה... ⁵ וַיָּבֹא בֵית־אָבִיו (read) עָפְרָתָה וַיַּהֲרֹג אֶת־אֶחָיו בְּנֵי־יְרֻבַּעַל שִׁבְעִים אִישׁ עַל־אֶבֶן אֶחָת... ⁶ וַיֵּאָסְפוּ כָּל־בַּעֲלֵי שְׁכֶם וְכָל־בֵּית מִלּוֹא וַיֵּלְכוּ וַיַּמְלִיכוּ אֶת־אֲבִימֶלֶךְ לְמֶלֶךְ... בִּשְׁכֶם:

a) _____ b) _____ c) _____   וַיְדַבְּרוּ

a) _____ b) _____ c) _____   וַיָּבֹא

3 ⁷ וַיַּגִּדוּ לְיוֹתָם וַיֵּלֶךְ וַיַּעֲמֹד בְּרֹאשׁ הַר־גְּרִזִים וַיִּשָּׂא קוֹלוֹ וַיִּקְרָא
וַיֹּאמֶר לָהֶם שִׁמְעוּ אֵלַי בַּעֲלֵי שְׁכֶם וְיִשְׁמַע אֲלֵיכֶם אֱלֹהִים: ⁸ הָלוֹךְ
הָלְכוּ הָעֵצִים לִמְשֹׁחַ עֲלֵיהֶם מֶלֶךְ (Judg. 9:1–3, 5–8)

a) _____ b) _____ c) _____ וַיַּגִּדוּ

28.11 *Match* each grammatical phenomenon (from Exercise 28.10 above) with
the Hebrew construction that illustrates it. *Read* and *translate* orally. Observe
that the same grammatical phenomenon may appear more than once, but
only one instance is to be noted. Each Hebrew construction is to be used
once!

1 Particle of request *Often follows an imperative*   ( ) וַיֵּלֶךְ אֲבִימֶלֶךְ... שְׁכֶמָה

2 Formula indicating reported speech   ( ) מִשְׁפַּחַת בֵּית־אֲבִי אִמּוֹ
'The verb נגד (3mp, הִפְעִיל H) + לְ + noun'

3 Noun chain *With four nouns*   ( ) בַּעֲלֵי שְׁכֶם

4 Hardening dagesh is omitted *Preceding*   ( ) דַּבְּרוּ־נָא
word ends in a vowel

5 Quotation marker 'לְ + *infinitive*'   ( ) הֲמְשֹׁל בָּכֶם
שִׁבְעִים אִישׁ

6 Phrase expressing purpose   ( ) וַיַּגִּדוּ לְיוֹתָם
'לְ *(in order to)* + infinitive'

7 Question marker *Introduces a yes-or-no question* ( ) וַיָּבֹא בֵית־אָבִיו

8 Direction marker ה ָ *Rendered by 'to/towards'* ( ) הָלוֹךְ הָלְכוּ הָעֵצִים

9 Infinitive-as-intensifier *Precedes a finite verb* ( ) הָלְכוּ הָעֵצִים לִמְשֹׁחַ

10 The noun בַּעַל as the first term in a noun   ( ) לֵאמֹר
chain *'Owner of...'*

28.12 *Translate* into English. Proper names are enlarged.

1 ¹ וַיֹּסִפוּ בְּנֵי יִשְׂרָאֵל לַעֲשׂוֹת הָרַע בְּעֵינֵי יהוה וַיִּתְּנֵם יהוה
בְּיַד־פְּלִשְׁתִּים אַרְבָּעִים שָׁנָה: ² וַיְהִי אִישׁ אֶחָד מִצָּרְעָה מִמִּשְׁפַּחַת
הַדָּנִי וּשְׁמוֹ מָנוֹחַ...

2 ⁶ וַתָּבֹא הָאִשָּׁה וַתֹּאמֶר לְאִישָׁהּ לֵאמֹר אִישׁ הָאֱלֹהִים בָּא אֵלַי וּמַרְאֵהוּ
כְּמַרְאֵה מַלְאַךְ הָאֱלֹהִים נוֹרָא מְאֹד וְלֹא שְׁאִלְתִּיהוּ שְׁאִלְתִּיהוּ (read
אֵי־מִזֶּה הוּא וְאֶת־שְׁמוֹ לֹא־הִגִּיד לִי: ⁷ וַיֹּאמֶר לִי הִנָּךְ הָרָה וְיֹלַדְתְּ
וְיָלַדְתְּ (read בֵּן וְעַתָּה אַל־תִּשְׁתִּי יַיִן...

3 ⁹ וַיִּשְׁמַע הָאֱלֹהִים בְּקוֹל מָנוֹחַ וַיָּבֹא מַלְאַךְ הָאֱלֹהִים עוֹד אֶל־הָאִשָּׁה

וְהִיא יוֹשֶׁבֶת בַּשָּׂדֶה וּמָנוֹחַ אִישָׁהּ אֵין עִמָּהּ: ¹⁰ וַתְּמַהֵר הָאִשָּׁה

וַתָּרָץ וַתַּגֵּד לְאִישָׁהּ וַתֹּאמֶר אֵלָיו הִנֵּה נִרְאָה אֵלַי הָאִישׁ אֲשֶׁר־בָּא

בַּיּוֹם אֵלָי:

4 ¹¹ וַיָּקָם וַיֵּלֶךְ מָנוֹחַ אַחֲרֵי אִשְׁתּוֹ וַיָּבֹא אֶל־הָאִישׁ וַיֹּאמֶר לוֹ הַאַתָּה

הָאִישׁ אֲשֶׁר־דִּבַּרְתָּ אֶל־הָאִשָּׁה וַיֹּאמֶר אָנִי: ¹² וַיֹּאמֶר מָנוֹחַ עַתָּה

יָבֹא (read יָבֹאוּ) דְבָרֶיךָ מַה־יִּהְיֶה מִשְׁפַּט־הַנַּעַר וּמַעֲשֵׂהוּ: ¹³ וַיֹּאמֶר

מַלְאַךְ יהוה אֶל־מָנוֹחַ מִכֹּל אֲשֶׁר־אָמַרְתִּי אֶל־הָאִשָּׁה תִּשָּׁמֵר:

(Judg. 13:1–2, 6–7, 9–13)

28.13 *Match* each grammatical phenomenon (from Exercise 28.12 above) with
the Hebrew construction that illustrates it. *Read* and *translate* orally. Observe
that the same grammatical phenomenon may appear more than once, but
only one occurrence is to be noted. Each Hebrew construction is to be
used once!

1 Negative command 'אַל + *shortened imperfect*' ( ) וַיֵּסְפוּ בְּנֵי יִשְׂרָאֵל לַעֲשׂוֹת

2 Relative clause describing a noun in a   ( ) וּמָנוֹחַ אִישָׁהּ אֵין עִמָּהּ
   main clause *Introduced by the particle* אֲשֶׁר

3 Verbless clause is negated by אֵין   ( ) אַל־תִּשְׁתִּי יָיִן

4 Hardening dagesh is omitted *Preceding*   ( ) וְהִיא יוֹשֶׁבֶת בַּשָּׂדֶה
   word ends in a vowel

5 Mappiq *Marks that* ה *at the end of a word is a* ( ) אֵי־מִזֶּה הוּא
   consonant (often an attached pronoun, 3fs 'her, its')

6 Question marker *Introduces yes-or-no question* ( ) הָאִישׁ אֲשֶׁר־בָּא בַּיּוֹם
                                                            אֵלָי

7 זֶה *intensifying a question*   ( ) בָּא בַּיּוֹם

8 הִפְעִיל verb functioning as an adverbial ( ) וַתָּבֹא הָאִשָּׁה וַתֹּאמֶר
   Followed by 'לְ + *infinitive', rendered by 'again, more'* לְאִישָׁהּ

9 Verbless clause *With a participle as predicate,* ( ) הַאַתָּה הָאִישׁ
   the time reference is determined by the context

28.14 In Exercises 28.8, 28.10 and 28.12 above *identify* five inverted imperfect
forms of פָּעַל (G), in which the stress is thrown back from the last to the
next-to-last (penultimate) syllable. *Write* the verbs. *Indicate* the root
consonants of each verb. *Remember*:

> - The stress is thrown back from the last to the next-to-last syllable in פָּעַל forms (without a following ending) of II-י/ו, III-י/ו (III-ה) and a few I-י/ו-verbs (and also the verbs הלך and אמר).
> - A closed syllable with a short vowel (segol or qamets) at the end of a word signals that the stress falls on the next-to-last syllable.

28.15 In Exercise 28.12 above *identify* one inverted imperfect form of הִפְעִיל (H) without a following ending and *write* it. *Indicate* the corresponding ordinary imperfect. *Remember*:

> - There are two distinct imperfect forms in הִפְעִיל (unchangeable root types, שְׁלֵמִים), ordinary and shortened.

28.16 *Translate* into Hebrew. *Use* the perfect tense.
  1   The king died when he was seventy-three years old (= in his being son of seventy-three year).
  2   After all these matters, his son returned (שׁוּב) to the city.
  3   The priest put (שִׂים) his hand on the man's head and blessed him, saying, "May the LORD keep you."
  4   On that day the master went out of (= from) the house and said to his servant, "Take me to the land of my fathers."
  5   The man walked with his brother on (= בְּ) the road to Jerusalem.
  6   The woman was on the mountain. The man went up to (אֶל) her and built a house for her there. The man dwelt in this house many years. The woman bore him (= to him) two children.

28.17 *Check* (and *correct* if needed) your translation of Exercise 28.16 above. Then *transform* the verbs from the perf into the inverted imperfect. *Note*:

> - The transformation of the verbs from the perfect into the inverted imperfect does not change the meaning of the verbs.
> - In many of the inverted forms above the stress is thrown back from the last to the next-to-last syllable.

28.18 *Check* (and *correct* if needed) Exercise 28.17 above. Then *transform* the clauses (with the inverted imperfect forms) from the singular into the plural (verbs as well as nouns and pronouns).

☆ HEBREW VIA HEBREW NAMES (Appendix I)

Please proceed now to the exercises based on Hebrew names in Appendix I and *do* all the exercises. Then turn back to the text samples in the FOUR STYLES OF BIBLICAL PROSE.

FOUR STYLES OF BIBLICAL PROSE: TEXT SAMPLES

There are four types of texts in Biblical Hebrew prose:[1]

I *Narrative texts,* which primarily include stories of a historical character from the creation of the world and forwards. Many narrative texts are found in the books of Genesis, Exodus, Joshua, Judges, Samuel, Kings and Chronicles.

II *Legal texts,* in which laws and regulations are gathered. Legal texts are found mainly in the books of Exodus (chapters 20–23), Leviticus and Deuteronomy.

III *Parables* and *proverbs*: Parables are scattered throughout the Bible, e.g., in Judg. 9:8–15, 2 Sam. 12:1–9 and Ezek. 37. Most of the proverbs are found in the books of Proverbs, Job and Ecclesiastes.

IV *Prophetic speeches,* which often contain various poetic features.

The following texts are included in the text samples below:

I *Narrative texts*
 1 Gen. 15:1–10, 13–14, 18–21
 2 Gen. 16:15–16, 17:1–10
 3 Gen. 22:1–19

II *Legal texts*
 1 Dt. 5:1–33, 6:1–18
 2 Dt. 11:13–21

III *Parables* and *proverbs*
 1 2 Sam. 12:1–9
 2 Ecc. 1:4, 7, 9; 3:1–3, 6, 8

IV *Prophetic speeches*
 1 Isa. 2:1–4

Note:

- ◆ Chapter and verse numbers are indicated in the titles of the following text units by letters (see Numerical value of the letters of the alphabet on page 1). This usage is often found in editions of the Hebrew Bible printed in Israel. Observe that the combinations יה (10 + 5) and יו (10 + 6) which occur in the divine name יהוה (YHWH) are replaced by טו (9 + 6) and טז (9 + 7).
- ◆ Words that are not included in the general Alphabetical Hebrew–English Vocabulary are listed after each unit of text in the order in which they appear in the text, preceded by the verse number (in a reduced and raised form). Words that appear more than once in the same text are not repeated.
- ◆ Proper names are enlarged.

THIS IS HOW YOU ARE EXPECTED TO WORK WITH THE TEXTS, *verse by verse*:

1 *Read* each verse at least twice.

2 *Write* the *lexical forms* of all the nouns, adjectives, numerals and particles in the verse.

3 *Rewrite* the words in pause which undergo vowel changes. Then *write* the normal form of the words in pause (see Exercises 12.8 and 17.8).

---

[1] 'Prose' refers to ordinary language not in verse form.

4 *Analyze* the *verb forms* as follows: **a**) verb type (stem) **b**) root consonants **c**) tense. *Identify* deviant verb forms systematically, that is, by the application of the regular sound change rules which can be found in *Appendix II*.

5 *Translate* the verse, staying as close as possible to the original Hebrew text.

6 *Check* your translation against a Bible translation/s. *Pay attention* to the interpretation of the particles אֲשֶׁר ,כִּי ,וְ and the tense of the verbs.

I *Narrative texts*

Text I.1: *The Covenant with Abram* (Gen. 15:1–10, 13–14, 18–21)

הַבְּרִית עִם אַבְרָם (בְּרֵאשִׁית טו: א–י, יג–יד, יח–כא)

¹ אַחַר הַדְּבָרִים הָאֵלֶּה הָיָה דְבַר־יהוה אֶל־אַבְרָם בַּמַּחֲזֶה לֵאמֹר אַל־תִּירָא אַבְרָם אָנֹכִי מָגֵן לָךְ שְׂכָרְךָ הַרְבֵּה מְאֹד: ² וַיֹּאמֶר אַבְרָם אֲדֹנָי יֱהוִה (= אֱלֹהִים special reading) מַה־תִּתֶּן־לִי וְאָנֹכִי הוֹלֵךְ עֲרִירִי וּבֶן־מֶשֶׁק בֵּיתִי הוּא דַּמֶּשֶׂק אֱלִיעֶזֶר: ³ וַיֹּאמֶר אַבְרָם הֵן לִי לֹא נָתַתָּה זָרַע וְהִנֵּה בֶן־בֵּיתִי יוֹרֵשׁ אֹתִי: ⁴ וְהִנֵּה דְבַר־יהוה אֵלָיו לֵאמֹר לֹא יִירָשְׁךָ זֶה כִּי־אִם אֲשֶׁר יֵצֵא מִמֵּעֶיךָ הוּא יִירָשֶׁךָ: ⁵ וַיּוֹצֵא אֹתוֹ הַחוּצָה וַיֹּאמֶר הַבֶּט־נָא הַשָּׁמַיְמָה וּסְפֹר הַכּוֹכָבִים אִם־תּוּכַל לִסְפֹּר אֹתָם וַיֹּאמֶר לוֹ כֹּה יִהְיֶה זַרְעֶךָ: ⁶ וְהֶאֱמִן בַּיהוה וַיַּחְשְׁבֶהָ לּוֹ צְדָקָה: ⁷ וַיֹּאמֶר אֵלָיו אֲנִי יהוה אֲשֶׁר הוֹצֵאתִיךָ מֵאוּר כַּשְׂדִּים לָתֶת לְךָ אֶת־הָאָרֶץ הַזֹּאת לְרִשְׁתָּהּ: ⁸ וַיֹּאמַר אֲדֹנָי יֱהוִה בַּמָּה אֵדַע כִּי אִירָשֶׁנָּה: ⁹ וַיֹּאמֶר אֵלָיו קְחָה לִי... ¹⁰ וַיִּקַּח־לוֹ אֶת־כָּל־אֵלֶּה וַיְבַתֵּר אֹתָם בַּתָּוֶךְ... ¹³ וַיֹּאמֶר לְאַבְרָם יָדֹעַ תֵּדַע כִּי־גֵר יִהְיֶה זַרְעֲךָ בְּאֶרֶץ לֹא לָהֶם וַעֲבָדוּם וְעִנּוּ אֹתָם אַרְבַּע מֵאוֹת שָׁנָה: ¹⁴ וְגַם אֶת־הַגּוֹי אֲשֶׁר יַעֲבֹדוּ דָּן אָנֹכִי וְאַחֲרֵי־כֵן יֵצְאוּ בִּרְכֻשׁ גָּדוֹל:...

New vocabulary (not included in the general vocabulary list)

מַחֲזֶה, חֹזֶה¹	*m*, vision	נבט⁵	*hiph* הִבִּיט look: *imperf* יַבִּיט
מָגֵן¹	*m*, shield	חָשַׁב⁶	consider, reckon: *imperf* יַחְשֹׁב
שָׂכָר¹	*m*, reward	בָּתַר בַּתָּוֶךְ¹⁰	*pi* בִּתֵּר cut in in the middle:
הַרְבֵּה¹	much, great		*imperf* יְבַתֵּר
עֲרִירִי²	*m*, childless	גֵּר¹³	*m*, sojourner, alien
בֶּן־מֶשֶׁק²	the one in charge of	עָנָה¹³	*pi* עִנָּה oppress: *imperf* יְעַנֶּה
כִּי אִם⁴	but (rather)	דוּן¹⁴	*perf* דָּן judge: *imperf* יָדוּן
מֵעַיִם⁴	*pl*, bowels, inward parts	רְכוּשׁ¹⁴	*m*, possessions
חוּץ⁵	outside		

¹⁸בַּיּוֹם הַהוּא כָּרַת יהוה אֶת־אַבְרָם בְּרִית לֵאמֹר לְזַרְעֲךָ נָתַתִּי אֶת־הָאָרֶץ

הַזֹּאת מִנְּהַר מִצְרַיִם עַד־הַנָּהָר הַגָּדֹל נְהַר־פְּרָת: ¹⁹ אֶת־הַקֵּינִי וְאֶת־הַקְּנִזִּי

וְאֵת הַקַּדְמֹנִי: ²⁰ וְאֶת־הַחִתִּי וְאֶת־הַפְּרִזִּי וְאֶת־הָרְפָאִים: ²¹ וְאֶת־הָאֱמֹרִי

וְאֶת־הַכְּנַעֲנִי וְאֶת־הַגִּרְגָּשִׁי וְאֶת־הַיְבוּסִי:

Text I.2: *Circumcision* (Gen. 16:15–16, 17:1–10)

בְּרִית מִילָה (בְּרֵאשִׁית טז: טו–טז, יז: א–י)

^{16:15} וַתֵּלֶד הָגָר לְאַבְרָם בֵּן וַיִּקְרָא אַבְרָם שֶׁם־בְּנוֹ אֲשֶׁר־יָלְדָה הָגָר

יִשְׁמָעֵאל: ¹⁶ וְאַבְרָם בֶּן־שְׁמֹנִים שָׁנָה וְשֵׁשׁ שָׁנִים בְּלֶדֶת־הָגָר אֶת־

יִשְׁמָעֵאל לְאַבְרָם: ^{17:1} וַיְהִי אַבְרָם בֶּן־תִּשְׁעִים שָׁנָה וְתֵשַׁע שָׁנִים וַיֵּרָא

יהוה אֶל־אַבְרָם וַיֹּאמֶר אֵלָיו אֲנִי־אֵל שַׁדַּי הִתְהַלֵּךְ לְפָנַי וֶהְיֵה תָמִים:

² וְאֶתְּנָה בְרִיתִי בֵּינִי וּבֵינֶךָ וְאַרְבֶּה אוֹתְךָ בִּמְאֹד מְאֹד: ³ וַיִּפֹּל אַבְרָם

עַל־פָּנָיו וַיְדַבֵּר אִתּוֹ אֱלֹהִים לֵאמֹר: ⁴ אֲנִי הִנֵּה בְרִיתִי אִתָּךְ וְהָיִיתָ לְאַב

הֲמוֹן גּוֹיִם: ⁵ וְלֹא־יִקָּרֵא עוֹד אֶת־שִׁמְךָ אַבְרָם וְהָיָה שִׁמְךָ אַבְרָהָם כִּי

אַב־הֲמוֹן גּוֹיִם נְתַתִּיךָ: ⁶ וְהִפְרֵתִי אֹתְךָ בִּמְאֹד מְאֹד וּנְתַתִּיךָ לְגוֹיִם וּמְלָכִים

מִמְּךָ יֵצֵאוּ: ⁷ וַהֲקִמֹתִי אֶת־בְּרִיתִי בֵּינִי וּבֵינֶךָ וּבֵין זַרְעֲךָ אַחֲרֶיךָ לְדֹרֹתָם

לִבְרִית עוֹלָם לִהְיוֹת לְךָ לֵאלֹהִים וּלְזַרְעֲךָ אַחֲרֶיךָ: ⁸ וְנָתַתִּי לְךָ וּלְזַרְעֲךָ

אַחֲרֶיךָ אֵת אֶרֶץ מְגֻרֶיךָ אֵת כָּל־אֶרֶץ כְּנַעַן לַאֲחֻזַּת עוֹלָם וְהָיִיתִי לָהֶם

לֵאלֹהִים: ⁹ וַיֹּאמֶר אֱלֹהִים אֶל־אַבְרָהָם וְאַתָּה אֶת־בְּרִיתִי תִשְׁמֹר אַתָּה וְזַרְעֲךָ

אַחֲרֶיךָ לְדֹרֹתָם: ¹⁰ זֹאת בְּרִיתִי אֲשֶׁר תִּשְׁמְרוּ בֵּינִי וּבֵינֵיכֶם וּבֵין זַרְעֲךָ אַחֲרֶיךָ

הִמּוֹל לָכֶם כָּל־זָכָר:

שַׁדַּי¹	Almighty	פָּרָה⁶	*hiph* הִפְרָה make fruitful:
רָבָה²	*hiph* הִרְבָּה make many:		*imperf* יַפְרֶה
	imperf יַרְבֶּה	מְגוּרִים⁸	*pl*, place of residence (of גֵּר 'sojourner, alien')
הָמוֹן⁴	multitude, crowd	אֲחֻזָּה⁸	*f*, possession (landed property)

Text I.3: *Offering of Isaac, lit., 'The Binding of Isaac'* (Gen. 22:1–19)

עֲקֵדַת יִצְחָק ‹בְּרֵאשִׁית כב: א–יט›

וַיְהִי אַחַר הַדְּבָרִים הָאֵלֶּה וְהָאֱלֹהִים נִסָּה אֶת־אַבְרָהָם וַיֹּאמֶר אֵלָיו אַבְרָהָם ¹

וַיֹּאמֶר הִנֵּנִי: ² וַיֹּאמֶר קַח־נָא אֶת־בִּנְךָ אֶת־יְחִידְךָ אֲשֶׁר־אָהַבְתָּ אֶת־יִצְחָק

וְלֶךְ־לְךָ אֶל־אֶרֶץ הַמֹּרִיָּה וְהַעֲלֵהוּ שָׁם לְעֹלָה עַל אַחַד הֶהָרִים אֲשֶׁר אֹמַר

אֵלֶיךָ: ³ וַיַּשְׁכֵּם אַבְרָהָם בַּבֹּקֶר וַיַּחֲבֹשׁ אֶת־חֲמֹרוֹ וַיִּקַּח אֶת־שְׁנֵי נְעָרָיו אִתּוֹ

וְאֵת יִצְחָק בְּנוֹ וַיְבַקַּע עֲצֵי עֹלָה וַיָּקָם וַיֵּלֶךְ אֶל־הַמָּקוֹם אֲשֶׁר־אָמַר־לוֹ הָאֱלֹהִים:

בַּיּוֹם הַשְּׁלִישִׁי וַיִּשָּׂא אַבְרָהָם אֶת־עֵינָיו וַיַּרְא אֶת־הַמָּקוֹם מֵרָחֹק: ⁵ וַיֹּאמֶר ⁴

אַבְרָהָם אֶל־נְעָרָיו שְׁבוּ־לָכֶם פֹּה עִם־הַחֲמוֹר וַאֲנִי וְהַנַּעַר נֵלְכָה עַד־כֹּה

וְנִשְׁתַּחֲוֶה וְנָשׁוּבָה אֲלֵיכֶם: ⁶ וַיִּקַּח אַבְרָהָם אֶת־עֲצֵי הָעֹלָה וַיָּשֶׂם עַל־יִצְחָק

בְּנוֹ וַיִּקַּח בְּיָדוֹ אֶת־הָאֵשׁ וְאֶת־הַמַּאֲכֶלֶת וַיֵּלְכוּ שְׁנֵיהֶם יַחְדָּו: ⁷ וַיֹּאמֶר יִצְחָק

אֶל־אַבְרָהָם אָבִיו וַיֹּאמֶר אָבִי וַיֹּאמֶר הִנֶּנִּי בְנִי וַיֹּאמֶר הִנֵּה הָאֵשׁ וְהָעֵצִים

וְאַיֵּה הַשֶּׂה לְעֹלָה: ⁸ וַיֹּאמֶר אַבְרָהָם אֱלֹהִים יִרְאֶה־לּוֹ הַשֶּׂה לְעֹלָה בְּנִי וַיֵּלְכוּ

שְׁנֵיהֶם יַחְדָּו: ⁹ וַיָּבֹאוּ אֶל־הַמָּקוֹם אֲשֶׁר אָמַר־לוֹ הָאֱלֹהִים וַיִּבֶן שָׁם אַבְרָהָם

אֶת־הַמִּזְבֵּחַ וַיַּעֲרֹךְ אֶת־הָעֵצִים וַיַּעֲקֹד אֶת־יִצְחָק בְּנוֹ וַיָּשֶׂם אֹתוֹ עַל־הַמִּזְבֵּחַ

מִמַּעַל לָעֵצִים: ¹⁰ וַיִּשְׁלַח אַבְרָהָם אֶת־יָדוֹ וַיִּקַּח אֶת־הַמַּאֲכֶלֶת לִשְׁחֹט

אֶת־בְּנוֹ: ¹¹ וַיִּקְרָא אֵלָיו מַלְאַךְ יהוה מִן־הַשָּׁמַיִם וַיֹּאמֶר אַבְרָהָם אַבְרָהָם

וַיֹּאמֶר הִנֵּנִי: ¹² וַיֹּאמֶר אַל־תִּשְׁלַח יָדְךָ אֶל־הַנַּעַר וְאַל־תַּעַשׂ לוֹ מְאוּמָה כִּי

עַתָּה יָדַעְתִּי כִּי־יְרֵא אֱלֹהִים אַתָּה וְלֹא חָשַׂכְתָּ אֶת־בִּנְךָ אֶת־יְחִידְךָ מִמֶּנִּי:

יָחִיד²	only	מַאֲכֶלֶת⁶	*f,* slaughtering knife
עֹלָה²	*f,* burnt offering	יַחְדָּו⁶	together
שכם³	*hiph* הִשְׁכִּים rise early in	שֶׂה⁷	*m,* lamb
	the morning: *imperf*	עָרַךְ⁹	lay in order:
	יַשְׁכִּים		*imperf* יַעֲרֹךְ
חָבַשׁ חֲמוֹר³	saddle an ass	עָקַד⁹	bind: *imperf* יַעֲקֹד
בָּקַע³	*pi* בִּקַּע cut:	מִמַּעַל⁹	upon
	imperf יְבַקַּע	שָׁחַט¹⁰	slay: *imperf* יִשְׁחַט
שְׁלִישִׁי⁴	third	מְאוּמָה¹²	anything
רָחֹק⁴	far off	חָשַׂךְ¹²	withhold: *imperf* יַחְשֹׁךְ

¹³ וַיִּשָּׂא אַבְרָהָם אֶת־עֵינָיו וַיַּרְא וְהִנֵּה־אַיִל אַחַר נֶאֱחַז בַּסְּבַךְ בְּקַרְנָיו וַיֵּלֶךְ
אַבְרָהָם וַיִּקַּח אֶת־הָאַיִל וַיַּעֲלֵהוּ לְעֹלָה תַּחַת בְּנוֹ: ¹⁴ וַיִּקְרָא אַבְרָהָם
שֵׁם־הַמָּקוֹם הַהוּא יהוה יִרְאֶה אֲשֶׁר יֵאָמֵר הַיּוֹם בְּהַר יהוה יֵרָאֶה: ¹⁵ וַיִּקְרָא
מַלְאַךְ יהוה אֶל־אַבְרָהָם שֵׁנִית מִן־הַשָּׁמָיִם: ¹⁶ וַיֹּאמֶר בִּי נִשְׁבַּעְתִּי נְאֻם־יהוה
כִּי יַעַן אֲשֶׁר עָשִׂיתָ אֶת־הַדָּבָר הַזֶּה וְלֹא חָשַׂכְתָּ אֶת־בִּנְךָ אֶת־יְחִידֶךָ:
¹⁷ כִּי־בָרֵךְ אֲבָרֶכְךָ וְהַרְבָּה אַרְבֶּה אֶת־זַרְעֲךָ כְּכוֹכְבֵי הַשָּׁמַיִם וְכַחוֹל אֲשֶׁר
עַל־שְׂפַת הַיָּם וְיִרַשׁ זַרְעֲךָ אֵת שַׁעַר אֹיְבָיו: ¹⁸ וְהִתְבָּרְכוּ בְזַרְעֲךָ כֹּל גּוֹיֵי
הָאָרֶץ עֵקֶב אֲשֶׁר שָׁמַעְתָּ בְּקֹלִי: ¹⁹ וַיָּשָׁב אַבְרָהָם אֶל־נְעָרָיו וַיָּקֻמוּ וַיֵּלְכוּ
יַחְדָּו אֶל־בְּאֵר שָׁבַע וַיֵּשֶׁב אַבְרָהָם בִּבְאֵר שָׁבַע:

¹³אַיִל	*m*, ram	¹⁷הִרְבָּה רָבָה	*hiph* make many:
¹³אָחַז	*niph* נֶאֱחַז be caught:		*imperf* יַרְבֶּה
	imperf יֵאָחֵז	¹⁷חוֹל	sand
¹³סְבַךְ	thicket	¹⁷שְׂפַת הַיָּם	seashore
¹³קֶרֶן	*f*, horn: *dual* קַרְנַיִם	¹⁷אֹיֵב	*m*, enemy
¹⁵שֵׁנִית	second time (adverb)		

II *Legal texts*

Text II.1: *Giving the Law, The Ten Commandments* (Dt. 5:1–33, 6:1–18)

מַתַּן תּוֹרָה, עֲשֶׂרֶת הַדִּבְּרוֹת (דְּבָרִים ה: א–לג, ו: א–יח)

^{5:1} וַיִּקְרָא מֹשֶׁה אֶל־כָּל־יִשְׂרָאֵל וַיֹּאמֶר אֲלֵהֶם שְׁמַע יִשְׂרָאֵל אֶת־הַחֻקִּים
וְאֶת־הַמִּשְׁפָּטִים אֲשֶׁר אָנֹכִי דֹּבֵר בְּאָזְנֵיכֶם הַיּוֹם וּלְמַדְתֶּם אֹתָם וּשְׁמַרְתֶּם
לַעֲשֹׂתָם: ² יהוה אֱלֹהֵינוּ כָּרַת עִמָּנוּ בְּרִית בְּחֹרֵב: ³ לֹא אֶת־אֲבֹתֵינוּ כָּרַת
יהוה אֶת־הַבְּרִית הַזֹּאת כִּי אִתָּנוּ אֲנַחְנוּ אֵלֶּה פֹה הַיּוֹם כֻּלָּנוּ חַיִּים: ⁴ פָּנִים
בְּפָנִים דִּבֶּר יהוה עִמָּכֶם בָּהָר מִתּוֹךְ הָאֵשׁ: ⁵ אָנֹכִי עֹמֵד בֵּין־יהוה וּבֵינֵיכֶם
בָּעֵת הַהוּא לְהַגִּיד לָכֶם אֶת־דְּבַר יהוה כִּי יְרֵאתֶם מִפְּנֵי הָאֵשׁ וְלֹא־עֲלִיתֶם
בָּהָר לֵאמֹר: ⁶ אָנֹכִי יהוה אֱלֹהֶיךָ אֲשֶׁר הוֹצֵאתִיךָ מֵאֶרֶץ מִצְרַיִם מִבֵּית
עֲבָדִים: ⁷ לֹא יִהְיֶה־לְךָ אֱלֹהִים אֲחֵרִים עַל־פָּנָי: ⁸ לֹא־תַעֲשֶׂה־לְךָ פֶסֶל
כָּל־תְּמוּנָה אֲשֶׁר בַּשָּׁמַיִם מִמַּעַל וַאֲשֶׁר בָּאָרֶץ מִתָּחַת וַאֲשֶׁר בַּמַּיִם מִתַּחַת
לָאָרֶץ: ⁹ לֹא־תִשְׁתַּחֲוֶה לָהֶם וְלֹא תָעָבְדֵם כִּי אָנֹכִי יהוה אֱלֹהֶיךָ אֵל קַנָּא פֹּקֵד

עֲוֹן אָבֹת עַל־בָּנִים וְעַל־שִׁלֵּשִׁים וְעַל־רִבֵּעִים לְשֹׂנְאָי: 10 וְעֹשֶׂה חֶסֶד לַאֲלָפִים לְאֹהֲבַי וּלְשֹׁמְרֵי מִצְוֹתָו: 11 לֹא תִשָּׂא אֶת־שֵׁם־יְהוָה אֱלֹהֶיךָ לַשָּׁוְא כִּי לֹא יְנַקֶּה יְהוָה אֵת אֲשֶׁר־יִשָּׂא אֶת־שְׁמוֹ לַשָּׁוְא: 12 שָׁמוֹר אֶת־יוֹם הַשַּׁבָּת לְקַדְּשׁוֹ כַּאֲשֶׁר צִוְּךָ יְהוָה אֱלֹהֶיךָ: 13 שֵׁשֶׁת יָמִים תַּעֲבֹד וְעָשִׂיתָ כָּל־מְלַאכְתֶּךָ: 14 וְיוֹם הַשְּׁבִיעִי שַׁבָּת לַיהוָה אֱלֹהֶיךָ לֹא תַעֲשֶׂה כָל־מְלָאכָה אַתָּה וּבִנְךָ־וּבִתֶּךָ וְעַבְדְּךָ־וַאֲמָתֶךָ וְשׁוֹרְךָ וַחֲמֹרְךָ וְכָל־בְּהֶמְתֶּךָ וְגֵרְךָ אֲשֶׁר בִּשְׁעָרֶיךָ לְמַעַן יָנוּחַ עַבְדְּךָ וַאֲמָתְךָ כָּמוֹךָ: 15 וְזָכַרְתָּ כִּי עֶבֶד הָיִיתָ בְּאֶרֶץ מִצְרַיִם וַיֹּצִאֲךָ יְהוָה אֱלֹהֶיךָ מִשָּׁם בְּיָד חֲזָקָה וּבִזְרֹעַ נְטוּיָה עַל־כֵּן צִוְּךָ יְהוָה אֱלֹהֶיךָ לַעֲשׂוֹת אֶת־יוֹם הַשַּׁבָּת: 16 כַּבֵּד אֶת־אָבִיךָ וְאֶת־אִמֶּךָ כַּאֲשֶׁר צִוְּךָ יְהוָה אֱלֹהֶיךָ לְמַעַן יַאֲרִיכֻן יָמֶיךָ וּלְמַעַן יִיטַב לָךְ עַל הָאֲדָמָה אֲשֶׁר־יְהוָה אֱלֹהֶיךָ נֹתֵן לָךְ: 17 לֹא תִּרְצָח: 18 וְלֹא תִּנְאָף: 19 וְלֹא תִּגְנֹב: 20 וְלֹא־תַעֲנֶה בְרֵעֲךָ עֵד שָׁוְא: 2 (see footnote 2)

21 וְלֹא תַחְמֹד אֵשֶׁת רֵעֶךָ וְלֹא תִתְאַוֶּה בֵּית רֵעֶךָ שָׂדֵהוּ וְעַבְדּוֹ וַאֲמָתוֹ שׁוֹרוֹ וַחֲמֹרוֹ וְכֹל אֲשֶׁר לְרֵעֶךָ: 22 אֶת־הַדְּבָרִים הָאֵלֶּה דִּבֶּר יְהוָה אֶל־כָּל־קְהַלְכֶם בָּהָר מִתּוֹךְ הָאֵשׁ הֶעָנָן וְהָעֲרָפֶל קוֹל גָּדוֹל וְלֹא יָסָף וַיִּכְתְּבֵם עַל־שְׁנֵי לֻחֹת אֲבָנִים וַיִּתְּנֵם אֵלָי:

¹דִּבֶּר	speak (compare דָּבָר)	¹⁵נָטָה	stretch out: *pass part*
⁸פֶּסֶל	*m*, carved image		נָטוּי outstretched
⁸תְּמוּנָה	*f*, form	¹⁶ארך	*hiph* הֶאֱרִיךְ prolong:
⁸מִמַּעַל	upon		*imperf* יַאֲרִיךְ
⁹קַנָּא	jealous	¹⁸נָאַף	commit adultery:
⁹שִׁלֵּשִׁים	*third* generation (from שָׁלֵשׁ)		*imperf* יִנְאַף
⁹רִבֵּעִים	*fourth* generation (from אַרְבַּע)	¹⁹גָּנַב (אַרְבַּע)	steal: *imperf* יִגְנֹב
¹¹לַשָּׁוְא	in vain	²⁰תַּעֲנֶה עֵד שָׁוְא	bear false witness
¹¹נקה	*pi* נִקָּה hold guiltless:	²¹חָמַד	desire: *imperf* יַחְמֹד
	imperf יְנַקֶּה	²¹אָוָה	*hitp* הִתְאַוָּה crave:
¹³מְלָאכָה	*f*, work, task		*imperf* יִתְאַוֶּה
¹⁴שׁוֹר	*m*, ox	²²קָהָל	*m*, assembly
¹⁴חֲמוֹר	*m*, ass	²²עָנָן	*m*, cloud
¹⁴בְּהֵמָה	*f*, cattle, domestic animal	²²עֲרָפֶל	*m*, thick gloom
¹⁴גֵּר	*m*, sojourner, alien	²²לוּחַ	*m*, tablet: *pl* לוּחֹת
¹⁴נוּחַ	*perf* נָח rest: *imperf* יָנוּחַ		

---

² In some editions of the Hebrew Bible verses 17–20 are included in one verse, i.e., verse 17, thus chapter 5 includes only 30 verses.

^{5:23} וַיְהִי כְּשָׁמְעֲכֶם אֶת־הַקּוֹל מִתּוֹךְ הַחֹשֶׁךְ וְהָהָר בֹּעֵר בָּאֵשׁ וַתִּקְרְבוּן אֵלַי

כָּל־רָאשֵׁי שִׁבְטֵיכֶם וְזִקְנֵיכֶם: ²⁴ וַתֹּאמְרוּ הֵן הֶרְאָנוּ יְהוָה אֱלֹהֵינוּ אֶת־כְּבֹדוֹ

וְאֶת־גָּדְלוֹ וְאֶת־קֹלוֹ שָׁמַעְנוּ מִתּוֹךְ הָאֵשׁ הַיּוֹם הַזֶּה רָאִינוּ כִּי־יְדַבֵּר אֱלֹהִים

אֶת־הָאָדָם וָחָי: ²⁵ וְעַתָּה לָמָּה נָמוּת כִּי תֹאכְלֵנוּ הָאֵשׁ הַגְּדֹלָה הַזֹּאת

אִם־יֹסְפִים אֲנַחְנוּ לִשְׁמֹעַ אֶת־קוֹל יְהוָה אֱלֹהֵינוּ עוֹד וָמָתְנוּ: ²⁶ כִּי מִי

כָל־בָּשָׂר אֲשֶׁר שָׁמַע קוֹל אֱלֹהִים חַיִּים מְדַבֵּר מִתּוֹךְ־הָאֵשׁ כָּמֹנוּ וַיֶּחִי: ²⁷ קְרַב

אַתָּה וּשֲׁמָע אֵת כָּל־אֲשֶׁר יֹאמַר יְהוָה אֱלֹהֵינוּ וְאַתְּ תְּדַבֵּר אֵלֵינוּ אֵת כָּל־אֲשֶׁר

יְדַבֵּר יְהוָה אֱלֹהֵינוּ אֵלֶיךָ וְשָׁמַעְנוּ וְעָשִׂינוּ: ²⁸ וַיִּשְׁמַע יְהוָה אֶת־קוֹל דִּבְרֵיכֶם

בְּדַבֶּרְכֶם אֵלָי וַיֹּאמֶר יְהוָה אֵלַי שָׁמַעְתִּי אֶת־קוֹל דִּבְרֵי הָעָם הַזֶּה אֲשֶׁר דִּבְּרוּ

אֵלֶיךָ הֵיטִיבוּ כָּל־אֲשֶׁר דִּבֵּרוּ: ²⁹ מִי־יִתֵּן וְהָיָה לְבָבָם זֶה לָהֶם לְיִרְאָה אֹתִי

וְלִשְׁמֹר אֶת־כָּל־מִצְוֹתַי כָּל־הַיָּמִים לְמַעַן יִיטַב לָהֶם וְלִבְנֵיהֶם לְעֹלָם:

בָּעַר²³	burn: *imperf* יִבְעַר	שְׁבָטִים²³	*m*, tribe: *pl* שֵׁבֶט

^{5:30} לֵךְ אֱמֹר לָהֶם שׁוּבוּ לָכֶם לְאָהֳלֵיכֶם: ³¹ וְאַתָּה פֹּה עֲמֹד עִמָּדִי וַאֲדַבְּרָה

אֵלֶיךָ אֵת כָּל־הַמִּצְוָה וְהַחֻקִּים וְהַמִּשְׁפָּטִים אֲשֶׁר תְּלַמְּדֵם וְעָשׂוּ בָאָרֶץ אֲשֶׁר

אָנֹכִי נֹתֵן לָהֶם לְרִשְׁתָּהּ: ³² וּשְׁמַרְתֶּם לַעֲשׂוֹת כַּאֲשֶׁר צִוָּה יְהוָה אֱלֹהֵיכֶם

אֶתְכֶם לֹא תָסֻרוּ יָמִין וּשְׂמֹאל: ³³ בְּכָל־הַדֶּרֶךְ אֲשֶׁר צִוָּה יְהוָה אֱלֹהֵיכֶם אֶתְכֶם

תֵּלֵכוּ לְמַעַן תִּחְיוּן וְטוֹב לָכֶם וְהַאֲרַכְתֶּם יָמִים בָּאָרֶץ אֲשֶׁר תִּירָשׁוּן: ^{6:1} וְזֹאת

הַמִּצְוָה הַחֻקִּים וְהַמִּשְׁפָּטִים אֲשֶׁר צִוָּה יְהוָה אֱלֹהֵיכֶם לְלַמֵּד אֶתְכֶם לַעֲשׂוֹת

בָּאָרֶץ אֲשֶׁר אַתֶּם עֹבְרִים שָׁמָּה לְרִשְׁתָּהּ: ² לְמַעַן תִּירָא אֶת־יְהוָה אֱלֹהֶיךָ

לִשְׁמֹר אֶת־כָּל־חֻקֹּתָיו וּמִצְוֹתָיו אֲשֶׁר אָנֹכִי מְצַוֶּךָ אַתָּה וּבִנְךָ וּבֶן־בִּנְךָ כֹּל יְמֵי

חַיֶּיךָ וּלְמַעַן יַאֲרִכֻן יָמֶיךָ: ³ וְשָׁמַעְתָּ יִשְׂרָאֵל וְשָׁמַרְתָּ לַעֲשׂוֹת אֲשֶׁר יִיטַב לְךָ

וַאֲשֶׁר תִּרְבּוּן מְאֹד כַּאֲשֶׁר דִּבֶּר יְהוָה אֱלֹהֵי אֲבֹתֶיךָ לָךְ אֶרֶץ זָבַת חָלָב וּדְבָשׁ:

סוּר³²	*perf* סָר	turn: *imperf* יָסוּר	^{6:3}רָבָה	become numerous: *imperf* יִרְבֶּה
יָמִין³²	right		³זוּב	*perf* זָב flow: *imperf* יָזוּב
שְׂמֹאל³²	left		חָלָב³	*m*, milk
אָרַךְ³³	*hiph* הֶאֱרִיךְ prolong: *imperf* יַאֲרִיךְ		דְּבַשׁ³	*m*, honey

^{6:4} שְׁמַע יִשְׂרָאֵל יְהוָה אֱלֹהֵינוּ יְהוָה אֶחָד: ⁵ וְאָהַבְתָּ אֵת יְהוָה אֱלֹהֶיךָ
בְּכָל־לְבָבְךָ וּבְכָל־נַפְשְׁךָ וּבְכָל־מְאֹדֶךָ: ⁶ וְהָיוּ הַדְּבָרִים הָאֵלֶּה אֲשֶׁר אָנֹכִי
מְצַוְּךָ הַיּוֹם עַל־לְבָבֶךָ: ⁷ וְשִׁנַּנְתָּם לְבָנֶיךָ וְדִבַּרְתָּ בָּם בְּשִׁבְתְּךָ בְּבֵיתֶךָ וּבְלֶכְתְּךָ
בַדֶּרֶךְ וּבְשָׁכְבְּךָ וּבְקוּמֶךָ: ⁸ וּקְשַׁרְתָּם לְאוֹת עַל־יָדֶךָ וְהָיוּ לְטֹטָפֹת בֵּין עֵינֶיךָ:
⁹ וּכְתַבְתָּם עַל־מְזוּזֹת בֵּיתֶךָ וּבִשְׁעָרֶיךָ:

(Dt. 6:4–9 above and Dt. 11:13–21 in Text II.2 below form the Jewish Confession)

⁵מְאֹד	might	⁸טֹטָפֹת	sign
⁷שׁנן	pi שִׁנֵּן repeat: imperf ⁹יְשַׁנֵּן	מְזוּזָה	doorpost
⁸קָשַׁר	tie: imperf יִקְשֹׁר		

^{6:10} וְהָיָה כִּי־יְבִיאֲךָ יְהוָה אֱלֹהֶיךָ אֶל־הָאָרֶץ אֲשֶׁר נִשְׁבַּע לַאֲבֹתֶיךָ לְאַבְרָהָם
לְיִצְחָק וּלְיַעֲקֹב לָתֶת לָךְ עָרִים גְּדֹלֹת וְטֹבֹת אֲשֶׁר לֹא־בָנִיתָ: ¹¹ וּבָתִּים
מְלֵאִים כָּל־טוּב אֲשֶׁר לֹא־מִלֵּאתָ וּבֹרֹת חֲצוּבִים אֲשֶׁר לֹא־חָצַבְתָּ כְּרָמִים
וְזֵיתִים אֲשֶׁר לֹא־נָטָעְתָּ וְאָכַלְתָּ וְשָׂבָעְתָּ: ¹² הִשָּׁמֶר לְךָ פֶּן־תִּשְׁכַּח אֶת־יְהוָה
אֲשֶׁר הוֹצִיאֲךָ מֵאֶרֶץ מִצְרַיִם מִבֵּית עֲבָדִים: ¹³ אֶת־יְהוָה אֱלֹהֶיךָ תִּירָא וְאֹתוֹ
תַעֲבֹד וּבִשְׁמוֹ תִּשָּׁבֵעַ: ¹⁴ לֹא תֵלְכוּן אַחֲרֵי אֱלֹהִים אֲחֵרִים מֵאֱלֹהֵי הָעַמִּים
אֲשֶׁר סְבִיבוֹתֵיכֶם: ¹⁵ כִּי אֵל קַנָּא יְהוָה אֱלֹהֶיךָ בְּקִרְבֶּךָ פֶּן־יֶחֱרֶה אַף־יְהוָה
אֱלֹהֶיךָ בָּךְ וְהִשְׁמִידְךָ מֵעַל פְּנֵי הָאֲדָמָה: ¹⁶ לֹא תְנַסּוּ אֶת־יְהוָה אֱלֹהֵיכֶם
כַּאֲשֶׁר נִסִּיתֶם בַּמַּסָּה: ¹⁷ שָׁמוֹר תִּשְׁמְרוּן אֶת־מִצְוֹת יְהוָה אֱלֹהֵיכֶם וְעֵדֹתָיו
וְחֻקָּיו אֲשֶׁר צִוָּךְ: ¹⁸ וְעָשִׂיתָ הַיָּשָׁר וְהַטּוֹב בְּעֵינֵי יְהוָה לְמַעַן יִיטַב לָךְ וּבָאתָ
וְיָרַשְׁתָּ אֶת־הָאָרֶץ הַטֹּבָה אֲשֶׁר־נִשְׁבַּע יְהוָה לַאֲבֹתֶיךָ:

¹¹טוּב	m, good things	¹⁴סָבִיב	all around,
¹¹חָצַב	hew: imperf יַחֲצֹב		neighbourhood
¹¹כֶּרֶם	m, vineyard: pl כְּרָמִים	¹⁵קַנָּא	jealous
	(☆ Carmel)	¹⁵קֶרֶב	midst: with suff קִרְבִּי
¹¹זַיִת	m, olive (tree): pl זֵיתִים	¹⁵חָרָה אַף	become angry:
¹¹נָטַע	plant: imperf יִטַּע		imperf יֶחֱרֶה
¹¹שָׂבַע	be/become full/satisfied (with	¹⁵שׁמד	hiph הִשְׁמִיד destroy:
	food): imperf יִשְׂבַּע		imperf יַשְׁמִיד
		¹⁷עֵדָה	f, testimony

Text II.2: *This is the Law* (Dt. 11:13–21)

זֹאת הַתּוֹרָה (דְּבָרִים יא: יג–כא)

¹³ וְהָיָה אִם־שָׁמֹעַ תִּשְׁמְעוּ אֶל־מִצְוֹתַי אֲשֶׁר אָנֹכִי מְצַוֶּה אֶתְכֶם הַיּוֹם לְאַהֲבָה אֶת־יְהוָה אֱלֹהֵיכֶם וּלְעָבְדוֹ בְּכָל־לְבַבְכֶם וּבְכָל־נַפְשְׁכֶם: ¹⁴ וְנָתַתִּי מְטַר־אַרְצְכֶם בְּעִתּוֹ יוֹרֶה וּמַלְקוֹשׁ וְאָסַפְתָּ דְגָנֶךָ וְתִירֹשְׁךָ וְיִצְהָרֶךָ: ¹⁵ וְנָתַתִּי עֵשֶׂב בְּשָׂדְךָ לִבְהֶמְתֶּךָ וְאָכַלְתָּ וְשָׂבָעְתָּ: ¹⁶ הִשָּׁמְרוּ לָכֶם פֶּן־יִפְתֶּה לְבַבְכֶם וְסַרְתֶּם וַעֲבַדְתֶּם אֱלֹהִים אֲחֵרִים וְהִשְׁתַּחֲוִיתֶם לָהֶם: ¹⁷ וְחָרָה אַף־יְהוָה בָּכֶם וְעָצַר אֶת־הַשָּׁמַיִם וְלֹא־יִהְיֶה מָטָר וְהָאֲדָמָה לֹא תִתֵּן אֶת־יְבוּלָהּ וַאֲבַדְתֶּם מְהֵרָה מֵעַל הָאָרֶץ הַטֹּבָה אֲשֶׁר יהוה נֹתֵן לָכֶם: ¹⁸ וְשַׂמְתֶּם אֶת־דְּבָרַי אֵלֶּה עַל־לְבַבְכֶם וְעַל־נַפְשְׁכֶם וּקְשַׁרְתֶּם אֹתָם לְאוֹת עַל־יֶדְכֶם וְהָיוּ לְטוֹטָפֹת בֵּין עֵינֵיכֶם: ¹⁹ וְלִמַּדְתֶּם אֹתָם אֶת־בְּנֵיכֶם לְדַבֵּר בָּם בְּשִׁבְתְּךָ בְּבֵיתֶךָ וּבְלֶכְתְּךָ בַדֶּרֶךְ וּבְשָׁכְבְּךָ וּבְקוּמֶךָ: ²⁰ וּכְתַבְתָּם עַל־מְזוּזוֹת בֵּיתֶךָ וּבִשְׁעָרֶיךָ: ²¹ לְמַעַן יִרְבּוּ יְמֵיכֶם וִימֵי בְנֵיכֶם עַל הָאֲדָמָה אֲשֶׁר נִשְׁבַּע יהוה לַאֲבֹתֵיכֶם לָתֵת לָהֶם כִּימֵי הַשָּׁמַיִם עַל־הָאָרֶץ:

מָטָר ¹⁴	*m*, rain	סוּר ¹⁶	*perf* סָר turn aside:
יוֹרֶה ¹⁴	*m*, early (autumn) rain		*imperf* יָסוּר
מַלְקוֹשׁ ¹⁴	*m*, late (spring) rain	חָרָה אַף ¹⁷	become angry: *imperf* יֶחֱרֶה
דָּגָן ¹⁴	*m*, grain	עָצַר ¹⁷	shut up: *imperf* יַעֲצֹר
תִּירוֹשׁ ¹⁴	*m*, wine	יְבוּל ¹⁷	*m*, produce (of the soil)
יִצְהָר ¹⁴	*m*, oil	אָבַד ¹⁷	perish: *imperf* יֹאבַד
עֵשֶׂב ¹⁵	*m*, grass	מְהֵרָה ¹⁷	quickly
בְּהֵמָה ¹⁵	*f*, cattle, domestic animal	קָשַׁר ¹⁸	tie: *imperf* יִקְשֹׁר
שָׂבַע ¹⁵	be full/satisfied (with food): *imperf* יִשְׂבַּע	טוֹטָפֹת ¹⁸	sign
		מְזוּזָה ²⁰	doorpost
פָּתָה ¹⁶	deceive: *imperf* יִפְתֶּה	רָבָה ²¹	become numerous: *imperf* יִרְבֶּה

III *Parables*

Text III.1: *The Poor Man's Ewe Lamb* (2 Sam. 12:1–9)

כִּבְשַׂת הָרָשׁ (שְׁמוּאֵל ב, יב: א–ט)

וַיִּשְׁלַח יהוה אֶת־נָתָן אֶל־דָּוִד וַיָּבֹא אֵלָיו וַיֹּאמֶר לוֹ שְׁנֵי אֲנָשִׁים הָיוּ בְּעִיר ¹
אֶחָת (= אַחַת of pausal form) אֶחָד עָשִׁיר וְאֶחָד רָאשׁ (= רָשׁ): ² לְעָשִׁיר הָיָה צֹאן
וּבָקָר הַרְבֵּה מְאֹד: ³ וְלָרָשׁ אֵין־כֹּל כִּי אִם־כִּבְשָׂה אַחַת קְטַנָּה אֲשֶׁר קָנָה
וַיְחַיֶּהָ וַתִּגְדַּל עִמּוֹ וְעִם־בָּנָיו יַחְדָּו מִפִּתּוֹ תֹאכַל וּמִכֹּסוֹ תִשְׁתֶּה וּבְחֵיקוֹ תִשְׁכָּב
וַתְּהִי־לוֹ כְּבַת: ⁴ וַיָּבֹא הֵלֶךְ לְאִישׁ הֶעָשִׁיר וַיַּחְמֹל לָקַחַת מִצֹּאנוֹ וּמִבְּקָרוֹ
לַעֲשׂוֹת לָאֹרֵחַ הַבָּא לוֹ וַיִּקַּח אֶת־כִּבְשַׂת הָאִישׁ הָרָאשׁ וַיַּעֲשֶׂהָ לָאִישׁ הַבָּא אֵלָיו:

עָשִׁיר¹	rich	יַחְדָּו³	together
רָשׁ¹	poor	פַּת³	f, morsel (of bread):
צֹאן²	small cattle (sheep and goats)		*with suff* פִּתִּי
בָּקָר²	cattle	כּוֹס³	f, cup
הַרְבֵּה²	many	חֵיק³	m, bosom
כִּי אִם	except, but (rather)	הֵלֶךְ⁴	m, visitor
כִּבְשָׂה³	f, ewe lamb	חָמַל⁴	spare: *imperf* יַחְמֹל
קָנָה³	buy	אֹרֵחַ⁴	m, traveller, wanderer

וַיִּחַר־אַף דָּוִד בָּאִישׁ מְאֹד וַיֹּאמֶר אֶל־נָתָן חַי־יהוה כִּי בֶן־מָוֶת הָאִישׁ הָעֹשֶׂה ⁵
זֹאת: ⁶ וְאֶת־הַכִּבְשָׂה יְשַׁלֵּם אַרְבַּעְתָּיִם עֵקֶב אֲשֶׁר עָשָׂה אֶת־הַדָּבָר הַזֶּה וְעַל
אֲשֶׁר לֹא־חָמָל: ⁷ וַיֹּאמֶר נָתָן אֶל־דָּוִד אַתָּה הָאִישׁ כֹּה־אָמַר יהוה אֱלֹהֵי
יִשְׂרָאֵל אָנֹכִי מְשַׁחְתִּיךָ לְמֶלֶךְ עַל־יִשְׂרָאֵל וְאָנֹכִי הִצַּלְתִּיךָ מִיַּד שָׁאוּל:
וָאֶתְּנָה לְךָ אֶת־בֵּית אֲדֹנֶיךָ וְאֶת־נְשֵׁי אֲדֹנֶיךָ בְּחֵיקֶךָ וָאֶתְּנָה לְךָ אֶת־בֵּית ⁸
יִשְׂרָאֵל וִיהוּדָה וְאִם־מְעָט וְאֹסִפָה לְּךָ כָּהֵנָּה וְכָהֵנָּה: ⁹ מַדּוּעַ בָּזִיתָ אֶת־דְּבַר
יהוה לַעֲשׂוֹת הָרַע בְּעֵינוֹ (= בְּעֵינַי special reading) אֵת **אוּרִיָּה** הַחִתִּי הִכִּיתָ
בַחֶרֶב וְאֶת־אִשְׁתּוֹ לָקַחְתָּ לְּךָ לְאִשָּׁה וְאֹתוֹ הָרַגְתָּ בְּחֶרֶב בְּנֵי עַמּוֹן:

חָרָה אַף⁵	become angry:	אַרְבַּעְתָּיִם⁶	fourfold
	imperf יֶחֱרֶה	מְעָט⁸	little
שׁלם⁶	*pi* שִׁלֵּם pay; compensate:	כָּהֵנָּה⁸	like these
	imperf יְשַׁלֵּם	מַדּוּעַ⁹	why
		בָּזָה⁹	despise: *imperf* יִבְזֶה

III *Proverbs*

Text III.2: *The Words of the Preacher* (Ecc. 1:4, 7, 9; 3:1–3, 6, 8)

דִּבְרֵי קֹהֶלֶת (קֹהֶלֶת א: ד, ז, ט; ג: א–ג, ו, ח)

1:4 דּוֹר הֹלֵךְ וְדוֹר בָּא וְהָאָרֶץ לְעוֹלָם עֹמָדֶת:

1:7 כָּל־הַנְּחָלִים הֹלְכִים אֶל־הַיָּם וְהַיָּם אֵינֶנּוּ מָלֵא אֶל־מְקוֹם שֶׁהַנְּחָלִים הֹלְכִים
שָׁם הֵם שָׁבִים לָלָכֶת:

1:9 מַה־שֶּׁהָיָה הוּא שֶׁיִּהְיֶה וּמַה־שֶּׁנַּעֲשָׂה הוּא שֶׁיֵּעָשֶׂה וְאֵין כָּל־חָדָשׁ תַּחַת הַשָּׁמֶשׁ:

3:1 לַכֹּל זְמָן וְעֵת לְכָל־חֵפֶץ תַּחַת הַשָּׁמָיִם: 3:2 עֵת לָלֶדֶת וְעֵת לָמוּת...

3:3 עֵת לַהֲרוֹג וְעֵת לִרְפּוֹא... 3:6 ...עֵת לִשְׁמוֹר וְעֵת לְהַשְׁלִיךְ:

3:8 עֵת לֶאֱהֹב וְעֵת לִשְׂנֹא עֵת מִלְחָמָה וְעֵת שָׁלוֹם:

1:7 נַחַל	*m,* stream, small river	3:1 זְמָן	*m,* specific time
1:7 יָם	*m,* sea	3:1 חֵפֶץ	*m,* matter, affair
1:9 □ שֶׁ (= אֲשֶׁר) which, that		3:3 רָפָא	heal: *imperf* יִרְפָּא

IV *Prophetic speeches*

Text IV.1: *The Latter Days* (Isa. 2:1–4)

אַחֲרִית הַיָּמִים (יְשַׁעְיָהוּ ב: א–ד)

2:1 הַדָּבָר אֲשֶׁר חָזָה יְשַׁעְיָהוּ בֶּן־אָמוֹץ עַל־יְהוּדָה וִירוּשָׁלָם: 2 וְהָיָה
בְּאַחֲרִית הַיָּמִים נָכוֹן יִהְיֶה הַר בֵּית־יְהוָה בְּרֹאשׁ הֶהָרִים וְנִשָּׂא מִגְּבָעוֹת וְנָהֲרוּ
אֵלָיו כָּל־הַגּוֹיִם: 3 וְהָלְכוּ עַמִּים רַבִּים וְאָמְרוּ לְכוּ וְנַעֲלֶה אֶל־הַר־יְהוָה
אֶל־בֵּית אֱלֹהֵי יַעֲקֹב וְיֹרֵנוּ מִדְּרָכָיו וְנֵלְכָה בְּאֹרְחֹתָיו כִּי מִצִּיּוֹן תֵּצֵא תוֹרָה
וּדְבַר־יְהוָה מִירוּשָׁלָם: 4 וְשָׁפַט בֵּין הַגּוֹיִם וְהוֹכִיחַ לְעַמִּים רַבִּים וְכִתְּתוּ
חַרְבוֹתָם לְאִתִּים וַחֲנִיתוֹתֵיהֶם לְמַזְמֵרוֹת לֹא־יִשָּׂא גוֹי אֶל־גּוֹי חֶרֶב וְלֹא־יִלְמְדוּ
עוֹד מִלְחָמָה:

1 חָזָה	see, vision: *imperf* יֶחֱזֶה	4 יכח	*hiph* הוֹכִיחַ set (matters) right: *imperf* יוֹכִיחַ
2 גִּבְעָה	*f,* hill: *pl* גְּבָעוֹת		
2 נָהַר	flow, stream: *imperf* יִנְהַר	4 כתת	*pi* כִּתֵּת beat: *imperf* יְכַתֵּת
3 ירה	*hiph* הוֹרָה teach, instruct: *imperf* יוֹרֶה	4 אֵת	*f,* plowshare: *pl* אִתִּים
		4 חָנִית	*f,* spare
3 אֹרְחָה	*f,* path	4 מַזְמֵרָה	*f,* vine-knife

APPENDIX I: HEBREW VIA HEBREW NAMES
☆ עִבְרִית בְּעֶזְרַת הַשֵּׁם[1]

The following units of HEBREW VIA HEBREW NAMES are included in the book:

EXERCISES

1 *Read* the following Hebrew names. Then *fill in* the blanks with the correct lexical forms[2] from the lists of words given below.

I לָבָן צוה (צִוָּה) (pi חַי שָׁקַל שָׁמַע שָׁלוֹם

Lexical form	Lexical form: Meaning	Name: English pronunciation	
_____	hear	Simeon	שִׁמְעוֹן 1
_____	command	Bar mitzvah	בַּר מִצְוָה 2
_____	white	Lebanon	לְבָנוֹן 3
_____	living	Eve	חַוָּה 4
_____	weigh	Ashkelon	אַשְׁקְלוֹן 5
_____	peace, well-being	Solomon/Absalom	שְׁלֹמֹה/אַבְשָׁלוֹם 6

---

[1] עִבְרִית בְּעֶזְרַת הַשֵּׁם literally means 'Hebrew with the help of the name'. The word הַשֵּׁם 'the Name' is used by orthodox Jews as a substitute for the sacred name YHWH (the LORD), thus עִבְרִית בְּעֶזְרַת הַשֵּׁם also means 'Hebrew with the help of the LORD'.

[2] The forms with no inflection ending which are listed in lexicons and vocabularies.

II עֶם חָבֵר עַם חַג מַלְאָךְ לָמַד בַּת שָׁנָה מֶלֶךְ אָב

Lexical form	Lexical form: Meaning	Name: English pronunciation	
_____	king	Abimelech	אֲבִימֶלֶךְ 1
_____	nation, a people	Ammon	עַמּוֹן 2
_____	father	Abraham	אַבְרָהָם 3
_____	messenger, angel	Malachi	מַלְאָכִי 4
_____	with	Immanuel	עִמָּנוּאֵל 5
_____	daughter	Bathsheba	בַּת שֶׁבַע 6
_____	feast, festival	Haggai	חַגַּי 7
_____	friend/comrade	Hebron	חֶבְרוֹן 8
_____	study (verb)	Talmud	תַּלְמוּד 9
_____	repeat	Mishnah	מִשְׁנָה 10

III נֹעַם אָבִיב יָרַד רַב שַׂר שֶׁמֶשׁ אָח אִישׁ שָׁמַר בֶּן שֶׁבַע

Lexical form	Lexical form: Meaning	Name: English pronunciation	
_____	kindness	Naomi	נָעֳמִי 1
_____	seven; oath	Beer-sheba	בְּאֵר שֶׁבַע 2
_____	son	Benjamin	בִּנְיָמִין 3
_____	spring (Mar/Apr)	Tel Aviv	תֵּל אָבִיב 4
_____	great, numerous	Rabbi	רַב 5
_____	sun	Samson	שִׁמְשׁוֹן 6
_____	man	Judas Iskariot	אִישׁ קְרִיּוֹת 7
_____	keep	Samaria	שֹׁמְרוֹן 8
_____	brother	Ahimelech	אֲחִימֶלֶךְ 9
_____	go down	Jordan	יַרְדֵּן 10
_____	official, leader	Sarah	שָׂרָה 11

2 The following Hebrew names are *verb forms*. *Read* and *fill in* the blanks with the missing data in the table below. *Remember*:

> ◆ When a verb form is used as a proper name, the short /a/-vowel in a stressed closed syllable (e.g., the verb form נָתַן) is lengthened (e.g., the name נָתָן).

Meaning: Lexical form	Tense	Root type	Verb type (stem)	Verb root	Name: English pronunciation	Name: Verb form	
					Amen	אָמֵן	1
					Cohen	כֹּהֵן	2
					Isaac	יִצְחָק	3
					Jerusalem	שָׁלֵם	4
					Hosea	הוֹשֵׁעַ	5
					Hosianna	הוֹשִׁיעָה	6
					Joseph	יוֹסֵף	7
					Hallelujah	הַלְלוּ	8
					Noah	נֹחַ	9
					Obed	עוֹבֵד	10
					Amos	עָמוֹס	11
					Jacob	יַעֲקֹב	12
					Nathan	נָתָן	13
					Jephthah	יִפְתָּח	14
					Asaph	אָסָף	15
					Nimrod	נִמְרֹד	16
					Dan	דָּן	17
					Saul	שָׁאוּל	18

3 The following Hebrew names are *verbless clauses,* most of them with the divine name as subject, either אֵל (God) or יְה/יָהוּ/יוֹ (elements denoting YHWH, the LORD). *Read* and *identify* the predicate in each clause. Then *fill* in the blanks with the correct lexical forms from the list given below.

עֵזֶר צֶדֶק שֵׁם (גִּבּוֹר) גֶּבֶר עֹז אוֹר אָב אָדוֹן מֶלֶךְ אֵל
יֵשַׁע מֶלֶךְ טוֹב

Lexical form	Lexical form: Meaning	Name: English pronunciation	
_____	salvation, help	Joshua	יְהוֹשֻׁעַ 1
_____	God	Elijah	אֵלִיָּהוּ 2
_____	king	Malchiel	מַלְכִּיאֵל 3
_____	king	Elimelech	אֱלִימֶלֶךְ 4
_____	good	Tobija	טוֹבִיָּה 5
_____	master	Adonijah	אֲדֹנִיָּה 6
_____	strength	Uzziah	עֻזִּיָּה 7
_____	father	Joab	יוֹאָב 8
_____	name	Samuel	שְׁמוּאֵל 9
_____	justice	Zedekiah	צִדְקִיָּהוּ 10
_____	help	Eliezer	אֱלִיעֶזֶר 11
_____	light	Uriah	אוּרִיָּה 12
_____	young strong man (vigorous, hero)	Gabriel	גַּבְרִיאֵל 13

4 The following Hebrew names are *verbal clauses,* most of them with the divine name as subject, either אֵל (God) or יָה/יָהוּ/יוֹ (elements denoting YHWH). *Read* and *identify* the verbs. Then *fill in* the blanks with the correct lexical forms from the lists of verbs given below.

I רוּם חָנַן יִשׁע קָנָה חָזַק (pi) שָׁמַע עָזַר דּוּן קוּם (hiph) רָפָא

Lexical form	Lexical form: Meaning	Name: English pronunciation	
_____	be gracious to someone	Hananiah	חֲנַנְיָה 1
_____	set up	Jehoiakim	יְהוֹיָקִים 2
_____	judge	Daniel	דָּנִיֵּאל 3
_____	cure	Rephael	רְפָאֵל 4
_____	acquire, buy	Elkanah	אֶלְקָנָה 5
_____	help, save	Isaiah	יְשַׁעְיָהוּ 6
_____	be high, exalted	Jeremiah	יִרְמְיָהוּ 7
_____	hear	Ishmael	יִשְׁמָעֵאל 8
_____	strengthen	Ezekiel	יְחֶזְקֵאל 9
_____	help	Azariah	עֲזַרְיָה 10

II נָתַן שָׂרָה זָכַר יָדה (huph) גָּדֵל/גָּדַל נחם (pi) שָׁפַט זָרַע חָנַן עָזַר

	Lexical form: Meaning	Name: English pronunciation	
_____	help	Eleazar	אֶלְעָזָר 1
_____	comfort	Nehemiah	נְחֶמְיָה 2
_____	contend, strive (with)	Israel	יִשְׂרָאֵל 3
_____	remember	Zechariah	זְכַרְיָה 4
_____	give	Jonathan	יְהוֹנָתָן 5
_____	sow	Jezreel	יִזְרְעֵאל 6
_____	be gracious to someone	Johanan	יוֹחָנָן 7
_____	judge	Jehoshaphat	יְהוֹשָׁפָט 8
_____	thank	Judah	יְהוּדָה 9
_____	be/become great/big	Gedaliah	גְּדַלְיָה 10

APPENDIX II: REGULAR SOUND CHANGES IN HEBREW

There are four types of regular sound changes in Hebrew, formulated below as sound change rules (also summarized in Grammatical cornerstones 2–5):

A Vowel changes related to the *position of the stress* in the word.
B The softening of the hard sound of the *BeGaDKeFaT-consonants*.
C Vowel change due to the presence of a *guttural/s* in the word.
D Sound change due to the presence of a *changeable consonant/s* in the word (the changeable consonant may be omitted or altered).

The knowledge and application of the sound change rules give the deviant word patterns and inflections a see-through structure.

It is easiest to detect the deviant feature/s of a given form by placing the consonants of the deviant form, e.g., בָּחֲרוּ 'they chose', in the corresponding normal pattern, that is, ‏ָ ‏ְ ‏וּ, and ask, "Why is it בָּחֲרוּ and not בָּחְרוּ as it is in the normal form שָׁמְרוּ)?" Sound change rule C1a below answers this question.

		A	B	C	D
		Vowel changes	BeGaDKeFaT-consonants	Gutturals (ר) – the vowel-changers	Changeable (i.e., weak) consonants
1		Reduction (**unstressed** open syllables)	Undergo softening of the hard sound after a vowel or a reduced vowel	Take supporting vowels: a) Chateph (instead of shva) b) Glide-/a/ (additional /a/-vowel)	א *Aleph* at the end of a syllable is **silenced**; preceding vowel is lengthened
2		Lengthening (**unstressed** open syllables)		Take special insertion vowels a) Before/after a guttural with a chateph – the vowel of chateph b) At the end of a word – /a/-vowel	ה *He* after a shva is often **omitted**, its vowel being transferred to the preceding consonant
3		Shortening (**unstressed** closed syllables)		Prefer the /a/-vowel (instead of an I/E- or U/O vowel)	י/ו *Vav/Yod* at the end of a syllable forms a diphthong, thus it **becomes a vowel letter**
4		Breaking up of clusters (by inserting a vowel)		Bring about compensatory lengthening of the preceding vowel (since gutturals and ר cannot be doubled)	י/ו *Vav/Yod* with vowels on either side forms a triphthong, hence it is usually **omitted**
5		Raising (**unstressed** closed syllables, /a/ becomes /i/)		Avoid vowel raising (original /a/-vowel in an unstressed closed syllble is retained)	נ *Nun* at the end of a syllable is **assimilated** to the next consonant, which is doubled
6		Lowering (**stressed** closed syllables, I/E becomes /a/)		Permit vowel raising only halfway (original /a/-vowel in an unstressed closed syllable becomes /e/)	A **voiceless doubled consonant** is often **simplified** (loses its doubling)

A. REGULAR VOWEL CHANGES (refers to simple vowels. Full vowels are not changeable)

1 *Vowel reduction*: When the word stress is moved from its original position, the vowel in an *unstressed open syllable* either one or two steps (i.e., syllables) before the stress is reduced (shown in writing by the shva sign): 'שֹׁפֵט + the ending ים ָ ' results in the hypothetical form שֹׁפֵטִים which becomes שֹׁפְטִים 'judges'; 'גָּדוֹל + the ending ה ָ ' results in גָּדוֹלָה which becomes גְּדוֹלָה 'big'.

2 *Vowel lengthening*: When the word stress is moved from its original position, the vowel in an *unstressed open syllable* one step before the stress is lengthened, when it is not reduced (shown in writing by being transformed into a long vowel within the same vowel category):[1] זְכָרַנִי 'he remembered me' becomes זְכָרַנִי.

3 *Vowel shortening*: When the word stress is moved from its original position, the long vowel in an *unstressed closed syllable* is shortened (shown in writing by being transformed into a short vowel within the same vowel category): 'דָּבָר + the ending כֶם' results in the hypothetical form דָּבָרְכֶם which becomes דְּבַרְכֶם 'your word'; 'וַ (the inverting-Vav) + יֵשֵׁב' results in וַיֵּשֶׁב 'he dwelt' (not וַיֵּשֵׁב)

4 *Insertion vowel*: Two vowelless consonants in succession are not permitted. An impermissible sequence of consonants (*cluster*) is broken up by the addition of a vowel between the vowelless consonants in the sequence.

a The insertion vowel added between two vowelless consonants at the beginning of a syllable is normally /i/: 'לְ + שְׁמֹר' results in the hypothetical form לְשְׁמֹר which becomes לִשְׁמֹר 'to guard'.[2]

b The insertion vowel added between two vowelless consonants at the end of a word is normally /e/: 'שֹׁפֵט + the ending ת' results in שֹׁפֵטְת which becomes שֹׁפֶטֶת 'judge' (*f*).

5 *Vowel raising (Law of attenuation)*: An original /a/-vowel in an *unstressed* originally *closed syllable*, e.g., יַשְׁמֹר, is ordinarily changed into an /i/-vowel: יִשְׁמֹר 'he will guard'.

6 *Vowel lowering (Philippi's law)*: An original I/E-vowel in a *stressed* originally *closed syllable*, e.g., דִּבֵּרְתִּי, is ordinarily changed into an /a/-vowel: דִּבַּרְתִּי 'I talked'.[3]

---

[1] This sound change rule is traditionally called *pretonic lengthening* (tone = stress).

[2] This rule is known in some grammars of Biblical Hebrew as *The Rule of Sheva*.

[3] Philippi's law applies both to the main and the secondary stress of a word.

B. BEGADKEFAT-CONSONANTS: ב, ג, ד, כ, פ, ת

Softening: The hard sound of the BeGaDKeFaT-consonants becomes soft after an immediately preceding vowel or a reduced vowel (shown in writing by the absence of the hardening dagesh). In modern Hebrew the sound is softened only in פ, כ, ב: יִבְחַר 'he will choose' (compare בָּחַר), יְבַקֵּשׁ 'he will request' (compare בִּקֵּשׁ), יִכְתֹּב 'he will write' (compare כָּתַב), יִפְתַּח 'he will open' (compare פָּתַח).

C. GUTTURALS (VOWEL-CHANGERS): א, ה, ח, ע (ר is sometimes included)

1 *Supporting vowels*: Vowelless gutturals require supporting vowels.

a *Chateph*: A guttural takes a chateph (shva-plus-vowel) instead of a shva
   – at the beginning of a syllable (instead of a vocal shva): אֲהַבְתֶּם 'you loved' (not אְהַבְתֶּם), בָּחֲרוּ 'they chose' (not בָּחְרוּ)
   – often also at the end of a syllable (instead of a silent shva): יַעֲבֹד 'he will serve' (not יַעְבֹד), נֶהֱרַג 'he was killed' (not נֶהְרַג).

b *Glide-/a/*: A vowelless ח *Chet*, ע *Áyin* and ה *He* (the consonant ה!) at the end of a word that is not preceded by an /a/-vowel takes an additional (unstressed) /a/-vowel. The glide-/a/ is written under the guttural but pronounced before it: שֹׁמֵעַ šōmēₐʕ 'listening' (not שֹׁמֵע).

2 *Special insertion vowels*: Gutturals take special insertion vowels.

a The insertion vowel added to break up an impermissible consonant sequence before and after (i.e., under)[4] a guttural with a chateph matches the vowel of the chateph (instead of an /i/-vowel): לַחֲכָמִים (instead of לְחֲכָמִים, from the hypothetical form לְחַכָמִים) 'for the wise [ones]', יַ-עֲבְדוּ (not יִ-עֲבְדוּ) 'they will serve'.

b The insertion vowel added to dissolve an impermissible consonant sequence before and after a guttural at the end of a word is /a/ (instead of an /e/-vowel): שֶׁבַע 'seven' (not שֶׁבֶע), יֹודַעַת 'knowing' (not יֹודֶעַת).

3 *Preference for the /a/-vowel*: A guttural that is not preceded by an /a/-vowel may take an /a/-vowel instead of an original I/E- or O/U-vowel: יִשָּׁלַח 'he will be sent' (instead of יִשָּׁלֵח), יִשְׁלַח 'he will send' (instead of יִשְׁלֵח).

4 *Compensatory lengthening of vowels*: Gutturals and ר *Resh* cannot be doubled. Instead, the preceding short vowel may be lengthened according to the following scheme:

a Always before א and ר, e.g., הָאִישׁ 'the man' (instead of הַאִישׁ), מְבָרֵךְ 'blessed' (not מְבַרֵךְ).

b Never before ח, e.g., נִחַם 'comfort'.

c Sometimes before ה and ע, e.g., יֵעָבֵד 'he will be served' (not יֵעַבֵד).

---

[4] 'The vowel after (i.e., under) the guttural' means that the vowel is *pronounced after* but *written under* the guttural.

5 *No vowel raising ("attenuation")*: The original /a/-vowel in an unstressed originally closed syllable is sometimes retained due to the presence of a neighbouring guttural: יַעֲבֹד 'he will serve' (instead of יַעְבֹד), compare יִשְׁמֹר.

6 *Vowel raising ("attenuation") realized only halfway*: The original /a/-vowel in an unstressed originally closed syllable is sometimes raised halfway, that is, to an /e/-vowel due to the presence of a neighbouring guttural: נֶהֱרַג 'he was killed' (not נַהֱרַג), אֶשְׁמֹר 'I will guard' (not אַשְׁמֹר), compare נִשְׁמֹר.

D. CHANGEABLE CONSONANTS: א, ה, ו, י, נ and a *doubled consonant*. Note:

> ♦ א, ה, ו, י, נ and the doubled consonant are changeable mostly when there is no vowel preceding or following them (shva is regarded as no-vowel!). However, when they are surrounded by vowels, no sound changes occur.

1 א *Áleph*: The consonant א at the end of a syllable is *silenced*. That is, א disappears in pronunciation but is retained in writing as a silent letter. The silencing of א is compensated by the lengthening of the preceding vowel (if it is not already long): קָרָאנוּ 'we called' (instead of קָרַאְנוּ).

2 ה *He*: The consonant ה after a vowelless consonant (i.e., a consonant with a shva) *tends to disappear*, its vowel being "inherited" by the preceding vowelless consonant: בַּמִּדְבָּר 'in the wilderness/desert' (instead of בְּהַמִּדְבָּר)

3 י/ו *Vav/Yod (in a diphthong)*: The consonant י/ו at the end of a syllable forms a diphthong and is usually *silenced*, being retained in writing as a vowel letter: בָּנִינוּ 'we built' (instead of בָּנַיְנוּ *bānaynû); נוֹלַד 'he was born' (not נַוְלַד *nawlad).[5]

4 י/ו *Vav/Yod (in a triphthong)*: The consonant י/ו with vowels on either side forms a triphthong and is usually *omitted*, the triphthong being pulled together to one vowel, either simple or full.

a Within a word the triphthong usually becomes a simple vowel: קָם 'he stood up' (from the hypothetical form קָוַם *qāwam).

b At the end of a word the triphthong normally becomes a full vowel (with either the vowel letter י/ו or ה): בָּנוּ 'they built' (from the hypothetical form *bānayû), יִבְנֶה 'he will build' (from the hypothetical form *yivnayu).[6]

---

[5] Historically, the contraction of diphthongs took place before vowel raising occurred.

[6] Historically, most of the words in Hebrew ended in a vowel, either short or long, but at a certain stage in the history of the language the short vowels at the end of words fell away. The contraction of triphthongs took place before the short vowels at the end of words were lost.

5   נ *Nun*: The consonant נ at the end of a syllable is generally *assimilated to* (absorbed in) the sound of the next consonant, which in turn is doubled (shown in writing by the doubling dagesh): יִשָּׁמֵר 'he will be guarded' (instead of יִנְשָׁמֵר), יִתֵּן 'he will give' (not יִנְתֵּן). *Note* the following exceptions to this rule:

   – The consonant נ at the end of a syllable is *not* assimilated when נ is the third consonant in the word root: זָקַנְתִּי 'I am/I have grown old'.

   – The consonant נ at the end of a syllable is not assimilated when the following consonant is a guttural: יִנְחַל 'he will inherit'.

6   A *doubled consonant*: A doubled consonant is often *simplified* (i.e., loses its doubling, which is shown in writing by the absence of the doubling dagesh):

a   A vowelless doubled consonant at the end of a word is normally simplified: קַל (instead of קַלּ, the word root is קלל).

b   A vowelless doubled consonant with a shva within a word tends to lose its doubling (except for the BeGaDKeFaT consonants that never lose their dagesh): וַיְדַבֵּר 'he spoke' (instead of וַיְדַבֵּר).

7   ו *Vav*: The consonant ו *Vav* at the beginning of a word is normally *replaced by* י *Yod*. However, the original ו is retained, when ו occurs within a word, e.g., יִוָּלֵד 'he will be born' (the root letters are ילד).

APPENDIX III: GUIDE TO GRAMMATICAL TERMS

Name in this book	*Corresponding name/s*	*Section*
Hardening dagesh	Dagesh lene	2
BeGaDKeFaT-consonants: Hard versus soft pronunciation/sound	BeGaDKeFaT-consonants: Stops versus spirants	
Doubling dagesh	Dagesh forte	
Vowel letters	Matres lectionis, mater letters, vowel indicators	
Silent א *Áleph*	Quiescent Áleph	
Stress	Accent, tone	
Chateph, shva-plus-vowel	Composite/compound sheva	3
Glide-/a/	Furtive patach	
Verbless clause	Nominal clause/sentence	
Qamets-/o/	Qamets chatuf	4
Lexical form	Base form, citation form	5
Unchangeable consonant	Strong consonant	7
Changeable consonant	Weak consonant	
Unchangeable root types, שְׁלֵמִים	Strong/regular roots	
Root types with changeable consonants	Weak/irregular roots	
Noun types	Declensions	8
Penultimate nouns	Segholates	
Twin-consonant nouns	Geminate/reduplicated nouns	9
Noun: Free/independent form	Noun: Absolute state/form	10
Noun: Bound form	Noun: Construct state/form	
Noun chains	Construct relationship/construct chains	
Attached pronouns	Pronominal suffixes	11
Question marker הֲ	Interrogative He הֲ	
Verb types, stems	Verbal patterns, conjugations	13
Suffixed pronouns	Sufformatives	
Prefixed pronouns	Preformatives	
Twin-consonant verbs	Geminate/reduplicated/double Áyin verbs	
Direction marker ָה	He directive, He locale, locative ה, directive -āh	14
"Redundant" attached pronoun	Resumptive pronoun	15
Lengthened imperfect	Cohortative	17
Shortened imperfect	Jussive, apocopated verb forms	
Ordinary infinitive/infinitive	Infinitive construct	19
Infinitive-as-intensifier	Infinitive absolute	
Inverting-Vav	Vav/Waw-consecutive/conversive	20
Verb chains	Verb sequences, coordinate relationships of verbs	

HEBREW–ENGLISH VOCABULARY

- ◆ The number in parentheses refers to the section in which the word is introduced.
- ◆ Particles-as-intensifiers can be rendered by various intensifying adverbs/adverbial constructions.

א

אָב	(3) *m*, father: *bound form* אֲבִי, *pl* אָבוֹת
אָבִיב	(24) *m,* ears (of grain); month of year (March/April)
אֶבֶן	(9) *f*, stone: *pl* אֲבָנִים, *with suff* אַבְנִי
אָדוֹן	(4) *m*, lord, master: אֲדֹנָי the Lord
אָדָם	(6) *m*, person, man; mankind
אֲדָמָה	(7) *f,* ground, soil; earth
אָהַב	(13) love: *imperf* יֶאֱהַב
אַהֲבָה	(20) loving, love
אֹהֶל	(27) *m*, tent: *pl* אֹהָלִים, *with suff* אָהֳלִי
אוּלַי	(28) perhaps
אוֹר	(11) *m*, light
אוֹת	(20) *f,* sign, omen
אָז	(13) then (= at that time)
אזן	(24) *hiph* הֶאֱזִין listen: *imperf* יַאֲזִין, *inver imperf* וַיַּאֲזֵן
אֹזֶן	(12) *f*, ear: *dual* אָזְנַיִם, *with suff* אָזְנִי
אָח	(6) *m*, brother: *bound form* אֲחִי, *pl* אַחִים
אֶחָד	(9) *m*, one: *bound form* אַחַד, *f* אַחַת
אָחוֹת	(12) *f*, sister: *pl* אֲחָיוֹת
אַחֵר	(15) another, other
אַחַר/אַחֲרֵי	(12) after, behind: *with suff* אַחֲרֵי
אַחֲרִית	(27) *f,* end
אַחַת	(11) *f,* one: *bound form* אַחַת, *m* אֶחָד
אֵי/אַיֵּה	(12) where?
אֵי־זֶה	(12) which? אֵי־מִזֶּה from which
אֵיךְ	(15) how?
אַיִן	(9) nothing, naught
אֵין	(9) [there is/are] not/no (*non-existence*): אֵין לְ someone has not
אֵיפֹה	(12) where?
אִישׁ	(5) *m*, man: *pl* אֲנָשִׁים
אַךְ	(14) only; surely (intensifier)
אָכַל	(14) eat: *imperf* יֹאכַל, *hiph* הֶאֱכִיל cause to eat, feed
אָכֵן	(14) truly, indeed (intensifier)
אֵל	(4) *m*, god; God
אֶל־	(11) to, toward
אַל	(17) no, not (followed by the shortened imperf)

אֵלֶּה (8) *c*, these

אֱלֹהִים (5) *m*, God; gods

אֶלֶף (12) *m*, thousand: *dual* אַלְפַּ֫יִם, *pl* אֲלָפִים, *with suff* אַלְפֵּי

אֵם (9) mother: *with suff* אִמִּי

אִם (14) if; surely (intensifier)

אָמָה (28) *f*, female slave

אמן (24) *niph* נֶאֱמַן be confirmed, trustworthy, verified: *imperf* יֵאָמֵן, *hiph* הֶאֱמִין believe

אָמְנָם (14) surely (intensifier)

אָמַר (13) say: *imperf* יֹאמַר, *inver imperf* וַיֹּאמֶר

אֱמֶת (12) *f*, truth

אָן/אָ֫נָה (14) where to?

אֱנוֹשׁ (21) *m*, man

אֲנַ֫חְנוּ (5) we

אֲנִי/אָנֹכִי (3) I

אָסַף (16) gather: *imperf* יֵאֱסֹף

אֵ֫צֶל (22) near, beside, by: *with suff* אֶצְלִי

אַרְבַּע (28) *f*, four: *m* אַרְבָּעָה; אַרְבָּעִים forty

אָרוֹן (19) *m*, chest, ark (of the covenant): *with defin art* הָאָרוֹן

אֶ֫רֶץ (7) *f*, earth; land, country: *with defin art* הָאָ֫רֶץ, *pl* אֲרָצוֹת, *with suff* אַרְצִי

ארר (18) curse: *passive part* אָרוּר

אֵשׁ (20) *f*, fire: *with suff* אִשִּׁי

אִשָּׁה (5) *f*, woman, wife: *bound form* אֵ֫שֶׁת, *pl* נָשִׁים, *with suff* אִשְׁתִּי

אֲשֶׁר (15) who, whom, whose, which, that (corresponds to English relative pron); the one who/whom etc.; what, where

(18) for, because (conj)

אַתְּ (3) *f singular*, you

אֵת/אֶת־ (11) with, together with: *with suff* אִתִּי

(14) marker of a direct definite object: *with suff* אֹתִי

אַתָּה (3) *m singular*, you

אַתֶּם (5) *m plural*, you

אַתֵּן/אַתֵּ֫נָה (5) *f plural*, you

ב

בְּ (בּ, בֶּ, בֵּ, בַּ, בָּ) (6) in, at, within, among; with, by: *with suff* בִּי

בדל (24) *hiph* הִבְדִּיל separate, distinguish: *imperf* יַבְדִּיל, *inver imperf* וַיַּבְדֵּל

בּוֹא (15) come, enter, go in: *perf* בָּא, *imperf* יָבוֹא, *hiph* הֵבִיא bring

בּוֹר   (24) *m*, pit; cistern

בָּחַר   (14) choose (followed by בְּ)

בֵּין   (16) between: *with suff in sing* בֵּינִי, *with suff in pl* בֵּינֵינוּ

בַּיִת   (9) *m*, house: *bound form* בֵּית, *pl* בָּתִּים, *with suff* בֵּיתִי

בָּכָה   (19) weep: *imperf* יִבְכֶּה, *inver imperf* וַיֵּבְךְּ

בִּלְתִּי/לְבִלְתִּי   (19) not (negates an infinitive)

בֵּן   (9) son: *pl* בָּנִים

בָּנָה   (15) build: *imperf* יִבְנֶה, *inver imperf* וַיִּבֶן

בַּעֲבוּר   (20) in order that/so that; for the sake of: *with suff* בַּעֲבוּרִי

בְּעַד   (23) for (the sake of), on behalf of: *with suff* בַּעֲדִי

בַּעַל   (3) *m*, lord, master; owner (of), husband: *pl* בְּעָלִים, *with suff* בַּעֲלִי

בֹּקֶר   (12) *m*, morning: *pl* בְּקָרִים, *with suff* בָּקְרִי

בקש   (22) *pi* בִּקֵּשׁ seek; require: *imperf* יְבַקֵּשׁ

בָּרָא   (15) create: *imperf* יִבְרָא

בָּרַח   (19) flee: *imperf* יִבְרַח

בְּרִית   (4) *f*, covenant

ברך   (18) bless: *in G-stem only passive part* בָּרוּךְ, *niph* נִבְרַךְ be blessed, *pi* בֵּרַךְ bless, *imperf* יְבָרֵךְ

בְּרָכָה   (12) *f*, blessing

בָּשָׂר   (19) *m*, flesh, meat

בַּת   (9) daughter: *pl* בָּנוֹת, *with suff* בִּתִּי

ג

גָּאַל   (13) redeem: *imperf* יִגְאַל

גָּדוֹל   (5) big, great; important

גָּדֵל/גָּדַל   (16) be/become great/big, grow: *imperf* יִגְדַּל

גּוֹי   (13) *m*, nation, a people: *pl* גּוֹיִם

גּוּר   (27) stay as foreigner/guest: *perf* גָּר, *imperf* יָגוּר, *inver imperf* וַיָּגָר

גָּלָה   (24) uncover, reveal; go into exile: *imperf* יִגְלֶה, *hiph* הִגְלָה send into exile

גַּם   (14) also, too, even; moreover (intensifier)

ד

דבר   (22) *pi* דִּבֶּר speak, talk: *imperf* יְדַבֵּר, *niph* נִדְבַּר speak with one another

דָּבָר   (7) *m*, word; thing; matter, affair

דּוֹר   (20) *m*, generation: *pl* דּוֹרוֹת

דָּם (19) *m,* blood

דֶּרֶךְ (7) *c,* way, road: *pl* דְּרָכִים, *with suff* דַּרְכִּי

דָּרַשׁ (16) seek; inquire: *imperf* יִדְרשׁ

ה

הֲ (12) question marker: ...הֲ אִם whether... or

הַ ⊡ (הָ, הֶ, הֶ) (5) the

הוּא (3) he

הִיא (3) she

הָיָה (15) be; become (followed by לְ); happen: *imperf* יִהְיֶה, *inver imperf* וַיְהִי

הֵיכָל (12) *m,* palace, temple: *pl* הֵיכָלוֹת

הָלַךְ (14) go, walk: *imperf* יֵלֵךְ, *inver imperf* וַיֵּלֶךְ, *pi* הִלֵּךְ walk around, wander, *hitp* הִתְהַלֵּךְ walk around

הלל (22) *pi* הִלֵּל praise: *imperf* יְהַלֵּל

הֵם/הֵמָּה (5) *m,* they

הֵן/הִנֵּה (14) indeed (intensifier); behold! look! here! *with suff* הִנֵּנִי/הִנְנִי

הֵנָּה (5) *f,* they

הַר (10) *m,* mountain: *with defin art* הָהָר, *pl* הָרִים, *with suff* הָרִי

הָרַג (21) kill, slay: *imperf* יַהֲרֹג

הָרָה (28) conceive, be pregnant: *imperf* תֶּהֱרֶה, *inver imperf* וַתַּהַר

ו

וְ (וּ, וֶ, וִ, וַ, וָ) (8) and (also 'but; or')

ז

זֹאת (8) *f,* this

זֶבַח (19) *m,* sacrifice: *pl* זְבָחִים, *with suff* זִבְחִי

זֶה (8) *m,* this

זָהָב (11) *m,* gold

זָכַר (13) remember: *imperf* יִזְכֹּר, *niph* נִזְכַּר remember, be remembered, *hiph* הִזְכִּיר make someone remember, remind

זָכָר (28) *m,* male

זֵכֶר (20) *m,* mention (of a name): *with suff* זִכְרִי

זָקֵן (13) be/become old: *imperf* יִזְקַן

(5) old; elder (*noun*): *bound form* זְקַן

זְרוֹעַ (19) *f,* arm; strength

זֶרַע (12) *m,* seed, offspring: *pl* זְרָעִים, *with suff* זַרְעִי

ח

חַג (12) *m*, feast, festival: *with defin art* הֶחָג, *pl* חַגִּים, *with suff* חַגִּי

חֹדֶשׁ (24) *m,* new moon, month: *pl* חֳדָשִׁים, *with suff* חָדְשִׁי

חָדָשׁ (7) new

חוה (26) *hisht* הִשְׁתַּחֲוָה bow down, prostrate oneself, worship: *imperf* יִשְׁתַּחֲוֶה, *inver imperf* וַיִּשְׁתַּחוּ

חָזַק (22) be/become strong, hard: *imperf* יֶחֱזַק, *pi* חִזֵּק make strong

חָזָק (12) strong, mighty

חָטָא (20) sin: *imperf* יֶחֱטָא/יְחַטָּא

חַטָּאת (26) *f,* sin; pardon, sin-offering

חַי (9) living (also 'alive'): *pl* חַיִּים

חָיָה (15) live: *imperf* יִחְיֶה, *inver imperf* וַיְחִי, *pi* חִיָּה keep alive

חַיָּה (20) *f,* living thing, beast, animal

חַיִּים (4) *pl,* life

חַיִל (12) *m*, strength, army; capacity, valour: *bound form* חֵיל, *pl* חֲיָלִים *with suff* חֵילִי

חָכָם (5) wise, clever; skilful

חָכְמָה (22) *f,* wisdom

חָמֵשׁ (28) *f,* five: *m,* חֲמִשָּׁה; חֲמִשִּׁים fifty

חֵן (17) agreeableness, charm, favour: *with suff* חִנִּי

חִנָּם (26) without compensation, for nothing, in vain

חֶסֶד (10) *m*, goodness, kindness, grace; faithfulness: *pl* חֲסָדִים evidences of kindness, *with suff* חַסְדִּי

חֹק (10) *m*, statute, law: *with suff* חֻקִּי

חֻקָּה (20) *f,* statute

חָרַב (25) be/become dried up, wasted, desolated: *imperf* יֶחֱרַב, *hiph* הֶחֱרִיב dry up, desolate

חֶרֶב (7) *f,* sword: *pl* חֲרָבוֹת, *with suff* חַרְבִּי

חֹשֶׁךְ (26) *m,* darkness

ט

טָהֵר (23) be/become clean, pure: *imperf* יִטְהַר, *hitp* הִטַּהֵר cleanse, purify oneself

טוֹב (5) good

טוֹבָה (9) *f,* kindness, goodwill

י

יָד (9) *f,* hand: *dual* יָדַיִם

יָדַע (14) know: *imperf* יֵדַע, *hiph* הוֹדִיעַ make known, inform, announce

יהוה	(6) YHWH: the Lord, pronounced אֲדֹנָי ?ᵃdōnāy
יוֹם	(7) *m*, day: *pl* יָמִים
יוֹמָם	(26) by day, during the day
יוֹנָה	(14) *f*, dove: *pl* יוֹנִים
יטב	(26) be/become good (perf is not used; טוֹב serves as perf to פָּעַל): *imperf* יִיטַב, *hiph* הֵיטִיב make good, treat kindly, before infinitive 'well'
יַיִן	(10) *m*, wine: *with suff* יֵינִי
יָכֹל	(19) be able/capable: *imperf* יוּכַל
יָלַד	(20) bear (child), give birth: *imperf* תֵּלֵד, *inver imperf* וַתֵּלֶד, niph נוֹלַד be born, *hiph* הוֹלִיד beget, become the father of
יֶלֶד	(9) *m*, child, boy: *pl* יְלָדִים, *with suff* יַלְדִּי
יָסַף	(26) add, continue: *hiph* הוֹסִיף add, continue; before infinitive 'again, more', *imperf* יוֹסִיף, *inver imperf* וַיֹּסֶף/וַיּוֹסֶף
יַעַן	(18) because (often followed by כִּי/אֲשֶׁר)
יָפֶה	(10) beautiful, handsome: *f* יָפָה
יָצָא	(14) come/go out/forth: *imperf* יֵצֵא, *hiph* הוֹצִיא bring out
יָרֵא	(14) fear, be afraid: *imperf* יִירָא
יִרְאָה	(14) *f*, fear
יָרַד	(22) go down, descend: *imperf* יֵרֵד, *inver imperf* וַיֵּרֶד, huph הוּרַד be brought down
יָרַשׁ	(24) inherit: *imperf* יִירַשׁ, *hiph* הוֹרִישׁ make someone inherit
יֵשׁ	(9) there is/are (*existence*): יֵשׁ לְ someone has (*possession*)
יָשַׁב	(14) sit; dwell, reside: *imperf* יֵשֵׁב, *inver imperf* וַיֵּשֶׁב, hiph הוֹשִׁיב make someone sit/dwell, set, settle, populate (a city)
יְשׁוּעָה	(26) *f*, salvation, deliverance
ישע	(24) *hiph* הוֹשִׁיעַ save, deliver: *imperf* יוֹשִׁיעַ, *inver imperf* וַיּוֹשַׁע
יָשַׁר	(13) be/become straight, upright: *imperf* יִישַׁר
יָשָׁר	(5) straight, upright, honest

כ

כְּ (כּ, כֶ, כֶּ, כַּ, כָּ)	(6) like, as, according to: *with suff* כָּמוֹנִי, כָּכֶם
כַּאֲשֶׁר	(18) as; when
כָּבֵד	(18) be/become heavy: *imperf* יִכְבַּד, *pi* כִּבֵּד make weighty, honour
כָּבוֹד	(14) *m*, glory, honour
כֹּה	(14) so, thus
כֹּהֵן	(3) *m*, priest
כּוֹכָב	(10) *m*, star
כון	(27) *niph* נָכוֹן be firm, established, *polel* כּוֹנֵן establish, found

כִּי	(14) undoubtedly (intensifier)
	(18) that; because, since, for; when (conj)
כֹּל/כָּל־	(10) totality, everything; all, the whole, each, every
כְּלִי	(7) *m*, vessel, utensil: *pl* כֵּלִים
כלם	(21) *niph* נִכְלַם be/feel ashamed: *imperf* יִכָּלֵם
כְּמוֹ	(11) as, like (= כְּ): *with suff* כָּמוֹנִי, כָּכֶם
כֵּן	(14) so, thus; rightly
כִּסֵּא	(12) *m*, throne, seat: *pl* כִּסְאוֹת
כסה	(22) *pi* כִּסָּה cover, conceal: *imperf* יְכַסֶּה
כֶּסֶף	(11) *m*, silver; money: *with suff* כַּסְפִּי
כפר	(22) *pi* כִּפֶּר atone for: *imperf* יְכַפֵּר
כָּרַת	(13) cut; כָּרַת בְּרִית make a covenant: *imperf* יִכְרֹת, *niph* נִכְרַת be cut off, *hiph* הִכְרִית eliminate
כָּתַב	(13) write: *imperf* יִכְתֹּב

ל

לְ (לִ, לֶ, לֵ, לָ, לְ)	(6) to, for; of
לֹא	(6) no, not
לֵב	(10) *m*, heart: *pl* לִבּוֹת, *with suff* לִבִּי
לֵבָב	(15) *m*, heart: *pl* לְבָבוֹת, *with suff* לְבָבִי
לְבַד	(18) alone: *with suff* לְבַדִּי
לְבִלְתִּי/בִּלְתִּי	(19) not (negates an infinitive)
לוּ	(26) if only! O that… might
לוּלֵא/לוּלֵי	(28) if not, unless
לחם	(21) *niph* נִלְחַם fight: *imperf* יִלָּחֵם
לֶחֶם	(7) *m*, bread, food: *with suff* לַחְמִי
לַיְלָה	(14) *m*, night: *pl* לֵילוֹת, *with suff* לֵילִי
לָכֵן	(22) therefore
לָמַד	(16) learn: *imperf* יִלְמַד, *pi* לִמֵּד make learn, teach
לָמָּה/לָמֶה	(13) why?
לְמַעַן	(20) in order that/so that; for the sake of
לִפְנֵי	(12) before, in front of: *with suff* לְפָנַי
לָקַח	(14) take: *imperf* יִקַּח
לִקְרַאת	(27) towards, against, to meet: *with suff* לִקְרָאתִי

מ

מִ (מֵ) מִן/◌ּ	(6) from, out of; than: *with suff* מִמֶּנִּי (מִכֶּם)
מְאֹד	(7) very, exceedingly
מֵאָה	(28) *f*, hundred; *dual* מָאתַיִם

מֵאַיִן   (12) where from? whence?

מֵאֵן   (22) *pi* מֵאֵן refuse: *imperf* יְמָאֵן

מִדְבָּר   (20) *m*, wilderness; desert

מָה, מַה־ ⊡   (12) what?

מהר   (26) *pi* מִהֵר hurry: *imperf* יְמַהֵר, before infinitive 'quickly'

מול   (28) circumcise: *perf* מָל, *imperf* יָמוּל, *inver imperf* וַיָּמָל
niph נָמוֹל be circumcised

מוֹלֶדֶת   (20) *f*, birth: *with suff* מוֹלַדְתִּי

מוֹעֵד   (27) *m*, appointed time

מות   (19) die: *perf* מֵת, *imperf* יָמוּת, *inver imperf* וַיָּמָת

מָוֶת   (7) *m*, death: *bound form* מוֹת: *with suff* מוֹתִי

מִזְבֵּחַ   (10) *m*, altar: *pl* מִזְבְּחוֹת

מַחֲנֶה   (28) *m*, camp: *pl* מַחֲנִים/מַחֲנוֹת

מָחָר   (27) *m*, tomorrow

מִי   (12) who?

מַיִם   (10) *pl*, water: *bound form* מֵי, *with suff* מֵימַי

מַכָּה   (24) *f*, stroke; plague; defeat

מָכַר   (15) sell: *imperf* יִמְכֹּר

מָלֵא   (14) be full/filled (with): *imperf* יִמְלָא, *pi* מִלֵּא fill

מַלְאָךְ   (11) *m*, messenger; angel

מִלְחָמָה   (16) *f*, war, battle: *bound form* מִלְחֶמֶת, *with suff* מִלְחַמְתִּי

מלט   (21) *niph* נִמְלַט escape: *imperf* יִמָּלֵט

מָלַךְ   (13) reign (as king): *imperf* יִמְלֹךְ, *hiph* הִמְלִיךְ make someone
king, crown

מֶלֶךְ   (5) *m*, king: *pl* מְלָכִים, *with suff* מַלְכִּי

מַמְלָכָה   (28) *f*, kingdom

מְעַט   (12) a little, few: *pl* מְעַטִים

מַעֲשֶׂה   (12) *m*, deed, act: *pl* מַעֲשִׂים

מָצָא   (14) find: *imperf* יִמְצָא, *niph* נִמְצָא be found

מַצָּה   (28) *f*, unleavened bread

מִצְוָה   (6) *f*, commandment: *pl* מִצְוֹת

מִצְרַיִם   (12) *f*, Egypt

מִקְדָּשׁ   (10) *m*, sanctuary

מָקוֹם   (9) *m*, place: *pl* מְקוֹמוֹת

מַרְאֶה   (10) *m*, sight; appearance: *pl* מַרְאוֹת

מָשַׁח   (13) anoint: *imperf* יִמְשַׁח

מָשִׁיחַ   (3) *m*, anointed (one)

מִשְׁכָּן   (14) *m*, dwelling-place; tabernacle: *pl* מִשְׁכָּנוֹת

מָשַׁל   (19) rule: *imperf* יִמְשֹׁל (followed by בְּ)

מָשָׁל   (10) *m,* proverb, parable

מִשְׁמָר   (26) *m,* guard(ing)

מִשְׁפָּחָה   (21) *f,* family, clan: *bound form* מִשְׁפַּחַת, *with suff* מִשְׁפַּחְתִּי

מִשְׁפָּט   (8) *m,* judgement, legal decision, ordinance; justice

נ

נָא   (17) please, I/we pray (intensifier)

נְאֻם   (25) *m,* utterance, oracle

נָבִיא   (5) *m,* prophet

נגד   (24) *hiph* הִגִּיד tell, report: *imperf* יַגִּיד, *inver imperf* וַיַּגֵּד
              (followed by לְ), *huph* הֻגַּד be told/reported

נֶגֶד   (22) before, in front of, opposite to: *with suff* נֶגְדִּי

נָהָר   (19) *m,* river: *pl* נְהָרוֹת

נָחַל   (26) inherit, take possession: *imperf* יִנְחַל, *hiph* יַנְחִיל cause to
              inherit

נחם   (22) *pi* נִחַם comfort, console: *imperf* יְנַחֵם

נכה   (24) *hiph* הִכָּה hit, strike, smite; defeat: *imperf* יַכֶּה, *inver imperf*
              וַיַּךְ

נכר   (27) *hiph* הִכִּיר recognize: *imperf* יַכִּיר, *inver imperf* וַיַּכֵּר

נסה   (26) *pi* נִסָּה test, try: *imperf* יְנַסֶּה

נַעַר   (8) *m,* lad, young man: *pl* נְעָרִים, *with suff* נַעֲרִי

נָפַל   (25) fall: *imperf* יִפֹּל

נֶפֶשׁ   (9) *f,* soul, living thing, person; life: *pl* נְפָשׁוֹת, *with suff* נַפְשִׁי

נצל   (25) *hiph* הִצִּיל save, rescue: *imperf* יַצִּיל, *inver imperf* וַיַּצֵּל

נָשָׂא   (25) lift up, raise, carry: *imperf* יִשָּׂא, *niph* נִשָּׂא be lifted up,
              raised

נָתַן   (13) give; set, put; appoint; allow, permit: *imperf* יִתֵּן

ס

סבב   (27) turn; go around, surround: *perf* סָבַב/סַב, *imperf* יִסֹּב/יָסַב,
              inverted imperf וַיִּסֹּב/וַיָּסָב

סָגַר   (25) shut, close: *imperf* יִסְגֹּר

סָפַר   (22) count: *imperf* יִסְפֹּר, *pi* סִפֵּר recount, tell

סֵפֶר   (6) *m,* book: *pl* סְפָרִים, *with suff* סְפָרִי

סֹפֵר   (18) *m,* scribe

סתר   (23) *hitp* הִסְתַּתֵּר hide oneself: *imperf* יִסְתַּתֵּר, *hiph* הִסְתִּיר hide,
              conceal

ע

עָבַד	(13) work, serve: *imperf* יַעֲבֹד
עֶבֶד	(8) *m*, servant, slave: *pl* עֲבָדִים, *with suff* עַבְדִּי
עֲבוֹדָה	(18) *f*, work, service
עָבַר	(15) cross, pass over; transgress: *imperf* יַעֲבֹר
עִבְרִי	(14) *m*, a Hebrew (also Hebrew): *f* עִבְרִיָּה, *pl* עִבְרִים
עַד	(12) to, up to, until: *with suff* עָדַי
עֵדָה	(20) *f*, congregation, assembly
עוֹד	(11) again, yet, still: *with suff* עוֹדֶנִּי/עוֹדִי
עוֹלָם	(12) *m*, eternity: עַד־עוֹלָם/לְעוֹלָם ,וָעֶד לְעוֹלָם forever
עָוֹן	(21) *m*, offence, sin: *pl* עֲוֹנוֹת
עַז	(9) strong, mighty: *pl* עַזִּים
עָזַב	(20) leave, abandon: *imperf* יַעֲזֹב
עָזַר	(19) help: *imperf* יַעֲזֹר (followed by לְ)
עַיִן	(8) *f*, eye: *bound form* עֵין, *dual* עֵינַיִם, *with suff* עֵינִי
עִיר	(9) *f*, city: *pl* עָרִים
עַל	(10) on, over, upon: *with suff* עָלַי
עָלָה	(15) go up, ascend: *imperf* יַעֲלֶה, *inver imperf* וַיַּעַל, *hiph* הֶעֱלָה bring/lead up
עַם	(9) *m*, nation, a people: *with defin art* הָעָם, *with suff* עַמִּי
עִם	(11) with, together with: *with suff* עִמִּי
עָמַד	(14) stand: *imperf* יַעֲמֹד, *hiph* הֶעֱמִיד set upright, set someone standing
עָנָה	(25) answer, respond: *imperf* יַעֲנֶה, *inver imperf* וַיַּעַן
עָפָר	(24) *m*, dust
עֵץ	(15) *m*, tree, wood, stick: *pl* עֵצִים
עֵקֶב	(18) because (often followed by אֲשֶׁר/כִּי)
עֶרֶב	(25) *m*, evening: *pl* עֲרָבִים, *with suff* עַרְבִּי
עָשָׂה	(15) do, make: *imperf* יַעֲשֶׂה, *inver imperf* וַיַּעַשׂ, *niph* נַעֲשָׂה is done
עֶשֶׂר	(28) *f*, ten: עֶשְׂרֵה -teen; *m* עֲשָׂרָה ;עָשָׂר -teen; עֶשְׂרִים twenty
עֵת	(11) *f*, time: *pl* עִתִּים/עִתּוֹת: *with suff* עִתִּי
עַתָּה	(18) now

פ

פֶּה	(11) *m*, mouth: *bound form* פִּי, *pl* פִּיּוֹת, *with suff* פִּיךָ
פֹּה	(12) here
פלט	(22) *pi* פִּלַּט let escape: *imperf* יְפַלֵּט
פלל	(23) *hitp* הִתְפַּלֵּל pray: *imperf* יִתְפַּלֵּל

פֶּן   (20) lest, in order not, so that not

פָּנִים   (10) *pl*, face

פַּעַם   (27) *f*, step, time (= occurrence): *dual* פַּעֲמַיִם twice, *pl* פְּעָמִים

פָּקַד   (19) remember; pay attention, take care of; watch over: *imperf* יִפְקֹד

פרד   (27) *hiph* הִפְרִיד separate, part: *imperf* יַפְרִיד, *inver imperf* וַיַּפְרֵד

פְּרִי   (11) *m*, fruit: *pl* פֵּרוֹת, *with suff* פִּרְיִי

פָּתַח   (21) open: *imperf* יִפְתַּח, *niph* נִפְתַּח be opened

פֶּתַח   (8) *m*, opening, entrance: *pl* פְּתָחִים, *with suff* פִּתְחִי

צ

צָבָא   (6) *m*, army, host: *pl* צְבָאוֹת

צַדִּיק   (5) righteous

צָדַק   (23) be just, righteous: *imperf* יִצְדַּק, *hitp* הִצְטַדֵּק prove oneself to be right, innocent

צֶדֶק   (12) *m*, righteousness, justice: *with suff* צִדְקִי

צְדָקָה   (12) *f*, righteousness

צוה   (22) *pi* צִוָּה command, order: *imperf* יְצַוֶּה, *inver imperf* וַיְצַו

צָחַק   (28) laugh: *imperf* יִצְחַק

ק

קָבַר   (19) bury: *imperf* יִקְבֹּר, *niph* נִקְבַּר be buried

קָדוֹשׁ   (5) holy

קִדֵּשׁ   (22) *pi* קִדֵּשׁ sanctify: *imperf* יְקַדֵּשׁ, *hitp* הִתְקַדֵּשׁ sanctify oneself

קֹדֶשׁ   (10) *m*, holiness: *pl* קֳדָשִׁים/קָדָשִׁים, *with suff* קָדְשִׁי

קוֹל   (10) *m*, voice, sound: *pl* קוֹלוֹת

קוּם   (15) stand up, rise up: *perf* קָם, *imperf* יָקוּם, *inver imperf* וַיָּקָם, *hiph* הֵקִים set up

קָטַל   (13) kill, slay: *imperf* יִקְטֹל

קָטֹן   (13) be/become small, unimportant: *imperf* יִקְטַן

קָטֹן, קָטָן   (12) small, young, unimportant: *f* קְטַנָּה

קָלַל   (15) be/become light, unimportant, despised: *perf* קַל, *imperf* יֵקַל/יָקֹל

קָרָא   (13) call, proclaim, name (followed by לְ), summon; read: *imperf* יִקְרָא, *niph* נִקְרָא be called, be read

קָרַב   (24) come/draw near, approach: *imperf* יִקְרַב, *hiph* הִקְרִיב bring (near), offer

קָרוֹב   (21) near, close

ר

רָאָה   (15) see: *imperf* יִרְאֶה, *inver imperf* וַיַּרְא, *niph* נִרְאָה become visible, appear, *hiph* הֶרְאָה show

רֹאשׁ   (9) *m*, head: *pl* רָאשִׁים

רִאשׁוֹן   (10) first

רֵאשִׁית   (15) *f*, beginning

רַב   (9) numerous, many; great: *pl* רַבִּים

רֶגֶל   (12) *f*, foot: *dual* רַגְלַיִם, *with suff* רַגְלִי

רָדַף   (18) pursue, persecute: *imperf* יִרְדֹּף

רוּחַ   (8) *f*, spirit; wind: *pl* רוּחוֹת

רוּץ   (28) run: *perf* רָץ, *imperf* יָרוּץ, *inver imperf* וַיָּרָץ

רָם   (10) high

רֵעַ   (26) *m*, friend; companion, neighbour: אִשָּׁה.... רְעוּתָהּ/אִישׁ... רֵעֵהוּ 'one... another

רַע   (9) evil, bad, wicked: *pl* רָעִים

רָעָב   (28) *m*, hunger, famine

רָעָה   (11) *f*, evil, trouble, disaster

רעע   (27) be/become bad/displeasing רַע: *imperf* יֵרַע, *hiph* הֵרַע cause evil, harm

רָצַח   (16) kill: *imperf* יִרְצַח

רַק   (14) only, except; surely (intensifier)

רָשָׁע   (7) wicked, criminal, impious, sinful

שׂ

שָׂדֶה   (10) *m*, field: *pl* שָׂדוֹת

שִׂים   (15) put, set; appoint: *perf* שָׂם, *imperf* יָשִׂים, *inver imperf* וַיָּשֶׂם

שָׂנֵא   (20) hate: *imperf* יִשְׂנָא

שִׂנְאָה   (20) *f*, hatred

שָׂרַף   (20) burn: *imperf* יִשְׂרֹף

שׁ

שָׁאַל   (16) ask, inquire; request: *imperf* יִשְׁאַל

שְׁבִיעִי   (28) seventh

שבע   (21) *niph* נִשְׁבַּע swear, take an oath: *imperf* יִשָּׁבַע *hiph* הִשְׁבִּיעַ make swear

שֶׁבַע   (10) *f*, seven: *m* שִׁבְעָה; שִׁבְעִים seventy

שָׁבַר   (21) break: *imperf* יִשְׁבֹּר, *niph* נִשְׁבַּר be broken

שַׁבָּת   (20) *f*, day of rest, Sabbath

שׁוּב   (15) return, come back: *perf* שָׁב, *imperf* יָשׁוּב, *inver imperf* וַיָּשָׁב, *polel* שׁוֹבֵב bring back, restore, refresh

שׁוֹפֵט	(5) *m*, judge
שִׁיר	(6) *m*, song
שָׁכַב	(18) lie down: *imperf* יִשְׁכַּב
שָׁכַח	(19) forget: *imperf* יִשְׁכַּח
שָׁכֵן	(15) dwell: *imperf* יִשְׁכֹּן, *pi* שִׁכֵּן let/make someone dwell
שָׁלוֹם	(12) *m*, peace; well-being
שָׁלַח	(14) send; שָׁלַח יָד stretch out one's hand: *imperf* יִשְׁלַח, *pi* שִׁלַּח send away, let go
שׁלך	(24) *hiph* הִשְׁלִיךְ throw, cast: *imperf* יַשְׁלִיךְ, *inver imperf* וַיַּשְׁלֵךְ
שָׁלֵם	(5) perfect, whole, complete, sound
שָׁלֹשׁ	(24) *f,* three: *m* שְׁלֹשָׁה; שְׁלֹשִׁים thirty
שֵׁם	(10) *m*, name: *pl* שֵׁמוֹת
שָׁם	(14) there
שָׁמַיִם	(10) heaven/s, sky
שְׁמֹנֶה	(28) *f,* eight: *m* שְׁמֹנָה; שְׁמֹנִים eighty
שָׁמַע	(13) hear, listen; understand: *imperf* יִשְׁמַע; שָׁמַע בְּקוֹל/לְקוֹל obey, *hiph* הִשְׁמִיעַ cause to hear, announce
שָׁמַר	(13) guard, keep, watch: *imperf* יִשְׁמֹר, *niph* נִשְׁמַר be guarded, be on one's guard, be careful, *hitp* הִשְׁתַּמֵּר be on one's guard
שֶׁמֶשׁ	(11) *f,* sun: *with suff* שִׁמְשִׁי
שָׁנָה	(11) *f,* year: *pl* שָׁנִים/שָׁנוֹת
שֵׁנִי	(27) second, *f* שְׁנִיָּה
שְׁנַיִם	(9) *m*, two: *bound form* שְׁנֵי, *f* שְׁתַּיִם; שְׁנֵים עָשָׂר twelve (*m*)
שַׁעַר	(8) *m*, gate: *pl* שְׁעָרִים, *with suff* שַׁעֲרִי
שָׁפַט	(16) judge: *imperf* יִשְׁפֹּט
שׁרת	(22) *pi* שֵׁרֵת serve, minister: *imperf* יְשָׁרֵת
שֵׁשׁ	(28) *f,* six: *m* שִׁשָּׁה; שִׁשִּׁים sixty
שָׁתָה	(28) drink: *imperf* יִשְׁתֶּה, *inverted imperf* וַיֵּשְׁתְּ
שְׁתַּיִם	*f,* two: *bound form* שְׁתֵּי, *m* שְׁנַיִם; שְׁתֵּים עֶשְׂרֵה twelve (*f*)

ת

תָּוֶךְ	(21) *m*, midst, middle: *bound form* תּוֹךְ, בְּתוֹךְ in the midst of
תּוֹרָה	(5) *f,* instruction, teaching, law: Law
תַּחַת	(11) under; instead/in place of: *with suff* תַּחְתַּי
תָּמִים/תָּם	(15) perfect, complete, whole: *pl* תְּמִים
תמם	(27) be finished/completed: *perf* תַּם, *imperf* יִתַּם/יִתֹּם
תְּפִלָּה	(17) *f,* prayer
תִּקְוָה	(9) *f,* hope
תֵּשַׁע	(28) *f,* nine: *m* תִּשְׁעָה; תִּשְׁעִים ninety

ENGLISH–HEBREW VOCABULARY

The number in parentheses refers to the section in which the word is introduced in a translation exercise from English into Hebrew

about (13)	עַל	call (13)	קָרָא
add, continue *hiph* (26)	הוֹסִיף	carry (25)	נָשָׂא
afraid (18)	יָרֵא	child (9)	יֶלֶד
after (21)	אַחֲרֵי	choose (14)	בָּחַר
all (10)	כָּל־	city (9)	עִיר
also (15)	גַּם	come (15)	בּוֹא
among (7)	בְּ	command *pi* (22)	צִוָּה
and (8)	וְ	commandment (7)	מִצְוָה
angel (20)	מַלְאָךְ	country (11)	אֶרֶץ
anoint (16)	מָשַׁח	covenant (13)	בְּרִית
appearance (10)	מַרְאֶה	cut (13)	כָּרַת
army (6)	צָבָא		
as (7)	כְּ	daughter (10)	בַּת
as follows (23)	לֵאמֹר	day (7)	יוֹם
ask (20)	שָׁאַל	death (15)	מָוֶת
ask for (request) (23)	שָׁאַל	desert (22)	מִדְבָּר
at (13)	בְּ	die (27)	מוּת
		do (18)	עָשָׂה
battle (21)	מִלְחָמָה	dwell (reside) (15)	שָׁכַן/יָשַׁב
be (was/were) (15)	הָיָה		
bear (child) (24)	יָלַד	each (11)	כָּל־
beautiful (10)	יָפֶה	ear (20)	אֹזֶן
because (21)	עֵקֶב כִּי/אֲשֶׁר	eat (14)	אָכַל
before (16)	לִפְנֵי	Egypt (13)	מִצְרַיִם
beget (24)	הוֹלִיד	elder *noun* (7)	זָקֵן
big (6)	גָּדוֹל	entrance (19)	פֶּתַח
bless *pi* (22)	בֵּרַךְ	escape *niph* (21)	נִמְלַט
book (13)	סֵפֶר	every (10)	כָּל־
bread (14)	לֶחֶם	evil (23)	רַע
brother (6)	אָח	eye (9)	עַיִן
build (15)	בָּנָה		
bury (21)	קָבַר	father (10)	אָב
by (21)	בְּ	favour (27)	חֵן

fear (14)	יָרֵא
field (10)	שָׂדֶה
fill *be/become full* (14)	מָלֵא
find (14)	מָצָא
for (14)	לְ
forever (12)	עַד־עוֹלָם
forget (21)	שָׁכַח
from (7)	מִ/⬚/מִן
gate (8)	שַׁעַר
give (13)	נָתַן
glory (14)	כָּבוֹד
go (14)	הָלַךְ
go back (27)	שׁוּב
go into exile (24)	גָּלָה
go out (14)	יָצָא
go up (25)	עָלָה
God (6)	אֱלֹהִים
gods (17)	אֱלֹהִים
gold (13)	זָהָב
good (6)	טוֹב
great (6)	גָּדוֹל
guard (18)	שָׁמַר
guard *noun* (21)	שֹׁמֵר/שׁוֹמֵר
hand (10)	יָד
have (9)	(יֵשׁ) לְ
he (6)	הוּא
head (28)	רֹאשׁ
hear (13)	שָׁמַע
heart (15)	לֵב
heaven (13)	שָׁמַיִם
Hebrew *noun* (14)	עִבְרִי
help *verb* (19)	עָזַר
here (12)	פֹּה
hide oneself *hitp* (23)	הִסְתַּתֵּר
holy (6)	קָדוֹשׁ

house (10)	בַּיִת
husband (14)	בַּעַל
I (6)	אֲנִי/אָנֹכִי
if (27)	אִם
in (7)	בְּ
in order that (23)	לְמַעַן אֲשֶׁר
	בַּעֲבוּר אֲשֶׁר
in order that not (21)	פֶּן
inherit (24)	יָרַשׁ
it *m* (7)	הוּא
judge *verb* (18)	שָׁפַט
judge *noun* (7)	שֹׁפֵט/שׁוֹפֵט
keep (16)	שָׁמַר
kill (21)	הָרַג
kindness (10)	חֶסֶד
king (6)	מֶלֶךְ
know (25)	יָדַע
land (7)	אֶרֶץ
law (11)	תּוֹרָה/חֹק
Law (7)	תּוֹרָה
learn (16)	לָמַד
life (20)	חַיִּים
like (9)	כְּ
listen (13)	שָׁמַע
look! (14)	הִנֵּה
Lord = YHWH (6)	יהוה
love *verb* (18)	אָהַב
make (19)	עָשָׂה
man (7)	אָדָם
man/person (8)	אִישׁ
many (9)	רַב
master (7)	אָדוֹן

matter (28)	דָּבָר	request (23)	שָׁאַל
messenger (20)	מַלְאָךְ	rescue *hiph* (26)	הִצִּיל
money (15)	כֶּסֶף	return (21)	שׁוּב
morning (14)	בֹּקֶר	righteous (6)	צַדִּיק
mother (10)	אֵם	road (7)	דֶּרֶךְ
mountain (14)	הַר	rule (as king) (13)	מָלַךְ
nation, a people (10)	עַם	sanctuary (10)	מִקְדָּשׁ
new (7)	חָדָשׁ	say (13)	אָמַר
night (14)	לַיְלָה	see (18)	רָאָה
not (8)	לֹא	seek *pi* (23)	בִּקֵּשׁ
now (18)	עַתָּה	send (14)	שָׁלַח
		send *pi* (22)	שִׁלַּח
old (6)	זָקֵן	servant (19)	עֶבֶד
on (14)	עַל	serve (17)	עָבַד
ordinance (17)	מִשְׁפָּט	serve (minister) *pi* (22)	שֵׁרֵת
other (15)	אַחֵר	seventy (28)	שִׁבְעִים
over (13)	עַל	she (10)	הִיא
		silver (13)	כֶּסֶף
palace (14)	הֵיכָל	sinful (9)	רָשָׁע
pass through (26)	עָבַר	sister (12)	אָחוֹת
people/nation (13)	עַם	sit (18)	יָשַׁב
persecute (18)	רָדַף	sky (14)	שָׁמַיִם
place (9)	מָקוֹם	slave (15)	עֶבֶד
please (17)	נָא	soil (7)	אֲדָמָה
praise (22)	הִלֵּל	son (9)	בֵּן
pray *hitp* (23)	הִתְפַּלֵּל	soul (11)	נֶפֶשׁ
priest (19)	כֹּהֵן	speak *pi* (23)	דִּבֶּר
prophet (6)	נָבִיא	stand (14)	עָמַד
prophetess (18)	נְבִיאָה	statute (11)	חֹק
pursue (21)	רָדַף	strong (9)	עַז
put (27)	שִׂים	swear *niph* (21)	נִשְׁבַּע
		sword (7)	חֶרֶב
read (13)	קָרָא		
refuse *pi* (22)	מֵאֵן	tabernacle (14)	מִשְׁכָּן
reign (as king) (20)	מָלַךְ	take (14)	לָקַח
remember (16)	זָכַר	talk *pi* (27)	דִּבֶּר

teach *pi* (22)	לִמֵּד	we (6)	אֲנַ֫חְנוּ
temple (12)	הֵיכָל	well-being, peace (23)	שָׁלוֹם
than (6)	מִ ·/מִן	what? (12)	מָה, מַה־·
that (man, thing) *m* (8)	הַהוּא	when (+ *infin*) (19)	בְּ
the (6)	הַ ·	where from? (12)	מֵאַ֫יִן
then (13)	אָז	where? (12)	אִיפֹה/אַיֵּה
there (14)	שָׁם	where to? (14)	אָן/אָ֫נָה
there is/are (9)	יֵשׁ	which *relative pron* (15)	אֲשֶׁר
there is/are not (9)	אֵין	while (+ *infin*) (26)	בְּ
these (8)	אֵ֫לֶּה	who *relative pron* (17)	אֲשֶׁר
they *m* (6)	הֵם/הֵ֫מָּה	who? (12)	מִי
thing (15)	דָּבָר	whole (10)	כָּל־
this *m* (8)	זֶה	why (13)	לָ֫מָּה/לָמָה
this *f* (9)	זֹאת	wife (9)	אִשָּׁה
three (28)	שָׁלֹשׁ	wilderness (22)	מִדְבָּר
throne (12)	כִּסֵּא	wise (6)	חָכָם
thus (14)	כֹּה	with (11)	אֵת־/עִם
to (13)	לְ	woman (9)	אִשָּׁה
today (18)	הַיּוֹם	word (7)	דָּבָר
towards (14)	אֶל־	work (13)	עָבַד
tree (15)	עֵץ	write (16)	כָּתַב
two *m* (28)	שְׁנַ֫יִם		
two *f* (15)	שְׁתַּ֫יִם	year (28)	שָׁנָה
		you *m singular* (6)	אַתָּה
until (15)	עַד	you *f singular* (14)	אַתְּ
upon (10)	עַל	you *m plural* (6)	אַתֶּם
upright (7)	יָשָׁר	young man (25)	נַ֫עַר
very (7)	מְאֹד		
vessel (25)	כְּלִי		
vicious (17)	רַע		
voice (13)	קוֹל		
walk (28)	הָלַךְ		
war (21)	מִלְחָמָה		
water (21)	מַ֫יִם		
way (11)	דֶּ֫רֶךְ		

KEY TO THE EXERCISES[1]

SECTION 1

Page 3, **Exercise 1.2**

1 ʔlf byt gyml dlt hʔ ww zyn ḥyt ṭyt ywd kf
2 lmd mym nwn smx ʕyn pʔ ṣdy qwf ryš śyn šyn tw
3 ʔdm yʕqv dvwrh ḥwh yśrʔl šmwʔl qyn lʔh ʔsf
4 rḥl byt ʔl šm šmʕwn ḥnh yft gd šʔwl ʕvr lwy
5 dwd ʔvrhm yhwdh ʔvšlwm lwṭ ywsf ntn śrh bnymyn

Page 7, **Exercise 1.5**

1 נחום, ירושלים, אמן, עמרם, שלם, צבאות, שלם, יוכבד, יוסף, כהן, יהונתן,
יהושפט, קבוץ, פתח תקוה, בעל, חברון, אחימלך, עזה, ראש פנה.

2 הללויה, עמנואל, טבריה, שלום, אפרים, באר שבע, הר סיני, משנה,
חזקיה, שומרון, תלמוד, עזיה, יעל, יהודית, כפר נחום, הבה נגילה,
בית חסדא.

3 ישי, אל על, יזרעאל, ירדן, לוי, ברית מילה, לחיים, מסורה, בת שבע,
יהודה איש קריות, שדה בוקר, בני ברית, בר מצוה, גלגלת (גלגתא),
למה עזבתני.

Page 10, **Exercise 1.7**

1 Adam Jacob Deborah Eve Israel Samuel Cain
2 Leah Asaph Abel Rachel Bethel Simeon Shem
3 Hannah Japhet Abraham Saul Eber Moses Gad
4 Judah Absalom Joseph Solomon Sarah Benjamin Nathan
5 Hagar Abimelech Isaac Pharaoh Hezekiah Lamech Levi
6 Johanan Laban Miriam Zedekiah Rebekah Canaan Esau
7 Michael Manasseh Ishmael Bethlehem

SECTION 2

Page 15, **Exercise 2.3**

1 דבר אל אהרן ואל בניו לאמר כה תברכו את בני ישראל אמור להם.
יברכך יהוה וישמרך. יאר יהוה פניו אליך ויחנך. ישא יהוה פניו אליך
וישם לך שלום. ושמו את שמי על בני ישראל ואני אברכם. (Num. 6:23–27)

2 לכל זמן ועת לכל חפץ תחת השמים. עת ללדת ועת למות. עת להרוג
ועת לרפוא. עת לשמור ועת להשליך. עת לאהב ועת לשנא. עת מלחמה
ועת שלום. (Ecc. 3:1–3, 6, 8)

---

[1] The word stress is normally not marked in the Key.

3 וְהָיָה בְּאַחֲרִית הַיָּמִים נָכוֹן יִהְיֶה הַר בֵּית יְהוָה בְּרֹאשׁ הֶהָרִים וְנִשָּׂא מִגְּבָעוֹת וְנָהֲרוּ אֵלָיו כָּל הַגּוֹיִם. וְהָלְכוּ עַמִּים רַבִּים וְאָמְרוּ לְכוּ וְנַעֲלֶה אֶל הַר יְהוָה אֶל בֵּית אֱלֹהֵי יַעֲקֹב וְיֹרֵנוּ מִדְּרָכָיו וְנֵלְכָה בְּאֹרְחֹתָיו כִּי מִצִּיּוֹן תֵּצֵא תוֹרָה וּדְבַר יְהוָה מִירוּשָׁלִָם. וְשָׁפַט בֵּין הַגּוֹיִם וְהוֹכִיחַ לְעַמִּים רַבִּים וְכִתְּתוּ חַרְבוֹתָם לְאִתִּים וַחֲנִיתוֹתֵיהֶם לְמַזְמֵרוֹת. לֹא יִשָּׂא גוֹי אֶל גּוֹי חֶרֶב וְלֹא יִלְמְדוּ עוֹד מִלְחָמָה. (Isa. 2:2–4)

Page 15, **Exercise 2.4**

Hardening dagesh (dagesh lene)

1 וְ|תָּ|רָה, |דְּ|בָרִים, |בְּ|רֵאשִׁית, |דְּ|בְרֵי הַיָּמִים.

2 |תְּ|הִלִּים, |בַּ|מִּ|דְבָּ|ר, אֶסְ|תֵּ|ר.

Doubling dagesh (dagesh forte)

1 שִׁיר הַ|שִּׁ|ירִים, חֲבַ|קּ|וּק, דִּבְרֵי הַ|יָּ|מִים.

2 תְּהִ|לּ|ים, חַ|גַּ|י, וַ|יִּ|קְרָא, אִ|יּ|וֹב, בַּ|מִּ|דְבָּר.

Page 16, **Exercise 2.5**

1 יְה|וּ|דְ|י|ת, כְּפַר נַ|חַ|וּ|ם, י|וֹ|ם, |יוֹ| כֶבֶד, צִדְקִ|יָּ|ה |וּ|, צְפַנְ|יָ|ה, שֶׁמֶשׁ |וֹ| ן

2 פֶּתַח תִּקְוָ|ה| |וָ|ת, צָבָ|וֹ|א, אָחִ|י| מֶלֶךְ, לֵוִ|י|, מִשְׁנָ|ה|, שָׁל|וֹ| ם

3 יְה|וֹ| נָתָן, מְנַשֶׁ|ה|, י|וֹ| נָ|ה|, שְׁ|י| ר הַשּׁ|י| רִ|י| ם.

Page 16, **Exercise 2.7**

1 Jerusalem Amen Bathsheba Masorah Salem Cohen Jonathan
2 Jehoshaphat Kibbutz Baal Bar mitzvah Ahimelech Gaza Immanuel
3 Ephraim Beer-sheba Sinai Mishnah Samaria Talmud Uzziah
4 Jael Judith Capernaum Hávah nagílah Jesse El Al Jordan
5 Brith milah Hebron Lamah azavtáni (think of 'Eli, Eli, lama sabachthani')

SECTION 3

Page 21, **Review & Application I**

← 7 וְדָ| ד |ְ 3 ט| ל |וֹ 8 ה| ֶ |עַ 6 חַ| כֹ 1 ד| ְ |יָ 4 מוּאֵל |שׁ 10 סִ| נַ |י

5 לוּל אָ| ֲ 2 ר| עַ |שׁ 9 שׁ אָ| ר

Page 22, **Review & Application II:** 9, 10, 8, 7, 2, 4, 3, 5, 1, 6

Page 23, **Exercise 3.1**

1 yᵉrûšālayim ʔāmēn bat ševa ʕ māsôrā h šālēm kōhēn yᵉhônātān
2 yᵉhôšāfāṭ qibbûṣ baʕal bar miṣwā h ʔᵃhîmelex ʕazzā h ʕimmānûʔēl
3 ʔefrayim bᵉʔēr ševaʕ sînay mišnā h šômrôn talmûd ʕuzziyyā h
4 yāʕēl yᵉhûdît kᵉfar naḥûm hāvā h nāgîlā h yišay ʔel ʕal yardēn
5 bᵉrît mîlā h ḥevrôn lāmā h ʕᵃzavtanî

Page 23, **Exercise 3.2**

1 ḥᵃvaqqûq ʔᵃḥîmelex ʔᵃnî ʔᵃnaḥnû ʔᵃdāmāʰ ḥᵃxāmîm
   ʔᵃrāṣôt ḥᵃrāvôt ʕᵃvādîm ḥᵃxāmāʰ ʔᵃlāfîm ʔᵃḥāyôt
   ʔᵃvîmelex ʕᵃvôdāʰ ʕᵃrāvîm ḥᵃzāqāʰ ḥᵃdāšôt ḥᵃsādîm
2 ʔahᵃvāʰ ʔaḥᵃrê yaʕᵃqōv maʕᵃśeʰ maḥᵃneʰ
3 ʔᵉnôš ʔᵉlōhîm ʔᵉmet ʔᵉmûnāʰ ʔᵉlûl
4 ḥᵒdāšîm ʔᵒḥālîm
5 hôšēₐʕ rûₐḥ zᵊrôₐʕ māšîₐḥ mizbēₐḥ rēₐʕ

Page 23, **Exercise 3.3**

1 yáḥad báʕal náʕar šáʕar táḥat kᵊnáʕan lᵊmáʕan
   páʕam yáʕan pétaḥ šévaʕ pésaḥ zéraʕ śóvaʕ
2 qáyin ḥáyil ʔáyin báyit máyim ʕáyin
   yáyin ʕênáyim šᵊnáyim šāmáyim miṣráyim yômáyim
   yādáyim yᵊrûšāláyim ʔefráyim

Page 24, **Exercise 3.4**

1 He [is] Abraham **2** I [am a] lord **3** I [am a] father **4** He [is] Amram
5 He [is a] priest **6** She [is] Judith **7** You [are] Satan **8** Absalom [is a]
priest **9** You [are] Messiah **10** You [are] Peninnah

SECTION 4

Page 27, **Review & Application I**

→ 8 ⟨ת⟩ ⟨לֵ⟩ ⟨לְ⟩ קֻה 7 כִּי ⟨נ⟩ אָ 9 תְּר ⟨ס⟩ אֶ 6 ⟨א⟩ א הוּ 11 אָ סְנָת ⟨א⟩ בִּיאִם 3 ⟨נ⟩
5 ה ⟨ת⟩ א 4 ⟨א⟩ נִי 1 הֶן ⟨כ⟩ 2 ⟨ח⟩ פְּת 10 ⟨דַ⟩ יְ

Page 27, **Review & Application II:** 3, 9, 1, 2, 10, 4, 7, 5, 6, 8

Page 28, **Exercise 4.1**

Silent shva (the original no-vowel)

1 ⟨כ⟩ לָה 2 וַיִּ ⟨ק⟩ רָא, ⟨ד⟩ בָּר, יִ ⟨ר⟩ מְיָהוּ 3 יֵשׁ ⟨ע⟩ יָהוּ.

Vocal shva (shva-reduced-vowel)

1 ⟨אֱ⟩ ⟨ס⟩ פוּ, ⟨נ⟩ בִיאִם, ⟨כ⟩ תוּבִים, ⟨בּ⟩ רֵאשִׁית, ⟨יְ⟩ הוֹשֻׁעַ, ⟨שׁ⟩ מוֹת.
2 שׁוֹ ⟨פ⟩ טִים, ⟨תְּ⟩ הִלִּים, ⟨שׁ⟩ מוּאֵל, ⟨מְ⟩ לָכִים, יִרְ ⟨מְ⟩ יָהוּ.
3 ⟨דְ⟩ בָרִים, ⟨יְ⟩ שַׁעְיָהוּ, אָ ⟨כ⟩ לָה.

1 ʔāsᵊfû ʔoxlāʰ nᵊvîʔîm kᵊtûvîm bᵊrēʔšît yᵊhôšuₐʕ šᵊmôt
2 šôfᵊṭîm tᵊhillîm wayyiqrāʔ šᵊmûʔēl bammidbār mᵊlāxîm yirmᵊyāhû
3 dᵊvārîm yᵊšaʕyāhû ʔāxᵊlāʰ

Page 28, **Exercise 4.2**

1 חֲבַק-קוּק (ק=קק), אֲחִי-מֶ-לֶךְ, אֲנִי, אֲנַחְ-נוּ, אֲדָ-מָה, חֲכָ-מִים,

אֲרָ-צוֹת, חֲרָ-בוֹת, עֲבָ-דִים, חֲכָ-מָה, אֱלָ-פִים, אֲחָ-יוֹת,

אֲבִי-מֶ-לֶךְ, עֲבוֹ-דָה, עֲרָ-בִים, חֲזָ-קָה, חֲדָ-שׁוֹת, חֲסָ-דִים.

3   אֱנוֹשׁ, אֱלֹ-הִים, אֱמֶת, אֱמוּ-נָה, אֱלוּל.

4   חֳדָ-שִׁים, אֳהָ-לִים.

5   הוֹ-שֵׁעַ, רוּחַ, זְרוֹעַ, מָ-שִׁיחַ, מִזְ-בֵּחַ, רֵעַ.

Page 28, **Exercise 4.3**

Abbreviations: **UC** = unstressed closed syllable (**always** takes a **short** vowel).
UO = unstressed open syllable, **SC** = stressed closed syllable and **SO** =
stressed open syllable (**generally** take a **long** vowel).

1 šā-lēm: šā (UO), lēm (SC) -- ʔav-šā-lôm: ʔav (UC), šā (UO), lôm (SC) --
nim-rōd: nim (UC), rōd (SC) -- yiṣ-ḥāq: yiṣ (UC), ḥāq (SC) --
ʕim-mā-nû-ʔēl: ʕim (UC), mā (UO), nû (UO), ʔēl (SC) -- ʔel-qā-nā^h: ʔel
(UC), qā (UO), nā^h (SO) -- gᵊdal-yā^h: gᵊdal (UC), yā^h (SO).

2 yô-nā^h: yô (UO), nā^h (SO) -- yā-ʕēl: yā (UO), ʕēl (SC) -- yif-tāḥ: yif (UC), tāḥ
(SC) -- bᵊnê bᵊrît: bᵊnê (UO), bᵊrît (SC) -- dᵊvô-rā^h: dᵊvô (UO), rā^h (SO) --
ʕam-rām: ʕam (UC), rām (SC) -- dān: dān (SC) -- yô-ḥā-nān: yô (UO), ḥā
(UO), nān (SC).

3 sᵊdôm: sᵊdôm (SC) -- ʕᵃmō-rā^h: ʕᵃmō (UO), rā^h(SO) -- rā-ḥēl: rā (UO), ḥēl
(SC) -- šā-ṭān: šā (UO), ṭān (SC) -- ʔā-sāf: ʔā (UO), sāf (SC) -- yô-sēf: yô
(UO), sēf (SC) -- nā-tān: nā (UO), tān (SC) -- yᵊhû-dā^h: yᵊhû (UO), dā^h (SO).

Page 29, **Exercise 4.4**

1 יְ-חַד   בַּ-עַל   נַ-עַר   שַׁ-עַר   תַּ-חַת   כְּנַ-עַן   לְמֶ-עַן
פַּ-עַם   יַ-עַן   פֶּ-תַח   שֶׁ-בַע   פֶּ-סַח   זֶ-רַע   שַׁ-בַע

2 קַ-יִן   חַ-יִל   אַ-יִן   בַּ-יִת   מַ-יִם   עַ-יִן
יַ-יִן   עֵי-נַ-יִם   שְׁנַ-יִם   שָׁ-מַ-יִם   מִצְ-רַ-יִם   יוֹ-מַ-יִם
יָ-דַ-יִם   יְרוּ-שָׁ-לַ-יִם   אֶפְ-רַ-יִם.

The common feature of syllables with deviant vocalization: A stressed open
syllable with an /e/- or /a/-vowel in words with the stress on the next-to-last
syllable has a short instead of a long vowel.

Page 29, **Exercise 4.5**

2 אַ-הֲבָה, אַ-חֲרֵי, יַ-עֲקֹב, מַ-עֲשֶׂה, מַ-חֲנֶה.

The common feature of syllables with deviant vocalization: An unstressed
open syllable immediately before a chateph (shva-plus-vowel) has a short
instead of a long vowel.

Page 29, **Exercise 4.6**

1 I [am] God/[a] god   **2** She [is] Deborah   **3** You [are] Leah   **4** I [am]
Jonah **5** David [is a] father **6** Moses [is a] priest **7** He [is a] lord
8 It [is a] covenant.

Page 30, Exercise 4.7 (Gen. 17:3–8)

1 וַיִּפֹּל אַבְרָם עַל פָּנָיו וַיְדַבֵּר אִתּוֹ אֱלֹהִים לֵאמֹר.

2 וְהָיִיתָ לְאַב הֲמוֹן גּוֹים (Gen. 17:4, the first part of the verse is omitted).

3 וְלֹא יִקָּרֵא עוֹד אֶת שִׁמְךָ אַבְרָם וְהָיָה שִׁמְךָ אַבְרָהָם כִּי אַב הֲמוֹן גּוֹים נְתַתִּיךָ.

4 וְהִפְרֵתִי אֹתְךָ בִּמְאֹד מְאֹד וּנְתַתִּיךָ לְגוֹים וּמְלָכִים מִמְּךָ יֵצֵאוּ.

5 וַהֲקִמֹתִי אֶת בְּרִיתִי בֵּינִי וּבֵינֶךָ וּבֵין זַרְעֲךָ אַחֲרֶיךָ לְדֹרֹתָם לִבְרִית עוֹלָם לִהְיוֹת לְךָ לֵאלֹהִים וּלְזַרְעֲךָ אַחֲרֶיךָ.

6 וְנָתַתִּי לְךָ וּלְזַרְעֲךָ אַחֲרֶיךָ אֵת אֶרֶץ מְגֻרֶיךָ אֵת כָּל אֶרֶץ כְּנַעַן לַאֲחֻזַּת עוֹלָם וְהָיִיתִי לָהֶם לֵאלֹהִים.

SECTION 5

Page 34, Review & Application I

→ 10 ת עַ שׁוֹמֵ 4 לְמִים שָׁ 6 לוֹמוֹת חָ 9 ת בְ כּוֹת 7 בָה וֹ ט

הֵ הֵיכָל 3 קוֹ רְ אִים 5 הָ 2 אֵל קָ יְ ז 11 רְ אָ שִׂים 8 הַ צְ דִיק 1

Page 36, Exercise 5.3

1 שְׁלֵמָה, שְׁלֵמִים, שְׁלֵמוֹת 2 זְקֵנָה, זְקֵנִים, זְקֵנוֹת 3 קְדוֹשָׁה, קְדוֹשִׁים, קְדוֹשׁוֹת 4 טוֹבָה, טוֹבִים, טוֹבוֹת 5 חֲכָמָה, חֲכָמִים, חֲכָמוֹת 6 צַדִּיקָה, צַדִּיקִים, צַדִּיקוֹת 7 יְשָׁרָה, יְשָׁרִים, יְשָׁרוֹת

Page 36, Exercise 5.4

1 nᵊvî-ʔîm ʔᵃnaḥ-nû 2 ḥᵃxā-mîm hēm 3 ʔat-tēn haš-šô-fᵊtôt
4 ʔᵃdô-nîm hēm 5 ʔē-lîm ʔat-tem 6 ṣad-dî-qîm ʔᵃnaḥ-nû 7 ʔat-tem
hā-ʔā-vôt 8 ʔᵃnaḥ-nû hak-kō-hᵃnîm 9 ṭô-vôt hēn-nāʰ 10 šᵊlē-mîm
ʔat-tem 11 yᵊšā-rîm hān-nᵊvî-ʔîm 12 ham-mᵊlā-xîm zᵊqē-nîm hēm
13 gᵊdô-lîm ʔᵃnaḥ-nû 14 qᵊdô-šîm hēm hā-ʔē-lîm 15 han-nᵊvî-ʔôt
ṭô-vôt hēn-nāʰ

Page 37, Exercise 5.5 (אֲנִי = אָנֹכִי)

I [am a] prophet נָבִיא אָנִי 1	She [is] good טוֹבָה הִיא 9
He [is] wise חָכָם הוּא 2	You [are] perfect שָׁלֵם אַתָּה 10
You [are] the judge אַתְּ הַשּׁוֹפֶטֶת 3	The prophet [is] honest יָשָׁר הַנָּבִיא 11
He [is a] lord אָדוֹן הוּא 4	The king [is] old הַמֶּלֶךְ זָקֵן הוּא 12
You [are] God/[a] god אֵל אַתָּה 5	I [am] great גָּדוֹל אֲנִי 13
I [am] righteous צַדִּיק אֲנִי 6	God (= the god) [is] holy קָדוֹשׁ הוּא הָאֵל 14
You [are] the father אַתָּה הָאָב 7	The prophetess [is] good הַנְּבִיאָה טוֹבָה הִיא 15
I [am] the priest אֲנִי הַכֹּהֵן 8	

SECTION 6

Page 40, **Review & Application I**

➡ 9 ס $\boxed{\text{יִ}}$ עֵינַ֫ 1 בִיא $\boxed{\text{נְ}}$ מְ 10 $\boxed{\text{א}}$ לֹ 8 ר $\boxed{\text{עַ}}$ נַ 6 שׁ $\boxed{\text{וֹ}}$ קָד 5 רים $\boxed{\text{מְ}}$ שׁ

7 ר $\boxed{\text{פְּ}}$ סְ 3 פָּרִים $\boxed{\text{סְ}}$ 4 בודות $\boxed{\text{עַ}}$ 2 אָדָם $\boxed{\text{מֵ}}$

Page 41, **Exercise 6.1**

1 [A] great man [is] in Israel. The great man [is] in Israel. **2** Solomon [is a] great king **3** The law [is] holy. **4** Noah [is a] righteous man. **5** The hosts [are] big. **6** Solomon the great [is a] king. **7** The wise [one/man is] from Bethlehem. [A] wise [one/man is] from Bethlehem. **8** The wise king [is] upright. **9** The righteous [one/man is a] good man. The good man [is] righteous. **10** The old master [is] from Beer-sheba. The master from Beer-sheba [is] old.

Page 42, **Exercise 6.2**

1 -- הַצַּדִּיקִים -- מֵהַמְּלָכִים --

The prophets [are as] righteous as the kings. The prophets [are more] righteous than the kings. The prophets [are] (the) [most] righteous.

2 -- הַחֲכָמִים -- מִמְּלָכִים --

The judges [are as] wise as kings. The judges [are] wiser (= wise) than kings. The judges [are] (the) wisest (= wise).

3 -- בַּתּוֹרוֹת הַגְּדוֹלָה -- מֵהַתַּלְמוּד --

The Law [is as] important as the Talmud. The Law [is more] important than the Talmud. The Law [is] the [most] important of laws (= among the laws).

4 -- הֶחָכָם -- מִדָּוִד --

Solomon [is as] wise as David. Solomon [is] wiser (= wise) than David. Solomon [is] (the) wisest (= wise).

5 -- הַשָּׁלֵם -- מֵהָאָדָם --

(The) man [is as] perfect as [a] god. God [is more] perfect than (the) man. God [is] (the) [most] perfect.

6 -- בַּמְּלָכִים הַזָּקֵן -- מֵהַכֹּהֵן --

The king [is as] old as the priest. The king [is] old[er] than the priest. The king [is] the old[est] of kings (= among the kings).

7 -- הַקָּדוֹשׁ -- מֵאָדָם --

[A] god [is as] holy as [a] man. [A] god [is] holier (= holy) than [a] man. The god/God [is] (the) holiest (= holy). ·

8 -- סֵפֶר הַסְּפָרִים -- הַטּוֹב -- מִשִּׁיר --

The book [is as] good as [a] song. The book [is] better (= good) than [a] song. The book [is] (the) best (= good). It [is] the book [of] books = the best of books.

9 -- הַיָּשָׁר -- מִמֶּלֶךְ --

The prophet [is as] honest as [a] king. The prophet [is more] honest than [a] king. The prophet [is] (the) [most] honest.

10 -- מֵאַשְׁקְלוֹן -- הַגְּדוֹלָה
Jerusalem [is as] big as Ashkelon. Jerusalem [is] big[ger] than Ashkelon.
Jerusalem [is] (the) big[gest].

Page 43, Exercise 6.3

I. 1 He [is] the king.　**2** The man Moses [was] great.　**3** You [are] the man.
4 I [am] the Lord.　**5** Noah [was a] righteous man.　**6** The Lord [is] God
(= the god).　**7** We [are] wise.　**8** Holy, holy, holy [is] the Lord [of] hosts.
II. 9 David [was] old.　**10** We [are] brothers.　**11** Righteous [are] you, Lord.
12 They [are] wise.　**13** He [is a] prophet.　**14** God [is] not man.
15 I [am] holy.　**16** You [are] wiser (= wise) than Daniel.

Page 44, Exercise 6.4

➤ חְנוּ ‏‎ אַ ‎ נַ in pause: The short vowel in the stressed syllable is lengthened.

נִי ‏‎ אַ ‎ in pause: The reduced vowel (i.e., the chateph) reverts to a short vowel
and is lengthened. The stress is thrown back to the next-to-last syllable.

Page 44, Exercise 6.5

I. 1 צַדִּיק אֲנִי/אָנֹכִי.　2 מֶלֶךְ חָכָם אַתָּה.　3 אֱלֹהִים (הוּא) גָּדוֹל.
4 הַצְּבָאוֹת גְּדוֹלִים (הֵם/הֵמָּה).　5 קְדוֹשִׁים אֲנַחְנוּ.
II. 6 זְקֵנִים אַתֶּם.　7 זָקֵן הוּא מְדָוִיד.　8 הֵם/הֵמָּה הַנְּבִיאִים הַצַּדִּיקִים.
9 טוֹבִים אַתֶּם מֵהַמֶּלֶךְ.　10 יהוה (הוּא) הַטּוֹב.

SECTION 7

Page 47, Review & Application I

1 לִנְבִיאָה (1)　**2** כִּכְלִי (7 ,1)　**3** מִסֵּפֶר (3)　**4** בִּירוּשָׁלַיִם (4 ,1)
5 כָּאֲדָמָה (2)　**6** לַצָּבָא (5)　**7** בַּחֲרָבוֹת (2)　**8** מֵהַשִּׁיר (6 ,3)
9 לַעֲבָדִים (2)　**10** כָּאִישׁ (6 ,5)　**11** לִצְבָאוֹת (1)　**12** בִּבְרִית (7 ,1)

Page 48, Review & Application II

➤ 9 ת ‏‎ בֵּ ‎ כֹּתְ 11 זָ ‎ קֵן 1 מִ ‎ לָכִים 2 הַ ‎ לְ ‎ כִים 7 מָ ‎ לֹהִים ‎ אַ ‎ כְּ
3 זוּבִים ‎ עַ ‎ 6 הוּדָה לְ ‎ י ‎ 4 נְבִיאִים לְ ‎ 10 ל ‎ י ‎ לְ ‎ בַּ ‎ עַ ‎ 5 עֲבוֹדָה ‎ לַ
12 בַּשִּׁיר (not *) ‎ בְּהַשִּׁיר‎‎ 8 הַמֶּלֶךְ ‎ מֵ

Page 49, Review & Application III: 5, 1, 6, 7, 3, 2, 4, 8

Page 50, Exercise 7.1

1 lin-vî-ʔāʰ 'to [a] prophetess'　**2** kix-lî 'like [a] vessel'　**3** mis-sē-fer
'from [a] book'　**4** bî-rû-šā-la-yim 'in Jerusalem'　**5** ka-ʔᵃdā-māʰ 'like soil'
6 laṣ-ṣā-vāʔ 'to the army'　**7** ba-ḥᵃrā-vôt 'with swords'　**8** mē-haš-šîr 'from
the song'　**9** la-ʕᵃvā-dîm 'to slaves'　**10** kā-ʔîš 'like the man'
11 liṣ-vā-ʔôt 'to armies'　**12** biv-rît 'in [a] covenant'

Page 50, **Exercise 7.2**

1 הַמְּלָכִים הַצַּדִּיקִים זְקֵנִים. הַמְּלָכִים הַצַּדִּיקִים זְקֵנִים מֵהָאֲנָשִׁים הָרְשָׁעִים. הַמְּלָכִים הַצַּדִּיקִים זְקֵנִים מְאֹד.

The righteous kings [are] old. The righteous kings [are] old[er] than the sinful men. The righteous kings [are] very old.

2 הַבְּרִית בִּירוּשָׁלַיִם טוֹבָה. הַבְּרִית טוֹבָה מֵהַמָּוֶת. הַבְּרִית בִּירוּשָׁלַיִם הַקְּדוֹשָׁה טוֹבָה מְאֹד.

The covenant in Jerusalem [is] good. The covenant [is] better (= good) than (the) death. The covenant in the holy [city of] Jerusalem [is] very good.

3 הַנָּשִׁים חֲכָמוֹת כִּנְבִיאִים. הַנָּשִׁים מִיהוּדָה יְשָׁרוֹת מִנְּבִיאִים. הַנָּשִׁים הַיְשָׁרוֹת מִיהוּדָה בַּצָּבָא.

The women [are as] wise as prophets. The women from Judah [are more] upright than prophets. The upright women from Judah [are] in the army.

4 הָאִשָּׁה הַגְּדוֹלָה בָּאָרֶץ. הָאִשָּׁה בָּאָרֶץ הַגְּדוֹלָה. הָאִשָּׁה בָּאָרֶץ הִיא הַגְּדוֹלָה בַּנָּשִׁים.

The important/great woman [is] in the land. The woman [is] in the big land. The woman in the land [is] the [most] important of women (= among the women).

5 הַדָּבָר קָדוֹשׁ מְאֹד. הַדָּבָר קָדוֹשׁ מֵהַשִּׁיר. הַדָּבָר הוּא הַקָּדוֹשׁ בַּדְּבָרִים.

The word [is] very holy. The word [is] holier (= holy) than the song. The word [is] the holiest (= holy) of words (= among the words).

Page 51, **Exercise 7.3** (אַתֵּנָה = אַתֵּן, הֵמָּה = הֵם)

1 הֵם אָבוֹת זְקֵנִים   They [are] old fathers.

2 הָאָבוֹת הַזְּקֵנִים בָּאֲרָצוֹת הַטּוֹבוֹת   The old fathers [are] in the good countries.

3 אַתֶּם לֹא צַדִּיקִים. אַתֶּם רְשָׁעִים מְאֹד.   You [are] not righteous. You [are] very sinful.

4 אַתֵּן הַשּׁוֹפְטוֹת הַגְּדוֹלוֹת מִיִּשְׂרָאֵל   You [are] the great prophetesses from Israel.

5 אֲנַחְנוּ נְבִיאִים בִּירוּשָׁלַיִם הַקְּדוֹשָׁה   We [are] prophets in the holy [city of] Jerusalem

6 הֵנָּה דְּרָכִים חֲדָשׁוֹת   Those (= they) [are] new roads.

7 הַדְּרָכִים הַחֲדָשׁוֹת טוֹבוֹת מְאֹד   The new roads [are] very good.

8 הֵם כֵּלִים גְּדוֹלִים   Those (= they) [are] big vessels.

9 הָאֲנָשִׁים הָרְשָׁעִים מֵאֲרָצוֹת טוֹבוֹת   The sinful men [are] from good countries.

10 קְדוֹשִׁים הָאֵלִים   The gods [are] holy.

Page 51, **Exercise 7.4**

1 הַדְּבָרִים טוֹבִים מְאֹד.   **2** חָכָם אֱלֹהִים מֵאָדָם.   **3** הַחֶרֶב הַחֲדָשָׁה גְּדוֹלָה.

4 הָאֲדָמָה הַקְּדוֹשָׁה גְּדוֹלָה מְאֹד.   **5** הַדֶּרֶךְ בָּאָרֶץ הַקְּדוֹשָׁה טוֹבָה.   **6** יוֹם גָּדוֹל הוּא.   **7** הַמִּצְוֹת בַּתּוֹרָה טוֹבוֹת מְאֹד.   **8** יָשָׁר הַשֹּׁפֵט כְּמֶלֶךְ.

9 הַזְּקֵנִים מִצִּיּוֹן צַדִּיקִים.   **10** הָאָדוֹן (הוּא) הַטּוֹב בָּאֲדוֹנִים.

SECTION 8

Page 55, **Review & Application I**

➤ 4 רָצוֹת ‎ אֵ ‎ 8 לֹהִים ‎ א ‎ | וַ ‎ א ‎ | 11 זָ ‎ ? ‎ עָ 14 בַּדֶּרֶךְ (not דְּ ‎ רֶ ‎ הָ 9 (*בְּהַדֶּרֶךְ

10 אֶרֶץ ‎ מֶ ‎ 2 נִים ‎ הָ ‎ כָ 7 הוֹדָה ‎ י ‎ וְ ‎ 13 ח ‎ בַ ‎ זְ ‎ 12 נְבִיאִים ‎ וּ

5 פַּרְעֹה ‎ וּ ‎ 6 עֲבוֹדָה ‎ וַ ‎ 1 טוֹת ‎ פְ ‎ שָׁ ‎ 3 רָכִים ‎ הַ

Page 56, **Review & Application II:** 5, 7, 4, 3, 6, 1, 8, 10, 9, 2

Page 56, **Review & Application III:** 4, 7, 5, 3, 8, 2, 6, 1

Page 57, **Exercise 8.1**

This [is a] sword. This sword [is] big.	1 זֹאת -- הַחֶרֶב הַזֹּאת
This [is a] road. This road [is] straight.	2 זֹאת-- הַדֶּרֶךְ הַזֹּאת
These [are] commandments. These commandments [are] good.	3 אֵלֶּה -- הַמִּצְוֺת הָאֵלֶּה
This [is] soil. This soil [is] good.	4 זֹאת -- הָאֲדָמָה הַזֹּאת
These [are] winds. These winds [are] good.	5 אֵלֶּה -- הָרוּחוֹת הָאֵלֶּה
These [are] judges. These judges [are] sinful.	6 אֵלֶּה -- הַשּׁוֹפְטִים הָאֵלֶּה
This [is a] lad. This lad [is] honest.	7 זֶה -- הַנַּעַר הַזֶּה
This [is a] gate. This gate [is] complete.	8 זֶה -- הַשַּׁעַר הַזֶּה
This [is a] vessel. This vessel [is] new.	9 זֶה -- הַכְּלִי הַזֶּה
This [is a] country. This country [is] holy.	10 זֹאת -- הָאָרֶץ הַזֹּאת

Page 58, **Exercise 8.2** (הָהֵמָּה = הָהֵם)

1 That master [is] old. הַבְּעָלִים הָהֵם זְקֵנִים
2 The word [is] perfect. שְׁלֵמִים הַדְּבָרִים
3 The prophetess [is] (the) great[est]. הַנְּבִיאוֹת הֵנָּה הַגְּדוֹלוֹת
4 This good book [is] holy. הַסְּפָרִים הַטּוֹבִים הָאֵלֶּה קְדוֹשִׁים
5 The judge [is more] honest than the prophet. הַשּׁוֹפְטִים יְשָׁרִים מֵהַנְּבִיאִים
6 This prophet [is] good. הַנְּבִיאִים הָאֵלֶּה טוֹבִים
7 That covenant [is] holy. קְדוֹשׁוֹת הַבְּרִיתוֹת הָהֵנָּה
8 The country [is] good. טוֹבוֹת הָאֲרָצוֹת
9 This prophet [is] wiser (= wise) than that king.

הַנְּבִיאִים הָאֵלֶּה חֲכָמִים מֵהַמְּלָכִים הָהֵם

10 This entrance [is as] big as that entrance.

הַפְּתָחִים הָאֵלֶּה גְּדוֹלִים כַּפְּתָחִים הָהֵם

Page 59, **Exercise 8.3**

I. 1 And the king [was] very old. **2** [A] very skilful/wise man **3** The man Moses [was] very great. **4** The day [is] holy. **5** This [is] he.
6 This [is a] book. **7** This [is] the day. **8** This [is] the gate of/to (= לְ) the LORD. **9** This [is a] good man. **10** These [are] the things.

II. 11 The thing [is] good.　**12** These [are] the commandments and the ordinances.　**13** The land [is] exceedingly (= very very) good.　**14** God [is] good to Israel.　**15** Good and upright [is] the LORD.　**16** Righteous and upright [is] he.　**17** I [am] God and not man.　**18** I [am] not [a] prophet.

Page 59, **Exercise 8.4**

I. 1 זֶה אִישׁ. זָקֵן הוּא.　2 הַיּוֹם הַזֶּה טוֹב.　3 הַמְּלָכִים הָאֵלֶּה חֲכָמִים מְאֹד.
4 גְּדוֹלִים הַשְּׁעָרִים.　5 הַדְּבָרִים הָאֵלֶּה קְדוֹשִׁים מְאֹד.

II. 6 לֹא מֶלֶךְ אֲנִי/אָנֹכִי.　7 הָאִישׁ הַזֶּה צַדִּיק.　8 הַמֶּלֶךְ וְהַנָּבִיא יְשָׁרִים.
9 הַמֶּלֶךְ הַהוּא וְהַנָּבִיא הַהוּא זְקֵנִים.　10 יָשָׁר וְקָדוֹשׁ יהוה.

SECTION 9

Page 62, **Nouns via the names of the books in the Hebrew Bible I (4)**

I Doubling dagesh (2), hardenening dagesh (6), silent shva (1), vocal shva (6), silent א (1), omitted ה (1).

Page 63, **Exercise 9.1** (הֵמָּה = הֵם)

1 The son [is] wicked. הַבַּת הִיא רָעָה The daughter [is] wicked.
הַבָּנִים הֵם רָעִים The sons [are] wicked. הַבָּנוֹת הֵנָּה רָעוֹת The daughters [are] wicked.

2 The people [is] numerous. רַבָּה הַטּוֹבָה The kindness [is] great.
רַבִּים הַבָּתִּים The houses [are] many. רַבּוֹת הֶעָרִים The cities [are] many.

3 The son [is] alive. חַיָּה הַנֶּפֶשׁ The soul [is] alive. חַיִּים הָאַחִים
The brothers [are] alive. חַיּוֹת הַנְּפָשׁוֹת The souls [are] alive.

4 The vessel [is] big. גְּדוֹלָה הָעִיר The city [is] big. גְּדוֹלִים הָרָאשִׁים
The heads [are] big. גְּדוֹלוֹת הַנָּשִׁים The women [are] big.

5 The day [is] good. הָאֵם טוֹבָה הִיא The mother [is] good. הַיָּמִים טוֹבִים הֵם
The days [are] good. הַבָּנוֹת טוֹבוֹת הֵנָּה The daughters [are] good.

Page 64, **Exercise 9.2** (אַתֵּנָה = אַתֵּן, הֵמָּה = הֵם)

1	He [is] the strong son.	הֵם הַבָּנִים הָעַזִּים
2	The eye [is] big.	הָעֵינַיִם גְּדוֹלוֹת הֵנָּה
3	This [is] the good father.	אֵלֶּה הָאָבוֹת הַטּוֹבִים
4	I [am a] living person.	נְפָשׁוֹת חַיּוֹת אֲנַחְנוּ
5	This place [is] holy.	הַמְּקוֹמוֹת הָאֵלֶּה קְדוֹשִׁים הֵם
6	This [is a] new house.	אֵלֶּה בָּתִּים חֲדָשִׁים
7	This [is] the evil spirit.	אֵלֶּה הָרוּחוֹת הָרָעוֹת
8	The city [is] holy.	הֶעָרִים הֵנָּה קְדוֹשׁוֹת
9	This [is a] big head.	אֵלֶּה רָאשִׁים גְּדוֹלִים
10	You [are] the sinful man.	אַתֶּם הָאֲנָשִׁים הָרְשָׁעִים
11	You [are a] wicked woman.	נָשִׁים רָעוֹת אַתֵּן
12	You [are] better (good) than [a] son or (= וְ) daughter.	טוֹבִים אַתֶּם מִבָּנִים וּמִבָּנוֹת
13	The day [is] perfect.	שְׁלֵמִים הַיָּמִים

14 He [is an] old man. הֵם אֲנָשִׁים זְקֵנִים

15 She [is] the wise daughter. הֵנָּה הַבָּנוֹת הַחֲכָמוֹת

16 You [are a] wicked brother. אַחִים רָעִים אַתֶּם

17 You [are] the new wife. אַתֵּן הַנָּשִׁים הַחֲדָשׁוֹת

18 I [am an] honest servant. עֲבָדִים יְשָׁרִים אֲנַחְנוּ

19 This [is] the good country. אֵלֶּה הָאֲרָצוֹת הַטּוֹבוֹת

20 He [is a] living god. אֵלִים חַיִּים הֵם

Page 64, **Exercise 9.3**

1 The man [is] not in the city. 2 There is (= יֵשׁ) [a] woman in the city.
3 The woman has (= to the woman) [a] son. 4 The man has no daughter
(= there is not to the man daughter). 5 There is no (= אֵין) woman in the
house. 6 The man has (= to the man) [a] son. 7 There is no (= אֵין) nation
in the land. 8 The woman has (= to the woman) [a] husband (man) within/at
(= בְּ) the gate. 9 There is (= יֵשׁ) [a] stone at the entrance. 10 There is no
(= אֵין) book on (= בְּ) the road. 11 The king has (= יֵשׁ to the king) [a]
sword. 12 The LORD has (= to the LORD) [a] nation. 13 The prophet has
(= יֵשׁ to the prophet) [a] book. 14 There is no (= אֵין) servant in the place.

Page 65, **Exercise 9.4**

1 And David [is] old. This [is] David. 2 [An] important woman. And the
stone [is] big. 3 The day [is] holy. The place [is] holy.

Page 65, **Exercise 9.5**

I. 1 You [are a] holy people to the LORD. 2 That (= it) [is] the big city.
3 Two [are] better than one (= the two good than the one). 4 The LORD
[is] (= יֵשׁ) in this place. 5 The LORD [is a] great God. 6 And we [are]
many. 7 These [people are] sinful/wicked. 8 There is no [one] (= אֵין)
like the LORD. 9 And there are (= יֵשׁ) eyes.

II. 10 The LORD [is] one. 11 In those days there was no (= אֵין) king in Israel.
12 Israel has (= יֵשׁ to Israel) [a] God. 13 There is (= יֵשׁ) [a] prophet in
Israel. 14 Peninnah had (= to Peninnah) children and Hannah had no
(= אֵין to Hannah) children. 15 There is no (= אֵין) good to man/mankind.
16 And there is not (= אֵין) [a] man on (= בְּ) (the) earth.

Page 66, **Exercise 9.6**

I. 1 הֵם/הֵמָּה רַבִּים. 2 יֵשׁ אֲנָשִׁים רַבִּים. 3 אֵין אֲנָשִׁים גְּדוֹלִים בַּמָּקוֹם
הַזֶּה. 4 יֵשׁ מָקוֹם קָדוֹשׁ בָּעִיר. 5 אַתֶּם רְשָׁעִים. 6 יֵשׁ אֲנָשִׁים רְשָׁעִים
בָּעִיר הַזֹּאת. 7 אֵין נָשִׁים רַבּוֹת כְּלֵאָה.

II. 8 לַבָּנִים אֵין עֵינַיִם. 9 יֵשׁ מְלָכִים טוֹבִים בַּמָּקוֹם. 10 אֵין נְבִיאִים רַבִּים
בְּיִשְׂרָאֵל. 11 (יֵשׁ) לְיִשְׂרָאֵל בָּנִים עַזִּים. 12 (יֵשׁ) לָאִישׁ יְלָדִים.
13 (יֵשׁ) לַשֹּׁפְטִים נָשִׁים טוֹבוֹת. 14 הַיֶּלֶד הַזֶּה גָּדוֹל מֵהַיֶּלֶד הַהוּא.

SECTION 10

Page 70, Exercise 10.1

Note: The column '*Insertion vowel dissolving cluster*' is not included since none of the words below takes an insertion vowel.

Translation	ו/י becomes a vowel letter	Shortened vowel	Reduced vowel	Unchangeable vowel	Noun: Attached form	
the ordinance of the Law		paṭ		miš	מִשְׁפַּט	5
the parable of Solomon		šal	mᵊ		מְשַׁל	6
the death of the prophet	môt				מוֹת	7
the son of Abraham		ben			בֶּן	8
every lad		kol			כָּל	9
wise of/at heart		xam	ḥᵃ		חֲכַם	10
the hope of the people		wat		tiq	תִּקְוַת	11
the law of (the) man		rat		tô	תּוֹרַת	12
the prophet of (the) God			nᵊ	vî'	נְבִיא	13
the host of God			ṣᵊ	vā'	צְבָא	14
the word of the Lᴏʀᴅ		var	dᵊ		דְּבַר	15
the holy spirit				rû_a h	רוּחַ	16
the eye of the man	ʕên				עֵין	17

Page 72, Exercise 10.2

Translation	Insertion vowel which dissolves cluster	Reduced vowel	Unchangeable vowel	Noun: Attached form	
two men			šᵊnê	שְׁנֵי	3
the voices of the people			qô-lôt	קוֹלוֹת	4
the proverbs of Solomon	miš		lê	מִשְׁלֵי	5
the tops (heads) of the mountains			rā'-šê	רָאשֵׁי	6
the daughters of Jerusalem		bᵊ	nôt	בְּנוֹת	7
the commandments of the Law			miṣ-wōt	מִצְוֹת	8
the eyes of the woman			ʕê-nê	עֵינֵי	9
the lands of the nations	'ar		ṣôt	אַרְצוֹת	10
the souls of the prophets	naf		šôt	נַפְשׁוֹת	11
allies (= sons of covenant)		bᵊ	nê	בְּנֵי	12
the words of the judge	div		rê	דִּבְרֵי	13
the wise [men] of/in the place	ḥax		mê	חַכְמֵי	14
the water of the city			mê	מֵי	15
the mountains of Judah			hā-rê	הָרֵי	16
the sky of (the) earth		šᵊ	mê	שְׁמֵי	17
the hands of Esau		yᵊ	dê	יְדֵי	18
the nations of the lands			ʕam-mê	עַמֵּי	19

Page 74, **Exercise 10.3** (there is/are יֵשׁ =, there is/are not/no = אֵין)

1 The son [is] bold-faced/shameless (adj עַז): הַבָּנִים עַזֵּי פָּנִים

There is no son on (= בְּ) the road: אֵין בָּנִים בַּדְּרָכִים

There is no shameless son on the road: אֵין בָּנִים עַזֵּי פָנִים בַּדְּרָכִים

2 The woman [is] good-looking (= beautiful in appearance, adj יָפֶה):

הַנָּשִׁים יְפוֹת מַרְאֶה

There is [a] woman in the city: יֵשׁ נָשִׁים בֶּעָרִים

There is [a] good-looking woman in the city: יֵשׁ נָשִׁים יְפוֹת מַרְאֶה בֶּעָרִים

3 The man [is] wise (= wise of/at heart, adj חָכָם): הָאֲנָשִׁים חַכְמֵי לֵב

The man has (= יֵשׁ to the man) [a] sword: יֵשׁ לָאֲנָשִׁים חֲרָבוֹת

The wise man has (= יֵשׁ to the wise man) [a] sword: יֵשׁ לָאֲנָשִׁים חַכְמֵי הַלֵּב חֲרָבוֹת

4 The man has beautiful eyes (= The man [is] beautiful of eyes = with beautiful eyes, adj יָפֶה): הָאֲנָשִׁים יְפֵי עֵינַיִם

There is no man in this place: אֵין אֲנָשִׁים בַּמְּקוֹמוֹת הָאֵלֶּה

There is no man with beautiful eyes in this place:

אֵין אֲנָשִׁים יְפֵי עֵינַיִם בַּמְּקוֹמוֹת הָאֵלֶּה

5 The servant [is] upright (= upright at heart, adj יָשָׁר): הָעֲבָדִים יִשְׁרֵי לֵב

There is no servant in the field: אֵין בַּשָּׂדוֹת עֲבָדִים

There is no upright servant in the field: אֵין בַּשָּׂדוֹת עֲבָדִים יִשְׁרֵי לֵב

6 The daughter [is] ugly (= bad in appearance, adj רָעָה): הַבָּנוֹת רָעוֹת מַרְאֶה

There is [a] daughter in the house: יֵשׁ בָּנוֹת בַּבָּתִּים

There is [an] ugly daughter in the house: יֵשׁ בָּנוֹת רָעוֹת מַרְאֶה בַּבָּתִּים

Page 75, **Exercise 10.4**

1 Every day [is a] new day.   2 All the houses [are] new.   3 The LORD has/possesses (= to the LORD) the whole earth.   4 Every man [is] in the field. 5 Every woman [is] in the house. 6 All the women [are] in the place. 7 The whole house [belongs] to the man. 8 All the sanctuaries [belong] to God. 9 All the statues and the ordinances [are] good.

10 Every living person (= נֶפֶשׁ) [is] in the country.

Page 75, **Exercise 10.5**

I. 1 And this [is] the law for mankind. תּוֹרָה   2 The voice [is] the voice of Jacob, but (= וְ) the hands [are] Esau's hands. קוֹל, יָדַיִם   3 And these [are] the words of the letter (lit., 'book'). דְּבָרִים   4 And the word of the LORD [is] from Jerusalem. דָּבָר   5 And there was no (= אֵין) sword in the hand of David. יָד   6 The words of Qohelet/the Preacher, the son of David דְּבָרִים, בֶּן   7 The heart of the king [was] merry (= good) with (the) wine. לֵב   8 This (= הִיא) [is] from the hand of God. יָד   9 The LORD of hosts, the God of Israel אֱלֹהִים

II. 10 This (= הִיא) [was] the commandment of the king. מִצְוָה **11** And these [are] the names of the Israelites (= sons of Israel). שֵׁמוֹת, בָּנִים **12** Moses, the man of God אִישׁ **13** They [are] kind kings. מְלָכִים **14** She [was] good-looking (= good in appearance). טוֹבָה **15** You, [O] Lᴏʀᴅ, [is] good... and very kind/ (= great in kindness). רַב **16** The Lᴏʀᴅ in Zion [is] great and he [is] high over all the peoples. כֹּל **17** This [is] the whole [duty of a] person. כֹּל **18** The Lᴏʀᴅ [is] great[er] than all (the) gods. כֹּל

Page 76, Exercise 10.6

I. 1 דָּוִד מֶלֶךְ. הוּא מֶלֶךְ יְרוּשָׁלַיִם. 2 וַיהוה (הוּא) אֱלֹהֵי יִשְׂרָאֵל. 3 הִיא בַּת־מֶלֶךְ. 4 טוֹבִים הָאֲנָשִׁים. הֵם/הֵמָּה טוֹבֵי מַרְאֶה. 5 הָאִישׁ נָבִיא. הוּא נְבִיא יהוה. 6 הַחֶרֶב בִּידֵי הָאִישׁ. 7 דִּבְרֵי אֱלֹהִים בְּמִקְדַּשׁ אֱלֹהִים. 8 צִבְאוֹת יהוה עַזִּים.

II. 9 חֶסֶד אֱלֹהִים עַל־הָעָם הַזֶּה. 10 זֹאת מִצְוַת הָאָב. 11 הַבָּתִּים יָפִים (יְפֵי מַרְאֶה). 12 יָפָה כָּל־הַשָּׂדֶה. 13 כָּל־הַנָּשִׁים טוֹבוֹת מַרְאֶה. 14 כָּל־מִצְוֹת יהוה טוֹבוֹת. 15 בְּנֵי יִשְׂרָאֵל בְּצִיּוֹן. 16 לְכָל־עַם (יֵשׁ) מֶלֶךְ. 17 (יֵשׁ) לְכָל־יֶלֶד אֵם וָאָב.

SECTION 11

Page 79, Exceptions to the basic rule of vocalization via Hebrew names I (6)

1 מְעַט, חַג, עֲדִי 2 אַחֲרֵי, לְפָנַי, רֶגֶל, צֶדֶק, זֶרַע, אֶלֶף 4 none

5 מֵאַיִן, רַגְלַיִם, מִצְרַיִם, חַיִל, אַלְפַּיִם, אָזְנַיִם 6 אַחֲרֵי, אַחֲרֵי, מַעֲשֶׂה

Other categories: Particles עַד, אִם, אַחַר. *Odd exceptions*: אֱמֶת.

Page 79, Review & Application I

1 (1, 3) I [am] Qohelet/the Preacher... [a] king over Israel, in Jerusalem.

2 (4) For everything [there is a]... time... under (the) heaven.

3 (5) There is (= יֵשׁ) [an] evil [thing]... under the sun and it [is] heavy (= רַבָּה) upon (the) man/mankind. **4** (5) The former (= first) days [were]... better than these. **5** (1,6) Peninnah had (= to Peninnah) children.

6 (4, 5) In those days [there was] no king in Israel. **7** (2) But (= וְ) we [are] many. **8** (4, 5) And [there is] not [a] man on (= בְּ) (the) earth.

Page 81, Exercise 11.1 (הֵם = הֵמָּה, אַתֶּן = אַתֵּנָה, אֲנִי = אָנֹכִי)

2 אֲנִי, בְּ in/via me	9 אֲנִי, כְּ/כְּמוֹ like me	16 הוּא/אֲנַחְנוּ, אֵין he [is]/we [are] not
3 אַתֶּם, לְ to/for you	10 אַתֶּן, אֵין you [are] not	17 הֵם, בְּ in/via them
4 הוּא, לְ to/for him/it	11 אֲנַחְנוּ, אֵת with us	18 הוּא, כְּ/כְּמוֹ like him/it
5 אַתְּ, מִן from/than you	12 הִיא, מִן from/than her/it	19 הוּא/אֲנַחְנוּ, מִן from him/us
6 הֵם, לְ to/for them	13 אַתָּה, לְ to/for you	20 הוּא, אֵת with him/it
7 הוּא, אֵין he/it [is] not	14 הִיא, בְּ in/via her/it	
8 הִיא, עִם with her/it	15 אֲנַחְנוּ, לְ to/for us	

Page 83, **Exercise 11.3** (אָנֹכִי = אֲנִי, אַתֶּנָה = אַתֶּן, הֵמָּה = הֵם)

2 מָוֶת, אֲנַחְנוּ our death מוֹת (1)

3 חֹק, הִיא her statute חֹק (4)

4 אֲדָמָה, אַתָּה your soil אַדְמַת (2, 3)

5 בְּרִית, הוּא his/its covenant בְּרִית (1)

6 מָשִׁיחַ, הֵם their Messiah מְשִׁיחַ (1)

7 מִצְוָה, הִיא your commandment מִצְוַת (2,3)

8 אוֹר, אַתְּ your light אוֹר (1)

9 אָדוֹן, אַתֶּם your master אֲדוֹן (1)

10 סֵפֶר, אַתֶּם your book סִפְרְ (5)

11 נָבִיא, אַתָּה your prophet נְבִיא (1)

12 תּוֹרָה, הוּא his/its law תּוֹרַת (1, 2)

13 רֹאשׁ, הֵם their head רֹאשׁ (1)

14 מֶלֶךְ, אֲנַחְנוּ our king מֶלֶךְ (5)

15 תִּקְוָה, אֲנִי my hope תִּקְוַת (2, 3)

16 קֹדֶשׁ, אַתָּה your holiness קֹדֶשׁ (5)

17 עַיִן, הִיא her eye עֵין (1)

18 עַם, אֲנִי my nation עַם (4)

Page 84, **Exercise 11.4**

1 your **2** his **3** she, you **4** you, our **5** him **6** them **7** she, her
8 you, my **9** he, my **10** she (her), her **11** we (us) **12** I (me), I (me)
13 she (her) **14** I, your

Page 85, **Exercise 11.5**

1 Our father [is] old. **2** The Lord of hosts [is] with us. **3** God [is] with us.
4 The whole earth [is] mine (= to me). **5** And in my house [there is] no
bread. **6** You [are] my father. **7** Your kindness [is] better (= good) than life.
8 This [is] the word of the Lord to Zerubbabel. **9** This [is] the law of the
house. **10** She [was] very beautiful. **11** And all the men of/in his house
12 He has (= to him) no son or (= וְ) brother. **13** In the year of the king's
death **14** The God of my father Abraham **15** The ways of the Lord [are]
upright.

Page 85, **Exercise 11.6**

1 אָבִיךָ עִמָּנוּ/אִתָּנוּ. **2** תּוֹרַת יהוה (הִיא) תּוֹרָתֵנוּ. **3** יֵשׁ לְךָ בָּנִים וּבָנוֹת
בְּבֵיתֶךָ. **4** יֵשׁ לִי בֵּן כָּמוֹהוּ. אֵין לוֹ אַחִים. **5** צָבָא הַמֶּלֶךְ עָז. יֵשׁ לוֹ צָבָא
עָז. **6** אֱלֹהִים (הוּא) הַגָּדוֹל. גָּדוֹל חַסְדּוֹ עַל־עַמּוֹ. **7** לְכָל־עַם מִקְדָּשׁ.
כָּל־הַמִּקְדָּשִׁים קְדוֹשִׁים. **8** כָּל־הָאֲנָשִׁים בַּשָּׂדֶה הַגָּדוֹל. **9** אֵין אֲנִי/אֵינֶנִּי
בְּבֵיתָהּ הַיָּפֶה. **10** אֵין אַתֶּם/אֵינְכֶם בְּעִירֵנוּ הַטּוֹבָה. **11** זֹאת אֶרֶץ גְּדוֹלָה.
(יֵשׁ) בָּהּ אֲנָשִׁים רַבִּים. הִיא גְּדוֹלָה מֵאַרְצְכֶם. **12** זְקַן אֲבִיהֶם מֵאָמָּם. הוּא
זָקֵן מִמֶּנָּה. **13** דְּבָרְךָ (הוּא) חֶקְנוּ. **14** דֶּרֶךְ אֱלֹהִים טוֹבָה. נַפְשִׁי בִּידֵי
אֱלֹהִים. **15** אֵין אֲחִיכֶם/אֲחִיכֶם אֵינֶנּוּ עִמִּי/אִתִּי.

SECTION 12

Page 89, **Exercise 12.1** (אָנֹכִי = אֲנִי, הֵמָּה = הֵם)

2 עָלַי, אֲנִי, עַל on/over me — 8 לְפָנֵינוּ, אֲנַחְנוּ, לִפְנֵי before us

3 אֵלָיו, הוּא, אֶל to/towards him/it — 9 עָלֶיהָ, הִיא, עַל on/over her/it

4 עֲלֵיכֶם, אַתֶּם, עַל on/over you — 10 אַחֲרֶיךָ, אַתָּ, אַחַר after/behind you

5 אֲלֵיהֶן, הֵנָּה, אֶל to/towards them — 11 תַּחְתַּי, אֲנִי, תַּחַת under/instead of me

6 עָלָיו, הוּא, עַל on/over him/it — 12 לְפָנֶיךָ, אַתָּה, לִפְנֵי before/in front of you

7 עָלֶיךָ, אַתָּה, עַל on/upon you — 13 אַחֲרֶיהָ, הִיא, אַחַר after/behind her/it

14 תַּחְתֶּיךָ, אַתָּה, תַּחַת **16** instead of you   לִפְנֵיכֶם, אַתֶּם, לִפְנֵי before/in front of you
15 אַחֲרָיו, הוּא, אַחַר after him/it   **17** אַחֲרֵיהֶם, הֵם, אַחַר after/behind them
18 לְפָנַי, אֲנִי, לִפְנֵי before/in front of me

Page 91, **Exercise 12.2** (אָנֹכִי = אֲנִי, אַתֵּנָה = אַתֵּן, הֵמָּה = אַתֶּן, הֵם = הֵמָּה)

2 אֲנִי, מְקוֹמוֹת, מָקוֹם my places   **11** הֵם, מִצְוֹת, מִצְוָה their commandments
4 אַתֶּם, מְשָׁלִים, מָשָׁל your proverbs   **12** הוּא, חֻקִּים, חֹק his statues
5 אֲנַחְנוּ, עַמִּים, עַם our nations   **13** אֲנַחְנוּ, אָזְנַיִם, אֹזֶן our ears
6 הוּא, אָבוֹת, אָב his fathers   **14** הֵם, עֵינַיִם, עַיִן their eyes
7 אַתֶּם, שָׂדוֹת, שָׂדֶה your fields   **15** אַתָּה, בָּתִּים, בַּיִת your houses
8 הִיא, שִׁירִים, שִׁיר her songs   **16** אַתְּ, רַגְלַיִם, רֶגֶל your feet
9 אַתָּה, כּוֹכָבִים, כּוֹכָב your stars   **17** אֲנַחְנוּ, פָּנִים, פָּנִים our faces
10 אַתְּ, בְּקָרִים, בֹּקֶר your mornings   **18** אֲנִי, הֵיכָלוֹת, הֵיכָל my temples

Page 92, **Exercise 12.3:** 6, 15, 12, 16, 11, 1, 14, 9, 7, 8, 13, 4, 10, 3, 2, 5

Page 93, **Exercise 12.4**

➤ **1** הַאַתָּה [Are] you the man of God?   **2** הַעוֹד [Is] your father still alive?
3 הַבְרָכָה Do you have (= to you) [only] one blessing, my father?
4 הֲלוֹא [Is] not Esau Jacob's brother (= brother to Esau)!   **5** הֲטוֹבָה [Is] it good or bad?   **6** הֲזֹאת [Is] this Naomi?   **7** הַמְעַט [Is] it few or many?
8 הַאֵין [Is there] no prophet here?   **9** הַאֱלֹהִים [Am] I God?   **10** הֶחָזָק [Is] it strong?

Page 93, **Exercise 12.5**

➤ **1** מַה־הִיא What [is] it?   **2** מַה־שְּׁמוֹ וּמַה־שֶּׁם־ What [is] his name and what [is] his son's name?   **3** מַה־שְּׁמֶךָ What [is] your name?
4 מָה הֶעָרִים What [kind of] cities [are] these?   **5** מַה־הַדָּבָר What [is] this bad thing?   **6** מָה־אָדָם What [is] man?   **7** מָה אַרְצֶךָ What [is] your country?

Page 94, **Exercise 12.6**

1 our   **2** your   **3** our, (he), us   **4** you   **5** your, your   **6** them   **7** you, yours   **8** your, me   **9** his   **10** we (us)   **11** your   **12** I, you   **13** you, me   **14** his, his   **15** her, her   **16** your, your   **17** our, us

Page 95, **Exercise 12.7**

1 To me the Israelites (= sons of Israel) [are] servants.   **2** [Is] not the whole country before you?   **3** All the servants of Pharaoh, the elders of his house[hold] and all the elders of the land of Egypt   **4** Absalom, Absalom, my son, my son!   **5** LORD, who [is] like you?   **6** Whom have I (= who to me) in (the) heavens?   **7** [Are] you not [a] man! And who [is] like you in Israel?

Page 96, **Exercise 12.8**

➤ **1** אַרְצְךָ (3) What [is] your land?   **2** שָׁמַיִם (1) Whom do I have (= who to me) in the heavens?   **3** שֶׁמֶשׁ (6) There is (= יֵשׁ) [an] evil under the sun and it

[is] heavy **(= רָבְה)** upon (the) man.   **4** שְׁמֶךָ (3) What [is] your name?
5 (4) עִמְּךָ Who [are] these men with you?   **6** יֶלֶד (6) [Is] it well with
(= הֲשָׁלוֹם לְ) you? [Is it] well with your husband (= man)? [Is it] well with the
child?   **7** עָלַי (1) Your kindness [is] great toward **(= עַל)** me.   **8** יָדְךָ (3) All
his holy [ones are] in your hand.   **9** כֶּסֶף (6) Your law (= the law of your
mouth) [is] better (= good) for me than thousands [pieces] of gold and silver.
10 אַתְּ (1) You [are a] woman of valour.   **11** בַּיִת (1) This [is] the law of the
house.   **12** אַתָּה (2) You [are] my father.   **13** אֲנִי (5) I [am a] great king.
14 אֲנַחְנוּ (1) We [are] brothers.   **15** יְרוּשָׁלַם (1) And the word of the LORD
from Jerusalem.

Page 97, **Exercise 12.9**

1 אַיֵּה/אֵיפֹה הַיְלָדִים?   **2** מֵאַיִן הָאֲנָשִׁים הָאֵלֶּה?   **3** מַה־תּוֹרָתְךָ?   **4** מִי
אֲדוֹנֶךָ? הֲטוֹב הוּא?   **5** מִי פֹה וּמִי בְהֵיכַל אֱלֹהִים?   **6** הֲלוֹא אָחִיךָ הוּא!
7 הֲיֵשׁ לָכֶם אָחוֹת? אֵיפֹה/אַיֵּה הִיא?   **8** הֲכֹל־בְּנוֹתֶיךָ בְּבֵיתְךָ?   **9** כִּסְאִי
בָּאָרֶץ עַד־עוֹלָם/לְעוֹלָם.   **10** אַיֵּה/אֵיפֹה כָּל־יְלָדַי?

SECTION 13

Page 101, **Review & Application I:**   4, 1, 7, 6, 2, 9, 3, 5, 8

Page 102, **Review & Application II** (ג = guttural, שְׁלֵמִים = unchangeable)

1 not קָרָאתִי 4, 5 --> א, ל"א	**5 not** כָּרַתְתָּ 1 --> שְׁלֵמִים
2 not מָאְסָה 2 --> ע"ג, II-ג	**6 not** קָרָאתֶן 4, 5 --> א, ל"א
3 not שָׁמַעְתְּ 3 --> ג, III-ג	**7 not** גָּאֲלוּ 2 --> ע"ג, II-ג
4 not עֲבַדְתֶּם 2 --> ג, I-ג	**8 not** נָתַנְנוּ 1 --> irregular

Page 103, **Exercise 13.1**

Meaning	אֲנַחְנוּ	אַתְּ	אַתָּה	אֲנִי	Lexical form
write	כָּתַבְנוּ	כָּתַבְתְּ	כָּתַבְתָּ	כָּתַבְתִּי	כָּתַב 1
guard, keep	שָׁמַרְנוּ	שָׁמַרְתְּ	שָׁמַרְתָּ	שָׁמַרְתִּי	שָׁמַר 2
reign (as king)	מָלַכְנוּ	מָלַכְתְּ	מָלַכְתָּ	מָלַכְתִּי	מָלַךְ 3
love	אָהַבְנוּ	אָהַבְתְּ	אָהַבְתָּ	אָהַבְתִּי	אָהַב 4
say	אָמַרְנוּ	אָמַרְתְּ	אָמַרְתָּ	אָמַרְתִּי	אָמַר 5
redeem	גָּאַלְנוּ	גָּאַלְתְּ	גָּאַלְתָּ	גָּאַלְתִּי	גָּאַל 6
work, serve	עָבַדְנוּ	עָבַדְתְּ	עָבַדְתָּ	עָבַדְתִּי	עָבַד 7

Page 104, **Exercise 13.2**

Meaning	אַתֶּן	אַתֶּם	הֵם/הֵנָּה	הִיא	Lexical form
cut	כְּרַתֶּן	כְּרַתֶּם	כָּרְתוּ	כָּרְתָה	כָּרַת 1
guard, keep	שְׁמַרְתֶּן	שְׁמַרְתֶּם	שָׁמְרוּ	שָׁמְרָה	שָׁמַר 2
reign (as king)	מְלַכְתֶּן	מְלַכְתֶּם	מָלְכוּ	מָלְכָה	מָלַךְ 3
work, serve	עֲבַדְתֶּן	עֲבַדְתֶּם	עָבְדוּ	עָבְדָה	עָבַד 4
love	אֲהַבְתֶּן	אֲהַבְתֶּם	אָהֲבוּ	אָהֲבָה	אָהַב 5

English					
redeem	גְּאַלְתֶּן	גְּאַלְתֶּם	גָּאֲלוּ	גָּאֲלָה	6 גָּאַל
hear, listen	שְׁמַעְתֶּן	שְׁמַעְתֶּם	שָׁמְעוּ	שָׁמְעָה	7 שָׁמַע

Page 105, Exercise 13.3

Translation	Lexical form	Independent pronoun		
I remembered	זָכַר	אֲנִי	זָכַרְתִּי	2
you worked, served	עָבַד	אַתָּה	עָבַדְתָּ	3
you heard, listened	שָׁמַע	אַתְּ	שָׁמַעַתְּ	4
she loved	אָהַב	הִיא	אָהֲבָה	5
you called, read	קָרָא	אַתֶּם	קְרָאתֶם	6
we called, read	קָרָא	אֲנַחְנוּ	קָרָאנוּ	7
they said	אָמַר	הֵם/הֵנָּה	אָמְרוּ	8
you heard, listened	שָׁמַע	אַתֶּם	שְׁמַעְתֶּם	9
you guarded, kept	שָׁמַר	אַתָּה	שָׁמַרְתָּ	10
she gave, placed	נָתַן	הִיא	נָתְנָה	11
she said	אָמַר	הִיא	אָמְרָה	12
we worked, served	עָבַד	אֲנַחְנוּ	עָבַדְנוּ	13
they reigned (as kings)	מָלַךְ	הֵם/הֵנָּה	מָלְכוּ	14
I called, read	קָרָא	אֲנִי	קָרָאתִי	15
you gave, placed	נָתַן	אַתָּה	נָתַתָּ	16
she anointed	מָשַׁח	הִיא	מָשְׁחָה	17
you loved	אָהַב	אַתֵּן	אֲהַבְתֶּן	18

Page 106, Exercise 13.4

I anointed מָשַׁחְתִּי	1	you said אָמַרְתָּ	8
you said אֲמַרְתֶּן	2	we reigned (as kings) מָלַכְנוּ	9
you called, read קָרָאת	3	he remembered זָכַר	10
he heard, listened שָׁמַע	4	I guarded, kept שָׁמַרְתִּי	11
she loved אָהֲבָה	5	they called, read קָרְאוּ	12
they wrote כָּתְבוּ	6	you heard, listened שְׁמַעְתֶּם	13
you worked, served עֲבַדְתֶּם	7	she worked, served עָבְדָה	14

Page 106, Exercise 13.5

1 Why did you not obey (= listened in the voice of) the LORD?   2 And out of
(= from) Egypt I called (= called to) my son.   3 The LORD, our God, made
(= cut) [a] covenant with us at Horeb.   4 My people did not listen to me (= to
my voice).   5 They did not keep the covenant of God.   6 You did not obey
(= listened in the voice of) the LORD, your God.   7 I have said to the LORD,
'You [are] my God'.   8 You have called me (= to me).   9 Then the king
listened to them.   10 God has become king over [the] nations.

Page 107, **Exercise 13.6**

1 אָמַרְנוּ לוֹ, 'אַתָּה מַלְכֵּנוּ'.   2 שָׁמְעָה הָאִשָּׁה קוֹל מִן־/מֵהַשָּׁמַיִם.   3 שָׁמַע
הָאִישׁ בְּקוֹל אֱלֹהִים.   4 קָרָאתִי סֵפֶר עַל־אִישׁ חָכָם.   5 אָז מָלַךְ הַמֶּלֶךְ
עַל־אֲרָצוֹת רַבּוֹת.   6 בַּיּוֹם הַהוּא קָרָאתָ לִי מֵעִיר דָּוִד.   7 כָּרַת אֱלֹהִים
עִם/אֶת־עַמּוֹ בְּרִית.   8 לָמָה/לָמָּה נָתַן לִי יהוה זָהָב וָכֶסֶף.   9 עָבַדְתָּ בְּעִירִי.
10 עָבְדוּ בְּנֵי יִשְׂרָאֵל בְּמִצְרַיִם.

SECTION 14

Page 109, **Review & Application I:** 2, 4, 11, 8, 3, 9, 10, 7, 6, 5, 12, 1

Page 110, **Review & Application II** (ג = guttural, שְׁלֵמִים = unchangeable)

1 א not audible 4 --> III-א, לי"א   5 not עֲזַרְתֶּם 2 --> I-ג, פ"ג
2 not עֲמַדְתֶּן 2 --> I-ג, פ"ג   6 not שָׁלַחְתְּ 3 --> III-ג, לי"ג
3 not כָּרַתָּ 1 --> שְׁלֵמִים   7 not בָּחֲרוּ 2 --> II-ג, עי"ג
4 not בָּחֲרָה 2 --> II-ג, עי"ג   8 not יָצָאתִי 4, 5 --> I-י, פי"י + III-א, לי"א

Page 111, **Review & Application III**

→ 5 א קָ‌רַ‌ר 6 תַב כ 8 תִ‌תַ‌ה י 1 נָ‌תַ רָה 3 שָׁ‌מַ רוּ חַ‌ה בָּ 7 רְתִ‌שָׁמַ
2 תבתֶם כ 4 בַדְתֶּם עַ

Page 112, **Exercise 14.1**

Meaning	אֲנַחְנוּ	אַתְּ	אַתָּה	אֲנִי	Lexical form
cut	כָּרַתְנוּ	כָּרַתְּ	כָּרַתָּ	כָּרַתִּי	כָּרַת 2
eat	אָכַלְנוּ	אָכַלְתְּ	אָכַלְתָּ	אָכַלְתִּי	אָכַל 3
know	יָדַעְנוּ	יָדַעַתְּ	יָדַעְתָּ	יָדַעְתִּי	יָדַע 4
go	הָלַכְנוּ	הָלַכְתְּ	הָלַכְתָּ	הָלַכְתִּי	הָלַךְ 5
fear	יָרֵאנוּ	יָרֵאת	יָרֵאתָ	יָרֵאתִי	יָרֵא 6
go out	יָצָאנוּ	יָצָאת	יָצָאתָ	יָצָאתִי	יָצָא 7
sit, dwell	יָשַׁבְנוּ	יָשַׁבְתְּ	יָשַׁבְתָּ	יָשַׁבְתִּי	יָשַׁב 8
choose	בָּחַרְנוּ	בָּחַרְתְּ	בָּחַרְתָּ	בָּחַרְתִּי	בָּחַר 9
anoint	מָשַׁחְנוּ	מָשַׁחְתְּ	מָשַׁחְתָּ	מָשַׁחְתִּי	מָשַׁח 10
give, put	נָתַנּוּ	נָתַתְּ	נָתַתָּ	נָתַתִּי	נָתַן 11
be/become little	קָטֹנּוּ	קָטֹנְתְּ	קָטֹנְתָּ	קָטֹנְתִּי	קָטֹן 12
call, read	קָרָאנוּ	קָרָאת	קָרָאתָ	קָרָאתִי	קָרָא 13
hear, listen	שָׁמַעְנוּ	שָׁמַעַתְּ	שָׁמַעְתָּ	שָׁמַעְתִּי	שָׁמַע 14
take	לָקַחְנוּ	לָקַחַתְּ	לָקַחְתָּ	לָקַחְתִּי	לָקַח 15
send	שָׁלַחְנוּ	שָׁלַחַתְּ	שָׁלַחְתָּ	שָׁלַחְתִּי	שָׁלַח 16
find	מָצָאנוּ	מָצָאת	מָצָאתָ	מָצָאתִי	מָצָא 17

Page 113, **Exercise 14.2**

Meaning	אַתֵּן	הֵם/הֵנָּה אַתֶּם	הִיא	Lexical form	
stand	עֲמַדְתֶּן	עֲמַדְתֶּם עָמְדוּ	עָמְדָה	עָמַד	2
eat	אֲכַלְתֶּן	אֲכַלְתֶּם אָכְלוּ	אָכְלָה	אָכַל	3
choose	בְּחַרְתֶּן	בְּחַרְתֶּם בָּחֲרוּ	בָּחֲרָה	בָּחַר	4
send	שְׁלַחְתֶּן	שְׁלַחְתֶּם שָׁלְחוּ	שָׁלְחָה	שָׁלַח	5
know	יְדַעְתֶּן	יְדַעְתֶּם יָדְעוּ	יָדְעָה	יָדַע	6
find	מְצָאתֶן	מְצָאתֶם מָצְאוּ	מָצְאָה	מָצָא	7
be full/filled (with)	מְלֵאתֶן	מְלֵאתֶם מָלְאוּ	מָלְאָה	מָלֵא	8
hear, listen	שְׁמַעְתֶּן	שְׁמַעְתֶּם שָׁמְעוּ	שָׁמְעָה	שָׁמַע	9
take	לְקַחְתֶּן	לְקַחְתֶּם לָקְחוּ	לָקְחָה	לָקַח	10
give	נְתַתֶּן	נְתַתֶּם נָתְנוּ	נָתְנָה	נָתַן	11
be/become little	קְטָנְתֶּן	קְטָנְתֶּם קָטְנוּ	קָטְנָה	קָטֹן	12
love	אֲהַבְתֶּן	אֲהַבְתֶּם אָהֲבוּ	אָהֲבָה	אָהַב	13
call, read	קְרָאתֶן	קְרָאתֶם קָרְאוּ	קָרְאָה	קָרָא	14

Page 114, **Exercise 14.3** (ג = guttural, שְׁלֵמִים = unchangeable)

Translation	Root type	Lexical form	Independent pronoun		
you ate	פ"א, א-I	אָכַל	אַתֶּם	אֲכַלְתֶּם	2
you remembered	שְׁלֵמִים	זָכַר	אַתָּה	זָכַרְתָּ	3
we cut	שְׁלֵמִים	כָּרַת	אֲנַחְנוּ	כָּרַתְנוּ	4
you took (irregular)	ג"ל	לָקַח	אַתְּ	לָקַחַתְּ	5
she sat, dwelt	פ"י, ו/י-I	יָשַׁב	הִיא	יָשְׁבָה	6
they chose	ע"ג, ג-II	בָּחַר	הֵם/הֵנָּה	בָּחֲרוּ	7
he knew	ו/י-I + ג-III	יָדַע	הוּא	יָדַע	8
you went out	ו/י-I + א-III	יָצָא	אַתֵּן	יְצָאתֶן	9
we ate	פ"א, א-I	אָכַל	אֲנַחְנוּ	אֲכַלְנוּ	10
she went	irregular	הָלַךְ	הִיא	הָלְכָה	11
you chose	ע"ג, ג-II	בָּחַר	אַתְּ	בָּחַרְתְּ	12
you sent	ל"ג, ג-III	שָׁלַח	אַתֶּם	שְׁלַחְתֶּם	13
they found	ל"א, א-III	מָצָא	הֵם/הֵנָּה	מָצְאוּ	14
you were/became full (with)	ל"א, א-III	מָלֵא	אַתָּה	מָלֵאתָ	15
I stood	פ"ג, ג-I	עָמַד	אָנֹכִי/אֲנִי	עָמַדְתִּי	16
he feared	ו/י-I + א-III	יָרֵא	הוּא	יָרֵא	17
you knew	ו/י-I + ג-III	יָדַע	אַתֵּן	יְדַעְתֶּן	18

Page 115, **Exercise 14.4**

10 מָלֵאתָ you were/became full (with)	1 יָדַ֫עְתִּי I knew
11 נָתַ֫נּוּ we gave	2 כָּרַ֫תָּ you cut
12 עָמַד he stood	3 יָצָאת you went out
13 יָרֵ֫אתִי I feared	4 יָשַׁב he sat/dwelt
14 אָכַ֫לְתְּ you ate	5 בָּחֲרָה she chose
15 אֲמַרְתֶּם you said	6 זָכַ֫רְנוּ we remembered
16 לָקְחָה she took	7 שְׁלַחְתֶּם you sent
17 אָהֲבוּ they loved	8 אֲכַלְתֶּן you ate
18 מְצָאתֶן you found	9 הָלְכוּ they went

Page 116, **Exercise 14.5**

1 you, what, these **2** his, his **3** you, your **4** I, you (your), his **5** his **6** you, my, my **7** them **8** I, they **9** you, your, they, your **10** you, him (his) **11** he, his **12** I **13** I, my **14** what, you

Page 117, **Exercise 14.6**

I 5, 10, 8, 9, 2, 3, 4, 1, 7, 6   **II** 4, 8, 1, 5, 10, 7, 9, 2, 6, 3

Page 118, **Exercise 14.7**

1 You have not kept the commandment of the LORD, your God.
2 Our fathers did not keep the word of the LORD.   **3** But (= וְ) his father kept the matter (= word) [in mind].   **4** And we have heard his voice.   **5** The LORD has given you (= to you) the land.   **6** They gave him (= to him) the city.
7 Their father loved him [more] than all his brothers.   **8** I have loved you.
9 My master does not know (= יָדַע) what [is] with me in the house.   **10** And [there was] with us there [a] Hebrew lad/young man.   **11** We [are] wise and the law of the LORD [is] with us.   **12** They had anointed him king (= to king) in place of his father.   **13** But (= וְ) Jacob did not send Benjamin, Joseph's brother, with his brothers.   **14** On (= בְּ) that day the LORD made (= cut) [a] covenant with Abram.   **15** You have said, 'We have made (= cut) [a] covenant with death'. **16** Not with our fathers did the LORD make (= cut) this covenant.   **17** And all his brothers I have given him (= to him) for servants. **18** Your voice I heard.   **19** I did not send the prophets.   **20** Hilkiah, the priest, found the book of the law of the LORD.   **21** And the LORD [is] with us.

Page 119, **Exercise 14.8**

1 you **2** you, your **3** you **4** your, us **5** this **6** you **7** this **8** he **9** you **10** you, my **11** you, my **12** who **13** you **14** I, you (your)

Page 121, **Exercise 14.9**

1 אָכַל הָאִישׁ אֶת־לַחְמוֹ בַּלַּ֫יְלָה וְאִשְׁתּוֹ אָכְלָה אֶת־לַחְמָה בַּבֹּ֫קֶר.

2 אָכַל הָעָם בְּאֶ֫רֶץ מִצְרַ֫יִם לֶ֫חֶם וְהָעִבְרִים בְּאֶ֫רֶץ כְּנַ֫עַן לֹא אָכְלוּ לָ֫חֶם.

3 הָלְכָה הָאִשָּׁה אֶל־הַבַּ֫יִת/הַבַּ֫יְתָה.   4 לָקַ֫חְתָּ אֶת־הַלֶּ֫חֶם וְאָכַ֫לְתָּ אֹתוֹ.

5 עֲמַדְתֶּם עַל הָהָר וּשְׁלַחְתֶּם אֶת־יְדֵיכֶם הַשָּׁמַיְמָה/אֶל־הַשָּׁמַיִם.   6 אֵת בַּהֵיכָל אִתָּם/עִמָּם.   7 יָצְאָה אִשָּׁה עִבְרִיָּה מִן־הַבַּיִת/מֵהַבַּיִת אֶל־בַּעְלָהּ/אִישָׁהּ בַּשָּׂדֶה.   8 בָּחַר בּוֹ אֱלֹהִים לְנָבִיא שָׁם.   9 מָלֵא הַמִּשְׁכָּן בִּכְבוֹד יהוה. יֵרָאֲנוּ אֶת־יְהוה.   10 כֹּה אָמַר יהוה, 'שָׁלַחְתִּי אֶתְכֶם לְמִצְרַיִם/מִצְרַיְמָה אֶל־אֲחִיכֶם'.   11 אָן/אָנָה הָלַךְ עַמִּי בַּיּוֹם הַהוּא?   12 הִנֵּה מָצָאתִי לְךָ אִשָּׁה.

SECTION 15

Page 123, **Review & Application I:** 8, 7, 5, 10, 2, 1, 3, 6, 4, 9

Page 124, **Review & Application II** (III-י/ו , לו״י = III-ה, ל״ה; ג = guttural)

1 not עָשִׂיתִי* 3, 5 --> I-ג + III-י/ו   **5** not עָלַי* 4 b --> I-ג + III-י/ו
2 not עֲלִיתֶם 1, 3, 5 --> I-ג + III-י/ו   **6** not מְצָאֲנוּ 2 --> III-א, ל״א
3 not קַוָמָה 4 a --> II-י/ו , עו״י   **7** not קָוַם 4 a --> II-י/ו , עו״י
4 not עָלִיו 4 b --> I-ג + III-י/ו   **8** not רְאִיתֶם 3, 5 --> II-ג + III-י/ו

* The original form of the 3ms (הוּא) ended in a short /a/-vowel.

Page 125, **Review & Application III**

➡ **8** וּ ל ל ל ק 6 נו א בָּ 5 תִי סַבּ 9 תִי קַם 4 קָם (not *qawam)
7 בָּנ ה בָּנ 3 תִי בָּנ י 10 נִיתֶם בְּ 2 לִיתֶם עָ 1

Page 126, **Exercise 15.1** (III-י/ו , לו״י = III-ה, ל״ה; ג = guttural)

Meaning: Lexical form		Root type	הֵם/הֵנָּה	אַתֶּם/אַתֶּן	הִיא	הוּא	
stand/rise up		II-י/ו , עו״י	קָמוּ	קַמְתֶּם/תֶּן	קָמָה	קָם	1
go up		III-י/ו + I-ג	עָלוּ	עֲלִיתֶם/תֶן	עָלְתָה	עָלָה	2
build		לו״י , III-י/ו	בָּנוּ	בְּנִיתֶם/תֶן	בָּנְתָה	בָּנָה	3
be		irregular	הָיוּ	הֱיִיתֶם/תֶן	הָיְתָה	הָיָה	4
come		ו-II + III-א	בָּאוּ	בָּאתֶם/תֶן	בָּאָה	בָּא	5
see		ו-II + III-י/ו	רָאוּ	רְאִיתֶם/תֶן	רָאֲתָה	רָאָה	6
be/become light		twin-cons ע״ע,	קַלּוּ	קַלּוֹתֶם/תֶן	קַלָּה	קַל	7
do, make		ו-I + III-י/ו	עָשׂוּ	עֲשִׂיתֶם/תֶם	עָשְׂתָה	עָשָׂה	8
live		irregular	חָיוּ	חֲיִיתֶם/תֶן	חָיְתָה	חָיָה	9
return		ו-II-י/ , עו״י	שָׁבוּ	שַׁבְתֶּם/תֶן	שָׁבָה	שָׁב	10
put, place		ו-II-י/ , עו״י	שָׂמוּ	שַׂמְתֶּם/תֶן	שָׂמָה	שָׂם	11

Page 127, **Exercise 15.2** (III-י/ו , לו״י = III-ה, ל״ה; ג = guttural)

Translation	Root type	Lexical form	Pers pron		
you built	לו״י , III-י/ו	בָּנָה	אַתָּה	בָּנִיתָ	2
she stood up	II-י/ו , עו״י	קוּם	הִיא	קָמָה	3
he went up	III-י/ו + I-ג	עָלָה	הוּא	עָלָה	4
she did/made	III-י/ו + I-ג	עָשָׂה	הִיא	עָשְׂתָה	5
we saw	III-י/ו + II-ג	רָאָה	אֲנַחְנוּ	רָאִינוּ	6
you put	II-י/ו , עו״י	שִׂים	אַתֶּם	שַׂמְתֶּם	7

you went up	ג-I / ו-III	עָלָה	אַתֶּן	8 עֲלִיתֶן
they returned	עו"י, ו-II-י	שׁוּב	הֵם/הֵנָּה	9 שַׁבוּ
she went around	twin-consonant ע"ע	סבב	הִיא	10 סָבְבָה
you came	ו-II-י / א-III	בּוֹא	אַתְּ	11 בָּאת
we were	irregular	הָיָה	אֲנַחְנוּ	12 הָיִינוּ
you lived	irregular	חָיָה	אַתֶּם	13 חֲיִיתֶם
I am/became light	twin-consonant ע"ע	קלל	אֲנִי	14 קַלּוֹתִי
you created	ל"א, III-א	בָּרָא	אַתָּה	15 בָּרָאתָ
you did, made	ג-I / ו-III	עָשָׂה	אַתֶּן	16 עֲשִׂיתֶן
they went up	ג-I / ו-III	עָלָה	הֵם/הֵנָּה	17 עָלוּ

Page 128, Exercise 15.3

she was הָיְתָה 13	you lived חֲיִיתֶם 7	I went up עָלִיתִי 1
we went up עָלִינוּ 14	you came בָּאתֶן 8	you were הָיִיתָ 2
I lived חָיִיתִי 15	they were הָיוּ 9	you built בָּנִיתָ 3
you put שַׂמְתָּ 16	you did עָשִׂיתָ 10	he stood up קָם 4
	you saw רְאִיתֶם 11	she returned שָׁבָה 5
	he built בָּנָה 12	we saw רָאִינוּ 6

Page 129, Exercise 15.4: **I** 6, 5, 4, 7, 1, 3, 2   **II** 8, 3, 1, 2, 6, 5, 4, 7

Page 130, Exercise 15.5

1 She gave me (= to me) from the tree.   **2** I have said to the LORD, 'You [are] my God'.   **3** And he did not walk in the way of the LORD. **4** Where [is] Abel, your brother?   **5** And his wife you took to [be] your wife (= took for yourself to wife).   **6** God heard (= שָׁמַע אֶל־) the voice of the boy/lad.
7 And Jacob gave Esau bread.   **8** Jacob saw Rachel. **9** Abram dwelt in the land of Canaan. **10** What do you know (= יָדַעְתָּ)?   **11** What have you done?
12 In the beginning God created the heavens and the earth.

Page 131, Exercise 15.6

1 I, your, you **2** you, him, all **3** everything, all, his, I, your **4** this, your, you **5** you **6** this **7** you, yourself/you, I **8** -- (=none) **9** I, you (your), everything, you, me **10** your **11** you, your **12** I, all, all, you, your

Page 132, Exercise 15.7

1 him **2** his **3** that **4** all (all) **5** this, your, your **6** we, what, him
7 what, this **8** these **9** I, my, your **10** him, him, all, his, all, his
11 them **12** he

Page 134, Exercise 15.8

1 שָׁכַנְתָּ/יָשַׁבְתָּ בָּאָרֶץ הַזֹּאת. אָבִיךָ הָיָה עֶבֶד. שָׁכַנְתָּ/יָשַׁבְתָּ בָּאָרֶץ אֲשֶׁר בָּהּ הָיָה אָבִיךָ עֶבֶד.   **2** בָּאתִי אֶל־מָקוֹם קָדוֹשׁ. הָיוּ עֵצִים רַבִּים בַּמָּקוֹם הַהוּא. הָיוּ עֵצִים רַבִּים בַּמָּקוֹם אֲשֶׁר אֵלָיו בָּאתִי/בָּאתִי אֵלָיו.   **3** בָּנָה הַמֶּלֶךְ הַזָּקֵן בַּיִת

לַיהוה. בֵּית יהוה הָיָה יָפֶה מְאֹד. הָיָה הַבַּיִת אֲשֶׁר (אֹתוֹ) בָּנָה הַמֶּלֶךְ לַיהוה
יָפֶה מְאֹד.   4 לֹא הָיוּ לָאִישׁ יְלָדִים. הָיוּ לוֹ שְׁתֵּי נָשִׁים. לָאִישׁ אֲשֶׁר הָיוּ לוֹ
שְׁתֵּי נָשִׁים לֹא הָיוּ יְלָדִים עַד־יוֹם מוֹתוֹ.   5 נָתַן לְךָ אֱלֹהִים לֵב חָכָם. הָיוּ לְךָ
גַּם דְּבָרִים אֲחֵרִים. נָתַן אֱלֹהִים לָאִשָּׁה אֲשֶׁר הָיוּ לָהּ דְּבָרִים רַבִּים גַּם לֵב טוֹב.
6 הָיָה לְכָל־עַם כֶּסֶף. הַכֶּסֶף הָיָה בַּהֵיכָל. הָעָם אֲשֶׁר הָיָה לוֹ כֶּסֶף הוּא
עַם יהוה.

SECTION 16

Page 137, Review & Application I (ג = guttural)

1 not יִשְׁלַח 2 --> III-ג, ל״ג	5 not יִקְרָא 2, 6 --> III-א, ל״א
2 not יַעֲמֹד 1, 4 --> I-ג, פ״ג	6 not תַּעַבְדְנָה 1, 4 --> I-ג, פ״ג
3 not יֶאֱסֹף 1, 5 --> I-ג, פ״ג	7 not תִּבְחֲרוּ 1 --> II-ג, ע״ג
4 [1] not תַּעֲבְרִי 4 --> I-ג, פ״ג	8 not נִבְחֹר 2 --> II-ג, ע״ג
3 תַּ־עֲבְרִי [2] not 1, [3] not תַּעֲבְרִי	

Page 138, Exercise 16.1 (שְׁלֵמִים = unchangeable, ג = guttural)

	Root type	אַתֶּן/הֵנָּה	אֲנַחְנוּ	אַתָּה/הִיא	אֲנִי	הוּא
1	יִכְתֹּב	אֶכְתֹּב	תִּכְתֹּב	נִכְתֹּב	תִּכְתֹּבְנָה	שְׁלֵמִים
2	יִכְרֹת	אֶכְרֹת	תִּכְרֹת	נִכְרֹת	תִּכְרֹתְנָה	שְׁלֵמִים
3	יִשְׁפֹּט	אֶשְׁפֹּט	תִּשְׁפֹּט	נִשְׁפֹּט	תִּשְׁפֹּטְנָה	שְׁלֵמִים
4	יִזְכֹּר	אֶזְכֹּר	תִּזְכֹּר	נִזְכֹּר	תִּזְכֹּרְנָה	שְׁלֵמִים
5	יַעֲבֹר	אֶעֱבֹר	תַּעֲבֹר	נַעֲבֹר	תַּעֲבֹרְנָה	I-ג, פ״ג
6	יִשְׁלַח	אֶשְׁלַח	תִּשְׁלַח	נִשְׁלַח	תִּשְׁלַחְנָה	III-ג, ל״ג
7	יַעֲבֹד	אֶעֱבֹד	תַּעֲבֹד	נַעֲבֹד	תַּעֲבֹדְנָה	I-ג, פ״ג
8	יִגְדַּל	אֶגְדַּל	תִּגְדַּל	נִגְדַּל	תִּגְדַּלְנָה	שְׁלֵמִים
9	יִרְצַח	אֶרְצַח	תִּרְצַח	נִרְצַח	תִּרְצַחְנָה	III-ג, ל״ג
10	יִשְׁאַל	אֶשְׁאַל	תִּשְׁאַל	נִשְׁאַל	תִּשְׁאַלְנָה	II-ג, ע״ג
11	יֶאֱסֹף	אֶאֱסֹף	תֶּאֱסֹף	נֶאֱסֹף	תֶּאֱסֹפְנָה	I-ג, פ״ג
12	יִקְרָא	אֶקְרָא	תִּקְרָא	נִקְרָא	תִּקְרֶאנָה	III-א, ל״א

Page 139, Exercise 16.2 (שְׁלֵמִים = unchangeable, ג = guttural)

	Base form הוּא	אַתְּ	אַתֶּם	הֵם	Root type	Meaning: Lex form
1	יִכְתֹּב	תִּכְתְּבִי	תִּכְתְּבוּ	יִכְתְּבוּ	שְׁלֵמִים	write
2	יִכְרֹת	תִּכְרְתִי	תִּכְרְתוּ	יִכְרְתוּ	שְׁלֵמִים	cut
3	יִזְכֹּר	תִּזְכְּרִי	תִּזְכְּרוּ	יִזְכְּרוּ	שְׁלֵמִים	remember
4	יִשְׁפֹּט	תִּשְׁפְּטִי	תִּשְׁפְּטוּ	יִשְׁפְּטוּ	שְׁלֵמִים	judge
5	יִשְׁלַח	תִּשְׁלְחִי	תִּשְׁלְחוּ	יִשְׁלְחוּ	III-ג, ל״ג	send
6	יֶאֱסֹף	תַּאַסְפִי	תַּאַסְפוּ	יַאַסְפוּ	I-ג, פ״ג	gather
7	יַעֲבֹד	תַּעַבְדִי	תַּעַבְדוּ	יַעַבְדוּ	I-ג, פ״ג	work/serve
8	יַעֲבֹר	תַּעַבְרִי	תַּעַבְרוּ	יַעַבְרוּ	I-ג, פ״ג	pass, cross
9	יִשְׁאַל	תִּשְׁאֲלִי	תִּשְׁאֲלוּ	יִשְׁאֲלוּ	II-ג, ע״ג	request

Page 140, **Exercise 16.3**

Translation	Lexical form: 3ms perf	Base form: 3ms imperf	Independent pers pron	Pronoun-plus-verb	
I will guard, keep	שָׁמַר	יִשְׁמֹר	אֲנִי	אֶשְׁמֹר	2
you/she will reign (as king/queen)	מָלַךְ	יִמְלֹךְ	אַתָּה/הִיא	תִּמְלֹךְ	3
you will remember	זָכַר	יִזְכֹּר	אַתְּ	תִּזְכְּרִי	4
we will call, read	קָרָא	יִקְרָא	אֲנַחְנוּ	נִקְרָא	5
you will work, serve	עָבַד	יַעֲבֹד	אַתֶּם	תַּעַבְדוּ	6
you/they will send	שָׁלַח	יִשְׁלַח	אַתֵּן/הֵנָּה	תִּשְׁלַחְנָה	7
they will hear	שָׁמַע	יִשְׁמַע	הֵם	יִשְׁמְעוּ	8
you/they will choose	בָּחַר	יִבְחַר	אַתֵּן/הֵנָּה	תִּבְחַרְנָה	9
you/she will grow	גָּדַל/גָּדֵל	יִגְדַּל	אַתָּה/הִיא	תִּגְדַּל	10
he will find	מָצָא	יִמְצָא	הוּא	יִמְצָא	11
you will request, ask	שָׁאַל	יִשְׁאַל	אַתְּ	תִּשְׁאֲלִי	12
I will judge	שָׁפַט	יִשְׁפֹּט	אֲנִי	אֶשְׁפֹּט	13
you will anoint	מָשַׁח	יִמְשַׁח	אַתֶּם	תִּמְשְׁחוּ	14
you/they will guard, keep	שָׁמַר	יִשְׁמֹר	אַתֵּן/הֵנָּה	תִּשְׁמֹרְנָה	15
they will call, read	קָרָא	יִקְרָא	הֵם	יִקְרְאוּ	16
we will send	שָׁלַח	יִשְׁלַח	אֲנַחְנוּ	נִשְׁלַח	17
you will gather	אָסַף	יֶאֱסֹף	אַתְּ	תַּאַסְפִי	18

Page 141, **Exercise 16.4**

she will write תִּכְתֹּב	5		I will judge אֶשְׁפֹּט	1
we will cut נִכְרֹת	6		you will guard, keep תִּשְׁמֹר	2
you will write תִּכְתְּבוּ	7		you will remember תִּזְכְּרִי	3
they will remember יִזְכְּרוּ	8		he will reign (as king) יִמְלֹךְ	4

Page 142, **Exercise 16.5**

I will call, read אֶקְרָא	6		he will choose יִבְחַר	1
you will listen תִּשְׁמְעוּ	7		we will send נִשְׁלַח	2
she will choose תִּבְחַר	8		you will redeem תִּגְאַל	3
they will anoint יִמְשְׁחוּ	9		you will call, read תִּקְרְאִי	4
we will find נִמְצָא	10		I will request, ask אֶשְׁאַל	5

Page 143, **Exercise 16.6**

1 this, my, which, you, me, you, your, you   **2** this, which, I, those
3 it, you, my   **4** they, your   **5** his, you   **6** who, your (your)   **7** who
8 whom, he   **9** which, you, your, their   **10** I, my, you

Page 144, **Exercise 16.7:** 10, 3, 9, 2, 8, 1, 7, 5, 6, 4

Page 145, **Exercise 16.8**

Verbs from Exercise 16.6

1 שְׁמַרְתֶּם **2** כָּרַתִּי **3** שָׁאַלְתָּ **4** שָׁמְעוּ **5** מָשַׁחְתָּ **6** שָׁכַן **7** מָצָא

8 בָּחַר   9 כָּתַבְתָּ   10 שָׁלַחְתִּי

Verbs from Exercise 16.7

1 שְׁמַרְתֶּם   2 לָמְדוּ   3 שָׁמְעוּ   4 גָּדַל   5 שָׁלַח   6 מָלַךְ   7 קָרָאתִי

8 גָּדַל   9 זָכַר   10 שָׁמַע

Page 145, Exercise 16.9

1 יִכְרֹת יהוה בְּרִית אֶת־עַמּוֹ עַד־עוֹלָם/לְעוֹלָם.   2 יִזְכְּרוּ בָּנָיו אֶת־דְּבָרָיו וְיִשְׁמְרוּ אֶת־מִצְוֹת אֱלֹהִים.   3 אֶכְתֹּב לִילָדַי סֵפֶר אֲשֶׁר בּוֹ יִקְרְאוּ כָּל־יוֹם. יְלַמְּדוּ יְלָדַי אֶת־חֻקֵּי יהוה וְיִזְכְּרוּ אֹתָם.   4 תִּשְׁמַע קוֹל מִשָּׁמַיִם.   5 כֹּה אָמַר יהוה, 'אֹתְךָ אֶשְׁלַח לְמִצְרַיִם/מִצְרַיְמָה וְאַתָּה תַּעֲמֹד לִפְנֵי הַמֶּלֶךְ'.   6 אַתֶּם תִּבְחֲרוּ מֶלֶךְ וַאֲנִי אֶמְשַׁח אֹתוֹ.

SECTION 17

Page 147, Review & Application I (ג = guttural)

1 not שָׁלַח 2 --> III-ג, לי״א
2 not עָמַד 1 --> I-ג, פ״ג
3 not שָׁאֲלִי 1, 3 --> II-ג, ע״ג
שָׁאֲלִי [3) שְׁאָלִי [1)

4 not קָרָא 2, 4 --> III-א, לי״א
5 not עֶבְדָנָה 1 --> I-ג, פ״ג
6 not בְּחֲרוּ 1, 3 --> II-ג, ע״ג
בַּחֲרוּ [3) בְּחֲרוּ [1)

Page 148, Exercise 17.1

	Meaning	אַתֵּן	אַתֶּם	אַתְּ	אַתָּה	
send!		שְׁלַחְנָה	שִׁלְחוּ	שִׁלְחִי	שְׁלַח	1
work/serve!		עֲבֹדְנָה	עִבְדוּ	עִבְדִי	עֲבֹד	2
gather!		אֱסֹפְנָה	אִסְפוּ	אִסְפִי	אֱסֹף	3
cut!		כְּרֹתְנָה	כִּרְתוּ	כִּרְתִי	כְּרֹת	4
judge!		שְׁפֹטְנָה	שִׁפְטוּ	שִׁפְטִי	שְׁפֹט	5
request/ask!		שְׁאַלְנָה	שַׁאֲלוּ	שַׁאֲלִי	שְׁאַל	6
call/read!		קְרֶאנָה	קִרְאוּ	קִרְאִי	קְרָא	7

Page 148, Exercise 17.2

			Ordinary imperfect					
Lengthened imperfect								
אֲנַחְנוּ	אֲנִי	הֵם	אַתֶּם	אַתְּ	*Base form* הוּא			
נִשְׁמְעָה	אֶשְׁמְעָה	יִשְׁמְעוּ	תִּשְׁמְעוּ	תִּשְׁמְעִי	יִשְׁמַע	1		
נִבְחֲרָה	אֶבְחֲרָה	יִבְחֲרוּ	תִּבְחֲרוּ	תִּבְחֲרִי	יִבְחַר	2		
נִקְרְאָה	אֶקְרְאָה	יִקְרְאוּ	תִּקְרְאוּ	תִּקְרְאִי	יִקְרָא	3		
נִדְרְשָׁה	אֶדְרְשָׁה	יִדְרְשׁוּ	תִּדְרְשׁוּ	תִּדְרְשִׁי	יִדְרֹשׁ	4		
נִלְמְדָה	אֶלְמְדָה	יִלְמְדוּ	תִּלְמְדוּ	תִּלְמְדִי	יִלְמַד	5		
נִגְאֲלָה	אֶגְאֲלָה	יִגְאֲלוּ	תִּגְאֲלוּ	תִּגְאֲלִי	יִגְאַל	6		

Page 149, Exercise 17.3: 3, 8, 10, 9, 1, 2, 5, 6, 4, 7

Page 150, Exercise 17.4

1 שָׁמַרְתָּ   2 עָבַרְתִּי   3 כָּרַתְנוּ   4 שָׁלַחְתָּ   5 זָכַרְתִּי   6 שְׁמַעְתֶּם   7 כָּרַתָּ

8 שָׁמַעְתָּ   9 אָמַרְתְּ   10 עָמַדְתָּ

Page 150, **Exercise 17.5**

Ask [for] the peace of Jerusalem.	אַל תִּשְׁאֲלוּ	1
Listen, Israel, the Lᴏʀᴅ [is] our God, the Lᴏʀᴅ [is] one.	אַל תִּשְׁמַע	2
[O] earth, earth, earth, hear the word of the Lᴏʀᴅ.	אַל תִּשְׁמְעִי	3
[O] God, judge the earth.	אַל תִּשְׁפֹּט	4
Send to me David, your son.	אַל תִּשְׁלַח	5
[O] Lᴏʀᴅ, God [of] hosts, hear my prayer.	אַל תִּשְׁמַע	6
Son of man, stand upon your feet.	אַל תַּעֲמֹד	7
And write on it all the former (= first) words.	אַל תִּכְתֹּב	8
Observe (= keep) and seek [out] all the commandments of the Lᴏʀᴅ.	אַל תִּשְׁמְרוּ, אַל תִּדְרְשׁוּ	9

Page 150, **Exercise 17.6**

1 Behold, I have become/I am old, I do not know (= יָדַעְתִּי) the day of my death.   **2** If I have found favour in your sight (= eyes), please do not pass by (= מֵעַל) your servant.   **3** Look, I shall certainly do (= עָשִׂיתִי) this thing.   **4** Now (= הִנֵּה־נָא) I open (= פָּתַחְתִּי) my mouth.   **5** 'Let me pass, I pray, [through] your land'; but (= וְ) the king of Edom did not listen.   **6** Please, let my lord pass [through] before his servant.

2 אִם־נָא מָצָאנוּ חֵן בְּעֵינֵיכֶם אַל־נָא תַעַבְרוּ מֵעַל עַבְדֵּיכֶם. **3** הִנֵּה־נָא עָשִׂינוּ אֶת־הַדְּבָרִים הָאֵלֶּה. **4** הִנֵּה־נָא פָּתַחְנוּ פִינוּ. **5** נַעְבְּרָה־נָּא בְאַרְצוֹתֵיכֶם וְלֹא שָׁמְעוּ מַלְכֵי אֱדוֹם. **6** יַעַבְרוּ־נָא אֲדֹנֵינוּ לִפְנֵי עַבְדֵּיהֶם.

Page 151, **Exercise 17.7**

➡ **7** מֵעַל **1** הַדָּבָר אֶת־ **8** יַעֲבָר־נָא **4** אַל־תַּעֲבֹר **6** אֶעְבְּרָה־נָּא
5 עַבְדְּךָ **2** מָצָאתִי **3** פִּי פָּתַחְתִּי

Page 151, **Exercise 17.8**

1 Let us pass, please, through (= בְּ) your land. אַרְצְךָ (2)   **2** The Lᴏʀᴅ, our God, we will serve and him we will obey (= listen in his voice). נִשְׁמַע (1)
3 And also the nation which they serve יַעֲבֹדוּ (3)   **4** Please, do not pass by (= מֵעַל) your servant. עַבְדְּךָ (2)   **5** [It was] the Lᴏʀᴅ I remembered. זָכַרְתִּי (1)
6 She had no (= were not to her) child to (= עַד) the day of her death. יֶלֶד (4)
7 You said, 'I will not listen'. אֶשְׁמַע (1)   **8** And his commandments you should keep, and him you should obey (= listen in his voice) and him you should serve. תִּשְׁמְרוּ, תִּשְׁמְעוּ, תַּעַבְדוּ (3)   **9** Your words, I myself heard. שָׁמַעְתִּי (1)   **10** And you yourself (= you – you) would hear from heaven תִּשְׁמַע (1)   **11** But (= וְ) in all the land of Egypt [there] was bread. לֶחֶם (4)
12 By me kings reign. יִמְלְכוּ (3)

Page 152, **Exercise 17.9**

1 עָבַרְנוּ 2 עָבַדְנוּ, שְׁמַעְנוּ 3 עָבְדוּ 4 לֹא עָבַרְתָּ 5 אֶזְכֹּר 7 שָׁמַעְתִּי

8 שְׁמַרְתֶּם, שְׁמַעְתֶּם, עֲבַדְתֶּם 9 אֶשְׁמַע 10 שָׁמַעְתָּ 12 מָלְכוּ

Page 152, **Exercise 17.10**

1 עֲבֹד אֶת־יהוה. אַל־תַּעֲבֹד אֱלֹהִים אֲחֵרִים. 2 שְׁמַע לְדִבְרֵי הַנָּבִיא אֲשֶׁר יִשְׁכֹּן בְּאַרְצֶךָ. 3 זְכְרִי־נָא אֶת־אַרְצֵךְ וְאֶת־עַמֵּךְ. אַל־תִּשְׁמְעִי לָאִישׁ הָרָע הַהוּא. 4 יִזְכֹּר יהוה אֹתְךָ וְאֶת־יְלָדֶיךָ. 5 נִכְרְתָה בְּרִית עִם/אֶת־הַמֶּלֶךְ הַזֶּה. 6 כִּתְבוּ־נָא אֵת כָּל־הַחֻקִּים וְהַמִּשְׁפָּטִים הָאֵלֶּה בְּדִבְרֵי הַיָּמִים. 7 יִמְלֹךְ הַמֶּלֶךְ עָלֵינוּ וְעַל־כָּל־עַם יִשְׂרָאֵל. 8 שִׁלְחוּ־נָא אֹתָנוּ אֶל־הָאָרֶץ אֲשֶׁר נָתַן אֱלֹהִים לַאֲבוֹתֵינוּ. נַעַבְדָה אֶת־יהוה שָׁם.

SECTION 18

Page 155, **Review & Application I** (III-ה = III-י/ו; ג = guttural)

1 not שֶׁלַח 4 <-- III-ג, ל"ג   5 not בְּנַיִם 6 <-- III-י/ו, ל"י

2 א not audible 5 --> III-א + I-י/ו   6 not שׁוֹמַעַת 2, 3 --> III-ג, ל"ג

3 not עֲזוּבָה 1 --> I-ג, פ"ג   7 not עֲשׂוּיִם 1 --> III-י/ו + I-ג, ל"י

4 א not audible 5 --> III-א, ל"א   8 not שְׁאֵלוֹת 1 --> II-ג, ע"ג

Page 156, **Review & Application II**

→ 4 זובים עֹ 5 ת כוֹתֵֹ 6 ת בֵֹ לֹ מֹ 3 מוֹרה שֹׁ   שׁוֹמֵעַ 2 כות

1 רים חֹ בֹ 10 ת קֹרֹ 9 ס נֹי בֹ 8 (בָּנָֹים not) וֹי בֹ נֹ 7 ע שֹׁמֹ

Page 157, **Exercise 18.1** (III-ה = ל"ה; ג = guttural)

	Root type	Lexical form	Meaning: participle	Voice	fp	mp	fs	ms
2	פ"א	אָכַל	eating	active	אֹכְלוֹת	אֹכְלִים	אֹכֶלֶת	אֹכֵל
3	פ"ג+ע"ג	אָהַב	beloved	passive	אֲהוּבוֹת	אֲהוּבִים	אֲהוּבָה	אָהוּב
4	irregular	לָקַח	taking	active	לֹקְחוֹת	לֹקְחִים	לֹקַחַת	לֹקֵחַ
5	עו"י	קוּם	rising	active	קָמוֹת	קָמִים	קָמָה	קָם
6	פ"י+ל"א	יָרֵא	fearing/afraid	active/passive	יְרֵאוֹת	יְרֵאִים	יְרֵאָה	יָרֵא
7	irregular	נָתַן	giving	active	נֹתְנוֹת	נֹתְנִים	נֹתֶנֶת	נֹתֵן
8	פ"י+ל"ג	יָדַע	"knowing"	active	יֹדְעוֹת	יֹדְעִים	יֹדַעַת	יֹדֵעַ
9	פ"ג+לו"י	עָשָׂה	doing	active	עֹשׂוֹת	עֹשִׂים	עֹשָׂה	עֹשֶׂה
10	ל"א	קָרָא	calling	active	קֹרְאוֹת	קֹרְאִים	קֹרֵאת	קֹרֵא
11	עו"י+ל"א	בּוֹא	coming	active	בָּאוֹת	בָּאִים	בָּאָה	בָּא
12	ל"ג	שָׁמַע	listening	active	שֹׁמְעוֹת	שֹׁמְעִים	שֹׁמַעַת	שֹׁמֵעַ
13	ע"ג+לו"י	רָאָה	"seeing"	active	רֹאוֹת	רֹאִים	רֹאָה	רֹאֶה
14	לו"י	בָּנָה	built	passive	בְּנוּיוֹת	בְּנוּיִים	בְּנוּיָה	בָּנוּי
15	שְׁלֵמִים	זָקֵן	aged/old	passive	זְקֵנוֹת	זְקֵנִים	זְקֵנָה	זָקֵן

Page 158, **Exercise 18.2**

Lexical form	Participle: Meaning	Participle: Gender & number	Participle: Free form
רָדַף	pursuing	mp	1 רֹדְפִים
סָפַר	used only as noun	ms	2 סֹפֵר
שָׁפַט	judging	ms	3 שֹׁפֵט
רָדַף	pursuing	mp	4 רֹדְפִים
בּוֹא	coming	ms	5 בָּא
שָׁמַר	guarding	ms	6 שֹׁמֵר

Page 159, **Exercise 18.3**

1 who has done (= doing) this   **2** who came (= coming) up out of (= from) Egypt   **3** who comes (= coming) up   **4** who lay (= lying) with the woman **5** who reigned (= reigning) instead of

Page 160, **Exercise 18.4**

1 you, my   **2** it (= הִיא)   **3** I, you   **4** I, you, that   **5** you, I, this   **6** — **7** I, my, your   **8** you, your   **9** my, his   **10** you, you

Lexical form	Participle: Basic meaning	Participle: Voice	Participle: Gen & num	Participle: Free form
ברך	blessed	passive	fs	1 בְּרוּכָה
כָּתַב	written	passive	fs	2 כְּתוּבָה
שָׁלַח	sending	active	ms	3 שׁוֹלֵחַ
עָמַד	standing	active	ms	4 עֹמֵד
כָּרַת	cutting	active	ms	5 כֹּרֵת
כָּתַב	written	passive	ms	6 כָּתוּב
נָתַן	giving	active	ms	7 נֹתֵן
שָׁכַב	lying	active	ms	8 שֹׁכֵב
רָדַף	pursuing	active	ms	9 רֹדֵף
ארר	cursed	passive	ms	10 אָרוּר

Page 161, **Exercise 18.5**

1 These [are] the names of the Israelites who (= הַ) came (coming) to Egypt with Jacob.   **2** [O] LORD, the God of Israel, [there is] no God like you in the heavens… or (= וְ) on the earth beneath, keeping the covenant and the kindness toward (= לְ) your servants who (= הַ) [are] walking before you with all their heart.   **3** The place on which you [are] standing [is] holy ground. **4** And all the people perceived/witnessed the thunders (= "seeing" the sounds). **5** The king of Babylon of whom (= אֲשֶׁר from his face) you [are] afraid. **6** Abraham went (going) with them.   **7** [May] you [be] blessed by/of (= לְ) the LORD.   **8** [Will] they keep (keeping) the way of the LORD?   **9** What [is] this thing that you [are] doing for the people?   **10** Now (= וְ) Deborah, [a] prophetess (= woman prophetess), the wife of Lappidoth, [was] judging Israel at that time.   **11** After whom [are] you pursuing?   **12** Samuel [was] lying in the temple of the LORD.

Page 162, **Exercise 18.6**

I (singular) 1 זֶה שֵׁם בֶּן־יִשְׂרָאֵל הַבָּא...   7 בָּרוּךְ אַתָּה לַיהוה.
8 הֲשֹׁמֵר הוּא ... ?

II (plural) 3 הַמְּקוֹמוֹת אֲשֶׁר אַתֶּם עֹמְדִים עֲלֵיהֶם אַדְמַת קֹדֶשׁ הֵם.   9 מָה־הַדְּבָרִים הָאֵלֶּה אֲשֶׁר אַתֶּם עֹשִׂים לָעַמִּים?   11 אַחֲרֵי מִי אַתֶּם רֹדְפִים?

Page 162, **Exercise 18.7**

◄ 8 הַבָּאִים 1 אֶת־דֶּרֶךְ 5 הַשֹּׁמְרִים 7 מִצְרָיְמָה 2 הַהֹלְכִים
3 וְעַל־הָאָרֶץ 4 אֲשֶׁר 6 הַקּוֹלֹת (instead of הַקּוֹלוֹת).

Page 162, **Exercise 18.8**

1 הָאֲנָשִׁים בָּאִים אֶל־הַבַּיִת/הַבַּיְתָה עִם נְשֵׁיהֶם.   2 הֵם הֹלְכִים לְהֵיכַל אֱלֹהִים וְעַתָּה אֲנַחְנוּ שֹׁמְרִים עַל־בָּתֵּיהֶם.   3 אֶת־מִי אַתָּה שֹׁפֵט הַיּוֹם?   4 לָמָה/לָמָּה אַתֶּם יְרֵאִים אֶת־יְהוה? יהוה אֹהֵב אֶתְכֶם.   5 מָה הוּא עֹשֶׂה בָּאָרֶץ הַזֹּאת?
6 הִיא רֹאָה אֶת כָּל־הָעָם עֹמְדִים/עֹמֵד שָׁם.   7 מִי הָאִישׁ הָרֹדֵף אֹתָךְ?
8 הָאִשָּׁה הַיּוֹשֶׁבֶת בְּהֵיכַל אֱלֹהִים (הִיא) נְבִיאָה.

Page 163, **Exercise 18.9**: 10, 7, 8, 2, 1, 3, 12, 5, 4, 11, 6, 9

SECTION 19

Page 166, **Verb roots and particles via Hebrew names (14)**

I 1 ישע (פו״י, ו/י-I + ל״ג, III-)   help, save, rescue   2 רום (עו״י,
ו/I-II)   be high/exalted   3 חזק (פ״ג, I-)   be/become strong   4 עמס
(פ״ג, I-)   load   5 עבד (פ״ג, I-)   work, serve   6 נחם (ע״ג, II-)
treasure up (unchangeable שְׁלֵמִים)   7 צפן   comfort, console
8 זכר (שְׁלֵמִים)   remember   9 דון (עו״י, ו/I-II)   judge
10 נחם (ע״ג, II-)   comfort, console

II 1 בְּ   in   2 וְ   and (see Section 20)   3 בְּ, in, הַ   the   4 מִי, who, כְּ   like
5 אֵיךְ/אֵיכָה   how

Page 167, **Exercise 19.1** (III-י/ ו = III-ה; ג = guttural)

Infinitive-as-intensifier	Infinitive: Ordinary	Imperative: Base form	Root type	Meaning: Lexical form	Lexical form	
אָמוֹר	אֱמֹר	אֱמֹר	פ״א, א-I	say	אָמַר	3
עָלֹה	עֲלוֹת	עֲלֵה	פ״ג + לו״י	go up	עָלָה	4
עָשֹׂה/עָשׂוֹ	עֲשׂוֹת	עֲשֵׂה	פ״ג + לו״י	make	עָשָׂה	5
קָרוֹא	קְרֹא	קְרָא	ל״א, א-III	call, read	קָרָא	6
רָאֹה/רָאוֹ	רְאוֹת	רְאֵה	ע״ג + לו״י	see	רָאָה	7
שָׁלוֹחַ	שְׁלֹחַ	שְׁלַח	ל״ג, III-	send	שָׁלַח	8
שָׁמוֹעַ	שְׁמֹעַ	שְׁמַע	ל״ג, III-	listen	שָׁמַע	9

מוֹת	מוּת	מוּת	עו״י, ו/י-II	die	מוּת	10
בָּנֹה	בְּנוֹת	בְּנֹה	לו״י, ו/י-III	build	בָּנָה	11
זָכוֹר	זְכֹר	זְכֹר	שְׁלֵמִים	remember	זָכַר	12
כָּתוֹב	כְּתֹב	כְּתֹב	שְׁלֵמִים	write	כָּתַב	13
מָצוֹא	מְצֹא	מְצֹא	ל״א, א-III	find	מָצָא	14
עָבוֹד	עֲבֹד	עֲבֹד	פ״ג, ג-I	work	עָבַד	15
שׁוֹב	שׁוּב	שׁוּב	עו״י, ו/י-II	return	שׁוּב	16

Page 168, Exercise 19.2

1 take care of/remember **2** be king/reign, rule **3** keep **4** walking **5** learn **6** listen **7** keep

Page 169, Exercise 19.3: 2, 6, 1, 9, 7, 8, 5, 10, 4, 3

Page 170, Exercise 19.4

➤ 8 כְּשָׁכַב 3 בְּרִית 9 עֲשׂוֹת 5 אֶרֶץ 4 וְשָׁמַיִם 10 כִּי 6 אָכַל לְבִלְתִּי
2 הֱיוֹת הָאָדָם 7 עַמְּךָ 1 אֶת־אָבִיו

Page 170, Exercise 19.5

Translation	Infinitive-plus-pronoun		Translation	Infinitive-plus-pronoun	
her calling/reading	קָרְאָהּ	8	our guarding	שָׁמְרֵנוּ	1
their listening/hearing	שָׁמְעָם	9	my judging	שָׁפְטִי	2
their standing up	קוּמָן	10	your help (helping)	עֶזְרְךָ	3
your death (dying)	מוּתְךָ	11	your remembering	זָכְרֶךָ	4
his forgetting	שִׁכְחוֹ	12	his eating	אָכְלוֹ	5
our doing	עֲשׂוֹתֵנוּ	13	her writing	כָּתְבָהּ	6
your coming	בּוֹאֲכֶם	14	your building	בְּנוֹתְכֶם	7

Page 171, Exercise 19.6

1 he (his), these **2** him, us, our, us **3** you (your), it **4** he (his), his **5** I (my) **6** we, we, we (our) **7** you (your), all, your **8** all, that, you, you (your), this **9** he (his), his

Page 172, Exercise 19.7

I (plural): 1 בְּכָתְבָם 3 אֲכָלְכֶם 4 בְּבָרְחָם 5 שׁוּבֵנוּ 7 לְשָׁמְרְכֶם 9 רָדְפָם
II (singular): 2 לְעֶזְרִי 6 בְּזָכְרִי 8 בֹּאֲךָ

Page 172, Exercise 19.8

1 To guard the way to (= of) the tree of life **2** When Joshua was (= in Joshua's being) by/near (= בְּ) Jericho **3** To write the words of this law in (= עַל) [a] book **4** When/as he heard (= as/in his hearing) these words **5** The LORD – he hears when I call (= in my calling) to him **6** When you lie down (in your lying down), it will watch (stand guard) over you **7** Not to keep his commandments and his ordinances **8** If you do (= שָׁכַח) forget the Lord, your God **9** Remember this day [in] which you went out of (= מִ) Egypt, from [the] house of slaves. **10** Go... to David, 'Thus said the Lord' **11** And if [it is] bad in your sight (= eyes) to serve the Lord, choose for yourself today whom (= אֶת־מִי) you will serve, whether (= אִם) [the] gods that your fathers served ... or (= וְאִם) the gods of the Amorite[s] in whose land (= אֲשֶׁר + in their land) you dwell (= dwelling). But (= וְ) [as for] me (= אָנֹכִי) and my house, we shall serve the Lord. **12** You know (= יָדַעְתָּ) yourself (= additional אַתָּה) David, my father, that he could not build (= to build) [a] house for the name of the Lord, his God. **13** And when he heard (= as his hearing) the words of Rebekah, his sister, saying (= לֵאמֹר)

14 Look, you are old (= זָקַנְתָּ) and your sons have not walked in your ways. Now appoint (= שִׂימָה) for us [a] king to judge us like all the nations.

Page 173, **Exercise 19.9**

a) 1 הֹלֵךְ going (irregular) **2** בָּא coming II-י/ו, עו״י, + III-א, ל״א **3** עֹמֶדֶת standing I-ג, פ״ג **4** הֹלְכִים going (irregular) **5** מָלֵא full III-א, ל״א **6** הֹלֵךְ going (irregular) **7** שָׁבִים returning II-י/ו, עו״י

b) 1 מוּת die/dying II-י/ו, עו״י (מֵת) **2** הָרֹג kill/killing I-ג, פ״ג (הָרֹג, הָרוּג) **3** רָפוֹא cure/curing III-א, ל״א (רָפֵא) **4** שָׁמוֹר guard/guarding, unchangeable (שָׁמֵר, שָׁמוּר) **5** אֱהֹב love I-ג, פ״ג + II-ג, ע״ג (אָהַב, אָהוּב) **6** שְׂנֹא hate III-א, ל״א (שָׂנֵא, שָׂנוּא)

Page 173, **Exercise 19.10**

1 בְּכִתְבִי סֵפֶר עַל הַנְּבִיאִים, לֹא הָיָה עַבְדִּי בַּבַּיִת. **2** יַעֲזֹר לְךָ אָבִיךְ בְּשָׁמְרְךָ אֶת־מִצְוֹת יהוה. **3** בְּשָׁלְחָהּ אֶת־בַּעֲלָהּ/אִישָׁהּ אֶל־הַכֹּהֵן, עָמַד הַכֹּהֵן בְּפֶתַח הַהֵיכָל. **4** כְּבוֹאֵךְ נָתְנָה לָךְ הָאִשָּׁה לֶחֶם. **5** בַּעֲשׂוֹתוֹ אֶת־הַשַּׁעַר, לֹא הָיָה אָבִיו בָּעִיר. **6** בָּאתִי לַעֲזֹר לְעַמִּי. **7** יָצָאתָ מִן/מֵהָאָרֶץ לִמְצֹא לְבִנְךָ אִשָּׁה.

Page 173, **Exercise 19.11**

1 בְּכָתְבֵנוּ סְפָרִים עַל הַנְּבִיאִים, לֹא הָיוּ עֲבָדֵינוּ בַּבָּתִּים. **2** יַעַזְרוּ לָכֶם אֲבוֹתֵיכֶם בְּשָׁמְרְכֶם אֶת־מִצְוֹת יהוה. **3** בְּשָׁלְחָן אֶת־בְּעֲלֵיהֶן אֶל־הַכֹּהֲנִים, עָמְדוּ הַכֹּהֲנִים בְּפִתְחֵי הַהֵיכָלוֹת. **4** כְּבוֹאֲכֶן נָתְנוּ לָכֶן הַנָּשִׁים לֶחֶם. **5** בַּעֲשׂוֹתָם אֶת־הַשְּׁעָרִים, לֹא הָיוּ אֲבוֹתֵיהֶם בֶּעָרִים. **6** בָּאנוּ לַעֲזֹר לְעַמֵּנוּ (לְעַמֵּינוּ pl). **7** יְצָאתֶם מִן/מֵהָאֲרָצוֹת לִמְצֹא לִבְנֵיכֶם נָשִׁים.

SECTION 20

Page 176, **Exercise 20.1**

	Perf Imperf	Inverted perf Inverted imperf	Deviant forms: Relevant sound change rule	Translation
1	קָרָאתִי	וָאֶקְרָא	1	I called
2	תִּקְרְאוּ	וּקְרָאתֶם	2	you will call

you will work	3	וַעֲבַדְתֶּם	תַּעַבְדוּ	3
he will reign (as king)	4	וּמָלַךְ	יִמְלֹךְ	4
you/she will lie down		וְשָׁכַבְתָּ/וְשָׁכְבָה	תִּשְׁכַּב	5
he wrote		וַיִּכְתֹּב	כָּתַב	6
you wrote		וַתִּכְתֹּב	כָּתַבְתָּ	7
they cut		וַיִּכְרְתוּ	כָּרְתוּ	8
he dwelt		וַיִּשְׁכֹּן	שָׁכַן	9
I will stand		וְעָמַדְתִּי	אֶעֱמֹד	10
they passed		וַיַּעַבְרוּ	עָבְרוּ	11
we will hear		וְשָׁמַעְנוּ	נִשְׁמַע	12
you remembered		וַתִּזְכְּרִי	זָכַרְתְּ	13
you guarded		וַתִּשְׁמְרוּ	שְׁמַרְתֶּם	14
you will hear	2	וּשְׁמַעְתֶּן	תִּשְׁמַעְנָה	15
I remembered	1	וָאֶזְכֹּר	זָכַרְתִּי	16
he guarded		וַיִּשְׁמֹר	שָׁמַר	17
we will burn		וְשָׂרַפְנוּ	נִשְׂרֹף	18

Page 177, Exercise 20.2

1 And the LORD God called to the man (קָרָא)   **2** And the LORD will reign (as king) over them in Mount Zion from now and forever (יִמְלֹךְ)   **3** You shall be servants to us (= you will serve us) (תַּעַבְדוּ)   **4** He had written in the name of the king (כָּתַב)   **5** And he wrote in the book (כָּתַב)   **6** So (= וְ) they made (= cut) [a] covenant at Beer-sheba (כָּרְתוּ)   **7** And I have remembered my covenant (זָכַרְתִּי)   **8** And they burnt her and her father with fire (= the fire) (שָׂרְפוּ)   **9** Then (= וְ) David slept (= lay down) with his fathers (שָׁכַב)   **10** He kept his commandments (שָׁמַר)   **11** The glory of the LORD resided (= dwelt) on Mount Sinai (שָׁכַן)   **12** He burnt the house of the LORD and the house of the king and all the houses of Jerusalem (שָׂרַף)
13 After that (= וְ) God remembered Noah (זָכַר)

Page 178, Exercise 20.3

1 he, his   **2** I, you   **3** I, your   **4** you, your, his, his, his   **5** whole
6 your

Page 179, Exercise 20.4

Translation	Object pronoun	Verb		
I knew you	אֹתְךָ	יָדַעְתִּי	יְדַעְתִּיךָ	2
she bore me	אֹתִי	יָלְדָה	יְלָדַתְנִי	3
he sent you	אֹתְךָ	שָׁלַח	שְׁלָחֲךָ	4
he took me	אֹתִי	לָקַח	לְקָחַנִי	5
I anointed you	אֹתְךָ	מָשַׁחְתִּי	מְשַׁחְתִּיךָ	6
she/it ate him/it	אֹתוֹ	אָכְלָה	אֲכָלַתְהוּ	7

they left me	אֹתִי	עָזְבוּ	עֲזָבוּנִי 8
I sent you	אֹתְךָ	שָׁלַחְתִּי	שָׁלַחְתִּיךָ 9
you left me	אֹתִי	עָזַבְתָּ	עֲזַבְתַּנִי 10
he hated her	אֹתָהּ	שָׂנֵא	שְׂנֵאָהּ 11
he loved her	אֹתָהּ	אָהֵב (אָהַב)	אֲהֵבָהּ 12
I chose you	אֹתְךָ	בָּחַרְתִּי	בְּחַרְתִּיךָ 13
I sent him	אֹתוֹ	שָׁלַחְתִּי	שְׁלַחְתִּיו 14
I sent them	אֹתָם	שָׁלַחְתִּי	שְׁלַחְתִּים 15
you loved us	אֹתָנוּ	אֲהַבְתָּ	אֲהַבְתָּנוּ 16
he sent me	אֹתִי	שָׁלַח	שְׁלָחַנִי 17

Page 180, Exercise 20.5

1 your, me, all   **2** I (I, I), you   **3** you   **4** who, me, my, my   **5** I, myself, you   **6** him   **7** this, you, I (I, I), you   **8** he, her, he, her   **9** you, my, I, (you), my (me)   **10** I (I, I), him   **11** I (I, I), them   **12** I, you, you, you, us   **13** me, you

Page 181, Exercise 20.6

1 My God, my God, why have you left me?   **2** Look, [if/supposed] I come to the Israelites (= sons of Israel) and say to them, 'The God of your fathers has sent me to you', and they say to me, 'What [is] his name?'   **3** The LORD, the God of your fathers, the God of Abraham, the God of Isaac and the God of Jacob has sent me to you; this [is] my name forever…   **4** I have indeed (= פָּקוֹד) paid attention [to] you and [to] what (= הַ) [is] being done (= עָשׂוּי) to you in Egypt.   **5** And the Israelites shall keep the sabbath, observe (= לַעֲשׂוֹת) the sabbath throughout (= לְ) their generations [as an] everlasting covenant.   **6** I will open your mouth and you will say to them, 'Thus says (= אָמַר) the LORD God!' He who listens (= the listening [one]), let him listen'   **7** For the whole assembly, all of them, [are] holy.   **8** The Israelites listened to him…. And never again (= לֹא עוֹד 'not more') did arise in Israel [a] prophet like Moses, whom the LORD knew (= knew him) face to face. For all the signs… that the LORD sent him to do in the land of Egypt to Pharaoh and to all his servants and to his whole land.   **9** Lest we burn you and the house of your father with fire (= the fire).

Page 182, Exercise 20.7

→ **4** עֲזָבְתָּנִי   **11** אָנֹכִי בָא   **7** שְׁלָחַנִי   **8** אֲבֹתֵיכֶם (instead of אֲבוֹתֵיכֶם)
12 זֶה־שְּׁמִי   **6** פָּקֹד פָּקַדְתִּי   **9** הֶעָשׂוּי   **3** לַעֲשׂוֹת   **2** אֲשֶׁר יָדְעוּ
1 אֶתְכֶם   **10** כִּי   **5** אַרְצוֹ

Page 182, **Exercise 20.8:** 32 cases of וְ.

Page 183, **Exercise 20.9:** 29 cases of inverted imperfect.

Page 183, **Exercise 20.10**

1 הָלַךְ הַנָּבִיא אֶל־הָעָם וַיִּקְרָא בְּאָזְנָיו/בְּאָזְנֵיהֶם אֶת־תּוֹרַת יהוה. וַיַּעֲמֹד הַנָּבִיא וַיִּבְחַר לָעָם מֶלֶךְ וַיִּמְשַׁח אֹתוֹ. וַיִּשְׁמַע הַמֶּלֶךְ בְּקוֹל יהוה אֱלֹהָיו וַיִּזְכֹּר אֶת־כָּל־מִצְוֹתָיו כָּל־יְמֵי חַיָּיו וַיִּמְלֹךְ יָמִים רַבִּים.   2 כָּתַב הַשֹּׁפֵט אֶת־כָּל־חֻקֵּי יהוה וּמִצְוֹתָיו וַיַּעֲבֹד הָעָם אֶת־יהוה וַיִּשְׁמֹר אֶת־מִצְוֹתָיו.   3 מָצָא הַמַּלְאָךְ אֶת־הָאִשָּׁה בַּשָּׂדֶה וַיִּשְׁאַל אַתָּה מִי נָתַן לָהּ לֶחֶם.

Page 183, **Exercise 20.11**

1 הָלְכוּ הַנְּבִיאִים אֶל־הָעַמִּים וַיִּקְרְאוּ בְּאָזְנֵיהֶם אֶת־תּוֹרַת יהוה. וַיַּעַמְדוּ הַנְּבִיאִים וַיִּבְחֲרוּ לָעַמִּים מְלָכִים וַיִּמְשְׁחוּ אֹתָם. וַיִּשְׁמְעוּ הַמְּלָכִים בְּקוֹל יהוה אֱלֹהֵיהֶם וַיִּזְכְּרוּ אֶת־כָּל־מִצְוֹתָיו כָּל־יְמֵי חַיֵּיהֶם וַיִּמְלְכוּ יָמִים רַבִּים.

2 כָּתְבוּ הַשֹּׁפְטִים אֶת־כָּל־חֻקֵּי יהוה וּמִצְוֹתָיו וַיַּעַבְדוּ הָעַמִּים אֶת־יהוה וַיִּשְׁמְרוּ אֶת־מִצְוֹתָיו.

3 מָצְאוּ הַמַּלְאָכִים אֶת־הַנָּשִׁים בַּשָּׂדוֹת וַיִּשְׁאֲלוּ אֹתָן מִי נָתַן לָהֶן לֶחֶם.

SECTION 21

Page 186, **Review & Application I** (III-ה; ‎III-‎ו/‎‎י = ‎‎ג = guttural)

A 1 not נִשְׁמֶעֶת ‎2, 3 --> ‎III-‎ג, ‎ל"ג   5 א not audible 5 --> III-‎א, ‎ל"א
2 not נִגְאֲלוּ ‎1 --> ‎II-‎ג, ‎ע"ג   6 not יִשְׁלַח ‎2 --> ‎III-‎ג, ‎ל"ג
3 not הֻשְׁבַּע ‎2 --> ‎III-‎ג, ‎ל"ג   7 not תֶּחֱשַׁב ‎4 --> ‎I-‎ג, ‎פ"ג
4 not הַלֶּחְמִי ‎1 --> ‎II-‎ג, ‎ע"ג

B 1 not נֶחְשַׁב ‎1 --> ‎I-‎ג, ‎פ"ג   5 not נִבְנַי* ‎5 --> ‎III-‎י/‎ו, ‎לו"י
2 not נִבְנֵיתָ ‎4, 6 --> ‎III-‎י/‎ו, ‎לו"י   6 not תִּבְנִיי ‎5 --> ‎III-‎י/‎ו, ‎לו"י
3 not נֶאֱכַל ‎1, 2 --> ‎I-‎א, ‎פ"א   7 not נֶעֶמְדוּ ‎1, 2, 3 --> ‎I-‎ג, ‎פ"ג
4 not נַוְלְדָה ‎4 --> ‎I-‎י/‎ו, ‎פו"י   נֶ-עֶמְדוּ ⁽³⁾ נֶ-עָמְדוּ ⁽²⁾ נֶ-עָמְדוּ ⁽¹⁾

* The original form of the 3ms (הוּא) ended in a short /a/-vowel.

Page 187, **Exercise 21.1**

Imperf	Perf	Imperf	Perf	
יִלָּחֵם	נִלְחַם	יִזָּכֵר	נִזְכַּר	הוּא
תִּלָּחֵם	נִלְחֲמָה	תִּזָּכֵר	נִזְכְּרָה	הִיא
תִּלָּחֵם	נִלְחַמְתָּ	תִּזָּכֵר	נִזְכַּרְתָּ	אַתָּה
תִּלָּחֲמִי	נִלְחַמְתְּ	תִּזָּכְרִי	נִזְכַּרְתְּ	אַתְּ
אֶלָּחֵם	נִלְחַמְתִּי	אֶזָּכֵר	נִזְכַּרְתִּי	אֲנִי
יִלָּחֲמוּ	נִלְחֲמוּ	יִזָּכְרוּ	נִזְכְּרוּ	הֵם
תִּלָּחַמְנָה	נִלְחֲמוּ	תִּזָּכַרְנָה	נִזְכְּרוּ	הֵנָּה
תִּלָּחֲמוּ	נִלְחַמְתֶּם	תִּזָּכְרוּ	נִזְכַּרְתֶּם	אַתֶּם
תִּלָּחַמְנָה	נִלְחַמְתֶּן	תִּזָּכַרְנָה	נִזְכַּרְתֶּן	אַתֶּן
נִלָּחֵם	נִלְחַמְנוּ	נִזָּכֵר	נִזְכַּרְנוּ	אֲנַחְנוּ

Page 188, Exercise 21.2

Translation: Imperative	אַתֵּן	אַתֶּם	אַתְּ	אַתָּה	
be on your guard/be careful!	הִשָּׁמַרְנָה	הִשָּׁמְרוּ	הִשָּׁמְרִי	הִשָּׁמֵר	1
feel ashamed!	הִכָּלַמְנָה	הִכָּלְמוּ	הִכָּלְמִי	הִכָּלֵם	2
fight!	הִלָּחַמְנָה	הִלָּחֲמוּ	הִלָּחֲמִי	הִלָּחֵם	3
swear!	הִשָּׁבַעְנָה	הִשָּׁבְעוּ	הִשָּׁבְעִי	הִשָּׁבַע	4
remember!	הִזָּכַרְנָה	הִזָּכְרוּ	הִזָּכְרִי	הִזָּכֵר	5
escape!	הִמָּלַטְנָה	הִמָּלְטוּ	הִמָּלְטִי	הִמָּלֵט	6

Page 189, Exercise 21.3

Translation: Participle	fp	mp	fs	ms	
being guarded	נִשְׁמָרוֹת	נִשְׁמָרִים	נִשְׁמֶרֶת	נִשְׁמָר	1
fighting	נִלְחָמוֹת	נִלְחָמִים	נִלְחֶמֶת	נִלְחָם	2
being cut off	נִכְרָתוֹת	נִכְרָתִים	נִכְרֶתֶת	נִכְרָת	3
being buried	נִקְבָּרוֹת	נִקְבָּרִים	נִקְבֶּרֶת	נִקְבָּר	4
being found	נִמְצָאוֹת	נִמְצָאִים	נִמְצֵאת	נִמְצָא	5
remembering	נִזְכָּרוֹת	נִזְכָּרִים	נִזְכֶּרֶת	נִזְכָּר	6
swearing	נִשְׁבָּעוֹת	נִשְׁבָּעִים	נִשְׁבַּעַת	נִשְׁבָּע	7
being opened	נִפְתָּחוֹת	נִפְתָּחִים	נִפְתַּחַת	נִפְתָּח	8
being written	נִכְתָּבוֹת	נִכְתָּבִים	נִכְתֶּבֶת	נִכְתָּב	9
being judged	נִשְׁפָּטוֹת	נִשְׁפָּטִים	נִשְׁפֶּטֶת	נִשְׁפָּט	10

Page 189, Exercise 21.4

pers/gen/num	Root	Tense		
3ms הוּא	זכר	imperf	יִזָּכֵר	1
3mp הֵם	כרת	imperf	יִכָּרְתוּ	2
3mp הֵם	זכר	imperf	יִזָּכְרוּ	3
mp הֵם/אַתֶּם/אֲנַחְנוּ	שבר	participle	נִשְׁבְּרֵי	4
3ms הוּא	לחם	imperf	יִלָּחֵם	5
2mp אַתֶּם	לחם	imperf	תִּלָּחֲמוּ	6
–	כלם	infinitive	הִכָּלֵם	7
2ms אַתָּה	מלט	imperf	תִּמָּלֵט	8
ms הוּא/אַתָּה/אֲנִי	שבר	participle	נִשְׁבָּר	9
3cp הֵם/הֵנָּה	מצא	perf	נִמְצְאוּ	10
3ms הוּא	קרא	perf	נִקְרָא	11
3cp הֵם/הֵנָּה	ברך	inverted perf	וְנִבְרְכוּ	12

Page 191, Exercise 21.5

Translation	Independent objet pronoun	Verb		
serve him!	אֹתוֹ	עֲבֹד	עָבְדֵהוּ	1
judge me!	אֹתִי	שְׁפֹט	שָׁפְטֵנִי	2

send me!	אֹתִי	שְׁלַח	שְׁלָחֵנִי 3
write them!	אֹתָם	כְּתֹב	כָּתְבֵם 4
remember me!	אֹתִי	זְכֹר	זָכְרֵנִי 5
keep them!	אֹתָם	שְׁמֹר	שָׁמְרֵם 6
bury her!	אֹתָהּ	קִבְרוּ	קִבְרוּהָ 7
you/she will bury him/it/us.	אֹתָנוּ/אֹתוֹ	תִּקְבֹּר	תִּקְבְּרֶנּוּ 8
you/she will bury me.	אֹתִי	תִּקְבֹּר	תִּקְבְּרֵנִי 9
he/it will guard you.	אֹתְךָ	יִשְׁמֹר	יִשְׁמָרְךָ 10
he will send me.	אֹתִי	יִשְׁלַח	יִשְׁלָחֵנִי 11
they will bury him.	אֹתוֹ	יִקְבְּרוּ	יִקְבְּרוּהוּ 12

Page 192, Exercise 21.6

1 me   **2** he, it   **3** you, me   **4** what, you, him, you, him   **5** them
6 me, my   **7** I, you   **8** you, me   **9** they, them   **10** me   **11** you, him, that   **12** them, your   **13** you, her

Page 192, Exercise 21.7

1 And there you shall be buried, you and all your friends (= those who love you).   **2** The heavens were opened.   **3** He shall be cut off from his people.
4 And you shall not fight against (= עִם) your brothers.   **5** And the name of Israel will be remembered no more.   **6** ²⁹ The events/affairs/acts of Rehoboam and all that he did, [are] they not written in (= עַל) the book of the Chronicles (= events/ words of the days) of (= לְ) the kings of Judah!   ³⁰ And [there] was a war between Rehoboam and (between) Jeroboam all the time (= the days).
³¹ And Rehoboam slept [lay down] with his fathers and was buried with his fathers in the city of David. His mother's name [was] Naamah the Ammonitess. Then Abijam his son reigned after (= תַּחַת 'instead of') him.   **7** Please, take care of this cursed [woman] and bury her for she [is a] king's daughter.
8 They buried him in his house.   **9** And God sent me before you.
10 The LORD will keep you from all evil; he will keep your life (= soul).
11 And you, write with regard to (= עַל) the Jews as you please (= as good in your eyes), in the king's name… for… what (= אֲשֶׁר) [is] written in the name of the king…

Page 193, Exercise 21.8

2 נִכְתָּב   10 הֲלֹא   5 סֵפֶר דִּבְרֵי הַיָּמִים   4 (אֹהֵב) לֹא־תִלָּחֲמוּ   11 אֹהֲבֶיךָ ◄

9 פִּקְדוּ־נָא   6 הָאֲרוּרָה   8 וְנִכְרַת   3 וַיִּקְבְּרֻהוּ   7 כִּי בַת־מֶלֶךְ הִיא

12 וַיִּשְׁלָחֵנִי   1 יִשְׁמָרְךָ

Page 194, Exercise 21.9

1 אַחֲרֵי הַמִּלְחָמָה נִמְצְאוּ בָנָיו. בְּהִמָּצְאָם לֹא הָיָה לָהֶם מַיִם וָלֶחֶם. לֹא נֶהֶרְגוּ בָנָיו בִּידֵי רֹדְפֵיהֶם כִּי נִמְלְטוּ מִן־הַמָּקוֹם בַּבֹּקֶר. נִשְׁבְּעוּ הַבָּנִים לָשׁוּב אֶל־שְׂדֵה

הַמִּלְחָמָה.　2　נֶהֶרְגוּ הָאֲנָשִׁים וְנִקְבְּרוּ/וַיִּקָּבְרוּ עִם־אֲבוֹתֵיהֶם.　3　נִמְצְאוּ
הַסְּפָרִים בְּהֵיכַל יהוה וְנִקְרְאוּ/וַיִּקָּרְאוּ בְּאָזְנֵי הָאֲנָשִׁים בַּהֵיכָל.　4　מָצְאוּ
אֹתָנוּ/מְצָאוּנוּ הַשּׁוֹמְרִים בִּהְיוֹתֵנוּ שָׁם.　5　הִשָּׁמְרוּ לָכֶם פֶּן/לְמַעַן לֹא/בַּעֲבוּר
לֹא תִּשְׁכְּחוּ אֶת־יהוה.

Page 194, **Exercise 21.10**

1　אַחֲרֵי הַמִּלְחָמָה נִמְצָא בְּנוֹ. בְּהִמָּצְאוֹ לֹא הָיָה לוֹ מַיִם וָלָחֶם. לֹא נֶהֱרַג בְּנוֹ
בִּידֵי רֹדְפוֹ כִּי נִמְלַט מִן־הַמָּקוֹם בַּבֹּקֶר. נִשְׁבַּע הַבֵּן לָשׁוּב אֶל־שְׂדֵה הַמִּלְחָמָה.
2　נֶהֱרַג הָאִישׁ וְנִקְבַּר/וַיִּקָּבֵר עִם־אָבִיו.　3　נִמְצָא הַסֵּפֶר בְּהֵיכַל יהוה וְנִקְרָא/וַיִּקָּרֵא
בְּאָזְנֵי הָאִישׁ בַּהֵיכָל.　4　מָצָא אֹתִי/מְצָאַנִי הַשּׁוֹמֵר בִּהְיוֹתִי שָׁם.　5　הִשָּׁמֶר לְךָ
פֶּן/לְמַעַן לֹא/בַּעֲבוּר לֹא תִּשְׁכַּח אֶת־יהוה.

Page 194, **Exercise 21.11**

1　יִמָּצֵא, יֵהָרֵג, יִמָּלֵט, יִשָּׁבַע　2　יֵהָרֵג　3　יִמָּצֵא　4　יִמְצָא, יִמְצָאֵנִי

SECTION 22

Page 196, **Review & Application I** (III-י/ו = III-ה; ג = guttural, including ר)

1 not יְכַסָּיו <-- 5　III-י/ו, לו״י	6 not מְשַׁלֶּחֶת <-- 2　III-ג, ל״ג
2 not מְבָרֵךְ <-- 3　II-ג, ע״ג	7 not מֵאָנוּ <-- 1, 3　II-ג, ע״ג
3 not כִּסִּינוּ <-- 4　III-י/ו, לו״י	8 א not audible, 6 <-- III-א, ל״א
4 not שַׁלַּח <-- 2　III-ג, ל״ג	9 not מְבַקְשִׁים <-- 7　unchangeable שְׁלֵמִים
5 not בְּרֵךְ <-- 2, 3　II-ג, ע״ג	

Page 197, **Review & Application II**

→ 9　לים לְ מַה 10　נוּ אָ מִלֵּ רָה דָּ בָּ דִ 7　תִי בַּרְ דַּ 3　אן מָ יְ

5　דָרְ בַ מְ 8　תָּ סִי כְּ 2　מוּ נִ חַ 4　אָר פֶּ 6　חַ מְשַׁלַּ

Page 197, **Review & Application III**

→ 1　נַשׁ מַ עַת (2a)　2　בִּ קְ שָׁה (3b)　3　יְ עֲבֹד (3a)　4　וַ יֶּחֱזַק (3b)

5　אָבוֹ תִי (1a)　6　נָ אֱכַל (3a)　7　עֲ בַ נִי (2b)　8　מְדַ בֵּ רֶת (2a)

9　זְכָ רְ נוּ (2b)　10　יְ דְּ הָ (2b)　11　יְ דַּע נוּ (1b)　12　הַ לְלוּ (3b)

13　יֵשׁ כַּב (1b)　14　טְ הַר (3b)　15　יְ אֱסֹף (3a)

Page 199, **Exercise 22.1**

	Imperf	Perf	Imperf	Perf	Imperf	Perf
הוּא	יְבַקֵּשׁ	בִּקֵּשׁ	יְדַבֵּר	דִּבֶּר	יְקַדֵּשׁ	קִדֵּשׁ
הִיא	תְּבַקֵּשׁ	בִּקְשָׁה	תְּדַבֵּר	דִּבְּרָה	תְּקַדֵּשׁ	קִדְּשָׁה
אַתָּה	תְּבַקֵּשׁ	בִּקַּשְׁתָּ	תְּדַבֵּר	דִּבַּרְתָּ	תְּקַדֵּשׁ	קִדַּשְׁתָּ
אַתְּ	תְּבַקְּשִׁי	בִּקַּשְׁתְּ	תְּדַבְּרִי	דִּבַּרְתְּ	תְּקַדְּשִׁי	קִדַּשְׁתְּ
אֲנִי	אֲבַקֵּשׁ	בִּקַּשְׁתִּי	אֲדַבֵּר	דִּבַּרְתִּי	אֲקַדֵּשׁ	קִדַּשְׁתִּי
הֵם	יְבַקְּשׁוּ	בִּקְּשׁוּ	יְדַבְּרוּ	דִּבְּרוּ	יְקַדְּשׁוּ	קִדְּשׁוּ

תְּבַקֵּשְׁנָה	בִּקְּשׁוּ	תְּדַבֵּרְנָה	דִּבְּרוּ	תְּקַדֵּשְׁנָה	קִדְּשׁוּ	הֵנָּה
תְּבַקְּשׁוּ	בִּקַּשְׁתֶּם	תְּדַבְּרוּ	דִּבַּרְתֶּם	תְּקַדְּשׁוּ	קִדַּשְׁתֶּם	אַתֶּם
תְּבַקֵּשְׁנָה	בִּקַּשְׁתֶּן	תְּדַבֵּרְנָה	דִּבַּרְתֶּן	תְּקַדֵּשְׁנָה	קִדַּשְׁתֶּן	אַתֵּן
נְבַקֵּשׁ	בִּקַּשְׁנוּ	נְדַבֵּר	דִּבַּרְנוּ	נְקַדֵּשׁ	קִדַּשְׁנוּ	אֲנַחְנוּ

Page 200, Exercise 22.2

Translation	אַתֶּן	אַתֶּם	אַתְּ	אַתָּה	
speak!	דַּבֵּרְנָה	דַּבְּרוּ	דַּבְּרִי	דַּבֵּר	1
sanctify (make holy)!	קַדֵּשְׁנָה	קַדְּשׁוּ	קַדְּשִׁי	קַדֵּשׁ	2
recount! tell!	סַפֵּרְנָה	סַפְּרוּ	סַפְּרִי	סַפֵּר	3
seek!	בַּקֵּשְׁנָה	בַּקְּשׁוּ	בַּקְּשִׁי	בַּקֵּשׁ	4
honour (make weighty)!	כַּבֵּדְנָה	כַּבְּדוּ	כַּבְּדִי	כַּבֵּד	5
praise!	הַלֵּלְנָה	הַלְלוּ	הַלְלִי	הַלֵּל	6
teach (let learn)!	לַמֵּדְנָה	לַמְּדוּ	לַמְּדִי	לַמֵּד	7

Page 200, Exercise 22.3

Translation	fp	mp	fs	ms	
strengthening	מְחַזְּקוֹת	מְחַזְּקִים	מְחַזֶּקֶת	מְחַזֵּק	1
honouring	מְכַבְּדוֹת	מְכַבְּדִים	מְכַבֶּדֶת	מְכַבֵּד	2
recounting, telling	מְסַפְּרוֹת	מְסַפְּרִים	מְסַפֶּרֶת	מְסַפֵּר	3
seeking	מְבַקְּשׁוֹת	מְבַקְּשִׁים	מְבַקֶּשֶׁת	מְבַקֵּשׁ	4
teaching	מְלַמְּדוֹת	מְלַמְּדִים	מְלַמֶּדֶת	מְלַמֵּד	5

Page 200, Exercise 22.4

Imperf	Perf	Imperf	Perf	Imperf	Perf	
יְכַפֵּר	כִּפֵּר	יֶחֱזַק	חָזַק	יִכְבַּד	כָּבֵד	הוּא
תְּכַפֵּר	כִּפְּרָה	תֶּחֱזַק	חָזְקָה	תִּכְבַּד	כָּבְדָה	הִיא
תְּכַפֵּר	כִּפַּרְתָּ	תֶּחֱזַק	חָזַקְתָּ	תִּכְבַּד	כָּבַדְתָּ	אַתָּה
תְּכַפְּרִי	כִּפַּרְתְּ	תֶּחֶזְקִי	חָזַקְתְּ	תִּכְבְּדִי	כָּבַדְתְּ	אַתְּ
אֲכַפֵּר	כִּפַּרְתִּי	אֶחֱזַק	חָזַקְתִּי	אֶכְבַּד	כָּבַדְתִּי	אָנֹכִי
יְכַפְּרוּ	כִּפְּרוּ	יֶחֱזְקוּ	חָזְקוּ	יִכְבְּדוּ	כָּבְדוּ	הֵם
תְּכַפֵּרְנָה	כִּפְּרוּ	תֶּחֱזַקְנָה	חָזְקוּ	תִּכְבַּדְנָה	כָּבְדוּ	הֵנָּה
תְּכַפְּרוּ	כִּפַּרְתֶּם	תֶּחֶזְקוּ	חֲזַקְתֶּם	תִּכְבְּדוּ	כְּבַדְתֶּם	אַתֶּם
תְּכַפֵּרְנָה	כִּפַּרְתֶּן	תֶּחֱזַקְנָה	חֲזַקְתֶּן	תִּכְבַּדְנָה	כְּבַדְתֶּן	אַתֵּן
נְכַפֵּר	כִּפַּרְנוּ	נֶחֱזַק	חָזַקְנוּ	נִכְבַּד	כָּבַדְנוּ	אֲנַחְנוּ

Page 201, Exercise 22.5

1 my, me   **2** whole, his, which, his   **3** your (your), you (your), me
4 she (her), he, her, her   **5** I, I, you   **6** I (my), you, I, your, you, them
7 he (his), me, this, I   **8** my, I   **9** our, all, him   **10** me, I   **11** you,
yourself (= you), I, you

Page 202, **Exercise 22.6**

Person/gender/number	Root	Tense	
הוּא 3ms	כבד	imperfect	יְכַבֵּד 1
אֲנִי 1cs	דבר	inverted perfect	וְדִבַּרְתִּי 2
אַתָּה 2ms	כבד	imperative	כַּבֵּד 3
הוּא 3ms	צוה	perfect	צִוָּה 4
mp הֵם/אַתֶּם/אֲנַחְנוּ	בקש	participle	מְבַקְשִׁים 5
אַתְּ 2fs	בקש	imperative	הַלְלִי 6
ms הוּא/אַתָּה/אֲנִי	דבר	participle	מְדַבֵּר 7
הוּא 3ms	ברך	perfect	בֵּרַךְ 8
הוּא 3ms	צוה	perfect	צִוָּה 9

Page 204, **Exercise 22.7:** 9, 6, 10, 5, 1, 3, 4, 11, 2, 7, 8

Page 204, **Exercise 22.8**

➤ 9 דַּבֶּר־נָא   8 וַאֲדַבְּרָה   5 וַיְבַקֵּשׁ   6 הַלְלוּ   4 וְרָדְפֵהוּ   (רְדֹף) 2 מְלַמֵּד
3 כַּבְּדֵנִי (כַּבֵּד) 1   בְּקָדְשׁוֹ 7   יָהּ

Page 205, **Exercise 22.9**

1 And bless your people Israel and the soil which you have given us as you did swear to our fathers… This day the LORD, your God, [is] commanding you to do these statutes and (the) ordinances. You shall keep [them] and do them with all your heart and (with) all your soul.

2 Later (= וְ) [a] man found him… in the field and the man asked him (saying), "What are you seeking?" He said, "[It is] my brothers I [am] seeking."

3 [Is] this not the word which we spoke to you in Egypt, saying

4 For all the men who (= הַ) [were] seeking your life (= soul) are dead (= died).

5 Was [anything] heard like it? Has [any other] people heard [the] voice of God speaking out of (= מִ) the midst of the fire, as you yourself have heard?

6 "[Are] you the man who spoke (= you spoke) to this (= הַ) woman?" He said, "I [am]."

7 And the Levites and the priests [were] praising the (= for the) LORD day by (= בְּ) day.

8 And Abraham [was] walking with them to send them away. The LORD said, "[Am] I concealing from Abraham what (= אֲשֶׁר) I [am] doing?"

9 Therefore, by this the sin of Jacob will be atoned [for].

Page 205, **Exercise 22.10**

➤ I 6 עֹשֶׂה   9 לֵאמֹר   2 נָתַתָּה   8 הַמְבַקְשִׁים   4 וַיִּמְצָאֵהוּ   10 וּבָרֵךְ
3 הַלְוִיִּם (instead of   7 (לְשַׁלֵּחַ) לְשַׁלְּחָם   5 מְצַוְּךָ (מְצַוֶּה) 1 הַלְוִיִּם (instead of
(הַלְוִיִּים

9 הֲלֹא   5 הֲנִשְׁמַע   אֲשֶׁר דִּבַּרְנוּ 1   הַאַתָּה 7   הָלַךְ 4   כִּי 8   הַמְבַקְשִׁים 3 II

אֲשֶׁר אֲנִי עֹשֶׂה 2   הַמְכֻסֶּה 6

Page 206, **Exercise 22.11**

1   צִוָּה אֹתִי/צִוַּנִי אָבִי לְבִלְתִּי עֲשׂוֹת אֶת־הַדְּבָרִים הָאֵלֶּה וַאֲנִי לֹא שָׁמַעְתִּי
בְּקוֹלוֹ.

2   בֵּרַךְ יהוה אֶת־עַמּוֹ וְהָעָם מֵאֵן לִזְכֹּר אֶת חֻקָּיו וְלִשְׁמֹר אֶת־מִצְוֹתָיו.

3   שִׁלַּח מֶלֶךְ מִצְרַיִם אֶת־בְּנֵי יִשְׂרָאֵל מֵאַרְצוֹ וַיְלַמֵּד אֹתָם/וַיְלַמְּדֵם מֹשֶׁה
אֶת־הַתּוֹרָה בַּמִּדְבָּר בְּסִינַי.

4   הִלֵּל הָאִישׁ אֶת־יהוה אֱלֹהָיו וַיְשָׁרֶת אֹתוֹ/וַיְשָׁרְתוֹ בְּכָל־לִבּוֹ וּבְכָל־נַפְשׁוֹ.

SECTION 23

Page 209, **Sound change rules via Hebrew names I (15)**

1 *Abraham* אַבְרָהָם (B1)   6 *Jacob* יַעֲקֹב (C1a)   11 *Joseph* יוֹסֵף (D7[2])

2 *Ezra* עֶזְרָא (D1)   7 *Jacob* יַעֲקֹב (C5)   12 *Jonathan* יוֹנָתָן (D2)

3 *Abimélech* אֲבִימֶלֶךְ (C1a)   8 *Messiah* מָשִׁיחַ (C1b)   13 *Michael* מִיכָאֵל (B1)

4 *Baal* בַּעַל (C2b)   9 *Tel Aviv* תֵּל אָבִיב (D6)   14 *Bethlehem* בֵּית לֶחֶם (D3)

5 *Dan* דָּן (D4)   10 *Sarah* שָׂרָה (C4)   15 *Mazal Tov* מַזָּל טוֹב (D5).

Page 209, **Review & Application I** (III-י/ו = III-ה; ג = guttural, including ר)

1 not תִּתְכַּסִּי 4 --> III-ו/י, לו״י   5 א not audible, 5 --> III-א, ל״א

2 not מִתְבָּרֵךְ 2 --> II-ג, ע״ג   6 not מִתְפַּתֵּחַ 1 --> III-ג, ל״ג

3 not הִתְכַּסִּיתָ 3, 7 --> III-ו/י, לו״י   7 not הִתְפַּתַּח 1 --> III-ג, ל״ג

4 not מִתְהַלְלִים 6 -> ע״ע twin-consonant   8 הִתְכַּסַּי* 4 --> III-ו/י, לו״י

* The original form of the 3ms (הוּא) ended in a short /a/-vowel.

Page 210, **Review & Application II**

7 נוּ בִּי התע   התה 5 לְ 1 כוּ ישׁ תַ מֵר 5 התפ לַל תִּי 9 התנ חֵ 2 מוּ

מתפתֵּ חַ 6 מתפ חַ ת 8 התמֵל א תי 10 התה לֵ לי 4 הת פַּ אר 3

Page 211, **Exercise 23.1**

Perf	Imperf	Perf	Imperf	Perf	Imperf	
הִתְפַּלֵּל	יִתְפַּלֵּל	הִסְתַּתֵּר	יִסְתַּתֵּר	הִתְהַלֵּךְ	יִתְהַלֵּךְ	הוּא
הִתְפַּלְּלָה	תִּתְפַּלֵּל	הִסְתַּתְּרָה	תִּסְתַּתֵּר	הִתְהַלְּכָה	תִּתְהַלֵּךְ	הִיא
הִתְפַּלַּלְתָּ	תִּתְפַּלֵּל	הִסְתַּתַּרְתָּ	תִּסְתַּתֵּר	הִתְהַלַּכְתָּ	תִּתְהַלֵּךְ	אַתָּה
הִתְפַּלַּלְתְּ	תִּתְפַּלְּלִי	הִסְתַּתַּרְתְּ	תִּסְתַּתְּרִי	הִתְהַלַּכְתְּ	תִּתְהַלְּכִי	אַתְּ
הִתְפַּלַּלְתִּי	אֶתְפַּלֵּל	הִסְתַּתַּרְתִּי	אֶסְתַּתֵּר	הִתְהַלַּכְתִּי	אֶתְהַלֵּךְ	אָנֹכִי
הִתְפַּלְּלוּ	יִתְפַּלְּלוּ	הִסְתַּתְּרוּ	יִסְתַּתְּרוּ	הִתְהַלְּכוּ	יִתְהַלְּכוּ	הֵם
הִתְפַּלֵּלְנָה	תִּתְפַּלֵּלְנָה	הִסְתַּתֵּרְנָה	תִּסְתַּתֵּרְנָה הִתְהַלַּכְנָה	תִּתְהַלֵּכְנָה	הֵנָּה

---

[2] For D7, see Appendix II, page 296.

תִּתְהַלְּכוּ הִתְהַלַּכְתֶּם הִתְהַלַּכְתֶּם תִּסְתַּתְּרוּ הִסְתַּתַּרְתֶּם תִּתְפַּלְלוּ הִתְפַּלַּלְתֶּם			אַתֶּם
תִּתְהַלֵּכְנָה הִתְהַלַּכְתֶּן תִּסְתַּתַּרְנָה הִסְתַּתַּרְתֶּן תִּתְפַּלֵּלְנָה הִתְפַּלַּלְתֶּן			אַתֵּן
נִתְהַלֵּךְ הִתְהַלַּכְנוּ נִסְתַּתֵּר הִסְתַּתַּרְנוּ נִתְפַּלֵּל הִתְפַּלַּלְנוּ			אֲנַחְנוּ

Page 211, **Exercise 23.2**

Translation	fp	mp	fs	ms	
blessing	מְבָרְכוֹת	מְבָרְכִים	מְבָרֶכֶת	מְבָרֵךְ	1
hiding oneself	מִסְתַּתְּרוֹת	מִסְתַּתְּרִים	מִסְתַּתֶּרֶת	מִסְתַּתֵּר	2
praising	מְהַלְלוֹת	מְהַלְלִים	מְהַלֶּלֶת	מְהַלֵּל	3
seeking	מְבַקְשׁוֹת	מְבַקְשִׁים	מְבַקֶּשֶׁת	מְבַקֵּשׁ	4
praying	מִתְפַּלְלוֹת	מִתְפַּלְלִים	מִתְפַּלֶּלֶת	מִתְפַּלֵּל	5

Page 212, **Exercise 23.3**

Translation	אַתֵּן	אַתֶּם	אַתְּ	אַתָּה	
go/walk around!	הִתְהַלֵּכְנָה	הִתְהַלְּכוּ	הִתְהַלְּכִי	הִתְהַלֵּךְ	1
hide yourself!	הִסְתַּתֵּרְנָה	הִסְתַּתְּרוּ	הִסְתַּתְּרִי	הִסְתַּתֵּר	2
pray!	הִתְפַּלֵּלְנָה	הִתְפַּלְלוּ	הִתְפַּלְלִי	הִתְפַּלֵּל	3
fill!	מַלֶּאנָה	מַלְאוּ	מַלְאִי	מַלֵּא	4
strengthen!	חַזֵּקְנָה	חַזְּקוּ	חַזְּקִי	חַזֵּק	5
send away!	שַׁלַּחְנָה	שַׁלְּחוּ	שַׁלְּחִי	שַׁלַּח	6
atone for!	כַּפֵּרְנָה	כַּפְּרוּ	כַּפְּרִי	כַּפֵּר	7

Page 212, **Exercise 23.4**

Person/gender/number		Root	Tense		
2ms	אַתָּה	פלל	shortened imperfect	תִּתְפַּלֵּל	1
3ms	הוּא	הלך	inverted imperfect	וַיִּתְהַלֵּךְ	2
ms	אֲנִי/אַתָּה/הוּא	סתר	participle	מִסְתַּתֵּר	3
3ms	הוּא	פלל	inverted perfect	וְהִתְפַּלֵּל	4
2ms	אַתָּה	פלל	imperative	הִתְפַּלֵּל	5
3ms	הוּא	הלך	inverted perfect	וְהִתְהַלֵּךְ	6
ms	אֲנִי/אַתָּה/הוּא	הלך	participle	מִתְהַלֵּךְ	7
2mp	אַתֶּם	קדשׁ	imperative	הִתְקַדִּשׁוּ	8
1cs	אָנֹכִי	שׁמר	inverted imperfect	וָאֶשְׁתַּמְּרָה	9
2mp	אַתֶּם	הלך	imperative	הִתְהַלְּכוּ	10

Page 214, Exercise 23.5: 9, 4, 8, 3, 10, 2, 7, 5, 6, 1

Page 214, **Exercise 23.6**

1 Now (= וְ) Abraham [was] old, well advanced (= בָּא) in years (= days) and the LORD had blessed Abraham in everything. Hence (= וַ) Abraham said to his servant, the old[est one] of his house, who (= הַ) [was] managing (= ruling) all that he had (= to him) (perf, בֵּרך, D פִּעֵל)

2 And he will eat, in order that/so that he may bless you before his death (inverted perf, אכל, G/Qal פָּעַל)

3 And by (= בְּ) your seed/offspring all nations of the earth shall bless themselves because you have obeyed me (= listened in my voice) (perf, שמע, G/Qal פָּעַל)

4 The Lord, before whom (= אֲשֶׁר לְפָנָיו) I have walked, will send his angel with you (imperf, שלח, G/Qal פָּעַל)

5 I promised (= אָמוֹר אָמַרְתִּי) [that] your house and the house of your father will walk before me forever (infinitive-as-intensifier, אמר, G/Qal פָּעַל)

6 You were on (= בְּ) God's holy mountain (mountain of holiness); in the midst of fiery stones (stones of fire) you walked (perf, היה, G/Qal פָּעַל)

7 What can (shall) we speak and how (= מַה) can (shall) we prove ourselves righteous? God (= the God) has found out the guilt (= sin) of your servants. Here/Now (= הִנֵּה) we [are] slaves to my master (imperf, דבר, D פִּעֵל)

8 [Was] the sin of Peʿor, from which we have not cleansed ourselves until this day, not enough/a small thing (= מְעַט) to us (perf, טהר, HtD הִתְפַּעֵל)

9 Indeed I know (= יָדַעְתִּי) that [it is] so, but (= וְ) how (= מַה) can (shall) [a] man be just [in a case] with God? (perf, ידע, G/Qal פָּעַל)

10 And the Lord has greatly (= מְאֹד) blessed my master and he has become great.

11 And the Lord hardened the heart of Pharaoh, the king of Egypt, thus (= וְ) he pursued (lit., + אַחֲרֵי 'after') the Israelites while (= וְ) the Israelites [were] going out with uplifted (רָמָה 'high') hand. The Egyptians pursued them... (inverted imperf, חזק, D פִּעֵל; inverted imperf, רדף, G/Qal פָּעַל)

12 Listen to me, O (= הַ) Levites, now sanctify yourself and sanctify the house of the Lord, the God of your fathers (imperative, קדש, D פִּעֵל)

Page 216, **Exercise 23.7**

I 10, 4, 7 וְיִתְבָּרֲכוּ 2, 1, 9 אֲבֹתֵיכֶם (instead of אֲבוֹתֵיכֶם), 6, 11, 8 כִּי־כֵן

(שִׁמְעוּ אֹתִי) שְׁמָעוּנִי 3 וַיֶּחֱזַק 5

II 3 יֹצְאִים 7 עֵקֶב אֲשֶׁר 1/9 מִמֶּנּוּ... עֲוֺן פְּעוֹר אֲשֶׁר 5 הַמְעַט

בַּעֲבֻר אֲשֶׁר 2 יָדַעְתִּי כִּי 6 הַמָּשָׁל 4 אֲשֶׁר־לוֹ 8 יהוה אֲשֶׁר־הִתְהַלַּכְתִּי לְפָנָיו 1/9

Page 217, **Exercise 23.8** (the number of the entry is indicated)

(נִצְטַדָּק) 10 וַיִּגְדַּל (וַיִּגְדָּל) 7 נִצְטַדָּק 6 הִתְהַלַּכְתָּ (הִתְהַלָּכְתְּ) 4 אִתָּךְ (אִתְּךָ) 2 וְאָכַל (וָאֹכַל)

Page 217, **Exercise 23.9**

1 הָלַךְ הַכֹּהֵן אֶל־הַהֵיכָל/לַהֵיכָל/לָהֵיכָל לַעֲבֹד/לְשָׁרֵת אֶת־יהוה וּלְהִתְפַּלֵּל. וַיִּשְׁאַל מֵיהוה שָׁלוֹם לוֹ, לְאִשְׁתּוֹ, לִבְנוֹ, לְבִתּוֹ וּלְעַמּוֹ.

2 הָרַג הָאִישׁ אֶת־נְבִיא יהוה וַיִּשְׁלַח הַמֶּלֶךְ שֹׁמֵר לִמְצֹא אֶת־הָאִישׁ אֲשֶׁר הָרַג אֶת־הַנָּבִיא וְלֹא מָצָא אֹתוֹ/מְצָאוֹ. וַיִּסָּתֵר הָאִישׁ אֲשֶׁר־עָשָׂה אֶת־הַדָּבָר הָרַע הַזֶּה בְּבֵית אָחִיו יָמִים רַבִּים כִּי/עֵקֶב אֲשֶׁר בִּקֵּשׁ הַמֶּלֶךְ אֶת־נַפְשׁוֹ.

3 דִּבְּרוּ הַנְּבִיאִים אֶל־עַמֵּיהֶם לֵאמֹר בָּרְכוּ אֶת־אֱלֹהִים וְהַלְלוּ אֹתוֹ/וְהַלְלוּהוּ.
לַמְּדוּ אֶת־בְּנֵיכֶם אֶת־מִצְוֹת יהוה לְמַעַן/בַּעֲבוּר אֲשֶׁר יִשְׁמְרוּ אֹתָם כָּל־יְמֵי
חַיֵּיהֶם.

Page 217, Exercise 23.10

1 הָלְכוּ הַכֹּהֲנִים אֶל־הַהֵיכָלוֹת/לַהֵיכָלוֹת לַעֲבֹד/לְשָׁרֵת אֶת־יהוה וּלְהִתְפַּלֵּל.
וַיִּשְׁאֲלוּ מֵיהוה שָׁלוֹם לָהֶם, לִנְשֵׁיהֶם, לִבְנֵיהֶם, לִבְנוֹתֵיהֶם וּלְעַמֵּיהֶם.

2 הָרְגוּ הָאֲנָשִׁים אֶת־נְבִיאֵי יהוה וַיִּשְׁלְחוּ הַמְּלָכִים שֹׁמְרִים לִמְצֹא
אֶת־הָאֲנָשִׁים אֲשֶׁר הָרְגוּ אֶת־הַנְּבִיאִים וְלֹא מָצְאוּ אֹתָם/מְצָאוּם. וַיִּסְתַּתְּרוּ
הָאֲנָשִׁים אֲשֶׁר־עָשׂוּ אֶת־הַדְּבָרִים הָרָעִים הָאֵלֶּה בְּבָתֵּי אֲחֵיהֶם יָמִים רַבִּים
כִּי/עֵקֶב אֲשֶׁר בִּקְשׁוּ הַמְּלָכִים אֶת־נַפְשָׁם.

3 דִּבֶּר הַנָּבִיא אֶל־עַמּוֹ לֵאמֹר, "בָּרֵךְ אֶת־אֱלֹהִים וְהַלֵּל אֹתוֹ/וְהַלְלוּ. לַמֵּד
אֶת־בִּנְךָ אֶת־מִצְוַת יהוה לְמַעַן/בַּעֲבוּר אֲשֶׁר יִשְׁמֹר אַתָּה כָּל־יְמֵי חַיָּיו."

SECTION 24

Page 221, Sound change rules via Hebrew names II (16)

→1 *Naomi* נָעֳמִי (C1a)   6 *Zephaniah* צְפַנְיָה (B1)   11 *Nimrod* נִמְרֹד (A5)

2 *Noah* נֹחַ (C1b)   7 *Eliézer* אֱלִיעֶזֶר (C1a)   12 *Ephraim* אֶפְרַיִם (C6)

3 *Ham* חָם (D6)   8 *Joshua* יְהוֹשֻׁעַ (C1b)   13 *Hallelujah* הַלְלוּיָהּ (D6b)

4 *Obadiah* עוֹבַדְיָה   9 *Bathsheba* בַּת שֶׁבַע   14 *Isaac* יִצְחָק (A5)
  (A6[3], B1)   (B1, C2b)

5 *Hosea* הוֹשֵׁעַ (D3, D7[4]) 10 *Torah* תּוֹרָה (D3, D7) 15 *Joseph* יוֹסֵף (D3)

Page 221, Review & Application I (III-י/ו = III-ה; ג = guttural)

A 1 not מְשַׁמֶּעֶת 2 --> ל"ג, ג-III   5 not הַשְׁמֵעַ 2 --> ל"ג, ג-III
  2 not תַּאְזִינִי 1 --> פ"ג, ג-I   6 not הָעֳמָדָה 3 ,1 --> פ"ג, ג-I
  3 not הַאְזִינָה 4 ,1 --> פ"ג, ג-I   הָ־עֳמָדָה[3] הָ־עָמְדָה[1)
  4 not הֶעְמִידוּ 4 ,1 --> פ"ג, ג-I   7 not הַשְׁמִיעַ 2 --> ל"ג, ג-III
                          8 א not audible 5 --> ל"א, ג-III

B 1 not הִגְלֵינוּ 1 --> III-י/ו, לו"י   6 not יַעֲלִיו A1, B2 --> I-ג + III-י/ו
  2 not מַוְשִׁיעִים 1 --> III-ג + ו/י-I יַעֲלוּ[B2] יַעֲלוּ[A1)
  3 not תַּוְלִידוּ 1 --> ו/י-I, פו"י   7 not יַיְטִיב 1 --> ו/י-I, פו"י
  4 not תַּגְלְיִי 2 --> III-י/ו, לו"י   8 not יַנְכִּיו 3 ,2 --> III-ג + נ-I + ו/י-I
  5 not הִנְגַּדְתָּ 3 --> נ-I, פ"נ   יַכּוּ[2] יַכּוּ[3)
                          9 not אָוְרִישׁ 1 --> ו/י-I, פו"י

---

[3] See Appendix II, footnote 3.
[4] For D7, see Appendix II, page 296.

Page 223, **Exercise 24.1**

	Imperf: Ordinary	Imperf: Shortened	Imperf: Ordinary	Imperf: Shortened	Imperf: Ordinary	Imperf: Shortened
הוּא	יַמְלִיךְ	יַמְלֵךְ	יַסְתִּיר	יַסְתֵּר	יַזְכִּיר	יַזְכֵּר
הִיא	תַּמְלִיךְ	תַּמְלֵךְ	תַּסְתִּיר	תַּסְתֵּר	תַּזְכִּיר	תַּזְכֵּר
אַתָּה	תַּמְלִיךְ	תַּמְלֵךְ	תַּסְתִּיר	תַּסְתֵּר	תַּזְכִּיר	תַּזְכֵּר
אַתְּ	תַּמְלִיכִי	as ord. imperf	תַּסְתִּירִי	as ord. imperf	תַּזְכִּירִי	as ord. imperf
אֲנִי	אַמְלִיךְ	אַמְלֵךְ	אַסְתִּיר	אַסְתֵּר	אַזְכִּיר	____
הֵם	יַמְלִיכוּ	as ord. imperf	יַסְתִּירוּ	as ord. imperf	יַזְכִּירוּ	as ord. imperf
הֵנָּה	תַּמְלֵכְנָה	as ord. imperf	תַּסְתֵּרְנָה	as ord. imperf	תַּזְכֵּרְנָה	as ord. imperf
אַתֶּם	תַּמְלִיכוּ	as ord. imperf	תַּסְתִּירוּ	as ord. imperf	תַּזְכִּירוּ	as ord. imperf
אַתֶּן	תַּמְלֵכְנָה	as ord. imperf	תַּסְתֵּרְנָה	as ord. imperf	תַּזְכֵּרְנָה	as ord. imperf
אֲנַחְנוּ	נַמְלִיךְ	נַסְתִּיר	נַזְכִּיר

Page 224, **Exercise 24.2**

	אַתָּה	אַתְּ	אַתֶּם	אַתֵּן	Translation
1	הַמְלֵךְ	הַמְלִיכִי	הַמְלִיכוּ	הַמְלֵכְנָה	crown!
2	הַשְׁלֵךְ	הַשְׁלִיכִי	הַשְׁלִיכוּ	הַשְׁלֵכְנָה	cast!
3	הַכְרֵת	הַכְרִיתִי	הַכְרִיתוּ	הַכְרֵתְנָה	eliminate!
4	הַבְדֵּל	הַבְדִּילִי	הַבְדִּילוּ	הַבְדֵּלְנָה	distinguish!
5	הַקְרֵב	הַקְרִיבִי	הַקְרִיבוּ	הַקְרֵבְנָה	bring near/offer!
6	הַסְתֵּר	הַסְתִּירִי	הַסְתִּירוּ	הַסְתֵּרְנָה	hide!

Page 225, **Exercise 24.3**

	Perf	Imperf	Perf	Imperf	Perf	Imperf
הוּא	הִכְרַת	יַכְרַת	הִקְרַב	יַקְרַב	הִבְדִּיל	יַבְדִּיל
הִיא	הִכְרַתָה	תַּכְרַת	הִקְרִבָה	תַּקְרַב	הִבְדִּילָה	תַּבְדִּיל
אַתָּה	הִכְרַתָ	תַּכְרַת	הִקְרַבְתָ	תַּקְרַב	הִבְדַּלְתָ	תַּבְדִּיל
אַתְּ	הִכְרַתְ	תַּכְרִתִי	הִקְרַבְתְ	תַּקְרִבִי	הִבְדַּלְתְ	תַּבְדִּילִי
אֲנִי	הִכְרַתִי	אַכְרַת	הִקְרַבְתִּי	אַקְרַב	הִבְדַּלְתִּי	אַבְדִּיל
הֵם	הִכְרַתוּ	יַכְרִתוּ	הִקְרִבוּ	יַקְרִבוּ	הִבְדִּילוּ	יַבְדִּילוּ
הֵנָּה	הִכְרַתוּ	תַּכְרַתְנָה	הִקְרִבוּ	תַּקְרַבְנָה	הִבְדִּילוּ	תַּבְדֵּלְנָה
אַתֶּם	הִכְרַתֶּם	תַּכְרִתוּ	הִקְרַבְתֶּם	תַּקְרִבוּ	הִבְדַּלְתֶּם	תַּבְדִּילוּ
אַתֵּן	הִכְרַתֶּן	תַּכְרַתְנָה	הִקְרַבְתֶּן	תַּקְרַבְנָה	הִבְדַּלְתֶּן	תַּבְדֵּלְנָה
אֲנַחְנוּ	הִכְרַתְנוּ	נַכְרַת	הִקְרַבְנוּ	נַקְרַב	הִבְדַּלְנוּ	נַבְדִּיל

Page 226, **Exercise 24.4**

	ms	fs	mp	fp	Translation
1	מָשְׁלָךְ	מָשְׁלֶכֶת	מָשְׁלָכִים	מָשְׁלָכוֹת	casted
2	מַשְׁלִיךְ	מַשְׁלִיכָה	מַשְׁלִיכִים	מַשְׁלִיכוֹת	casting

offering	מַקְרִיבוֹת	מַקְרִיבִים	מַקְרִיבָה	מַקְרִיב 3
eliminated	מָכְרָתוֹת	מָכְרָתִים	מָכְרֶתֶת	מָכְרָת 4
distinguishing	מַבְדִּילוֹת	מַבְדִּילִים	מַבְדִּילָה	מַבְדִּיל 5
hiding	מַסְתִּירוֹת	מַסְתִּירִים	מַסְתִּירָה	מַסְתִּיר 6
being set upright	מָעֳמָדוֹת	מָעֳמָדִים	מָעֳמֶדֶת	מָעֳמָד 7

Page 226, Exercise 24.5

Pers/gen/num	Root	Tense	
3cp	נגד	perfect	הִגִּידוּ 1
mp	נכה	participle	מַכִּים 2
—	ישע	infinitive	הוֹשִׁיעַ 3
3ms	נגד	perfect	הִגַּד 4
2ms	סתר	imperfect	תַּסְתִּיר 5
2ms	בדל	imperfect	תַּבְדִּיל 6
2mp	שלך	imperative	הַשְׁלִיכוּ 7
1cs	זכר	lengthened imperfect	אַזְכִּירָה 8
—	סתר	infin-as-intensifier	הַסְתֵּר 9
ms	עלה	participle	מַעֲלֶה 10
mp	יצא	participle	מוֹצִיאִים 11

Page 228, Exercise 24.6: 2, 6, 5, 9, 8, 1, 3, 4, 10, 7

Page 228, Exercise 24.7

1 me, myself (my), them   **2** your, you   **3** all, they, him, to, him, all
4 your, my, for/because, you (you – you), me, over   **5** himself (his), from
6 me, your (your)   **7** he, you, what, what, you   **8** I, your, your   **9** what, this, you, me, why, you, not, me, she, your   **10** you, his, you, your (you), him, you

Page 230, Exercise 24.8: 6, 3, 12, 11, 2, 10, 1, 4, 7, 8, 9, 5

Page 230, Exercise 24.9

1 And the Lord threw [down] on them great stones from the sky as far as/all the way to (= עַד) Azekah
2 The Lord will surely separate me from his people
3 I myself have told and (I have) saved and (I have) announced (= caused to hear) [it] (perf, ישע, H הִפְעִיל)
4 Now I do know (= יָדַעְתִּי) that the Lord will save (= הוֹשִׁיעַ) his anointed (perf, ידע, G/Qal פָּעַל)
5 Concerning you/in Your behalf (= לְךָ) I (= my heart) have said, 'Seek me (= my face)!' Your face, [O] Lord, I seek. Do not conceal/hide your face from me (imperf, בקש, D פִּעֵל)
6 Conceal your face from my sins.

7 The heavens told his righteousness and all the peoples have seen his glory
(perf, נָגַד, H הִפְעִיל)

8 Do not hide your commandments from me (shortened imperf, סתר, H
הִפְעִיל)

9 Samuel said to all Israel, "Here/look, I have listened to you (= in your voice),
in (= לְ) all that you have said to me, and (I) have set a king (= וָאַמְלִיךְ) over
you. And now, look, the king walks (= walking) before you. As for me
(= וַאֲנִי), I have grown old… but (= וְ) my sons [are] with you; and I – I have
walked before you…" (participle, הלך, HtD הִתְפַּעֵל).

Page 231, **Exercise 24.10**

1 יָרַשׁ הַבֵּן אֶת־הַבַּיִת. הוֹרִישׁ לוֹ אָבִיו אֹתוֹ. הַבַּיִת הָיָה יָפֶה.

2 יָלְדָה הָאִשָּׁה יֶלֶד. נוֹלַד הַיֶּלֶד בָּעִיר. הוֹלִיד הַבֵּן יְלָדִים רַבִּים.

3 גָּלָה הָעָם מֵאַרְצוֹ. יהוה הִגְלָה אֶת־הָעָם.

4 אָכַל הַבֵּן. הֶאֱכִילָה הָאִשָּׁה אֶת־בְּנָהּ.

5 לֹא זָכַר הָאִישׁ אֶת־מִצְוַת יהוה. הִזְכִּיר לוֹ הַכֹּהֵן אֶת־הַמִּצְוָה הַזֹּאת.

6 יָשַׁב הָעָם בָּאָרֶץ הַטּוֹבָה הַזֹּאת. אֱלֹהִים הוֹשִׁיב אֶת־הָעָם שָׁם.

Page 231, **Exercise 24.11**

1 יָרְשׁוּ הַבָּנִים אֶת־הַבָּתִּים. הוֹרִישׁוּ לָהֶם אֲבוֹתֵיהֶם אֹתָם. הַבָּתִּים הָיוּ יָפִים.

2 יָלְדוּ הַנָּשִׁים יְלָדִים. נוֹלְדוּ הַיְלָדִים בֶּעָרִים. הוֹלִידוּ הַבָּנִים יְלָדִים רַבִּים.

3 גָּלוּ הָעַמִּים מֵאַרְצוֹתֵיהֶם. יהוה הִגְלָה אֶת־הָעַמִּים.

4 אָכְלוּ הַבָּנִים. הֶאֱכִילוּ הַנָּשִׁים אֶת־בְּנֵיהֶן.

5 לֹא זָכְרוּ הָאֲנָשִׁים אֶת־מִצְוֹת יהוה. הִזְכִּירוּ לָהֶם הַכֹּהֲנִים אֶת־הַמִּצְוֹת הָאֵלֶּה.

6 יָשְׁבוּ הָעַמִּים בָּאֲרָצוֹת הַטּוֹבוֹת הָאֵלֶּה. אֱלֹהִים הוֹשִׁיב אֶת־הָעַמִּים שָׁם.

SECTION 25

Page 234, **Review & Application I**

➤ 10 כָּל‎ ‎ י‎ ‎ו‎ 5 ‎ י‎ ‎בְ‎ ‎ז‎ 1 ‎ וַיִּ‎ ‎ שׁ‎ ‎ יָ‎ 9 ‎ ל‎ ‎ י‎ ‎ פְּ‎ ‎ יָ‎ 12 יִבְּנוּ (not ‎ו‎) (יִבְנֶ‎

11 ‎ עָ‎ ‎ וַ‎ 6 מְרִי ‎ א‎ ‎ ת‎ 3 ‎ שָׁתְּ‎ ‎ וַיִּ‎ 2 לוֹ ‎ חָ‎ ‎ תִּנָ‎ ‎ טַב‎ 8 ‎ י‎ ‎ י‎ עָנוּ 7 ‎ יָ‎

4 ‎ ת‎ ‎ רֶד‎

Page 234, **Review & Application II**

1 not וַיְדַבֵּר (D6, he spoke), not מָצָאתִי (D1, B1, I found), not מָוֶת (D4,
dying), not אֶעֱלֶה (C6, let me go up), not קְבֹר (B1, burying),
not וַיַּעַל/וַיַּעֲל (C2a/b, he went up), not וַיַּעֲלוּ (D4, they went up)

2 not וַיַּעֲנוּ (C1a, they answered), not הֻגַּד (D5, it was told),
not וַנִּירָא (D3, D1, we feared), not וַיַּעַשׂ/וַיַּעַשׂ (C2a/b, he did),
not וַיַּצֵּל (D5, he delivered), not הֲרָגוּם (C1a, they killed them)

3 not וְעָשִׂיתָ (D3, B1, you shall do)

4 not וַיִּשָּׁבַע (C3, B1, he swore)

Page 235, Exercise 25.1: I 5, 6, 4, 1, 7, 8, 3, 2 **II** 3, 5, 4, 2, 1, 7, 8, 6

Person/gender/number	Tense	Root	Verb type	
הוּא 3ms	inver imperf	אמר	פָּעַל G	**I** 1 וַיֹּאמֶר
הוּא 3ms	inver imperf	ראה	הִפְעִיל H	2 וַיַּרְא
אַתָּה 2ms	shortened imperf	לקח	פָּעַל G	3 תִּקַּח
אַתָּה 2ms	imperf	ראה	פָּעַל G	4 תִּרְאֶה
אָנֹכִי/אֲנִי 1cs	imperf	ירד	פָּעַל G	5 אֵרֵד
הֵם 3mp	imperf	הלך	פָּעַל G	6 יֵלְכוּ
אָנֹכִי/אֲנִי 1cs	imperf	נתן	פָּעַל G	7 אֶתֵּן
הוּא 3ms	shortened imperf	היה	פָּעַל G	8 יְהִי
הוּא 3ms	imperf	יכל	פָּעַל G	**II** 1 יוּכַל
אָנֹכִי/אֲנִי 1cs	imperf	היה	פָּעַל G	2 אֶהְיֶה
—	infinitive	נתן	פָּעַל G	3 תֵּת
הוּא 3ms	shortened imperf	עלה	פָּעַל G	4 יַעַל
הוּא 3ms	imperf	ראה	נִפְעַל N	5 יֵרָאֶה
הוּא 3ms	inver imperf	נגד	הֻפְעַל Hp	6 וַיֻּגַּד
הוּא 3ms	imperf	נשא	פָּעַל G	7 יִשָּׂא
הוּא 3ms	perf	ירד	הֻפְעַל Hp	8 הוּרַד

Page 236, Exercise 25.2: I 5, 3, 2, 7, 1, 8, 9, 4, 6 **II** 8, 5, 1, 2, 6, 4, 3, 7

Page 237, Exercise 25.3 (הִפְעִיל H, הִתְפַּעֵל HtD, נִפְעַל N, פָּעַל G)

Missing words	Meaning	Tense	Root	Verb type	
your, which, he, you	active simple	perf	שמר	G	**I** 1 שָׁמַרְתָּ
lest, you	reflexive	imperative	שמר	N	2 הִשָּׁמְרוּ
my	reflexive	inver imperf	שמר	HtD	3 וָאֶשְׁתַּמְרָה
he, after, he (his)	active simple	inver perf	סגר	G	4 וְסָגַר
he, not, until	passive	imperf	סגר	N	5 יִסָּגֵר
not, to, his	active causative	imperf	סגר	H	6 תַּסְגִּיר
they, out of (= from), to	active simple	inver imperf	מכר	G	7 וַיִּמְכְּרוּ
to	passive	perf	מכר	N	8 נִמְכַּר
to, in	reflexive	inver imperf	מכר	HtD	9 וַיִּתְמַכְּרוּ
to	active simple	inver imperf	קרב	G	**II** 1 וַיִּקְרַב
to	passive	inver perf	קרב	N	2 וְנִקְרַב
to, as, in	active causative	infinitive	קרב	H	3 הַקְרִיב
to, his, he	active simple	inver imperf	קרא	G	4 וַתִּקְרֶאנָה
their	passive	inver imperf	קרא	N	5 וַיִּקְרָא
him, him, in, his	active simple	inver perf	שמע	G	6 וּשְׁמַעְתֶּם

thus, this, you	passive	imperf	שמע	N	7 יִשָּׁמַע
out of (= from), his	active causative	perf	שמע	H	8 הִשְׁמִיעַ

Page 240, Exercise 25.4

1 ⁴Joseph spoke to Pharaoh's house saying (= לְ + saying'), "If, please, I have found favour in your eyes, speak, please, to (= in the ears of) Pharaoh, saying, ⁵'My father made me swear, saying, 'Look, I [am] about to die (= dying)… In the land of Canaan, there you shall bury me'. Now therefore (= וְ) let me go up, please, and bury my father'"…. ⁶And Pharaoh said, "Go up and bury your father as he made you swear." ⁷So (= וְ) Joseph went up to bury his father; and with him went up all the servants of Pharaoh, the elders of his household (= בַּיִת) and all the elders of the land of Egypt ⁸as well as (= וְ) all the household of Joseph and his brothers' and his father's household.

2 ²⁴Then (= וְ) they answered Joshua and said, "Because your servants were clearly (= הֻגַּד) told (= told to) [the things] that the LORD, your God, had commanded Moses, his servant, to give you all the land…. So (= וְ) we feared greatly (= מְאֹד) for our lives (= souls) because of you (= from your faces) and did this thing. ²⁵And now here (= הִנֵּה) we [are] in your hand, do to us as you please (= as good and right in your eyes)." ²⁶Thus (= וְ) he did to them so (= כֵּן) and delivered them from (the hand of) the Israelites and they did not kill them.

3 ¹¹At the place that the LORD, your God, will choose to make his name dwell there. ¹²You shall remember that you were [a] slave in Egypt. Therefore (= וְ) you shall observe (= keep) and carry out (= do) these statutes.

4 ²¹And he swore that I should not cross (= not my crossing) the Jordan and that I should not enter (= entering) to the good land which the LORD, your God, [is] giving you…. ²²For I should die (= dying) in this land. I shall not cross (= crossing) the Jordan, but (= וְ) you will cross (= crossing) and take possession of (= inherit) this good land. ²³Be careful (= watch out for yourselves) that you may not (= lest you) forget the covenant of the LORD, your God, which he made (= cut) with you.

Page 240, Exercise 25.5

1 (a **פָּעַל** G: אָמֹר (לֵאמֹר), מָצָאתִי, אָמַר, אָמַר, מֵת, תִּקְבֹּר, אֶעֱלֶה, אֶקְבְּרָה, וַיֹּאמֶר, עָלָה, קְבֹר, וַיַּעַל, קָבַר, וַיַּעֲלוּ (14 cases) (b **פָּעֵל** D: וַיְדַבֵּר, דַּבְּרוּ (2 cases) (c **הָפְעִיל** H: הִשְׁבִּיעַ, הִשְׁבִּיעַ (2 cases).

2 (a **פָּעַל** G: וַיַּעֲנוּ, וַיֹּאמְרוּ, תֵּת, וַנִּירָא, וַנַּעֲשֶׂה, עֲשׂוֹת, עָשָׂה, וַיַּעַשׂ, הָרְגוּ (9 cases). (b **פָּעֵל** D: צִוָּה (1 case) (c **הָפְעִיל** H: וַיַּצֵּל (1 case). (d **הָפְעַל** Hp: הֻגַּד, הֻגַּד (2 cases).

3 (a **פָּעַל** G: יִבְחַר, וְזָכַרְתָּ, הָיִיתָ, וְשָׁמַרְתָּ, וְעָשִׂיתָ (5 cases). (b **פָּעֵל** D: שַׁכֵּן (1 case)

4 (a **פָּעַל** G: עָבַר, בֹּא, נָתַן, מֵת, עָבֵר, עֹבְרִים, וִירִשְׁתֶּם, תִּשְׁכְּחוּ, כָּרַת (9 cases). (b **נִפְעַל** N: וַיִּשָּׁבַע, הִשָּׁמְרוּ (2 cases).

Page 241, **Exercise 25.6**

1 הִשְׁבִּיעַנִי – הִשְׁבִּיעַ אֹתִי (הִפְעִיל H), תִּקְבְּרֵנִי – תִּקְבֹּר אֹתִי (פָּעַל G),
הִשְׁבִּיעֶךָ – הִשְׁבִּיעַ אֹתְךָ (הִפְעִיל H).   2 הֲרָגוּם – הָרְגוּ אֹתָם (פָּעַל G)

Page 241, **Exercise 25.7**

1 אָמֹר (פָּעַל G), קְבֹר (G), 2 תֵּת (G), עֲשׂוֹת (G), 3 שַׁכֵּן (פִּעֵל D) 4 עֲבֹר
(G), בֹּא (G)

Page 241, **Exercise 25.8**

1 וַיְדַבֵּר D (שְׁלֵמִים unchangeable), וַיֹּאמֶר G (א-I), וַיַּעַל G (ו/י-III + ג-I),
וַיַּעֲלוּ G (ו/י-III + ג-I)

2 וַיִּעָנוּ G (ו/י-III + ג-I), וַיֹּאמְרוּ G (א-I), וַיִּירָא G (א-III + ו/י-I), וַנַּעֲשֶׂה
G (ו/י-III + ג-I), וַיַּעַשׂ G (ו/י-III + ג-I), וַיַּצֵּל H (נ-I)

4 וַיִּשָּׁבַע N (ג-III)

Page 241, **Exercise 25.9**

1 בְּעֵינֵיכֶם (in your *eyes*), בְּאָזְנֵי פַרְעֹה (in the *ears* of Pharaoh)

2 לְנַפְשֹׁתֵינוּ (for our *souls*), מִפְּנֵיכֶם (from your *face*), בְּיָדֶךָ (in your *hand*),
בְּעֵינֶיךָ (in your *eyes*), מִיַּד בְּנֵי יִשְׂרָאֵל (from the *hand* of the Israelites)

Page 241, **Exercise 25.10:** 5, 12, 11, 7, 6, 8, 1, 2, 10, 3, 9, 4

Page 242, **Exercise 25.11**

1 אָכַל הָאִישׁ לֶחֶם.   2 אָמְרָה הָאִשָּׁה לַבַּעֲלָהּ/לְאִישָׁהּ, ''הֲלֹא/הֲלוֹא אִשְׁתְּךָ
אָנִי?''   3 הָיָה לַכֹּהֵן סֵפֶר.   4 הָלַכְתָּ אֶל־הָעִיר/הָעִירָה לִרְאוֹת אֶת־הַמֶּלֶךְ.
5 יָלְדָה הַנְּבִיאָה שְׁנֵי בָנִים.   6 יָדַע אָבִי אַיֵּה/אֵיפֹה הַכֶּסֶף.   7 יָצָא הָעָם
מִן־/מֵהָאָרֶץ.   8 יָשַׁב הַנָּבִיא בְּמִקְדַּשׁ אֱלֹהִים.   9 נָשָׂא הָעֶבֶד אֶת־כְּלֵי אֲדֹנוֹ.
10 לָקַחְתָּ אֶת־הַיֶּלֶד אֶל־הַבַּיִת/הַבַּיְתָה.   11 עָלָה בְּנוֹ מֵאֶרֶץ מִצְרַיִם.
12 עָשָׂה הַנַּעַר אֶת־כָּל־הַדְּבָרִים הָאֵלֶּה.   13 רָאֲתָה בִתִּי אֶת־צְבָא הַמֶּלֶךְ.

SECTION 26

Page 244, **Review & Application I**

26.1) 1 Not וַיְהִי (D6, it was), not רָאִיוּ (D4, they saw) 2 Not וְיִשְׁאֲלוּ
(C1a, they will ask) 4 Not וְנִלְחֲמוּ (C1a, they will fight) 5 Not וְהוֹדַעְתִּי
(D3, I will make known)

26.5) 1 Not וַעֲבַדְתַּנִי (C1a, you will serve me) 3 Not הֶחֱרִיבוּ (C6, C1a, they
devastated/made dry up) 4 Not לְהוֹשִׁיעַ (D3, C1b, to save) 5 Not הֵיטַבְתָּ
(D3, you did well)

26.10) 1 Not וַתִּתֵּן (D5, you let/gave), not הָיִיתָ (D3, B1, you were), not יֵאָמֵן
(C4, may it be confirmed/verified), not גָּלִיתָ (D3, B1, you revealed), not
לִבְנוֹת (B1, to build), not מָצָא (D1, he found)

Page 245, **Exercise 26.1**

1 in, all, one another (his brother), all (G פָּעַל, ראה, perf)   **2** his neighbour, her neighbour (D פִּעֵל, דבר, imperative)   **3** with one another, with his companion (N נִפְעַל, דבר, perf)   **4** they, one another (man/person, his brother, man, his friend/companion), city, city (N נִפְעַל, לחם, inver perf)   **5** (to) me, I, between, another (between his neighbour), I, his (G פָּעַל, היה, imperf)

Page 246, **Exercise 26.2**

1 you (you – you), this people, the land which I, their   (N נִפְעַל, שׁבע, perf)   **2** you, the manna which, not (H הִפְעִיל, אכל, inver imperf)   **3** they, me, righteous judgements (judgements of justice) (G פָּעַל, שׁאל, imperf)   **4** he (he – he), them, the land (H הִפְעִיל, נחל, imperf)

Page 246, **Exercise 26.3**

1 While/when Israel dwelt (= in Israel's dwelling) in that land (G פָּעַל, הלך, inver imperf)   **2** After these things (G פָּעַל, אמר, inver imperf)   **3** In that day (G פָּעַל, היה, imperf)   **4** As [soon as] his master (= masters, pl of majesty) heard (= as his master's hearing) the words of his wife (G פָּעַל, שׁמע, infinitive)   **5** Now (= וֹ) when David dwelt in his house (G פָּעַל, ישׁב, participle)

Page 247, **Exercise 26.4**

1 said, be (G פָּעַל, היה, shortened imperf)   **2** their, very, go down, see (G פָּעַל, ירד, lengthened imperf)   **3** wish, all, his, them (G פָּעַל, נתן, imperf)   **4** wish, from   **5** said, let, be, you (your) (G פָּעַל, אמר, invert imperf)   **6** if only/that, my, me, in my (D פִּעֵל, הלך, imperf)

Page 248, **Exercise 26.5**

1 חִנָּם you, me   **2** יוֹמָם וָלַיְלָה we, our, them   **3** אָמְנָם their
4 אוֹסִיף I, you   **5** הֵיטַבְתָּ you   **6** מִהַרְתָּ you, my   **7** וַיֵּאָסְפוּ

Page 248, **Exercise 26.6**

1 And you will worship (= bow down to) other gods and serve them.
2 You [are] the LORD, you alone. You made the heavens, the heaven of heavens, and all their host, the earth and all that [is] on it … And you keep (= keeping) all of them alive, and the host of heavens bows (= bowing) down to you
3 Then (= וֹ) Abraham bowed down before the people of the land.
4 Joab fell on (= אֶל) his face to the ground, prostrated himself and blessed the king. Joab said: "Today your servant knows (= יָדַע) that I have found favour with you (= in your eyes), my lord the king, for (= אֲשֶׁר) the king has granted (= done) the request (= word) of his servant (your servant)."
5 She fell at (= עַל) his feet and bowed down to the ground. Afterwards (= וֹ) she lifted up her son and went out. Now (= וְ) Elisha returned to Gilgal.

6 And in that day... they will worship (bow down to) the LORD on (= בְּ) the holy mountain (mountain of holiness) in Jerusalem.

7 Your father's sons shall bow down to you.

Page 249, **Exercise 26.7** (H) הִפְעִיל HtD, הִתְפַּעֵל N, נִפְעַל G, פָּעַל

Missing words	Meaning	Tense	Root	Verb type	
their, from your, to	active simple	imperative	גלה	G	גְּלֵה 1 **I**
	active simple	inver perf	גלה	G	וְגָלִיתָ
to, in	reflexive	perf	גלה	N	נִגְלָה 2
by, his	active simple	inf-as-intens	גלה	G	גָּלֹה 3
	active simple	imperf	גלה	G	יִגְלֶה
from his, to, until, this	active simple	inver imperf	גלה	G	וַיִּגֶל 4
from, to	active causative	perf	גלה	H	הִגְלֵיתִי 5
and, to	passive	part	גלה	Hp	מֻגְלִים 6
him	active simple	perf	ראה	G	רָאָה 1 **II**
my	passive	imperf	ראה	N	יֵרָאוּ 2
(as/like), which	active causative	perf	ראה	H	הֶרְאָה 3
which	passive	perf	ראה	Hp	הָרְאֵיתָ 4
that, my, to, me	active simple	perf	ידע	G	יְדַעְתֶּם 5
how, which, (it)	active simple	imperf	ידע	G	נֵדַע 6
who, him	passive	perf	ידע	N	נוֹדַע 7
your	active causative	inver perf	ידע	H	וְהוֹדַעְתֶּם 8
who, in	active simple	participle	ישב	G	יֹשֵׁב 1 **III**
I (my), you from all your	active causative	inver perf	ישב	H	וְהוֹשַׁבְתִּי 2
yourselves	passive	perf	ישב	Hp	הוּשַׁבְתֶּם 3
from/out of	active simple	infinitive	יצא	G	צֵאת 4
his, his, and his, him	active simple	inver imperf	יצא	G	וַיֵּצֵא 5
not, to you, my, my, my, from	active causative	inver perf	יצא	H	וְהוֹצֵאתִי 6

Page 252, **Exercise 26.8**

1 אָכַל (וַיֹּאכַל) 2 אָמְרָה (וַתֹּאמֶר) 3 הָיָה (וַיְהִי) 4 הָלַכְתְּ (וַתֵּלֶךְ) 5 יָלְדָה
(וַתֵּלֶד) 6 יָדַע (וַיֵּדַע) 7 יָצָא (וַיֵּצֵא) 8 יָשַׁב (וַיֵּשֶׁב) 9 נָשָׂא (וַיִּשָּׂא)
10 לָקַחְתָּ (וַתִּקַּח) 11 עָלָה (וַיַּעַל) 12 עָשָׂה (וַיַּעַשׂ) 13 רָאֲתָה (וַתֵּרֶא)

Page 252, **Exercise 26.9**

1 וַיֹּאכְלוּ הָאֲנָשִׁים לֶחֶם. 2 וַתֹּאמַרְנָה הַנָּשִׁים לְבַעְלֵיהֶן, "הֲלֹא נָשֵׁיכֶם
אֲנַחְנוּ!" 3 וַיִּהְיוּ לַכֹּהֲנִים סְפָרִים. 4 וַתֵּלְכוּ אֶל־הֶעָרִים לִרְאוֹת אֶת־הַמְּלָכִים.
5 וַתֵּלַדְנָה הַנְּבִיאוֹת שְׁנֵי בָנִים. 6 וַיֵּדְעוּ אֲבוֹתֵינוּ אַיֵּה הַכֶּסֶף. 7 וַיֵּצְאוּ
הָעַמִּים מִן־/מֵהָאֲרָצוֹת. 8 וַיֵּשְׁבוּ הַנְּבִיאִים בְּמִקְדְּשֵׁי אֱלֹהִים. 9 וַיִּשְׂאוּ
הָעֲבָדִים אֶת־כְּלֵי אֲדוֹנֵיהֶם. 10 וַתִּקְחוּ אֶת־הַיְלָדִים אֶל־הַבָּתִּים. 11 וַיַּעֲלוּ
בָנָיו מֵאֶרֶץ מִצְרַיִם. 12 וַיַּעֲשׂוּ הַנְּעָרִים אֶת־כָּל־הַדְּבָרִים הָאֵלֶּה. 13 וַתִּרְאֶינָה
בְּנוֹתַי אֶת־צִבְאוֹת הַמְּלָכִים.

Page 252, **Exercise 26.10**

1 [22] And you have established/made/constituted (= נָתַן) your people Israel to [be] your people (= to you to people) forever and you, [O] LORD, you became (= הָיִיתָ לְ) their (= לָהֶם 'to them') God. [23] And now, [O] LORD, let the word which you have spoken concerning (= עַל) your servant and (concerning) his house be confirmed forever, and do as you have spoken. [24] And let your name be confirmed and be great forever, saying, 'The LORD of hosts, the God of Israel, [is] God to Israel'.... [25] Because you, my God, you has revealed to your servant (= the ear of your servant) [that you will] build (= to build) [a] house for him. Therefore, your servant has found [courage] to pray to you (= toward/before your face). [26] And now, [O] LORD, you [are] the God (N נִפְעַל, אמן, imperf; G פָּעַל, בנה, infinitive)

2 [14] He said, "[O] LORD, God of Israel, [there is] no God like you in the heavens or (= וְ) on (= בְּ) the earth, keeping the covenant and the kindness toward (= לְ) your servants who walk (= הַ + walking) before you with all their heart. [15] [You] who has kept toward your servant David, my father, what (= אֲשֶׁר) you promised him (= spoke to him); you promised (= spoke with your mouth) and has fulfilled (= with your hand has fulfilled) as [at] this day. [16] And now, [O] LORD, God of Israel, keep toward your servant David, my father, what you promised him (= spoke to him), saying, '[There] will not be cut off [a] descendant (= man to/of you) before me sitting on the throne of Israel if only your sons will take care of (= יִשְׁמְרוּ) their way, to walk in my law, as you have walked before me (= my face)'. [17] And now, [O] LORD, God of Israel, let your promise (= word) which you have promised (= spoken) to your servant, to David, be confirmed/trustworthy. [18] For does really God dwell with man (= the man) on the earth?" (G פָּעַל, הלך, infinitive; G פָּעַל, ישב, imperf)

Page 253, **Exercise 26.11**

1 (a פָּעַל G: וַתִּתֶּן, הָיִיתָ, עָשָׂה, יִגְדַּל, אָמֹר, גָּלִיתָ, בָּנוֹת, מָצָא (8 cases).
(b נִפְעַל N: יֵאָמֵן, יֵאָמֵן (2 cases). (c פִּעֵל D: דִּבַּרְתָּ, דִּבַּרְתָּ (2 cases).
(d הִתְפָּעֵל HtD: הִתְפַּלֵּל (1 case).

2 (a פָּעַל G: וַיֹּאמַר, שָׁמֵר, הַלְכִים, שָׁמַרְתָּ, שָׁמֹר, אָמֹר, יוֹשֵׁב, יִשְׁמְרוּ, לֶכֶת, הָלַכְתָּ, יֵשֵׁב (11 cases). (b נִפְעַל N: יִכָּרֵת, יֵאָמֵן (2 cases).
(c פִּעֵל D: דִּבַּרְתָּ, וַתְּדַבֵּר, מִלֵּאתָ, דִּבַּרְתָּ, דִּבַּרְתָּ (5 cases).

Page 253, **Exercise 26.12**

1 אָז יָצְאוּ הָאֲנָשִׁים מִן־/מֵהַבַּיִת וַיֹּאמְרוּ אִישׁ אֶל־אָחִיו, "יַצֵּל יהוה אֹתָנוּ/יַצִּילֵנוּ יהוה מִיָּדָם". **2** אַחַר הַדְּבָרִים הָאֵלֶּה הוֹסִיפוּ הַנְּבִיאִים לְדַבֵּר אֶל־הָעָם לֵאמֹר "אֱלֹהִים אִתְּכֶם/עִמָּכֶם". **3** בַּיּוֹם הַהוּא אָמְרוּ בְּנֵי יִשְׂרָאֵל "מִי יִתֵּן וְעָבַרְנוּ בְּאַרְצְךָ יוֹמָם". **4** בְּהִסָּתְרוּ הָלְכוּ הַשֹּׁמְרִים אֶל־שַׁעַר הָעִיר.

Page 253, **Exercise 26.13**

‏1 וַיֵּצְאוּ (וַיֵּצֵא)   2 וַיּוֹסִיפוּ (וַיּוֹסֶף)   3 וַיֹּאמְרוּ (וַיֹּאמֶר)   4 וַיֵּלְכוּ (וַיֵּלֶךְ)

SECTION 27

Page 255, **Review & Application I**

→ 6 ‏יֹסׁ בׁ   9 ‏גָ ר   8 ‏שֵׁם   ‏וַ ‏יְ   10 ‏וֹן   ‏כֻ   ‏יְ   4 ‏בְ ‏רֵ   ‏וַ   1 ‏קֻ ‏מוּ   ‏יוֹ

3 ‏הַ ‏קִימֹתִי   ‏וַ   2 ‏סַבּוֹתִי   ‏נְ   5 ‏תֶם   ‏סַ ‏בּ ‏וֹ   7 ‏תִי ‏וְכוֹנֵן

Page 256, **Review & Application II**

1 not ‏יִנְתֶּן (D5, he/it will give/permit)   **2** not ‏וַיְצַו (D6, he ordered/commanded)
3 not ‏וַיַּעְבְרוּ (C5, C1a, C2a they passed)   **5** not ‏וַיַּנְכֵּר (D5, he recognized),
not ‏עָשִׂיתִי (D3, B1, I did), not ‏יִשְׁמַע (C3, he will hear/may he hear)
6 not ‏תּוּכַל (D3, you will be able), not ‏שָׁוֻב (D4, he returned)
7 not ‏וַיְהִי (D6, it was), not ‏וַיֹּאמְרוּ (D1, they said), not ‏מָצָאנוּ (D1, we found)

Page 256, **Exercise 27.1** (H ‏הִפְעִיל HtD, ‏הִתְפַּעֵל N, ‏נִפְעַל G, ‏פָּעַל)

Missing words	Pers/gen/num	Tense	Root	Verb type	
who, in your, who, your	3ms	imperf	‏גור	G	1 ‏יָגוּר I
in, you (in, your), from it, you	___	infin-as-intensifier	‏מות	G	2 ‏מוֹת
before you, there, him (him), he (he, he) it	3ms	imperf	‏בוא	G	3 ‏יָבֹא
this, in, land	3ms	inver imperf	‏שׂים	G	4 ‏וַיָּשֶׂם
in, days, house	ms	participle	‏כון	N	5 ‏נָכוֹן
they (in their), in, his brother, him	3ms	inver imperf	‏קום	G	6 ‏וַיָּקָם
your, to me, your words, you, not, they, they, one another (his brother)	2mp	imperf	‏בוא	H	7 ‏תָּבִיאוּ
he (he, he), house for me, his	1cs	inver perf	‏כון ‏פּוֹלֵל		8 ‏וְכֹנַנְתִּי
my, with you	1cs	inver perf	‏קום	H	1 ‏וַהֲקִימֹתִי II
thus says/said the Lord	ms	participle	‏בוא	H	2 ‏מֵבִיא
she, son, thing that, eyes	3ms	inver imperf	‏רעע	G	3 ‏וַיֵּרַע
to, why, to your servant	2ms	perf	‏רעע	H	4 ‏הֲרֵעֹתָ
day, city	3mp	inver imperf	‏סבב	G	5 ‏וַיָּסֹבּוּ
on(= in) that day, city, seven	3cp	perf	‏סבב	G	6 ‏סָבְבוּ
in this, they, there	3mp	imperf	‏מות	G	7 ‏יָמֻתוּ
my	3ms	imperf	‏שׁוב ‏פּוֹלֵל		8 ‏יְשׁוֹבֵב

Page 259, **Exercise 27.2:** 12, 10, 13, 7, 6, 3, 5, 11, 4, 9, 2, 8, 1

Page 260, **Exercise 27.3**

1 saw ("seeing"), going out, said, said, know   **2** die, die, buried   **3** learn, swear, taught, swear, built   **4** done, die (death), watch (= ‏שָׁמַר)

Page 261, **Exercise 27.4:** 7, 8, 2, 3, 1, 4, 5, 6

Page 261, **Exercise 27.5**

1 He wept and so he said as he went (= in his going/walking), "My son Absalom, my son, my son Absalom! If only (= who will give/permit) I had died (= מוּתִי 'my dying') instead of you!" (G פָּעַל, בכה, inverted imperf)

2 So (= וַ) the men got up and went [away]. Joshua ordered those who (= הַ) [were] going to write [a description of] the land, as follows (= לֵאמֹר), "Go and walk about in the land and write [a description of] it. Then (= וְ) return to me." (D פִּעֵל, צוה, inverted imperf)

3 The men went and passed through (= בְּ) the land and wrote [a description of] it town by town (= to towns)… in (= עַל) [a] book. Then (= וַ) they came to Joshua in (= אֶל) the camp [at] Shiloh (G פָּעַל, הלך, inverted imperf)

4 Then (= וַ) Pharaoh said to him, "Go [away] from me! Be on your guard, do not see me (= my face) again, for the day you see (= in day of your "seeing") me (= my face) you shall die." Moses said, "You have spoken rightly (= כֵּן). I shall not see your face again." (H הִפְעִיל, יסף, shortened imperf)

5 Saul recognized David's voice and said, "[Is] this your voice, my son David?" And David said, "[It is] my voice, my lord the king." After that (= וַ) he said, "Why actually (= זֶה) does my lord pursue (= pursuing) after his servant? For what have I done and what badness [is there] in my hand? Now therefore (= וְ) let my lord the king, please, hear the words of his servant." (H הִפְעִיל, נכר, inverted imperf)

6 Saul said to David, "Blessed [may] you [be], my son David! You will without doubt (= עָשֹׁה, יָכֹל: infinitives-as-intensifiers) both do [things] and (= גַם… וְגַם 'both… and') achieve (= תּוּכַל) [them]". So (= וַ) David went his way (= to his way) and Saul – he returned to his place (G פָּעַל, יכל, imperf)

7 They took oath with one another (= man to his brother). Isaac sent them away and they went from him in peace. Now (= וַיְהִי) on (= בְּ) that day Isaac's servants came and reported to him… . They said to him, "We have found water!" Hence (= וַ), he called it Shibah. Therefore, the name of the city [is] Beer-sheba to this day. (N נִפְעַל, שבע, inverted imperf)

Page 262, **Exercise 27.6:** 3, 9, 8, 5, 6, 4, 11, 1, 10, 7, 2

Page 263, **Exercise 27.7**

▶**1** (כָּתֹב) לִכְתֹּב ;הָלַךְ part :(לֶכֶת) בְּלֶכְתּוֹ :part מֵת (מוּת) מוּתִי **2** (2 cases) (כְּתֹב) לִכְתֹּב;

(רָאֹות): part אָמֹר/אָמוּר (2 cases) **4** אָמַר/אָמוּר (אָמֹר): part כְּתֹב/כָּתוּב; לֵאמֹר part

part עָשֹׂה (infin-as-intensifier): part עָשֹׂה **6** (3 cases) רָאֹות + רְאֹתְךָ + רָאָה ;

יָכֹל (infin-as-intensifier): part יָכֹל (2 cases); עָשׂוּי◀

Page 263, **Exercise 27.8**

1 (בָּכָה) וַיֵּבְךְּ 2 (קָמוּ) וַיָּקֻמוּ, (הָלְכוּ) וַיֵּלְכוּ, (צִוָּה) וַיְצַו 3 (הָלְכוּ) וַיֵּלְכוּ, ➤
וַיַּעַבְרוּ (עָבְרוּ), וַיִּכְתְּבוּהָ (כְּתָבוּהָ), וַיָּבֹאוּ (בָּאוּ) 4 וַיֹּאמֶר (אָמַר), וַיֹּאמֶר
5 וַיַּכֵּר (הִכִּיר), וַיֹּאמֶר (אָמַר), וַיֹּאמֶר 6 וַיֹּאמֶר, וַיֵּלֶךְ
7 (הָלַךְ) וַיִּשָּׁבְעוּ (נִשְׁבְּעוּ), וַיִּשְׁלְחֵם (שְׁלָחָם), וַיֵּלְכוּ (הָלְכוּ), וַיְהִי (הָיָה),
וַיָּבֹאוּ (בָּאוּ), וַיַּגִּידוּ (הִגִּידוּ) וַיֹּאמְרוּ (אָמְרוּ), וַיִּקְרָא (קָרָא).

Page 263, **Exercise 27.9**

1 דִּבֶּר הָאִישׁ אֶל־הַמֶּלֶךְ וְאָמַר, "אִם־נָא מָצָאתִי חֵן בְּעֵינֶיךָ..."
2 בָּאָה הָאִשָּׁה לִרְאוֹת אֶת־בְּנָהּ בַּהֵיכָל.
3 שָׁלַח יהוה אֵלֵינוּ אֶת־הַנָּבִיא הַזֶּה. מֵת הַנָּבִיא הַזָּקֵן.
4 נָתַן אֱלֹהִים לְעַמּוֹ אֶת־הַתּוֹרָה.
5 קָרָא בְּנוֹ אֶת־הַסֵּפֶר וְשָׁם אֹתוֹ בַּבַּיִת.
6 שָׁב הָעֶבֶד אֶל־אֲדוֹנוֹ/אֲדוֹנָיו (plural of majesty).
7 רָאָה אֹתִי/רָאַנִי אָחִי יוֹשֵׁב בַּשַּׁעַר עִם־זִקְנֵי הָעִיר.

Page 263, **Exercise 27.10**

1 וַיְדַבֵּר, וַיֹּאמֶר, וָאֶמְצָא 2 וַתָּבוֹא 3 וַיִּשְׁלַח, וַיָּמָת 4 וַיִּתֵּן 5 וַיִּקְרָא, וַיָּשֶׂם
6 וַיֵּשֶׁב 7 וַיַּרְא

Page 263, **Exercise 27.11**

1 דִּבְּרוּ הָאֲנָשִׁים אֶל־הַמְּלָכִים וְאָמְרוּ, "אִם־נָא מָצָאנוּ חֵן בְּעֵינֵיכֶם..."
2 בָּאוּ הַנָּשִׁים לִרְאוֹת אֶת־בְּנֵיהֶן בַּהֵיכָלוֹת.
3 שָׁלַח יהוה אֵלֵינוּ אֶת־הַנְּבִיאִים הָאֵלֶּה. מֵתוּ הַנְּבִיאִים הַזְּקֵנִים.
5 קָרְאוּ בָּנָיו אֶת־הַסְּפָרִים וְשָׂמוּ אֹתָם בַּבָּתִּים.
6 שָׁבוּ הָעֲבָדִים אֶל־אֲדוֹנֵיהֶם.
7 רָאוּ אֹתָנוּ/רָאוּנוּ אַחֵינוּ יוֹשְׁבִים בַּשְּׁעָרִים עִם־זִקְנֵי הָעִיר.

SECTION 28

Page 265, **Review & Application I**

28.8) 1 Not וַיָּקֹם (D4, he rose up) **2** Not וַיֻּגַּד (D5, it was reported), not
לְבַקְשׁוֹ (B1, D6, to seek him) **3** Not מָצָאתִי (D1, B1, I found), not יִתְּנוּ
(D5, may they give)

28.10) 1 Not וַיְדַבֵּר (D6, he spoke) **2** א not audible (D1, he came), not וַיַּהֲרֹג
(C5, C1a, he killed), not וַיֵּאָסְפוּ (C4, they gathered themselves) **3** Not
וַיַּגִּידוּ (D5, they reported), not וַיַּעֲמֹד (C5, C1a, he stood), not וַיִּנָּשֵׂא
(D5, D1, he raised), not וַיִּקְרָא (D1, he called), not יִשְׁמַע (C3, may he listen),
not לִמְשֹׁחַ (C1b, to anoint)

28.12) 1 Not לַעֲשׂוֹת (C2a, to do), not וַיְהִי (D6, it was), not בָּא (D4, D1 he
came), not נוֹרָא, the א not audible (D3, D1, frightening), not הִגִּיד (D5, he
told), not תִּשְׁתְּיִ (D4, you drink), not וַיִּשְׁמַע (C3, he heard)

Page 266, **Exercise 28.2**

1 in, first, in, you, eat, until, day, in the (G פָּעַל, אכל, imperf)   **2** blessed, seventh, it (D פִּעֵל, ברך, invert imperf)   **3** thirty (thirty), he (his), forty, in, he, over, seven, six, thirty-three (thirty, three), all (G פָּעַל, מלך, infinitive)   **4** he, he said, forty, there, he said, do, forty (H הִפְעִיל, יסף, invert imperf)

5 eighty-six (eighty, six), to (G פָּעַל, ילד, infinitive)   **6** on his face, he said, born, hundred (hundred), ninety (ninety) (N נִפְעַל, ילד, imperf)   **7** to me they, given, thousands (G פָּעַל, נתן, perf)   **8** (these, days, years, life, which), hundred, seventy-five (hundred, seventy, five) (G פָּעַל, חיה, perf)

Page 268, **Exercise 28.3:** 4, 7, 9, 6, 3, 5, 8, 11, 1, 2, 10

Page 268, **Exercise 28.4**

1 Supposed (= perhaps) there are (= יֵשׁ) fifty righteous within (= in the midst of) the city   **2** We [are] twelve brothers, the sons of our father. One [is] no more (= the one, he not) and the youngest (= the young) [is] today (= הַיּוֹם) with our father in the land of Canaan.   **3** Six days you shall work … but (= וְ) the seventh day [is a] sabbath of (= לְ) the Lord, your God.   **4** And sixteen thousand persons (= soul of man)   **5** And he said to them, "I [am one] hundred and twenty year[s] old today."   **6** Moses (= and Moses) [was one] hundred and twenty year[s] old when he died (= in his death)   **7** For your servant knows (= יָדַע) that it was I who (= I – I) has sinned. Therefore (= וְ), look/here, I have come today, [the] first   **8** He uttered (= וַיְדַבֵּר) three thousand (= thousands) proverb[s] and his songs were (= his song was) [a] thousand and five   **9** And the years of Levi's life [were a] hundred and thirty-seven year[s].

Page 269, **Exercise 28.5: 1** (צַדִּיקִ"ם) צַדִּיקִם 5 אֱלֵהֶם (אֲלֵיהֶם) 6 (מוֹתוֹ) מֹתוֹ

Page 269, **Exercise 28.6**

1 he, you, you, say, speak, your, listening   **2** to her, go, me, I, go, you, go with me, I, go   **3** they said (to his friend), we sitting here, we, died, we say, enter/go into, in, we, die, there, sit, here, we, die, now, they, live, we, live, they, die, die   **4** you, like us, every, we, give our, to you, your, we, take, we dwell with you, people, you, listen to us, we, take our, we, go   **5** you, you, him, you, you, him   **6** be with me, keep me, this, going, give me, eat, I, to, house, my father, my (me)   **7** man, his, she   **8** to you, he, you six, seventh, you, him, from you   **9** to you, I, from you, you, your, you, you, take   **10** (takes, wife), he, army

Page 271, **Exercise 28.7**

➡ **3** יְחַיֵּנוּ (יְחַיּוּ אֹתָנוּ), יְמִיתֵנוּ (יָמִיתוּ אֹתָנוּ)

5 תְּבָרְכֵנוּ (תְּבָרֵךְ אֹתוֹ), יְבָרְכְךָ (יְבָרֵךְ אֹתְךָ), תַּעֲנֶנּוּ (תַּעֲנֶה אֹתוֹ)

6 אֹהַבְךָ (אָהַב/אֹהַב אֹתְךָ)   **9** תְּשַׁלְּחֶנּוּ (תְּשַׁלַּח אֹתוֹ)   **8** וּשְׁמָרַנִי (וְשָׁמַר אֹתִי)

Page 271, **Exercise 28.8**

1 [2] So (= וַ) David rose up and crossed over, he and [the] six hundred men (= man) who [were] with him, to Achish, the son of Maoch, king of Gath.
[3] And David dwelt with Achish at Gath, he and his men, [each] man with (= וְ) his house[hold], David and his two wives, Ahinoam the Jezreelitess and Abigail, Nabal's wife, the Carmelitess. (G פָּעַל, קוּם, inver imperf; G פָּעַל, עבר, inver imperf)

2 [4] When (= וַ) it was reported to Saul that David had fled [to] Gath, he did not seek him any more (= עוֹד + יָסַף) (Hp הָפְעַל, נגד, inver imperf)

3 [5] Then (= וַ) David said to Achish, "If, please, I have found favour in your eyes, let [a] place be given me (= יִתְּנוּ לִי, lit., 'they will give to me') in one of the towns of the countryside (= שָׂדֶה), that (= וְ) I may dwell there. For (= וְ) why should your servant dwell in the royal city (city of the kingdom) with you?" [6] So (= וַ) Achish gave him Ziklag on (= בְּ) that day. Therefore, Ziklag has belonged to (= was to) the kings of Judah to this day (G פָּעַל, נתן, imperf; G פָּעַל, ישׁב, lengthened imperf)

Page 272, **Exercise 28.9:** 6, 3, 9, 2, 4, 8, 1, 5, 7

Page 272, **Exercise 28.10**

1 [1] Now (= וַ) Abimelech, the son of Jerubbaal, went to Shechem, to his mother's brothers and spoke to them and to the whole family of the house of his mother's father as follows (= לֵאמֹר), [2] "Speak, please, to (= in the ears of) all the [land]owners of Shechem, 'Which [is] better (= what good) for you; [will] seventy men (= man), all the sons of Jerubbaal, [be] ruling over (= בְּ) you or one man [will be] ruling over (= בְּ) you?'..." (G פָּעַל, הלך, inver imperf).

2 [3] So (= וַ) his mother's brothers spoke all these words on his behalf (= עָלָיו) in the hearing (= ears) of all the [land]owners of Shechem... [5] After that (= וַ) he came [to] his father's house, to Ophrah, and killed his brothers, the sons of Jerubbaal, seventy men (= man), upon one stone... [6] Subsequently (= וַ) all the [land]owners of Shechem and all the house of Millo gathered themselves and went and made Abimelech king (+ לְמֶלֶךְ 'to king' which is redundant in English translation)... at Shechem (D פָּעַל, דבר, inver imperf; G פָּעַל, בוא, inver imperf).

3 [7] When (= וַ) they reported [it] to Jotham, he went and stood at the top (= head) of Mount Gerizim, raised his voice, called [out] and said to them, "Listen to me, [land]owners of Shechem, so that (= וְ) God may listen to you. [8] Once upon a time (= הָלוֹךְ) the trees went to anoint [a] king over them..." (H הִפְעִיל, נגד, inver imperf).

Page 273, **Exercise 28.11:** 8, 3, 10, 1, 7, 2, 4, 9, 6, 5

Page 273, **Exercise 28.12**

1 [1] And the Israelites (= sons of Israel) again did what (= הַ) [was] evil in the sight (= eyes) of the LORD, so that (= וַ) the LORD gave them into the hand of the Philistines [for] forty years. [2] And [there] was a certain (= one) man from Zorah, of (= מִ) the family of the Danite[s], whose name (= and his name) [was] Manoah.

2 [6] Then (= וַ) the woman came and said to her husband as follows (= לֵאמֹר), "The man of (the) God came to me, and his appearance [was] like the appearance of the angel of (the) God, very frightening. And I did not ask him where actually (= זֶה) he [was] from, neither (= וְלֹא) did he tell me (= to me) his name. [7] He said to me, 'Look! You [will be] pregnant and you will give birth [to a] son, and now do not drink wine...' "

3 [9] And (the) God listened to (= in the voice of) Manoah, and the angel of (the) God came again to the woman, while (= וְ) she [was] sitting in the field and Manoah her husband [was] not with her. [10] The woman quickly ran (= hurried and ran) and told (= told to) her husband. She said to him, "Look! The man who came to me the [other] day (= in the day) has appeared (= was seen) to me."

4 [11] Manoah arose and went after his wife and came to the man and said to him, "[Are] you the man who spoke to this (= הַ) woman?" And he said, "I [am]." [12] Then (= וַ) Manoah said, "Now may your words come [true]! What rules will be [observed] for the boy (= what legal decision/ordinance will be for the boy and his work/deed)?" [13] So (= וַ) the angel of the LORD said to Manoah, "From everything that I said to the woman, she should keep herself."

Page 274, **Exercise 28.13:** 8, 3, 1, 9, 7, 2, 4, 5, 6

Page 274, **Exercise 28.14**

◄— וַיָּקָם (קום), וַיֵּשֶׁב (ישב), וַיֹּאמֶר/וַתֹּאמֶר(אמר), וַיֵּלֶךְ (הלך), וַתָּרָץ (רוץ)

Page 275, **Exercise 28.15:** וַתַּגֵּד. The ordinary imperfect is תַּגִּיד.

Page 275, **Exercise 28.16**

1 מֵת הַמֶּלֶךְ בִּהְיוֹתוֹ בֶּן־שִׁבְעִים וְשָׁלֹשׁ שָׁנָה.

2 אַחַר כָּל־הַדְּבָרִים הָאֵלֶּה שָׁב בְּנוֹ אֶל־הָעִיר/הָעִירָה.

3 שָׂם הַכֹּהֵן אֶת־יָדוֹ עַל־רֹאשׁ הָאִישׁ וּבֵרַךְ (וּבֵרֶךְ) אֹתוֹ/וּבֵרְכוּ לֵאמֹר, "יִשְׁמֹר אֹתְךָ/יִשְׁמָרְךָ יהוה."

4 בַּיּוֹם הַהוּא יָצָא הָאָדוֹן מִן־/מֵהַבַּיִת וְאָמַר לְעַבְדּוֹ, "קַח אִתִּי/קָחֵנִי אֶל־אֶרֶץ אֲבוֹתַי."

5 הָלַךְ הָאִישׁ עִם/אֶת־אָחִיו בַּדֶּרֶךְ לִירוּשָׁלַיִם/יְרוּשָׁלַיְמָה.

6 הָיְתָה הָאִשָּׁה עַל־הָהָר. עָלָה הָאִישׁ אֵלֶיהָ וּבָנָה לָהּ בַּיִת שָׁם. יָשַׁב הָאִישׁ בַּבַּיִת הַזֶּה שָׁנִים רַבּוֹת. יָלְדָה לוֹ הָאִשָּׁה שְׁנֵי יְלָדִים.

Page 275, **Exercise 28.17**

1 וַיָּמָת 2 וַיֵּשֶׁב 3 וַיָּשֶׂם, וַיִּבְרֶךְ 4 וַיֵּצֵא, וַיֹּאמֶר 5 וַיֵּלֶךְ 6 וַתְּהִי, וַיַּעַל,
וַיִּבֶן, וַיֵּשֶׁב, וַתֵּלֶד

Page 275, **Exercise 28.18**

1 וַיָּמוּתוּ הַמְּלָכִים בִּהְיוֹתָם בְּנֵי שִׁבְעִים וְשָׁלֹשׁ שָׁנָה.

2 (וַיְהִי) אַחַר כָּל־הַדְּבָרִים הָאֵלֶּה וַיָּשׁוּבוּ בָּנָיו אֶל־הֶעָרִים.

3 וַיָּשִׂימוּ הַכֹּהֲנִים אֶת־יָדָם עַל־רָאשֵׁי הָאֲנָשִׁים וַיְבָרְכוּ אֹתָם/וַיְבָרְכוּם לֵאמֹר,
"יִשְׁמֹר אֶתְכֶם/יִשְׁמָרְכֶם יהוה."

4 (וַיְהִי) בַּיָּמִים הָהֵם וַיֵּצְאוּ הָאֲדוֹנִים מִן־/מֵהַבָּתִּים וַיֹּאמְרוּ לְעַבְדֵיהֶם, "קְחוּ
אֹתָנוּ אֶל־אֶרֶץ אֲבוֹתֵינוּ."

5 וַיֵּלְכוּ הָאֲנָשִׁים עִם/אֶת־אֲחִיהֶם בַּדֶּרֶךְ לִירוּשָׁלַיִם/יְרוּשָׁלַיְמָה.

6 וַתִּהְיֶינָה הַנָּשִׁים עַל־הֶהָרִים. וַיַּעֲלוּ הָאֲנָשִׁים אֲלֵיהֶן וַיִּבְנוּ לָהֶן בָּתִּים שָׁם.
וַיֵּשְׁבוּ הָאֲנָשִׁים בַּבָּתִּים הָאֵלֶּה שָׁנִים רַבּוֹת. וַתֵּלַדְנָה לָהֶם הַנָּשִׁים שְׁנֵי
יְלָדִים.

APPENDIX I

Page 287, **Exercise 1**

I   1 שָׁמַע 2 צַוֵּה 3 לָבָן 4 חַי 5 שֶׁקֶל 6 שָׁלוֹם

II   1 מֶלֶךְ 2 עַם 3 אָב 4 מַלְאָךְ 5 עִם 6 בַּת 7 חַג 8 חָבֵר 9 לָמַד
10 שָׁנָה

III 1 נֹעַם 2 שֶׁבַע 3 בֵּן 4 אָבִיב 5 רַב 6 שֶׁמֶשׁ 7 אִישׁ 8 שָׁמַר
9 אָח 10 יָרַד 11 שַׂר

Page 289, **Exercise 2**

	Meaning: Lexical form	Tense	Root type	Verb type	Verb root	
1	be/become confirmed	perf/part	פ״ג, ג-I	G פָּעַל	אמן	אָמֵן
2	be/become priest	active part	ע״ג, ג-II	פָּעַל	כהן	כֹּהֵן
3	laugh	imperf	ע״ג, ג-II	פָּעַל	צחק	יִצְחָק
4	be/become whole/perfect	perf/part	שְׁלֵמִים	פָּעַל	שׁלם	שָׁלֵם
5	save, deliver	infin-as-intensifier	ו-I/־י + ג-III	H הִפְעִיל	ישׁע	הוֹשֵׁעַ
6	save, deliver	imperative	ו-I/־י + ג-III	הִפְעִיל	ישׁע	הוֹשִׁיעָה
7	add	active part	פו״י, ו-I/־י	פָּעַל	יסף	יוֹסֵף
	add	shortened imperf			הִפְעִיל		
8	praise	imperative	ע״ע twin-cons	D פִּעֵל	הלל	הַלְלוּ
9	rest	infin-as-intensifier	ו-I/־י + ג-III	פָּעַל	נוח	נֹחַ
10	work, serve	active part	פ״ג, ג-I	פָּעַל	עבד	עוֹבֵד
11	load	infin-as-intensifier	פ״ג, ג-I	פָּעַל	עמס	עָמוֹס
12	grasp by the heel; cheat	imperf	פ״ג, ג-I	פָּעַל	עקב	יַעֲקֹב

13 נָתַן	נתן	פָּעַל	נ-I irregular	perf	give, set, permit
14 יִפְתַּח	פתח	פָּעַל	ל"ג, III-ג	imperf	open
15 אָסַף	אסף	פָּעַל	פ"ג, I-ג	perf	gather
16 נִמְרֹד	מרד	פָּעַל	שְׁלֵמִים	imperf	revolt, rebel
17 דָן	דון	פָּעַל	עו"י, II-ו/י	perf/part	judge
18 שָׁאוּל	שאל	פָּעַל	ע"ג, II-ג	passive part	request, ask

Page 290, **Exercise 3**

1 יֵשַׁע   2 אֵל   3 מֶלֶךְ   4 מֶלֶךְ   5 טוֹב   6 אָדוֹן   7 עֹז   8 אָב   9 שֵׁם
10 צֶדֶק   11 עֵזֶר   12 אוֹר   13 גֶּבֶר (גִּבּוֹר)

Page 291, **Exercise 4**

I   1 חָנַן   2 קוּם   3 דוּן   4 רָפָא   5 קָנָה   6 ישׁע   7 רוּם   8 שָׁמַע
9 חָזַק   10 עָזַר

II   1 עָזַר   2 נחם   3 שָׂרָה   4 זָכַר   5 נָתַן   6 זָרַע   7 חָנַן   8 שָׁפַט
9 ידה   10 גָּדֵל/גָּדַל